*f*P

LOOK AWAY!

*A History
of the Confederate
States of America*

WILLIAM C. DAVIS

THE FREE PRESS
New York   London   Toronto   Sydney   Singapore

THE FREE PRESS
A Division of Simon & Schuster, Inc.
1230 Avenue of the Americas
New York, NY 10020

THE FREE PRESS and colophon are trademarks
of Simon & Schuster, Inc.

For information regarding special discounts for bulk purchases,
please contact Simon & Schuster Special Sales:
1-800-456-6798 or business@simonandschuster.com

Designed by Katy Riegel

Manufactured in the United States of America

1   3   5   7   9   10   8   6   4   2

Library of Congress Cataloging-in-Publication Data

Davis, William C.
    Look away! : a history of the Confederate States of America / William C. Davis.
        p.   cm.
    Includes bibliographical references and index.
    1. Confederate States of America—History. I. Title.

E487 .D278 2002   2001059778
973.7'13—dc21

    ISBN 0-684-86585-8

What ish my nation?
Ish a villain and a bastard and a knave and a rascal.
. . . Who talks of my nation?

William Shakespeare, *Henry V*

CONTENTS

Preface   ix

The Foretelling   1

Dixie's Land   7

1. Guiding the Whirlwind   12

2. Shadowy Words, Shadowy Meanings   35

3. Visions of Breakers Ahead   55

4. The Struggle for a Confederate Democracy   85

    The Opening Guns   125

5. Men but Not Brothers   130

6. Law and Disorder   163

    The Season of Lee   189

7. "Proving Our Loyalty by Starvation"   194

8. "We Are Done Gone Up the Spout"   225

    The Year of Decision   254

  9. The Enemy Within   259

10. Cotton Communism, Whiskey Welfare, and Salt Socialism   280

    The Struggle to Hold On   317

11. The States in Their Sovereignty   323

12. The Power and the Ignominy in Richmond   341

13. "Growlers & Traitors"   365

    An End to Valor   397

14. The End?   401

    Abbreviations Used in the Source Citations   429

    Notes   430

    Bibliography   468

    Index   479

PREFACE

A GOOD STORY DESERVES retelling often, and every generation will find new subtleties and new meanings to an old tale, meanings that reflect as much about ourselves as they do of the story itself, perhaps. The Confederacy has always been a great story. Even before its brief life winked out, people North and South and in much of the rest of the world found it fascinating, even if they opposed the motives and imperatives that brought the would-be nation into being. Certainly it is an oft-told story. Edward A. Pollard began publishing his multi-volume history of the Confederacy and its war in 1862 when the subject itself was scarcely a year old. Since then the Confederacy has been the platform for a score and more of histories, some quite good, many undistinguished. With notable exceptions they have all looked not so much at the Confederacy itself as at its war with the Union, certainly a vital part of the tale but not the whole story. There were other wars within that war, other battlegrounds than Gettysburg and Vicksburg, where men and women, white and black, children even, leavened the epic with labors and sacrifices of their own. And most of all, the conflict was a political and social battle from beginning to end, at first to establish the Confederacy, but then for the next four years to define what sort of democracy that Confederacy was or ought to be.

That is the story of *Look Away!* The campaigns and battles are here, to be sure, but they have been recounted in such detail and so often elsewhere that it would be redundant to go into them in great depth here. Indeed, the quality of Confederate military history has never been greater than it is in the hands of today's historians. We all must never forget that, after all, it was a war. Everything that happened behind the lines North or South was in some measure informed or influenced by events on the battlefield. To look at events on the home front or in legislative halls without taking into account the course of the war is more than myopic, it is pointless. While paying heed to events on the battlefields, however, *Look Away!* seeks to present a comprehensive view of everything else that went into making the Confederate national experience, from the political turmoil that led to its creation to the social and economic devastation left in its wake. Civilian life, civil law and justice, disloyalty, the affairs in the state legislatures and governors' mansions, the relations between state and nation, and the Confederate government itself, including its not-too-loyal opposition, are the meat of the story. Throughout there runs the thread of a people whose rulers were trying to bring a link from their past into a new nation in a modern world, to create what they thought they wanted without giving up what they thought they needed. In short, it is the story of how the Confederates faced the perpetual dilemmas of all peoples who want a democracy, while realizing that there are many kinds of democracies, some of them quite unpleasant to the Southern taste.

The sources of Confederate history are myriad. No one could hope to master them all, and *Look Away!* has not tried the impossible. However, to capture as much of the immediacy of the moment as possible, to speak for them in terms of how they felt and what they knew and thought at the moment, the Confederate story appears here almost exclusively drawn from the actual primary documents of the time, especially the correspondence of the common people. Their spelling and punctuation were often as not idiosyncratic, but unless there is a danger of meaning being clouded, their words appear here undoctored. If they are to be allowed to speak as they spoke, then they should be read and heard as they were heard by their contemporaries. The later literature by historians of the Confederate experiment is staggering, much of it of a high caliber. Many of their works have been used, and not a few of their interpretations presented, but in the main the story of *Look Away!* comes from the people themselves.

Many friends and colleagues have assisted in assembling the research for this book, notably Robert K. Krick, Richard McMurry, Gary W. Gallagher, Emory Thomas, James I. Robertson, Jr., Douglas L. Gibboney, Deborah Petite, Shinaan Krakowsky, and Katherine Breckinridge Prewitt.

Archivists across the country have been generous, and all deserve thanks, most particularly Rickie Brunner at the Alabama Department of Archives and History; David Cole of the Florida State Archives; Ann Lipscomb-Webster at the Mississippi Department of Archives and History; Kate Adams at the Center for American History of the University of Texas at Austin; Donaly E. Brice of the Texas State Library, Austin; J. Tracy Power at the South Carolina Department of Archives and History; John Coski of the Museum of the Confederacy in Richmond, Virginia; Allen Stokes of the South Caroliniana Library, University of South Carolina; Richard Shrader of the Southern Historical Collection, University of North Carolina; and the great benefactor to all who work in the field, Michael Musick at the National Archives in Washington. Many may disagree with the portrait of the Confederacy that emerges from *Look Away!*, but if so, their argument will be with the author and not with these fine servants of posterity.

The Foretelling

WILLIAM JAHNSENYKES OF BOSTON employed a facile pen, though one inclined to spill rather more ink than necessary in flights of stylistic display. It was a tendency certainly dissonant with the prevailing cultural myth of the terse and constrained Yankee. Yet when he decided to limn his own history of the road to secession in the American South, and the ill-starred Confederate quadrennium that followed, he rapidly exceeded even his own limits for hyperbole. But then it was a hyperbolic age. Americans North and South breathed a cultural atmosphere redolent of their own mythology, made more fragrant still as their need to be a distinct people impelled them to make up for their youth as a nation by taking their brief past all the more seriously. If their household gods were few, they only loomed that much larger thanks to the need to create an American pantheon; their myths and sagas, though not many, lay the more deeply ingrained in the public consciousness. Peoples of the Old World chiefly found amusement in their particular myths. Americans, especially Southerners, actually chose to believe theirs.

Certainly Jahnsenykes saw all of this at work as he wrote his brief history of secession, the Confederacy, and the civil war that followed, even as his own pen unwittingly revealed that those myths were acting on him, too. His narrative reached print in a 1901 compilation of six letters to his son Julius, said to have been written many years before in 1872 while the war was still fresh in his memory and the people of the South still resisted the

1

Reconstruction that followed. He wrote in an attempt to explain to the boy why the "divided and distracted people" of the old Union had come to such a tragic pass. "These letters faithfully paint the miseries of former times," declared the son, and in publishing them now he hoped that they might persuade Southerners that destiny and common sense had always dictated that Americans be one people rather than two. Animated by "an antient grudge, and still more by a desire of attracting to themselves individually the management of the State," the onetime Confederates had kept alive four decades of bickering since the outbreak of the war, and he thought it was time for them to stop. His recounting of "the deadly feuds of civil war" might, he hoped, remind them of the advantages of unity over separatism.

"Nations act on a plan totally selfish," his father's first letter began. "The very essence of patriotism consists in preferring the good of our own country to the good of any other." The purpose of erecting a government over a country was surely that it might promote the good of its people. Yet "confiding in their own blind vanity, and patriotick partialities," ante-bellum Southerners convinced themselves that their government no longer protected their interests. Such a belief naturally placed them in opposition to the ruling majority, and the very act of opposition itself, he said, strengthened opinions and prejudices. Soon some Southern leaders "embarked with their vilest passions on the tumultuous sea of politicks, and had been driven by malice and contention."

The senior Jahnsenykes granted that differences of character created some natural division between the states of the old Union, contrasts dictated by birth and national origin among their ancestors, religion, and, of course, politics. Some Americans felt ancient tugs of republicanism derived from admiration for ancient Greece and consular Rome. They harbored instinctive antipathy for anything smelling of aristocracy by birth. Yet there were others, calling themselves republicans, who did so only because such a posture opened doors to the favor of the people, from whom alone they could gain preferment, office, and power. Indeed, Jahnsenykes saw all too many, especially in the South, whose "pride and vanity, which in other circumstances would hardly have allowed them to acknowledge an equal, absolutely forbad their submitting to a superior." Pretending republicanism allowed them a cover for instincts so aristocratic that such men decried real democracy, and tried to subvert the very system by which an electorate they distrusted and disdained held power over them with the ballot. If they mouthed the platitudes of democracy, it was only because a system that ostensibly kept everyone equal at least prevented anyone from becoming superior to themselves. To them the French Revolution had been farcical with its naive platitudes of liberty, equality, and fraternity among all classes. These men were oligarchs in all but open avowal, and claimed republican sympathies simply "because circumstances precluded them from being kings, dukes or lords," according to Jahnsenykes.

Jahnsenykes was no fool. He did not question whether "most of the Republicks, which have been constituted in the world, did not take their origin from the ambition, jealousy, envy and pride of leading men." He blamed much of Southern attitudes on "the illustrious Jefferson—for I will not call him great"—and on Southerners who formed "the party called democratick" that grew around him, openly showing their preference for leadership by aristocracy over the vox populi. And always there had been the complicating factor of the one institution that peculiarly set the South apart from the North, slavery. More and more Jahnsenykes saw that Southern states had embraced the Union only insofar as it served to protect their rights to hold property in slaves, and to spread slavery as the nation expanded and the institution itself became intertwined as a defining element in the struggle for national power itself. If slavery could not spread as new states were formed, then the existing slave states would be doomed to perpetual minority in representation in Congress, guaranteeing that if the day came when Northern antipathy to slavery itself became hot enough, the majority could use the government to subvert the Constitution and abolish the institution where it already existed. In short, the South could not afford to lose any battle over slavery, nor even over issues on its periphery. "The disputants seemed to have forgotten, that the government was decidedly and legally a creation of the majority," Jahnsenykes recalled in dismay, "and that of course it was the duty of a minority to submit with cheerful loyalty." But simple human nature dictated otherwise.

That was why the Founding Fathers had created a system mandating an opportunity for a change of administration in Washington every four years. Rather than easing tensions between minority and majority, however, Jahnsenykes believed that "it tended rather to imbitter domestick and civil life [and] party rancour prevailed." Instead of the democratic utopia envisioned by the Revolutionary generation, there arose two aristocracies, one in the North born out of new wealth from industry and commerce, and another in the South founded on old wealth derived by birth and sustained through long years of national political dominance. Sadly he lamented that, "could there have been an aristocracy of honour, to check and balance these two parties, possibly the form of government might have subsisted much longer." But, alas, "men love distinction; and distinction they will obtain, though in some instances it be by the hardihood of villainy." In the South especially, "rank and titles were eagerly courted, and pertinaciously kept." Bred as they were in habits of assumed social superiority, "and accustomed to deference from early years, owing to the great prevalence of slavery in those times," Jahnsenykes declared, "the planters were, in fact, a kind of lords."

Before long that fear over slavery and all that it entailed brought on the crisis. Soon North and South both uttered defiance to one another, the former accusing the latter of willfully seeking to dissolve the Union, and the slave states did not deny the charge. A presidential election briefly distracted the march toward secession, but not for long, and in the end the ambitions of petty men used events for their own ends. "It was now too late to recede, and the cry of war resounded from the South," recalled Jahnsenykes. "No sooner did it appear, from the measures of Virginia and her associates, that a political sovereignty, of whatever name, was about to be formed in the South," he went on, than attitudes hardened on both sides of Mason and Dixon's line. Soon there appeared what he called, in his quaint phrase, "the Southern Division of the States, which had seceded from the late Union." Led by Virginia, they "cast the gauntlet of civil war at the feet of the yet confederated states."

The new confederation elected a "respectable chief" and looked to Europe for aid and succor in its battle with the North. "I will not enter into a detail of the debates of that eventful period," Jahnsenykes protested. "I look on all the scenes I have related with horror." It was only with profound reluctance that he mentioned to his son at all the "long and violent" conflict that followed, a narration that "awakens unheeded and ineffectual regrets, and will ever be the theme of mortification and sorrow." He recoiled from relating "the murders, sieges, devastations and cruelties of a mode of warfare ever the most bloody," Jahnsenykes went on. "Why paint to you the rage, barbarity and brutal violence of a contest so deplorable and fatal?" As the war raged, its focus gradually shifted westward, and there, far from where it all began, the Confederacy met its end.

After losing its bid for independence, the Southern nation found itself subjected to occupation by the victor's armies for long and painful years, retreating for solace into romanticized recollections of what the South once had been that soon framed a fresh corpus of mythology, all of it serving only to keep alive old passions. Still Jahnsenykes hoped that "quiet may be restored to this unhappy country in all its parts." Southerners, "a people, who had neither the wisdom nor virtue to protect the government of their first and deliberate choice," had been forced as Confederates to submit to what he called "a system imposed by arms," and in memory rendered dear, by a remembrance of their wartime sacrifices. Only if they abandoned their cherished myths about themselves, however, were they likely to find a happy home once more as a part of the Union.

As an actual recollection of the events that surrounded the brief life of the Confederacy, Jahnsenykes's epistolary history was unremarkable and surely too general to command much interest. But it was not a recollection. It was a prediction. The author's real name was William Jenks, and though he was a Bostonian, he wrote not in 1872, nor was his oddly titled *Memoir of the Northern Kingdom* published in 1901. It sprang from his pen and press in November 1808, fifty-two years and one month before South Carolina seceded from the Union and set in train the events that led to the Confederacy and the Civil War.

In fact, Jenks's forty-eight-page tract was an attack on incumbent President Thomas Jefferson and his affinity for France over Britain. Jenks actually went far beyond his predictions of a confederacy, concluding with the South allying itself with France and eventually accepting a new monarchy born of the son of a French king by an American wife. Somehow, over a half century in advance, Jenks anticipated Southern secession over issues surrounding slavery and the bitter divisions on the nature of republican democracy. He saw right to the heart of forces that made many of his predictions come true years after his death. Most perceptive of all, Jenks realized that at the core of the dominant Southern society and leadership there lay an instinct not for true democracy but for a democratic form of oligarchy, for rule by the few from an aristocracy of wealth and birth, chosen by their own class in a process that only paid lip service to republicanism. He might even have grasped that however much Southern leaders would and did deplore the idea of a monarchy itself, they craved and would fight to preserve the sort of hereditary aristocracy that only an absolute monarch could keep in place, and that only slavery or a serf labor class could sustain. In anticipating a king for the South, Jenks merely followed those aspirations to a perfectly logical conclusion. The only alterna-

tive was for Southern oligarchs somehow to cling to the forms of democracy within a system that allowed them to retain their traditional unchallenged control in their states, while keeping the powerless and largely
disfranchised multitude of Southern people content, persuaded that they
were enjoying the fruits of enlightened democracy.

With or without a king, however, Jenks and that generation of Southern
leaders who came half a century later stood unanimous on one paramount
point. The Union, with its inevitable momentum toward ever greater centralization of power, and the broadening expansion of the franchise necessary
to sustain it, posed not promise but threat, not only to their domination
over their states' destinies but even to the social and labor systems on
which they wove their social fabric. The only way to achieve their aspirations, while protecting themselves, was in a nation of their own.[1]

Dixie's Land

They would never even agree on who fired the first shot and when. Some maintained that the fighting went back to 1856 and the days of "Bleeding Kansas," when free state and slave state advocates clashed in the bloodiest sort of bushwhacking and rangering in the name of their separate causes. In the main, however, those men—Jayhawkers, Redlegs, Border Trash, Missouri Pukes, and all the other names they called themselves or were called by their enemies—had been thugs, or terrorists like John Brown, with little more genuine grasp of the sophisticated issues that propelled the sections apart than they had of so-called civilized modes of warfare. Others would say that the first blows were those that struck down Senator Charles Sumner of Massachusetts when Preston Brooks of South Carolina assaulted him in a cowardly attack from behind with a cane while Sumner was in his seat in the Senate, unable to rise or defend himself. Or was it Brown's October 1859 attack on the Federal arsenal at Harpers Ferry, Virginia, in his crack-brained plot to start a slave insurrection across the South? Still more argued for those shots fired at the Star of the West *in January 1861 in her abortive supply mission to the garrison at Fort Sumter. Or was it the hostile act of those citizens and state forces in every state as it seceded, when they took, usually at gunpoint, possession of fortifications, customshouses, arsenals, post offices, and more Federal property?*

Maybe they were all just echoes of the first shots fired from harquebuses and matchlocks a quarter of a millennium earlier, when settlers in 1607 made their first tentative westward push up the James River for more land and encountered a native obstacle. From the outset, colonists North and South were set on different paths, in part thanks to geography and in part to their own motives and inclinations. New England was never destined to go under the plow of the large-scale planter. Its soil and topography decreed that it would be the realm of small farmers and town dwellers, awaiting the rise of future industry to harness its rivers for power and its natural resources to feed shops and factories. In the South, however, the land encouraged expansive thinking and planting, and that suited the mind of its settlers. Most of those who emigrated from England to the New World came as Englishmen, bent on remaining such and preserving the social and cultural world they knew. Yet those who went to New England came largely just to live in peace, to find religious and intellectual freedom; the ones who landed at Jamestown, and those who followed, came as well to prosper. Prosperity required land, and continued or expanded prosperity needed a constant diet of new territory. Both, of course, also required a lot of cheap labor. Rarely in history did opportunity and need arise so perfectly—and ultimately tragically—timed for one another as in the seventeenth and eighteenth centuries when North American expansion and the burgeoning of the African slave trade came together.

Planting and slavery built a culture and society in the American South that was hardly unique. Variations could be found elsewhere in the British and Spanish empires of the era, with many of the same dynamics in play. Planting and slavery created a ruling planter elite, the usual small and rather stunted middle class of professionals to be found in any agrarian society, and an enormous body of smallholders farming chiefly for subsistence, and scarcely a significant producing or consuming component of a broad economy that came to be dominated by cotton, rice, tobacco, and sugar. Neither were the divisions of class and caste that emerged, based on bloodlines and wealth, anything out of the ordinary. What was different, however, was that unlike Jamaica or Cuba, this culture existed side by side with the different aspirations and values and usages of the North, and after the Revolution actually in the same nation state. There lay the seeds of future discord, for as the two sections each sought its own destiny, they were bound to come into conflict. How could one Federal republican government serve both masters? Could it?

The answer, of course, was that increasingly it could not. Their differences emerged in the Continental Congress's deliberations before declaring independence, and then again more seriously when they framed their Constitution. They came down to two fundamental and contrasting points of view over the nature of government, between those who favored a stronger central authority ideally to promote the strength, security, and prosperity of all, and those who preferred limited government to favor greater local control in the individual states, so that people who best knew their own interests could better serve them. Inextricably intertwined in the question was slavery, and it only became the more so in the years that followed. Socially and culturally North and South were not much different. They prayed to the same deity, spoke the same language, shared the same ancestry, sang the same songs. National triumphs and catastrophes were shared by both. For all the myths they would create to the contrary, the only significant and defining difference between them by the dawn of the nineteenth century was slavery, where it existed and where it did not, for by 1804 it had virtually ceased to exist north of Maryland. Slavery demarked not just their labor and economic systems, but power itself in the new republic. By the nature of their Constitution, there was a natural protection of Southern interests built into the provision for a Senate. No matter how much Northern population outstripped its neighbor's, or how great the imbalance of representation accordingly became in the House of Representatives, so long as the number of slave states was the same as or greater than the number of free states, then in the Senate the South had a check on the government.

Not surprisingly, then, the first great controversies were over settlement and expansion. The South heavily favored Thomas Jefferson's purchase of the Louisiana Territory from France in 1803, and then backed the 1812 war with Britain, seeing the opportunity in both to acquire more territory and new slave states in the Louisiana, Mississippi, and Alabama territories. Then in 1820, with the admission of Missouri as a slave state in the face of Northern opposition, the so-called Missouri Compromise ensured that there would be future slave states below an established line, and at the same time implied that in future admissions there would be a parity between free and slave to preserve an even balance in the Senate.

That calmed the slavery question long enough for economic issues to take the fore, chiefly Henry Clay's American System. An ardent nationalist, he proposed a high protective tariff to encourage domestic manufactures and products, and at the same time a program of spending on "Internal Improvements" such as roads and canals that would encourage

*manufacturing and transportation, and further reduce foreign depen-
dence. Popular in the North and the border states like Clay's Kentucky, his
program outraged many in the South, who ignored the protection the tariff gave to their agricultural produce against cheaper imports and cried out
at having to pay higher prices for Northern manufactures. At the same
time they decried seeing revenue raised in their Southern customshouses
spent on improvements in the North. Even though the great South Carolinian John C. Calhoun had stood with Clay in 1824, many in his state
and elsewhere in the South began to break with him, and by 1827 there
was a growing outcry against the tariff especially. It led, after an even
higher tariff in 1828, to Calhoun's own break with Clay, and the nullification crisis of 1832, when South Carolina declared that a state should have
the right to nullify the operation of a law within its own borders, or else exercise the option of secession. Threats and compromises calmed the waters,
even though the tariff especially would be a sore point for another quarter
century.*

*By then it no longer mattered. Even in 1832 there were those in the
South who confessed that the tariff was only a battlefield, not the war. If
they did not fight their ground and win on the tariff, soon enough they
would be fighting for something even closer to their hearths, slavery itself.
In 1846 the nation went to war with Mexico. Once again the South eagerly
promoted the conflict in the hope of acquiring territory all the way to the
Pacific, and perhaps even all of Mexico itself. Under the terms of the Missouri Compromise, that would provide enough territory for slave states to
guarantee the balance of power. But Pennsylvanian David Wilmot proposed in Congress legislation to prevent slavery from being introduced
into territory taken in the war, since Mexico itself had abolished slavery
decades earlier. That set the fires blazing, and even the group of enactments
constituting the Compromise of 1850, including a Fugitive Slave Law to
return runaways to their masters, could not completely mollify Southern
fears, for California was admitted as a free state at the same time, giving
the free states a majority of one. The balance was broken.*

*Pro-slavery men believed they managed to redress the balance in 1854
when they got President Franklin Pierce to back a repeal of the Missouri
Compromise. Now any new territory could be a slave state, but the reaction in the North was predictable. Anti-slave elements that had always
been a part of the body politic coalesced into a new Republican Party, its
chief tenet opposition to extension of slavery into the territories or the ad-*

mission of any more slave states. What followed became known as Bleeding Kansas, as both sides poured men and money and weapons into the territory, hoping to influence its decision on slavery when it applied for statehood. There were skirmishes, many no better than ambushes, each side charging the other with barbarities, and place names like Lawrence and Osawatomie took on grim meaning. By 1856 the violence reached the floor of the Senate and Charles Sumner. It continued through 1858 as partisans of both sides still fought and cheated and maneuvered to affect the Kansas outcome, and with it the balance of power. As late as 1859 the issue was still in doubt, when one of the men who had helped to make Kansas bloody came east. Out of the pre-dawn gloom of an October morning in 1859, John Brown of Osawatomie and his followers rode out of the night to capture the arsenal at Harpers Ferry, Virginia, their dream being to foment an uprising among Virginia slaves and arm them to take their freedom by force, and then to spread the uprising through the slave states generally. Captured and soon hanged, Brown became a martyr despite his harebrained scheme and its pathetic management. Yet in a way he achieved part of his object, though it would be someone else who rebelled and took arms. Harpers Ferry was the last electric shock sent through the South. It galvanized slave state leaders as nothing before it. Here was proof that with an anti-slave Republican Party now dominant in the North, and men like Brown ready to attack Southern interests with secret, if well-known, backing from the North, the South was no longer safe within the Union. With a presidential election coming in 1860 the danger was even more pressing. Should the Republicans win the White House, what would they not do to prosecute their fell purpose of forever marginalizing the South in national councils?

More to the point, what alternative lay before the South but to seek another home for its loyalty and allegiance? Fifty years earlier William Jenks had imagined what that alternative might be, and during the past half century there had been occasional voices suggesting the same thing, their chorus growing with each new challenge to Southern values and interests. They had been talking, more often shouting, for decades. At last, perhaps, it was time to act.

1

Guiding the Whirlwind

A WAG MIGHT ARGUE that the origins of the Confederacy dated to the philosophy of Aristotle, who proposed that differences arising from race and regional origin and birth created natural distinctions between peoples and their inherent abilities.[1] Yet there is substance in the case beyond Aristotle's speculations on human variations. Writing twenty-two centuries before the breakup of the Union, the Greek philosopher penned in his *Politics* a discussion of what he called "one of the true forms of government," a limited monarchy. There were four varieties, he suggested. The first was that of the Spartans, wherein the king held office, but not absolute power, by birth or election. The second more closely resembled tyranny, yet it was legal and hereditary, established by ancient ancestry, and unchallenged by the people, indeed willingly accepted by them. A third was the dictatorship elected by the people, and thus willingly imposed upon themselves, an office held sometimes for life or else only for a stated term of years. The dictator's power might be despotic, even absolute, yet still he held it at the will of the people. The last form of limited monarch was the hereditary "heroic" king, who held office by virtue of his being able to provide for the people what they could not provide for themselves: organization, land perhaps, leadership in war, community, and more.

The only difference among them was in their degree of sovereignty. All fit in with most of the ideas of the new democracy that appeared in Greece 150 years earlier. No king wielded unlimited power, yet each ruled by

some democratic acknowledgment of his superior skills or accomplish-
ments. All were elected (or at least popularly accepted) and in three of
Aristotle's scenarios the kingship was hereditary, suggesting that certain
families were destined to rule by bloodline and natural gifts. All of the
philosopher's leaders, in short, were elective dictators either for set terms
or for life, yet under their rule the people had some rights, could speak
out, even remove their king if they so chose, and by legal rather than revolutionary means. Authority was questionable, and kings needed to persuade or demonstrate to their subjects that they deserved to rule. Of the
four, the last, the heroic monarchs, seemed clearly Aristotle's preference,
for they were benefactors of the people in return for their high status.
They took command in war, and presided over the sectarian ceremonies as
their societies worshipped their own household gods. "They also decided
causes," said Aristotle, and "their power extended continuously to all
things whatsoever, in city and country." Yet with the passage of time, the
ancient heroic kings had voluntarily relinquished some of their prerogatives, while their people gradually took away others, "until in some states
nothing was left to them but the sacrifices."[2]

Virtually every founding father of the Confederacy who was educated
spent his formative years poring over Aristotle's *Politics,* and by 1861
would have recognized the philosopher's fourth monarch as the model of
the oligarchs who wielded acknowledged social and political rule in the
South, elected and given power in recognition of their superior blood and
ability. Four years later their power would be gone, some of it willingly
ceded to their new government in the interest of its survival, and some
wrested from them by an electorate no longer willing to be led by an elite
who had brought them to disaster. In the end, for those "heroic monarchs"
of the Confederacy, as for Aristotle's elective dictator, "nothing was left to
them but the sacrifices."

A cynic would look for premonitions of the Confederacy at a slightly less
distant date in antiquity, when the Roman statesman Cicero decried the
civil war that broke out in 48 B.C. He blamed the rivals Pompey and Caesar as men who "put personal power and private advantage before the
safety and honour of their country." After his success Caesar paid due service to the forms of republicanism, but in fact chose to rule as an autocrat.
Yet he so persuaded the citizens that he was a democrat that they all but
begged him to take more power as their champion. He quite happily
obliged. Caesar exemplified Aristotle's fourth king, but it is more to the

point that Rome tested the philosopher's musings on human inequality. Virtually all Roman citizens were members of one of thirty-five extended families or tribes, each originally the equal of the other in political decisions. But before long the wealthy and landed tribes acquired greater influence and power than the others, and soon their "colleges," the divisions whereby they voted for their consuls, were redistributed into so-called *classis,* literally "classes." Quickly the wealthier classes aggrandized their power, so the top two classes, though less than 46 percent of the colleges, controlled a majority of the votes in an election. At the other end of the economic spectrum, those with no property at all constituted the bottom class, the *proletarii,* and when it came time for their votes to be counted, they no longer mattered as the upper classes had already decided who the consuls should be. In time the *proletarii* simply became accustomed to following the minority upper classes without their voices even being heard. As Cicero himself argued, "when both the best and worst are given equal honours, equality itself is most unequal," something that could not happen "in states which are governed by the best people." The will of the majority was dying, and the oligarchy was born.

The most bitter observer of the Confederacy might advance half a millennium to the fifth century A.D., when Rome realized that it could no longer administer its empire in the West in the face of barbarian advances, and pulled back, leaving the bulk of a once united Europe to be divided and ruled by local chieftains whose allegiances had traditionally been tribal rather than political, and to kings rather than senates. To them power came by heredity and natural right, not from a popular mandate, and the place in society of the king and the nobles he sustained was unquestioned. No one could hold them to account. Aristotle's monarchs were dead.

The true family tree of the Confederacy, however, fed from much shallower tendrils, and shared a common taproot with conservatism as a political movement and philosophical idea. In Western democracies, potent political parties and ideologies emerged only in the wake of the collapse of the absolute monarchies beginning in the seventeenth century, a collapse that restless, disfranchised populations helped to bring about. Of course the shift to constitutional monarchies, especially in England, did not suddenly give real power to any more than a small percentage of the people, chiefly white male landowners. But far more important, it did remove the protection afforded by an absolute crown to an aristocracy of birth, making it vulnerable for the first time to social inroads and economic competition from the now-franchised middle class, and to the erosion of its hereditary rights to position and power. The ballot box and the suppressed aspirations of commoners posed a greater threat to the security of the landed aristocracy than anything in its history, and the further the franchise spread among the population at large, the more it endangered the rights and privileges of the upper class.

Denied the protection once afforded by an all-powerful monarch, that elite had no choice but to fight back in the same political arena that threatened its position if not its extinction. Thus was born conservatism as an active political idea, though adherents actually referred to themselves as "conservatory" until the early nineteenth century. Conservative or conservatory, the only syllable that really mattered in both was the first, for their inevitable posture in the political whirl was oppositional. From the Glorious Revolution onward, the slow spread of rights and opportunity and the growing power of national legislatures posed an ever greater danger to the aristocrats' status quo. For the protection of their class and their fortunes, their natural position was to resist change. Thus, while forces of the center and left might increasingly use parliaments as forums for active programs to spread rights and wealth—though still only to the middle classes—conservative parties, whatever their names, had no real platforms and no need for them. Their role was simply to oppose legislation that endangered the privileged class they represented. In England "conservatory" was eventually abandoned, to remain in vestige as Tory. The Tories were never proponents of an ideology. They had no real political philosophers, no grand ideas. Instead they represented a tradition of continuity and stability, of sensible government by those who had the greatest interest in good government, the upper classes.

This struggle came to the new colonies in America. Distance from England and slow communications made them slower to react to forces of change, and in some places allowed longer-lasting footholds of aristocratic power. Even though the king appointed royal governors in most of the colonies, still a few like South Carolina under its Lord Proprietors commenced and for some years operated almost as feudal states run by a few powerful families. For all the rhetoric about rights and freedom, the American Revolution, when it came, was largely a conservative movement to protect upper- and middle-class property, including the right to break free of British containment east of the Appalachians in order to obtain cheap or free new land to the west, and for Southerners especially to spread plantation slavery to the wide arable expanses of the Deep South. Even Edmund Burke, in seeking to alleviate the gnawing issue of taxation that helped propel the colonists to revolution, argued that the solution lay in the wisdom gleaned from past experience rather than future innovation. Indeed, genuine ideologues of liberty like Thomas Paine found the results of the Revolution dismaying in their failure to be innovative enough. A disillusioned Paine complained that any kind of government that observed some of the forms of democracy could get away with calling itself republican; he saw that in the years following independence, rights for most Americans were expanded little beyond what they had achieved before the war, the chief difference being that capital and wealth and commercial interests no longer faced the threat of onerous taxation.

The Constitution, at least in the mind of one of its principal architects, James Madison, failed to dent the hold of the landed gentry on power in the states and in the Congress. It left the central government too weak to impose taxes or regulate commerce, unable apparently to overcome the retained sovereignty in such areas held by the states, which were themselves, in the South at least, firmly in the hands of a planter oligarchy. For all their preaching of republicanism during the Revolution, the Americans, Madison feared, had largely only succeeded in making their own aristocracy more secure, and now with the power in the states to stall the spread of real democracy. A substantial body of citizens, again in the slave states especially, had no vote because they had no significant property, and so long as the oligarchs controlled most of the land and slaves, they could contain the democratic threat. At the same time, the middle class, the lawyers and doctors and merchants, who did emerge as a political force, very quickly began to demonstrate how quickly "have-nots" can adopt the values of the "haves" when they begin to acquire a little wealth themselves.

Suddenly throughout the United States, legislatures began pandering to a host of groups promoting parochial interests. Madison complained in 1786 that state legislatures had enacted more laws in the three years since independence than had been passed in the previous hundred, a staggering number of them designed solely to serve special entrenched interests. Ideologically, he feared, the Revolution had been a failure. Republicanism in the Union, as Paine declared before abandoning America altogether, was a sham. Just as in a courtroom no man could act as a judge in his own case, argued Madison, so in politics there could be no equity when the men making the laws were the ones who benefited from them, yet in Virginia and South Carolina, as well as in the Northern states, such was precisely the case. When legislation was proposed dealing with the problem of widespread debt, the creditors who stood to gain composed one party, while the debtors belonged to the other, neither arguing for universal justice, but both pressing for personal benefit. Naively Madison had hoped that under the Constitution the new government would stand above partisan politics to act solely in the national interest. That could happen only if the Congress and president enjoyed ultimate power over the states, however, and that the Constitution failed to provide.

Indeed, had such power been on the table in Philadelphia during the framing convention, the Constitution surely never would have been ratified. By then the dominant figures in the several oligarchies who ruled the slave states especially had already adopted a certain cant of republicanism that allowed them to use the vernacular of freedom, independence, and liberty to denounce absolute authorities whether they be kings or central governments, seemingly allying themselves with the general population while they really acted only in the cause of protecting themselves. In short, they sought the best of both worlds. If they had no supreme authority like a king to protect them, neither could he infringe their own rights. If they had to live in a more democratic society, at least by preaching the religion of liberty they could attract and win the votes of the broader electorate and use them to limit the spread of real democracy, while keeping power to themselves. Instead of solving a problem, democracy, as it was being practiced, had itself become a part of the problem.[3] No wonder that in 1808 William Jenks could see the difficulties arising in the new system, and at the same time discern through his parody the underlying desire of Southern men of property to return to a form of monarchy.

Meanwhile many people of the South, like the North, fed on the rhetoric of the Revolution and the euphoria of new independence, and embarked on the world of new possibilities presented by their ownership of a seemingly horizonless continent. The sons of the founders, growing up in an atmosphere of self-conscious independence and individualism, did not have to face the issue of severing old loyalties as had their fathers. Instead, they had before them new attachments to form, and of their own choosing. Not limited to what their old world had been, they could dream of what they might make of their new one.[4] Though Paine and even Madison despaired, the Revolution had succeeded in unleashing an idea of a republic, an idea that would eventually overwhelm all conservatives who resisted its

implications. Southern leadership stood apart by being the only oligarchs
in history to hold power by means other than military might. Instead they
had the strength of democracy working for them, but only so long as they
could control the direction that democracy took. In the first decades of the
nineteenth century, politics in almost every Southern state was dominated
by a few families. In Virginia it was the Masons, the Randolphs, and other
descendants of those they self-consciously referred to as the first families.
In South Carolina it was the Rhetts, the Calhouns and their cousins, the
Hugers and more. Louisiana divided its leadership between old Creole
families like the Héberts and Anglo dynasties like the Livingstons and
Claibornes. Even the more recently settled and organized states like Mississippi and Tennessee had their new aristocracies, often defined by their
blood ties to family in the older original states.

As the new century progressed, and in the face of one challenge after
another to the Southern oligarchy's control of Southern affairs, the danger
even of limited democracy became more and more apparent. Looking as
they did to England as a conservative model, Southerners were not unaware of the Tory member of Parliament William Mackworth Praed, once
a radical, but a man who had become increasingly conservative as he saw a
spreading franchise threaten entrenched interests. He bought his seat in
Parliament by spending a thousand pounds to buy the "rotten borough" of
St. Germans. In 1831 when Parliament considered legislation abolishing
most of the rotten boroughs and putting their seats up for general election,
Praed supported the spirit of the act, but then made the decidedly undemocratic protest that allowing too many people to vote risked giving the governed too much say in their own affairs. He predicted that a time might
come when a vital question would arise in which "a minority of number,
but a majority of property and intelligence" might be pitted against "a
large majority, of number, but a minority, perhaps an insignificant minority, of property and intelligence." In short, men who did not own property
were not intelligent enough to act in the best interests of the entire community. Oligarchies based on wealth and property and heredity, on the
other hand, produced men worthy to make public decisions. Absolute
democracy posed a positive danger to a republic. True democracy threatened the whole idea of "the great man," and the longer a society like the
one that grew up in the South flourished, the more individualistic it became. And such a society positively encouraged men of ambition to con-

fuse their own ends with those of the state, for what preserved the one served the other.

It all depended on conflating the old conservative economic and class systems with the trappings and forms of a very limited democracy. At first, almost all of the new American states did so. Limitation of the franchise to white males who owned property—sometimes even a required minimum net worth—was practically universal before, during, and immediately after the Revolution. Gradually the free states and newer states formed in the Old Northwest liberalized voting, but still by the middle of the nineteenth century most states, and all of them in the South, did not allow the voters themselves to elect senators to Congress. The legislatures kept that power to themselves. Being largely composed of an elite, they could thus choose their own men to the Senate to represent their own interests, if necessary, against delegates sent to the House of Representatives by the general electorate. Some states like South Carolina went farther, retaining the election of state cabinet officials and even of governors in the legislature as well. The control of power had become so cozy and clubbable that the leading men openly discussed trading the chief offices on a sort of rotation from attorney general to governor to senator, among the Calhouns and Pickens, the Rhetts and Elmores, the Hammonds and the Elliotts. Others used the property requirements to ensure that men sent to the House were likely to come from and represent the propertied classes. Virginia land west of the Appalachians was worth very little, being unsuitable for much more than subsistence farming, or for the slaves needed for large-scale planting, and thus became the domain chiefly of small farmers. The state's constitution demanded that a voter hold property valued to such an extent that a landowner in the western counties could have hundreds of acres and still not reach the qualifying benchmark. Yet a Tidewater or Piedmont planter east of the mountains, with even modest holdings of that much more valuable acreage, easily reached the threshold. Moreover, a man with little or no land at all could still vote if he owned just three or four slaves, for the market value of a single prime black could be greater than that of a hundred acres of flinty western soil. As a result, from the foundation of the Old Dominion right to the moment of secession in 1861, not a single Virginian from west of the mountains was ever elected governor or senator.

The longevity of such a system depended heavily on the preservation of a social order in which the opportunity to rise stopped at the middle class.

Even the later slave states to come into the Union, those like Mississippi and Alabama and Tennessee, which had no long history of settlement and thus no old oligarchy bent on self-preservation, also followed the pattern as immigrant planters from the older states quickly took hold and brought the old system with them. Louisiana, of course, came into the Union with an old Creole oligarchy already well entrenched, and of all the slave states, only Arkansas and Texas west of the Mississippi were really free of rule by an elite of birth. It is not just coincidental that of all of the various collective and socialist utopian communities that tried their new order experiments in America in the half century before the Civil War, not one attempted to take root in the lower South. It was soil that grew cotton and tobacco and rice, but not egalitarian democracy or social reformation. To the Rhetts and others who stood solidly for minority rule of a compliant populace, the Enlightenment was just something that happened to other people.

This political order was supported by the other pillars of Southern society. Religion, especially the stern Presbyterianism and the even sterner Baptism, encouraged a conservative outlook, while the Catholic and Episcopal Churches mirrored in their hierarchy the sort of authoritarian minority rule that suited the oligarchs. Indeed, long before the final eruption of the sectional controversy, some Southern spokesmen proclaimed that the features of their society and culture were sufficiently distinct that they were in effect a separate people from the North—that they were, in fact, a Southern race that deserved their own nation state.

What they failed to learn from history was that race had never been a defining element in successful nation states. The true definitions always depended far more on distinctions in language, culture, and political institutions. Southerners spoke precisely the same language as Northerners, so there was no distinction there. As for their cultures, despite certain isolated pockets like the Creoles of Louisiana—and ignoring the distinct cultures of the aboriginal Americans and free and slave blacks, who were not a part of the body politic in any case—virtually no differences existed between the sections. They were all, by 1850, solidly in the mainstream of western Victorian culture. They read the same books, listened to the same songs, ate predominantly the same foods despite some regional variations, and buried and mourned their dead in precisely the same fashion. The only substantial difference between them, and the one that divided them politically almost since birth, was their systems of labor. Nevertheless, the idea of being inherently different proved attractive to Southerners. Ideas of nationhood were historically more appealing to agricultural peoples like Southerners, whose lack of mobility made them more personally involved with their place and tradition, but without a distinct language and culture, and without some special liberality in their political institutions to set them apart from the North, they were nothing more than citizens of a region. They might have been dogs with some different spots from their Northern brethren, but that did not make them a separate breed.[5]

Besides, if Southerners had paid more attention to Alexis de Tocqueville, whose *Democracy in America* and *The Old Regime* they certainly read, they would have seen that it was not in the oligarchs' interest for the South to be a separate nation. One of the lessons Tocqueville drew was that nation states inevitably tended to aggrandize themselves and centralize power. The South and Southern political and social traditions only flourished because power was not concentrated in Washington, though the tendency appeared to be in that direction. Becoming a nation state themselves only risked accelerating the process because the region to be involved would have been dramatically smaller, and history demonstrated to the French observer that geography was itself an inhibitor to centralization. In short, the South had a far better chance of preserving its institutions and quirks of culture by remaining a part of a larger nation.

Another Southern advantage, from the oligarchs' point of view, was its modest middle class, which extended little beyond members of the professions like physicians and lawyers. Even Tocqueville declared that lawyers were not democrats, and thus no threat to an elitist order. Only a larger and ambitious capitalist class or the overwhelming pressure of labor seeking more entitlement and a rise to power could really pose a threat to the oligarchy. Thanks to slavery, in the South capital and labor were combined in nearly four million sweating field hands picking cotton and planting rice. They were numerous enough to pose a serious threat to the elite, but they had no power whatever. Free white property owners had a right to the political power to offer such a challenge but not the numbers.

Not a few Southern statesmen representing the common people tried to highlight the way they were being used. "How long will you suffer politicians to flatter you as sovereigns and *use you as victims,* without awakening your resentment?" Benjamin H. Hill asked a Georgia audience. "How often shall they *settle* and *unsettle* the slavery question before you discover the *only meaning* they have, is to excite your prejudices and get your votes? For how many years shall changing demagogues shuffle you as the gambler shuffles his cards—to win a stake—and still find you willing to be shuffled again?"[6] Taken altogether, Southern leaders enjoyed the best they could hope for in both the worlds they inhabited by the 1850s. At home their domination of statehouse and courthouse was unchallenged, while in Washington, even though the slave states were by now a minority, still as a bloc they were more than strong enough to stop any legislation that threatened themselves or their "institutions"—meaning slavery—in their own bailiwicks. Only two things could afford them better protection in the current circumstances, and Jenks had put his finger on both—a monarch at home and independent nationhood from the North. Their own generations-old protestations against kings and the republican rhetoric they preached precluded the former. As for the latter, the march of events made independence seem inevitable to many.

Robert Barnwell Rhett, in fact, had raised the shadow of a Southern nation as far back as the 1830s, and others, mostly extremists like himself, turned to it again and again during the sectional turmoil of the next two decades. In 1858, Alabama's leading "fire-eating" secessionist, William L. Yancey, was predicting "a Southern Confederacy," even suggesting that the giant state of Texas might be its leading element (though he said that to prominent Texan and fire-eater Senator Louis T. Wigfall, no doubt to flatter him into staying in line on secession).[7] Martin Crawford of Georgia thought that the contest for the Speakership in the House of Representatives in the spring of 1860 might be the catalyst to send slave states out of the Union, but lamented that though the South had men willing to take the risk, none of them had the general confidence of the country. They had no coordination among themselves. Indeed, so focused were secessionists on the independence of their individual states that no one seemed to make the effort to get them working together. Too many remembered that only ten years before, when South Carolina's Rhett was discovered trying to conspire with Mississippi's Governor John A. Quitman to promote secession in both states, each resorted to lying in the resultant furor over someone from one state interfering in the internal affairs of another, and Quitman abandoned his efforts altogether. "We might possibly be supported by the public judgment," Crawford lamented now, "but as it is I fear the people would be disgusted and we should be disgraced."[8]

Yancey hoped to solve that problem by uniting the slave states in one movement that could quickly be transformed into another. He did a lot of cajoling of men like Wigfall in the months leading up to the Democratic National Convention in Charleston in 1860. The best hope for precipitating secession was the election of a Republican president that year. With the Republicans still a minority party, however, the only way to ensure their victory was to split the Democrats. The candidate of the Northern wing of the Democratic Party, Stephen A. Douglas, had provided the issue with his doctrine of "popular sovereignty," declaring that the people in a newly formed territory could decide for themselves whether to embrace or exclude slavery prior to forming their constitution and applying for statehood. Southern pro-slave men argued that the question could only be settled at the actual time of achieving statehood. The difference was crucial. If settlers—or "squatters," as the condescending Southern elite called them—could prohibit slavery prior to statehood, then slaveowners could not move to the territory and bring their slaves with them, virtually guaranteeing that it would become a future free state. Only if the decision were made at achieving statehood would slave proponents have the opportunity to settle the territory and have their voice heard in deciding the issue, and perhaps bring another slave state into the Union. At stake was a balance of power in the Senate in Washington, the only place the South could hope to protect itself as Northern population rapidly outstripped that of the South, placing the House of Representatives increasingly in the hands of free state men. The issue was critical enough that it could divide the Democratic Party, the only truly national political organization left, and that is what Yancey and Rhett and other hopeful secessionists wanted. If Southern Democrats refused to support the almost certain candidacy of Douglas in 1860, then their bolting from the party would hand the election to the exclusively Northern Republicans, and the election of a president who represented strictly a sectional constituency could be enough to propel slave states into action.

There was nothing sophisticated in the scheme, nor was its operation a secret. It was a case of simple mathematics and, ironically, democracy. A generation earlier radicals like Rhett had decried political nominating conventions as being undemocratic, in that they gave undue influence to the larger states that naturally enough sent bigger delegations. Now, however, they could use that same system to their advantage, especially since a number of Northern Democrats also opposed "popular sovereignty," and would side with their more conservative Southern brethren. Assuming that the Republican candidate carried most or all of the Northern states, all the Democratic dissidents had to do was deny Douglas a handful of the smaller Southern states to hand the election to the Yankees. "I very much regret myself the divisions in the Democratic Party," complained Alexander H. Stephens of Georgia, whose own name was briefly bandied about as a possible candidate before he scotched the idea. A Unionist, he had no desire to become one of the pawns in the radicals' game.[9] When the Charleston convention did, as predicted, break up in a Southern walkout, the delegates determined to convene again in June in Baltimore. But when state Democratic conventions were held to choose delegates to Baltimore, disruption was all but guaranteed. In Yancey's Alabama the president of the convention could not even get a delegation selected at first, and predicted that Southerners would pull out of the Baltimore meeting, too, and form their own sectional convention to put forward their own candidate. "The split is now inevitable," James Saunders lamented to his wife, and in the whole mess he saw a lot of personal ambition involved. "A disinterested man is very much admired," he declared, "and excites some wonder."[10]

As the election fall approached, some attempted to reconstitute the old Democratic Party in states like Georgia, yet even they, men like Henry Cleveland in Augusta, feared it was to no point. Worse, he expected that in the wake of the election of the Republican nominee Abraham Lincoln, a clash between state militia and United States troops would be inevitable that winter as seceding states tried to reclaim property at Federal forts and arsenals within their borders.[11]

The likelihood of such a clash became ever greater with the formation of local defense associations. In October a number of distinguished South Carolinians including former governor James Adams, Maxcy Gregg, Langdon Cheves, and others organized themselves "with a view to the defense of the rights of the South," as one put it. They drafted a constitution, and then started liaison with other similar committees in Georgia and elsewhere, mirroring their forefathers' committees of correspondence on the eve of the Revolution. Their goal was to "perhaps accomplish something towards putting the South in a state of preparation for the issue that is almost upon us."[12] Soon thereafter similar organizations sprang up in all of the other slave states. Newspaperman Charles E.L. Stuart was a member of one of the Virginia "hives," as he called them. "These manufactured, as circumstances suggested with regard to time and topic, flaming dispatches, which were sent off and paraded at a convention, a public meeting or through the local journals." The communications were almost always unsigned, merely attributed to "high authority," and as Stuart himself, one of the authors, freely admitted, "were chiefly inflammatory fabrications, suited to the provocations wanted." Of course they were remedying the very problem that Crawford had decried earlier that year, but they were doing more. They were also making the first organized moves toward interstate cooperation in the crisis, moves that presaged a day when the slave states might consider some more formal organization for their "state of preparation." Moreover, the personal associations that brought their authors and promulgators together began an informal and unnamed "party," and saw the first signs of an even less organized opposition among those who either did not favor secession at all, or who wanted only to threaten to secede in order to get concessions from the North, or those "cooperationists" who would accept secession but only if several states "cooperated" by going out at the same time.[13]

The issue hit them as they predicted—indeed, wanted—when Lincoln achieved less than 40 percent of the popular vote, but took enough states—all in the North—to capture an electoral college victory. The immediate furor in the slave states was as intense as it was predictable. In Virginia all guests at the home of politician James Seddon had to listen to him talk ceaselessly of secession and revolution. At once a Virginia journalist named Littleton B. Washington began writing anonymous secession editorials for the Richmond *Examiner,* and "syndicating" them to papers as far away as Charleston and Montgomery, Alabama.[14] In Alabama itself Governor A. B. Moore told citizens there was no alternative now to secession, and called for the formation of a new "Southern Confederacy," while the press in the state capital declared that "the religious institution of slavery" deserved its own nation.[15] Yancey exulted that "nothing can long keep the cotton States in this Union." Just a week after Lincoln's election, he declared that only one state seceding would "by all natural laws" lead others to follow, "until in process of no distant day, there will be a Confederacy of Southern Atlantic and Gulf States, doing justice to others and securing peace, justice and independence to its own members."[16]

In Mississippi, Governor John J. Pettus summoned the state's congressional delegation to the capital for a special conference to discuss "the safety of Mississippi in the present emergency."[17] Next door in Louisiana, Governor Thomas Moore seemed to apprehend more fully than most the consequences of what was about to happen. He still felt an abiding affection for the old Union despite all the provocations. Barely a week before the election, broadsides proclaiming "The Indications of the Coming Storm" appeared on Louisiana streets. "The slavery agitation will soon make the North and the South *two separate nations,* unless it can cease, of which we have little hope," they declared. "We can never submit to Lincoln's inauguration; the shades of Revolutionary sires will rise up to shame us if we shall do that," they proclaimed. "Let us drop all discussions and form a Union of the South."[18] Certainly Moore decried the election of a purely sectional candidate like Lincoln who was a dedicated enemy of slavery. Nevertheless, "I so value the Union of these States, and would regard its dissolution as so great a calamity, that I cannot obtain the assent of my mind and heart to the adoption of a measure, or the execution of any project, which would cast us off," he declared, "without giving the Northern people one more opportunity."

He sent a message to his legislature suggesting a convention of all the slave states to settle on an ultimatum to the North that would set forth the conditions on which they would consent to remain thereafter in the Union. But it should be an ultimatum, he said, and not a basis for negotiation. "We have had enough, and too much, of compromises already," he warned. What they proposed to the North should be all or nothing. They must have a promise that Yankees would stop impeding the enforcement of the Fugitive Slave Law by harboring runaways who escaped to the North. They must have a guarantee of their right to move into the new territories with their slaves and thus have a say in the final makeup of future states. "I am not an advocate for the immediate secession or withdrawal of Louisiana from the Federal Union," he assured his assembly. "I maintain the right of secession and do not admit the right of the government at Washington City to obstruct the exercise [of] that right." Ironically, he wrote his message on paper carrying a watermark of the old Stars and Stripes, and the motto "Don't Tread on Me."[19] As far north as New York City, Southern sympathizers spoke of organizing themselves into the "Metropolitan Minute Men" to be ready to offer themselves to the Southern states in the event of secession and a conflict.[20]

All of this was before the first state seceded. Indeed, even before South Carolina, the first to move, could convene a state convention to act on secession, men were laying plans, and many counseled caution. In Washington representatives from the slave states had been meeting in groups large and small repeatedly for some time. At the same time a host of lesser

lights—clerks, newspapermen, businessmen, and simple political dilet-
tantes—caught up in a sort of comic opera romanticism over what they
were doing, formed little clubs for which they adopted names like the
Spartan, the Dixie, the Calhoun, and the Southern. Their goal was twofold:
to get information out of Washington to feed the secession movement at
home, while applying pressure on the slave state representatives in Congress to propel them toward definitive action. The outright secessionists
like Robert Toombs of Georgia, Wigfall of Texas, and Thomas Clingman of
North Carolina were their champions, though each stood well ahead of his
state on the secession issue at the moment. These so-called Coral Reefers
directed much of their attention toward moderates like Senators Jefferson
Davis of Mississippi and Clement Clay of Alabama, men still professing attachment to the Union, even while admitting that the South enjoyed the
right of secession, and that the time *might* be at hand. Of greatest concern
to the Reefers were men like Alexander H. Stephens of Georgia, Toombs's
best friend, who positively opposed secession, and James Mason of Virginia, who continued to counsel caution and moderation and concilia-
tion.[21]

Meanwhile, Howell Cobb and Toombs of Georgia met regularly with
Davis and Jacob Thompson of Mississippi, Benjamin Fitzpatrick and Clay
of Alabama, Wigfall and John Reagan of Texas, Mason and R.M.T. Hunter
of Virginia, John Slidell of Louisiana, and other leading men from all of the
slave states. The Reefers bombarded them with views, information, and
pressure of none too subtle a nature, some of it coming from the society
hostesses. "They struggled strenuously and unceasingly to edge the Congressional extremists on to the last stretch of violence," said the journalist
Stuart, "and to promt, prop up and incite the moderates." Ultimately their
goal was to persuade all of the slave state delegates to walk out of Congress, but most were unwilling to do so without being so instructed by
their own state governors or legislatures. Significantly, the South Carolina
delegates in Congress were not participating in the high-level meetings
because for the moment these gatherings, despite the efforts of the Reefers,
chiefly hoped to prevent the Palmetto State from moving precipitately.
Only South Carolina had the unanimity within the state leadership to be
able to pass a secession ordinance right away, and immediately after Lincoln's election the governor had summoned a special convention to debate
that very act. It would meet in mid-December and no one doubted the
outcome. But the other states were not as ready, facing as they did much

more reluctance within their electorates. For that reason, these men thought it best that South Carolina postpone seceding until February 1, 1861. By that time, they felt, Alabama, Mississippi, and Georgia would also be ready to move, and then the four states could secede in a bloc, to greater effect not only in the North but also with other slave states not yet galvanized for action.

Among the most insistent on this policy was Jefferson Davis, even though it won for him a growing suspicion and even distrust among some of the most ardent fire-eaters.[22] Unfortunately, the presence of journalists among the Reefers also meant that the reluctance of these men to act quickly became fairly common knowledge. That created the earliest signs of rift in the secessionist ranks, for more dedicated radicals like Rhett suspected that this was a sign that Davis especially, the acknowledged leading statesman in the South, did not have his heart in the cause, and wanted delay in the hope of compromise. Worse, some feared that Davis was at heart a Unionist and was willing to submit to Yankee domination. Therein lay the seeds of the one dangerous divide in the Southern leadership. If a new slave state nation were to be formed after secession, some idealists hoped that it might be a government without parties and partisan politics, since in seceding they would be leaving behind them most, if not all, of the issues that had been contentious. Many like Rhett believed along with Madison and others that political parties were at root evil because they encouraged men to act for the benefit of the party rather than the people, promoted demagoguery, and inevitable compromises of rights and liberties for the sake of gaining or keeping power. Of course, just such actions had characterized Rhett's entire political life, but utterly blind to failings in himself, he was completely unaware of his hypocrisy as he called for reform in others. This fundamental matter of just who was sound on secession, and at what point, inserted a small wedge between the ultras, like Rhett and Toombs and Wigfall, and the more cautious, like Davis. If time produced more issues that widened the crack, then the emergence at least of factionalism in any new nation would be inevitable, with opposing parties quite possible as a consequence, and that did not bode well for a movement that would need all the unanimity it could get.

Despite their apparent desire to keep their meetings secret, the Southern leaders in the capital unwisely allowed sympathetic journalists like Stuart and Washington to be fully apprised of their discussions, perhaps hoping that their pens would advance the cause. "I was kept advised of all the moves on the board," Washington would boast, while Stuart later attested, "I know of their organizations and of their influences." Stuart recoiled from calling them conspirators and preferred to refer to the several such groups meeting in the capital as "combiners." They met in several places, usually the rented rooms of one or another, but most often they gathered at the convivial home of well-placed society widow Rose O'Neal Greenhow, not far from the White House. "It was there that their devisements received the finishing touch," he recalled. They sent working committees out most evenings after congressional business was done, to sound support, solicit advice, and send more "from the highest authority" information south to the state committees who were working on propaganda. They also began to note those Southerners in Washington who were reliable in the cause and those who seemed to waver. Society even had its influence within this nascent "combination," for Southern congressmen who were bachelors or whose families were not with them in the capital, and who thus had no distractions of keeping house, were able to spend more time at the work than men like Davis who lived with his wife and children in the city. Indeed, the number of men without wives present inevitably meant that a lot of their work was conducted on social occasions at the homes of fellow Coral Reefers whose wives could entertain them. "Not one of these faithful 'fair ones' was winning to look at," said an unchivalrous Stuart, "but, though not at all personally captivating, they were not deficient in the arts of capturing the men or the matters upon which the Coral Reefers set them." Greenhow, especially, proved successful in flattering and cajoling information out of members of President James Buchanan's cabinet and Northern senators.[23]

The effort to reach a consensus also failed, for no one was going to be able to control the secessionist impulse in South Carolina, or in other states for that matter, and several of them were closer to action than their representatives in Washington realized. Florida was raising militia companies and commissioning officers by the middle of December even before its state convention convened, while Mississippi and South Carolina already had commissioners traveling as ambassadors to other slave states to promote secession even before they seceded themselves.[24] William L. Harris of Mississippi appeared before Georgia's legislature on December 17 and declared that it was time to act. The election of Lincoln was a virtual declaration of political and social war on the South, he told them. In outrageous exaggeration and outright lies, Harris said that the North was demanding abolition, political suffrage, and social equality for slaves, and worse, that it wanted to destroy the white race by forcing Southern white women to marry black men. "To-day our government stands *totally revolutionized,* in its main features," he declared, "and our Constitution broken and overturned." Their ancestors had made the Union for the white man, "rejecting the negro, as an ignorant, inferior, barbarian race, incapable of self-government, and not, therefore, entitled to be associated with the white man upon terms of civil, political, or social equality." Mississippi, for its part, was "sick and tired of the North, and pants for some respite from eternal disturbance and disquiet." It would secede and press for a new confederation under the existing Constitution.[25]

Even before Harris spoke, J.L.M. Curry of Alabama had warned his people that Lincoln intended to send an abolition army of half a million to subjugate the South, free their slaves, and force them to "amalgamate the poor man's daughter and the rich man's buck-nigger."[26] They might not be able to inflame poor non-slaveholding whites to secession and possible war to protect the planter's investment in slaves, but an appeal to fears of racial amalgamation cut across class lines. Many of the yeomen could not vote, but they could fight if the aristocracy managed to persuade them that it was in their own interest to defend Southern democracy as it existed. Economic arguments afforded little incentive in that direction, but racial and social ones did. A poor man might count for very little, but he was still free and white, which at least made him better than a free black or a slave, and in a society deeply dominated by class and caste, that was something worth fighting for.

Even before the first secession convention met in Charleston on December 17, Howell Cobb of Georgia lent his voice to the call for unity of action. As soon as a few states had seceded, he said, they should send delegates to a convention. For several weeks now others called for a meeting of delegates from the slave states. Some wanted to do it before the secession ball rolled, but Cobb saw that as a waste of precious time. They should secede first. Afterward would be the time for meetings, but when they did confer, he said, it must be in order to take action. What he meant, of course, was that they must form a government.

South Carolina would be first, as it had always been at the forefront of the movement for a different democracy. The fever rose to such a pitch that merely being nominated to serve in the forthcoming secession convention was tantamount to election.[27] The hotheads almost looked forward to a confrontation with the North that might follow. Rumors circulated that at a secession rally a few days before the election, Rhett had boasted that he would eat the bodies of everyone slain in any war resulting from secession, while Senator James Chesnut declared that he would join Rhett at the banquet by drinking all the blood shed.[28] There were calmer appetites, to be sure, more cautious heads, but too few ears to listen, especially among the younger men reared on decades of rhetoric of confrontation and bluster. Years later one of them asked Christopher G. Memminger of Charleston, himself a secessionist, "why did not you older men take all of us young enthusiasts and hold us down?" Memminger's reply spoke not just for South Carolina but for the slave South itself during these months of upheaval. "Oh! it was a whirlwind," he said, looking back, "and all we could do was to try to guide it."[29]

It took only a few hours after the South Carolina convention heard the first gavel for the delegates to decide unanimously for secession. Indeed, the debates were a mere formality. Three days later they solemnly signed the ordinance of secession before a cheering crowd. Rhett himself fell to his knees and lifted his hands heavenward in prayer and thanks when he approached the table to sign. The citizens at large reacted with enthusiasm. South Carolina "has acted nobly and history will accord to her the noble part she has played," wrote T. H. Spann of Woodlawn. "We have been grossly cheated by the North and I would rather that every soul of us would be exterminated than we should be allied to her again." Moreover, he knew that there were many truehearted men in the North who would sympathize with them and help protect them from Yankee malice. "When our Southern Confederacy is formed and in full operation, we will be the gainers and the North the losers." Should the Union attempt to coerce them back into its cold embrace, Southerners would fight to the death. "Let them commence the war," he declared, "and we will wage it with them until the last drop of blood is spent before we will submit."[30]

The same day that the ordinance passed, December 20, Rhett reiterated a call made the day before to send an invitation to the other slave states to meet for the purpose of forming a new confederation, and a few days later added the suggestion that they all meet in February 1861 in Montgomery, the home of his spiritual protégé Yancey. On December 31 the convention agreed to the call for a meeting and elected commissioners to travel to sister slave states as apostles. They further proposed that every seceding state should send a number of delegates to the planned conven-

tion, equal to the size of the congressional delegation formerly sent to
Washington. That guaranteed a degree of proportional representation in
the debate, but then in a quick retreat to the oligarchy's fundamental distrust of simple majority rule, they also called for states to vote as units in
the convention, one state one vote. Thus the smallest state, Florida, under
this scheme entitled to only three delegates, would carry the same weight
on a ballot as the largest, Georgia, with ten. Every state was certain to send
a few less propertied men to such a convention, men whose personal interests might not impel them to stand behind the planter elite. If each delegate had an individual vote, the possibility for mischief would exist,
whereas they would usually be secure in expecting that a majority within
any state delegation would fall in line in determining that state's one vote.
South Carolina wanted to be certain that no misguided egalitarianism led
to an excess of democracy. After all, that was partially what they were seceding from.[31]

Even before sending their missionaries out on January 3, 1861, determined to seek a Montgomery meeting on February 4, the convention went
on with its own revolution, for at the moment South Carolina was an independent nation in its own eyes, and thus far the only one of the slave states
to secede. This new nation, whether one state or many, intended to hold
onto as much as possible of the fabric of the old Union. Judicial power immediately concerned them, and here they wanted no reform, for the old
system had served their interests well. The delegates passed ordinances
maintaining the existing courts, keeping admiralty and maritime jurisdiction in Charleston, adopting the United States statutes at large for the time
being, and retaining all currently serving Federal employees in their positions for the convenience of the state. They passed an ordinance reverting
all state power formerly ceded to Congress back to the legislature, with the
notable exception of the authority to impose duties and customs, management of a postal service, and the power to make alliances with other states
and treaties with foreign nations, and to declare war. That authority the
convention kept to itself. In effect that meant there were two assemblies
wielding power in South Carolina: the legislature, elected conventionally
to run the day-to-day affairs of the state, and the convention, also popularly
elected, but for the specific purpose of charting its course regardless of the
legislature. Whereas the legislature represented the people at large and
was therefore a more conservative body, the convention consisted of delegates all elected on the basis of their stand on secession alone, and their

unanimity when they voted for the ordinance evidenced their like minds on other issues affecting the interests of the planters who had guided the movement from the start.

Further to cement its hold on the state's destiny, the convention went on to define citizenship in the new state. Everyone resident on the date of secession should be a citizen, as should every free white person born within its borders in the future, or the child of any male citizen born elsewhere. Furthermore, citizens of other states still a part of the United States could achieve citizenship if they moved to South Carolina within twelve months and took an oath of allegiance, and after that any resident for seven months or longer who took such an oath might become a citizen. Any man serving in the state's military or naval forces could also qualify, as could aliens who underwent the customary naturalization process. All must swear an oath abjuring fealty "to every prince, potentate, State or Sovereignty whatsoever," except to South Carolina. At the same time, the convention also defined treason to South Carolina as being the levying of war against the state or aiding its enemies, making the offense punishable by death "without benefit of clergy."[32]

Outside the convention hall, other bodies were adjusting themselves to what was happening. The South Carolina synod of the "Old School" Presbyterian Church met to adopt a resolution declaring that resistance was their duty to God, who gave them their rights; to their ancestors, who had preserved those rights in the blood of the Revolution; to their own children, for whom those rights were an inheritance; and even to their slaves, "whom men that know them not, nor care for them as we do, would take from our protection."[33]

On January 1, 1861, Governor Francis Pickens issued commissions to the state's emissaries to the other secession conventions meeting in the remaining slave states, and soon the men were on their way.[34] Meanwhile he and others turned their eyes toward Charleston Harbor, in which sat an artificial island of rubble upon which the Union had constructed as-yet unfinished Fort Sumter. When secession passed, the United States garrison at nearby Fort Moultrie did not pack up and leave as had been hoped. Instead the Yankee soldiers shifted to Fort Sumter, where their very presence astride the main ship channel seemed an affront to the newly sovereign state's prickly sense of honor. Ardent secessionists as far away as Virginia regarded this act alone as one of "hostility and coercion," as Littleton Washington declared. The state convention sent commissioners to Washington, DC, to try to negotiate the turnover of the fort, but by December 31, Littleton Washington, his finger on a number of pulses in the Union capital, concluded that the Yankees would instead attempt to resupply and reinforce the fort. When the commissioners came to the same conclusion, they feared to use the telegraph to warn Pickens to prepare to resist such an attempt, and instead sent Washington to Richmond, from which he could safely send the word over a wire free from unsafe ears. In the days ahead Littleton Washington would be furnished more information to pass on, including warning that the ship *Star of the West* was being dispatched for a resupply.[35] "What do the authorities in Washington mean?" puzzled an outraged Alabamian at the news. "Will they persist in the attempt to co-erce sovereign states? If so we shall have war & to their hearts content."[36] When she arrived off Charleston, a few shells sent her way from shore bat-teries discouraged any effort to succor the garrison in Fort Sumter. In-stead, efforts at reaching some kind of negotiated settlement stumbled on. Meanwhile, Charleston soon teemed with Southern volunteers whom T. H. Spann described as "panting" for a shot at the foe. "When the time does come," he boasted, and regardless of the outcome of any politicians' talks, "we care not who fires the first gun."[37]

2

Shadowy Words,
Shadowy Meanings

SOON SOUTH CAROLINA would no longer be alone. The North had driven the slave states "into madness & desperation," lamented a Kentuckian just after the new year. "South Carolina has already seceded, and other cotton states seem determined to follow in their foolish and mad course."[1] Certainly at the first word of South Carolina's ordinance, the secessionists in Washington redoubled their efforts. Secretary of the Treasury Howell Cobb and Secretary of War John B. Floyd resigned their posts almost immediately to go home and promote the movement in Georgia and Virginia, respectively, to no little displeasure among Reefers in their cabinet departments who had looked to them not only for leadership, but also for "spoils" in any newly formed Southern confederation. The journalist Charles E.L. Stuart, himself a bitter Reefer who never got what he thought he deserved for his efforts, grumbled that "in the coalescence between the faithful Coral Reefers and the mammoths of place and power, the latter may not have thought the former trifles, but the former had good and painful reasons to denounce a few of the latter as triflers." Such bitterness and disappointed ambition among those of the civil servant stratum was just another blow on the wedge to widen existing divisions, now adding envy and spite as powerful divisive allies with policy differences.[2]

Though Jefferson Davis and the other senators in Washington continued to meet to try to arrange some control or coordination on the "whirlwind," in the end all they could do was issue a joint statement after a last conference on January 5. Even those reluctant to come to secession agreed that South Carolina's action and the apparent unwillingness of the Union authorities to give up Fort Sumter (and a few other installations within Southern boundaries) left their states with no other course. They drafted resolutions calling on conventions already sitting or pending in their own states to move for secession. At the same time, they seconded the call for a meeting in Montgomery to form a new confederation.[3]

Then Davis's own Mississippi acted, seceding on January 9 with a call for "a new union with the seceded States," and Florida followed one day later. Now the ball was rolling, and its momentum would surely take out the rest of the Deep South states in the days ahead. Alabama followed on January 11, but by a margin of just 61 to 39. A shift of only twelve votes in its convention would have defeated the measure and considerably embarrassed the movement in William Yancey's own state, yet the debate was largely harmonious. "Alabama is a unit and she will not present a divided front to the enemy," delegate James Dowdell told a friend just hours after the vote. "We are all in one heart here, and whatever wars may come from without will find us a united people." Alabamians would all be brothers, "aye the Southern states all will stand together."[4] Writing from Tuscaloosa two days later, Robert Rodes exulted that "Alabama is in a blaze, the State is now out of the Union, and we are all expecting a brush with the Federal troops."[5]

"Four states are now out of the Union, all recommending a similar basis for a provisional government, & the same hour & place," Dowdell was cheered to report. Georgia would soon follow, he was sure, and then more until every slave state stood with them. "A Southern Confederacy is our safety now." They would attain the goal, "but most likely we shall be baptized with sufferings."[6] He was not alone in looking to the more moderate border states with some confidence. Governor John Pettus of Mississippi sent envoys to North Carolina where, even though the legislature adjourned at Christmas without acting on secession, it had taken the encouraging step of appropriating $300,000 to buy arms for the state. Once it became apparent that there would be no satisfactory settlement of the issues over slavery with the North, said the governor's agent, he believed North Carolina would join them.[7] At the same time, word came from the man sent to Arkansas that signs were hopeful. "The question of secession is a new one in Arkansas," reported G. Hall on Christmas. "It has never yet been debated or considered there, and it is not therefore surprising that the people of that great state, should not be as familiar with it, and as ready to act upon it, as are the people of Mississippi, where it has been discussed for many years, and where her most eminent statesmen, cheerfully embracing this issue, have in more than one contest before the people been beaten down and driven to private life." Nevertheless, he saw a groundswell of local public meetings around the state that he predicted would move the governor and legislature in time to cooperate in "the formation of a Southern Confederacy."[8]

Then it was Georgia's turn. "We are all for Secession," one observer advised Governor Joseph Brown on New Year's Eve. Unionist candidates for the state convention were actually withdrawing from the race, yet it was not to be so simple.[9] A large and influential proportion of the population, led by Alexander H. Stephens, opposed secession, or at least thought the time had not come yet. Meanwhile, even before the convention could meet or take action, Brown anticipated its action by ordering state militia late on January 2 to secretly approach and take possession of unoccupied Fort Pulaski, guarding Savannah.[10] At once civil officials in charge of coastal roads resorted to old laws allowing them to draft slaves from the local planters for public work, and put gangs to improving the fort, essentially mobilizing labor for defense. Seemingly such an action stepped across the line of interference with private property, but it rested on an old precedent of collective contribution for maintenance and improvement of public works in times of need, and the state also paid to feed and house the slaves while they were working.[11] The difference now was that they were all to go to work not to improve a road but to ready Fort Pulaski for war. There were some kinds of interference with their rights as property owners that the planters would accept. They could see, at least for the moment, that allowing a compromise of their absolute rights in the immediate event worked to preserve their prerogatives in the long run. The mayor of Savannah spoke their mind when he visited Charleston just as the Georgia secession convention was to meet, and offered the toast: "*Southern Civilization*—It must be maintained at any cost and at all hazards."[12] The need was brought home to them soon enough, for at the end of the month the planters themselves had to mobilize at one plantation when a slave uprising threatened; they suppressed the rumored outbreak before it could occur.[13] By that time, Georgia had toed the line on January 18, though so divided was the state that a shift of only 19 out of 296 votes would have seen secession defeated.

Meanwhile, as the states gradually rolled out of the Union, they each agreed to send delegates to the proposed Montgomery meeting, and then began to grapple with some of the issues of independence. Indeed, it was with some difficulty that the governors kept a rein on their volunteers, especially those in and around Charleston who wanted to attack Fort Sumter now, and those gathering in Pensacola, Florida, where Fort Pickens also still lay in the hands of a small Yankee garrison. Senator Stephen Mallory of Florida, who had been opposed to secession but then went along with his state, attracted bitter criticism when he repeatedly counseled against a precipitate move against Fort Pickens.[14] In Washington, meanwhile, Jefferson Davis met with manufacturer Eli Whitney to inspect and contract for 1,000 rifles to be sent home to Mississippi. Absurdly in the circumstances, the United States Army ordnance office in Washington agreed to sell 5,000 guns from its Baton Rouge arsenal to the state of Mississippi despite the increasing possibility that they might be turned against the Union in the not-too-distant future.[15] Meanwhile, out in Fort Sumter itself, commanding officer Major Robert Anderson sent dispatches to Washington on January 12 suggesting that since three states had gone out, and more were sure to follow, it was pointless to think of attempting to coerce them back into the Union. Clearly Anderson did not want a collision, and openly discussing the content of his letters with visiting South Carolinians guaranteed that his views would become known to the public.[16]

The South was soon to unite in Montgomery, and everyone knew it. Montgomery would be the setting for an historic reprise of the Continental Congress, when sovereign states in rebellion against a large and powerful foe needed to form a confederacy in a hurry. Only this time the foe was a neighbor and its form of government more admired than most. Every day the likelihood of war increased. Hurried last meetings among the delegates in Congress took place before several of them formally took their leave on instructions from their states, Davis among them. Now the Coral Reefers applied a new kind of pressure, trying to get influential men to arrange to shift as much government materiel of war as possible into remaining Southern armories and arsenals so that it would be there when those facilities were seized as more states seceded, thus to provide the basis of a defense if secession led to war. The several clubs met together in what Stuart called a "committee of the whole" pledging to engineer such a transfer, though they would not succeed, for the congressmen and senators took instructions only from their states, while cabinet officers like Cobb and Floyd had not cooperated, unwilling to compromise themselves. A few like Davis acted to purchase arms from private manufacturers, but that was hardly enough. Moreover, the Reefers wanted more. They wanted to devise some dramatic and radical act that would precipitate a crisis at once, taking advantage of the excitement of the moment "for the completion of the disruption at the very outset, and carrying its immediate consumation by *coup d'état* after *coup d'état*," as Stuart confessed.

One member proposed a plan to kidnap Abraham Lincoln when he passed through Baltimore on the way to Washington and his inauguration. With the approval of the several clubs, a delegation went to Baltimore to offer the plan to sympathizers there, while at the same time another faction of Reefers came up with a plan to abduct Lincoln and his cabinet in Washington itself before the inauguration, and to kidnap with them as many Republican members of Congress as possible. The captives were to be taken south to a hideaway in the Blue Ridge Mountains of Virginia. That would create a vacuum in Washington that the South could somehow capitalize upon, or so they thought. The Reefers had their scheme complete just as Jefferson Davis was about to leave to return to Mississippi, having resigned his seat in the Senate. Though circumspect about their plans, especially with moderates, the Reefers decided to take Davis into their confidence. After all, he was the leading statesman in the slave states, and one of a very few men likely to be considered for chief executive if a new confederacy was formed. The Reefers hoped that he would lend advice to further their project. At a secret meeting they laid it all before him, but Davis balked. He immediately condemned the plot for what it was, a silly and impractical pipe dream that would make a mockery of their stand for independence on high constitutional principles. Moreover, it was wicked. Besides, as they should have known themselves, he pointed out to the conspirators that Virginia had not yet seceded, and was itself deeply divided, with a strong contingent very loyal to the Union. The idea of being able to keep Lincoln and the others securely in the Blue Ridge was ridiculous. "He was very resolute in his dissuasions," said Stuart, "and staggered their confidence." Davis's condemnation doomed the plot, though the Reefers thought they would only postpone their plan to a later date. A few years later Stuart was convinced that Davis himself had caused a warning to be sent to Union authorities alerting them to the plot. Certainly in February 1861 when Lincoln traveled to Washington, he was apprised of a kid-

napping plot in Baltimore and managed to slip past the conspirators, some
of whom were later arrested, though whether Davis himself was the cause
of their undoing is uncertain.[17]

As each state seceded, its convention sent copies of its ordinance to all
of the other slave states, along with yet more embassies to spread the enthusiasm. Louisiana became next on January 26, and Governor Thomas
Moore immediately drafted a form letter to transmit its ordinance. And
just three days later a South Carolina commissioner reached Texas and put
before its convention his state's ordinance and the resolution "respectfully
inviting your cooperation in the formation with us, & other Seceding
States; of a Southern Confederacy."[18] Cooperation was urgent. D. H. Hamilton, himself a South Carolina oligarch, had declared, "we must travel
through blood and carnage to some better and stronger form of Government than that which can be controlled by a popular majority—a Government strong enough to protect each valuable interest." It would be a
severe trial, he knew, for "the South is almost entirely hemmed in and
nothing is left to us but desperate fighting—the sooner it comes the better
after we are prepared for it."[19] Another Carolinian, T. H. Spann, almost
hoped that the North would start active hostilities. "Let them commence
the war and we will wage it with them until the last drop of blood is spent
before we will submit to be dictated to by them." Five states had seceded
by now, and Texas would follow soon. "With such mettle as compose those
states," boasted Spann, "we will defy the whole North." A Federal garrison
was only in Fort Sumter now thanks to typical Yankee trickery. "When the
time comes, we will have it, if we have to make the waters of the harbour
red with the blood of Carolinians."[20]

But before they made anything run red, they would have to be more
than a loose collection of independent entities sharing a piece of the continent. Within hours of Spann's declaration, the first delegates were packing for the trip to Montgomery. For a start, many, especially those from the
older and more affluent Atlantic seaboard states like South Carolina and
Georgia, brought with them a certainty that, at the outset, they were a distinct people from their recent confreres in the North, and altogether a superior race of men. Many fully accepted the comfortable myth that their
immigrant ancestors came from the Cavalier stock of old England, descended from aristocratic Norman adventurers who invaded in 1066 and
conquered a churlish Saxon rabble, whose own descendants later emigrated to populate the North. Robert Barnwell Rhett was a leading pro-

mulgator of this nonsense, happily oblivious of the fact that his own ancestors came from neither Cavalier nor Roundhead stock, which was true of most people in the North as well. In fact, until 1837 Rhett's actual surname had been Smith, and his thoroughly unaristocratic forebears had played both sides in the English Civil War, while the ancestor from whom he adopted his more patrician-sounding name had been a sometime Dutch slave trader before coming to colonial South Carolina.

By the time the 1860 crisis came, the mythology of separateness had become so fully developed as to be cited on its own by secessionists like Rhett and Yancey as a just cause for disunion. J.D.B. DeBow, then of New Orleans, had made his *Review* perhaps the most influential journal in the South by 1861, and in it he declared that "we have a theory of our own about the origin of races," a theory that "rests its basis on holy writ." Citing Genesis, DeBow maintained that all plants, animals, and humans were created in or around ancient Persia, and from there diffused to all points of the compass, but the most favorable locality for the full development of all things was naturally in the latitude of creation. Moreover, regions similar to that hot climate "differ least from it in capacity to produce the finest specimens of vegetable, animal and human life." "As you recede from the isothermal latitude of creation, and go north or south, all created things deteriorate," he went on, and the deterioration became progressive. Climate had not changed anywhere on the globe since the creation, and "everything in warm climates is superior to everything in cold climates." As for Southerners, they were a "composite race" made up from Mediterranean nations in the main, and he cited France, Greece, and Spain. But when it came to acknowledging the staggering predominance of British blood in their veins, he mentioned not England as a whole, but rather only the Normans. "It is from these Normans that we of the South are in great part descended," he declared, "reckless, adventurous fillibusters from every part of southern Europe."

Granting that there had been differences between the peoples who settled the South, DeBow went on to aver that intermarriage made them a harmonious and blended whole. "With small exceptions, there is a general concurrence of opinion among us, on all subjects relating to the public weal, which makes us pre-eminently one people," he concluded in utter disregard of the fact that for two generations Southerners had not achieved a single mind on the secession issue, or that in every state but South Carolina deep divisions emerged even in the act of seceding.

"This is the secret of our strength and national vitality," he went on. Significantly, DeBow spoke of Southerners as a "nationality." Nations were ruined by a diversity of interests pulling them apart, he said, and in the case of the North by too much immigration from inferior north European peoples such as Poles, Russians, shanty Irish, and especially Germans, who instead of assimilating into the population and being elevated by it, rather remained apart in their own ethnic communities and thus dragged down the whole.[21] Somehow, he failed to grasp that by his own logic the African root stock of Southern slaves would be superior to the whites' balmier Mediterranean origins.

Of course not all Southerners in late January agreed with DeBow's often ridiculous rationalizations. Still, he represented in hyperbole the dominant assumptions that drove the majority. Even a man like Davis, from less refined Mississippi, who maintained no foolish assumptions about his own distinctly Celtic yeoman ancestry, could embrace and endorse the notion of the superiority of a Southern race. Virtually all accepted as an article of faith, and a foundation of their superior society, the unchallenged fact of the inferiority of the people they owned, and of their natural fitness for servitude. Slavery was a God-given blessing, DeBow argued, one that came directly from the moral injunctions of the Bible itself. "Everybody knows that slavery finds justification and authority throughout the whole of the Old and New Testaments," he said, "and that the Devil himself could not 'find Scripture for his purpose,' if the Devil be an abolitionist." DeBow was neither perceptive nor knowledgeable enough to realize that many if not most of the bondsmen spoken of in the Bible were themselves not black Africans but Mediterraneans held by fellow Mediterraneans—even Semites enslaved by other Semites, the master race enslaving its own kind. To his mind, "all free society must reject the Bible if it approve its own institutions and disapprove slavery, because slavery is not only instituted and justified by the Christian God, but, much more, *because Christian morality can be practiced only in slave society.*" He went on to declare to his Southern readers that in fact it was impossible to live a moral life in a free society. In a society where all were free, the ethic must naturally be what he called "a system of selfishness, instead of a system of love." The wage earner was inevitably exploited "because, to deprive the free laborer of his die and punch his family for food and clothing, is consistent with the philosophy of universal liberty—'every man for himself.'"

With slavery the situation was exactly the reverse. Good Christians did unto others as they would be done unto themselves, and in the South, where labor and capital were one and the same, neither tried to get the advantage of the other. In DeBow's rosy portrait, the family circle consisted of "parent, husband, wife, children, brothers, sisters and slaves," and the "law of love, and not of selfishness" prevailed. Even in slave punishment, DeBow declared that the master exercised the Golden Rule, for to fail to punish a child or a slave in proportion to misconduct was to fail in the holy duty required of an adult white male. "He who punishes his negroes when they deserve it, and retains them in slavery, treating them humanely, fulfils the golden rule," he concluded. By working hard and behaving well, the slave naturally improved his own condition, eliciting kinder treatment at the same time that he enriched his master, each thus serving the interest of the other. Indeed, he expected that in the near future, England and France would think better of their own abandonment of slavery, see for themselves how the institution worked to the advantage of all, and reinstitute it themselves rather than continue to condemn it in the South.

Ironically, for a society that he declared to be far superior, DeBow complained that before they could achieve their destiny they must first disenthrall themselves of their sense of inferiority. "Disunion will teach us to respect ourselves," he said. Despite the fact that the act of rebellion in a slave was only proof of his unsuitability for freedom, the editor maintained that rebellion by white Southerners would be validating their manhood and their birthright of liberty. Now they would stop sending their sons to Yankee universities, stop hiring Northern tutors for their younger children, stop eschewing their own local fabrics to wear the broadcloths that came from New England mills. They would cease reading obscene and immoral Northern books and magazines, and instead elevate their own literature. "We have been Yankee imitators and worshippers until now," he declared. "We have been in a state of pupilage, and never learned to walk alone." Now they would take care of themselves, even in war if necessary, and they would gain their own respect and that of the other nations they must look to for recognition and support. "We of the South are about to inaugurate a new civilization," he proclaimed. "We shall have new and original thought; negro slavery will be its great controlling and distinctive element."[22]

Of course, that would depend on what the seceding states created in Montgomery, if anything, and how the world chose to view their creation.

Hundreds of miles from DeBow's New Orleans office, another man who was just as illogical, just as hyperbolic, but far less honest intellectually, pondered just how any new Southern nation should present itself to Europe, especially to England, since all recognized that the rest of Europe took its lead from Britain. Rhett had already drafted his own version of a constitution that he hoped to impose on any new confederation. Never hindered by modesty, on his own authority alone he had actually called on the British consul in Charleston just days after South Carolina seceded to begin setting Southern foreign policy and attempting to dictate the terms on which the South would give the blessing of its friendship and trade to Her Majesty and her subjects. The consul listened politely, then privately wrote him off as an arrogant crank.[23]

Rhett, who certainly expected to be secretary of state if not president in any new government, wrote down a series of arguments for the South to use with foreign powers. Typical of the closed mind that had propelled him through a political career marked by staggering hypocrisy, demagoguery, and outright lying, without ever once doubting his own rectitude, he constructed a fictional dialog between an Englishman and a Southerner, whom he was already calling a Confederate. In it he framed every question in order to set up what seemed to him an inarguable answer, and all designed to place the seceding states in the best possible light in the eyes of England and the world. Unwittingly, he also added dimension to DeBow's rosy rationalization:

> Englishman: There is one thing, we do not clearly understand—the *cause of the rebellion!*
>
> Confederate: Rebellion! Why that word, My Dear Sir! affords at once the clue to all your difficulties. You have been reading Yankee News Papers; and really have some belief in what Yankees say. Cut off from the rest of the world, by *their* possession of the seas, *we* are not heard. The idea, to a Southerner, of his being a Rebel to a Yankee is so farcical, that it is with difficulty he can realize that any one believes it.
>
> Englishman: Well, if you are not rebels, what are you?
>
> Confederate: Why, an independent People, defending an independent country!
>
> Englishman: Were you not a part of the United States?

Confederate:	Certainly of the United States—that is, of the *States United*. States, from the very meaning of the word, must be independent political entities. To be united, they must still be independent; and when disunited, (it matters not by what means), the allegiance of the citizens of each State follows the State. It cannot belong to another State—much less to all the other States as an aggregate. As rebellion is the violation of allegiance; of course the Southern People could only rebel against their own States, in defending those States.
Englishman:	This seems plain enough. How then does the whole world call you Rebels?
Confederate:	Because the Yankees have had the ear of the world, and the world is prone to believe the strong. It is their interest to deceive the world with the belief that we are the wrong-doers. To be so we must be Rebels.
Englishman:	Well, tell me how they make out that you are Rebels to them.
Confederate:	Why by hard lying! And nothing else.
Englishman:	Certainly no Englishman, with the Treaty [of Paris] in our Archives in London, can deny that you are sovereign and independent States.
Confederate:	The Articles of Confederation, being the first compact of government made by the States, distinctly affirms in its commencement that "each State retains its freedom sovereignty and independence." Now this is either true or false.
Englishman:	Such facts, it appears to me, do not admit of argument. . . . But come to the Constitution itself. What does it say on the subject?
Confederate:	Not a word.
Englishman:	Not a word?
Confederate:	Not one. You may read the Constitution from the first word to the last and there is not a word concerning either sovereignty or allegiance.
Englishman:	Why is this?
Confederate:	Simply because the Constitution has really nothing whatever to do with either.

Englishman: How then do the Northern States affirm that it transfers
                the sovereignty of the States, and the allegiance of their
                citizens, to the Government?

Confederate: By inference. Inference with our Yankee neighbors, like
                interest with Falstaff, "is a great matter." . . . Only think
                of a man, who from a compact made with a neighbor
                consisting of elaborate details to carry on their business
                together, should claim the right by inference to take his
                neighbors life?

Englishman: I should say that he was a fool or a madman.

Confederate: Or a Yankee!

Englishman: But what of the People of the United States as one Peo-
                ple? Have they not got the sovereignty surrendered by
                the States?

Confederate: No! for the simple reason that there is no such People.

Englishman: No such People? Are you not all called "People of the
                United States?"

Confederate: Oh! Yes! "of the United States"—*States United.* The ap-
                pellation "People of the United States" however is not
                found in the Constitution.

Englishman: Why, that leaves the citizens of the United States, noth-
                ing but citizens of the several States.

Confederate: Certainly—nothing more.

Englishman: And the States are the only sovereignty to whom alle-
                giance is due?

Confederate: Certainly. And you see now, how absurd is the preten-
                sion, that the citizens of the Southern States who sup-
                ported them in their secession, were traitors to the
                United States, and therefore Rebels.

Englishman: But how does all this elucidate the cause of secession?

Confederate: In the plainest manner. The North contended that it was
                a Government of the People of the United States, and
                extendable to all powers Congress by inference might
                claim to exercise—Congress being the judge of their
                powers. In the opinion of the Southern People, the
                Northern construction would grant over them a most re-
                morseless despotism—the despotism of a majority in
                Congress, totally irresponsible to them.

Englishman: But is it not an axiom of popular governments that a ma-
               jority should rule?
Confederate: Yes! And a very good one, where the interests are identi-
               cal. But over so vast a country as the United States, it is
               the most hideous of all despotisms.
Englishman: But slavery. You have said nothing about African slavery,
               which they say was the cause [of secession]. . . . Did it
               not have a great deal to do with bringing on [secession]?
Confederate: Yes! It was the *occasion,* but not *the cause.* . . . The real
               cause, was in the change of Government, the agitations
               concerning slavery, manifested. . . . A sectional President
               was elected on an unconstitutional issue respecting slav-
               ery and the Southern States seceded from the Union
               of the United States. Slavery . . . was the *occasion,* but
               not the *cause* of secession.
Englishman: But the North—will not the North also rise again?
Confederate: I think not for these reasons. 1. Because in history no
               People who have enslaved themselves, have ever re-
               established their liberties. 2. Because the South can only
               be kept in connexion with them by force; and the des-
               potism over us must be a despotism over them. 3. The
               whole United States Government is under the control of
               the money power. It is a vast brokerage of Manufactur-
               ers—Bankers—Government Debt-owners and capital-
               ists of all kinds. Such a Government naturally leans to
               despotism, to maintain their privileges. But one thing
               seems to be sure. If they regain their liberties, it must be
               by the same instrumentality which preserved it to them
               from the foundation of the Government . . . the influ-
               ence of the South.[24]

Southerners had seceded in order to preserve constitutional government, not destroy it. They would not be rebels but reformers. Indeed, if
free government were to survive at all in North America, it was they who
would be its saviors. Majority rule was a sham that meant only subjugation
of the minority in a diverse population, and as for slavery, it was merely the
catalyst that produced secession. Seceding states were really innocent victims of Northern treachery, now exercising rights they had possessed all

along, at the same time making of themselves a beacon of individual rights and liberty for all the world to admire. Unsaid but implied—by the same means of inference that Rhett so decried—was the assumption that Southerners were somehow superior to their craven, money-rooting neighbors to the north; moreover, Southerners were of like mind with interests that all shared identically, hence the implication that the South could live under majority rule within itself. Such a people must inevitably frame and maintain a genuinely "more perfect union" among themselves.

They began arriving in Montgomery the weekend of February 2 and 3, while behind them the crisis over the Federal garrison in Fort Sumter gradually grew. Charlestonians advised that matters would remain quiet for perhaps two weeks while they awaited the result of the Montgomery meeting, unless the Buchanan administration made another attempt to supply or reinforce the fort. With Texas having voted to secede on February 1, even as the first delegates boarded the trains to the conference, hopes for a peaceful resolution grew.[25] "The organization of the six seceding states into the Confederacy this week may convince the govt. that coercion is folly and madness," a Carolinian advised Langdon Cheves that Sunday, joining DeBow and Rhett and so many others in full expectation that a new nation would result from the Montgomery convention.[26]

Stephens and his bosom friend Robert Toombs attracted much attention when they arrived, as did fellow Georgian Howell Cobb. Fingers pointed to Rhett when he entered, as well as to other Carolinians like his cousin Robert Barnwell, William Porcher Miles and James Chesnut, Lawrence Keitt and Christopher G. Memminger. Already bystanders noticed that for all his pretensions to leadership, Rhett seemed to enjoy little good will from any of his fellow South Carolina delegates except his cousin. Only one of the Louisianians was there now, Alexander De Clouet, but he was a man of substance, wisdom, and moderation, and most of the Alabama delegation was present, including J.L.M. Curry, while Wiley Harris of Mississippi came clearly at the head of his delegation.

Few other than Stephens, Toombs, and Cobb had truly achieved national stature and reputation as statesmen in the old Union, but taken in their all, and including others yet to arrive, they were easily the finest assemblage of public men the seceded states had to offer. Even Rhett came with more than twenty years of congressional experience behind him. More important, most were seasoned politicians at least by avocation, if not by profession. That should have been a warning in itself that the kind of harmony that Rhett and DeBow tried to depict was an illusion. In his own South Carolina, Rhett had spent his whole career battling against disagreements and disaffections just among those who otherwise agreed with his basic desire for an independent South founded on slavery and free trade. It was folly to expect unanimity across the South as a whole, for the interests of South Carolina and Louisiana were no more homogeneous than those of Mississippi and Maine. It was even greater folly to expect, as some did, that in leaving the Union they would leave behind their instincts for partisanship and politics. Indeed, the seeds of new alignments, and perhaps of new parties, had been sown back in those Washington meetings earlier in the winter, in the several loose associations bundled into what the journalist Stuart dubbed the Reefers, and in the several state secession conventions. Now on the afternoon of February 3 they would have their first opportunity to see how much of their old ways they had left behind, where the new alignments if any would appear, and just which if any of them were capable of replacing partisanship with statesmanship.[27] The delegations from Mississippi, Alabama, and Georgia had already met in caucus prior to leaving home in order to agree on their course. That in itself began the maneuvering even before they first met with those from other states. On the other hand, the South Carolinians, nominally under Rhett as leader, had not caucused at all nor would they. Most other than Barnwell detested their chairman and would take no lead from him whatever, as he well knew, while for his part Rhett, with typical arrogance, seems to have assumed that everyone would simply lie down and follow his dictates.

From the moment the first delegate in Montgomery encountered another, discussion of what would happen when the convention gathered dominated all conversation. Whether by coincidence or design, however, the serious discussion did not begin until the Georgians arrived on Sunday. With ten delegates coming, Georgia's was the largest delegation, and the attainments on the national stage of Stephens, Toombs, and Cobb dwarfed all but Rhett's. Indeed, many—Rhett definitely not among them—assumed that if a new government was formed, Georgia ought as a matter of course to get the presidency. Clearly, it was pointless to discuss real policy for the morrow's meeting until the Georgians were there to be heard. Just as clearly, the mere fact that the delegates gathered in the Exchange Hotel that afternoon to plan their course after the opening gavel revealed that

they were politicians enough to leave little to chance. The more they could
decide now, the fewer divisions they risked becoming manifest later. As
they left their afternoon meals and the walnut-paneled saloon to file into
the hotel lobby, from which the management politely ejected spectators, they
already knew that there was only one great question for them to settle now,
but it was the most important single issue they would decide.

What were they to be, and how should they achieve that goal? In fact,
none of the delegations came to Montgomery with power from either their
state legislatures or sitting conventions to agree to the formation and establishment of any form of government. They were merely here to talk,
consult, and return to their states with recommendations. The only absolute instructions to any of them related to procedural matters for their
debates. At first they squared off in the lobby in pairs and small groups,
their cigar smoke rising in time with the din of their voices on what Rhett
himself called a "conversational parliament." It soon became evident that
of the five states represented—Texas's delegates would soon be on their
way—only their host delegation from Alabama did not come with a pet
plan of its own. De Clouet of Louisiana thought they ought to frame a provisional constitution and establish a central government that mirrored the
one in Washington, elect a provisional chief executive and vice president,
and then let that provisional government proceed to craft at more leisure
a permanent constitution. What Louisiana did not say was who should constitute the provisional congress. In the discussion over this plan, some suggested that when their convention adjourned, they should call for an
immediate election in the states for provisional representatives to frame
the permanent constitution, and afterward another election for congressmen under the new organic law.

Mississippi suggested a more direct approach. They were a convention,
not a congress, urged Harris, and they had no power to frame constitutions. They should simply recommend to their state conventions the adoption verbatim of the United States Constitution, decide among themselves
on a president to recommend as well, and go home. Since Mississippi had
already decided that its delegates to the old Congress in Washington
would be its representatives in any new government, they should then adjourn and wait for other states to select their own new congressmen. Only
when that was done could lawful legislation for the new nation begin. In
passing, Harris did not fail to observe that Mississippi thought the best
man for their presidency would be its own Jefferson Davis.

It was left to the Georgians to state the obvious, and they had discussed it among themselves beforehand. The critical moment was upon them. No one could know what Buchanan, or more likely Lincoln, would do about the garrisons in Forts Sumter and Pickens. Equally to the point, who knew how long the hotheads in Charleston could be restrained from acting on their own and precipitating a genuine war. In such a moment, delay might be fatal. If they simply came here, made a show of their convention, talked, and then went home to recommend actions that could take weeks or even months to effect, they risked losing control of events. The crisis before them justified taking radical steps. Having heard what were already called the Mississippi plan and the Louisiana plan, they moved through the knots of delegates pressing the Georgia plan. This convention had to usurp power unto itself. It had to declare itself a congress representing the states and assume full legislative authority, frame a provisional constitution under which it would act for a period of a year, elect and install a provisional president and vice president to serve for the same term, and set the new government in motion. Then, with the machinery in place to act for the nation in case of emergency, they could draft a more perfect permanent constitution to go into effect after ratification by the states, and after regularly elected senators and representatives were chosen in the fall, and with them popularly elected executive officers. That done, the provisional congress would cease to be.

It was the right solution for the problem before them, however radical, but it did not please all of the Carolinians, especially Rhett. They came expecting only to meet and frame a provisional government. Their own convention in Charleston had empowered its delegation only to go so far as agreeing on necessary proposed changes in the United States Constitution, and then to adjourn after sending them to the several states for ratification; Rhett himself had come armed with a draft of the revisions that he had decided were necessary. Certainly they had no authority to elect a president; only the state conventions could do that, or the people at large. Even the Mississippi plan was too radical for Rhett, and impractical as well. It did not stipulate the manner of choosing new congressmen, meaning that if they did choose a president and vice president, the men would be "powerless puppets" in his phrase, without a congress to confirm cabinet appointments, raise revenue, or wage war if need be.

Worse, adopting the United States Constitution was virtually a step on the road to reconstruction. In it he saw a design to appeal to the border states, heavily tainted with Unionism and several of the old ideas that he believed they had seceded to escape. Of course a mere five or six states were not going to be enough to resist the might of a Union committed to reunion. Beneath all the boast, thinking men in the South knew that. Thus from the first they cast anxious eyes northward toward Virginia and Kentucky, states whose northern boundaries were rivers that would make handsome natural defenses against invasion, and whose large population, wealth, and manufacturing could be critical. But if they joined a new confederation without proper reforms in any new constitution, they might bring with them the old heresies they shared with the North of a high tariff that protected Yankee manufactures at the expense of Southern buyers, and adherence to the doctrine of spending national revenues on so-called internal improvements that benefited only certain states or regions. They had been the driving issues behind earlier agitation for secession until slavery took over in the 1840s. Even worse than that, adopting the old Constitution unchanged would actually set up the possibility of free states seceding to join them in the future, and in that lay the genesis of eventual destruction. Clearly to Rhett and a few other radical state rights men, adopting the old framework—and in the case of Mississippi even the same old representatives—presented them with a wolf in sheep's guise, reconstruction and reunion. "After all, we will have run round a circle, and end where we started," he grumbled. "We will only have changed masters."[28]

To his supreme disgust, Rhett saw in that lobby parliament how quickly most of the other delegates rallied to the Georgia plan. Indeed, some of them might have already favored something of the sort themselves, but simply lacked either the daring or the authority of the Georgians to suggest it. Almost immediately the Alabama delegates moved behind it, while De Clouet, the only Louisiana delegate present, already stood close in principle. Sensing the growing security of numbers, Harris and Mississippi fell quickly in line in the face of the inarguable necessity for resolute action. Florida had only J. Patton Anderson present at the moment, and he could hardly resist such a tide even had he wished.

Then Rhett's cousin Robert Barnwell decided the matter. What they found facing them in Montgomery differed dramatically from what he expected, he argued. He reminded the South Carolinians, as no doubt did Stephens and Toombs and others, that the divisions in some states like Alabama and Georgia were so great that they risked destruction if putting a new government into operation had to depend on ratification in those states by popular referenda. These men had to assume power immediately or court disaster not only there, but perhaps all across the slave states.[29] The backing of the respected Barnwell brought South Carolina into line. If that were not enough, one of the South Carolina delegates, catching the spirit of the emergency, went even further to suggest that after establishing a provisional government, they should not wait for regular elections at home to choose their replacements under a permanent constitution, but that this convention ought itself to elect the future delegates from the several states. However much such action would have worked to ensure the firm grip of the old political oligarchies on power, even for Rhett that end did not justify such means. Calling the proposal "a monstrous commentary upon representation in government," he condemned the outrage of allowing men from other states to have a say in the choosing of representatives from South Carolina, and vice versa. The idea gained no support and died, as it should have, for it was a repudiation not only of state rights but of basic tenets of democracy itself.[30]

"Words are certainly very shadowy in their meaning," Rhett complained bitterly.[31] When he suggested that the seceding states meet to confer, he contemplated nothing about what they were to do. When other states accepted the invitation, however, they clearly had something quite different in mind. There was danger here, and not just from the Georgia plan, which now he knew could not be stopped. Something in Harris's proposition disturbed him just as much, if not more. "Jefferson Davis and Mississippi have acted very meanly," he complained that evening. "Instead of being here to give all the weight possible to the proceedings of the Convention, they cook up offices for themselves, and send tools here, to carry out their selfish policy." He remembered how Davis had cautioned against secession for years beforehand. He remembered what he had heard of the meeting on January 5 in Washington, when Davis finally came out in favor of secession. Barnwell had been there, too, and soon Rhett concluded that his cousin had been duped then into making a corrupt bargain with Davis to support him for president of any new confederacy.[32] Instead of calmly and methodically creating a new and perfect republic, they were being manipulated into establishing something they had no power to create, making it more powerful than it ought to be, and perhaps also being manipulated into turning it over to an unscrupulous man whose ambitions—to Rhett's hardly impartial way of thinking—could lead him to use their creation as a dictator. It was almost too much, and Rhett feared that this unexpected state of affairs would leave his own delegation with little to do. "The Poor South!" he moaned. "If I had no trust in God, I would despair, utterly."[33]

Rhett had no intention of leaving the fate of their movement to any deity. Politics was the work of men, not gods. On this dramatic afternoon in the Exchange, with the cold late winter rain beating the windows outside, and the aroma of cigar smoke and whiskey and tobacco juice filling the lobby, the men inside took a long yet unwitting further step toward turning those tentative associations of earlier months into something more defined. Without either a government or an executive in existence to support, an administration party began to congeal. In Rhett, however, there flashed the first glimmers of an opposition. In a new democratic experiment that everyone had hoped would leave partisanship behind and need no parties, they were already divided.[34]

3

Visions of Breakers Ahead

WHILE ALABAMA'S CAPITAL BUZZED with interest in its newcomers, across the rest of the South people held their breath. In a few weeks Abraham Lincoln would be inaugurated in Washington, and all wondered what, if anything, that would bring. Despite the fact that six states had seceded, that still left nine other slave states in the Union, and for the old adage of safety in numbers to have real meaning for Southerners, they needed more numbers represented in their new confederation. There were hopeful signs in the border states, even Virginia and North Carolina, where the Union grip was strong. Still concerned chiefly with parochial matters, students at the University of Virginia in Charlottesville and their parents worried that if the state did not secede, then pupils from the other seceded states would leave and the university would wither. Meanwhile, the volunteer military companies paraded on the grounds of Mr. Jefferson's college.[1] A woman in Halifax County, North Carolina, condemned her own kin for adhering to the Union. "Now it is no longer glorious— when it ceases to be voluntary, it degenerates into a hideous oppression," she declared on February 10. "Regret it heartily, mourn over it as for a lost friend, but do not seek to enforce it; it is like galvanizing a dead body!"[2]

In Montgomery, the secessionists' convention knew that time was short and they must "galvanize" themselves. Having settled easily the most important question they would face in this convention, even before they convened, the delegates went on to other decisions nearly as significant. The

idea of moving quickly that propelled the Georgia plan took hold in the
rest of their discussions, all of which passed more easily with the big hur-
dle out of the way. The convention would need a presiding officer and a
secretary, but they could not waste time on opposing nominations and perhaps multiple ballots, not to mention the risk of partisanship appearing to
mar the all-important posture of unanimity that they had to present to the
North, the world, and more particularly their own South. They decided to
choose the men now. It might have seemed to an outsider to run counter
to democratic principles to settle such issues in what was literally a smoke-
filled room, but in fact their action was entirely harmonious with Southern democracy. Coming from states whose legislatures elected senators
and governors without reference to the populace, the delegates saw nothing discordant in a portion—a minority, in fact—of the convention pre-
selecting its own officers in advance of the gavel. Since the president of
this convention—or Congress to be—would essentially act in the role of
speaker, and Howell Cobb had served as Speaker of the House a few years
before, he seemed a natural choice. Yet already there was politics in it as
well. Many, including Cobb himself, understood that making him president of the convention would remove him from contention for a higher
presidency to come. Most of them distrusted Cobb, who had abandoned a
nascent secession movement in 1851 to seek Georgia's governorship on a
Union ticket. Mississippi made it clear from the first that it wanted Jefferson Davis as chief executive, and would happily eliminate Cobb for that
reason as well.[3] The only men with a real chance of being nominated by
Georgia were Robert Toombs and Alexander Stephens, presumably in that
order, and though South Carolina's delegates had agreed to advance no
one for any position in a new government, still Robert Barnwell Rhett had
his private hopes.[4] That done, the delegates quickly dispensed with choosing a secretary, "all according to previous arrangement," as Stephens wryly
commented two days later.[5] They might be about to establish a new government, but there was no need to change the way they had been managing public affairs for generations.

Then someone made a far more controversial proposal. Only fools
would deny that there would be disagreement among them in the days
ahead. They were already forestalling some of that by virtually deciding
the election of convention officers in advance. To prevent even more potentially acrimonious and dispiriting discord from becoming public, it was

proposed that they conduct all of their truly important debate behind closed doors in secret session. Almost all agreed on the wisdom of such a course, as had the delegates in Philadelphia some seventy years before, but Rhett fumed. The public had a right to know what its representatives were saying and doing. More particularly, he wanted South Carolina to know what he was doing. Combined with the Georgia plan, the apparent movement for Davis, and his growing suspicion about that January 5 meeting in Washington, secret sessions presented to his own calculating mind just one more evidence that unscrupulous men could well be combining to frame the new government to serve their own ambitions.[6]

Finally the long afternoon ended, and the delegates left the Exchange lobby to return to their rooms and their suppers. It had all gone so speedily that Thomas Cobb, Howell's brother and fellow delegate, thought they might finish their work in two weeks at this pace.[7] Rhett was far less sanguine. He was depressed at what had happened thus far, not only to his own ambitions but also to the vision he had for the new Southern slave nation. He smelled reconstruction in the air. Indeed, from the outset of the secession movement there had been those who favored seceding solely as a bluff to force the Yankees into constitutional concessions on slavery in the territories that would then allow the seceders to come back into the Union on their own terms. Howell Cobb he never trusted, and Toombs and Stephens could well be unsound. As for Davis, Rhett had already written him off as a schemer. To save his dream for an independent and perpetual Southern nation, he would have to watch them all, especially in their secret sessions. He would have to fight, and fighting inevitably meant faction. He would need supporters of his own, if he could find them. Perhaps without thinking it, and certainly without ever admitting it then or later, he needed a party of his own.

The next afternoon thirty-seven of them assembled in the Alabama statehouse. Several more delegates had arrived in past hours, but six had yet to come, and only Georgia and South Carolina floored their full delegations. Their composition showed the wisdom of agreeing on as much as possible in advance, for there was nothing approaching unanimity in their past. Almost half, like Stephens, had been soft on secession or opposed it outright up to the moment their state conventions acted. A third were planters, and only eight were not slaveholders. At least half were Democrats, and several more had been Southern rights Whigs. Only the most optimistic could hope that such a mixture, even though it included some of the best men in the South, could avoid falling into political infighting and battles for turf.

When they got started, however, it all went according to plan. Howell Cobb was elected, credentials were presented and accepted, and then Stephens introduced a motion to appoint the rules committee. It passed, but then Cobb appointed Stephens to its head, ignoring his request to be left out, and "Little Aleck" had no choice but to accept. Pending adoption of their rules of order, there was nothing else to do, and Cobb adjourned the meeting barely an hour after it began. Stephens went to his boarding house to prepare a draft to present to his committee when they met later that day, while most of the rest returned to the "conversational parliament" in the Exchange Hotel lobby, where cracks were already beginning to show. Seeing it all, Tom Cobb grumbled that same evening, "I fear we shall not be as harmonious at the beginning as we expected." Their unanimity was fragmenting before they were fairly started, he lamented. "The breakers ahead of us are beginning to appear."[8]

It lay in Stephens's hands now to create a machinery that could get them past as many breakers as possible. He began by providing that each state have but a single vote, determined by a majority in each delegation. When a caucus produced a tie among its delegates, that state would cast no vote. A simple majority of four votes out of the six present—the Texas delegation was yet to arrive—would be decisive, and any tie vote on a measure meant defeat. Such a simple system guaranteed a decision on every vote, a dramatic saving of time over the handling of debates in the old Congress. To speed affairs even more, Stephens provided that no time would be wasted by states being unable to cast their vote due to a lack of a quorum among a delegation in order to determine its vote. According to his rules, a single member of a delegation could constitute a quorum. In theory, that meant that even if thirty-nine of the forty-three current credentialed delegates were absent, just four men, one from each of four states, would be enough to make legislation.

As for debate itself, he provided for that, too, to pass more quickly to a decision by eliminating the device of calling for the "previous question," which parliamentarians had used for years to halt debate and amendment, and then stall movement. In its place he provided only for calling for "the question," which would yield a vote on whatever was currently under discussion without forestalling further amendment. And as a final blow aimed squarely at Rhett and other dissidents on the secret session issue, he included an article that anytime a member moved to close their doors and gained a second, it should be done, and any delegate who revealed what took place in secret session was liable to be expelled.[9] The convention next day adopted Stephens's rules in open session almost verbatim, which to his mind made the accomplishment of the Georgia plan now a foregone conclusion. Shortly after the passage, when Christopher Memminger of South Carolina introduced resolutions that the convention appoint a committee to report a plan for the formation of a provisional government on the basis of the old Constitution, Stephens stood immediately to correct him on the usage of the word "convention," saying, "we are a congress."[10]

There followed a number of counterresolutions and amendments and an evident disposition to debate. Their differences centered on whether the Constitution should be adopted verbatim or altered to suit their needs and situation. A few, like Francis Bartow of Georgia, felt the need to declare that they were empowered by their states to do this—which they were not—in order to relieve themselves ostensibly from charges of usurpation. Duncan Kenner of Louisiana suggested that they enact as part of the resolution an affirmation that this congress had full power to all legislation necessary to carry on the business of the new government. Having determined on a radical course, prudent politicians were already trying to garb themselves in a cloak of legitimacy, despite the transparent fact that the garment itself was of their own making. Others wanted to specify a time limit of no more than a year on the life of this provisional congress and the executives it should elect. Then William Boyce of South Carolina reintroduced his proposal that this body, instead of making itself a congress, take it on itself to elect members of a provisional body to take over. But Boyce also proposed something else. For years until the admission of California the United States Senate had been the only place where the slave states had been able to hold their own as a minority. So long as the number of slave states had been equal to the number of free states, the South could hope to stop hostile legislation by denying it passage in the Senate. Now this very day, in the rules of order just adopted, South Carolina had seen its strength as one of the larger delegations negated by adoption of the one state, one vote article, a situation that would continue if their provisional congress remained unicameral. Creating two houses would return to South Carolina—and other states, of course—some protection in a senate from small state desires. Much as he was out of favor with Rhett for the substance of his proposal, Boyce revealed that he, too, feared that they might need some protection from themselves. There was wisdom in the Founding Fathers' system of dividing power among branches, levels, and legislative bodies of government.[11]

Boyce's amendment was voted down, however, and Memminger's original resolutions passed 5 to 1. It remained only to appoint the committee, each state being allowed two members, and the importance attached to the matter showed as the delegations sent their best men, including Wiley P. Harris from Mississippi, Stephens from Georgia, Richard Walker and Robert Smith from Alabama, John Perkins and Kenner from Louisiana, and J. Patton Anderson from Florida. Of course Memminger represented South Carolina, and by protocol as introducer of the resolutions was entitled to the chairmanship. Again Rhett's absence proved fortuitous, for though none of the rest save Robert Barnwell really liked him, still enough others shared sufficient views in common with him that he might have been chosen as well. He always believed that he would have been selected had he been present, though he had a history of believing what he wanted to believe.

When the committee met that evening, it was not in Memminger's lodgings but in Stephens's boarding house. The venue might merely have been convenient, but still placing it in Little Aleck's parlor surely gave some subliminal advantage to his views and those who agreed with him. In fact, the committee was almost exactly evenly divided between hard-line secessionists like Harris and William S. Barry, and those like Stephens and Memminger who had opposed it to the last moment, with Barnwell and one or two others in between. In pre-secession politics they were also evenly divided between Democrats who had opposed a strong central government in Washington and former Whigs and Union Party members like Stephens who had supported a relatively more active and powerful central authority. The latter would be more likely to support taking as much of the old Constitution as possible, since they did not fear the strength it gave to a congress, while the former could be counted on to try to hold the line on supreme state sovereignty. With the balance so evenly set, even so little a thing as obligations of hospitality and deference to Stephens for hosting their meetings could be decisive.

What men like Stephens and Memminger probably did not anticipate was that the first issue to arise was not the constitution but the question they thought had been settled for two days now, namely the nature of this "congress" and what it had power to do. Harris had not given up after the afternoon session, and now spoke up again forcefully to argue that they had no authority either to make themselves a congress or to frame and adopt a constitution. He was not without support, but then Smith chimed in on the side of Stephens, Anderson, and others, to argue that they had no choice. Only the exercise of legislative power could frame the charter they needed immediately, he said, yet beyond that they would need laws to create the government and authorize its acts. To be effective in the crisis, their government had to "spring into strength," as he put it, "and to spread as if by magic touch, confidence to the pursuits of our people."[12] There he explicitly put his finger on a critical point that none had actually voiced before, and that was the need for decisive action in order to boost and maintain popular will and morale. Smith's colleague Walker and Stephens and Eugenius Nisbet of Georgia united with him in averring that if they did not stay ahead of the people in their states by leading, they would surely fall behind them. That settled the matter, for everyone else except the South Carolinians shared the fear of giving the people an opportunity to mandate or reject the new government. It might have been a sad reflection on the basic concept of democracy, but it certainly addressed the reality of democracy as practiced in the slave states until then. The unasked question was how much of a precedent it set for future Confederate democracy.[13]

A few blocks away at the Exchange, someone else worried about the future. Rhett fumed, ill or not. "Why are all these expedients brought forward?" he grumbled. Why did no one address the single paramount issue that what they were doing violated their instructions, went beyond their authority, and subverted the sovereignty of the states themselves? While the constitutional committee still debated, Rhett wrote a dispirited and disgusted report to his Charleston *Mercury*, warning Carolinians that "it is very doubtful whether you have not committed a great error in proposing any Provisional Government at all."[14]

But a provisional government was going to be created all the same. Harris finally "yielded to the necessity," as he explained, and when he did so all further opposition to going ahead in the committee collapsed.[15] Indeed, having made his case and lost, Harris went on to be one of the most able and productive members in the discussion. With the United States Constitution and Memminger's plan of adjustments before them, they went me-

thodically from paragraph to paragraph, conscious that they had to have
something for the Congress to consider within two days, if possible.

For now, they simply lumped everything into six articles, most in the
first, beginning with the empowering statement that all legislative authority therein should rest with the Congress until otherwise ordained. They
eliminated much that dealt with the election of president and Congress
and organizational matters that did not pertain to their particular condition. They did retain the prohibition on the African slave trade, not from
any opposition to slavery but simply as sound business policy. The South
no longer needed it, and introduction of new slaves from abroad served
only to act on supply and demand by reducing the value of those already
there.

The real challenge came in the changes they made. Stephens, long an
admirer of the British parliamentary system, eliminated the old proviso
that members of Congress could not serve concurrently in the cabinet. He
wanted the cabinet to come from the Congress, for that way, as in England, the executive would have direct representation in debate, and the
Congress could question department heads while legislation was being debated. Then they attacked old political enemies from whose wounds they
still bore scars. They specifically prohibited imposition of any protective
tariff for the furtherance of any branch of industry, and provided a limitation on import duties. To defeat internal improvements, they stipulated
that all appropriations had to originate with the president, through his cabinet officers, and that the Congress itself would have no power to appropriate money for anything other than its own expenses, which made it
impossible for any state to introduce an appropriation to benefit its own industry or produce.

To show just how much they viewed the provisional constitution as an
expedient to fit the immediate situation, they even inserted a clause aimed
directly at a currently pressing political reality. None of the border slave
states—Virginia, Maryland, Delaware, North Carolina, Kentucky, Tennessee, Missouri, and Arkansas—had seceded yet, though conventions to
debate the issue were soon to meet in Virginia and Missouri, and Arkansas
had a statewide referendum scheduled. In order to edge them on, the new
Congress would be empowered to prohibit trade with any slave state not a
member of the confederation. Since the last four of those states were
entirely dependent on the Mississippi River for their trade with foreign
markets, and with Mississippi and Louisiana between them containing vir-

tually all of the wholesalers and commission houses necessary for shipping abroad, this single provision could be powerfully coercive. For the first time these founding fathers manifested a willingness to distinguish between "good Southerners" and those who were not yet so good, and to use the power of their government against those who did not fall in line. It was also yet another example of how men who maintained that they left the old Union in order to protect the sovereignty of their states were quite willing, when the occasion arose, to trample on the right of a state to decide its course for itself free from outside interference. It could be a dangerous precedent, but then in the past, as well as the future, men like Rhett who crowed the sovereignty line the loudest also showed the greatest inclination to disregard the sovereignty of other states when it conflicted with their own pet projects.

They devoted a second article to the president, mandating salary and reaffirming his appointive powers. Despite some argument for and against holding a popular election to choose the man, in the end, as expected, they provided that their provisional executive should be elected by the delegates present just as all other matters were to be decided, voting in blocs by state. They required that their president be a native-born American, or else a citizen of one of their states at the time the constitution was adopted, and at least fourteen years a resident of one of the seceded states there represented. All of the men being spoken of as potential presidents at the moment were either natives or longtime residents of their states.

Many in Montgomery would agree that the best candidates to be president of a Southern republic were men whose states had not yet seceded. The incumbent vice president of the United States, John C. Breckinridge of Kentucky, was probably the most popular statesman in the South. In November 1860, as candidate of the Southern rights wing of the Democratic Party, he had carried every one of the states now represented in Montgomery. He was moderate, universally liked, diplomatic, and to some degree charismatic. These attributes combined in none of the current candidates. However, he was still loyal to his oath of office and trying to encourage compromise to achieve reunion. Then there was Robert M.T. Hunter of Virginia, a former senator and Speaker of the House, whose hard state-rights stance made him more appealing to some. Yet he was something of a chameleon, changing his views and allegiances according to expediency. He definitely wanted Virginia to secede and made little secret of his ambition to be a president.

But the radicals here feared men from the border states, or rather they
feared border state influence, for Virginia and Kentucky, though slave
states, were not cotton states. Slavery was far less essential to their economy and society. Moreover, many here, Rhett most loudly, distrusted the
instinct toward compromise inherent in the border states thanks to their
location and history. Many feared that if those states gained influence in
their new government, it would only result in an attempt to shift the seceded states back toward reunion. Having taken the step of declaring independence, most of these men wanted it to be not a gesture or a bluff but
the birth of a perpetual new nationality. By requiring that their president
be a citizen of one of the Confederate states at the time of adoption of this
constitution—not ratification, significantly—they ensured that even if Virginia or Kentucky, or Maryland or Missouri, or other border states should
subsequently secede and be admitted, still no border state man would be
able to assume the presidency if a vacancy occurred prior to the election of
a regular president under their later permanent constitution. Inevitably
there had to be some politics in this document, some of what Barnwell referred to as "a spice of policy."[16]

The fact that the committee devoted sufficient time and thought to
make such an insertion spoke eloquently of an awareness of the possibility
of presidential misuse of power. And it is just possible that some might
have pressed for the removal clause with a more immediate, and entirely
political, end in sight. There was no question that Harris and Barry and
their delegation wanted Davis for president. Yet there was another eligible
man among them, and because of where he was from and the general assumptions in some delegations as to which state ought to get the presidency, he would be a potent obstacle to their designs: Mr. Toombs. Yet he
was already manifesting a certain weakness there in Montgomery, one that
would certainly be an embarrassment in a president. Such a clause in Article II would afford a perfect mechanism for getting rid of him quickly if
occasion demanded or opportunity afforded, clearing the way for another—and perhaps Davis—after all.

They adopted most of the old provisions for the judiciary, but the
Supreme Court they mandated would sit only when and if Congress summoned them. They wanted no powerful high court deciding constitutional
issues or interpreting the powers of president and Congress for them.
They had seen enough mischief from such a bench in the old Union. Otherwise the presidentially appointed judges would serve as district justices,

one to each state, and even there the committee limited their power. Significantly, knowing just how widespread pro-Union or at least anti-secession sentiment ran in portions of all their states, they incorporated verbatim the United States Constitution's section covering treason, defining it as consisting solely of waging war against the Confederacy, or of giving aid and comfort to its enemies. That latter definition was so broad and open to interpretation, however, as to cover almost any sort of objectionable behavior.

In Article IV they naturally included a stronger fugitive slave law, but then they ducked entirely all of the necessary provisions for admission of new states and territories, an already contentious issue that they would leave for the permanent constitution to come. That done, they included a fifth article declaring nothing more than that this Congress could amend the provisional constitution at any time by a two-thirds vote, dispensing entirely with the usual procedure of ratification by state legislatures. Once again, for the sake of expediency, state sovereignty had to suffer. The Congress, if not all powerful, would still by this document set itself even further apart, as it did in its very self-transformation from convention to Congress, from the authority of the conventions that sent these men here merely to confer.[17]

Because they worked until midnight or later on February 6, none of the committee were able to attend a party that evening given by James Chesnut and his wife in the parlor of their lodgings at Montgomery Hall. Had they been there, they would have seen another decision being made. Howell Cobb never had any support, and though Stephens did, still there were problems with his not embracing secession until it became an accomplished fact. Toombs, on the other hand, had come over to secession at much the same time as the rest of them, yet without ever being a radical like Rhett or William Yancey. Thus Toombs's posture and views represented the mainstream among the men in Montgomery. The only other man who had a similar position was Jefferson Davis.

Davis was not here, of course, which Rhett at least resented, but then Mississippi had not chosen him as a delegate, and with good cause. Governor John Pettus summoned Davis back to Mississippi after he had resigned his Senate seat in January, and appointed him to organize and command the state militia. The delegates to Montgomery had already been elected well before Davis reached home; besides, he was slated by Pettus for much more important work at home. It would have been better for Toombs if *he* had been absent, not for his views but his behavior.[18] Bartow was a drinker, and drink only exaggerated his natural bent for bombast and posturing. Unfortunately, Toombs was too often in the same condition. "*Common* men cannot comprehend the reasons for some of his actions," a fellow Georgian would say of Toombs eighteen months later, but what was not attributable to his bombastic nature probably came from the bottle.[19] He was no alcoholic, though many years later he probably became one. But despite his stature and robust physique, his was a system that simply did not metabolize spirits as well as other men. The journalist and Reefer Charles E.L. Stuart referred pointedly to Toombs's drinking when, after himself reaching Montgomery, he spoke of him as the "Bibacious Georgian."[20] Even his best friend Stephens had to confess that Toombs was "tight" almost every evening. Now on February 6, when the constitutional committee took a brief recess that evening, Stephens dined with his friend, and naturally there was wine. When they finished Stephens rose to return to his work and saw that when Toombs stood he was already unsteady, "*tighter* than I ever saw him," thought Little Aleck, and "too tight for his character & reputation by far."[21]

Unfortunately, instead of going to his room to sleep it off, Toombs went on to Chesnut's party, and there probably had another glass or two, only to make a fool of himself. The result was disastrous to his hopes for the presidency. His behavior on previous evenings might already have eroded confidence in him, but now too many could see in a drawing room setting just how much of an embarrassment Toombs would be as chief executive. There was no way they could risk presenting such a face to the world. "I think that evenings exhibition settled the Presidency," Stephens said a few days later.[22]

If Toombs was out of contention, the gainer under the circumstances had to be either Davis or another Georgian. Stephens accrued much benefit from Toombs's self-destruction, though he claimed that he did not want that office and that, having opposed secession down to the last minute, he could not possibly be acceptable to the people at large. Still, in the next forty-eight hours a small parade of men would approach him, drawn by his intellect, his temperance, and the fact that he had not been too radical. Stephens's moderation, in fact, ought to sit well with the large body of the Southern people who had had to be led to secession rather than demanding it.

It would take them two days to pass the provisional charter, yet pass it they did, almost unchanged in any significant component. There was some debate over exactly what to call themselves, but they settled on Stephens's suggested Confederate States of America. The only real attempt at substantive deletion came when Rhett tried to strike out the prohibition of the African slave trade. He believed that such a proscription on any aspect of slavery was a tacit condemnation of the institution that he regarded as one of divine ordination. Only South Carolina supported him, the first of many messages this congress would send that though slavery lay at the root of secession, and therefore of their new nation, they were not going to confuse what they chose to see as a stand for state sovereignty with a crusade for slavery itself.

Substantive additions included giving the president a line item veto on appropriations bills, a significant reform reflecting their common opposition to pork barrel legislation and special riders attached to bills that, in the United States, the president had to accept or reject in their entirety. Perkins saw passed a clause vesting executive power in the Congress until their president could take office, and Thomas Withers of South Carolina actually succeeded in amending the clause on right of petition and redress. The committee had borrowed this unchanged from the Constitution, but ardent slave proponents like Withers and Rhett remembered all too well the early days of anti-slavery agitation, when the Congress in 1836 adopted a so-called gag rule to prohibit even the receipt or acknowledgment of petitions involving abolition. Rhett himself had helped author the rule, and fought to maintain it for eight years as one of his proudest achievements. Now Withers introduced an amendment that qualified what had been an unlimited right of petition and redress with a limitation "as the delegated powers of this Government may warrant it to consider and redress." In short, Congress should have the unquestioned power to install a "gag" whenever it chose, and on whatever issue.

After a final reading, the states voted 6 to 0 to adopt. If anything became evident in the discussion and amendments prior to adoption, it was that the more radical members like Rhett and Withers felt distrustful of too much executive power and privilege, and that to them a fundamental obligation of this new nation was the protection and advancement of slavery. A broader range of delegates was interested in genuine reform, especially in fiscal policy, and all were committed to ending the old abuses of internal improvements and protectionism. By the time they adjourned that evening they had been actively in discussion with each other in Montgomery for no more than six days for most, and actually in session just four days.

They had come bringing with them their old political associations and partisanships and personal relations. In the face of that spirit of community and compromise, many could and did speak of themselves as being all of one party, devoid of partisanship. "We shall go through the ordeal with a bold and united front," Tom Cobb crowed. "There will be no wavering." Boyce exulted, "I cant describe to you how much pleasanter it feels to sit in a Congress where you are surrounded by friends."[23]

Yet there were other dynamics than friendship already at work—ambition, jealousy, disappointment, suspicion, as well as deep-seated and fundamental philosophical differences on the reasons for secession and for forming a new confederation. To date they had yet to polarize delegates into opposing camps, and in fact to the extent that there were any consistent contestants so far, it was South Carolina against the other five, driven by the much deeper degree of secession ideology ingrained in many of the Carolinians, and by the assertive pro-slavery stance they had adopted as justification. There was no question that Rhett was the leading dissident in the Congress, nor that he had a few followers, chiefly the elderly Withers, Lawrence Keitt and Boyce on some issues, James B. Owens of Florida, and one or two in the Alabama and Georgia delegations, including at least some sympathy from Tom Cobb. But it was no real opposition, at least not yet, and they were all mainly leaving politics behind them on the big questions.

Next day they would face their biggest choice since the fundamental decision to make themselves a congress and assume power, a choice that would almost overnight inject partisanship and politics into Confederate government and thereafter accelerate them to the very end of its existence: the election of their president.

When the Constitutional Convention delegates had assembled in Philadelphia in 1787, they faced internal divisions between slave and nonslave—or more-slave and less-slave—states that resulted in the three-fifths compromise. But this natural division between North and South was greatly mollified by one question of leadership. The president was always to be George Washington. Absent a fight at the top, harmony was never seriously threatened. The new Confederates, though as yet from only six states, had no such luck in Montgomery. The selection of their president was destined by their very nature to be a murky and contested affair, revealing fault lines and exacerbating some of them. It suggested trouble

ahead, which could be suppressed, perhaps, but not eliminated, by the veneer of unanimity in which they cloaked themselves.

After Toombs unwittingly saw his hopes empty with his glass, speculation on the presidency only increased. Mississippi forthrightly wanted
Davis and let it be known. Alabama apparently still looked to Georgia for
a nominee, and recent discussions with Chesnut and Keitt had Stephens
convinced that a majority in South Carolina still wanted a Georgian. Only
two of Florida's three delegates were present, and Owens made it clear
that he would follow South Carolina, though he also might have intimated
that he hoped South Carolina itself would field a candidate for him to
back, meaning Rhett.[24] Louisiana still kept its own counsel, though there
were hints that Davis could be its favorite, and Georgia, of course, still expected everyone to fall in line behind its own nominee. The unspoken but
commonly understood removal of Toombs as an acceptable candidate certainly opened the door for Davis, yet Mississippi did not actively attempt
to press him on other delegations, other than by making its own preference no secret.[25] That alone was enough for Rhett to conclude that the
Mississippians had come under orders from their governor or convention
to "get Davis elected President," and as early as February 6, perhaps even
before Toombs's misstep, Rhett predicted that Davis would probably take
the prize.[26]

During the day on February 7, while waiting for the provisional constitution to be printed and distributed for the debates, there was leisure for
the speculation to escalate briefly, and it was now that Stephens suddenly
seemed likely to fill Toombs's place. Louis T. Wigfall, the Texas fire-eater
still in Washington but soon to be a delegate here, sent a telegram to
Montgomery that found its way into much of the Southern press before it
got there, urging them to elect Little Aleck as the best man available, one
who would promote unity rather than division, and a man who would win
favor in the border states that they all hoped to see join them, on the right
terms. Then Benjamin Hill, a fellow Georgian, began trying to advance
Stephens's cause within the delegation. He detested Howell Cobb and
feared that he saw Cobb's star rising as Toombs's fell. The only answer was
to push another, even though he and Stephens had been personal enemies
for years. If Hill could win enough support to get them to nominate
Stephens, then common wisdom said the other states would follow. Hill
was probably not unaware that fear of Cobb was motivating others as well.

Word came to the Carolina delegation from friends in Charleston that they
expected either Cobb or Davis to be elected. Yet Cobb was so unaccept-
able to Rhett's delegation that instead Barnwell began to politick actively
for Davis, while Keitt tried to promote Stephens to his colleagues.

Whenever a few minutes of respite from the constitution allowed, there
were visits in hotel rooms and whispered conversations in the statehouse
lobby. Keitt called Stephens out of the hall on the evening of February 8
shortly before final passage. He had watched him in the debate, thinking
him like a spider that spun its web and then quietly watched and waited,
craftily manipulating the threads to snare its prey. "His speech is the concentrated sense of the whole house," Keitt told friends of Stephens, "the
brains of Congress double-distilled."[27] Now Keitt forthrightly told Stephens
that South Carolina expected Georgia to provide the president. Too many
opposed Cobb for his past for him to be viable, and though Keitt himself
had favored Toombs, now that was out of the question. He asked Stephens
if he would accept the presidency. He knew that Barnwell was stumping
for Davis, but Keitt disliked the Mississippian and was trying to promote
Stephens to stop Davis, though he did not say that to the Georgian. Rather
he implied that his state wanted Little Aleck.[28] Stephens gave a politician's
response, showing that he was not immune after all to the lures of ambition. Knowing Toombs to be out, and himself entirely opposed to Cobb,
Stephens might have seen the road clear to an easy win, and himself as the
only alternative available if Georgia were to have the presidency. He still
favored Toombs personally, he told Keitt, but at any event they had to stop
Cobb. If Toombs was truly out of contention, and if his own election could
be made unanimous in order to bind rather than divide the moderates and
the radicals, and if he could have a free hand in choosing a cabinet that
shared his views, then he would accept.[29] The conversation had not gone
unnoticed, nor had Little Aleck's suddenly rising prospects. "Stephens is
looming up for President," Tom Cobb grumbled that evening, still hoping
to see his brother in the executive chair.

The only good news for Tom Cobb that night was that he thought Davis
stood an even better chance of victory than Stephens.[30] If so, it was because Barnwell was the other Carolinian actively politicking, both more
energetically and effectively than Keitt. Moreover, passive and benign as
the bespectacled old gentleman appeared, he also read the political geography in Montgomery far better than Cobb's few supporters or even Keitt.
Mississippi was for its favorite son. Louisiana showed some lean in that di-

rection. Florida would go with South Carolina. That made South Carolina key to a Davis victory, for by bringing Florida with it, they would have four states for Davis. Consequently, instead of trying to influence other delegations, Barnwell concentrated all his effort within his own delegation, and it was no easy task. Old Withers bore some ancient animosity toward the Mississippian, though they had never met. Boyce and Keitt both knew Davis from Congress in Washington, and neither liked him personally. Rhett, of course, disliked him without knowing almost anything of him firsthand, and even liked to claim that the two had never met, a typical Rhett lie, since they were on record for an amicable exchange or two on the floor of the old Senate. The good news was that Chesnut, who had expressed some feeling for Stephens, was also known to be friendly to Davis, and William Porcher Miles appeared positively disposed. Memminger had expressed no preferences. Since Cobb had no hope of a majority of the delegation, Barnwell reasoned that with Miles and Chesnut in his camp for a start, he needed only overcome two of the three—Rhett, Withers, and Keitt—and that would make a majority of the delegation even if Memminger remained noncommittal.

Securing Chesnut's support for a start, Barnwell turned to Withers. He made a total of four visits to Withers, who finally came over after much persuasion very likely involving a play on prejudices against Stephens as unsound and Cobb as a former traitor. Added to himself, Chesnut, and Miles, that was four Davis votes already. Then he went to Keitt and apparently intimated disingenuously that Memminger, too, had come over, making the majority to cast the delegation's vote for Davis. It would be pointless, therefore, for Keitt to vote for Stephens or Cobb or anyone else. Better to vote with the rest for the sake of unanimity. He might even have lied in saying that Rhett was also ready to vote for Davis. Keitt saw the logic, unaware until later that he might have been duped, but he apparently did not make a commitment. So it was still four votes for Davis, and one more needed. That one would be the toughest of all, Barnwell's cousin Rhett. He called on him initially and came away empty-handed, Rhett protesting that he found none of the candidates acceptable. When Barnwell called again, probably during the day on February 7, Rhett frankly stated his objections to Davis. Barnwell countered that he knew Davis well as an able and honest man, and if not brilliant, still he would make good appointments. It took a lot of persuading, but finally Rhett came around, realizing at last, if he had not beforehand, that he stood no chance himself.

He agreed to Davis, though still only in preference to Cobb. Rhett's was the fifth vote for Davis in the delegation, and that was enough. Keitt would come over easily now, and Memminger, and probably only Boyce held out to no point.[31]

The final argument came from Davis himself. Alexander Clayton, a Mississippi delegate, had been held up and only arrived on the afternoon of February 7. With him he brought a letter from Davis in which, replying to a question from Clayton, he said he would not turn down the presidency if offered. Many had assumed that, in the event of war, he would naturally be appointed to chief command of the armies they would have to raise, the best use for the Mississippian's acknowledged military talents. Indeed, he made it clear that this would be his preference as well. But the constitution they were then debating included the old commander-in-chief clause unchanged, meaning that their president would have ultimate authority over their armed forces just as in the United States. If there was any lack of unanimity for Davis in the Mississippi delegation, this quenched it entirely. Moreover, Clayton must have learned somehow that South Carolina and Florida were in the Davis camp now, too, though that knowledge certainly was not general. However it happened, by late that day, no doubt while the constitutional debate resumed, the delegation got word back to Governor Pettus that Davis would almost certainly be elected, and that same night Pettus sent Davis a cryptic telegram advising him to come immediately to the state capital in Jackson, "prepared to go to Montgomery."[32]

Thus matters stood when they passed the provisional constitution and Boyce made his motion to hold the election at noon the next day, followed by his fellow Carolinian Miles's motion to conduct the election immediately. Knowing the current for Davis in his own delegation and elsewhere, Boyce could have been hoping for time to curb the momentum, and at least rally three states against Davis to stop him. Miles, on the other hand, saw the same groundswell and no doubt thought it best to capitalize upon it by taking the vote now. His motion lost by an unrecorded vote, but under the rules at least three states had to vote against it for defeat. One would have been Georgia, which still had not met to decide which of its men to nominate, and which in any event was certainly not part of the Davis tide. Alabama and Louisiana were probably the others, not yet having determined where their support should go. They needed to meet first.

Mississippi already knew where its vote would go, and now so did South Carolina, so neither needed to have a late-night caucus after the midnight adjournment on February 8. If Florida did, it was apparently only to decide to go along with the determination to stand behind South Carolina. Georgia, meanwhile, somehow still unaware of the shift in current toward Davis, decided not to meet until the morning, still secure in the belief that whoever they put forward would be elected. Alabama and Louisiana, however, had a serious decision to make. With Toombs unelectable, and Stephens diffident and not acceptable to many, a new Georgian candidate was needed who would appeal to these two states.

When Alabama and Louisiana caucused that night, surely they did not expect a visit to one from Tom Cobb, and to the other from Cobb's compatriot Bartow. It is certain that they also did not expect what the two told them. Georgia had already met and decided to nominate Tom's brother Howell Cobb, they lied. They even went to South Carolina and Florida with the same news, perhaps unaware of just how solid support there was now for Davis. That done, they went to their lodgings, full in the expectation that when Tom Cobb visited the other delegations in the morning, before Georgia met, he would hear the news that the groundswell for Howell was decisive. Then he could take that back to his own delegation, which he would thus have maneuvered into nominating the one man who otherwise never had even a remote chance of being put forward.[33]

They reckoned without the depth of the distrust of Howell Cobb, thanks to his defection from Southern rights ranks ten years earlier. South Carolina's resolution for Davis only stiffened, and thus Florida's as well. Louisiana had still been leaning toward Stephens, perhaps, but Davis was always acceptable to them, and with their own economy tied to the Mississippi, they preferred a more western man of similar interests to an Atlantic seaboard president who might favor the eastern cotton states. There were also complaints about Cobb's management of national funds when he was secretary of the Treasury. Thus the bluff by his brother and Bartow only propelled Louisiana in a different direction. Mississippi being for Davis, they would stand with their neighbor. Alabama, meanwhile, had been even less decided, some wanting favorite son Yancey, others Toombs. They, too, did not like Howell Cobb. More moderate than any other delegation, Alabama wanted the safety of numbers most of all, and always had its eye on the border states. For days they had been getting word that Davis enjoyed great favor in Virginia, which could be a powerful lure in securing secession in the Old Dominion, and perhaps North Carolina and even Davis's native Kentucky. Making Cobb president, they feared, would do nothing to advance that end. Thus, again the bluff backfired, and the Alabama delegation, though still divided, decided for Davis in a close vote.[34]

It was only the next morning that a crestfallen Toombs learned that no Georgian would be president. He could only respond that Georgia should have the vice presidency, proposing Stephens for the office, with most of the delegation's assent. Being neither too conservative nor too radical, Stephens would at least suggest harmony, and send a conciliatory message to the border states. That was too much for Howell Cobb, who left the room with Bartow and Tom Cobb silently following. The remainder sent an emissary on his rounds, soon returning with the word that Davis indeed had the majority, and the other delegations agreed to Stephens in the second spot.[35]

At least now they had the beginnings of a government. But it had no laws and little time to make them, so Harris rose to press a battle he had lost in the Provisional Constitution. He introduced a bill that all of the current statutes in effect in the United States that did not conflict with their new Constitution should be adopted and continued in force, subject to subsequent repeal or alteration. It was eminently sensible and soon passed, with only South Carolina in opposition. Purists like Rhett and Boyce wanted a more complete break with everything that smacked of the old Union, especially since those statutes contained the 1857 tariff, which conflicted with Rhett's pet hobbyhorse of free trade, and the abolition of the foreign slave trade that he and others still felt left a stigma on slavery itself. Ironically, then, the very first law passed by the Confederate Congress was to adopt virtually all of the laws of the United States.[36]

While word went off to Mississippi telling Davis of his selection, and Howell Cobb sent out the news that they had adopted their provisional constitution unanimously, the news spread rapidly, first through Montgomery and then to the rest of the South.[37] Church bells rang and locomotive and steamboat whistles hooted to celebrate, while a cannon on the Alabama statehouse grounds began a salute that would be echoed all across the new Confederacy. "We have started a govt, and I do not see any thing to mar our unity," Keitt wrote home in the excitement of the moment.[38] Alabama delegate J.L.M. Curry would write happily that "we are getting along quietly and harmoniously," and proclaimed Davis a "noble fellow" and the best selection that could have been made.[39] Toombs, swallowing his disappointment, seconded the declaration of harmony, and a

Mississippi delegate wrote home within hours of the election that "the word Confederate truly expresses our present condition."[40]

There was real bitterness in one room at the Exchange, however. Nothing was going as Rhett had forecast. Davis was president. The provisional constitution was puny and objectionable, and he believed that some of South Carolina's delegates on the framing committee behaved "abominably" in allowing it to get by without a reform of the tariff and with the insult to slavery intact. The only good news was that he perceived the Congress was genuinely bent on a new nation, and he saw little evidence of a desire for reconstruction. Even then, however, Alabama, Louisiana, and Georgia were so worried about divisions in their states that their delegates did not want the Constitution put to popular referenda, and felt especially solicitous of the border states, needing the security of larger numbers. Everyone was so timid, he complained, and it only made him the more incensed when word came a few hours earlier that Governor Francis Pickens had positively refused a suggestion that he should attack Fort Sumter and drive out the Yankee garrison before the Confederate government had formed itself. Rhett wanted it done at once, fearing that there would be delay if left to the newly organizing administration, yet that is precisely what Pickens wanted, and he had already sent word to Memminger—not to Rhett, the head of the delegation, by the way—to hurry forming the government so that it could take over the matter of Fort Sumter. Only Rhett's own strenuous exertions prevented Keitt from actually introducing before the Congress on February 8 an appeal for aid and protection for Charleston. To do so would have disgraced the state, Rhett declared. "For heavens sake, cannot a fight be got up in Charleston Bay?" he complained this day. "We are here shorn of our usefulness, by the cowardly submission and inactivity of our Executive authority." He wanted Pickens burned in effigy, if nothing else, to save them from "the shame and dishonor in which we are."[41]

In the week that followed, there was little to do until Davis could take office. The Congress installed Stephens in the interim, began investigating availability of quarters in Montgomery for the necessary government offices, and in fact did turn their attention to Fort Sumter. Delegates passed a resolution to send commissioners to Washington to try to negotiate recognition of their independence, and a peaceful settlement of all issues between them, including Forts Sumter and Pickens. At the same time they passed a resolution assuming full responsibility for the question of the forts and any other disputed places. Rhett, of course, wanted action, not talk, but all he could do was rant in editorials sent off for his son to publish in the *Mercury*. Memminger was already complaining that Rhett used his ownership of the newspaper to get around the secrecy injunction with un-signed letters and editorials whose origin was an open secret, even while Rhett and his son both lied repeatedly when denying his authorship. "He has already brought himself into evil odor with some of the Delegations as well as our own," Memminger complained the same day they installed Stephens. Unfortunately, none of the other delegates had the time or in-clination to undertake a campaign to counter Rhett in some rival press, "so we have to stand misrepresented."[42]

Davis arrived on February 16 after a roundabout train trip via Chat-tanooga, made necessary by the lack of a more direct connection between Jackson, Mississippi, and Montgomery. That in itself was a lesson to Davis, if he needed one, that should war come, the South's rail system was woe-fully unprepared for the needs of rapid movement of men and materiel. By the time he stepped off his train, the Congress had already passed the en-abling legislation creating the executive departments he would need to conduct his administration—state, war, navy, Treasury, justice, and post of-fice. "Slow and painful is the growth of a good man—still more that of the great Nation," Keitt advised his wife while they worked.[43] Yet they moved with admirable alacrity. The Texas delegates began arriving on February 15 and presented their credentials, but they could not be admitted to their seats on the floor nor their state to the Confederacy until a February 21 referendum in Texas made its secession official. Bills had been introduced and passed for organizing an army and navy, purchasing ships and arms, and creating a diplomatic commission to go to Europe. Typically, Rhett tried to pre-empt Davis's prerogative in appointing emissaries to go abroad by introducing a resolution for the Congress to choose the men and send them off before the president arrived. With Davis not yet in office, Rhett was already making a clear bid to undermine his authority, one that Davis himself was not likely to forget.[44] Indeed, on hearing the news of Davis's election, James Hammond in South Carolina, himself no friend to Rhett, remarked that "he is not the man ever to forgive."[45]

On February 18, Jefferson Davis sat in an open barouche drawn by six white horses, accompanied by Stephens and other dignitaries, and joined a slow procession from the Exchange Hotel up Market Street toward the capitol. As the presidential party approached, a shout went up from several thousand spectators packed around the statehouse and on stands specially erected, while cannon on the grounds boomed out a salute. Inside, the Congress had just finished signing the formal copy of the Provisional Constitution on a roll of parchment more than ten feet long. Soon came word of the approach of the carriage, and they stopped their business to receive Davis.[46]

At one o'clock Howell Cobb introduced Davis to the crowd, and the president-elect began to speak. Like most inaugurals, his would not be memorable either for eloquence or substance, but at least it was brief, no more than eighteen minutes. History would vindicate their cause, he declared. They were not revolutionaries but men true to the original promise and intent of the U.S. Constitution. In seceding they but exercised their undeniable rights. They wanted nothing not theirs, had no designs on the rightful property or rights of the Union, and did not wish for war, but if forced upon them, they would accept it in defense of their own rights. "Our true policy is peace," Davis said, and averred that North and South ought, in fact, to coexist amicably as mutually complementary and mutually dependent nations. But he dismissed all idea of eventual reconstruction. This separation was perpetual, and if the North tried to coerce them back into the old association, then he promised that "the suffering of millions will bear testimony to the folly and wickedness of our aggressors."[47] That done, Davis laid his left hand on a Bible held by Cobb, raised his right, and took the brief oath of office.

Many observers expressed pleasure, and even some wonder, at the harmony with which they had come this far. Howell Cobb complimented them all on holding their voluble tempers in debate, and their secretary noted their coolness. Looking beyond the ultras, Nisbet thought the majority were bent on doing good, and even Rhett paid tribute to the patriotism of the members. Stephens, ever the pessimist, actually confided a few days after the inauguration that "I am not without hope," though at the same time admitting that he was on tenterhooks waiting to see how long the harmoniousness and unity would last.[48]

Its first test would be Davis's cabinet appointments. No one knew his mind in this regard, and whatever thoughts he may have had he kept just as secret as Congress's deliberations. There had been rumors for days before the inauguration, of course, most of it in the press, and all of it ill-informed. Some said Memminger, or Toombs, or even Yancey would get state, or Charles Conrad of Louisiana or Stephen Mallory of Florida—not even a delegate—the navy portfolio, and Georgia's Martin Crawford or Bartow the War Department. One rumor even mentioned Rhett's name in connection with the Treasury, while another spoke of Memminger.[49] As in any new administration, there would be favors to return, and even though Davis had not sought the presidency nor campaigned for it, and therefore came to Montgomery unfettered by debts to redeem, still he would not have a hand entirely free from political considerations when it came to filling his cabinet. For a start, there were still just six states in the Confederacy, for Texas still awaited the February 21 referendum. There were also six executive departments, and that alone applied the first and most obvious restriction on Davis's choices. Each state was entitled to one cabinet position as its share of the political largesse. Should any appointee from either Mississippi or Georgia decline a preferment, then it ought to go to Texas, since those other two states already held the presidency and vice presidency, respectively.

Certain things were obvious to mature minds even before Davis took his hand from the Bible. He was a moderate himself and would be most comfortable with fellow moderates. There was no logic at all in expecting him to hand a portfolio to one of the radicals. Davis was intelligent enough to realize that in any revolution the greatest security lay in the political center with the greatest numbers. There was nothing to gain by the gesture of putting a radical in his cabinet, yet not naming one could be counted on only to inflame further the wounded pride and ambition of a man like Rhett who had already been passed over for so much, and no one had cabinet office more on his mind than Rhett. While his aspirations for the presidency might have been tempered somewhat by the realization even on his part that he was unelectable, he felt much greater claim—even right—to a premier cabinet post. After all, South Carolina had been first to secede, first to take the risk while others only followed, and that alone entitled it to an important seat at the cabinet table. Rhett's preference would have been secretary of state, the senior and certainly most prestigious post in the old Union, and one in fact more often considered a stepping-stone to the presidency than even Stephens's office. Rhett had no diplomatic experience, but he had been to England and France twice, met with leading men, dealt with British importers and businessmen, and taken an active role in foreign relations issues when serving in the old Congress in Washington. He also considered himself an authority on tariff policy, and had

been the most outspoken advocate of free trade for years. Surely that qualified him for the cabinet post from which he might well exert even more
influence than Davis, or so he thought.

But once he lost the initial battle in the Exchange that first weekend
over what the convention ought to do, Rhett saw himself steadily reminded of just how little influence he had here. He knew his colleagues
would do nothing to advance him for appointment. "I expect nothing
therefore from the delegation, lifting me to position," he complained on
February 11. "I have never been wise in pushing myself forward to office
or power." Already crushing the juice from sour grapes, he self-righteously
declared, "I will do my duty as the occasion requires, and leave office to be
intrigued for by others." Yet there was no doubt that he was wretchedly
unhappy at his lack of a prospective portfolio. "Prepare for disappointment," he warned his family. "Life is nothing but a continual series of disappointments."[50] A few years later he would write: "Mine was a singular
fate, in the affairs of the Southern Confederacy. I built the ship; and with
my own hands, put into it, its best ribs and soundest planks—and then was
turned out of it to be navigated by others, some of whom shed tears at its
construction. Well!—wise men did not do this."[51]

Certainly it was a wise man who prepared himself for the jealousies and
disappointed ambitions inevitable in any new government formed by men
who were, after all, in the main politicians, prominent men in their own
states who naturally could feel an aspiration to strut on a larger stage.
Moreover, where all saw themselves as founding fathers, many would feel
themselves entitled to recognition for their services and an opportunity to
shine. That Jefferson Davis was a man of some wisdom, surely, few would
doubt, but those who knew him best would well doubt that he would take
cognizance of anything other than his duty as he saw it in making his appointments. He had never been a man to worry over the feelings and sensibilities of others. Just as convinced of his own moral and political
rectitude as was Rhett, Davis could be just as obstinate, and just as unfor-
giving of opposition, though otherwise an eminently more reasonable
man. In short, ambitions, feelings, and, most of all, the political expedi-
ence of taking men like Rhett and Cobb into account simply would not occur to Davis. In association with men far more ambitious than himself,
such an attitude was certain to create enemies without his ever intending
to do so, or even being aware of what he had done.

Significantly, the first real hint of the kind of cabinet Davis would appoint came in a sarcastic remark made in Montgomery within hours of the inauguration. Asked whom Davis would appoint, a wag replied: "For Secretary of State, Hon. Jeff. Davis of Miss.; War and Navy, Jeff. Davis of Miss.; Interior, ex-Senator Davis, of Miss.; Treasury, Col. Davis, of Miss.; Attorney General, Mr. Davis, of Miss."[52] Setting aside the fact that Congress had not created an interior department, and would not, and omitting the Post Office Department, which the joker presumably assumed even Davis would not want, still he put his finger on the salient point. Davis had always been his own man, by nature more autocratic than collegial. When secretary of war under President Franklin Pierce, he became noted for his unwillingness to delegate, and for a compulsion to do everything himself. He told his wife that he wanted to surround himself now with the best men, regardless of their viewpoints, admitting that there could be other ideas than his own of merit. Yet Varina Davis, who knew her husband better than he did, saw through the pose of open-mindedness with which Davis fooled himself. He was not by temperament cut out to be an executive, of that she was certain. Davis himself would have agreed in more introspective moments, but having been given a job of trust, he knew only one way to approach its execution, and that was his way.[53]

In fact, Davis showed some sensitivity to the several constituencies assembled in Montgomery, while at the same time taking the prudent decision to write off the ultras. Within hours of the inauguration he sent messages to Yancey and Barnwell asking them to see him. He met with Yancey first, and offered him any post in the cabinet he might choose other than state, or else the post as head of the diplomatic mission he would soon send abroad. Yancey replied that he preferred his position in the Alabama state convention at the moment, but agreed to make a choice within a day or two.[54] It was perhaps no more than an hour before Barnwell made his call, and on his arrival Davis forthrightly offered him the premier chair as secretary of state, the one post he withheld from his offer to Yancey. Davis had fixed on Barnwell for the position sometime earlier. Politically it was expedient, recognizing South Carolina's leadership by giving the state the most important cabinet spot, and even though Barnwell was nowhere near as radical as his cousin, still he had been among the secession leaders for some time, which meant that faction would be recognized. More to the point, Davis knew and trusted Barnwell as a man of reason whose sense transcended doctrine, as he had shown here already. Unfortunately, Barnwell was sick of the political world, or so he felt at the moment. He wanted to serve out his current term as congressman and then retire. He declined the offer. Instead he suggested that Howell Cobb or Toombs would be good in the state office, and went on to say that if South Carolina was to have a seat at the cabinet table, then he would suggest Memminger for secretary of the Treasury. Davis made no commitment, but did ask Barnwell to keep their discussion private.[55]

Unfortunately, for a man who had shown sufficient guile to gambit his delegation into voting for Davis, Barnwell proved remarkably naive about keeping Davis's confidence. Within hours he told Keitt the result of the conversation, and worse, told Rhett, who mingled shock that his own name was not put forward for the state portfolio by his cousin with renewed resentment toward Davis for failing to recognize Rhett's own claim to high appointment. That the despised Memminger might get a cabinet slot made it only worse.[56] Rhett told his son in a few days that "I was too sick of heart" to ask any more detail of Barnwell. This was certain confirmation that Rhett was to be ignored entirely. "The course of things appear to consign me to retirement," he complained. "My uncompromising Southernism and anti-Tariffism, I suppose, renders me unfit for the councils of the Provisional Government," he sighed.[57] Already primed for two weeks now to be hostile to anyone who gained power in his place, Rhett let this turn of affairs only propel him further along the road to opposition. Indeed, before long Barnwell would be complaining that his cousin inaugurated the opposition party before Davis even had an opportunity to do anything objectionable.[58]

Before making any more offers, Davis met with Stephens in a harmonious session that led the new vice president to think that their relations would be cordial and that his views would carry some weight. The president was thinking most immediately of Toombs, mindful that the Georgian had missed the top spot himself, and aware as well of Toombs's ability and influence. The two had never been especially close, and eight years earlier a misunderstanding led to Davis calling Toombs "radically false and corrupt" and Toombs responding in kind that Davis was a "swaggering braggart and cunning poltroon." A rumored duel never happened, but they were cool toward each other for three years until mutual associates got them to drop their animosity and meet as friends.[59] Southern society and politics had always been fueled in large degree by personality and temperament as much as policy. Though much more reasonable than Rhett, Davis could and would allow personal animus to choose his political

friends. Certainly Davis showed good will now when he asked Stephens if
Toombs would accept a cabinet appointment. It was "the highest compli-
ment" to Toombs, as Stephens acknowledged, and he agreed to go to his
friend to sound out his feeling.[60]

Now Davis believed that he had at least the two top positions lined up,
and South Carolina and Georgia taken care of. Memminger accepted as
soon as Davis sent an offer, but Toombs suddenly had to leave Montgomery to see a seriously ill daughter at home and in the rush could not
call on the president, so Davis sent a telegram to catch up with him in
Georgia. Meanwhile Davis wired to his old friend Clement C. Clay of Alabama offering him the War Department, but Clay declined because of his
health. Interestingly, hereafter Davis did not invite suggestions from any
others, nor did he ask the remaining state delegations to propose candidates. He seems to have consulted only with Stephens, which just further
irritated both brothers Cobb that they were left out. "Davis acts for himself," Tom complained, "and receives no advice."[61]

The day after their first meeting, Yancey called and proposed that Alabama would be pleased to see the War Department go to Leroy Pope
Walker of Huntsville, whose younger brother Richard Walker now sat in
the Congress. The elder Walker had been Yancey's closest compatriot in
bringing Alabama to secession. He was chairman of the state delegation at
the Democratic convention in Charleston in 1860 and led the walkout that
precipitated the breakup of the meeting. Significantly, he had never held
any sort of executive position, but he wanted one. Indeed, Walker was the
first man to mount a real campaign to win an appointment, politicking
Clay, Yancey, and others for support.[62] Walker himself went to Montgomery to campaign for the position personally, and asked friends to send
telegrams to Davis endorsing him. Naturally he met with his old friend
Yancey, and Yancey was happy to back him for office.[63] Davis at first
replied that he could not give Alabama two places in the cabinet, but then
Yancey finally and firmly declined any seat himself, and asked that Alabama's appointment go to Walker.[64]

One thing Davis had to have been immediately aware of was Walker's
complete lack of experience for a cabinet position of that importance. That
Walker knew nothing at all of military matters was a concern, or certainly
ought to have been. His own brother would testify that Walker "was *no*
politician," but then, Davis himself had served four years as secretary of
war from 1853 to 1857.[65] He knew better than anyone else the require-

ments of the office, and could well rationalize that Walker's inexperience would be no problem since Davis, being Davis, would likely manage the affairs of that department himself in the main.

With the big three states and the big three offices taken care of, Davis made the rest of his selections. He wanted Senator Judah P. Benjamin to be his attorney general. They were friends—though they, too, nearly fought a duel some years before—and Benjamin, lately a senator from Louisiana, was an able attorney and noted authority on the law. It was an insignificant office, but Louisiana's was a small delegation and it should not expect more. Florida, as the smallest of all, might have expected the least significant portfolio, the postmaster general, but Davis was well acquainted with Senator Stephen R. Mallory from their days in Washington, and knew his command of naval affairs, something that few Southerners were familiar with, coming as they did from a section with little maritime industry. As for the postmastership, a job few if any would even want, it seemed most fitting that it go to Mississippi, which could hardly expect an important cabinet position after getting the presidency itself. Davis chose Henry Ellett for that thankless job, and then sent telegrams to all three notifying them of their appointments and summoning them to Montgomery should they accept.

Davis would not get his cabinet in place without some difficulty. He had to lean on Toombs to get him to accept, with Stephens's help. The bluff Georgian did not have the temperament of an administrator, nor did he like taking an office second to the one he hoped to have. Besides, he had been appointed to the committee to frame the permanent constitution, and there he could do some real good, he felt. In the end he accepted only on the condition that he would hold the office temporarily.[66] Mallory proved to be a problem, too, for Jackson Morton of his own delegation rekindled an old prewar grudge and held up his confirmation, charging that Mallory was unsound on secession, when in fact it was Morton who had once opposed secession. Nevertheless, the hold on Mallory's confirmation afforded the first pretext for focusing opposition to Davis, and predictably Rhett's was the active hand. Through the *Mercury,* Rhett tried to make capital on the embarrassing opposition from Florida delegates, and Mallory's confirmation hung fire for two weeks before finally being acted on on March 8.[67]

As for the post office, Ellett turned it down flat, even though Congress confirmed the appointment before he could do so. Davis tried another

Mississippian, Wirt Adams, but he finally declined as well, and it seemed that no one would take the spot. Fortunately, by then there was another state. Delegates from Texas finally got the word that the February 21 referendum resulted in a more than three-to-one majority for secession, close to the largest voter turnout in the state's history even though the referendum had been announced only twelve days before the balloting.[68] The strains of Unionism ran deep in some parts of the Lone Star State all the same. "In the name of God and our country," one citizen begged Governor Sam Houston "to never forsake the Union, but oppose with your great powers the secession men."[69] He had tried and failed, and now the Texans were admitted to the floor and to the Confederacy. If no Mississippian would take the Post Office Department, Davis could prevail on his old friend John H. Reagan of Texas to do so, but only after he, too, twice tried to turn it down.[70]

Generally the cabinet appointments met with public favor, though every one of them aroused objections in one quarter or another. Perhaps the greatest criticism was a perceived lack of variety. In 1860 all of the appointees had supported Breckinridge, the Southern rights Democratic nominee, but then so had the overwhelming majority of those who were now citizens of the Confederate States. "It is objectionable on the score of its exclusive party character," said a Montgomery critic. Davis had not included anyone representative of the Stephen Douglas or John Bell following in 1860, but then those factions were almost exclusively active in the border states, where Bell carried Virginia, Tennessee, and Kentucky, and Douglas took Missouri—states still in the Union and not represented in Montgomery. "Partisanship . . . appears to have influenced their own selection," complained a Georgia editor. Yet a Montgomery commentator thought that this same group represented sufficient diversity to be evidence that "the last vestige of party is being rapidly swept away."[71] It was all in what they wished to see. Most important of all, however, where there was disgruntlement at any of the appointments, it focused not on the appointee but on the man responsible, Jefferson Davis.

4

The Struggle for a Confederate Democracy

THE WAR TALK WAS HEARD everywhere, both in Montgomery and from the Confederacy at large. "During Buchanan's administration we shall have peace," a Louisianian advised Governor Thomas Moore, "but that of Lincoln will be a bloody one." The Confederacy "should be prepared to *bide the shock*."[1] Jabez L.M. Curry, delegate from Alabama, agreed that James Buchanan would do nothing. "Lincoln may and may not," he advised two days after Jefferson Davis's inauguration. "The interests in favor of peace are so great that war can hardly be unnecessarily attempted. If the Black Republicans force it upon us, of course we must defend ourselves."[2] From every quarter came similar expressions of resolution. "I ask not to breathe an atmosphere so putrid as the one corrupted by northern tread," a Georgian assured Governor Joseph Brown, "but to fall among Chivalrous Georgians if fall we must struggling with that execrated horde for our rights."[3]

Talk of the possibility of war dominated Davis's first cabinet meeting on March 4, timed to coincide with the inauguration of Abraham Lincoln in Washington. There was division among them. Davis, Alexander Stephens, and Judah Benjamin agreed that war was highly probable, while Christopher Memminger and Leroy Pope Walker thought it unlikely, and Robert Toombs, for all his former bluster, seemed equivocal. Benjamin argued that they must raise an army and find money to buy weapons and munitions, that they needed to win the formal recognition of England and

85

France, and that their principal asset for achieving both was Southern cotton, which the government ought to acquire immediately from growers and ship abroad in quantity to purchase what they needed and build up future credit, especially now while there were no hostilities. If war did start, Lincoln could be expected to blockade Southern ports, which would make export far more difficult, with a corresponding impact on credit and purchasing power. Memminger pointed out that it would take special legislation to allow the government to go into the cotton business, and even then it would have the effect of putting the government in competition with private growers. Moreover, had they not seceded in part to get away from a government that they thought too willing to interfere in the private market? The meeting broke up with no decision made, yet the basic objects discussed were those that would dominate much of Confederate politics for the next four years.

Personally Davis had little expectation that foreign powers would recognize the Confederacy until it had proven that it could win and maintain its independence on its own. Still, Congress had called for sending a diplomatic mission to England and France, and certainly there was no harm in the effort. Davis's choice of emissaries revealed how little he expected from it, however, or else spoke to a woeful judgment. Of all people, he asked William Yancey to head the mission. Wanting to send to the world the message that the Confederates were not radicals or revolutionaries, he nevertheless selected one of the South's two most radical revolutionaries. Indeed, the selection of Yancey might have been more political than anything else on Davis's part, for sending the Alabamian abroad would get him out of the country, removing his influence from the small ultra party that Yancey himself had admitted he still felt duty-bound to represent.[4] Just as amazing, Yancey accepted, without explanation and against the advice of friends and family. Adding further weight to the argument that Davis expected little from the mission, he filled it out with two nonentities, Pierre Rost of Louisiana and his old friend Ambrose Dudley Mann of Virginia, the only one of the three with any diplomatic experience.

Making the mission's efforts even more pointless, Davis would give them no unilateral power at all to negotiate and conclude treaties. They were empowered only to meet foreign heads of state and present their case for independence and recognition. Implicit, of course, was the veiled threat that there might be a cut in the supply of cotton to Europe's mills otherwise. Even Toombs thought it pointless. He wanted to offer Europe positive lures like favored-nation trading status, and for the first time he found himself in agreement with Robert Barnwell Rhett, who chaired the foreign relations committee. Rhett wanted the lowest possible import duties to be imposed at guaranteed rates for twenty years for nations that recognized the Confederacy, as well as free entry into Confederate ports. When Rhett found out that Davis's instructions to Yancey embraced nothing of the sort, he stormed to his friend's house and told him he had no business even going abroad if he had nothing to offer. "You carry no argument which Europe wishes to hear," he said. He fruitlessly urged Yancey either to refuse the mission or else demand that the president give him the power to present real inducements.[5] For Rhett, however, it was another affirmation that Davis was opposed to free trade, and was in fact wedded to high tariffs and protectionism. The Carolinian's effort to sway Yancey's course was his first active attempt to thwart the president but hardly the last. Rather, it was the first move of an opposition. Though Toombs was not involved or aware, now at least one issue had initiated agreement—it was too soon to call it an alliance—between an ultra and one of the more mainstream members of the administration. There had already been other issues promoting division but they had only established lines between the mainstream majority and the more ultra minority. But this issue was different.

Davis had another commission to appoint, this one to go to Washington to attempt to adjust differences short of war. The new Confederacy was willing to negotiate on compensation for the Federal installations taken over, and those like Forts Sumter and Pickens still in Union hands, even if it was bargaining under the gun. Davis asked Stephens to head a delegation, but the vice president politely but firmly declined, and not for the last time. A few days later, on March 2, when the president asked Stephens to head a commission to Arkansas to encourage its state convention toward secession, Stephens again declined. Instead, he pleaded ill health, as he would frequently when asked to take on a task he did not want. This hardly put the vice president in an opposing camp, but it gave Davis good cause to wonder just how much support he could expect from this quarter. And when Stephens instead offered suggestions of others for the embassies, he felt chagrined that Davis did not follow his advice and appointed his own men, without further consultation. This remarkable, brilliant yet diffident Georgian did not accept well the rejection of his advice. "I fear that the appointing power will not act with sufficient prudence, discretion, and wisdom," he complained just a week after the inauguration, only days after declaring with some pride how much confidence Davis appeared to have in his advice.[6] This hardly soured his relationship with Davis, but it did not bode well that within a week there was already doubt and a hint of resentment. The fact that Stephens's closest friend, Toombs, was already more disenchanted with Davis, for personal and political reasons, was more ominous, for where one Georgian went, the other usually followed.

In the end Davis sent three men to Washington. Though technically they reported to Toombs, Davis made the appointments and gave them their directions, another reason for Toombs, like Stephens, to feel himself trapped in a pointless office with no power. The delegation to Washington, of course, would fail, for Davis had nothing to offer and Lincoln had nothing to give. The only question arising out of the negotiations would be how long they would prolong peace before action took over, and whether Davis could keep a lid on the hotheads in Charleston before they acted unilaterally and started a war. In this instance, even Yancey argued for caution. If Governor Francis Pickens's batteries opened fire before negotiations were concluded or broken off, it would embarrass the new Confederacy, make its government and administration appear weak and undecided, and cause trouble and confusion. "Victory even will not palliate the movement," he warned. Such an act would cause "an indignation & astonishment here in the Confederate Congress that will tend to break up the new government."[7] Davis soon appointed newly commissioned Brigadier General Pierre G.T. Beauregard to go to Charleston and personally assume command of its defenses. That took the heat off Pickens, and a grateful governor would not forget.

On the chance—or the expectation—that armed confrontation was inevitable, Congress passed legislation on February 27 to create a "provisional" army, and here again there was division. Davis, wiser than most in his assessment of Union determination, expected that any war could well be a long one. He wanted the enabling legislation to allow him to raise volunteers for enlistments of three years or the term of the war. Unfortunately, Montgomery teemed with self-proclaimed military wizards like Francis Bartow, chairman of the military affairs committee, who felt certain that the Yankees would back down in the face of any show by the South. Finally the best compromise Davis could get was authorization for up to 100,000 volunteers for twelve-month terms. But then the division in opinion became more acute, and began to combine with other issues. How many men should he call out immediately, the full 100,000 or only as many as appeared to be needed at the moment? The United States Army had barely more than 13,000 men actively under arms, spread in detachments all across the continent. Should the Confederacy build its forces judiciously just to keep parity with its potential foe, or should it raise a massive army overnight in the hope of intimidating the North away from any notion of coercion?

It was a question not just of strategic and political policy but also of economic feasibility. Not surprisingly, those in favor of the most aggressive possible policy, again led by Rhett and with some agreement from Toombs, wanted a huge army that could only be paid for and supported by precisely the sort of government cotton export scheme that these same critics also expounded. Yet Davis, seconded by Memminger, and urged on by his own conservative military and fiscal policy, thought it better to raise such an army as they could afford. Several states were giving the Confederate Treasury outright gifts of large sums, with Memminger arranging for more in the form of loans. It was enough to create an army to match the Union's at the moment, but not to overwhelm it. To do more would risk exhausting Confederate credit at home and abroad, necessitating sudden and dramatic calls on the public in taxes and sales of bonds or notes simply to fund the debt.

Moreover, to call out a massive force at once risked sending all the wrong signals to Washington and abroad. How could they present themselves as peaceable and non-belligerent on the one hand—Stephens had already said publicly that all they wanted was to be left alone, a line Davis would borrow soon enough—while on the other raising the largest army yet seen on the continent? Meanwhile, England and France already had several generations' experience witnessing the expansionist appetite of Americans, always most ravenous in the South with its dream of spreading slavery to Mexico, Cuba, and Central America. What could raising a huge army in the face of Lincoln's puny 13,000 suggest to London and Paris but that the Confederates had further designs in the hemisphere despite their protestations on wanting nothing not their own?

As Davis always did, he opted for the conservative approach, and on March 9 called for just 7,700 volunteers from five of the states, to be added to the several thousand South Carolina volunteers already in service around Charleston. That would put a total of just under 12,000 men in the field, certainly a fair equivalent to the Union army at the moment. Most of them he would assign to Charleston and Pensacola, and all but 1,000 east of the Mississippi, closer to the scene of potential action than much of the United States Army. It was no sort of field force to fight a battle with, but then there was still no war.[8]

Then came problems from an unexpected quarter. The several governors had largely been left out of the decision-making process in establishing the Confederacy. That had been almost exclusively the province of the state conventions through their representatives. For some of the governors, men of collegial character, this created little or no problem, but for one or two, especially the jealous and imperious Joseph Brown of Georgia, the removal of decision making from his hands rankled. Even a more reasonable man like Thomas Moore of Louisiana also found ground to stand on his own authority. When Davis made his first call for volunteers, it was the governors' first opportunity to insert themselves directly into Confederate policy, and Brown especially did not hesitate. The new Provisional Constitution did not give Davis or the government authority to raise troops directly in their states, these men argued, for it would be a clear violation of the sovereignty of the states. Only the governors had the power to do that, and any soldiers sent to the national service had to be raised and forwarded by the governors themselves.

Further complicating the issue was the matter of weapons. Some of the states already supplied arms to a number of private military companies. Those units, being private, were certainly free to offer themselves directly to Montgomery, but they could not take state weapons with them. However, if those units volunteered through the governors' offices, then the governors would allow them to take state weapons out of the state with them. In a clear bid to hold onto political patronage power, Brown made it even more difficult by insisting that only he had the authority to appoint officers for regiments Georgia raised. Thornier yet, Brown appointed his officers first before raising the troops, sent the officers out into the countryside to enlist the volunteers, and then tried to claim that he had filled his quota of regiments when, in fact, all he had was a full complement of officers. Necessity forced Montgomery to bend its own rules time and time again to accept whatever the governors would send. Secretary of War Walker, in one of his first decisions, compromised, no doubt only after securing Davis's blessing. "Technicalities must not stand in the way of harmony," he told Brown as he gave in to him.[9]

Interestingly enough, while men like Brown stood on their prerogatives to use military appointments to play the patronage game, some carped when the president exercised the same functions himself. The Constitution clearly mandated that it was his duty to appoint all officers of general rank, and he was, of course, not a man to shirk his duty to the letter. Besides, he had more practical military experience than anyone else in either state or national government. Logically, he first thought of seeking men with extensive military training and experience, which naturally led him to look for West Point graduates like himself. Yet Rhett immediately accused him privately of using his authority simply to take care of old friends from his army days, and to redeem yet more favors owed due to the same sort of corrupt agreements made in Washington that he believed had led to Davis getting elected in the first place.[10]

The problem was, they lived in a culture that, thanks to its own mythology, believed that every Southern man, as a descendant of those Norman lords who conquered the Saxons in 1066, was a born leader. No training or experience was necessary to lead men in battle, only bravery and the opportunity to let the natural leadership qualities inherent in them all come out. Still, compelling logic and common sense said that men with experience and training, especially training, were the best ones to train and lead a new army of volunteers raised from the canebrakes and pine woods and small villages of the Confederacy. Yet every state governor felt that he was due a fair proportion of general's stars for his favorite sons, regardless of aptitude.

At the same time, aspirants engaged members of their state delegations to put pressure on Davis, which made it a patronage matter. James Chesnut was often seen walking with Davis on Montgomery's streets in the evenings, pressing the claims of some Carolinian or another, while others lobbied Walker. As the commissions were forthcoming, governors and congressmen grumbled alike that there was too much West Point and not enough recognition of homegrown applicants. And even when local favorites did get commissions, some of them proceeded only to carp that their new rank was not high enough. Milledge L. Bonham, currently a general in the South Carolina state militia, actually expected state militia generals to be taken into the Confederate service at their same rank, regardless of the fact that many of them were nothing but lawyers who had never heard a hostile shot fired. Worse was W.H.T. Walker of Georgia, who was "insulted" by being offered a mere colonelcy. It was an affront to Georgia, he told his governor. He must be a general or nothing, warning the prickly Brown that "it is very important that the rights and dignity of Georgia should be maintained in this *scuffle* at Montgomery."[11] It is no wonder that Chesnut's wife mused in disgust that what had begun as a struggle for secession was rapidly becoming "a War for the Succession of Places."[12]

Just as Davis's approach to the military was prudent, meeting the current situation rather than anticipating the uncertain future, so his naval policy matched. Congress did not actually authorize creation of a navy until March 11, in itself an admission of the obvious, that the South was not a nautical country and never had been, and that its defense of its independence would rest on the land. They had captured a few Yankee ships when state forces overran United States naval bases at Pensacola, Mobile, and elsewhere, and as they took possession of some Coast Guard revenue cutters. With no shipbuilding facilities capable of producing warships, they could hardly hope to match the North hull for hull. In fact, Davis did not intend to try. The Confederacy had no desire to become a maritime power, nor any need to do so. All of its major harbors and river mouths were under the protection of strong masonry forts and shore batteries. Its only real naval need would be gunboats to augment the forts and to keep the Mississippi clear of enemy ships, and a few new ironclads to help guard those rivers and harbors and break any blockade should Lincoln try to impose one. As long as foreign and domestic shipping could get into and out of Southern ports, the Confederacy had no need for further naval force.

Clearly the administration sought to achieve the maximum that was practical on the limited resources available, suiting its program to the current state of affairs. Davis was reactive rather than proactive, but for a government and an administration in place for less than a month, it was the best he could do. Unfortunately, it brought him up against Rhett yet again. A navy was one of Rhett's first pet projects. He almost nagged Congress into the enabling legislation, and some ten days earlier, even before Secretary of the Navy Stephen Mallory reached Montgomery to take office, he attempted to make naval policy just as he had tried to pre-empt foreign policy. "It was upon the Ocean, that the United States was most vulnerable," he argued, "and the Confederate States, without shipping to be captured or sunk, could sweep that of the United States from the seas." The conclusion was puerile, even for Rhett, who never allowed complete ignorance of a subject to conflict with his declarations of certitude. He thought that an appropriation of $9 million or $10 million to buy cotton to ship abroad to be bartered for building a navy would give the South superiority. The president dismissed the idea, and rightly so, for as yet the Confederacy had neither several million dollars nor credit, and as Memminger pointed out already, their Constitution did not allow the government to enter private enterprise in the cotton trade.[13]

That was not what Rhett wanted to hear. Combined with Davis's modest military policy, it sounded almost as if the president did not want to be able to defend the Confederacy, and certainly that he had no desire to defeat the Union. That smacked of what Rhett and a few other ultras had feared all along, a desire for reconstruction. What could be the reason other than a secret desire to keep peace long enough to secure some constitutional guarantees from Washington to protect slavery in return for reunion?

It was one more reason for Rhett to conclude that if the Confederacy was to be saved from Davis and his ilk, it was up to him to do it in the Permanent Constitution. Unlike Davis, Rhett always preferred to strike the first blow, and though over the years he had lost almost all his political battles, he still believed that initiative meant advantage. In South Carolina's secession convention, when it was first suggested that delegates to Montgomery might frame a constitution, he felt personal outrage. "I send a Commissioner to make a Constitution for me!" he shouted. "I give a batch of men the right to make a Constitution for me!" South Carolina should dictate the terms of any new constitution, and the rest of the South would follow. Just as implicit was the suggestion that he expected himself to be the guiding hand in that constitution.[14]

When Rhett's framing committee of twelve first met, he declared that his intention would be to rise above party and faction, make no compromises, and produce a document closed to "constructive usurpations." It had to be a charter impervious to "doubt, dissatisfaction or revision here, in order to please others," he said, meaning the border states. If those states seceded, they were going to have to take a pure Southern rights document or none at all. "A failure now," he warned, "will probably be a failure forever."[15] He was also determined, if possible, to see that when he delivered the document, it would not be debated behind closed doors. "What took place on the provisional government satisfies me that we must have the Constitution considered in open session," he told his son Barnwell.[16]

Rhett proposed that they take the United States Constitution as a model and make only the most necessary changes. Their task should be "a matter of restoration, than of innovation," he said. Then he produced for them a bound copybook with his proposed changes, suggesting that they should use it as a basis for their deliberations.[17] He wanted no preamble with its unfounded talk of "the People of the United States," for as he maintained, there were no such people. Each state should retain "its sovereignty free-dom and independence and every power jurisdiction and right" except those explicitly delegated therein. He proposed that Congress be consti-tuted and elected just as before, but then he made his first bold departure. When it came to apportionment of representatives, he wanted every in-habitant except Indians to be counted in full, changing the old means by which slaves were numbered at three-fifths of their white counterparts. It was a clear bid for power for South Carolina. Among the existing seven Confederate states, four had greater total populations of white and black than his own. Yet South Carolina's proportion of free white population was the smallest of all, dramatically smaller than that of any of the border slave states that might secede in the future. At the same time, South Carolina had more slaves than all of the border states combined except Virginia. Counting slaves in full for apportionment would thus strengthen South Carolina and other slave-dominated Deep South states like Alabama and Louisiana in the Congress without materially doing the same for the bor-der states. That would give them representation commensurate with their stake in and commitment to a slave nation. It was nothing less than an at-tempt to guarantee that the Congress could not get out of the control of its original secessionist element, and a move to entrench the state oligarchies like his own into the fabric of national government. Such a move could be the foundation of a new Confederate democracy.

Rhett wanted to reform taxation by limiting taxes and duties solely to levels for raising revenue necessary to carry on the government, specifi-cally adding that "no tax duty impost or excise shall be laid to foster or pro-mote one branch of industry rather than another; nor shall any tax or duty be laid on importations from foreign Nations, higher than fifteen per cent on their value." However, in line with his foreign policy hopes for favored-nation status, he would allow Congress to set lower duties on imports from foreign nations of choice "to enduce friendly political relations." He also toyed with establishing a poll tax on slaves as on whites for raising revenue. The Confederacy, too, should have the right to accept from a state or states a district for the capital city, but he emphatically provided that Congress should have no power to interfere with slavery in that district. That and the gag rule provision already in the Provisional Constitution should pre-empt the introduction of any embarrassing anti-slavery petitions here. The old Constitution granted Congress complete authority over state land bought by the national government for forts, arsenals, and other such installations, but in his Confederacy the states would have the prerogative to retain possession of such places. If they surrendered them for defense in time of war, it should be only temporary, and possession was to be restored to the states upon demand. It was a policy that potentially crippled a new nation's ability to defend itself if state and national authorities fell out, but to Rhett's mind it was important to establish again and again the primacy of the states over any central regime.

Rhett, who never abandoned an idea, inserted again the proposal that Congress could if it chose prohibit the slave trade, but omitted an outright exclusion, and his apportionment gambit could help ensure that no such exclusion would ever pass. In Rhett's proposal, the president would serve for six years instead of four and be limited to a single term, though after an intervening term he might be eligible again. It was a reform born of reaction to the two-term Andrew Jackson, who had betrayed his Southern birth and become in Rhett's eyes a dictator who abused executive patronage and power in the quest for reelection. Rhett's attitude toward Davis made this especially important, for if Davis should succeed himself as president under the Permanent Constitution, they had to limit the damage he could do by limiting his incumbency. As another curb, he proposed to change the oath of office to add a promise to "preserve protect and defend the Sovereignty of the States," yet again reminding everyone just where the real power lay. He left presidential appointing power untouched, but in a blow against patronage abuse, provided that if the Senate rejected an appointee, the president could not simply reappoint that person again during the Senate's recess as had been done in the past.

Rhett took no chance of misunderstanding or interpretation when it came to a fugitive slave law. Governors were legally obligated to return runaways from other states, and in cases of abduction or rescue from slavery, the state in which it happened should owe the owner full compensation of his loss. Neither did he forget the searing issue that had precipitated the crisis of the 1850s, the territories. They belonged to the national government under the old Constitution, but he specified that in the new concern they should be the property of "all the states and the peoples thereof." Every Confederate citizen should have equal right to settle them with all "property" recognized as lawful in the state from which he came. There would be no "squatter sovereignty" in his Confederacy.

Rhett wanted it to be more difficult to overturn a presidential veto, and so would require a two-thirds vote of the entire membership of the House, rather than just two-thirds of those present for the ballot. And finally, to make certain that no state would ever have to suffer challenges to its dignity or sovereignty from sister states or the national government, he added that "any State whenever it deems it expedient may exercise its sovereign right of withdrawing peaceably from the Confederacy."[18] There should be no pussyfooting about the right of secession.

Aside from a few other minor changes, that was it, but so far as he was concerned, the injustices and abuses they had suffered in the old Union justified every one. However, Rhett soon discovered that his committee was not as malleable as a document that could not fight back. It was an excellent group of men aggregating several years of legal and political experience. Besides Rhett it included Toombs, Wiley Harris, Robert Smith, Tom Cobb, and Chesnut. Even the less experienced members like Alexander De Clouet, Alexander Clayton, and Richard Walker were still men of character, and some of them would have very definite ideas of their own. Toombs believed framing the permanent charter to be the most important single effort they would make in Montgomery, and could be expected to fight hard, and for all his foolishness otherwise, Cobb was an excellent legal scholar. As soon as Rhett presented his draft at their first meeting on February 11, he found that they were not to be overridden by his notorious arrogance and determination.

More than once the tyranny of the majority that so offended his autocratic nature overruled him now in his own committee. The result was much more discussion than he had expected. And for a start, instead of taking his draft as their starting point, they decided merely to use it for reference, and instead started with the United States Constitution itself. The committee was not merely going to lie back and endorse his vision. Bitterly he sent word to his son editing the *Mercury* that all hope for reform from his committee was about to be dashed, and typically predicted that failure to take his lead promised disaster for the Confederacy. "Let your people prepare their minds for a failure in the future Permanent Southern Constitution," he warned, "for South Carolina is about to be saddled with almost every grievance except Abolition." For a start, they retained the prohibition of the slave trade, thus leaving that stain on the holy banner of slavery and compromising the foundations of their cause itself. There was no telling what else he would lose in the days ahead. "The fruit of the labors of thirty odd long years, in strife and bitterness, is about to slip through our fingers," he wrote in disgust.[19]

By the time they finished, the committee reinserted a preamble that, though it strongly asserted the sovereignty of the states, still included those odious words "the people of the Confederate States," with their implication of a higher loyalty. The three-fifths clause remained, shattering Rhett's hope of making slavery a part of the democratic process by using the disfranchised and enslaved to ensure continued slaveholder domination. Gone, too, was his change in the veto override procedure. As in Stephens's Provisional Constitution, their final draft permitted cabinet heads to hold seats on the floor of Congress when invited but rejected Rhett's reforms of the taxing power, tariffs, and internal improvements. Where he wanted to limit Congress to raising money only for defense and the payment of debts, others softened that considerably, and Smith even managed to incorporate a line item veto for the president. There was still financial reform in Smith's proposal that Congress could appropriate money only for its own expenses, and that all other appropriations had to be requested by the president through one of the executive departments, thus quashing pork barrel. Cobb also inserted a requirement that no contractor should be paid more than the contract price for goods or services, putting an end to the potential for hidden extras when a job was done. Toombs actually inserted an explicit statement that their post office must be self-supporting within two years.

In the end Rhett's only significant changes that were retained were his six-year presidential term limit and the guarantee of slavery in the territories, though the committee provided this only during the territorial stage and thus left the door open to possible free states being formed. They also accepted his prohibition against the reappointment of rejected presidential appointees, a small victory at best.[20] A few matters they ignored, leaving them to the floor debates. For the moment the committee settled on a clause merely protecting slavery everywhere in their nation, regardless of state legislation. Significantly, in a movement that all declared to be predicated on the sovereignty of the states, the one area in which now and again in the future they would deny state sovereignty would be slavery. To the old Union they had said that Federal power had no authority to interfere with slavery issues in a state. To their new nation they would declare that the state had no power to interfere with a federal protection of slavery. Of all the many testimonials to the fact that slavery, and not state rights, really lay at the heart of their movement, this was the most eloquent of all. States had the right to embrace slavery but not to reject it once embraced. And as if further evidence were needed, after much discussion they also decided not to include any specific provision recognizing explicitly the right of a state to secede. None of their number should have the right to do to them what they had just done to the Union.[21]

As so often before, the rejection cast Rhett into a deep gloom. "My life," he said, "appears to me to be worthless to any body."[22] It hardly helped that just then came word of the death of a sick daughter in South Carolina. Rhett always put his family second to his obsession with politics, and he did so even now, setting his mourning aside to present his committee report and their draft on February 26.[23] At once he lost yet another fight when a majority on his committee went against him and said they wanted the Constitution considered behind closed doors. Rhett even lost when he proposed that when formal debate began on February 28, stenographers should make verbatim record of the proceedings to ensure that someday at least the people would know what transpired.[24] If that were not enough disappointment, that day came word that another of his daughters, a three-year-old, had died.[25] Rhett was the sort who needed to bury himself in activity to forget his grief, and the sort who needed an enemy on whom to focus blame for his losses. In the workings of his mind, he could make Jefferson Davis responsible for anything, and even the fatal watering down of his proposed constitution he could lay at the feet of those following Davis's policy of catering to the border states and avoiding a real confrontation with the Union. "Rhetts, &c," said Mary Chesnut, had "heated themselves into a fever that only bloodletting could ever cure—it was the inevitable remedy."[26]

If Rhett and other dissidents needed anything to further dispose them against Davis, it came on February 28, the very day and perhaps only an hour before the committee reported its draft for debate. In advance of any constitutional prohibition, a bill abolishing the foreign slave trade had been introduced six days earlier. It passed, but now Davis returned it with his first veto. The object of the prohibition was to prevent the introduction of any foreign slaves into the Confederacy, yet the bill provided that when any were caught, they were to be seized and sold by the president. That, in effect, resulted in importation after all, and as a result Davis sent the bill back unsigned.[27] It only confirmed the suspicions of Rhett that Davis was no friend to slavery, or he would have allowed the bill to pass with its loophole intact. That he did not raised the prospect that the president secretly favored emancipation. It was a thoroughly illogical conclusion, but it was thoroughly Rhett, and in a few days the *Mercury* would be casting dark hints about the president's loyalty to the South's most treasured institution.[28] The veto also outraged Tom Cobb because he had strenuously resisted South Carolina's efforts to dilute or kill the bill. Suddenly he was again in Rhett's camp, not on an issue, but united in disgust and ill feeling toward Davis. Resolving to get the bill passed over the president's veto, Cobb crowed privately that "it will do my very soul good to *rebuke* him at the outset of his *vetoing*."[29] Cobb's spite, Toombs's disappointed ambition, Rhett's jealousy, and perhaps even Stephens's still nascent discontent at being ignored were all tending in the same direction. There they would find others waiting for them—men like William Boyce and Laurence Keitt, whose personal dislike of Davis was of long standing; a crackpot like Withers, who condemned Davis because his inaugural carriage was drawn by white horses that seemed to smack too much of the regal; and one or two others. No policy or issue would bind them other than their personal antagonism to Davis. Rhett found cause in every aspect of what was happening in Montgomery, for Davis was actively or passively thwarting almost every one of the Carolinian's carefully matured political truths. Cobb, Toombs, and the others could hate Davis for something; Rhett could hate him for everything.

The debate that followed would last for ten days, much of it heated, even acrimonious, but within that exchange they revealed the full maturation of how they had come to see themselves during their weeks in Montgomery. Even seemingly minor semantic issues like the precise wording of the preamble displayed their attitudes. Half of the first day's debate turned on this single issue before they finally agreed to address the world as "We, the people of the Confederate States, each State acting in its sovereign and independent character." They were individual peoples of supreme states taking collective action, not a single people merely subdivided by artificial geographical boundaries. There would be no appeal for a Confederate nationalism here.

That done, they began to march through the document article by arti-

cle, and at a pace that quickly made it evident that it might take them
weeks to finish. Rather consistently the committee had gone along at least
with Rhett's determination to weaken the central government in favor of
the states, starting with a clause that the states did not "grant" power to
Congress—implying permanence—but only that they "delegated." The
Congress agreed. But then the first roadblock came over defining Confederate citizenship, and the matter was simply tabled until later. Then came
apportionment, and South Carolina stood to fight Rhett's battle anew, and
seemed not about to accept defeat as Keitt raised the issue again and
again. Seeing a logjam in the making, Stephens again stepped into the
breach and moved that this, too, should be postponed until they had settled the rest of the document. In the days ahead he would resort to this device again and again, revealing as he had before that he probably possessed
the greatest degree of practical political sense of any in the chamber. The
more they came to agreement on the less divisive issues, the more agreement should become a habit, and at the same time a momentum of accomplishment could take over.

For his part, Stephens, despite his success at keeping the Congress
moving, felt uncertain, seeing around him too many men who "lack statesmanship of what I consider of the highest order." Few of them seemed to
have the sort of long-range vision that he felt was necessary in the present.[30] After four days Stephens complained that all they wanted was
"debate debate—no end of debate."[31] He, too, lost favorite proposals,
including his wish to give cabinet officers seats in Congress. They did
agree on the line item veto and on an end to protective tariffs. Then they
stuck fast on Toombs's proposal of a prohibition on internal improvements.
There were quite proper exceptions, such as lighthouses and navigational
markers that ought to be built at government expense. Yet some men dug
in their heels, and Stephens had to engineer postponement yet again. At
least Toombs's proposal to require a self-sustaining post office department
after March 1, 1863, passed easily.

But again, anything that touched on slavery could produce an instant
slowdown. When the prohibition of the African slave trade came up, Rhett
tried yet again to remove the stigma from that glorious institution by soft-
ening the wording to allow that Congress "may" enact a prohibition, but
without making it a part of the organic law. South Carolina was virtually
alone on this, however, the overwhelming majority of delegates being
committed to an outright abolition, many on instructions from their state

conventions. The debate became hot and tempers flared, leading Tom Cobb, who stood with Rhett on this, to declare the entire Texas and Mississippi delegations nothing but conceited weaklings.[32]

By March 5, after almost a week of hard work and sometimes mind-numbing debate, the strain and weariness showed on many, and a few despaired of ever finishing. Then the next day Boyce, usually in the more ultra camp, tried to introduce the specific recognition of the right of a state to secede that had been left out by the committee over Rhett's objection. Duncan Kenner of Louisiana, who seemed to work in tandem with Stephens, immediately moved to table the motion, and only South Carolina opposed the action. Rhett struck back with a new proposition that any Confederate state that should abolish slavery in the future ought to be expelled from the nation. It was not only yet another assertion that for him and the radicals the whole movement was founded on slavery. The proposition also sought to pre-empt action by border states that were soft on slavery, especially Maryland, and even more so Delaware, which though a slave state legally, had practically seen the institution die out long before. Rhett's proposal also presaged a fight to come on the issue of admission of new states that all knew they would have to face, and soon. His motion, too, was tabled in spite of his state's objections, and the Congress went on.

That brought them to the presidency. They had no trouble agreeing on the proposed single six-year term, but they stumbled on the electoral college. None of them had been entirely happy with the system in the old Union. It gave too much power to the larger states. In their current situation, for instance, Georgia would have had more than three times the influence of Florida if they had mandated an electoral system for the election of Davis. Men like Rhett who carried a deep-seated mistrust of the will of the majority, almost any kind of majority, wanted a system that equalized the small and large states. Yet at the other extreme, almost all of the men here distrusted the idea of a simple popular vote, for they all came from state systems that had been crafted to resist the will of the majority of their citizens. Indeed, Curry of Alabama, a prime example of the more mediocre talents that Stephens feared in the Congress, actually said that popular elections encouraged the formation of political parties, which they all supposedly hoped to abolish.[33]

Yet again Stephens had to take the reins and move postponement of the whole issue. At the same time Harris of Mississippi, who seemed to strike straight to the heart of matters as well as any, foresaw that their growing list of postponed items could produce a dangerous, perhaps destructive bottleneck at the end of their consideration of the Permanent Constitution. He moved creation of a committee of seven men, one from each state, to begin a separate consideration of those issues. The House agreed, but that evening the South Carolinians somehow convinced Harris that his committee would not be needed after all, and the next morning when Keitt suggested that they dispense with the select committee, Harris himself withdrew his motion. He might have gotten promises that the ultras would be cooperative, or he might have been outmaneuvered by those who wanted a clear field for a floor fight without the weight of a committee report working against them.[34]

That there might have been some strategy involved in setting aside Harris's motion became evident when immediately afterward Benjamin Hill of Georgia and Chesnut took them by surprise when Hill reintroduced the postponed issue of secession, and with it the old nullification doctrine. Suggesting a prohibition of the idea of a state having the right to nullify within its borders any federal law that it found objectionable, Hill suggested that if a state questioned the constitutionality of a law, the Supreme Court ought to be convened to try the matter, or else the state should have the right to secede. The ultras shuddered. Part of the reason they did not want to provide for any mandated sessions of such a court was that they did not want a court interpreting their Constitution, one of the complaints they had with the Supreme Court in Washington. Then Chesnut, perhaps by prearrangement, proposed another version of the same idea, but fortunately the majority postponed both amendments.

Back on track again, they agreed on a measure of patronage reform by restricting the president's power to dismiss employees at will to just his cabinet unless he could justify dismissal of other confirmed appointees to the Senate. It was a blow at the old spoils system, and a genuine reform that was much needed. In another shot at reform, they agreed on an ironclad fugitive slave law, and adopted the clause guaranteeing any citizen the right to take his slaves with him to any part of the Confederacy.

Finally they had to face the issue that many dreaded most of all, and that Stephens would dub the "Great Debate." How should they admit new states, and just what sort of states should be welcomed into their Confederacy? Some actually believed that when the border states saw the perfection of their new Constitution and government, they would finally secede and come to join them. But that was not all. Not a few thought that eventually the remainder of the old Union would crumble under its own weight, and that more conservative free states, perhaps even all of them, would seek sanctuary in the new regime. Davis himself would speculate that New Hampshire might one day secede to join them! Should that happen, however, ought they to grant admission? The theoretical possibility lurked therein for themselves to find the slave states once again a minority in their own government just as they had been in the Union. In Rhett's expression, truly they would just have run around a circle to wind up where they began.

Foreseeing this, William Porcher Miles commenced the debate with a motion that only slave states ought to be admitted, which would protect slavery indefinitely, revealing yet again the black bedrock on which they were building their new temple. The debate continued into the next day, March 8, and so did the rising blood of partisans on both sides. South Carolina stood immovable on a free state ban, and Florida dutifully followed that lead, while four other states defeated them at every turn. Georgia deadlocked in a tie vote, infuriating Tom Cobb, who favored the free state prohibition. But it was much closer than that. In fact, despite the vote by states, a shift of just one vote each in Texas and Georgia would have sided them with South Carolina and Florida and the ban would have passed. After what Stephens thought to be the most tense and potentially dangerous debates of the whole business, they finally left the wording on admission to be settled later.

March 9 would be the last day of debate, and then all of the postponed matters came before them. It was a tense day throughout, for any one of them could explode, and there was always the possibility that something else already settled, especially admission policy, could erupt again with a new motion. Stephens and other hopefuls were on tenterhooks throughout the day, and predictably it was South Carolina that started the process as Keitt yet again proposed full accounting of slaves for apportionment. Happily, everyone else was weary of the issue, and it was defeated handily. Slaves would be counted at three-fifths, Indians not at all, and a state would be entitled to one representative for each adjusted 50,000 of population. Thus another challenge to border state influence was dampened. Then Toombs dropped his internal improvements amendment in favor of one now introduced by Rhett, and for a change Rhett got what he wanted.

Congress could raise money to take care of navigation in rivers and harbors, but for nothing else that would encourage industry or favor one over another.

Rhett still had an amendment in play to expel any state that should abolish slavery. Stephens tried to kill it by tabling but lost on a close vote that revealed scant backing for the measure itself, only to have William Barry of Mississippi introduce yet another version. Clearly the Rhett forces had this campaign well organized, but Stephens demanded the question which resulted in an immediate vote, and Little Aleck had counted heads well. Three states voted for and three against, and Louisiana was split, making a tie, and defeat.

The only victory that the Rhett camp could get on the free state issue came when they finally settled the admission question. Since this was intended as a vehicle for admitting states already formed and a part of the old Union, they dispensed with provisions for territorial status which were moot in this instance. Instead, they settled on a means by which a state would need a vote of two-thirds of the members of the House of Representatives, and two-thirds of the Senate, though in the Senate the balloting would be one state, one vote. The required concurrence in the Senate was the guarantee. Even if all the existing fifteen slave states eventually became a part of the Confederacy, as few as six in opposition could kill statehood in the Senate, and the Deep South states could be expected to stand firm on admitting only slave states. The important point to Stephens and others in defeating an outright ban on free states was essentially one of public posture. Already the more thoughtful were sensitive about their movement being perceived by the world at large as exclusively driven by slavery, and a ban would have reinforced that idea. But having accomplished this, they then went right on to provide in another clause that all territory that should be acquired in the future by the new nation, and any new states formed from that territory, should include slavery, not by the choice of the inhabitants, but by constitutional mandate. There would be no popular sovereignty to allow territorial governments to choose to become free states. Here as throughout, preservation of slavery was the driving force behind most of the variations from the Constitution of the United States.[35]

That left the manner of electing the president, and in the end they simply ignored the issue, leaving it for a later time by adopting the wording of the United States Constitution without alteration. Curry complained yet

again that this would inevitably encourage partisanship and party formation, but they were simply too tired to wrangle out another means when almost all admitted that they could think of nothing more perfect. And with
that, at last they were done.[36]

Many were well pleased with the result, most were glad just to be done,
and a few felt continuing dissatisfaction. Rhett, who had gotten some of
what he wanted, like all zealots, was never satisfied unless he got all. Even
Stephens thought their success, if any, lay in the new Constitution not being worse than he thought it would be. What disturbed him the most was
what the debates revealed about coalescing factions. "There are some very
bad passions and tempers beginning to develop themselves here," he observed the day after they finished. How could they hope to hold together
if a real crisis of war put them under even greater strains?

The moderates like himself were clearly the majority, men whose vision
saw safety in numbers and a temperate policy that looked outward. There
was more to them than slavery. They believed, too, that a strong government was vital to self-preservation, yet that it could be made compatible
with recognition of state sovereignty. Fortunately, the dissident elements—
the radical slavery proponents and the hard-core state sovereignty people—
were weak by comparison, and themselves fragmented. South Carolina lay
at the center of both. The dissidents had been stopped at almost every turn
in the debates, but if enough of them came to agree in time on enough issues to field a cohesive and comprehensive alternate policy to that being
pursued by the government, then they would have a party. Gifted with
more forecast than many of those present, Stephens lamented, "I see
many dangers and breakers ahead."[37]

Yet Stephens should have felt some sense of accomplishment as well,
and so should they all. Of course there were the specific reforms. They put
a curb on the spoils system, commenced the first civil service reform in
America, albeit modest, prohibited internal improvements and protective
tariffs, and denied themselves the power to spend public money on pork
barrel. While placing curbs on presidential power on the one hand, they
increased it on the other with the line item veto. Yet there was far more
woven even more deeply into the document. In ten days of intermittent
yet exhausting effort, they had come perhaps as close as they ever would to
defining their vision of republican government, what could best be termed
a Confederate democracy.

It rested on a couple of fundamental assumptions that reflected their

society and culture. All men were not created equal. Indeed, not even all
white men were created equal. There were the masses and an elite, the
one born to be led and unequipped to decide great issues and the other
destined by birth and breeding to lead. In such a world, the greatest
tyranny, worse even than that of a dictator, was the will of a majority that
did not, and perhaps could not, grasp the stakes raised by issues of state.
Moreover, the masses were not men of property, and thus did not even
have an equal risk in the affairs of a nation, wherefore no justification existed for their having equal influence. Unsophisticated, they could easily
be swayed by unscrupulous demagogues who would court them solely for
the power of their numbers if they were voters, and if two or more courted
them, then the rise of partisan political parties would ensue. Happily, sure
in the knowledge of this great truth, they made their Permanent Constitution provide security from majoritarian rule. Further, realizing that each
state, in its sovereignty, had the sole right to determine which of its citizens
should have the franchise, they recognized the possibility that some misguided state or states—most likely from the border—might allow power to
fall into the hands of the masses, and thus gain control of delegates in the
Congress.

But the oligarchs had a safeguard even there, for they made their most
vital issue, slavery, a part of their constitutional fabric and thus untouch-
able, while otherwise providing some protection from majority will even
on their own floor. Indeed, while the United States Constitution had
merely recognized slavery as an existing institution, their new charter entrenched it as a fundamental right, one of those "blessings of liberty" spoken of in their preamble. On this issue alone, they knowingly violated all
the arguments about state rights that their section had been making for
generations, for they set slavery above state sovereignty: inviolate, un-
touchable. Their fugitive slave law was ironclad. No Supreme Court could
touch it. In all practicality, no free state really stood a chance for admission. And to make the slave oligarchy's control even more secure, they provided that this Constitution could be amended much more easily than the
one in the Union. Only three states—already a minority—had to concur in
a call to convene a convention. Proposed amendments could come only
from the states, presumably those making the call, and once in the convention it would require just two-thirds rather than three-fourths of the
states to ratify. None of them publicly justified this provision, but it was not
hard to see the impulse at work. No one knew what the next months would

bring. Outbreak of war, secession and application for admission of border states, developments abroad, perhaps even dissatisfaction with their new administration, could all produce exigencies that required quick constitutional reaction in a new nation. The ultras especially persuaded themselves that there would be danger to slavery and the threat of a shift toward reconstruction when the border slave states came in. Only if they could revise their organic law speedily could they erect defenses, and as more states were added, it became all the more important that a minority of three still had the power to get remedy on the table.

It was a democracy different from the one they had recently departed, and it remained to be seen whether it could work. What had they gotten wrong? What had they overlooked? Did it give them the power to do what was necessary to preserve, protect, and defend their new nation? And most of all, would that great mass of people in the Confederacy, men and women, white and black, free and slave, willingly yield to the demands the future was going to place upon them, and accept the severely limited control over their own lives and fortunes in the crisis that their Constitution gave them? "For some minds, it is difficult to realize the fact that, in attaining an independent nationality we are to establish at the same time, a distinct individuality," maintained John Perkins of Louisiana.[38] It was now to be determined whether that emergent individual should be a new life form or just another of the dead ends of evolution.[39]

"The new government sprang forth as if by magic," Curry said with something approaching fatuousness.[40] If there was anything magical, it was that it got a unanimous vote on the final draft on March 11. Even then, Georgia, prodded by Stephens and Toombs, called for a voice vote in a crafty move to make every delegate present put himself on record as accepting the Permanent Constitution. Doing so would bind them to it and weaken the ability of those like Rhett who could be expected to try to cause trouble with their state conventions. Even then, Bartow, Tom Cobb, and Keitt left for home before the voting. Though they arranged for their affirmative votes to be cast for them, still their departure bespoke their unwillingness to actually say the word "yea."[41]

Other members began leaving even before the close of the session on March 16. There was still business to do, but they were all eager to get home to report to their conventions. One convention did not wait for them. Just the day after passage of the Permanent Constitution, and four days before the Congress even had the engrossed document to sign, Alabama ratified it by an overwhelming 87 to 5. After conducting a small flood of routine business, Howell Cobb brought down the final gavel and sent those who remained away, scheduled to reconvene on May 13. Almost at once the campaign for ratification commenced in the states, and the delegates and others took the stump, not just before their conventions, but before the people, to sell the new document.

Indeed, almost every opinion maker started to weigh in on the subject, and fortunately for the forces of ratification, J.D.B. DeBow of the New Orleans *Review,* easily the most influential editor in the new Confederacy, stood in their line, though not without qualifications. "We have separated from the States of the Union because we had not guarantees for our rights and liberties," he said in his *Review,* "and now the question is, have we secured them?" Secession alone could not accomplish that, he argued. Only by identifying the causes of secession could they determine if their new Constitution remedied the problems. They left the Union, he went on, because Washington had become too strong for them to resist its "usurpations," and had imposed protective tariffs. Moreover, Northern capitalists encouraged immigration by the pauper working class from Europe in order to keep their costs low. And when exploited labor complained, the moneyed interests and their political stooges diverted attention by promoting instead a hostility toward the even cheaper labor system of the South in slavery. The conflict was not between capital and labor, they said, but between free labor and slave labor. That led to anti-slavery agitation, and that led to secession. Thus, unjust taxation, and not a threat to slavery, really lay behind the breakup of the Union.

DeBow was never a very sophisticated observer, but knowingly or not in this instance he played to the needs of those like Stephens and others who sought to keep slavery's role in their new nation somewhat shadowed for public consumption. But then DeBow hit the underlying concept of Confederate democracy right on the head. The Union, he said, had been established on the principle that taxation and representation went together, but that had been perverted by the North into a wedding of population and representation. Worse, the South had denied to itself "the practical application" of the new principle by acquiescing in loss of representation for two-fifths of its slaves, and that in turn had allowed the more powerful North to pass unjust taxation in the form of the protective tariffs.[42]

In the next breath DeBow turned around and lamented the reluctance to embrace the social and moral good of slavery and proudly display it as a keystone of their culture and polity, rather than try to hide or disguise its centrality. Social life itself was a state of dependence, he argued. The benefits to one could be supplied only at the expense of another. "The majority of mankind serve in some inferior capacity," he argued, that higher powers might accomplish good ends. Blacks were by nature inferior and incapable of exercising the responsibilities of citizens, and therefore were not entitled to the rights of freeborn whites. Instead, the laws of the dominant race protected blacks in American society, and in return the blacks were obligated to provide the only thing they could, their labor. "Men are *not created equal*," he maintained in rejection of Jefferson and the Declaration of Independence, whether physically, morally, or intellectually, and slavery merely recognized this fact and offered a means whereby the inferior were prevented from having an opportunity to exercise rights they could not comprehend, while the superior gave them the care that they were equally incapable of providing for themselves, and at the cost of nothing more than compensatory work.

"It is the wisest and the best that generally govern everywhere," he argued, and it was designed by nature that they should govern. "The most intellectual portion of the political community possess not only the requisite abilities, but they have the natural right to establish rules and regulations, imperatively demanded to insure the safety of the State and the permanency of the existing political and social institutions," he continued, in the process justifying not only slavery, but also the sort of oligarchic rule over lower-class whites that the new Constitution helped to entrench. "It is utterly inconceivable upon what principle of reason, logic, or common sense, the social and legal subordination of an inferior race, protected by stringent laws, should be condemned and denounced," he added, especially when the enslavement was "sanctioned by the laws of necessity." "Domestic slavery in the South is nothing more nor less than the subordination of an inferior race," he said, "strictly conforming with the dictates of justice and right as the almost absolute dependence of the child on parental authority and parental support." Slavery made the black useful to society, kept him occupied and happy in his natural sphere. Indeed, the only unhappy Negroes were those who were free, and DeBow argued that Confederate leaders ought soon to address themselves to evicting all free blacks from their country before their natural penchant to debauchery and corruption spread to their docile slave brothers. Slavery was not a perfect system, he confessed, but it was ordained by nature, and protected the

Confederacy from the coming social upheavals that DeBow foresaw in Europe and elsewhere where exploited white labor would rise up. "As long as Southern statesmen act with wisdom and prudence, slavery will serve as the palladium of republican government," he averred. It united all members of the political community by common interest, in the face of common threat from freed blacks. Moreover, he recognized slavery as a vital element of social morale, for even the lowliest white still could stand with pride knowing that he was the superior of a black. Slavery gave poor whites a social status nowhere else enjoyed by the peasantry, and as proof he argued that some of the most ardent supporters of slavery were whites too poor themselves to own slaves. Slavery, said DeBow, "is a holy cause," a system that enriched the civilized by taming the "wild, useless, physical element of the most inferior race of mankind." Moreover, the produce of slave labor—sugar, rice, and cotton—was used to "feed the poor and clothe the masses of the civilized nations of the earth." Slavery was thus humanitarian in the best sense.[43]

Men trying to secure ratification would use DeBow's arguments, even in moderate Georgia, which was next after Alabama to act. The state convention sat in Savannah, and Tom Cobb, Stephens, and others hastened there. Cobb set aside his quibbles and supported the charter, and of course Stephens did, but in a startling aboutface Little Aleck changed his message to sell his product. Gone was his reluctance to downplay the importance of slavery in the movement. In Atlanta he declared that this new Constitution "made African *inequality* and subordination, and the *equality* of white men, the chief cornerstone of the Southern Republic." A few days later he went even further in Savannah, asserting that the Confederacy's "foundations are laid, its cornerstone rests, upon the great truth that the negro is not equal to the white man; that slavery, subordination to the superior race, is his natural and moral condition."[44] When reports of his speeches got back to Montgomery, Davis and other moderates were chagrined to see the vice president undermining the very posture they wanted to assume for the world. What they did not understand was that Stephens was playing to the audience, playing on race and the social standing that slavery accorded to the "crackers" to get them behind ratification, which in fact had already taken place on March 16.

Texas and Louisiana both ratified quickly, but then Mississippi stumbled, its convention doubting that it had the authority to ratify. Some suggested a popular referendum instead, complaining along with an editor that "for some months past all power has been rapidly passing from the many into the hands of a select few," an apt enough description of what, in fact, had been happening, and of a fundamental feature of Confederate democracy. That was all right for South Carolina or Louisiana, where oligarchy rule had been a way of life for centuries, but Mississippi, being newer, had experienced a much greater degree of popular democracy and a wider spread of the franchise, and the tendency of affairs now represented an unwelcome change. After two days of debate, some actually feared that ratification might fail, but Harris and others skillfully guided the convention away from a referendum and finally achieved a safe passage.

Everyone expected a real struggle in South Carolina, where Rhett tried to persuade the convention to make any ratification conditional on amendments to rectify his rejected provisions. Otherwise, South Carolina, the state that began the movement, should refuse to ratify, thus placing itself outside the Confederacy it had spawned. The moral blow to the whole movement, and its embarrassment before the world, would be staggering. Fortunately, better heads like Chesnut's countered all of Rhett's arguments, while in public editors referred to Rhett's efforts as those of "a wicked and suicidal opposition."[45] When the vote came, ratification passed handily, and another battle had been lost by the "Rhett & Co., Slave traders, free traders, fire eaters and extremists," as James Henry Hammond dubbed them.[46]

Oddly enough, little Florida took the longest, maybe because, of them all, its state convention had been the most suspicious of what might happen in Montgomery. Not until April 22 did they finally ratify, and then only with an expression of reservations on a number of points that they said ought to be corrected at an early day. They, too, wanted the three-fifths clause stricken. They also wanted a stipulation that "no State shall be admitted into this Confederacy, unless the Institution of slavery shall be distinctly and clearly recognized in its constitution and in actual operation under its laws."[47] It was still a ratification, but also a promise that those specters that had haunted the framers and Congress from the first had not gone to their rest, and would manifest themselves again in time.

So now they were genuinely a nation, their Constitution ratified. But by the time Florida gave its assent, they were also a nation at war. As many had expected, their commissioners to Washington had no hope of success. In his inaugural, while rattling no sword, Lincoln still made it clear that his

Constitution required him to be president of all the states. As a result, not recognizing the Confederacy as a legitimate authority, he refused to deal directly with its emissaries, but even if he had, his goals and Davis's were mutually exclusive. Thus compromise was impossible from the outset, but complicating the picture was undeniable ineptitude as both Lincoln and his secretary of state, William H. Seward, attempted to deal with the matter without speaking with one voice. As a result, the Confederates one moment thought that Federal troops would be withdrawn from Fort Sumter, only to find that Lincoln instead intended to resupply the garrison, and to reinforce it if the Confederates should try to stop the supply effort. Believing themselves deceived by Yankees merely stalling for time, they broke off their mission and reported it as hopeless. By April 6, Jefferson Davis knew that the control of events had now passed into his hands. The issue of peace or war was his to decide.

Two days later Davis ordered Beauregard, in command at Charleston, to close off Fort Sumter completely from outside contact, then met for several hours with his cabinet. He argued for giving Washington an ultimatum, and his ministers agreed. The refusal to evacuate the fort, which was in the sovereign territory of South Carolina and now under the jurisdiction of the Confederacy, constituted an act of war, he would say. It could still be forestalled if Lincoln reconsidered, but now they did not expect that. The ultimatum was simply an effort to put themselves on the right side of what they considered unstoppable, trying to shift to the Yankees the responsibility in the eyes of the world for what they now had to do. "We must have that fort if it costs us ten thousand men," declared one Carolinian the day of Lincoln's inauguration. "Our troops are all ready and anxious."[48]

Davis met repeatedly with his cabinet, and the majority stood behind him when he decided to order Beauregard to give the garrison a final ultimatum. He did so the next day, and though for a few hours there seemed hope of a last-minute accommodation, at 4:30 a.m. on the morning of April 12, Charleston's batteries opened fire. Davis had tried to cast Lincoln in the role of aggressor for his refusal to remove alien and unfriendly armed forces from Confederate territory, and years later would further advance his own rationalization that "he who makes the assault is not necessarily he that strikes the first blow or fires the first shot."[49]

Even before North and South really had time to react to news of the commencement of the bombardment, Davis was already predicting the positive benefit that had to accrue to the Confederacy the moment Lincoln made any effort to react. Now the border states would certainly secede and join the Confederacy. "Our cause is a common cause," he told journalist Charles E.L. Stuart, "as our ideas and interests are common ideas and interests, all so interwoven that they are naturally adhesive."[50] Even as the telegraph brought news on the afternoon of April 13 that Fort Sumter had surrendered after a bloodless bombardment, all eyes in Montgomery turned north toward the border, especially toward that great mother of states and of presidents, Virginia.

The Old Dominion felt rightly caught in the middle from the moment the secession crisis began. The legislature called for the election of a state convention to meet in Richmond on February 13, not necessarily to secede but to decide Virginia's course in the growing crisis. Secessionists were immediately disheartened by the complexion of the group, for the delegates in favor of the Union held a good majority when they convened. Nevertheless, "we had a powerful party for secession, a gaining cause, and I felt assured the border states would ere long secede," observed Virginia journalist Littleton Washington, who was writing pro-secession editorials from the national capital, "and we all struggled on hoping for the best."[51] After two weeks, while secessionist Jeremiah Martin delivered a "fierce fire-eating speech" only a few steps away from him, delegate John Echols wrote to a friend that the people of the state clearly were not ready for secession. "There must be something like unanimity before such a course would be safe," he argued. "I really believe if this state was taken out of the Union before the people were satisfied that all fair and honorable means were exhausted to avoid this step, that we would have a revolution in our midst." Even if they could pass a secession ordinance then, it would fatally divide the state. "Let us go where we may, either to the North or South," lamented Echols, "we have a dark future in view."[52]

In order to be where he could see the struggle firsthand, DeBow moved from New Orleans to Richmond just the day before the debates began, and he saw the same weakness for secession as did Echols, though he attributed it to entirely different causes. Nor did he content himself merely to observe, but actively tried to use his influence to sway the wavering toward separation. To his eyes, the majority of delegates were not loyal Southerners, "but were ready to barter away the honor, the dignity, the liberty and independence of Virginia, in order to obtain a little temporary ease, or a disgraceful truce with abolition." When the convention adopted a committee report proposing as a compromise between the sections that the repealed Missouri Compromise line should be reinstated, guaranteeing that slavery would be excluded from the northern half of the continent forever, DeBow and the secessionists exploded. "This is a distinct admission that slavery is wrongful," he exclaimed.[53]

No wonder the commissioners from the Confederate states worked so hard, and more than anything else they hammered on that "common interest" that the Old Dominion shared with the rest of the slave states. Georgian Henry Benning told them that they must leave affiliation with a people who hated slavery and condemned it morally. Yankees intended to destroy the institution in Virginia, and had plotted to do so for years, as John Brown's 1859 Harpers Ferry raid proved beyond a doubt. Worst of all, the Union would one day free slaves and give them the franchise, which meant that in the South in states where slaves were currently in the majority, there would be "black governors, black judges, black legislators, black juries, black witnesses—everything black." Whites would be literally exterminated and their beautiful paradise turned to a wasteland. The only prevention was to preserve slavery, and the only insurance of that was secession and admission to the Confederacy.[54]

In the hope of producing an eruption that would propel the Unionists and other conservatives into accepting secession, some of the old Reefers resurrected their harebrained plans to spark either a reaction from the North or an excitement in the South, but in the end all that remained for those secessionist denizens of Washington, like Littleton Washington, was to purloin as much as they could of the forms, books, and supplies of the several government offices they occupied, and take it south to be used in the new Confederacy. Almost a hundred of them did so, and for months to come, official correspondence of some of the bureaus in Montgomery would be written on United States stationery, with the heading crossed out and "Confederate States" scrawled in its place.[55]

Gradually events and emotions worked to the advantage of the secession party in Richmond, however, though as late as April 4, when they took a vote on submitting secession to a referendum of the people, the motion lost 88 to 45, virtually a vote on secession itself in the convention. But the Fort Sumter crisis produced a rapid shift in opinion as it appeared that Lincoln might initiate hostilities himself. All the while there came allurements from Montgomery to add to the weight of events. Boyce of South Carolina had advised Virginia's influential and very ambitious Senator

R.M.T. Hunter that the new Confederacy would give the Old Dominion "things exactly as she wants them capital included," if the state would act.[56] By early April former governor Henry A. Wise was promising Davis that he would be able to "stampede" his state into secession, and he certainly tried. After news of the firing on Fort Sumter, Wise tried to get Governor John Letcher to go along with his plans to seize government installations in the state. Letcher refused, but Wise went ahead to put his plot in motion and met late on April 16 with co-conspirators. The next morning he strode into the convention and pulled a huge pistol from his pocket and laid it on his desk as he proceeded to browbeat the convention as a set of cowards and poltroons, and then announced that while they sat there, Letcher's state militia was even then seizing the Yankee navy yard at Norfolk and the arsenal and armory at Harpers Ferry. The governor had finally come around, but only after assurance just hours before that the convention was going to secede. Now they had to make good that expectation. When the vote came, secession passed by just 88 to 55. It was a wrenching decision for many of those who finally went over to separation. So little did the ultras recognize conscience in anyone but themselves, and so little did they grasp the wisdom of moderation, that even after the vote the silly DeBow crowed that it came only after "repeated cringings and fawnings before the throne of Lincoln; after being insulted, cuffed and kicked from his footstool." Nor could he forgive that even then, the majority had voted reluctantly.[57]

Virginia's secession did not mean its automatic application for admission to the Confederacy. Some feared, and a few actually hoped, that Virginia and the other border slave states would form a new confederation of their own, perhaps as a buffer or stopgap whose intent would be to broker eventual reconstruction. Letcher was not so foolish. He knew, as did anyone who could read a map, that if Lincoln was going to put down the "rebellion," he would have to do it by land, and that meant Union armies marching across the border states to get to the Confederates. Yet when Letcher made an official overture to Davis, it was not for admission, but rather to conclude a defensive alliance as if between two nations. Davis would agree to that, for still it worked to his purpose, but he wanted and expected more. He met with Stephens and asked him to go to Richmond at once to negotiate with Letcher, and this time when the vice president yet again begged off, the president and cabinet insisted. He left immediately, and by April 22 he was in Richmond.

Following Letcher's lead, Stephens suggested an immediate treaty, but urged that it only be an expedient while the process of statehood was put in motion, requiring first Virginia's adoption of the Permanent Constitution. Soon he signed a treaty in conjunction with a committee from the convention, but observed an unfortunate tendency to delay and debate when it came to the next step. Indeed, he feared that the convention as a whole might not ratify the treaty. Now it was time for the more subtle political arts, of which the vice president had already shown himself an accomplished master. First he hinted that Davis might come to Richmond, without actually saying so, implying that the president would assume personal direction of any army formed to repel the Yankees. It was disingenuous, to say the least, for despite repeated rumors and speculation, Jefferson Davis neither now nor at any time in the future showed any sign that he seriously considered exercising his power as commander in chief to take command of an army in the field. Perhaps realizing that he had gone too far, Stephens retracted his speculation the next day.

Meanwhile Little Aleck dropped other hints, most potent of all the speculation that if Virginia joined the Confederacy, Congress might move the capital from Montgomery to Richmond. Undoubtedly it was something he had discussed thoroughly with Davis before leaving, and of course there had been suggestions since the first convening of Congress in February that it might happen if the Old Dominion should secede. It made sound strategic sense. Richmond was the South's greatest manufacturing center, second only to Atlanta as a rail hub and to Louisiana as a financial base. If Virginia joined the Confederacy and the Confederacy went to war, then Richmond had vital attributes that could not be removed in the face of Yankee arms. It would have to be defended, bitterly if need be. Further, with Virginia in the fold, and given the inescapable geographic fact that any Union army in the East that tried to invade the South would have first to pass through Virginia, it was obvious that the Old Dominion had to be the first line of defense. Circumstances dictated that it would be a major battleground, perhaps the decisive one. Despite the availability of rapid communications with Montgomery by means of the telegraph, still that was no substitute for the uppermost decision makers being within physical reach of the critical scene.

On April 25 the Virginia convention, responding to the vice president's subtle persuasions and their own wishes, ratified the treaty and two days later issued an invitation to Davis to move the capital to Richmond. The president, normally the most reserved of men, actually showed his elation at the word. Hard on Virginia's news, North Carolina said that surely it would follow. Now Davis sent messages and commissions to Missouri, Tennessee, and Arkansas in the hope that the dominoes would start falling. There was even cause to hope for Kentucky, too, and if the Bluegrass State seceded, then the formidable Ohio River itself would be the Confederacy's northern border, meaning that geography itself would be working in his favor. With events happening in a swirl, Lincoln declared a state of insurrection and decreed a blockade of Southern ports, and called for 75,000 volunteers to put down the uprising. Davis summoned the Congress back to Montgomery for an emergency session, and the Confederacy at large finally, seriously, faced the prospect of the war that until then so many of them had treated so cavalierly.

On April 29 they were back in the Alabama statehouse to receive Davis's special message. Most of all he spoke to the rest of the world. The Confederacy had no dreams of conquest or expansion. All they wanted was peace, he said; "all we ask is to be let alone." Two days later Rhett produced out of his foreign affairs committee the bill declaring a state of war with the Union, and it passed on May 3. Then Congress commenced a flurry of legislation that would begin the literal and symbolic tug of war between their cherished state sovereignty and military necessity. They passed a bill granting the president power to take over all of the telegraph lines in the country and to absorb staff into the government employ, a wise measure that yet raised seriously for the first time the specter of centralizing authority into the hands of the chief executive, and of subordinating the rights of private and state interests in the name of expediency. Already Confederate democracy showed that it could take a turn in a direction that some could term despotic. Yet Howell Cobb took heart that there was a high degree of unanimity in Congress.[58] On May 7 they formally admitted Virginia to statehood, but almost immediately there were complaints over some of the delegates the Old Dominion chose to send, for too many other than Hunter had been soft on secession and were now suspected of harboring secret desires for reconstruction. "They come to us for no good purposes," Tom Cobb complained.[59] At least one of them, Hunter, came with a purpose of his own in mind, for already he discussed with others the possibility that when the country elected a president in November under the Permanent Constitution, the man might be himself and not Jefferson Davis. They also came resolved to move the capital to Richmond.

As events continued to roll on their course, Tennessee voted to secede on May 6, and Arkansas seceded the next day even as Virginia was admitted. That made them ten states, with the certain promise of North Carolina soon. Ironically, the more states there were, the greater the potential for strain on Davis and their new Constitution, for they all had yet to test whether it was elastic enough to allow the states their full sovereignty, while yet strong enough to hold them all together—strains felt even within the states. Already the judiciary committee had grappled with the subject of control over public lands, forts, arsenals, navy yards, lighthouses, and other public works of the Union now in state hands, and had concluded that the national government had no control over such property. Instead it merely recommended that the states should voluntarily turn such installations over to the Confederacy, suggesting that if the national government should in the future pay the United States any compensation for that property, then the states should be willing to make restitution, a resolution that the Congress passed.[60] Meanwhile down in Florida a conflict arose with the Treasury when the state legislature passed a law exempting imported railroad iron for the state from the 24 percent duty imposed by statute in Montgomery. State law was trying to clash with federal law, and a few days later when the Florida railroad itself ignored Montgomery and removed the questioned iron without application to Congress, Secretary of the Treasury Memminger ordered the local district attorney to press the case.[61]

In fact it was already evident that cooperation from the governors was going to be a very individual and not always predictable affair. All of them certainly had their hearts in the cause. Governor Brown of Georgia found nothing too small to escape his notice if he thought it would help. And in a state that had more than its share of resistance, he worked hard at raising volunteers. "The Conservatism of our County is, and has been such as to keep down, to some extent, any Military Spirit amongst us," wrote a volunteer from Morgan County. "We are mostly men of business, & will go to war only at a Sacrifice of interest." They would do it, but they needed his encouragement, especially his promise that once their unit was raised, Montgomery would accept them into service.[62] Yet if they were not accepted, it was largely Brown's doing because he and others kept trying to impose their own conditions on Montgomery. Milton S. Perry of Florida, in addition to interfering in the railroad iron business, tried to place stipulations on the troops he forwarded, wanting assurance that at least one regiment would be sent to Virginia to have a chance to win glory for Florida in the coming great battle all expected. Governors Brown and Moore of Louisiana both bristled in May when Congress passed new legislation allowing the acceptance only of regiments raised for three-year terms. The governors had been raising, arming, and equipping men for only twelve months, had exercised their patronage by appointing officers, and now found that Secretary of War Walker would not accept them. Governors John Pettus of Mississippi and Francis Pickens of South Carolina grumbled about this, too, though they were more amenable to compromise solutions. Indeed, Pickens actually sent Andrew G. Magrath to Montgomery as an emissary to negotiate their differences and, if possible, meet directly with Davis, while at the same time seeking a role in organizing the operations of the Confederate courts that would be established in South Carolina.[63] Oddly enough, some of the greatest conflict came from Virginia, where Montgomery might least have expected it. Much of the problem was Governor Letcher, whose drinking made Toombs's look modest by comparison. Indeed, some thought it so bad that they recommended that the man in charge of Virginia's militia, General Robert E. Lee, ought to turn Letcher out of office and assume the governorship himself. Letcher simply refused to act or communicate, and Montgomery, faced with this first serious crisis in state relations, failed themselves to establish proper liaison with the governor. Instead, Walker made the mistake of bypassing Letcher in order to get things done, only to alienate the governor the more. It was hardly an auspicious beginning.[64]

Governor Brown was the worst from the first. He refused to transfer to the Confederacy seized Yankee arms from the forts and arsenals occupied by Georgia until he had gleaned the best to keep for his own militia. Thereafter he took every opportunity to keep any weapons from leaving his jurisdiction, and began to use the threat of holding them as leverage to coerce Montgomery into accepting units raised according to his own plan rather than meeting the new regulations. When Walker attempted to order what seemed rightfully Confederate munitions out of the state, Brown refused; when he agreed to sell materiel to the government, he made the purchase conditional on Montgomery buying other useless goods from him, even a defective steamboat. Moreover, all the while he sent his state delegates in Congress on a steady stream of patronage and special interest errands on his behalf. Even Tom Cobb thought Brown a disgrace, and accused him of doing "all he can to clog the Government." His brother How-

ell dismissed Brown, admittedly an old political foe, as a "miserable dem-
agogue."[65] Even more frustrating was Brown's own sanctimonious pose,
for to the world at large he presented himself as much put upon, one who
swallowed heaps of injustice rather than injure the cause. "I have rather
risk unjust censure than bring the government at Montgomery into disre-
pute," he told an editor with a straight face.[66]

All the while the cabinet and even the president began to come in for
increasing criticism, not just from the few like Rhett and Tom Cobb but
from observers more at large. Walker was slow and ineffective—as indeed
he was—and a failure at diplomatic relations with applicants and other officials. Toombs believed him an incompetent and, being Toombs, made no
effort to keep his feeling to himself. Even Stephens, so often more bal-
anced than most, believed Walker a mistake and regretted that Toombs
had not been put in his place from the outset, even at a time when Toombs
was blustering that if he had his way Confederate forces would invade the
North, a move that certainly would have put the lie to Davis's plea to be
left alone, and could not have helped the diplomatic effort that was supposedly Toombs's primary concern. Mallory came in for his share, too, and
once again his cabinet colleague Toombs was one of his chief critics, calling the navy secretary "good for nothing."[67] Benjamin appeared useless
and lazy, in large part because the attorney general's portfolio gave him
next to nothing to do, while many in that culture, obsessed with rigid ideas
of masculinity, found his effeminate nature suspicious. Toombs joined with
Rhett and others in deprecating Memminger's performance in office, and
Chesnut's wife, Mary, complained that "our *cabinet* [is] so dull and stupid."[68] Even Toombs was not immune from criticism, and only John Reagan at the Post Office Department escaped criticism entirely, perhaps
because his portfolio was of so little interest that no one cared to carp at
him.

That left Davis himself, and his standing now on the eve of war in
earnest was mixed. With the country as a whole he enjoyed wide regard
and perhaps the greatest quotient of good will and enthusiastic support yet
bestowed on any incoming president since Washington. Many in Congress
felt the same, including a good selection from all of the states and good
majorities in most delegations. Louis Wigfall of Texas, inebriated braggart
though he was, enthusiastically backed Davis in everything, and as a leading fire-eater, he was a powerful counter to Rhett and Yancey. Even Tom
Cobb did not oppose him on all things, and was capable of having a few

good things to say, while only Rhett and Withers maintained their adamant opposition at every turn. If there was cause for concern, it lay with the moderates who felt disgruntled. Toombs was already lost, more from personality and thwarted ambition than from policy. Harder still was the growing rift with Stephens, who charged the president with being too slow and deliberate, and even Davis's close friend Clement Clay was critical of the president's apparent difficulty at making decisions. Rhett was predictably the worst of all, and it was apparent that he already had some sense of building a hard opposition to Davis, for when the foolish old Withers announced his intention to resign, the only person attempting to dissuade him was Rhett, who even though he, too, thought Withers was a crackpot, still saw in him an ally against the president. Even a few men who once supported Davis were beginning to change their minds, men like Robert Smith of Alabama, always a moderate, who would support most of the president's policy, yet soon conclude that they had made a mistake in electing him.[69]

Alexander De Clouet of Louisiana saw clearly enough that even though the old organized pre-secession parties were dead, the effects of earlier partisan battles were still to be seen.[70] Even Tom Cobb, himself increasingly blinkered by his growing animosity toward the president, recognized now that "the atmosphere of this place is absolutely *tainted* with selfish, ambitious schemes for personal aggrandizement."[71] Certainly feelings and resentments were at work among the disappointed. "The time will come when we will be able to review the course pursued by those in authority," unsuccessful office seeker J.C.S. Blackburn groused to Governor Brown in May, "and from the deep toned thunder of free men, which ever and anon is heard, the retribution will be sure and overwhelming." Appointments were going to men who had opposed secession to the last minute, while original secessionists were seemingly being ignored. "This is not right, it is not just," he asserted. "To the extent of my poor ability I here advertise that some men *shall* feel my opposition. I expect soon to be in a position to wield some influence in this way. And rest assured that friends I remember, and enemies *I will not forget.*" Soon to become a newspaper editor now that his military hopes had been dashed, he promised, "I will let 'slip the dogs of war' upon those who little think that there is a 'storm a brewing.'"[72]

They would not meet that storm in Montgomery, however. Whether or not the vice president had been authorized to dangle the lure of moving the capital before Virginians, they intended to have it all the same, and the inevitable logic of the nascent war gave them support. "A directing head was absolutely needed at Richmond," the journalist Littleton Washington observed when he reached Montgomery on May 5. "Fresh from the border I realized the gravity of the struggle but few others did at Montgomery save the President."[73] Washington exaggerated his own prescience, to be sure, for even in framing their Permanent Constitution, Congress gave itself the authority to create a federal district like the District of Columbia somewhere, and several states had already offered land free of charge, attracted by the prosperity that the capital must inevitably bring. Virginia did so, too, almost immediately after seceding, and it was only four days later when Boyce of South Carolina introduced the first motion for relocating the capital. Indeed, there was widespread support for the idea, with only Alabama strongly opposed, for obvious reasons. Within a week it appeared that a vote to move was a certainty, and on May 11 a motion finally passed to reconvene in July in Richmond, but that only affected the Congress and not the government as a whole. Thus when the bill went to Davis, he vetoed it, pointing out that moving Congress without moving the executive departments and the rest of the government would be pointless, indeed crippling. He even noted the clear anomaly in the bill caused by three of his cabinet—Toombs, Memminger, and Reagan—also being members of Congress. How could they function with one job in Richmond and the other in Montgomery?

Quickly a revised bill covering the president's objections went on the floor, and on May 18 three separate resolutions for moving the capital to Richmond were introduced, it being clear that the forces for relocation intended to overwhelm Congress. They spent all day May 20 in debate, and finally hewed out a bill calling for their adjournment the next day, to reconvene in Richmond on July 20, and the immediate removal of the rest of the government in the meantime. Tennessee had not yet been formally admitted, meaning there were nine state delegations voting. Four voted in favor and four against. Louisiana's delegation split evenly and thus cast no vote, making a tie that signaled defeat for the legislation. The forces against the move were Alabama, which did not want to lose the capital; Mississippi, which feared its removal so far away; and South Carolina, which distrusted the inevitable border mentality influence if their seat of government were located in the midst of those considered prone to reconstruction. Florida, once again, simply followed South Carolina. The move

seemed dead, and with that several members from the opposing delegations, Rhett among them, decided to get a head start on the morrow's adjournment by leaving that afternoon. Within a few hours, only three states
had full delegations in the chamber. De Clouet, who had been absent,
came into the chamber, and one of the three Florida members present decided to change his vote in response to considerable persuasion. In what
was a last-minute yet carefully orchestrated maneuver, William Porcher
Miles of South Carolina called for another vote on the defeated bill. De
Clouet broke the tie in Louisiana, which voted for. The Florida vote
shifted in favor, too, while the original four favorable votes held. The measure passed 6 to 3, even though the actual head count stood a slender 24 to
20. Stephens's rules of order had produced a decision once again, and
Davis signed the new bill within hours. The capital was to be Richmond.[74]

"It has caused much remark here," said a politician in faraway Texas.
"As we cannot judge of its policy, without knowing anything of the reasons
that induced it, it is only just that Congress should be allowed to meet
emergencies as they arise." There were still those who feared Virginia's
motives and the dread specter of reconstruction, but in the main they
looked on the decision of Congress to move to Virginia as evidence that the
six states voting in favor of the move—representing Gulf, Atlantic, and
border states—felt secure in the change. "Is it not probable," asked the
Texan, "that Congress by meeting in Richmond would exert a strong influence over Virginia in favor of *absolute* secession, and the Southern
Confederacy?"[75]

Some more moderate heads felt uneasy, including Stephens's, who was
either absent when the final vote was taken or else abstained. "Whether it
was wise to do so or not the future must prove," he wrote two days later.[76]
"We have the elements of independence," he believed, and if wisdom and
prudence prevailed in their new government, then they should be successful. Yet he understood as well as, if not better than, anyone else that
the divisions within their ranks were deep. "I have considered it with us a
simple question of how much *quackery* we had strength of constitution to
bear and still survive," he would say a few years hence.[77] They had left a
system in which the old Constitution, for all its flaws, had begun to show
its strength in guarding freedom at large by encouraging flexibility. In its
place they had remolded their charter by erecting inflexible boundaries to
entrench specific freedoms for the few. To those like Stephens who were
observant enough, the root problem was evident. They had been a series

of greater or lesser oligarchies before secession, yet now they were artifi-
cially attempting to bind themselves together in a mongrel sort of democracy. But only a real democracy or an absolute monarchy was likely to have
the political power or resilience to bend every precious resource to the
task of winning independence. The divisions already apparent between
and among the founders were unsettling evidence of the deeper fissures
that ran through the whole Confederacy. Saddled with those fundamental
fault lines, were they even prepared to prosecute a war for independence,
and if so, what hope for success was there?

Still this new Confederate democracy of theirs reflected ideas that
Stephens saw changing. Some of them were what he called "ideas of
greatness," by which he could only mean the positive declaration of slavery
as the warp of their federal fabric and state sovereignty as the weft.[78] Now
as the statesmen abandoned Montgomery for their homes and the move to
Richmond, just how well they worked their new loom depended upon how
they could work together.[79]

The Opening Guns

Well before the bombardment of Fort Sumter, there were hostile acts that could have been interpreted as the onset of war—the armed seizure of Federal customshouses and arsenals, post offices, and, of course, forts like Pulaski and others that came into their hands without a fight, not to mention the firing on the Star of the West. And, of course, six states had seceded. All came before Lincoln's inauguration on March 4, and, of course, scores of cannon were loaded and aimed at the Stars and Stripes at Forts Sumter and Pickens. Then and later men would argue over at just what point North and South crossed the line between bombast and bullets, but all the arguing certainly came to an end when war began in earnest on April 12, 1861, in Charleston Harbor. It had to happen, the only question really being whether it would be here or at Fort Pickens off Pensacola, Florida, the only other military installation remaining in United States hands after its home state's secession. That it came at Charleston was largely due to Jefferson Davis and to the Carolinians themselves. Fort Pickens touched the same nerve with the Confederates, but it was not as susceptible to bombardment, nor did the ersatz state volunteers who soon came under control of the new War Department in Montgomery have the artillery or the manpower to attempt to take it. Young hotspurs had been gathering at the Charleston batteries for weeks before there even was a Confederacy, making the harbor the most heavily armed spot in the hemisphere. The problem for Davis once he was inaugurated lay in keeping them in check until he had no alternative but to open fire.

The task fell to a new brigadier general. In organizing his new army, Davis initially created but one rank, brigadier general, but in May 1861 he would revise the system to provide for full-rank generals, and eventually for lesser ranks of lieutenant, major, and then brigadiers. He gave a brigadiership and command of the Charleston batteries to a former superintendent of the United States Military Academy at West Point, Pierre Gustave Toutant Beauregard, who reputedly preferred to go by his initials or Gustave because he thought Pierre sounded too "foreign." But a corporal's guard could have taken the unfinished and barely armed Fort Sumter, and it fell on April 13 after thirty-six hours of bombardment. That made Beauregard the first hero of the war, and that put him in place to be one of the most difficult sources of disharmony for the president for the rest of the life of the Confederacy.

Meanwhile Davis created his other top command. The first full generals were to be, in order of seniority, Samuel Cooper—a desk soldier and War Department bureaucrat—Albert Sidney Johnston, Robert E. Lee, and Joseph E. Johnston. Later Beauregard would be promoted to their full rank as well. To Albert Sidney Johnston, the idol of Davis's youth, he assigned defense of the entire Mississippi Valley, virtually all of the Confederacy from the Appalachians to the great river and even beyond. Lee, the scion of a distinguished old Virginia family and himself a hero of the war with Mexico, would not get an important field command yet; he was kept as a military advisor and then later in 1861 wasted on minor assignments in western Virginia and South Carolina. Joseph E. Johnston, a proud, contentious, prickly Virginian with an unhealthy concern for rank and his reputation, was to go to Virginia itself and begin organizing the defenses of the Shenandoah Valley, a back door to the Old Dominion's heartland, while the new hero Beauregard was sent to northern Virginia to build and train an army in and around Manassas to protect Richmond.

Both Johnston and Beauregard did their work well, aided by subordinates who would make names for themselves in the days ahead. Johnston occupied the arsenal town of Harpers Ferry, then built a small army under commanders Barnard E. Bee, Edmund Kirby Smith, Thomas Jonathan Jackson, and others, while Beauregard organized and trained brigades of volunteers led by James Longstreet, Richard S. Ewell, Milledge L. Bonham, and others. Their mission was to keep the Yankees out of Virginia, *and they were placed so that a rail line connected the two armies. If one was threatened, the other might come speedily to its aid. In the first tactical use of the railroad in history, that is exactly what happened. When Washington sent two thrusts toward Virginia, Johnston easily feinted his opponent out of contention without even a fight, then put his brigades on cars for the trip to Manassas Junction, where they arrived on July 20–21 just in time to reinforce Beauregard in meeting a serious Union threat along the banks of Bull Run. Though there had been isolated skirmishes elsewhere, it was the first real battle of the Civil War, a near-run affair between two armed mobs in which the one that lost its nerve first was defeated. After a hard day's fighting, the Yankee mob was streaming back to Washington, Thomas Jackson had become "Stonewall," Beauregard was a hero twice over and worried that President Davis would try to deny him his due credit, Johnston was fretting over his rank, and the people of the Confederacy believed they had won the "war."*

For the next eight months in the East there followed a "phony war" in which almost nothing happened on the Virginia front. Johnston and Beauregard faced the Yankees, who were rebuilding and refitting, but there was no fighting. Beauregard feuded with Davis to such a degree that finally he asked to be assigned to the Western theater to get away, and Davis was glad to send him there. Johnston remained, but revealed increasingly his fear of initiative or responsibility, instead carping constantly about what he could not do. Finally, in the face of a tentative Yankee advance in the late fall, he simply abandoned northern Virginia without a fight, even further impairing the president's confidence in him. Then in the face of a bold Federal amphibious move down the Chesapeake to a landing on the Virginia peninsula below Richmond, Johnston pulled his army back to meet the threat and shield Richmond, at the same time sending Stonewall Jackson, now a general, to meet similar thrusts into the Shenandoah. Jackson performed brilliantly, creating a lasting legend as he defeated three separate Union armies one at a time, then raced back to aid in the defense of Richmond. Johnston, by contrast, faced a Union general just as cautious as he was, George B. McClellan, and still did nothing, nor did he seriously contest McClellan's glacial advance until late May when the Yankees were in sight of Richmond itself, and the capital was in a panic. At Seven Pines, Johnston stopped retreating and fought an inept action, but at least he fought until he took a serious wound. President Davis was on the field, and had been almost every day to ensure that something was done. At first he turned the command over to General G. W. Smith, but within hours Smith suffered an attack of nerves or fright that simply incapacitated him for further command. Only then did Davis ask his chief military advisor to take over, a man some thought too cautious for aggressive war, General Robert E. Lee. That single act changed the nature of the war and of Confederate history.

The change was desperately needed, too, for Lee came to power during the darkest days of the war to date. What had begun so auspiciously at Manassas was not matched out in the West. Instead, almost from the first it had been a tale of defeat and loss there. At least the Confederates almost took Missouri, which never really seceded, until spirited defense at heavy cost kept most of it under Federal control. Meanwhile, Albert Sidney Johnston's efforts to hold the Mississippi Valley were a tale of trying to do too much with too little. The ideal Confederate northern border would have been the Ohio River, a natural defense. But Kentucky, like Missouri, did not secede. Instead its legislature declared itself neutral, which worked to the South's benefit so long as the Yankees observed that neutrality, and they did in the main, for Lincoln feared to drive his native state into the enemy camp and give them that Ohio barrier. But then one of Johnston's own generals, Leonidas Polk, a longtime friend of Davis whose West Point education belied the fact that he had never done active duty in uniform, committed the first of what would be an unbroken string of costly blunders when he violated neutrality without orders by occupying Columbus, Kentucky, on the Mississippi. That was all it took to drive the Union faction in the state into the ascendancy. Kentucky abandoned neutrality, sided with the Union, and suddenly the Ohio was gone for good. Far worse, the Federals now had access to the Ohio's tributaries the Tennessee and Cumberland Rivers, each of which darted south into Tennessee, the latter then turning eastward to Nashville, while the former went on down into northern Mississippi and Alabama before turning back into Tennessee to run past Chattanooga. They offered natural highways of waterborne invasion, which is how Union General Ulysses S. Grant planned to use them.

All Albert Sidney Johnston had to stop Grant were the army he was hastily assembling from all across the Deep South and two unfinished forts on the rivers. The first, Fort Henry on the Tennessee, was in such poor shape that it fell to Grant in February 1862 almost without a fight. A few days later Grant struck Fort Donelson on the Cumberland, and this time he had a fight on his hands. Surrounding the fort by land and water, he *forced it to surrender, and with it more than 12,000 badly needed Confederate soldiers. Grant was free to use the rivers at will, and he would. Within days Nashville itself had to be evacuated, and before long most of central and west Tennessee had to be given up.*

Fortunately for the Confederacy, this Johnston was not like the other one. Immediately he began a concentration of forces to increase his army to the point that he could drive back north to push Grant out of Tennessee. Early in April he launched his campaign, and on April 6, 1862, he managed to launch an almost complete surprise attack on Grant's camps around Shiloh Church near Pittsburg Landing. Johnston pushed Grant back steadily through the day until late in the afternoon. At what might have been the pivotal moment of the battle, Johnston fell from his saddle, bleeding to death from a leg wound he might not even have noticed. There was a lull in the fighting as Johnston's second-in-command, Beauregard, took over. Unwell, uncertain, and off balance, Beauregard hesitated and then broke off the fight, expecting to continue drubbing Grant on the morrow. That night Grant received a massive reinforcement, and the next morning it was he who took the offensive, recovering all of the lost ground and forcing Beauregard to retreat back into Mississippi, where he would begin the task of defending his reputation, shifting the blame for his actions, and expanding his feud with the president.

Kentucky, west Tennessee, control of the Tennessee, Cumberland, and the upper Mississippi down to Memphis were gone, while at the other end of the river a complaisant reliance on old forts below New Orleans led Davis to denude the Crescent City of most of its defenders. That same April a Union fleet led by David G. Farragut boldly steamed past the forts almost unhurt and chugged right up to the waterfront of the undefended city, which had no choice but to surrender. Before many days Farragut would be on his way upriver toward Baton Rouge, then Natchez, and soon Vicksburg. The Confederacy was nearly cut in two, Texas, Arkansas, and western Louisiana almost isolated, and the war was only a year old. The phony war had become all too real, and there was but a single bright spot on the horizon.

Lee.

5

Men but Not Brothers

THE SECESSION and the Confederacy's existence were predicated on slavery, on preserving and defending it against containment, as virtually all of its founders from Robert Barnwell Rhett to Jefferson Davis unashamedly declared in 1861. Ironically, however, the very thing that the Confederates wanted most to protect would become by the end of the war perhaps the least controllable of its institutions, a runaway leviathan powered by internal disintegration at home and the tantalizing prospect of freedom cunningly proffered by Abraham Lincoln in 1862 in his Emancipation Proclamation. By 1864 the place of slavery in Southern society would be turned almost upside down, as it became a source of internal dissension and division, an object of resentment, eventually to find its own existence questioned and then threatened by its very protectors themselves.

That preservation of slavery and the control of the black in Southern society was interwoven into almost every significant new feature of the Permanent Constitution should hardly have surprised anyone, North or South, for Confederates were convinced that not only was slavery vital to their economy, but also to social control and even their domestic tranquility. And as the framers in Montgomery had declared time and time again, it was founded on the bedrock doctrine of racial inferiority. That had always been a given, not just in Southern society, but throughout Western culture, perhaps as far back as the earliest white contacts with black Africa. Men of letters and science had even theorized on the subject over the centuries, but more especially in the South during the generation leading up to secession, when the outside attacks on slavery put Southerners on the defensive and created the need to reinforce and defend their beliefs with the power of science and the authority of religion.

Of the many who sought to justify black bondage, one of the most influential had been Dr. Samuel Cartwright of the Medical Association of Louisiana, who addressed his group in New Orleans on March 12, 1851, with a discussion of "the diseases and physical peculiarities of our negro population." Admitting that blacks constituted nearly half of the Southern population, Cartwright confessed that whites knew little of them scientifically, a shortcoming he sought to resolve not by reference to medical books—which were themselves deficient on the subject—but by direct observation. For a start, the most obvious difference of color between black and white men went deeper than skin. Every segment of the Negro's body, from the tissue of his brain to his blood itself, was darker than the Caucasian's, he argued. According to Cartwright, their bones were different— whiter and more brittle, the head sat differently on the end of the spine, the neck was shorter, the legs more bowed. The Negro's brain was only 90 percent the size of the white's, the doctor maintained, yet his hearing was better, his sense of smell keener, his vision more acute. In short, said Cartwright, the comparisons between white and black were not unlike those between humans and wild mammals.

Then there was his physicality. "His imitative powers are very great, and he can agitate every part of the body at the same time," said Cartwright, "or what he calls *dancing all over*." His brain consisted much less of reasoning matter, and instead of a much higher proportion of nerves extending throughout his body, which made the Negro essentially a sensual creature "at the expense of intellectuality," the doctor explained. Hence his music was basic, rhythmic, but utterly lacking in the intellectuality of Mozart, with melody but no harmony, and composed of songs with no meaning whatever but merely collections of sounds pleasing to the ear. "The great development of the nervous system, and the profuse distribution of nervous matter to the stomach, liver and genital organs, would make the Ethiopian race entirely unmanageable," he went on, were it not for vascular and pulmonary deficiencies that, combined with his natural cerebral shortcomings, resulted in a "debasement of mind, which has rendered the people of Africa unable to take care of themselves." This was why they were lazy and apathetic, given up entirely to gluttony and lust if left to themselves, and why for centuries they were lost in "idleness, misery and barbarism." Africans had created no roads or cities, no lasting edifices or monuments, they had no written language, not even hieroglyphics, "to indicate that they have ever been awakened from their apathy and sleepy indolence." Even their spoken native languages were not capable of abstract ideas, nor had they ever conceived governments based on abstract ideas, but rather they habitually made themselves subject to a king or master. "Why, in America, if let alone, they always prefer the same kind of government, which we call slavery," he averred, without citing any instance in which blacks had been given the choice. Even had they not preferred slavery, their mental and moral deficiencies were such that, given liberty, they lacked the virtue, integrity, and industry to keep from sliding back into barbarism, or else back to slavery.

Even the diseases of the black were different. Negroes did not catch malaria, Cartwright said, somehow having overlooked the thousands that died in the periodic epidemics that swept the Mississippi Valley. They were prone to consumption—tuberculosis—but the chief cause was not infection nor anything to do with the lungs, but lay in the slave's mind, caused by superstition, and by dissatisfaction when they erroneously thought themselves ill-used by their masters. But the most interesting of all slave maladies was what Cartwright chose to call "drapetomania," the disease that made blacks want to run away from slavery. Western medical science had not yet recognized it, but its existence had long been known by its chief—indeed, only—symptom, "the absconding from service." Indeed, Cartwright proudly maintained that he was the first really to recognize this as a genuine disease, and to give it a name. The cause was a mental illness, but one that was curable. The remedy was simply good management.

Harkening back to the Bible, he maintained that the original name given to Negroes derived from a word that meant "submissive knee-bender," applied to one who by birth was meant to bow to higher authority. When the white man, out of generous but misguided philanthropy, sought to elevate the black's status to his own, or lowered himself to the level of the black, or mistreated his slaves, he upset the balance dictated by nature, and in that imbalance the Negro's mind impelled him to run away. Cartwright even laid out the progression of the disease, which first manifested itself in sulkiness and complaining. The way to treat that symptom and keep it from developing was the "preventive measure" of the lash, what he said some planters called "whipping the devil out of them." The way to keep slaves happy was to keep them warm, well fed and clothed, to allow them to have families, to keep them confined at night and cut off from slaves on other plantations, away from liquor, and not to overwork or overexpose them. Do that, and blacks were the most governable people on earth. But once a master had done all that, if a black should ever attempt to raise his head to a level with his master's, then "humanity and their own good require that they should be punished until they fall into that submissive state which it was intended for them to occupy in all after time."

There was another lesser disease also peculiar to blacks, which Cartwright chose to call dysaesthesia aethiopis, but which overseers and masters commonly knew as "rascality." It was much more prevalent among free blacks who lived together in groups than among slaves, and only attacked those slaves given sufficient liberty that they lived like freedmen. Indeed, almost all free Negroes were so afflicted, and he maintained that certain lesions were always present on the infected—he could as well have called them witch marks—along with a permanently half-awake state of lassitude. Made careless by the malady, blacks were prone to commit much mischief, not out of willful evil, but "owing to the stupidness of mind and insensibility of the nerves induced by the disease." Thus they broke dishes, wasted food, mistreated animals, stole from other slaves, and ruined their own meager property. Worse, when working they were lazy and intentionally damaged the master's crops when hoeing and cutting, and broke their tools. Some supposed that such behavior grew out of intentional mischief, but Cartwright showed that when not under the restraints of slavery, the black was too stupid even to conceive of premeditated mischief, nor was he sensate enough to be aroused by anger to such an act of courage as defying a master. A sure sign was that when punished, Negroes refused to allow those whipping them to see their pain, for the disease made them physically insensible. Northern doctors and others had seen these same signs, but "ignorantly attribute the symptoms to the debasing influence of slavery on the mind," whereas Cartwright maintained that "the disease is the natural offspring of negro liberty—the liberty to be idle, to wallow in filth, and to indulge in improper food and drinks." The cure was proper diet, and stimulation of the skin by a good washing followed by repeated applications of oil that was to be "slapped" into the skin with a stout leather strap. Then must come hard work, to stimulate the blood.

"The reason of this is founded in unalterable physiological laws," Cartwright said. Only under the exercise of slave labor imposed by the white man was the deficient blood of the black circulated properly, feeding and stimulating the brain to something approaching normal function. In short, slavery was the only real liberation for the mind of the slave. Adult blacks were like infant whites, all nervous system and no intellect. More importantly, white babies, nestled close to the mother's bosom, invariably breathed much of their own exhalation, thus depriving themselves of oxygen and stalling their intellectual development until they were grown enough to get around on their own, when finally they began breathing pure fresh air and began the development of their minds. Similarly, observation had shown that blacks always slept with something covering their faces, achieving the same deprivation of oxygen and producing the same effect. Indeed, they preferred this, said the doctor. Carrying the comparison to children even further, Cartwright noted also that blacks "are ungovernable, vicious and rude under any form of government whatever, not resting on love and fear as a basis." They need not be fearful of the whip, but only of disappointing their masters, for they were impelled by immutable natural law to love those in authority over them. Lacking courage or intellect, they felt instinctive dependence on others. Discipline was essential, whether in their eating, exercise, or even sleep, for without it they naturally ran to excess. "They often gorge themselves with fat meat, as children do with sugar," he added. If there was one overriding evidence of the inability of Negroes to live free in white society, it was the fact that on the plantation hundreds of them would docilely allow themselves to be governed by a single white overseer who could walk and sleep among them free of fear.

"Does he belong to the same race as the white man?" asked the doctor. Was he a son of Adam? Citing the old Biblical argument that the descendants of Ham, the son of Noah, were doomed to be the servants of mankind, Cartwright pointed out that according to Scripture Ham's descendants went to Africa and were the ancestors of the Negro. In fulfillment of the prophecy, the seed of Ham had shown themselves fitted to be servants and unfit to be free, and thus there was "both wisdom, mercy and justice in the decree dooming him to be servant of servants, as the decree is in conformity to his nature." The study of anatomy and physiology confirmed that the African was unfit to exercise the responsibilities or enjoy the freedoms of the white man, and history and Scripture confirmed that fact. His intellect was capable at best of grasping only a few simple moral truths, and even those had to be compulsory. "The black blood distributed to the brain chains the mind to ignorance, superstition and barbarism, and bolts the door against civilization, moral culture and religious truth." Only slavery opened that door to the extent that it could admit any intellectual improvement. The South and slavery accorded a great look on civilization and humanity alike, for keeping the black a slave gave him the opportunity to experience what little rise he was capable of, while at the same time the labor that he gave in return bestowed the agricultural blessings of cotton and rice and tobacco on the world. "A knowledge of the great primary truth, that the negro is a slave by nature, and can never be happy, industrious, moral or religious, in any other condition than the one he was intended to fill, is of great importance to the theologian, the statesman, and to all who are at heart seeking to promote his temporal and future welfare," concluded the doctor. If only Northern fanatics could understand that, there would be no need for sectional controversy or even, as Cartwright predicted ten years before the fact, "seeing the Union divided."[1]

Probably no other apologist for slavery managed to construct such a mountain of sophistries guised as science. What was important was not the flagrant nonsense of it all, the blatantly self-serving rationalizations, or the utter repudiation of the notion of forming conclusions based on evidence rather than the reverse. The real import of Cartwright's theories and others like them was that they supported in pseudo-science what religious and political arguments were also being marshaled to defend. What people believe or choose to believe can be far more meaningful than fact and what they ought to believe. Cartwright was only one of a vocal cadre of apologist-theorists whose sophistic arguments, couched in the trappings of scholarship, found ready acceptance in a society that wanted to believe that blacks were an inferior race that needed slavery for their own benefit. Their ideas permeated the arguments in Montgomery over issues touching on slavery, and echoed in every article of their new Permanent Constitution, allowing them to justify their movement not just on the grounds of protection of property and their political freedoms, but as the only true means available of protecting the Negro from himself, and their society from disintegration.

Thus it is hardly surprising that no sooner was the Confederacy launched in its new career than new apologists appeared to reinforce and strengthen orthodoxy, to reassure Confederates that having taken a giant step in the name of right, they were continuing in that just path. Indeed, in the actual act of secession, the Florida convention went on record not only to make protection of slavery the explicit reason for its action, but also to reaffirm Southern beliefs about the Negro, citing "their natural tendency every where shown where the race has existed to idleness vagrancy and crime." They could only flourish under slavery, said Florida's Declaration of Causes in January 1861, and offered as proof the fact that their numbers had increased in the South as "the highest evidence of the humanity of their owners." If the slave states could not expand, the blacks would soon be a glut, leading somehow to a decrease in the value of their labor and the deterioration of their material welfare. "Can anything be more impudently false than the pretense that this State of things is to be brought about from considerations of humanity to the slaves?" it asked.[2]

With the government only weeks old, J.D.B. DeBow published an article titled "The Right to Enslave," in which he argued that "emancipation can never give liberty." It merely substituted one kind of government for another where the slave was concerned. "Emancipation is a sin in many cases," he said, and certainly where those thus freed would slide back into barbarism and debauchery. If blacks were as hard-working as the Chinese, for instance, or as dedicated to making and saving money, then perhaps they could function as freedmen. But they were not, which meant that whites had to take care of them in any society in which the two shared the same polity. "What can be more just than for them to pay the expense of the very great benefit received when enslaved to those who govern them rightly?" he demanded to know. Stepping even closer to the heart of the matter as it related to the new nation, he asked just what was good government. "The first object of any possible government is to interfere with the freedom of men;" he said, "it is to compel them to do some things and refrain from other things." Was that necessarily not free government? Was not government the right and duty of the strong to interfere in or mediate the relations of men? "When a whole tribe continually does wrong, being worse than any two nations engaged in war, 'filled with all unrighteousness, fornication, wickedness, covetousness, maliciousness,'" and more, "it is manifestly not right for them to live so, and they have no right to live so a single day." Blacks would live so if left to themselves, and thus they forfeited any right to freedom, and demanded that whites impose government over them. Just as governments imposed taxes, duties, and other civic obligations on their citizens in return for the protections and benefits provided, so whites were entitled to the profits of a labor system that the inherent deficiencies of blacks forced the masters to impose to preserve order.[3]

President Davis himself added his own voice in March 1861, when he declared that "we recognize the negro as God and God's Book and God's Laws, in nature, tell us to recognize him—our inferior, fitted expressly for servitude." Freedom only injured the slave. "The innate stamp of inferiority is beyond the reach of change," he said. "You cannot transform the negro into anything one-tenth as useful or as good as what slavery enables him to be." Slavery had its evils and abuses, he admitted, and also granted that at some future date the black might even be capable of some limited freedom as a peasant or serf, but no more, and not now.[4] After two years of the war, the Confederate discussion of emancipation had advanced little beyond what DeBow and Davis had to say. In May 1863 a general assembly of the Presbyterian Church in Columbia, South Carolina, heard a report commissioned eighteen months earlier from a study of numerous large slaveholders in Alabama and Mississippi. "Should the force of circumstances compel [us], by gradual emancipation, to free the slaves," it concluded, then Confederates ought to be prepared to train former slaves "to become, what nature designs them to be, our hired servants, tho' nominally and legally free."[5]

More than justifications were needed for Confederates, though for the rest of slavery's existence Southern presses would continue to turn out from time to time the apologia for it needed to sustain certitude in the moral, religious, and scientific foundations of the institution. A whole literature began to appear—the continuation of a more sporadic press dating back for two generations—on the proper care and management of slaves. In part, of course, it was merely reinforcement. More importantly, however, as men went off to war in the early months, and as months turned to years and more and more men left home, it became increasingly necessary to address two new issues not previously concerns of slaveholders. With older experienced owners and overseers in the military, management of the slaves inevitably fell to the very young or the very old, or the women, none of them accustomed to handling blacks. Corollary to that was the increased possibility of runaways and "rascality," which demanded even closer management. Dr. Robert Collins of Macon, Georgia, turned his mind to the matter late in 1861, and published an essay on slave management that *DeBow's*, as the most widely circulated journal in the Confederacy, disseminated from Virginia to Texas.

Collins, like Cartwright, began with the Biblical history and justification of the institution, the vital reinforcement that always preceded every argument. "Slavery was established and sanctioned by divine authority," he averred, and then somehow concluded that the fact that the Confederacy currently had 3.5 million slaves in its midst had come about "providentially" and "without any agency on our part." It was a providence that gave them responsibilities as well as advantages, as they sought to find the best way to serve the welfare and interest of both races. Collins confessed that as a slaveowner for thirty years, he had tried many different experiments at management, treatment, labor, and living to find what worked the best. He concluded what many others had been saying long before, essentially what Cartwright maintained, that a combination of kindness and liberality, along with discipline and insistence on subordination, produced the desired effect. Nature gave the Negro an instinctive averse reaction to harshness and abuse, making the master who was kind but firm the more successful at maintaining control. "Every attempt to force the slave beyond the limits of reasonable service, by cruelty or hard treatment, so far from extorting more work only tends to make him unprofitable, unmanageable; a vexation and a curse." For that reason, Collins maintained that, in fact, cases of abuse of slaves seldom occurred, and when they did were universally condemned. It was more than merely an observation, whether accurate or not. It was a subtle admonition. In the current crisis, the Confederacy could not afford the risks attendant to a large population of unhappy blacks in its rear while the men accustomed to controlling them were away at the fronts.

Collins addressed everything conducive to slave contentment, starting with the Negro quarters on the plantation. Blacks should be housed under shade trees, close to good water, and with good ventilation. No more than one family ought to be housed in a single slave building, and buildings should be roomy, perhaps sixteen by twenty feet, for overcrowding was detrimental to their health and happiness. Every family ought to have proper bedding and blankets, and though it would cost a few dollars at the outset, the rewards in profit from increased labor from happy, well-tended blacks would be manyfold. The same applied to their food. Collins had experimented earlier with trying to feed slaves less meat and more cheap vegetables, but concluded that it did not work. Working adults must have bacon, molasses, lots of bread, and coffee in the morning to prepare them for work. Moreover, every slave house ought to be allowed a patch for a garden in which the family grew their own vegetables. As for children, they ought to have whatever they needed "as they pay a good interest upon the amount of care and expense bestowed upon them." For clothing they should have cotton in summer and wool in winter, with two suits of each, extra shoes and hats, and be required to dress themselves neatly. "The more pride and self-respect you can instill into them, the better they will behave," he added, suggesting that even a bit of individuality should be allowed by letting them indulge in some decoration for their apparel.

Of course they had to work, and should be started before sunrise and allowed no break until noon. In the winter they should have a breakfast, but otherwise their first meal would be their lunch, and after a break of an hour they should work again until nightfall. In the heat of summer the schedule should relax a bit, starting at dawn, eating breakfast after two hours, then working until noon and a two-hour break, and then toiling on to night. Saturdays they ought to work only until noon, however, then spend the rest of the day cleaning themselves and their homes in order to be neat for the Sabbath. Collins dismissed out of hand the recent practice of some planters of turning over a small parcel of land for the slaves to grow their own cotton or cane, in order to sell it for spending money. It encouraged trading among themselves and attempting to trade with whites, and moreover gave the slave an incentive to mix a little of his master's crop with his own to enhance his profit. Besides, with a war on, every bit of produce from the land was needed and none should be spared to the slaves. If masters gave their chattels something, it should be a little gift of money at the end of the year for good behavior.

And when it came to behavior, inevitably there had to be discipline, now more than ever. It should be systematic and regular, with rules clearly understood and rigidly enforced. Every slave should know his task and be required to perform it, the more so now that idle time could be dangerous. When punishment was necessary, moreover, lenience only worked against the system and actually disappointed the slave. Punishment, said Collins, "rather tends to win his attachment and promote his happiness and well-being." Slaves would not respect or love the master who indulged them or failed to enforce discipline. In return, the master ought to grant little indulgences and privileges when he could, but they should always be matters of special permission and not right, for blacks "are a people ever ready to practice upon the old maxim of 'give an inch and take an ell.'" There should be no cardplaying or gambling allowed to them, and certainly no liquor. Further, Negroes were tyrannical by nature. Left to themselves, the stronger would abuse the weaker, husbands their wives, mothers their children, and by maintaining discipline owners also kept the domestic peace. This was all the more reason to encourage religion among them, especially since they were much impressed by mysteries and miracles, loved a zealous and vehement style of preaching, and tended to hold tenaciously to faith once adopted. To cement their bonds to faith, master, and plantation, they should also be allowed to marry, though only with others from their own estate. Marrying the property of another master, with the enforced separation incumbent on such an arrangement, only led to discontent, and made even greater separation possible should one master or the other sell his property. "It is true they usually have but little ceremony in forming these connections; and many of them look upon their obligation to each other very lightly," Collins added, "but in others, again, is found a degree of faithfulness, fidelity and affection which owners admire." As for their physical health, masters and overseers ought always to commence treatment with some simple medicine as soon as symptoms of illness appeared. He had found in his own experience that red pepper could cure almost anything.[6]

As time wore on, presses also turned out guidelines for the conduct of overseers, especially as they became more and more important with the owners and their sons away from home. Moreover, with owners so often absent in the army, prudent people realized that the overseer came under much less direct scrutiny, and thus had more opportunity to slack off on his own effort, and at the same time to abuse the slaves. Being an overseer, said one advisor, "requires something more than your presence on the plantation, and that, at such times as suit your own pleasure and convenience." One printer of plantation account books even included a printed sheet with George Washington's instructions to his overseers, suggesting it as a form of contract or agreement. There was no other way to get work from blacks than by being constantly present, for when his back was turned they would be idle, and punishment after that could only make them sullen. Guidelines enjoined against overwork, too much exposure to the elements, inadequate food, even allowing the blacks to go on "night rambles." There must always be cool water for them in the heat of the day, and hands should not be allowed to carry their baskets of picked cotton on their head, "a most injurious practice." Immediately after advice on the care of the slaves, the guidelines went on to cover care of the mules and oxen.[7]

That such special precautions were going to be needed to manage the enormous slave population of the new Confederacy was early manifest to observers, and there were ample stories in circulation—most of them baseless rumors—to justify such concerns. Fears of slave insurrections dated back decades to the uprisings of Denmark Vesey and Nat Turner, and increased dramatically after John Brown's Harpers Ferry raid. On election day in 1860, Montgomery itself rocked to new hints of the sort of plots that had led years before to the creation of city night patrols all across the South. Rumors said Southern secessionists would be murdered by blacks when they went to vote, while their wives and daughters would be attacked. In fact, fearing the inevitable reprisals that such rumors led to, some slaves actually ran away to escape the hysteria, while Unionists used the emotional uproar to argue that after secession their slaves would rise up en masse, and Southerners would have to fight a two-front war against the Yankees before them and their own blacks in their rear. Then after Lincoln's election and the commencement of secession, new rumors surged across the country that Yankees were encouraging slaves to murder their owners and run away. Soon hysteria found concrete plots where they probably never existed, like the supposed scheme to poison flour in a mill at Autaugaville, Alabama, by putting strychnine in with the grist. More sinister was the story that unfolded at Pine Level of two white men who supposedly enticed local slaves to kill their masters and their families and take their livestock into hiding to await the coming of a Yankee army. Or were they actually supposed to march on Pine Level and destroy the town and kill its inhabitants? Or were they not, instead, supposed to take secretly fashioned pikes to attack some other community? One source said they were only to kill the white men and the old and ugly women, while keeping *"the young and handsome* white women *for their wives."* The problem with all of such stories was that they only came out after lawful and extralegal groups fanned across the countryside going from plantation to plantation to "interrogate" the slaves. "We are whipping the negroes taking them as they come," one vigilante declared. Under the lash the slaves often confessed to anything, even made up stories, to stop the whip, and then faced a rope and noose in its place. Every week there were hangings.[8]

Most Confederate cities of any size already had municipal codes that strictly controlled the movements and behavior of blacks within the city limits, whether slave or free. They could not sell crops of their own in town without written permission from their masters. They could not meet in groups, nor were free blacks allowed to remain within the city limits after nightfall, while out on the plantations slaves had to have passes from their masters to leave home, even to go to a neighboring plantation to visit a spouse. If blacks got into trouble, their punishment far outstripped that meted to whites for similar offenses. When a free black barber got into a fight with a slave, he received thirty lashes for injuring another man's property. An indiscreet oath in the hearing of a white could result in the lash, while attacking a white or a free black was asking for a hundred lashes whether done by freedman or slave. The least onerous penalty affecting blacks came when one free Negro assaulted another. No one caring about either damage or retribution, the offender merely got a fine of $10, thus at least doing some good for the city treasury. In fact, at an owner's request, whipping was often suspended by the authorities, though frequently only so the owner could do it instead, paying more heed not to damage his property and perhaps out of feeling that some of the code was unjust in the first place.[9]

Thus influences at every hand gave cause for Confederates to regard their black population with suspicion. All across the South citizens petitioned their governors for permission to use the arms of local militia units like the Davis Light Dragoons of Aberdeen, Mississippi, since there were few civilian guns in the area and the planters found themselves "in the midst of a numerous slave population."[10] Just two weeks after the firing on Fort Sumter, citizens of Bunker Hill, Mississippi, organized themselves for the purpose of "repelling insurrection among the negroes (if such thing should happen)," and even petitioned the governor to be allowed to set aside civil procedure in arresting and detaining suspects.[11] At the same time sudden fears that the proximity of Union soldiers would lead to a slave uprising on Amelia Island led citizens to petition the governor of Florida for permission to create a home guard, for fear that their slaves "would be led to commit acts of violence and cruelty upon the *defenceless females* and children."[12] Curiously, in Milledgeville, Georgia, local "loafers and vagabonds" even started rumors of a slave insurrection just in order to find some employment for themselves as guards against the uprising for local planters.[13]

Yet there were other quite different signs of black attitudes, ones more comforting if puzzling. From all across the new Confederacy there came stories of blacks, free and slave, who wanted to do their bit for the new nation. Even as the first elements of the new government reached Richmond, they could see a South Carolina slave who had come north with a Carolina regiment to defend the Virginia frontier, marching about the city wearing a sword with which he swore he would shave Lincoln's head. A free black descended from one of George Washington's slaves, now the owner of a small farm near Mount Vernon, offered twenty-eight acres, one-sixth of his property, to be sold at auction to raise money for Virginia's defense, leading the press to point out that "he is an intelligent negro."[14] More active efforts in Virginia came from other quarters, like the fifty free blacks in Amelia County, and two hundred more in Petersburg who offered themselves to the government either to perform labor or even to fight under white officers.[15] Slaves like a Tennessee barber named Jim donated money from their small savings to help raise companies; a Montgomery slave subscribed $150 of his own to the first call for loans from Secretary of the Treasury Christopher Memminger; not far from Mobile sixty slaves on one plantation practiced drilling every night after a full day's work, expressing their hope to fight the "damned buckram abolitionists" who had caused the crisis that now led to the fear of slave uprisings and the consequent curtailment of their few little freedoms.[16]

The motives behind the hundreds of proffers of support and even service that came from free and slave blacks were mixed and contradictory. Undoubtedly some were simply spurred by the excitement of the times, the desire for a little adventure, and the fact that they, too, were Southerners and Confederates, even if at the very bottom of the social order. Then, too, free blacks could hope that their lot in that society might improve if they showed themselves patriotic, while at the same time many of them who offered their labor at work or soldiering undoubtedly just needed employment. Slaves could hope that giving evidence of patriotism might lift some of the sanctions that the crisis imposed on them, and perhaps even lead to freedom in gratitude for service. And while many such offers were undeniably genuine as the mails brought them into Montgomery and then Richmond, surely, too, a number of those prominently circulated through the press were little more than rumors and exaggerations, and some even outright inventions, all to proclaim to Confederates and the world that their slaves stood with them in this contest. It was proof, if proof were needed, that this conflict was not about slavery, otherwise their blacks would hardly beg to risk their own lives in order to keep themselves in bondage. The message was simple. Slaves loved their masters and liked slavery, and knew what was good for them.

Once the war commenced in earnest, new strains and circumstances previously unimagined began rapidly wearing away at the Confederacy's early façade of complaisance and security in the righteousness of their institution, and the happiness of its inmates. With a certain fittingness, it was South Carolina's coastal rice planters who first felt the dislocations of war when Union naval forces took Port Royal in November 1861 and began to slowly spread out north and south, toward Charleston and Savannah, making Rhett's own rice plantations and large slaveholdings among the first threatened. That Port Royal could fall was only further proof to Rhett, if he needed any, of the inadequacy of Davis and his military policy. Stockpiled cotton and rice fell into Union hands, and families like his own had to be evacuated to the interior for their safety. With them had to go their slaves. Throughout November and December planters in an increasingly wide arc abandoned their homes, taking their blacks and their movable property with them. In Georgia, already feeling the financial straits that dislocation imposes, planters implored Governor Joseph Brown to order the railroads to transport them at the lowest possible rates. And South Carolina's Governor Francis Pickens issued an order that all livestock and slaves be "driven" off the coastal islands.[17]

Then in January 1862 the state convention in Georgia created a commission of planters to address the crisis, and it decided that all slaves should be removed out of the path of Union forces. This process would be repeated all across the Confederacy in the years ahead whenever invading Northern forces approached. Planter-statesman Langdon Cheves chose not to try Brown's railroads, but instead chartered a steamer called the *Manassas,* patriotically named for their first victory of the war. While he kept sixty of his blacks behind to protect his plantation as his furniture and valuables were packed for removal, he would send 250 others up the Savannah River to Augusta to safety.[18] The problems for men like Cheves did not end there, however. The *Manassas* made slow passage on the river, and one of the slaves, so disoriented at being removed from the only home he had ever known, simply got up during the night and walked off the deck to drown. Then when they reached Augusta the slaves were simply dumped on the wharf with no shelter and no one to assume the care and control of them at first before Cheves could arrange an overseer to take over. Then he had to find some employment for his slaves that would at least pay for their upkeep. At the same time, he worried that, finding themselves among strangers, they might feel that they had been "run out of the known world," as they complained. That could lead to demoralization of the sort that led one to drown himself.

It would take some time before Cheves could find a planter in South Carolina to allow the blacks to move in, and then they had to mill lumber to repair dilapidated cabins to house the slaves, while Cheves rented two hundred acres of poor land to try to put under cultivation in order to get his Negroes working again and supporting him and themselves. The plantation had to go on, for without it Cheves's fortune would be ruined, and his hundreds of unemployed and now unhappy slaves would be ripe for rascality and running away. Even then, the land he rented was not enough to keep all of them fully employed. Since the slaves worked less, his overseer concluded that they would need less to eat, and began to save on expenditure by cutting back on their meat, which the war and military demand was driving up in price. Then, as a result of being exposed to new people and new microbes in the relocation, the slaves came down with measles and some died. Before long one or two began to go missing, either simply avoiding work in the relaxed conditions with their master absent or actually running away. In this instance, all across the Confederacy, as legislature after legislature passed measures providing for removal of slaves from their states, the war was beginning to make the plantation system and slave control break down, in the process seemingly proving some of the warnings raised by Cartwright and Collins, even if for radically different causes.[19]

The influx of refugee planters and their slaves also caused considerable upheaval wherever they arrived. Missouri did not secede, despite the attempt of a rump secession convention to try to take the state out of the Union, and as a result many Confederate sympathizers left the state for Tennessee and Mississippi, taking their slaves with them. As early as September 1861 local authorities in Mississippi complained that the burden of caring for these extra slaves who had no plantation to work was becoming onerous. "As she is a non Confederate state we ought not to suffer her thousands of slaves to pour in upon our glorious soil," one planter urged Governor John Pettus of Mississippi. Their own slaves were remaining docile, "more Loyal than in former times," said one, but if the blacks from Missouri and Kentucky and Maryland kept coming in they risked seeing their own chattels incited to rebellion by the idle blacks.[20] Texans complained of the same influx by Louisiana planters, one slaveowner bringing more than three hundred with him as he fled advancing Union forces.[21]

Just as bad was what happened when Union forces arrived before slaves could be gotten away. Governor John Milton of Florida almost panicked in February 1862 when he perceived a threat to Tallahassee, in the middle of the largest concentration of slaves in the state. Yankee control would turn it into a haven for runaways from all over the state, as well as for disloyal whites, and frantically he tried to assemble men and arms to protect the town, but without success.[22] That inability to protect their blacks from being freed by Lincoln's armies, or to protect local whites from the depredations of slaves suddenly freed from the constraints of white control, caused more widespread fear and unrest in the Confederacy than perhaps any other matter, and from an early date. By June 1862 women in Adams County, Mississippi, complained to Governor Pettus that all the men were gone and there were none but boys aged six and seven years old to protect them. "In this neighborhood are many of the very vilest of negroes, who are constantly marauding the whole country," pleaded one farm wife. Repeatedly women begged for their husbands to be released from the army to come protect them, or else to send regular troops, and not skittish militia, to intimidate the blacks.[23]

Yet at the same time, others begged governors not to enforce the state militia draft in their counties.[24] After the first waves of enthusiastic enlistments by whites, national and state conscription slowly began to erode away the remaining white male population, taking even overseers until Congress passed the Twenty Negro Law, which granted exemption to one white male for every twenty slaves on a plantation. As early as September 1861, Carolina planters complained that the army had taken so many volunteers away that the men who remained could not maintain their "beats," the civilian patrols that kept an eye on the plantations.[25] As slaves in ever larger numbers escaped supervision by owners and overseers, they simply left plantations and found their way to Yankee lines, or stayed on the plantation only as they pleased, meanwhile exploiting the opportunities for plundering the locality. Marion County, Mississippi, pleaded in June 1862 that it needed white men to "keep the negroes in awe—who are getting quite impudent." The closer enemy forces came, the more unruly the blacks became. At the same time, the anger of the remaining citizens at this new Negro surliness was such that troops were needed to keep whites from retaliating on the blacks and injuring or killing them.[26] Patrols were constituted from the old men and boys to keep surveillance on the plantations and watch for signs of trouble. "I am truly sorry to hear that those negroes have so wilfully disobeyed my orders," an Alabama planter wrote home to his wife while he was away from home trying to find employment for them. "I will teach them how to disobey my orders so flatly," he concluded. "I am going to *sell* the last one of them."[27]

In the first year of the life of the Confederacy, more than forty slaves were hanged just in and around Natchez, Mississippi, and that many or more were put in irons for perceived threats of insurrection. Moreover, thanks to the constraints of the war, many planters were unable to care entirely for their slaves even when there was no threat of enemy proximity, leaving the blacks largely to fend for themselves by plundering other neighboring farms, and even foraging on helpless white communities. By the summer of 1862 there were sections in which slaves had such liberty that they roamed at will, acquired weapons, and even began harboring runaways from other plantations. They killed livestock, emptied corncribs and smokehouses, and even made a profit of sorts by selling some of what they stole at "negro markets" where barter was the rule and stolen goods the currency. Planters begged to have the local militia kept in its home counties rather than sent off for state defense.[28]

In Georgia's Wilkes County, the home of Toombs, after just one year there were over four hundred slaves on seven plantations utterly devoid of any oversight. This "will leave our wifes and children in a bad situation," a soldier complained to Governor Brown. "You know sufficiently well the nature and disposition of the negro race to perfectly understand what is necessary for their government," he said. "Leave them to govern themselves and they will soon go estray." Then there was the damage the uncontrolled blacks could do to their masters' crops. "The quantity of negroes above stated turned loose upon our wifes and children for one month would no doubt do us a very serious injury," he warned.[29] Mississippians actually sent their governor petitions begging him not to mobilize the militia. "As no white men would be left to control the Slaves," they implored, "its execution would be to turn at large the Slaves of the County and to expose all we hold dear and Sacred to their loosened passions and novel condition."[30] By the spring of 1863 even qualified overseers were in short supply when they could be exempted from service. In Florida an overseer could make $300 to $700 a year, but an able-bodied man over the draft age of forty-five could hire himself out as a substitute, going into the military in the place of another who had been conscripted, and be paid from $1,000 to $5,000. As a result, experienced overseers chose to enlist as substitutes, then take their money and buy cheap land and even slaves, preparing to set themselves up as planters when the war or their service ended. Meanwhile, civilians faced the prospect of their crops going to ruin with no one to drive the slaves, and the state itself could face starvation. It was a problem that repeatedly came to the eyes not just of the governors but of Davis and Congress as well.[31]

With the war barely two weeks old, Florida passed an ordinance amending its constitution in order to create special courts just for trying slaves, mulattos, and free blacks, the juries to consist entirely of slaveowners with authority to hand down capital sentences, and provide compensation for the owners thus deprived of their property.[32] Indeed, in several states, Louisiana for one, almost all cases involving slaves turned on their being property rather than people. Even the accidental or willful killing of a slave was more likely to wind up in a civil court than a criminal one.[33] By early 1864 the institution of special courts for trying blacks became commonplace. Curiously, in North Carolina it was even proposed that slaves should receive their trials immediately without having to wait in jail for the seasonal court to sit, not because the needs of justice were imperative, but because the longer a slave was in jail, the more of his work his owner lost.[34] By late 1864 the criminal court dockets were largely dominated by slave cases. The police court of Georgetown, South Carolina, found by late 1864 that it had not enough men to patrol the large slave population in the vicinity. "The constant presence & proximity of the enemy, exercise an unhappy influence over them & it has been the duty of the Police Court to resort to severe measures, in order to repress their demoralized spirit," reported a court member. Those measures included hanging eleven slaves, and though Georgetown was now peaceful, it was only because of the court, he added, hinting at the same time that its members ought to be exempted from conscription into the army.[35] In its way, the hysteria, justified and imaginary, actually worked to the ends of the less ardent men of the Confederacy. Keep alive the fears of uprising and violence, and especially of the rape of their women, and at least some men could stay out of the army and at home. By late 1864 governors like then sitting Andrew Magrath in South Carolina were inundated with petitions for exemption. One man wrote that he and one other were the only white men among a thousand slaves, and pleaded for exemption to protect their wives and daughters. When a man did successfully escape the draft by the Twenty Negro Law or some other means, he was said to have "greased out."[36]

It all seemed to be confirmation of Cartwright's, Collins's, and Jefferson Davis's pronouncements on the nature of the Negro and the need for slavery to keep him in check. It also appeared to be an endorsement of the necessity for founding their new Constitution so solidly on slavery and their racial beliefs. But at the same time it was evident that something within the rationale they had so carefully laid out over the years had to have been fundamentally flawed. Where was the loyalty on the part of their blacks that the masters held up to the world as a proof of the superiority of their system? Confederates went from protesting love and paternal affection for their slaves to finding themselves almost hysterically terrified of them. Within only a few months of the beginning of the war they needed men to protect them from their slaves, and to protect their slaves from angry civilians, hardly the happy and harmonious portrait of slavery in operation that Confederate propagandists liked to paint.

The national and state governments at least realized from an early date that the millions of slaves represented a source of energy that might be tapped in behalf of the cause if necessary. Certainly from the first, planters were willing, even eager, to loan or hire out their slaves for public works and military defenses. As the war dragged on the problem of unoccupied slaves added logic to the idea of employing their labor. As early as January 1861, even before the meeting in Montgomery, planters like Cheves loaned substantial numbers of their blacks to strengthen defenses at places like Fort Pulaski outside Savannah, and in some instances slaves from one state were even loaned to work across the border in another. Once the war commenced, local military commanders were empowered to levy a "tariff of assessment," essentially drafting up to one of every twenty slaves on a plantation to be put to temporary work on fortifications and road building.[37] In South Carolina a new statehouse was being built in Columbia, and though the outbreak of war forced the suspension of work, still slave quarrymen were kept at their work on hire from their owners.[38] By the fall of 1862 the public press began to support an actual conscription of slaves to relieve white soldiers from menial work for which they were not suited. "Dirt digging is not the proper business of Southern soldiers," proclaimed one editor, adding that drafting blacks could free up to 100,000 men for real soldiering.[39] Yet after the early enthusiasm for loaning or renting out their slaves, owners increasingly resisted military incursions on their property. By 1863 so many were refugees from their homes that their slaves were their only means of livelihood. One Louisiana planter who fled to

Mississippi got only 17 of his 250 slaves away with him, and then protested when the state drafted one of those to work on fortifications.[40] As the needs of the cause came more into conflict with the needs of the owners, the strains on commitment to the cause became ever greater.

The greatest loss to the planters came from those Cartwright probably would have called "drapetomaniacs," the slaves who simply disappeared. Governor Milton complained to Richmond in the fall of 1862 that large numbers of Florida's slaves were running away to the enemy every day, precipitating renewed fears of a general black uprising, even massacres of white civilians.[41] With so few white men left, there were not even enough to hold elections to choose officers for the local home guard he hoped to raise under his own control, exempt from the authority of Richmond, which would only order it away.[42] Winston County, Mississippi, already a seedbed of Unionism and so-called tory sentiment, was in such straits by February 1863 that women wrote to the governor begging him to "protect the wimmin and children from the outrages of the negroes." Rufinia Lawrence was "outraged" by a black and begged that her husband be sent home from the army to prevent it happening again. Jane Pattison of Port Gibson had no husband or overseer left, and had to manage 250 blacks on her own, with two neighboring plantations in the same condition. The slaves on all three came and went as they pleased, and took plantation horses at night to ride over the countryside committing nightly depredations.[43]

Provost officers complained that with the enemy nearby, the slaves were constantly going over to them, and soon the plantations would be deserted "if some steps are not taken to put a stop to it." Increasingly there were calls for the authorization of declarations of martial law to control the people black and white.[44] In May 1863, when a Union cavalry raid passed through Mississippi and Louisiana, neighborhood slaves turned out and "for the space of a week they had a perfect jubilee," complained a planter, stealing and killing hogs and cattle and sheep every day, including those belonging to Louisiana's governor, Thomas Moore. Then the slaves that did not run off with the Federals stayed behind "to do *much worse*," according to a report. They even confined a Confederate soldier, took Moore's furniture out of his house, and swarmed at will over the countryside. "Confound them," complained a friend of Moore's, "they deserve to be half starved and to be worked nearly to death for the way they have acted." Several were actually shot when they refused to go back to work.

Those that fled following the Yankees took with them everything they could carry, gathering some two thousand strong in a campground deep in the bayou country, and along the way they plundered every plantation they passed. "I must stop," protested Moore's informant, "for even now, as I bring up the scenes that met my eye and the tales of distress that I heard on that trip, the heart sickens."[45] In 1864 a Federal cavalry raid through North Carolina resulted in so many runaways that locals referred to it as "the Negro Raid," and this time only the women were left to manage the evacuation of the plantations and get their slaves to safety. One indomitable lady moved more than thirty miles, bought a new farm, paid $500 for a draft exemption for her overseer, and started planting again under a contract to sell her whole crop to the government, only to have her overseer conscripted in spite of his exemption.[46] Stories circulated soon after almost every Yankee incursion into Confederate territory that the enemy had come with written plans for inciting a general slave insurrection.[47] Just days after U. S. Grant's army crossed the Mississippi below Vicksburg and began its indirect march toward Jackson to cut off Vicksburg, a rumor spread through the state's interior that a slave revolt all across the Confederacy was planned for August 1 to aid Grant's campaign. The blacks intended to seize arms and destroy railroad track, bridges, and telegraph lines, and then disappear into the woods and swamps, shedding no blood except in self-defense.[48]

Worse, some of the slave men now showed enough impudence to stand up to their masters. When an overseer chastised one of Governor Moore's slaves, the man "showed fight" and threatened the white that he would strike back before the overseer beat him to the ground and put him in the stocks. Governor Pettus of Mississippi was told of two slaves who attacked and beat an elderly white woman before they were caught and one of them hanged.[49] When authorities finally caught up with the two thousand slaves who had escaped to the Louisiana interior, most of them died on the return to their plantations, in a cruel end to a brief bit of freedom. And by January 1864, when Moore delivered an annual message to the state assembly, he noted the startling number of trials pending in the courts involving slaves. The disruption of the courts, caused by the war, was leaving numbers of free blacks going untried for crimes, to the point that Moore suggested dispensing with jury trials for Negroes, posing a fundamental change in civil law. Likely impelled by the encouragement of the Emancipation Proclamation and the laxity of local white control, in August 1864 thirty or more Mississippi slaves brazenly took their masters' horses and guns and rode off cheering and shouting for Natchez and freedom. They were tracked by a few local men and stopped short of their goal, most of them being killed in the skirmish. One of the pursuers complained that if the militia were taken from the area, such attempts would increase, likely with similar results, and the loss of the "property" involved in killing the fugitives.[50] In Texas the problem of runaways became so great that in 1864 the governor issued mass broadsides pleading for their arrest. Ironically, with the shortage of paper, the circulars trying to apprehend one form of property were printed on the backs of leftover sheets carrying advertisements for stray horses.[51] It was simply no longer possible to keep the lid on a pot that had been boiling for generations.[52]

Not surprisingly, fear and instincts of self-preservation impelled white Confederates to begin to place sanctions on those who did not do enough to help maintain control, especially as late in the war the slaves substantially outnumbered the whites, as was the case in Florida by November 1864.[53] When a woman in Madison County, Mississippi, allowed three of her slaves to wander abroad trading with locals as if they were free men, she ran afoul of a new law that saw her fined $500 and even sentenced to a jail term until the judge in her case pleaded for clemency on account of her having given all her sons to the army and being herself unable to manage her slaves. Another woman was fined $1,500, $500 for each of three of her slaves who escaped her management, and also given a prison sentence. A widow whose sons were all in the army complained that her slaves were her only support, and the only way to turn a profit from them was to allow them to hire themselves out like free men. This was October 1864. Enemy raids had taken all of her best hands. It had been more than a year since the local circuit court had been able to meet, meaning there was no law or justice in the county, and in the legal vacuum the slaves had gotten "much demoralized & difficult of management," she protested. Her only alternative to simply watching them leave of their own accord was to let them work for others, and share their wages with her in return for providing them with homes. Even then, all the governor would do was remit her jail sentence. Courts applied the law to men as well, of course. No one was to allow a slave to go out in the countryside as a free man, and even though the law would be sporadically enforced, still it represented one more affront to the freedom of a property owner and recognition yet again that slavery was no longer under control in the Confederacy.

By early 1865 it seemed the law was striking out blindly, as if aware of its impotence in maintaining a situation long since beyond its control. In March a woman was caught allowing her female slave to live alone for several months in a house some two hundred yards away from the owner's townhouse in Canton, Mississippi. Unable or unwilling to prosecute the woman, authorities charged and fined her husband some $200, even though he knew nothing of the episode and was not even in the vicinity.[54] So fearful were the authorities of the threat to stability posed by uncontrolled blacks that even free Negroes faced legal action for nothing more than being free. In Prairie County, Arkansas, in March 1863, a black woman named July, born free in Tennessee but under indenture to a white man until she turned twenty-one, was brought before a circuit court when she was just short of reaching her age of freedom. There, thanks to a law passed two years before that banned free blacks in the state, the court gave her an ultimatum "to leave the state of Arkansas, be sold, or select her master and go into voluntary slavery." Faced with destitution on her own, she chose a man to be "her master for life" and voluntarily gave up her freedom as well as that of her two infant children.[55]

In fact, one of the rudest awakenings suffered by Confederates was the disillusionment of discovering just how quickly their slaves could turn on them. Lulled into complacency by their own self-generated mythology, they were stunned at the betrayal of their affection and care. "The recent trying scenes through which we have passed have convinced me," wrote one Louisianian, "that *no dependence is to be placed on the negro*—and they are the greatest hypocrites & liars that God ever made." In disgust one planter protested that his feelings toward the Negro had changed completely now: "I now care nothing for them save for 'their work.'"[56] No wonder that at least a few began to realize that their slaves had not been so happy after all, or as content with their lives. Most still would blame the turmoil on the Yankees and the inherent nature of blacks, but some started to entertain ideas that white Confederates needed to do more to quell the seething mass within their borders.

Examples like that of the slave woman Caroline of Spartanburg, South Carolina, provided constant reminders. Her owner, David Lipscomb, was notorious for his cruelty to his slaves, and he beat and whipped Caroline so badly that an examination of her body showed scars everywhere. In desperation, she set fire to his barn to divert his attention, not so that she could escape, but just for a respite from the beatings. Brought to trial in

March 1865, she was sentenced to death, and when a minister asked her if she would like to be pardoned and returned to Lipscomb, she replied simply that "death would be preferable." A petition from the white citizens of the community to the governor secured her release from her sentence, but not from her master.[57] Only the imminent death of the Confederacy and slavery a few weeks hence could do that, if she lived that long. "His rights as a human being demand recognition," declared a Baptist convention in Georgia in 1864, "his wrongs call for redress." Being in no legal position to claim justice for himself, the slave had to look to the white to grant him justice and mercy. "We are in condition to grant both," said the convention. For a start it advocated a universal law recognizing slaves' rights to marry as they chose, a small concession at best, but still a start, if much too late. More significantly, however, the convention's declaration, published in October as *Thoughts on Government,* actually went on to speculate that perhaps slavery itself was against divine law. They did not think so, but it was possible, and if so, then slavery had to fall.[58]

It was inevitable, therefore, that finally Confederate authorities addressed in a more formal fashion the twin problems of manpower shortages and uncontrolled slave populations. "The war has now on the part of the enemy assumed a position against the Slave interests of the country almost exclusively," said a resolution of citizens in Mississippi in 1864. "It is the duty of Slaveholders to devote their Slaves to the use of the armies to save their neighbors, brothers & sons from the performance of menial duties & services & thereby enable them to go into the ranks." They begged their governor to commence legislation to force slaves into noncombatant military service.[59] By the winter of 1863–64, General Joseph E. Johnston, commanding the Army of Tennessee in winter quarters around Dalton, Georgia, called on his political connections in Richmond to urge legislation allowing him to impress slaves in unlimited numbers to relieve all his white soldiers for front-line duty. Commanders had impressed slaves for limited periods before, just as they could commandeer axes and saws, wagons and harnesses, horses and mules, and all manner of provender. Such impressments were only temporary, and generally done under state law, thus preserving the sovereignty of the states over their citizens, though national impressment legislation came in time.[60] But now Johnston wanted authority to hold slaves indefinitely, despite the uproar he knew it would cause from the owners. "Is this not worth trying?" pleaded the general.[61]

In fact, the idea would rapidly become general. A quartermaster in Jackson, Mississippi, substituted conscripted slaves for his white teamsters. Tennessee infantry, engaged in tearing up Yankee railroad, found some local slaves who were willing to help them with the work. All through Confederate military lines by 1864, conscripted slaves were driving teams, digging earthworks, and tending livestock.[62] Somehow North Carolina even got away with conscripting a limited number of free blacks, which certainly would not outrage slaveowners, but it did irritate employers who had thought their cheap free black labor would be secure to them. At the same time, state and local authorities actually employed free Negroes when not conscripting them, once again soaking up some of the dwindling labor pool.[63]

At the same moment, similar suggestions were coming from all across the Confederacy, for with the face of defeat before them, the people were beginning to shift ideas and priorities. In November 1864, Governor Charles Clark of Mississippi received a proposal that slaves ought to be conscripted to accompany the cavalry, not to fight, but to hold the horses of the troopers in action. Cavalrymen mostly fought on foot, one of every four being detailed to hold his and the others' animals. Putting slaves at that task would increase the effective force of cavalry regiments by fully one-third. "If it be argued that the negroes are cowards, and might be stampeded," said the petitioner, "I answer, the same is true of white men." Blacks were not natural cowards. He had often seen them impervious to shot and shell when exposed to battle, and being less sensate and imaginative than whites, they were actually less susceptible to imagine dangers when not under fire. "Unaccustomed to think for themselves they place more confidence in the judgment of those commanding them, than do white men," he added. "Of course, I do not mean to say, that *any cornfield* negro would answer for such purpose; for they must be selected with regard to their intelligence, raising &c."[64] Certainly it was a crack in the door to yet another employment of blacks.[65]

The crack widened as the idea of somehow using the slaves gained wide currency by 1864, though with no real consensus on how to use them. In fact, the very fears of their blacks at home now argued to some Confederates that the slaves ought to be sent away to the armies. In Daleville, Mississippi, in August 1864 whites discovered a plot by slaves to arm themselves, steal horses, and fight their way across country to join the Yankees at Vicksburg. In the same town a few nights earlier, a slave man crept into the bedroom of his absent master's two daughters and groped one as she slept. When she awakened and screamed, he slapped her, then impudently returned to his cabin with little fear of retribution, and that was only one of several such outrages recently. "I think we ought to have men enough at home to protect our Families or else take all the negro fellows off and put them in the army so they can be controlled," asserted a citizen, adding that "I hear from other places and it seems as if the Negroes are in motion."[66] On many plantations, as on Louisiana Governor Moore's by the summer of 1863, slaves simply came and went at pleasure, using the master's place as a convenient domicile, while spending their days wandering the countryside scavenging.[67]

On October 17, 1864, the governors of North and South Carolina, Virginia, Georgia, Mississippi, and Alabama met in Augusta, Georgia, to discuss the crisis in Confederate affairs and compose recommendations to their states and the national government. One of the several resolutions they adopted was a call for the use of slaves in the military, with the government compensating their masters for them somehow, actually arming them as soldiers and promising them freedom after the war if they served well. Governor Thomas Watts of Alabama demurred from endorsing that notion. He had earlier opposed any conscription of slaves to work for the military, arguing that they did better service tilling the fields that fed the armies. In the end he had bent to the will of Congress, but regarded it as an intrusion on state sovereignty and a violation of the protection of private property rights.[68] But the governors' Augusta proposal was "utterly indefensible in principle and policy," Watts argued. Blacks could not be used as anything other than cooks and teamsters, laborers and perhaps nurses in their hospitals. "To permit the Confederate government to acquire property in them, and, ultimately, to emancipate such as faithfully perform service, would be as unconstitutional, as it would be destructive to the interests of the States," he went on. Alabama, for one, actually had a state constitution that prohibited emancipation.[69]

Then at the dawn of 1865 a South Carolinian suggested to his governor that in the manpower crisis, all exemptions should be withdrawn and those able-bodied men conscripted, their civil posts to be filled by invalids, while at the same time every slave between eighteen and forty-five should be drafted and sent into the army as a servant to wait on and even fight beside a soldier, "not as his equal but as his servant as Abrahams servants fought for him." It was not yet a suggestion actually to enlist slaves as soldiers.

That suggestion was socially revolutionary, and would have its day. This one, however, was perhaps more fundamentally subversive of the tenets of Confederate democracy, for it proposed that the government should take a planter's property, upturn a lifetime of teaching and inculcation, put that property under the control of other men, and risk its damage or even destruction, losing not only the property itself, but also the product of its labor that was neglected at home. "Is it not best to arm them & make them kill the foe than for that foe to arm them and make them kill us?" argued the Carolinian. The alternative seemed to be for their slaves to run away to the enemy anyhow. Since the Yankees began raising black regiments in earnest in 1863, their own Negroes would likely just turn around and enlist with the Union to come back and fight their masters. "If we fail to swell our ranks with the slaves," he warned, "the foe wil most surely swell his ranks with the slaves."[70]

The proposal of actually arming slaves as soldiers and sending them into the armies arose early in the war, and reappeared from time to time, but never met with a welcome reception. As Robert Toombs himself said, if a black man could be given a gun and made into a soldier, then that put him on a footing of equality with the white man, which would mean that their whole system was mistaken. Authorities from Davis on down simply dismissed such suggestions when they arose, but it might have been obvious that the gradual encroachments on slave property rights, from commandeering for menial labor in 1861 to outright impressment for noncombatant military work, were tending inevitably in one direction. Union authorities began enlisting black soldiers in 1862, and by 1864 Confederate soldiers were facing them on a growing number of battlefields, though often with disgraceful results. In the aftermath of battles at Fort Pillow, Tennessee, and Saltville, Virginia, wounded and surrendered black soldiers were simply murdered by some outraged Confederate soldiers, abetted and even aided by some of their officers. After a skirmish at Suffolk, Virginia, on March 9, 1864, one Southern soldier wrote home that he and his comrades "killed about thirty negrows but took no prisners but that is something that our souldiers are apt not to do to take any negro souldiers."[71] With that sort of murderous animosity widespread in the armies, how could Southern soldiers be expected to willingly serve alongside onetime slaves? In January 1864, perhaps more than coincidentally at the same time that his commander, Johnston, called for stronger slave impressment for military support, Major General Patrick Cleburne proposed the actual enlistment of slaves as soldiers in return for their freedom. The proposal died after arousing a storm of indignation, and Cleburne himself had his further advancement stunted, but at last some strong voices had brought the idea out in the open.

By the fall of 1864 the proposal made its way to the floor of Congress. Davis presented an annual message in which he argued that "the general levy and arming of the slaves for the duty of soldiers," as was increasingly suggested, would be "inexpedient." Bringing the subject into the public forum sparked a flurry of debate all across the Confederacy. Mississippi Congressman Ethelbert Barksdale asked his governor in November for guidance "in regard to the plan urged by some of placing negroes in the army as soldiers in the field," noting that "it involves consideration of the gravest import in its moral & political aspects, and in its bearing upon the great producing interests of the country."[72] Robert Hilton, congressman from Florida, found his constituents greatly agitated at the idea that fall before he returned to Richmond for a new session. He believed Floridians universally opposed to the idea. Thus when he returned to Congress he represented their views when Henry Foote of Tennessee introduced resolutions supporting the president's dismissal of the plan. Only if they reached such a pass that their choices were black enlistment or defeat should they risk such an act, they concluded. Even at that, Davis still outraged some with a proposal that the government should purchase some slaves from planters for employment in noncombatant roles, with the promise of freedom at a later date. It was a form of compensated gradual emancipation that clearly conflicted with several state laws prohibiting manumission of slaves. That it was not a policy that necessarily had to lead to general emancipation did not matter, for the mere fact that the president could broach the subject of such a violation of state sovereignty and Confederate social and political ideology was shock enough. It sparked new resolutions not only to oppose it, but also to close the door on what seemed the next logical step. "There is no purpose on the part of this House to introduce negro troops into our Army," declared Virginian Thomas Gholson on December 28.[73] Robert Barnwell Rhett, in forced retirement from politics in South Carolina, came out in the press with a condemnation, yet was prescient enough to observe that "emancipation, once begun, soon extends, or must be eradicated."[74]

Yet it was a tide that they could not resist. As Congressman Hilton observed, "our embarrassment from want of men rapidly increasing," and as more and more influential men came out in support of enlisting slaves, including General Robert E. Lee himself, it became apparent to him that the measure was a "necessity for our deliverance."[75] Finally it was Barksdale, having cleared himself with his governor, who on February 10, 1865, after several days of debate on the general subject, introduced a new bill "to increase the military force of the Confederate States." It proposed accepting the offer of slaves by their masters for military service, but said nothing about emancipation in return, nor of compensation to the owners. Indeed, even a resolution to ask the judiciary committee to look into the constitutionality of offering emancipation was tabled, and it was perhaps only the public support of Lee for the idea that kept emancipation alive. The logic was simple enough. Why should a slave fight and risk his life if there was nothing in it for him?

The timing was coincidental enough, for the United States Congress had just passed the Thirteenth Amendment to its own Constitution, abolishing slavery. In a symbolic move that showed that Washington continued to maintain that the Confederate states had never lawfully left the Union, Secretary of State William Seward even observed the formality of sending copies of the new amendment to the governors of the seceded states just as he sent them to the rest of the Union to be put before their legislatures. When the copy reached Governor Clark in Mississippi, he or someone in his office defiantly defaced the State Department seal and then filed the document.[76] But such bluster could not conceal the fact that some kind of emancipation was floating on the Southern breeze, too.

Confederates were terrified of what was happening to slavery. A week after submission of the Thirteenth Amendment in the North, and just the day after Barksdale's bill in Congress, a pamphlet appeared titled "On Slavery & the Duties Growing out of the Relations." Its author, James Lyons, made it clear that "*reformation,* and not *emancipation* is the duty of the South." Judicious reform of the undeniable evils of slavery was due to their slaves as to themselves, and to humanity. He called for legislatures to repeal their laws prohibiting slaves from being taught to read, to legalize slave marriages, to grant legal parental status to slave couples so that their children could not be sold away from them before the age of twelve, and to give better protection of slaves from the assaults of "low, vicious white men" by allowing slaves to testify in court in cases against their abusers, making their testimony the equivalent of circumstantial evidence on its own, or as valid testimony when there was corroboration. At last men who took a slave's life would be subject to criminal trial, affording at least some protection to blacks for their lives. "With these reforms, together with religious instruction, which must be enforced by *moral,* not *legal* means, slavery would be what the Bible recognizes," said Lyons, "and would be divested of its obnoxious features."[77]

It was too little, too late. Even the ranting of the Rhetts in their *Mercury* could not stop the inevitable. "We are fighting for our system of civilization," they declared, making it clear to all that their cause in the Confederacy had been the preservation of slavery. "We intend to fight for *that,* or nothing." South Carolina soldiers would not fight alongside blacks. "To talk of emancipation is to disband our army," they cried. "We are free men, and we choose to fight for ourselves," though it is worth noting that the younger editor Rhett, in fact, had chosen for four years not to fight at all.[78] The bill reached the Senate, and by February 21 seemed held up, perhaps fatally, but finally on March 13, 1865, it passed. The South would raise regiments of slave men, to be commanded by white officers, with the promise of freedom after good service. Ten days later the call went out for volunteers, who still must have their owners' permission and what amounted to a manumission from the owner. Even then, it had to await the action of the Virginia legislature and others to second the policy, thus getting around what was otherwise a clear and gross violation of state sovereignty by the national government inserting itself pre-emptively into the sacred relationship of owner and property. Not a few of the congressmen voting for it, like Hilton, felt great unease. "I felt constrained to give it my support," he confessed, "though at the time that I did so without any assurance that one in a hundred of my constituents would approve my vote."[79]

Passage found a number of whites who received the new opportunity happily. "Our population is becoming exhausted," complained one discharged soldier who wanted to raise a black company. "We may fight them through this campaign but must have men for the next." Where were they to get them? "I say take the negro," he concluded. Indeed, he felt that Congress had not gone far enough, no doubt for fear of outraging the states even more, "slavery being a state institution." He was in favor of conscription of blacks if necessary. "Negroes will make good soldiers," he maintained. "The difficulty with us is they are property and the owners of that Species of property have more influence in our legislatures and Congress than any other class in the Confederacy and they cling to their Slaves with a blind tenacity that will be their ruin." Six months before, as a slaveowner himself, he would not have countenanced the idea, but now he wanted every black man between eighteen and fifty enlisted or conscripted, with the promise of freedom. That would make them a part of the standing army of the Confederacy and thus, interestingly, remove them as an element of society. Then he turned philosophical. "If we don't succeed after arming the slaves we will be rid of the bulk of them anyhow, which will be better than to let them live to be our masters." They were going to lose them whether they won their independence or not, he reasoned, so why not gain something in the offing? Yet even at this late date, the soldier, writing with his proposal to Governor Pendleton Murrah of Texas, still did not sign the letter. "I have not the nerve to put my name to this," he explained.[80]

At the same time, however, other voices saw something happening before them that only made them the more cynical. On April 4, 1865, a Mississippian reported to his governor that "our negroes are again stampeding from the fear of Conscription." Made aware that they might be forced into the military, they saw the promise of freedom from the Confederacy as meaning little beside the certainty of it from the North. "The negroes know too well on which *side to fight,*" the complainant continued. The new law came too late, and would benefit the enemy without adding a single soldier in gray. "It seems at *this late date* like a drowning man catching at straws."[81] A North Carolina woman perhaps expressed best the conclusion that slavery itself was dead no matter what. "I believe slavery is doomed to dye out," she said in January, "that God is agoing to liberate niggars, and fighting any longer is fighting against God."[82]

It took a lot of nerve for all concerned, for it was nothing less than an assault on the sanctity of the property rights that underlay the Constitution and their movement itself. It had been one of the primary tenets backing their withdrawal from the Union that a congress had no authority of any kind over slavery. To be sure, the new legislation only provided that owners, and not the national government, should emancipate their slaves in return for service, yet that was a nicety that hardly concealed the enormous step they had taken. They had actually debated emancipation on the floor of Congress and created a mechanism to encourage slaveholders to willingly free their property. If Congress could do that, then what remained of their Constitution that was any better than the one they had left in Washington? All that was left of it were the somewhat stronger safeguards on state sovereignty, yet those were already severely eroded as well thanks to the pressure of the enemy without, and the fragile political and social tissue within.

Confederate democracy had been created to protect slave property and the pre-eminence of the planter oligarchy. In the interest of military necessity, Confederates themselves were intentionally eroding the sanctity of the master-slave relationship. More than that, they opened the door to wider emancipation, for even should they miraculously win their independence, what freed black soldier would not then want to see his wife and his children free as well, and to what lengths would he go toward that end? And what was to be the future of their agrarian nation if after independence, the prime of their labor force was free and could not be compelled to work, but rather had to be paid wages? Measures would be enlisted to declare that no more than one-fourth of the eligible slave male population from any state could be enlisted, but even that meant hundreds of thousands who theoretically could be freed after the war, and an enormous dent in an economy that would have incredible feats of financial rebuilding ahead. In short, the ramifications were almost too far-reaching to forecast entirely, but to many it was apparent that there was about to be a vital shift in the balance of the old order. The auguries were dire.

6

Law and Disorder

THE HEART OF DEMOCRACY is the civil law, the equal protection due to all regardless of station or estate. Certainly that belief lay always at the core of Southerners' arguments for the sovereign authority of the states, and was just as integral a part of their long-standing complaint against Washington for infringing on their lawful rights. Yet the story of the legal system of the Confederacy is one marked by an inability to protect its citizens from lawlessness, even as martial law in all but name steadily grew in power.

Initially, the Confederates felt their way as they evolved their concept of the courts, their provenance and powers. Of course, the state court systems were already established and in place at the time of secession, and thus Congress could do nothing to tamper with them nor did it wish to. It simply accepted all local law as in force, and then subsequently dealt with any conflicts between state and national statutes as they arose, and arise they did on impressment, conscription, and finally on emancipation. But on January 18, 1862, Congress got a chance to create a new legal system for a new entity when it passed an act organizing the Confederate "Territory of Arizona." Such a polity never really existed except as an idea, which quickly paled to insignificance after one brief, disastrously bungled, military invasion ending in March. However, since it did not have a prior civil organization, this territory, stretching theoretically from Texas to California, was going to represent the Confederacy's first territorial expansion by "conquest," and incidentally the first of many proofs that most Confederates including President Jefferson Davis himself did not take seriously his protests that they had no dreams of territorial aggrandizement and only wanted "to be let alone." They also had dreams of Cuba, and even northern Mexico, while in the years ahead they would attempt to take Maryland, Kentucky, and Missouri by invasion, despite the fact that the majority of the population in those states and their legislatures had made it clear they did not wish to secede. Once again, Confederate state sovereignty in concept and in practice were different things. A slave state's sovereignty included the right to embrace slavery but not to abolish it; a slave state had the power to secede and join the Confederacy but no right not to do so.

In framing a territorial government for its Arizona, Congress mandated an appointed governor to serve for six years, and a legislature consisting of a house of representatives and a council, each of thirteen members. They would have the authority to legislate on all matters consistent with the Confederate Constitution, but they could not legislate any issue that sold or transferred actual land, which was considered a part of the public lands under the jurisdiction of the Department of Justice. The Congress itself retained the power to annul or amend any law passed by the territorial legislature, and to pass any laws affecting the territory as it saw fit. Significantly, Congress said nothing about inhabitants framing a territorial constitution, which had been the crux of the old agitation over Kansas in the 1850s. Arizona could frame a charter only when applying for statehood. Thus, Congress did not even have to address the issue of slavery in creating the territory. All laws of the Confederacy being in effect in the territory, slavery would automatically be protected and encouraged, guaranteeing that when the citizens applied for statehood—should that day ever come—they would automatically come in as a slave state.

Congress devoted more time to the courts than to anything else in the territorial legislation, creating a state supreme court, district courts, probate courts, and justices of the peace, and outlining the powers and limitations of each. It also specified the line of appeal on decisions, providing that appeals from the territorial supreme court could be referred to the Supreme Court when the amount in question involved more than $1,000. Significantly, however, one class of legal property dispute could be referred from the territorial to the national court regardless of the value involved, and that, of course, was cases involving title to slaves. At the same time, any case involving the privilege of the writ of habeas corpus and the personal freedom of an accused also had the automatic right to appeal to the Confederate supreme court.[1]

Clearly, while bent on protecting slavery, Congress also intended to ensure a sensible and orderly system of justice modeled on what had been the norm in most of the states, North and South, with a special concern for the rights of property. Meanwhile the component states of the new Confederacy answered equal imperatives, though very quickly both state and national leaders found new pressures and demands that called for an alteration in their view of the sanctity of property. On the very day that the first real battle of the war was fought in Virginia at Manassas on July 21, the Mississippi legislature was called upon to consider a "stay" law to put a freeze on debts currently owed by its citizens. Claiming that many men who would otherwise enlist were staying out of the army because of debts and deeds of trust with payments due, attorneys for the petitioners argued that the only remedy was to suspend collection on certain classes of obligations. The same debt was also preventing planters from subscribing to the several loans advertised to raise funds for the Confederate government. "Let the private creditor have every security for the ultimate payment of his claims," it was argued, "but let him wait till our enemies are driven back and our Government firmly established."[2]

The idea quickly gained popularity, both because it made practical sense and because it would give perpetually debt-ridden planters a breather from their obligations, especially since the war was driving up prices and drying up the money supply. "The war is upon us," protested citizens' groups. Times were hard. Moreover, war profiteers were emerging to take advantage of shortages and inflation, or at least that was the argument used by many for seeking a stay. If the courts were forced to proceed on suits for debt it would work a tragic hardship on citizens, it was asserted: "their property will be sacrificed, their debts unpaid, their property from them gone, concentrated into the hands of a few—and in a comparative sense *extremely very few* Shilocks of the Country, whose God is gain, whether in war or peace."[3] Only legislatures suspending debt payment for some period of time, preferably the duration of the war, could prevent such an injustice, they argued, ignoring the injustice to the reputable merchants and stockholders who were now bundled with the "Shylocks" of the world. Citizens wanted what amounted to a breakdown of the old civil process for matters great and small, the only class of debt not being excluded being payments to guardians and administrators for widows and orphans, who would suffer otherwise.[4] Many even sought a stay law to escape small debts they were quite able to pay, like the superintendent of the Cassville Female College in Georgia, who discovered that one of his teachers came from a Unionist family in Maryland and wanted to go back, and hoped to seize on that as an excuse not to pay her wages on the grounds that she was not a Confederate citizen.[5]

A natural concomitant to petitions for freedom from domestic debt was a desire to take advantage of the war to repudiate prewar debts owed to individuals and firms in the Union, while at the same time confiscating Yankee-owned property in the Confederacy. Learning that the distinguished Massachusetts diplomat and cabinet officer Caleb Cushing owned substantial land in Texas, Governor Edward Clark came under early pressure to use the power of the government to seize it under sequestration. Others proposed that auditors cover the state examining the account books of business firms to identify amounts due to Northern concerns, and use legislation to make those debts due and payable to the Confederacy instead, leaving it to the national government to settle with the creditors at some future time after independence was achieved, if it so chose.[6] In Virginia surveys were to be made of land and deeds belonging to "Alien enemies" that were on the books in the several courthouses, especially those with any liens on them that could be cause for immediate foreclosure.[7] In Mississippi one man, who himself owed money that he could not pay to Northern firms, was so enthusiastic for such a policy that in addition to seeking to escape his debts, he tried to get a job as state agent to find the debtors and collect the money they would now owe to the Confederacy. By hiring him, the governor would actually enable him to pay his own debts, the money going right back to the state presumably.[8] The war might have been a terrible calamity, but it could also be a bonanza for a people already accustomed to putting off debt as long as possible.

With all this pressure building in the several states, it was inevitable that Congress would take some action. Sequestration was common enough among nations in time of war. Lincoln would seize Confederate-owned property in the North as a punitive measure and to defray the expense of his war effort, so it was natural that the Confederacy would do the same. Proposals for a national sequestration act emerged as early as June 1861, when Governor Thomas Moore of Louisiana proposed it in retribution for the Yankees seizing a Southern-owned merchant ship off New Orleans and refusing to hand it over. His own attorney general told him that the Confederate Constitution gave power for seizures of enemy property to Congress but not to the states. Faced with that, Moore had Duncan Kenner, one of his delegates in Congress at Montgomery, almost immediately introduce a resolution asking the judiciary committee to investigate crafting a sequestration bill.

Two weeks later the committee reported a bill, coincidentally on the same day that the United States Congress passed its own first confiscation act, though it was limited to seizure of property being used to make war on the Union, and aimed specifically at slaves caught being employed on Confederate military works. Two weeks later the Confederate bill passed, authorizing the taking of "estates, property, and effects of alien enemies." What was most interesting was what the law provided should be done with the confiscated property. Common usage had sequestered property for the purposes and benefit of the government. This act, however, required that when confiscated property was sold, the money should not go to the government, but into a separate fund "for the indemnity of citizens of the Confederate States and persons aiding the same." It was to reimburse people who themselves lost property to Yankee confiscation, and, of course, one of the chief forms of property being lost was those slaves being confiscated by Union military authorities.

Thus, unlike its operation anywhere else then or earlier, Confederate sequestration was to be yet another measure aimed to benefit not the many, but the few, the property holders and the slaveowners. The government was making it its business to indemnify slaveholders from loss. That very same day Congress also passed an act requiring the secretary of state's office to maintain testimony placed on file by slaveowners whose property had run away to the enemy or been abducted or forcibly removed. Though specifying that the act was not meant to imply that the government accepted liability for compensating for the loss, the fact of the bill being passed in tandem with the sequestration act made such an intent obvious all the same.[9]

The act excluded the property of people living in slave states not yet seceded, but made up for that by making the authorization for seizures retroactive to May 1861. Then in February 1862 it was amended, only further to qualify that proceeds would be used to provide an "equal indemnity of all persons" who were loyal citizens that suffered loss. However, in reaction to the pressure for stay laws, Congress specifically stated that the act could not be used to allow anyone to avoid payment of a lawful debt to an

alien enemy, nor could it be used to move against enemy property that had
been legally transferred to a Confederate citizen prior to August 30, 1861.
Rather, it required that all persons owing money to aliens had to file a report with the government's agents, and be prepared to make payment to
the Confederate Treasury instead, at the risk of legal action and garnish-
ment for failure to pay. Striking a further blow at those who hoped to escape payment, the amendment enacted that no state stay laws should
exclude persons from their obligation under the congressional act.[10] Except for minor changes, this remained the sequestration law for the rest of
the war, until January 1865 when Congress repealed the provision for payment of debts to alien enemies in Confederate bonds.[11]

In operation the acts intruded the national government into the lives of
state citizens in a way never attempted by Washington in the old Union.
Minions of the attorney general could summon citizens to give testimony
as to what alien assets they had in their possession, or might have had
retroactively, to list their debts owed to the North, and even to inform on
any other citizens who might have such property or liabilities. Failure to
respond could lead to trial, fine, even imprisonment. The amounts of confiscated property could be considerable. In Texas in the fall of 1862 alone
more than a quarter-million acres of sequestered real estate came into
Confederate hands to be auctioned. A single dry goods merchant in San
Antonio acknowledged debts to Yankee wholesalers totaling more than
$27,000, and was ordered to pay it to the Treasury instead, on the same
terms allowed by the wholesalers, but with the added imposition of 4 percent interest until the debt was settled.[12] Special handbooks of "Rules of
Practice" were published for distribution to the Confederate district
courts in each of the states, with the appointed collectors authorized to accept promissory notes for money due.[13] Having set its sights on a source of
desperately needed revenue, even though it was ostensibly earmarked for
distribution to injured citizens, the Confederate authorities were prepared
to go about the collection as systematically and persistently as all governments are when on the trail of money. As for that payment to compensate
parties for their loss of property, every such distribution required passage
of a private bill by the Congress, and no more than a handful were ever actually passed.

While the national government was taking an early start at inserting itself into the legal and financial affairs of private citizens, the individual

state courts were very much allowed to continue as they had before the war. Most counties had circuit courts that met twice a year, usually in spring and fall, and district attorneys and state attorneys general were anxious that the war not disrupt the continued speedy application of justice. If a vacancy appeared in the court, both citizens and counsel expected a quick replacement to avoid hardship to plaintiffs and defendants alike. Not yet realizing the challenges to their civil rights that were going to be coming from Montgomery and Richmond, citizens were concerned to keep their courts functioning smoothly.[14] In Texas early in 1862, when a sitting grand jury in Houston found itself acting too slowly, it actually called on Governor Francis Lubbock to leave the capital and come to Houston to speed its work and ensure greater efficiency.[15] At the same time, Governor John Milton in Florida authorized two district judges to switch certain courts between them in response to the disruptions caused by enemy forces.[16]

The governors especially, it seemed, were eager to make accommodation for justice in the face of shifting pressures and exigencies. They tried hard not to come into conflict with each other in legal matters, as for instance in the speedy extradition of fugitives taken in one state and returned to the place of offense. Cooperation between the states was essential to maintaining criminal justice, and would remain so.[17] They took pains, through their secretaries of state, to ensure that the proper roll books and forms were distributed to judges, especially urging neatness for the sake of accuracy.[18] A special problem arose as the conscription laws grew more and more demanding, and exemptions for civil officials came under attack. "It is certainly subversive of state sovereignty," complained one Georgian to Governor Joseph Brown. When justices of the peace found their exemptions endangered, they pointed out that it was their task to fill out the papers for the widows of thousands of slain soldiers whose pay the wives desperately needed. Most of them did it for nothing, whereas lawyers charged $5 for the service, money the widows could ill afford, and if the justices were drafted, there would be no one to keep the process running. It also affected other civil matters. "There is but little suing done," one lawyer declared, and that had been the mainstay of Southern courts for generations. When the courts could no longer handle such cases, one party or another naturally suffered. "Let there be no discrimination but equal Justice be awarded to all," pleaded one opponent of the effects of conscription on the courts. Brown himself vowed, "I shall do all in my power to maintain the sovereignty of the state," and so he would, but as the war began to impact the courts just as it did other aspects of society, a governor like Brown would be forced increasingly into conflict with Richmond.[19]

The collisions with national authority were inevitable, and came chiefly over issues of individual rights and liberties. Aliens were just as liable for difficulty as citizens, as a British resident of Texas discovered when a dozen soldiers came to his home one day and forcibly took him away to be enlisted in the army even though, as a foreign national, he was not liable to conscription. "He was taken away without warning or notice from his family of little children," pleaded his wife, "& I have nothing & no way to support them."[20] State authorities could trample on such rights just as easily, perhaps more so, since they assumed that ultimate sovereignty over inhabitants rested with the states. In 1862, Texas state militia arrested five British subjects and drafted them into the state forces, and continued to hold them for more than a year despite remonstrances from Whitehall itself.[21]

At the commencement of the Confederacy's life, citizens' groups had petitioned their governors to be allowed to bypass what one called "the tedious way" of administering justice by awaiting the action of legal officers to arrest suspected tories, begging instead to be allowed to arrest them themselves first.[22] Soon they were demanding the protection of that same civil law against the military as conflicts with civilian rights and civil authority became increasingly widespread, especially after Congress passed laws allowing for confiscation and impressment of farmers' produce and animals. In Mississippi in the fall of 1863 hard-up civilians began crossing the Tallahatchie River to buy needed provisions from civilians in Yankee-held territory on the other side. When they returned home, Confederate troops used the sequestration law to confiscate their purchases even though they had not been purchased from the foe. Even the issuance of civil writs could not make the military commanders give up the goods, probably because the soldiers needed the food and supplies themselves. "Can the civil law be enforced," protested one citizen, "or can the military authorities overrule and disregard all civil law?"[23]

Even more disturbing were arbitrary arrests of civilians. In Choctaw County, Mississippi, a Lieutenant Brock was sent to arrest deserters and those soldiers absent without leave. Instead, he soon tried to become a law unto himself in the legal vacuum caused by the war in the thinly populated county. He kept a pack of dogs and used them to run down those who ran afoul of him, and then used the whip on those he caught. One prisoner who shot one of the dogs was given his choice of a whipping or hanging. Naturally, he chose the former. "His cries under the torture were heard a mile," protested one civilian, who added that other Confederate cavalry nearby were said to be "practicing the same disgusting and degrading practices." Governor Clark referred the matter to General Joseph E. Johnston, overall commander in the region, but at the same time asked why the county sheriff did not arrest Brock. "Let the warrant issue and your sheriff *do his duty*," said the governor. "Let him call out, as he can, the force of the county and if that is not sufficient I will assist him. Do not let your civil officers say that they *cannot do their duty*. They *must do it or resign*."[24] In Perry County a tax collector protested that "it will be at the risk of my life to collect," citing the small hordes of deserters roaming the county. When cavalry were sent to arrest them, the soldiers themselves began to roam the countryside. "They prowl through the country frolicing & stealing too much," complained the collector. "There is no dicipline or order among them every one does near as he pleases." The cavalry actually wore out their horses, not in chasing deserters, but in the frolicking. "The civil Laws of this State have been trampled under foot by military power which has had a very demoralizing effect upon the minds of the citizens," the collector continued. "The citizens know not where to apply to have their rights protected."[25] Governor Thomas Watts of Alabama protested to the president in March 1864 that "a good cause is, frequently, in the eyes of the people, made odious, by the utter inefficiency, fraud, cruelty, or wantonness of the agents." Some of the military were even taking the soldiers' families' means of support.[26]

A woman in Texas watched helplessly when soldiers arrested her husband in the night without charges, and for a second time, at the same instance searching her house and even her "private drawers" after she objected to the arrest.[27] When the sheriff at Okolona incarcerated a man in jail for murder, Confederate soldiers came and removed him by force one night even though he was not in the military. Then their own provost incarcerated him and issued charges for murder despite martial law not being in effect and there being no military jurisdiction. On occasion military authorities even arrested and held people simply for the purpose of being witnesses in other cases, and kept them incommunicado as if they were under charges themselves.[28] Little matters like possession of a mule erupted into conflicts, as when the army took a civilian's animal that he held under authority from a local quartermaster. The county sheriff took possession of the mule pending adjudication, but then the army arrived to seize it from the sheriff. When his deputy tried to prevent the seizure, the soldiers bound him, broke into the stable, and left with the animal. Even though eventually the army returned the mule, the fact of the clash, and the soldiers' resort to force in conflict with legally constituted civil authorities, showed just how far the boundary between constitutional state law and martial power sanctioned by the national government could be overstepped. The sheriff spoke for many when he advised his governor to do something "to insure the dignity and sanctity of the law from being in future trampled under foot by military force."[29]

And yet under the pressure of the times, especially the farther removed from a center of civil power people found themselves, the more the military assumed to itself functions that incontestably violated the Constitution. This was especially the case west of the Mississippi in Texas, Arkansas, and western Louisiana, where isolation increasingly threw local civil authorities and the military into a competition. As early as 1862 a military commission was established in San Antonio that dealt with a range of cases extending far beyond the normal purview of the army. Civilians, including women, were routinely detained and even imprisoned on military authority, especially those suspected of being Union sympathizers. A German immigrant named Edward Degener was arrested and charged with being "a dangerous and seditious person and an enemy to the government," because he supposedly knew of a band of Unionists who were arming themselves to commit sabotage and then escape to Mexico, yet he failed to report them to the military. He was also charged with speaking critically of the Confederate government, and of corresponding with enemies of the nation. Degener immediately pled not guilty, and then challenged the jurisdiction of the military commission, which overruled his complaint. When his counsel pointed out that the statute law of the Confederacy contained no recognition of the crime of sedition—a sedition act having been passed and then repealed for being in conflict with rights of free expression—the commission again ignored the plea, thus virtually inventing on its own a civil crime that the government did not recognize, and that the military did not have lawful power to indict or punish. "Is it possible that the Defendant, may be condemned by this Court?" asked Degener's counsel. "If so, under what name? We look in vain through the catalogue of civil, military, or political offences to characterize it." Again Degener challenged the jurisdiction of the court as "an illegal and an unauthorized body," and again his challenge was dismissed. Found guilty of one charge, he was sentenced to post a bond of $5,000 that he would be a loyal and faithful citizen during the remainder of the war, again a species of sentence that the military had no lawful authority to impose on a civilian in the absence of martial law.

Another man, T. T. Taylor, was brought before the commission and when he could not defend himself, and there was insufficient evidence to try him, the officers decided instead to force him to be conscripted into the army. Ferdinand Simon was not so fortunate when he came before the commission charged as an enemy to the state. Found guilty of four specifications, he was sentenced to be hanged.[30]

Such exercise of civil justice functions in states where legally constituted civil authorities were in place and operating led to one conflict after another, though not having the power of soldiers and weapons behind them, and certainly being unwilling virtually to go to war with their own army, the civilian powers generally had to accept the humiliation of bowing to the army. West of the Mississippi after the summer of 1863, when communication with Richmond was all but cut off, President Davis did vest the department commander, General E. Kirby Smith, with all but absolute power, civil and military, especially as Confederates lost their hold on most of Arkansas and Louisiana and the civil governments of those states were driven into exile in Texas. In Texas itself, Governor Pendleton Murrah clashed repeatedly with General Smith over conscription issues, and actually propounded the theory that in cases where "the Confederate states and the state had concurrent jurisdiction, the party which occupied the ground first was entitled to exclusive jurisdiction."[31] That put state and federal authority in competition, and only further invited the military to step in to protect its own interest, since the chief point in contention was whether conscripts should go into the state militia or the national service, a point that Murrah finally gave up as lost. Yet the same conflict also arose over disposition of cotton, as the military inaugurated a policy of impressment or purchase at depressed rates, in order to sell the cotton itself to raise needed money, and again state authorities eventually had to yield to the military. Whereas the Davis administration had assumed the attitude at the outset that the government had no authority to go into the cotton business, now generals were doing so on their own despite the clearly understood constitutional subordination of the military to the civil power.

Once again, their Constitution simply could not protect the private property of the very planters whose needs, more than any others, lay behind secession and the Confederacy in the first place. Such clashes with the military revealed just how weak was Confederate democracy in the face of a crisis. In peacetime with no internal or external threat to raise the specter of necessity overriding constitutional provisions, their democracy could well have continued to function inviolate, but here as in so many other instances, it became manifest that Confederate democracy was too weak to protect itself in a crisis. By 1864 the public and press in Texas, for one, acknowledged that the civil authority in the state was all but overthrown by the generals.[32]

It required only the next step, the institution of martial law over civilians, to complete the apparent abrogation of civil law and rights. Even though circumstances often justified imposing military rule to preserve order, especially in the face of advancing Union armies, still the governors themselves were reluctant to impose it, and seldom did. In the fall of 1861 when Yankees threatened Apalachicola, Florida, Governor Milton resisted pressure to do so, declaring existing civil law sufficient for the emergency, and he proved to be right.[33] In fact, the Confederate Constitution did not provide for martial law, nor would it have been appropriate for it to do so. Although Congress adopted the United States Articles of War almost unchanged in March 1861, even they did not provide authority for martial law. Indeed, there lay the conundrum. The organic law of the Confederacy could not countenance handing civil law over to the military, while the regulations governing the military could not give them power to override the civil law. To have provided otherwise would have been to create the basis of possible future military despotism. In the end, only proclamation by President Davis could authorize the imposition of martial law, and that had to be approved by Congress.

He would actually do so a number of times, especially in the spring of 1862 in the face of the threat of a Yankee army almost within sight of Richmond, but applied it only to limited areas for limited periods. He much preferred meeting civil crises by suspending the privilege of the writ of habeas corpus, which at least still provided that accused civilians be tried before civil courts and not military tribunals. When his generals in the field attempted to impose martial law themselves on their own authority, Davis issued a proclamation canceling all such edicts. Yet there were arguments for martial law. "I have seen enough here to convince me that the civil authorities are wholly unfit to deal with a large class of offenders," complained a Mississippi judge. "To say that the military shall not punish them is virtually to say that they shall go unpunished."[34] In the end, subversive as they were of civilian morale, and trampling as they did on the good will and prerogatives of the state authorities, authorized impositions of military law on civilians were necessary at times in the crisis, and Davis acted wisely in using the precarious authority. Had he acted otherwise, Congress, ever jealous of challenges to rights, would have fought him rather than granting his repeated requests for extraordinary, though limited, powers. Yet a year after Davis first used martial law, many in the government regarded it as almost an artifact rather than a still pertinent issue. In fact, the original proclamation imposed in Richmond early in 1862 and drafted by Judah P. Benjamin, then acting as secretary of war, was taken from the War Department files and actually given in March 1863 to a young boy who wrote to the capital requesting a copy of Davis's autograph. "If we achieve our independence, which we will do so certainly that I ought not to have said 'if,'" wrote the clerk sending the boy the document, "this—the original document proclaiming martial law and the suspension of all civil process in Richmond will be an interesting muniment indeed, to any Citizen of Richmond to shew to his children, and his children's children!"[35]

Yet none would ever look back on the suspension of the privilege of the writ of habeas corpus as a curiosity. Strangely enough, though it represented not nearly as drastic an invasion of rights as martial law, still it excited a far more widespread and damaging outcry. All told, Confederates would spend almost one-third of their existence under some form of suspension in one area or another. The suspension extended for a year from February 1862 to February 1863, and again from February through the end of July 1864, and yet the restrictions on liberty were far more broad, encompassing the brief periods of martial law, and, of course, the virtual autocracy of Kirby Smith in Texas after 1864.[36]

Even before Congress and Davis produced the first suspension, there were already agents in the field as "habeas corpus commissioners," attorneys appointed by the War Department to specially investigate the cases of persons arrested on suspicion of disloyalty. The first were appointed in the fall of 1861, fully a year before Congress actually passed its Habeas Corpus Act authorizing their existence. It merely validated what the secretary of war had been doing for some time, and what they would continue to do even after the term of this act expired. Because they were not generally known, the habeas corpus commissioners attracted far less attention and outcry than did the formal passage of suspensions. Yet the effect of their actions was the same, investigating the cases of alleged traitors being held without bail for indeterminate periods without charges ever being preferred. The commissioner could act as judge and even jury, under no established order of procedure, nor was he answerable to higher authority for more than an infrequent report of his activities. In one of the greatest challenges to the concept of civil law and freedom, he did not even have to return a guilty finding in order to continue to hold a prisoner. If he simply failed to recommend release of a suspect, he could de facto keep the person in jail indefinitely.[37]

Once the arrests began, however, the outcry slowly grew. Chiefly the government interfered with due process in cases involving men trying to evade national conscription, and governors could themselves suspend the writ within their borders, often for the same reasons. Whether arrested by local or national authority, however, the victims protested loudly. "Now, it appears to me," complained a Mississippian arrested by Governor John Pettus and kept in "durance vile" for two months, "a Citizen of these Confederate States, struggling for their independence, that a man, being arrested, has a right to know the charges, if any, preferred against him and also, that a speedy trial be granted him in order that he may disprove the charges against him and regain his liberty."[38] So it would have seemed, and there were local judges who tried their best to counter what they regarded as an abuse. They tried to grant writs for people arrested as conscripts, but military authorities argued that the state judiciary had no power to attempt to override a national conscription act. The decision of army surgeons and examining boards on the fitness of a conscript was final. "This I consider amounts to a virtual suspension of the writ," protested Governor Clark of Mississippi late in 1863. If a judge freed a man on a writ, and then the military arrested him again in spite of that, state and federal law were in conflict. "I need not inform you of the demoralizing effects of these things upon our people," he complained. Admitting that conscription and impressment had become necessary, still he argued that "unless a wiser policy is pursued they will become odious," and indeed they did.[39]

They ought to allow Confederate authorities to prosecute appeals against the conscript or impressment laws, and allow the state supreme courts to determine whether they would agree "whether Congress has exceeded its own powers under the Constitution in conferring such a broad grant of authority," said Mississippi's attorney general. It was "a question for the consideration of the *judicial* and not the *Executive* department of the Government." The legislation by Congress authorizing the suspension smacked "very strongly of an interference with the right of Habeas Corpus and trial by jury," and he further called into doubt the legality of the rules established by the secretary of war in such cases, since he held no judicial role under the Constitution. The Alabama Supreme Court had issued a ruling endorsing Congress's act despite its questionable legality, and Mississippi's attorney general argued that "looking to the object to be accomplished, and the necessity for a liberal exercise of power by Congress to provide for the defense of the Country, I should *as a judge*, adopt the decision." In other words, since the government had decided that conscription and impressment were necessary, the states ought to act to accept their constitutionality, and thus put an end to any further habeas corpus cases arising under their operation. "The question is not free from doubt & difficulty," he added. If it was further asserted that only a Confederate government judge could have jurisdiction over writs applied for by injured parties, then it amounted to a virtual denial of the writ. "Whether State Courts have concurrent jurisdiction, by *Habeas Corpus*, over the question of unlawful imprisonment" by Confederate authorities was, he confessed, an unknown territory, and thus one that the states ought to settle to end the controversy.[40]

In capital after capital governors looked to their attorneys general to provide them some guidance or support in handling the conflict over habeas corpus. T. J. Wharton in Mississippi told Governor Clark that it was a subject of "vast importance," and he took a long time to ponder just where the power of a state's judiciary extended "in view of the alarming stretch of military authority, and the consequent danger of subverting the great principles of State Sovereignty." He suggested that there was a class of cases that arose under the acts of Congress in which state courts had a concurrent jurisdiction with Confederate courts, but maintained that in habeas corpus cases the state was supreme. Habeas corpus extended to all classes of illegal confinement by which any person was denied liberty, so long as the petition for a writ stated the probable cause for supposing that the arrest and detention were unlawful. That required something more than merely the judge's own personal knowledge of the applicant or the circumstances, however. Real evidence ought to be presented before a judge considered granting a writ to release a prisoner.[41]

Certainly the challenge to traditional concepts of justice and rights caused a lot of soul searching for those in Congress who had to accept or reject the president's calls for suspension, and then to face constituents afterward. Robert Hilton of Florida, one of the most sensible bellwether members of the House of Representatives, presented the case to Floridians in August 1863 after being attacked for voting to support suspension in February 1862 after the disasters at Forts Henry and Donelson, and again to sustain the imposition of martial law in Richmond in April and May. For a start, he pointed out that the chief sufferers under suspension were not law-abiding citizens, but those involved in the unlawful distillation and selling of liquor. After Davis first imposed the suspension and martial law in Richmond, military authorities immediately imposed prohibition to prevent disorderliness, and to keep soldiers from getting drunk and leaving their regiments. Before long the impetus for prohibition spread to all of the states, and even without martial law their legislatures began to pass laws prohibiting distillation for any purposes other than medicinal use. It was also a measure to conserve grain otherwise needed for the soldiers and their animals. "Hundreds of grog shops, engaged in exacting from our noble soldiers their small pay & in return poisoning them with vile liquor, were closed," argued Hilton. The Constitution specifically gave Congress power to do so. He granted that a few military commanders, mostly west of the Mississippi, had abused their authority and issued unlawful suspensions, but the president had revoked all of those. "I have felt it my solemn duty as a member of Congress to sustain the administration," he maintained. Doing so strengthened their army rather than "paralyzing it, to prolong the war until our present defenders should die of disease or on the battle field." If Davis and their generals "have been compelled for the defense of all that men hold dear—our wives, our homes, our children, our altars—to place temporary restraint at periods of great danger, upon the inhabitants of certain localities, the sufferers, if good citizens, will not complain; if disloyal to our cause, who shall sympathize with them?" To those like Rhett who complained that suspension and martial law were merely the first steps to a Davis despotism, Hilton sneered that they were fools to think that their own citizens' army would allow itself to be used to take away the very freedoms they were fighting for. Jefferson Davis would be as little capable of becoming a despot "as the sun is of becoming black."[42]

The issue of trying habeas corpus cases when they arose became increasingly difficult for judges as the list of those exempted from conscription shrank dramatically by 1864 in the face of the voracious appetite of the state militias and the army. At the same time, the volume of the cases increased steadily. By December 1864 former Virginia governor John Letcher was almost exclusively occupied with such cases in his law practice.[43] A Mississippi justice had to beg for a list of just which civil officers were exempt, down to the level of town officials like aldermen, selectmen, council members, and others. Even then, a governor could meet a crisis by calling out even all exempt state and local officials for thirty days or more, ordering them all to muster immediately at the county seat. Ironically, men who sought to evade national service by gaining state offices that were exempt from the Confederate draft found themselves liable to being conscripted by their own governors. That also meant, incidentally, that when the governor conscripted civil officers, the county courts could not meet if their clerks or justices of the peace were called up. In Kosciusko, Mississippi, the county records were removed for safekeeping from Yankee raids, but when the clerk was drafted, he was not available to bring them out of hiding, and without the records no court could be held. But at the same time, when a governor allowed men to enlist in his own militia, in the hope that this would exempt them from being taken away from home and drafted into the national service, time after time when Confederate authorities arrested the individuals as conscripts anyhow, their appeals on habeas corpus were denied.[44] Adding to the difficulty, especially for poor men who did not have the state willing to press their case, was the expense. It cost $15.70 in Louisiana in 1861 for all of the papers, applications, and filings for a habeas corpus case. For many citizens that was simply more than they could afford, and the cost only went up as the war progressed.[45] By January 1864 the Louisiana courts were so disrupted that dozens of slaves accused of crimes were going untried for want of available jurors, and Governor Thomas Moore actually suggested a radical change in legal precedent to allow trial without jury for Negro defendants. At the same time, Louisiana then being the only slave state that allowed free blacks to testify against whites in court, he proposed as well that this allowance be repealed, thus making a double reduction in legal protection for non-whites. Not even justice could escape the all-pervasive influence of slavery and race in Confederate democracy.[46]

Just one case in Louisiana late in the war showed how complex and frayed were the conditions between civil and military authority. E. Warren Moise was judge of the Confederate District Court for Louisiana, then located in Natchitoches in the western part of the state as a result of Yankees overrunning most of it to the east. To his bench came the case of a major charged with selling cotton to the enemy. He was arrested but then released on the issuance of a writ and posting of bond, but he immediately forfeited his bail by going over to the Yankees, only to be recaptured. An immediate outcry went up in Natchitoches that such a thief and traitor ought to be shot, no matter how, whether by civil or military law. "Poor fools!" Moise exclaimed. "They don't know how soon their time may come—when they will clamor for the protection of the law, as much as they now denounce it. They may learn some day, or other, that the law protects from violence the guilty as well as the innocent—and that if a man walk the streets with the brand of Cain upon him—he is as much protected from the rude hands of brute force, or illegal authority as is a virgin when she walks to church to take her first communion." Even though Moise knew that his judgment in granting habeas corpus to the major made him unpopular in light of the man's flight, still he maintained that "there never was a plainer question presented for solution than that involved in the trial of the Habeas Corpus."[47]

Very quickly the military itself got involved. Kirby Smith's headquarters directed that the major ought to be executed for treason without delay, but then learned that Moise was about to issue a writ to stay execution pending a proper trial before a civil court. In fact, Moise already had the procedure for issuing a writ under way when he learned that the order for execution had come down from headquarters, which he took as "evidence of a wilfull disregard of the sanctity of the judicial proceedings." The result was the beginning of a strained and publicized exchange of correspondence between Moise and Lieutenant General Simon B. Buckner, Smith's immediate subordinate in the area, turning upon the technicalities and niceties of habeas corpus procedure, and on the relations of the civil and military themselves. Buckner accused Moise of trying to impose justice in a military jurisdiction beyond his mandate, while Moise accused the army of the same violation. Buckner confessed that he found himself in conflict between obeying his military superior and following the judgment of the civil court, and sought to relieve himself of what he called the "embarrassment" of his position. "I regarded the civil authority as the superior of the two," he protested, but it was an attitude not distinctly shared by many in uniform. Moise even obtained the intercession of Congressman Duncan Kenner in his conflict with Buckner, but without much effect. Buckner himself professed that he desired "the establishment between the civil and military authorities of relations of confidence and mutual support so essential, under existing circumstances, to the maintenance of discipline in the army, and of civil liberty in the country."

As the controversy went on, neither side yielding, the offending major was quickly forgotten as the argument took on its own life. Even the judge concluded that on some topics he and the general ought to consider "the propriety of dropping the subject," but the main bone remained firmly in their teeth. Moise came down to quibbling with Buckner over the definitions of legal terms, and the general freely confessed his lack of grounding in the complexity of the judicial lexicon, though adding, "I am not yet a convert to the maxim that the purpose of language is to conceal ideas instead of to elucidate them." He even resorted to sarcasm when Moise at one stage denied that he had any more intention to insult Buckner than he would have Emperor Louis Napoleon of France. "As I am not advised of the personal relations existing between you and the Emperor of the French, or how you may have considered him responsible for the improper arrest," the general concluded, "it might be unsafe in me to hazard any deduction from this association of my name with that of so eminent a personage."[48] The controversy passed on into 1865 when the major was finally to be put on trial for treason in Moise's court thanks to the writ granted by the judge. Moise declared publicly that he "did not care a damn" about the public outcry that continued to demand the man's execution. The judge did not even countenance the accusations that he had been bribed to issue a writ to save the man's life. He reported that he was himself so destitute that he had no meat for his table, and no money to pay the $1 a pound required for bacon and beef, and was living on bread and water, which hardly suggested that he was receiving bribes. "You and I, who know his perfect integrity, can smile at such false judgment," a friend told Governor Moore. In the end even Buckner set aside his pique and tried to relieve Moise's hardship by issuing an order to allow him to buy provisions from the army commissary at army prices.[49] Unfortunately, very few such conflicts between civil and military law ended with such an act of charity.

On February 3, 1864, when the second habeas corpus suspension came before Congress, the issue was so loaded with emotion and bitterness that when Davis's message requesting the measure was read, the House of Representatives sat in unaccustomed and profound silence. It was immediately moved to refer the message to the judiciary committee while the message was printed for the House to consider in secret session. However, with the outcry on the habeas corpus issue so widespread now, John Baldwin of Virginia stood and moved that they debate the act in open session so that the people of the Confederacy could understand its import and why it might be necessary. To adopt another suspension in secret session, he said, "would be the last organized act of the Confederacy." Yet repeated attempts to get the House to agree to debate in open session were defeated. Others tried to get the normal rules of the House suspended so that they could deal with the matter at once, again unsuccessfully, and Henry Foote of Tennessee began to make conditions and ask for more information, even specific names of the kinds of people to whom the writ should be denied. The perpetually hypocritical Foote said he was "ready to become a martyr in defense of his principles. No one would dare call him a traitor," though before long the whole Confederacy would be doing just that. In the end, they passed a bill on February 15, but once again it was done in secret session, and without publishing to the nation the compelling argument laid down for the measure by Davis.[50] Loyal governors like Thomas Watts in Alabama, even though he opposed the suspension, abhorred even more a conflict between federal and state authorities, and acquiesced. In the end, almost everyone acquiesced, however much they grumbled.[51]

Nevertheless, the majority of the operations of the state and local justice system in the Confederacy did at least manage to continue without interference from Richmond or the army, but never without increasing hardship imposed by the war itself. Just electing court officials posed problems previously unimagined. In the election for judge of Hinds County, Mississippi, in October 1863, E. J. Goode won by a majority of just a hundred votes once all the returns came in to the office of the secretary of state. However, with the state partially overrun by Yankees, and Vicksburg in their hands no more than sixty miles away, everything moved slowly, and more returns arrived even after Goode was declared victor. By November 17 enough late precincts were heard from to reveal that Goode's opponent now had an actual majority of seven votes. Despite the fact that he had already been declared the winner, Goode wrote to the governor and resigned, "believing my election to be the result of the present distracted condition of our State which prevented the full returns from reaching their proper destination in time, and being unwilling to avail myself of such an accident."[52]

Mississippi represented a case in point of the steady disintegration of civil law. Tax collectors complained that the condition of the countryside prevented them from making their collections; moreover, in some regions the citizens would refuse to pay anyhow. Especially difficult were those densely anti-Confederate counties like Jones and Winston in Mississippi, where deserters and tories held virtual dominion. In Jones the disaffected met and resolved to pay no county, state, or national taxes, nor to allow collectors into their stronghold. When authorities managed to collect produce from the loyal—or submissive—farmers as payment of "tax in kind," the disloyal actually impressed wagons and teams from local civil authorities and used them to steal the supplies and haul them away for their own use. When two government agents ventured into Jones to collect livestock for the army, they were ambushed and murdered.[53] In Macon a justice complained that no attempt was even being made to preserve peace and order. "The city is infested with deserters of the worst class," he declared. "Peacible citizens are driven from their homes." He himself had survived an ambush attempt, and their sheriff had run off as a refugee. Tories made pro-Union and anti-Confederate speeches at will and "no man's life is safe who dares to speak out against them." Outright murder was on the increase, and lawlessness prevailed in many counties as the civil courts were unable to meet and the officers of the law like sheriffs and constables either simply did not do their duty or feared to make the attempt.[54]

The complaints against such men became an outcry by mid-1864. "The fact is that not one of these civil officers is attempting to discharge that duty, although the counties are full of deserters, and are often killing or outraging the persons & property of good citizens," complained Judge Robert Hudson of the Fifth Judicial District of Mississippi. If not for their offices, such sheriffs would be liable for conscription. They were shirking their civil duty out of fear or worse, spending their time speculating. "There is by them an utter & reckless disregard of said law & duty," continued JudgeHudson. Many of the officers actually had family who were themselves deserters. "They meet and sometimes feed & entertain without attempting to arrest, or even to reprimand them," Hudson went on. Of twenty "beat" officers patrolling the county, most treated the deserters with politeness rather than arrest. Hudson himself by May 1864 had not been able to hold a court in one county since the fall of 1861, and even he was so fearful of the deserters that when he reported their names to higher authority he begged that no one identify him as the informant. Leake, Attala, Neshoba, Winston, and other counties were "for the last six months emptying their filthy, base, disloyal, deserting, stealing, murdering population into Yazoo," he complained. "They ought to be hung." People pretended to go to those remote counties to buy corn for subsistence, but they never returned, remaining to escape the army and plunder. "They are all as rotten as Hell," he thundered. "Unless you get them out they will destroy you," he warned the governor.

> They are abolitionist spies, deserters, liars, thieves, murderers and everything foul & damnable. If you can manage to have them hung or put into our army, you will do Yazoo an immortal service. They are sly & shy and skilled in hiding and woodsing . . . put every element at work, that can arrest them & this hellish tide. They will tell lies, swear lies for each other and do any thing. Heed nothing they say or swear.[55]

Even in those counties where courts were being irregularly held, officers could not reach those who should be brought before the bench. Hudson attended several courts held by other judges and warned that when they were held, "they were rather nominal and farcical, they being unable to do any important business." The governor's response was to suggest revoking all exemptions for civil officials not in good faith doing their jobs.[56]

By April 1864, Alexander M. Clayton, the man so responsible for making Davis president, and now Confederate district judge for Mississippi, actually advised the governor not to attempt to hold a court, for the only business they could hope to attend to effectively was sequestration. There was even danger that state records would be captured or destroyed, and he recommended moving them to southwest Georgia. Separated from its mountains of precedent and records, a judicial system could not hope to function adequately.[57] Some places it was not even possible for police boards to assemble a citizens' meeting to choose commissioners to administer relief for the poor families of soldiers, as mandated by the legislature.[58] And yet there were those determined judges who would not be deterred by threat or hardship. In March 1864 one judge went to Corinth, Mississippi, immediately after the Federals evacuated the city, in order to try to hold a court, but the people were so destitute that he had to close it almost immediately. "No raid of the Yankees or Tories will drive me away," declared Judge William Kilpatrick of the Tishomingo County, Mississippi, circuit court. If he lived and the enemy did not return, he resolved to sit at his bench for a fall term in 1864 to dispense justice, though it would be the first time in three years that a civil court was held there. He had to ask for the furlough from the militia of the county district attorney so that he could prosecute cases. The people of the county were clamoring for a court after fully a year of civil disorder thanks to deserters. "Much good is being done to sustain public morals by holding the courts," said Kilpatrick, who fully appreciated the calming effect that the conduct of normal business could have on the population.[59]

By October 1864 the deterioration only worsened. In Attala County, which positively groaned under the weight of the population of deserters, the civil officers stopped trying to make arrests and the grand jury refused to risk the deserters' wrath by issuing any indictments, even when Judge Hudson lectured the jury at length on their duty. The police board chose the jury members, and the police themselves would have to make the arrests following indictments, being themselves subject to indictment if they did not. "Knowing their default & liability and looking to their own safety, they selected men, who approved their infidelity and sympathized with the deserters & tories, so far as to prevent any indictments," Hudson grumbled, suggesting a change in the law to prevent parties who were subject to indictment for malfeasance from themselves being able to select jury members, yet another change in the practice of justice and democracy forced by the pressures of war. The ruffians were so brazen that in the recent election of county officers in Leake County, the deserters ran their own candidates, and sent armed men—twenty-seven with pistols and bowie knives at one polling place—to vote for their men. In some counties they actually elected candidates to the police beats, selecting men pledged not to arrest them.[60] Eventually the circuit courts met so irregularly that their normal cases were sent to the governor for decision. At the same time, felons already convicted actually came to believe that the war gave them bargaining leverage, and a number sent petitions for pardon to the governor, promising to enlist if they were set free.

Mute testimony to the breakdown of justice is the fact that in the county jail at Linden, Texas, the iron "cage or Dungeon" was dismantled and turned over to the army so that the iron could be used for outfitting military wagons rather than holding malefactors.[61] By early 1865 everyone knew of some story of rank injustice. In Texas a soldier planning to desert took out a writ of habeas corpus for himself prior to his offense, thinking it would protect him.[62] A convicted man in Mississippi demanded remission of his penalty because the court records were hidden away for safekeeping after his conviction, and thus no transcript of his case was available for him to review for appeal.[63] In Lowndes County two young women were arrested for stealing a bolt of cloth, solely on the basis of a few scraps of similar cloth being found in their house, where they had been for months. One was the widow of a soldier, and the other's husband was still in the army. Moreover, one was a material witness in a rape charge against a slave who just happened to belong to the same man who accused her of theft, who brought the charges to keep her from appearing in court.[64] Less than two weeks before the surrenders began, a man saw two of his sons leave with soldiers to hunt deserters, but when an elderly tory who had threatened to kill any who came after him was himself killed, the sons and their captain were arrested by the same local police elected by the deserters. With no indictment preferred against them, the boys were simply incarcerated, leaving their father to beg the governor for a change of venue. "They could not have a fair trial—nor even a show of law & justice" in the hands of the deserters, he protested, "but they would be mobbed in revenge." In desperation the father begged the governor to allow the boys to resign their enlistments so that they could escape across the Mississippi to get away from the tories, without making themselves liable for arrest as deserters. For some, it seemed, there was no safety from one kind of justice or another.[65]

Confederate justice was crumbling at every level—national, state, and local—near the end of the war. The upheavals and dislocations of the war itself made local civil justice haphazard at best, while the erosion of local and state authority by national military power further weakened the consistent application of the rule of law. "Interruption in the administration of the laws of the country by the civil tribunals, is producing an alarming disintegration of all the usages and safeguards of Society," lamented a South Carolina judge at the end of March 1865, "and as it appears to me, driving the country with fearful velocity into a state of anarchy." The criminal courts sat paralyzed, offenders escaping justice, with some prosecutions on the docket from 1861 still untried. Indictments kept being handed down, but no trials took place, no juries could be impaneled, and the circuit justices did not have the authority to improvise in the crisis. Impotent jurists could only beg for harsher punishments for felons, when they could be tried and convicted.[66] Legislatures even overturned some of the building blocks of justice itself. In a dramatic shift in the basic presumption of innocence until proven guilty, Georgia decreed that anyone caught hoarding or speculating in vital goods under the pretense of purchasing it for the Confederate government should be forced in court to prove his innocence against the presumption of guilt.[67] It was Western law turned on its ear.

Confederate democracy had been engraved in their Constitution to preserve the sovereignty of the states in everything save slavery, and the individual rights of slave and other property owners against incursion. Implicit within the document, too, was recognition of the long and even exaggerated tradition of individual rights and liberties in the South, a tradition bound up in the old code of honor, the concept of being gentlemen, and firmly embedded in their populist prewar politics. What happened after 1861, however, revealed that the pressure of crisis gave president and Congress cause to be willing to override all of those rights, even slavery in some instances, and revealed as well that the population at large, for all their discontent, was not so outraged as to refuse to go along with their government, if for no other reason than that they felt powerless to stop it. Indeed, the greatest opponents of the administration on issues of civil law and liberty, men like Rhett, were repeatedly shown to be impotent in stopping Davis, and that being the case, what could private citizens do? As for the governors, the leaders of the sovereign states, they saw their own control of civil law collapsing under pressure from within and without. Davis and Congress had the power of their positions and the army behind them, a formidable tacit authority that only the combined wills of most or all of the governors could have hoped to counter. On other issues they would try, but there was sufficient division among them on justice, and sufficient acknowledgment of the exigencies of the war situation, that they could never hope to stand united against Richmond on habeas corpus or any other legal issue. And despite clear signs of divisions of class in the application of justice, just as the Constitution itself certainly made provision for the perpetuation of the propertied oligarchy, by the end Confederate courts were failing at every level of society. Indeed, and ironically, in those counties where the tory and deserter element managed to use a perverted version of the democratic process to gain some control of the civil justice system, it was actually the planters who had the most to fear. Even where law was applied fairly, with the slave impressments and the gradual erosion of the exemption system, near the end the old ruling class had seen its rights and prerogatives steadily diminished.

What can be said for Confederate democracy, through the president and Congress, is that in the face of the dramatic upheavals in the body politic, with widespread dissent, disruption, even treason by their definition, Jefferson Davis and the majority in his administration and Congress revealed a surprising degree of flexibility in attempting to deal with the issue. They had spent generations presenting themselves to the South and the world as true believers in a strict construction of a constitution, and had crafted theirs to be so perfect that some thought it would obviate the need for any future interpretation. Like the Bible, all answers could be found in the Constitution regardless of the question. But in practice they found they could and would reshape their democracy around that framework when necessary, even when it meant infringing or curtailing the rights it was built to protect. They made their government stronger to compensate for their own internal weakness. What they could not safeguard, however, was the sanctity and security of the common law and civil justice. As in so many other areas, in theory the Confederacy seemed to be working, but in practice its collapse commenced almost from the day of its birth.

The Season of Lee

When Robert E. Lee took over from the wounded Joseph E. Johnston, his grip was unsteady at first, and the army confused and lacking in coordination, but he knew what he had to do. He had to hold Richmond and drive the invader back, and that is what he did. Showing bold initiative and a sure grasp of the executive instincts necessary to manage an army, Lee stopped George B. McClellan at Seven Pines, and soon afterward began his own counteroffensive in a brilliant series of battles then and later known as the Seven Days. They were not all victories and they were not all brilliantly fought, especially the last one at Malvern Hill, but Lee stunned and then cowed McClellan as surely as if he had hit him on the head with a club. Stubbornly "Little Mac" refused to abandon the peninsula for several weeks more, but he was beaten and everyone in North and South alike knew it. Richmond was saved and the Confederacy had a hero to match or even eclipse the dynamic Stonewall.

Lee had little enough time to bask in his new glory—which would have been out of character for him in any event. Another Union army had moved south from Washington to threaten Richmond from the rear while McClellan confronted it from the peninsula, but McClellan's defeat left Lee free to turn to meet the new threat, and McClellan for his part would do nothing to stop him or to aid the approaching rival commander, General John Pope. As coincidence, and the dictates of geography and logistics, would have it, Lee met Pope on almost the same battleground around the

189

vital rail junction at Manassas, and there in a second battle just over a year from the first handed him a sound beating. This time the Federals did not retreat in a panic, however, and they gave a good account of themselves, but it was the eclipse of Pope in Virginia. McClellan withdrew from the peninsula and an angry and disappointed Lincoln had little choice but to put him in command of the two beaten but now united armies.

McClellan dallied and drilled and fretted about imaginary legions coming to get him as was his wont, but Lee had more practical things in mind. His army, newly dubbed the Army of Northern Virginia, was strong, high on victory, and most of the summer and fall campaigning weather was still ahead of him. Maryland, like Kentucky, was a slave state that did not secede, though there was much Confederate and secession sympathy there. Given the chance by a liberating army, its men and materiel might flock to the crimson banners of the South. At the same time, after the triumphs of Jackson in the Shenandoah and Lee on the peninsula and now against Pope, Confederate fortunes in the East were soaring. There might never be a better time to take the war to the enemy by invading the North, not for conquest—which was pointless and all but impossible in any case—but to throw the Yankees off their guard, show them the cost of the war on their own ground, relieve the pressure on Virginia by drawing McClellan away to follow, and perhaps even make the kind of impression on European powers that would make recognition a possibility. There were off-year elections coming in October and November, and a successful campaign on Lincoln's own turf could result in severe losses in his Republican governorships and his congressional coalition of Republicans and loyal Democrats. Politics was never far from the battlefield, and never closer than when Lee put his men into the Potomac fords that took them into the fields of Maryland.

It was a battle that Lee should have lost. He had to divide his army to take care of a Yankee garrison in his rear at Harpers Ferry. McClellan through incredible chance came into possession of a copy of Lee's campaign plan. Lee finally met the dilatory Little Mac along Antietam Creek around the village of Sharpsburg, and found himself outnumbered, almost cut off from the wing of his army marching from Harpers Ferry, and with his back to the impassable Potomac. Ulysses S. Grant would have destroyed him. Lee, if wearing the blue, would have destroyed him. McClellan all but let him emerge the victor. In the bloodiest day's carnage of the entire war, Lee held his ground until his reinforcements arrived, and Mc-

Clellan conducted such an uncoordinated and inept offensive that even though he was still in desperate straits, Lee actually held his ground the following day as if daring the Yankees to try him again. Finally he retreated, fortunate indeed to have been up against McClellan, and even more fortunate simply to be able to get away to Virginia intact. McClellan would never fight again, but thanks largely to his timidity, Lee would.

Meanwhile, off to the west Confederate fortunes still sagged, though the momentum of their decline slowed dramatically from the past spring. David G. Farragut took Baton Rouge and Natchez, and then with a small military force very nearly took Vicksburg itself in the summer before he was forced to retire. Upriver Memphis fell in June, and Federal gunboats got all the way south to Vicksburg before they, too, had to pull back. Still, there was now only a slender corridor of the Mississippi between Vicksburg and Port Hudson, Louisiana, connecting the Trans-Mississippi with the rest of the Confederacy. Grant would make Vicksburg his prime target for the next year, while the Confederates began turning it into the most heavily fortified spot on the globe.

The army that P.G.T. Beauregard led back south from Shiloh had a new commander, as Beauregard had left his command without permission and Davis promptly relieved him. Now these men in what was to become the Army of Tennessee would answer to General Braxton Bragg, irascible, narrow-minded, unstable even, yet despite his manifest shortcomings, the most aggressive army commander the Confederacy would field except for Lee himself. They had lost west Tennessee, but they might regain it if they could drive north into Kentucky again, all the way to the Ohio, claiming the Bluegrass State for the South, and putting themselves on the rear and flank of Grant's forces aiming for Vicksburg. At the same time, such a campaign coordinated with Lee's advance into Maryland would result in the two being mutually supportive, with the enemy both east and west too pressed in its own front to reinforce the other. Bragg moved with resolution, and by October had reached Lexington, and then the capital at Frankfort, where he spent a day installing a "Confederate" governor before turning back to meet the threat of a small Union army at his heels. They met on the banks of Doctor's Creek near Perryville, and even though Bragg largely won the battle that followed, he found he had no choice but to march back out of the state. The Kentucky dream had been an illusion. Instead of thousands of men flocking to enlist, and farmers handing over their fat cattle and corn cribs, the Confederates discovered little sympathy

for the Confederacy in the state, or at least not enough to make Kentuck-
ians risk their lives and their property. Confederates would never give up
the Kentucky dream, partly because so many in high station were Ken-
tuckians, including Davis himself by birth, but it would always be a fan-
tasy.

Instead, Bragg withdrew to south-central Tennessee to refit his army.
Then a Union force moved out from Nashville to strike south. Seeing an op-
portunity, Bragg planned to move north again and catch the Yankees
where he could thrash them. Late in December he encountered General
William S. Rosecrans's army near Murfreesboro, along the Stones River,
and there the two armies saw out the old year pounding one another inde-
cisively. Bragg did not manage a battle well. Worse, he had balky subordi-
nates, including the execrable Leonidas Polk, who spent more time
politicking with his friend Davis to undermine Bragg than he did in good
service to his cause. Someone who performed much better was John C.
Breckinridge, commander of a small corps at Shiloh even though he had no
experience in action. His prewar prominence as a politician made it politic
for Davis to give him a commission, as he would the Cobbs and others, but
Breckinridge was showing some genuine skill at midlevel command. Un-
fortunately, Bragg had also taken a dislike to him. In a high command al-
ready riddled with internal dissension and politics, Breckinridge, Polk,
and others would soon find themselves aligned against their army com-
mander. Polk actively conspired, Breckinridge tried to stay out of it, and
Bragg regarded them all as his enemies. Thus when a battle that had
seemed to be going his way ended in an equivocal defeat with the Confed-
erates leaving the field to Rosecrans, Bragg would soon begin another cam-
paign with Davis to shift the blame to his subordinates. The Army of
Tennessee was now at war with itself.

Thank Providence for Lee, Davis might well have said, and probably
did. It was not just that Lee brought him victories and did not foment trou-
ble with the administration or within his own army. Lee also happened to
be operating in the Virginia theater where the great majority of American
and world attention was focused. Most of the newspapers were there, and,
of course, the two capitals, always magnets of interest, were at either end
of a line no more than a hundred miles long, with Lee operating in be-
tween. His victories were thus magnified in importance tenfold, and helped
to eclipse the less noticed yet strategically much more important defeats in
the West. After eighteen months of war, the Confederacy had lost whole

states beyond the Appalachians, but world attention often saw no further than the battle to preserve a stalemate in Virginia, where neither side was gaining or losing much ground from where it had been at the beginning. But for the Confederates that was victory.

Lee built on it at the end of the year, just before Bragg's debacle at Stones River, another reason the defeat went less noticed. A new Federal commander, General Ambrose Burnside, took over McClellan's army. He planned an able campaign to get across the Rappahannock River and between Lee and Richmond, by so doing hoping either to take the Confederate capital or force Lee to fight him on ground of his own choosing, or both. But logistical snags ruined Burnside's plans, and faced with having to improvise, he turned pitifully clumsy and instead simply bludgeoned his own army by sending it across the river and up fortified heights into the guns of Lee's veterans. It was little better than murder. Lee himself was repelled by the horrible grandeur of it, yet once again he had won. And in the winter mud a few weeks later, when another Burnside campaign turned to a mired fiasco, Virginia and Richmond were safe yet again, and Lincoln was looking for another general. The Confederacy and Lee would never see such a season of triumph again. The trouble was, to survive, they needed it every season, but 1863 would be the season of Grant.

7

"Proving Our Loyalty by Starvation"

THE ENTHUSIASM for the war and the new cause on the part of those who stayed at home was truly remarkable at the outset. Indeed, some maintained that the most patriotic Confederates of all were the wives and mothers and sweethearts, perhaps because they saw a different sort of sacrifice from their men in the armies, and had to suffer the monotony of a crushing routine while living with the constant uncertainty that their lives and futures were being shaped by events beyond their sight.[1] Certainly the spirit of duty and self-subordination took early hold. "I shall endeavor to curtail domestic expenses and every dollar that we can raise beyond legitimate expenses shall be freely given to our soldiers," a Georgia wife declared in May 1861. "Their cause is our cause, their defeat would prove our ruin. While our sex are not allowed to mingle actively in the dire of conflict, we can work for those who go and pray kind Heaven's protection upon them while absent, thus proving that the blood which honored the women of the revolution has lost none of its patriotic fervor in us." Not surprisingly, the literate women of the South resorted to verse to express their determination:

> We scoff a like at art and word,
> A *despot's* stern decree,
> And fling our banner to the wind
> A nation *shall* be free.[2]

Some felt such a rush of patriotism at first that they could not content themselves to stay at home. "Oh what a glorious idea I have in mind!" young Eliza Moses confided to her diary on July 24, 1861. "It is to go to Virginia and be nurse for the wounded, for in that way I could be of use to somebody."[3] Despite the fact that nursing had been almost exclusively the province of men, especially in the military, still the stories—highly exaggerated—of Florence Nightingale and her lamp with the British soldiers in the Crimea a few years before had captivated the romantic sensibilities of American women. Hundreds of young would-be Confederate ministering angels dreamed of going to the armies, and not a few actually did, even though poor Eliza soon learned that she would not be needed. Married men applying for chaplaincies with the new regiments sometimes applied at the same time for an appointment for their wives as nurses, even though neither state nor national service recognized a formal role for women with the armed services.[4]

In the main, women simply appeared on the fringes of the army as self-appointed samaritans, doing what they could with no official sanction at all, but certainly appreciated none the less by the men and officers in the field. As the Confederacy's first real army took shape in northern Virginia, scores gathered in and around Manassas, bringing with them baskets of lamb and fried chicken, rice and custards, bread and pickles, milk and cherries, cakes and pies, and more, to augment the boxes being sent from homes all across the South. When they learned that a Union army was advancing from Washington, the women spent hours tearing bolts of red flannel into strips for Virginia soldiers to wear on their arms so that they could be distinguished, in their blue uniforms, from similarly clad Yankees. That done, they tore other cloth into strips for bandages, and picked cotton lint into daubs and dressings for the inevitable wounds. On July 21, during and after the fighting of the first battle along Bull Run, local women were up all night tending to the wounded and the dying in the face of the War Department's woeful lack of preparation for dealing with casualties. The victory won, they were also out in the field and beside the roads with coffee and water and what food they could hurriedly prepare to help the thirsty and exhausted soldiers. Elsewhere on the field, as the beaten Federals hastily retreated, Confederate women taunted them with songs and beat march time on their pots and pans to speed the enemy on their way.[5]

Yet these rather self-conscious heroines were then and would always be a distinct minority, as neither the armies nor the wounded came in close enough proximity for the vast majority of Confederate women to share their adventures. Rather, the real war burden for the woman of the South lay in watching her man or men go off to war, and then in trying to cope for four years with what that war did to her own circle and the world of her daily experience. "It seems hard that you could not be with me or I with you, until it is necessary to part, but I forget I must not complain of anything when it cannot be helped," the wife of former South Carolina governor John Manning wrote her husband in May 1861 as he was leaving for Virginia and the war. Though well-to-do, still she promised not to draw against their bank account until he had spent all he needed to for his comfort on the campaign to come.[6] As early as June 1861 so many regiments were leaving for the front on Sundays that the ministers complained that "the church going people talk about it," and asked authorities to select some other day that did not interfere with the Sabbath or so depress the people.[7] More than a few young couples who had just begun courting found themselves compelled to cut the courtship short and marry almost without notice before the man went off to war. Some, especially in the upper classes, even thought that such hurried nuptials, without waiting for extravagant ceremonies and fine wedding clothes to be made, revealed a new depth of common sense and serious purpose. Apparently a willingness to forgo all the show and "parade" of a society wedding had to mean that a couple of their station were really serious about each other.[8]

The waiting became all the more serious once the people at home heard the first news of a battle at Bull Run. After it there commenced days of anxiety and fear that were to be repeated time and time again throughout the war. "There are hundreds of hearts in pain here to-day," an older Carolinian wrote to a friend with the army when he heard that a regiment with many friends and family members had been exposed to heavy fire on July 21. Just as bad were the rumors that always preceded accurate news of casualties. Immediately after Bull Run, stories went out that General P.G.T. Beauregard himself had been killed, either by an enemy bullet or by his own horse falling on him in the battle, stories that people at home were much relieved to learn were unfounded. "How thankful we are that all of our friends are safe," became a universal expression, though increasingly infrequent as the war inevitably imposed a toll that approached every hearth.[9] Indeed, after almost every battle of the war the same progression of perceptions would sweep the home front. First came the vague rumors, almost always of a victory. Then came more definite news of the course of the battle accompanying the first rumors of casualties. Over the course of several days there followed confirmation of the killed and wounded, and then came the predictions that this latest victory would be the end of the war. "The gentlemen seem to think there will not be any more fighting," one young woman wrote the day after Bull Run, and they would keep uttering that hopeful sentiment right to the end.[10]

Many of the women made some show of wishing they could be more actively involved, even to the extent of taking up arms themselves. "It is wonderful how the ladies stand it here," a soldier wrote from Gloucester, Virginia, in May 1861. "Mary Lou Byrd is for the *ladies fighting;* she is exceeding anxious to kill Lincoln." Another older woman in the vicinity had composed and rehearsed a scathing speech she intended to deliver to any marauding party of Yankees who might approach her home to threaten her pigpen and chicken house. She actually advised all the rest of her family to move to a safer area and leave her to deal with the enemy alone.[11] More common were the wives and mothers who simply tried to sustain the spirits of their men in the field by assuring them that all was well at home, but even that was difficult. "I am at a loss to know what to write you as news," a Richmond woman wrote her husband in the army on the Manassas line, "for the reason that each moment crowds upon the mind something new in detail, but really of no leading importance in fact to the great struggle." Indeed, the predominant condition the home folk found was that they knew nothing of larger events to tell their soldiers. The authorities kept them largely in the dark about overall military movements, though most accepted that "this is all very proper and as it should be" in the interest of security. Even when military authorities imposed a requirement for civilians to obtain passports in order to leave Richmond to visit friends and relatives with the army, lest too free passage back and forth result in spies infiltrating Confederate works, civilians accepted the restriction as necessary.[12]

Instead of complaint at first, almost a cult of sacrifice arose, stimulated in part by recollection of the measures taken by grandparents during the Revolution. First citizens organized spontaneous gun drives. A friend of Manning's suggested the day after Bull Run that the authorities appoint commissioners for every county to receive contributions of weapons, and the people of Hinds County, Mississippi, took their rifles, shotguns, and pistols to the offices of the Raymond *Gazette* to be turned over to the state to help arm new regiments until the government could provide the men with regulation military arms.[13] Next they collected scrap iron to turn over to foundries to be made into cannonballs and shells, and were soon taking the bells from their churches. Even Vice President Alexander Stephens's church in Crawfordville, Georgia, gave up its musical peal to the cannon's roar.[14]

Not surprisingly, some of the women became the most strident of patri- ots. "Mother & the girls would like to see every one of you & recount to you her various adventures," wrote the son of an Alabama woman. "She has truly become a woman of the Revolution," he continued. "It is now the general opinion that she would make a good Brigadier General." Else- where "the feeling of hatred to the Nation of Wood Nutmegs & horn Gun- flints, Pumpkin pies & wooden Clocks, is growing intence," a soldier's wife wrote at the end of the first war year. "I would not have you at home frail as I am for my life," she declared, *Subject to the ridicule & contempt* of some that are here. If you die at your post doing your duty, I can honor your memory and teach it to your children, and mourn not as those with- out hope." She saw the same sentiments among the other women around her, and believed that "such wishes are not infrequent and the good they are doing our bleeding countrys cause is not fully estimated."[15] Inevitably the number of those who actually found themselves left with nothing but memory escalated after the casualty lists appeared in the newspapers with their doleful news. "My life is all a blank to me now," poor Eliza Moses cried when the battle death of her beloved turned her war suddenly and dramatically from euphoria to tragedy when his body came home. "It makes but little difference to me now, where I am or what I do, so long as I am near as possible to what remains of my lost treasure; and that I do what I feel and know would please him."[16]

That need became more pronounced as shortage and then hunger be- gan to gnaw at them. Immediately after Fort Sumter, when Lincoln insti- tuted a blockade of Confederate ports, the tightening began. Ineffective at first, and never completely effectual, the blockade gradually grew stronger, interdicting more and more of the goods that Southerners could not produce for themselves, and thus driving prices up dramatically in an economy already wildly inflationary because it had no sound currency and an overwhelming load of debt that only mounted as the war progressed. "Every thing looks very discouraging in your line of business," a Georgia coastal planter wrote to his father in the turpentine business in July 1861. "Though some seem to think the Blockade will be raised this fall," he warned, "if it is not you had as well hang up in my opinion." Indeed, turpentine being one thing Southerners could make for themselves from their abundant forests, too many suddenly turned to that trade, driving prices so low as to be unprofitable. "Times are getting hard here," said the son. "Nothing can be bought without the cash."[17]

The simplest articles of daily use rocketed in price. At the outset of the war a gallon of whiskey cost no more than a dollar, yet by July 1863 it had jumped to $60, while a simple toothbrush could cost $5. Sugar went for five cents a pound even when bought from the grower, and as Louisiana and Texas cane fields fell to advancing Yankees throughout 1862, the closure of sources drove the price up dramatically, forcing soldiers and civilians alike to resort to substitutes like watermelon juice. Governor Thomas Moore's wife blanched at what she called "a terrible price" of $8.50 for having a traveling dress made, while the high and mighty like Secretary of the Navy Stephen Mallory had to advise his wife on how to order shoes and clothing through the blockade via Nassau in the Bahamas. Even simple communications were not immune. Postmaster General John Reagan would keep postal rates low, though they still doubled during the war, while the demand of the military on the telegraph lines was so great that civilians had to pay dearly for access. Just a single word going from Milledgeville, Georgia, to New Orleans cost $1.65, while ten words or less to Richmond went for $1.90.[18]

It was in the face of such mounting expense that some communities turned even more to the military, petitioning their governors to locate regimental camps of instruction in or near their towns in the knowledge that inevitably some profit would accrue to them, and perhaps even employment.[19] "Times are hard" became an opening mantra in letters all across the Confederacy. A Louisiana editor complained as early as May 1861 that there were no editorial jobs open. "The military positions I might have sought are filled," he added, and "there is a general suspension of all lucrative employment."[20] Schools like the University of Mississippi suspended or greatly curtailed their classes, with all of the young men and many of the instructors going into the army, leaving the remaining professors without jobs, one even applying for a passport to go to Canada to seek work.[21]

Merchants, meanwhile, found themselves divided into at least two classes—those struggling to continue to do business in the old manner, and those more intent on capitalizing on the crisis by charging exorbitant rates and speculating. Some retailers continued to sell to their customers on credit, as they always had, while others demanded cash and thus made higher profits by not having to wait to be paid in inflated currency, if they got paid at all.[22] Much worse were the speculators, for whom shortages created opportunity. Late in 1861, Tennessee, for instance, laid an embargo on sales of home-produced pork and flour to other states, in order to try to meet its own demands for civilians and soldiers. New Orleans merchants, suddenly finding a major source of supply cut off, while at the same time seeing a rise in value due to the shortage, immediately went west into Texas to buy. "Our people are hard pressed for funds, and they will sell to these Sharpers, the last Beef, or Hog, and the last Sack of Flour, in our State," complained a Texan, when such goods ought to be going to the army and the Lone Star people themselves. Another warned Governor Francis Lubbock that "your Army and people will soon be without provisions unless you take immediate steps to stop the drain caused by New Orleans speculators." The buyers pretended to be acting on behalf of the army in order to play on growers' patriotism to sell at reasonable prices, but of course only took the livestock and flour back to the New Orleans markets to trade for unconscionable profits. "We must be protected or these shylocks will starve us," one Texan demanded. "What good will bushels of gold do us if we are out of food? Stop them, stop them at once."[23] Unfortunately, there was little the state authorities could do to stop such speculation, whether in domestically produced goods or merchandise brought through the blockade. Not only did it drive up the price of consumer articles, but it also tended more and more to concentrate the scarce supply of hard money in the hands of a small merchant class that could demand payment in specie and get it.

Before long the families at home began to send word to their men in the armies of how they had to struggle to cope with the prices and the shortages. Plantation managers scrambled to find shoes for the slaves in order to keep them working, while the mistresses of the houses put their hands to needles and sewing machines to make clothes not only for themselves but also for their blacks, an entirely new experience for most. "In spite of the scarcity of the articles generally, our servants will be even more *abundantly* clad than is usual," a Tennessee girl wrote to her father in the army, "for Mammas machine since Mr Graves rejuvinated it, spins most beautifully." The mother had become almost a clothing factory manager, organizing her daughters so that one traded her piano for a loom, another took up spinning, and all of them worked from 4 a.m. "You never saw so much cloth making in all your life," the girl said proudly. But it came at a price, for she also saw how her mother was being "just killed by inches" as she worried over trying to manage the whole plantation, especially the slaves. "Their tyranny over her is unparalleled," since there were no men left to enforce order. The mother would have preferred to hire the slaves out to relieve herself of the tension of watching over them, but no one in the neighborhood had work for them to do or money to pay.[24]

Some were less willing to suffer the sacrifice or to address the changes that the war required. Not a few planters found themselves charged with breaking the law merely for trying to supply their families, especially after Richmond placed an embargo on cotton. By 1864 the scarcity of goods was such that in limited circumstances the government actually allowed some cotton from the Mississippi Valley to be sold through the lines to Federal forces occupying Memphis, but quickly people from substantial planters to poor farmers tried to get into the trade in order to relieve the shortages. "We made every exertion to purchase these articles in the Confederacy but, at great expense, we met only with failure & disappointment," complained a Mississippi planter on behalf of himself and several others from Bolivar County who were thus stigmatized. "Necessity is said to have no law—we were compelled to save life, & to keep our people at home to purchase from Memphis," he protested. "We all have large families white & black to support—any other course pursued by us, would have brought *destitution & distruction* on us, our people would have decamped—our plantations today would have been barren, desolate wastes." By not allowing planters to sell their produce to someone, even the enemy, they charged that the government actually encouraged hardship and abetted the slaves in running away, since their masters would not have the wherewithal to provide for them, at the same time reducing once bountiful plantations, the backbone of the Southern economy, to fallow fields. "We don't think this the way to conquer a peace," argued one planter. "On the contrary, we believe it to be the opposite."[25] Significantly, however, the logical alternative of converting their fields to some other crop held little allure. Government authorities could impress foodstuffs, and local citizens had little enough money to buy produce. Even cotton could be impressed for military use for uniforms and more, but the driving dictate for such growers was that they were cotton planters, always had been, and felt they had a right to remain so. Had not the Confederacy been founded by cotton planters and slaveowners largely to protect the very interests they now found threatened?

Cotton growers had good cause to fear the destruction of their way of life. In Georgia by the summer of 1862, some eighty counties had suffered an average loss of half a million dollars in the taxable value of their land. All told, the state's capital value of cotton land was depressed by at least $70 million, which would reduce annual tax revenue by some $130,000, or almost 13 percent. Most patriotic planters converted as much of their cotton land as possible to corn for the war effort and to feed civilians, but corn was taxed at a lower rate, good for the planters but bad for their states. It seemed that no matter what course they pursued, there was some drawback awaiting them.[26]

The effect on other established industries was just as severe. Cities like Montgomery and Jackson, Mississippi, could no longer keep their gasworks operating. Telegraph lines, nationalized in everything but name, could scarcely take in enough genuine profit or cash to pay for upkeep, and the railroads suffered a constant deterioration almost from the first.[27] In Texas the president of the Southern Pacific Railroad actually took up old track and relaid it to connect Marshall, Texas, to Shreveport, Louisiana, in 1863 at an expense of $56,000, but only after being required to do so by General Kirby Smith as a military necessity. Smith drafted two hundred slaves and lent them for the work, but still it took a year to complete the job though the distance in new track was only twelve miles. They had but two engines, both in constant use, one passenger car, two boxcars, and four flatcars. In the course of a year in operation that little rolling stock covered 18,250 miles with passengers and freight, employed 21 white men and 200 blacks, carried 3 tons of cotton and 456 tons of produce, and still had to sell 56,320 acres of right-of-way land to cover operating expenses.[28]

The Mobile & Ohio, headquartered in Mississippi, had to pay for armed guards on its trains by late 1863 in order to prevent bands of deserters and tories from robbing its cars, which were so broken-down they could no longer be locked securely. When the railroad's guards were conscripted, it immediately suffered the theft of more than $30,000 in freight. As a result, civilians would no longer ship with it until it got more guards, but it could get none because of conscription. The company's only alternative was to charge even higher freight rates in order to cover its inevitable losses. Yet when it did that, local military authorities spread outrage about the apparent profiteering. Everyone seemed to forget that when the war started the railroads had patriotically halved all their haulage rates and had kept them low, in some cases below cost. Their track and rolling stock were almost ruined; many of their cars were commandeered by the army and transferred to other company lines and never returned. "It does seem to us that we deserve better things than to be held up to public indignation as extortioners," complained the Mobile & Ohio president. Worse, when Confederate forces were driven back, they destroyed the line's track and bridges to keep them from being used by the enemy. Yet for none of this was the company reimbursed. Instead, it was expected to repair and maintain its equipment at its own cost. "As to *profit* to us in running," lamented the president, "I am sure there will be none."[29] Clearly it was only having no alternative to the continued mounting and compounding debt that kept such businesses going, that and a mandate from the government and military that somehow they had to continue functioning. As late as 1865 some of the railroad companies continued the charade of submitting statements to their stockholders, with estimates of dividends due, when in fact the capital value of the companies had declined steadily, they had no money to pay their dividends, and what they did have was almost worthless.[30]

When any society is engulfed in war, peacetime endeavors beyond its economy inevitably suffer, but much more so in the case of an underdog like the Confederacy in which all resources are so strained and overtaxed that even fundamental functions like education are impaired.[31] From early in the war Southern officials and educators worried about the instruction of Confederate youth. "We must not yet lose sight of Educational interest," a teacher warned Governor John Pettus in Mississippi.[32] Yet all too soon the demands of the war machine directed school funds elsewhere, while at the same time the enthusiasm of early enlistment all but emptied many a classroom of the older boys, and later conscription began to erode male faculty. When the Mississippi legislature proposed making boys down to the age of fourteen eligible for military service, the protests rose from many quarters. "Let us, for Heavens sake, avoid an uneducated Government, after our Independence is achieved," complained one citizen. "I should fear vice and ignorance would predominate over virtue and intelligence."[33] Indeed, fears for the future after peace formed the basis of most of the concern over the interruption of education in the present. "There is no evil incident to the present calamitous war, greater than that of the frustration, of the education of the male youth of our land," lamented one of the Mississippi commissioners of education in January 1865. "A generation is soon to be introduced upon the great stage of action, who will not only control the elections, but fill all our civil offices, from the highest to the lowest, who will be uneducated in all that belongs to academical instruction, but deeply versed in the love of violence and arbitrary power." Their future doctors, lawyers, and even clergymen "will be, for the most part, destitute of mental culture."[34] President Davis himself expressed his concern over taking the young out of school and putting them on the battlefield. They should not "grind the seed corn," he said, else they risked devouring their own future.

Of course, there had always been a strain of anti-intellectualism in the South, with even leaders like Louis Wigfall and Robert Toombs declaring that they neither needed nor wanted universities in what they envisioned as a society founded on property and blood rather than intellect. Mississippi's state university at Oxford closed its doors in 1861, and for months thereafter a battle ensued over whether or not to turn it into a military hospital, a battle that some saw as merely an opportunistic continuation of a prewar fight by those who had always opposed the existence of the university in the first place. By late 1862 the battle was lost and invalid soldiers were being billeted in the lecture rooms.[35]

Yet elsewhere state and local authorities made special efforts to continue their universities and private academies. Governor John Milton turned over the Florida state arsenal at Chattahoochee for use as a school or military academy, while out in Texas in 1863 the legislature framed a constitutional amendment to allow the state to sell public lands to raise money to keep their schools going during the emergency.[36] By 1864 in Mississippi, Governor Charles Clark was trying to formulate plans for educating the orphaned children of dead soldiers, at the same time that he, like all other governors, dealt with petitions from hundreds—if not thousands—of teachers and schoolmasters begging for exemptions so that they could continue to teach their pupils. One educator was running his school free of charge to pupils by 1864, and even taught adult soldiers who had been sent home as invalids. By then there was often no more than a single teacher left in some counties, with the conscript officers after even them.[37]

Somehow most schools kept going in some degree, if compromised, with the result that there was a continuing demand for texts. Late in 1861 a group of teachers compiled and published in Nashville a set of new books including a *Confederate Primer* and two editions of a *Confederate Speller,* both of which not only included the customary rudiments, but also couched them in special illustrations designed to build Confederate patriotism in the young. Indeed, this "great and prevailing vice in our system," which the editor J.D.B. DeBow called "*Yankeeism,*" was one of the first educational reforms brought about by Confederate educators and publishers.[38] After generations of learning from texts written and published in the North, there was pride that "the Confederate States will very shortly be supplied with their whole school series by native writers and native presses."[39] Out in Houston another publisher issued a new "Texas Series of Readers" designed to promote patriotic as well as instructional learning, and some schoolbooks even came out in German to serve the German-speaking population in the state's interior.[40] As late as January 1865 a printer issued a new edition of his *Confederate Spelling Book* as well as a first reader, a grammar, a math book, more readers, and even a geography text that showed all the continents and the new Confederacy. The shortage of skilled printers caused delays, and problems were encountered especially in printing maps and illustrations that required chemicals for etching, yet still somehow he did it.[41] In the main, between what was newly published and the large supply of prewar texts still on hand, most students who were able to go to school had at least some rudimentary texts, and especially in the cities not under immediate threat from Yankee invasion, the public schools maintained some semblance of classes.

The private schools faced greater challenges, wholly dependent as they were on the subscriptions and tuition of parents. Many if not most cut back or simply closed. At the same time, the growing movement for education of young women that had been gathering momentum before the war continued, though stunted. After hostilities began, the move to continue creating private female academies continued, even as late as the end of 1864, and sometimes the organizers even used cotton sold through the lines to the enemy to raise the necessary funds.[42] In part they were driven now by the need to produce female schoolteachers to replace both drafted men and schoolmistresses who had for generations been imported from the North, "flimsy creatures" whom DeBow charged with teaching solely for show and sham. Although women were considered to be inferior to men in their capacity for learning, it was still argued that they deserved and of ne-

cessity ought to receive better education than they had been getting in the
South. DeBow, at least, reactionary though he was, argued in conditional
favor of the current women's rights movement that had burgeoned in the
North. "The woman's rights movement has some basis of truth," he confessed, as every reform movement had at least some grievance to address.
The problem came when they went too far, he said, as he warned of the
women's movement making the mistake of trying to achieve full equality
with men. But Southern women were not being equipped to realize their
full, if limited, potential as artists and composers, and more particularly as
teachers and even doctors and nurses for the wounded, DeBow argued.
They ought to be encouraged, though many were not prepared to assume
such a higher responsibility, and in order to take advantage of what the
Confederacy could do they would have to willingly postpone their urges to
marry and have children, he went on. But as to politics, the law, the min-
istry, and other more assertive professions, Southern women had no business attempting to participate. Those in the North who did so "are not
women," claimed DeBow; "they are horrible abortions, nondescripts, utter
perversions of human nature."[43]

In support of the schools and learning in general, libraries were few to
begin with, the principal ones being the state libraries in the capitols of the
several states. The one in Jackson, Mississippi, contained 10,912 volumes
covering everything from official state reports from many states North and
South, and even England, a law library, copies of civil codes, statutes, and
legislative journals and documents from much of the former Union, along
with a large body of world literature and philosophy. The Southern journals like DeBow's were on the shelf beside the *Edinburgh Review,* ency-
clopedias, histories, Smithsonian reports, maps, a number of newspapers
published in the state, and even a city directory of Nashville, Tennessee,
for some reason. Enemy raids presented an ever-present threat, of course.
The Jackson library lost much of its literary works and maps to Yankee
raids, with the most valuable books being carried away and some of the remainder mutilated. Worse, after locks were damaged by the raiders, local
people simply came into the library at all hours and took what they
wanted.[44]

Most prevalent of all in disseminating thought in the Confederacy was
their press. Hundreds of newspapers were being published in 1861, and
even in peacetime such enterprises were often fleeting, some new papers

lasting no more than a few issues. Wartime shortages forced many more to close their doors, especially after 1861. By 1863, Yazoo County, Mississippi, had only one man left who knew how to operate a press and he was just then conscripted, meaning his Yazoo *Banner* might have to cease operations. "It is indispensibly necessary to have a paper in this place," complained a citizen.[45] Especially with a war on, their press was the only source of news other than letters from the front and the swirl of wild rumor. Rhett's Charleston *Mercury* had to give up being a daily, and then cut back from four pages to two, and in the end reduced the size of its sheet before halting altogether in February 1865 on the eve of Charleston's fall. Yet some new papers also appeared, while others came and went. A few foreign language sheets were printed in Texas and Florida, and some regiments actually managed to publish a few issues of soldier newspapers when in the vicinity of a town with a printing press. Journals of opinion also felt the strain. DeBow had to reduce the frequency of his *Review,* then relocated it from New Orleans to Richmond after the Crescent City's fall, and finally he, too, ceased publication in August 1862 for two years before resuming it in Columbia, South Carolina, in July 1864.[46] There simply was not enough paper and ink, nor sufficient pressmen and machinery, to supply a demand that was itself curtailed for want of money in the readership.

Still a great deal of ink was being spilled throughout the war. Somehow the latest novels from England were reprinted, along with some new Southern literature, especially in Richmond, Columbia, and Mobile. The classics and especially histories and biographies remained vastly popular, particularly works on the current war, along with such works as the *Stonewall Jackson Song-Book,* the *Confederate Receipt Book* for cooks, and manuals of drill and tactics to be sold to the army.[47] Just as with the complaints against Yankee teachers educating their young, Confederate intellectuals raised an outcry against the domination of Northern literature over their reading. DeBow pleaded with Confederates to disenthrall themselves from the Yankee grip that corrupted their taste and filled their cultural life with sophistries and bigotry. Moreover, after independence was achieved, Southerners had to stop taking Northern newspapers and magazines. Intead, there must arise a new indigenous Confederate literature. "We may reasonably hope to rival in letters the most polished nations of the globe," he argued. Spurred by such admonitions, Confederate presses did begin to give birth to such historical works as *Morgan and His Men* and

The War and Its Heroes, as well as novels like *The Confederate,* all designed to promote patriotism and embed a distinctly Southern view of
their war for independence.[48]

Hardships seemed only to mount as the war dragged on, even nature con-
triving to make the lot of the home folk more severe. In the summer of
1862 some of the Mississippi tributaries, including the Yazoo River, over-
flowed their banks, ruining crops and spreading the breeding area for mos-
quitoes, leading to an outbreak of fevers.[49] Farther west Texas suffered
severe drought, leading the press to call on citizens to dig their wells down
as deep as thirty-five feet in order to find water.[50] Meanwhile, inland on
the Pearl River, too many years of cotton growing had finally exhausted the
soil, which farmers found almost sterile just when they most needed it for
subsistence. Then worms destroyed much of what corn they were able to
grow, while an undefined plague took much of their livestock. Yankees
were raiding in the region by the late summer of 1862, families were going
without food, the supply of inflated Confederate Treasury notes even dried
up, and many a farmer could produce nothing but tar, turpentine, and firewood, scarcely enough to sell to survive if they could find buyers with
money. The historian J.F.H. Claiborne found himself, he believed, the
only planter remaining in business between the Pearl and Mobile. "We
stand between starvation and execution," he told the governor. Still they
had provided some fresh companies of recruits and were managing to pay
most of their taxes. "We are now proving our loyalty by starvation—by the
tears of our women & the cries of our children for bread!" Their only hope
was to sell what they could to markets in New Orleans, but the city had
been in Yankee hands since April 1862, and state and national Confederate authorities had issued decrees prohibiting trading there, even if goods
could be gotten through the lines to loyal Southern people in the city. "No
government should reduce its people to such straights or lead them into
temptation, if it be possible to avoid it," Claiborne argued. "I take it for
granted that neither the State or Confederate authorities can feed or
clothe us, tho' you have cut off our trade, and it is for you we suffer."[51]

Before long governors not just in Mississippi, but in every state where
markets had been swallowed by advancing Union armies, began to feel
pressure from growers to allow them to trade through the lines, and eventually it would be allowed, even to include limited amounts of cotton,
while a brisk black market went on despite all sanctions. To try to lessen

the hardship, and at the same time reduce the necessity that drove citizens to risk defying the law, governors like John Milton of Florida issued decrees calling on planters to convert their fields to corn, peas, and sugarcane where possible, and give up cotton. Arguing that Confederate success depended upon abundant supplies, he warned that if they were not produced, then they would lose the war. Their slaves would be freed, the rest of their property would likely be confiscated by their enemies, and they and their families would be both destitute and disgraced by defeat.[52] But the planters refused. Not to plant cotton was tantamount to emancipating their slaves, the one just as much a violation of the rights they were fighting for as the other.

When it came to livestock, the voracious appetite of the army almost stripped the countryside, at first by purchase and later by impressment, contributing to a dangerous shortage of meat on civilian tables in many areas. Selling to the government ought at least to put some money in circulation, but the government paid far below what a raiser could get on the local market and took its time about reimbursement. Even Governor Moore of Louisiana got no special consideration. He sold a dozen beef cattle to the army for $540 in December 1861 and was not paid until February 1864, by which time the sum paid was so depreciated that it was scarcely enough to buy a single cow.[53] Langdon Cheves learned after the fact that army commissaries came onto his plantation in Georgia in May 1862 and told the overseer that they had his consent to take several of his oxen, which they promptly slaughtered. They had no such permission. Meanwhile they took all of a neighbor's cattle, and to protests from Cheves and others, the commissary officer's attitude was "characteristic of the contempt of all private rights which the existing practices are generating," Cheves complained. "There is no difficulty in getting beef honestly for the army," he told the commanding general, "but the department must either exert *itself*, or *seize* or *plunder* those who do." If growers' and planters' crops and animals were taken by such seizure, soon they would be unable to feed their slaves, while there would be famine for people and army alike. "The army after devastating a country which might have fed them, will be starved before mid-summer," he asserted, "while the systematic contempt of personal rights must foil all individual effort to avert the disaster."[54]

A Mississippi planter in the summer of 1863 promised his wheat crop to the state to be used for feeding the poor, but once it was harvested and loaded on railcars for shipment, a Confederate agent offered a better price that the grower accepted, and then the military actually took the cars into custody before paying. The railroad president bravely declared that Confederate soldiers could only have the wheat if they used force to take it, and so they did. *"Our unarmed agents cannot fight Bayonets,"* he protested to the governor in explaining why he could not deliver the state's wheat. This *"illegal* interference with the commerce of the country," as he called it, could only amplify public dissatisfaction and private impulses to hoard and speculate, while Governor John Pettus protested to General William J. Hardee, commanding in the area, about the "insolence of office" on the part of the petty commissary and impressment officers who abused their power in dealing with the people, and even insulted the governor himself when he tried to intervene on behalf of the original contract for the widows and children of soldiers in the field.[55]

No wonder growers often hoarded their produce. Cheves sold rice and grits to the military, but when he and others found the price being paid for corn hitting a profitable high, they decided to plant even more to store in anticipation of even higher prices as demand increased.[56] And no wonder some people resorted to speculation and usurious pricing in the civilian marketplace, either to make up for what they were losing on government contracts and impressments or from simple opportunism. In March 1862 the local market in Columbus, Georgia, could present only a meager supply of meat, going at twenty-eight to thirty-three cents a pound. But a Tennessean in the area had killed and packed an estimated 20,000 pounds or more of beef and pork sides the previous December, and was holding it off the market, knowing that the current supply would soon be exhausted and little or no more would be likely to come in from other sources. Then he announced his intention to sell his at forty to forty-five cents a pound, a clear case of taking advantage of the people in their hardship. Citizens begged Governor Joseph Brown to seize the meat for state use. "We had rather see it taken out of our market entirely than to be preyed upon by this Harpy," they declared, in the process actually asking government to trample on yet another property right, this time not out of necessity but retribution.[57]

The individual stories of hunger and hardship caused by shortages and impressment steadily mounted as the war churned onward.[58] "What am I to do with only daughters and old negroes and children at home for meat to use another year?" a Georgia wife begged to know after military authorities seized all of her corn and hogs. "I have since the very beginning of the war divided most cheerfully with the Poor Soldier and am still willing to do my part but to be deprived of all I have is neither Law nor justice."[59] In February 1864 a widow with children was forced to beg for corn, even though she had money to buy it if any had been available. "They all has sum money," protested a friend on behalf of several such women, "but they cant eat it."[60] Another woman wrote of having eight children and nothing to eat. "Dont no what to Doo only to rite to you," she moaned to her governor. If her husband could not be released from state service to come provide for them, "we will starve to Death."[61]

Compounding the problem by 1864 were the hoarders who, finding themselves in the likely path of Yankee armies, only sat on their goods the more, hiding them from impressment for worthless money that might never be paid, in favor of being able to make more from the enemy when it arrived. Planters in southwest Georgia had full corn cribs even after more than two years of war, but refused to open them. "They have plenty of corn, but solemnly declare they have none to spare and refuse to sell a bushel," complained a citizen. "Hundreds of thousands are now without a particle of bread, and under this state of things they must starve or, driven to desperation by hungry starvation, resort to the violence of *bread riots* and mobocracy." He could hear "the low deep mutterings of the coming strain" all around him, he said. "If something is not done, and quickly, to force these corn cormorants to open their cribs to the poor & the non producers it will burst in all its fury." There had to be some way for the state to force open those granary doors. "If you and the State are powerless," he warned Governor Brown, "we will go down in armed force & bring it out though it cost the blood of our own kith & kin."[62] He was right. All across the Confederacy the discontent approached the boiling point. "How cana pour man stand it?" asked a North Carolina soldier who had been three years without a furlough, whose wife wrote him of mounting hardship.

Fully two years earlier, as early as May 1862 when Secretary of the Navy Mallory had visited Danville, Virginia, he had felt troubled by what he saw of the attitude and condition of the women especially, "sad, gloomy, hungry, and without good bread."[63] The lack of uniform prices for commodities from state to state caused nearly as much dissatisfaction and fed the interest of those inclined to speculation. By the summer of 1863 the civil authorities had proposed a convention in Atlanta to be attended by impressment officers from all the states, its goal to set uniform prices, but that did no good to civilians forced to pay the inflated prices charged by some merchants.[64]

It was perhaps inevitable, then, that there would be some sort of explosion, and the overcrowding, compounded by the refugee problem, ensured that it would come in the cities. Richmond, most crowded of all by 1863, capital and center of attention, and so close to the army in Virginia that it could feel its sustenance being drawn off to the military, was naturally the most likely spot. It came on April 2 that year, driven by women whose husbands and sons were off in uniform, and whose money was so inflated it could not buy basic sustenance for themselves and their children.[65] Where it cost $6.55 to feed a family for a week in 1860, three years later it was $68.25 for the same staples. Day workers' wages did not keep up with that kind of inflation, only adding to the problem of ineffective organization of transportation by the military authorities, resulting in abundances sitting in warehouses in eastern Georgia or southern Virginia, while want prevailed elsewhere. Impressment by the army commissaries led only to further shortages and higher prices in the public markets, where basic foodstuffs brought double the price paid by the military.

The frustrated and hungry public had to blame somebody, and the most obvious and easy mark was the merchants, good and bad, whom the discontented tended to lump all together as speculators. For some days in late March a number of the poorer working-class women in Richmond planned a large public meeting to protest high prices. They gathered first on April 1, with the news fresh in their minds that a few days earlier in Salisbury, North Carolina, a similar group of women had stood up to local merchants, demanding a reduction in prices to sell to civilians at the same rates paid by the government. The Richmond women now decided to do the same thing on the morrow. The next morning they appeared in the square in front of the state capitol, which also housed the Confederate Congress, demanding to present their protest to Governor John Letcher. They left their children at home, and some of them came armed with knives and brickbats, and even a few pistols, clearly prepared for trouble if their demands were not met. Indeed, they were already resolved that if the governor did not give in to them, they would take their case directly to the shopkeepers' windows. Inevitably a number of idle teenage boys and a few street loungers also joined the crowd of several hundred, giving it something of the cast of a mob even before they made their demands.

Richmond, the seat of political, social, and industrial power in the Confederacy, with Jefferson's statehouse, capitol of the new nation, dominating the horizon.
Library of Congress

Capitol Square in Richmond, with its equestrian statue
of George Washington, reminding all Confederates
of their Revolutionary heritage.
Library of Congress

Jefferson Davis of Mississippi, somewhat reluctant president, as he appeared shortly before the war. Few executives ever faced greater challenges with more determination.
Library of Congress

An even more reluctant vice president, Alexander H. Stephens of Georgia, the dominant force in shaping seceding states into a new Confederacy that he would himself later wound by his own defection to Davis's opposition.
Library of Congress

The president's executive mansion on East Clay Street in Richmond. From his second-floor office Davis would conduct his wars—with the enemy and his opposition.
U.S. Army Military History Institute

The waterfront in Charleston, South Carolina, just one of the teeming
links to foreign trade that Confederates needed to keep alive
if they were to survive.
National Archives

"King Cotton" on the wharves at Charleston. Should
they use it, and if so, how? Weapon, vital resource, or
curse, cotton policy might decide Confederate fate.
Library of Congress

Industry, limited as it was, would be vital to Confederate survival, especially flour mills like these in Richmond, to feed Southern people and armies.
U.S. Army Military History Institute

Far from the cities, small rural industry could be just as important, like this water mill at Big Spring, Alabama, near Huntsville, as it appeared in 1863.
U.S. Army Military History Institute

Confederates did build some industry during the war, though very little, and almost all of it war related, like the giant Augusta Powder Works in Georgia.
Library of Congress

Amid the struggle to establish a new nation, Confederates
fought a desperate battle to continue old traditions, most
of all the law. Courthouses like the one in Warrenton,
Virginia, had an uphill battle to combat civil disintegration.
U.S. Army Military History Institute

The peaceful aspect of the courthouse in Bowling Green, Virginia, could not
belie the erosion of justice mirrored in broken windows and missing shutters.
U.S. Army Military History Institute

Education paid a price of its own. Many universities and academies in the South simply closed. The University of Virginia kept producing graduates, but competition with conscription officers made students few.
Valentine Museum, Richmond

In Beaufort, South Carolina, the college where fire-eating secessionist Robert B. Rhett was educated could no longer sustain itself even as a library, and would become a hospital for runaway slaves after Beaufort fell to the Yankees.
U.S. Army Military History Institute

Publishers could scarcely keep the libraries supplied in any case. Evans & Cogswell had printed Confederate money as well as books, but by 1865 its establishment was a ruin.
South Caroliniana Library, Columbia

For many Confederate communities, daily life went on as usual until
the coming of hardship and shortage. Country crossroads towns like
Warrenton, Virginia, were just as sleepy as they were before the war.
Library of Congress

In small cities like Norfolk, Virginia,
growers still came to town to set up their
stalls for the weekly farmers' markets.
U.S. Army Military History Institute

The ladies still gathered to sew and talk,
like these near Cedar Mountain, Virginia,
only now they were most likely to be
sewing socks and shirts for sons and
brothers in the Confederate army.
Library of Congress

Nor could the children escape the war's grip. Even the offspring of the prominent, like the son of General Joseph R. Anderson, found themselves involved in soldier play in miniature uniforms.
Valentine Museum, Richmond

Inevitably war's destruction came to their communities and even their own hearths, leaving ruined lives and homes like these in Hampton, Virginia, in 1862.
U.S. Army Military History Institute

The advance of Union armies forced hundreds of thousands to pack what
belongings they could and become refugees, placing unprecedented
burdens on already overtaxed public and private resources.
Library of Congress

Few Confederate communities had charitable institutions as grand as
the Richmond Alms House, and most would be exhausted by refugee
demands, or converted to soldier hospitals.
U.S. Army Military History Institute

Confederates had expected that one source of stability would be their slaves, and
hundreds of thousands would stay faithfully at their labors throughout the war.
Onondaga Historical Association

Perhaps just as many, however, took advantage of civil breakdown to wander from the
plantations, intimidate their owners, or run away to the Yankees like these
"contrabands" on the Joseph Davis plantation in Mississippi.
Kean Archives, Philadelphia

In what was supposed to be a one-party system, the Confederacy soon found itself riven by a growing opposition, founded in the disappointed ambitions and jealousies of men like Georgia's Robert Toombs.
Library of Congress

Governors jealous of the sovereign prerogatives of their states added their nettles to the pinpricks of the discontented, as did Governor Joseph Brown of Georgia, the most obstructive of all.
University of Georgia

More reasonable than Brown, but just as implacable in defense of his state's rights, was Governor Zebulon Vance of North Carolina, to whom Davis would turn in vain for support at the end.
North Carolina Department of Archives and History

Even former friends like Davis's early-wartime aide Louis T. Wigfall of Texas became ardent critics from their desks in Congress. Wigfall extended his political scheming into the army's high command.
Library of Congress

Some of the leading generals made easy converts to the opposition. The jealous failure General Joseph E. Johnston became, in his hatred of Davis, an easy pawn of Wigfall.
Library of Congress

General P.G.T. Beauregard's animosity toward the president matched Johnston's, making him, too, a darling of the largely ineffective cabal that hoped to thwart Davis, even to depose him. *National Archives*

The president's friends made him enemies, none more so than Judah Benjamin, whose unpopularity as secretary of war forced Davis to shift him to the State Department, only to spark renewed criticism. *National Archives*

One friend in particular, however, stood by the president unwaveringly, binding the army to Davis with himself. Yet even General Robert E. Lee, in the last months, considered breaking with the president's policy.
National Archives

By the last months of the war, the Confederacy was simply exhausted. When men old enough to be grandfathers were being conscripted into the ranks, Lee and others of mature cast were forced to face the inevitable.
Courtesy of Herb Peck, Jr.

By the spring of 1865, Confederate officers were meeting with their foes under truce flags all across the South, the only question now being not whether their cause should die, but how. *Vitolo-Rinhart Galleries, New York*

Some simply could not accept the end. Ardent old fire-eating secessionist Edmund Ruffin of Virginia blew out his brains with a shotgun rather than face reconstruction. *Library of Congress*

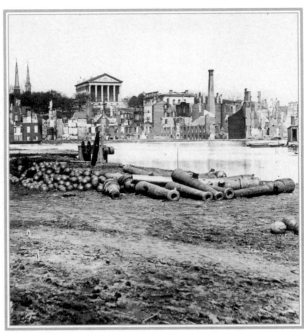

The ruins of the Confederate capital city, Richmond, were a metaphor for the destruction of the Confederacy, though the capitol itself miraculously escaped the holocaust.
Library of Congress

In South Carolina, where it all began, the new capitol in Columbia remained unfinished as it had been at the beginning of the war, but the bricks and determination were there to commence building again. The Confederacy might be gone, but so long as the states remained, the resistance could go on.
Library of Congress

The delegation sent to Letcher came back empty-handed, and though the governor made a brief address to the crowd, he failed to answer their demands with anything more than platitudes and calls for patriotism in the crisis. The next move already agreed, the crowd left the square and moved at first in an orderly fashion toward the principal shopping street. Along the way more unemployed men joined the crowd, and inevitably as they walked the talk became louder and louder, and a new and predictable mentality took over. By the time they reached Cary Street they had become a mob. Now there was not even an attempt at presenting a protest or a set of demands to the merchants, as at Salisbury. Instead, one woman with an axe in her hands simply started chopping at a storefront door, and with one of the men's assistance broke in. In moments the crowd had plundered the place, and simultaneously broke in the doors of several other businesses. Crying "bread" as they looted, in fact they took anything and everything, and when they finished with Cary Street they began to move to another block.

Before long the more responsible in the crowd realized things had gotten out of hand and began trying to calm the looters, while bystanders helped, and the late arrival of the city police began to break up the mob by arresting the leaders. Then Letcher sent state militia to the scene, while he and Mayor Joseph Mayo went there in person to try to calm the women. Mayo tried to shout over the noise to read the city riot act ordering them to disperse, but no one seemed to pay attention. Then Letcher stood on a wagon and spoke to them, with better, though mixed results. Backed now by the militia, he concluded by giving the mob five minutes to break up before he ordered the militia to open fire. That took care of those immediately in hearing of Letcher, and they disappeared, but other portions of the mob on other streets continued their looting until the militia appeared there, too, and arrested the leaders and put the rest to flight. Finally, two hours after the riot began, remnants of the crowd—most of them observers of the riot rather than participants—coalesced once more at the capitol, and there President Davis finally came out and spoke to them briefly, backed by the militia. He, too, warned that if they did not disperse he would order the militia to open fire. Davis was visibly shocked and dismayed, no doubt wondering how the Confederacy had come to such a pass that he was actually threatening to ask soldiers to shoot at civilians, mainly women.

Whether he actually would have given such an order is moot. More likely it would have been a volley over the heads of the mob, the noise and smoke enough to shock them to their senses. The real distress came in even having to make the threat. Several men and women were arrested and later brought to trial, but mainly released with fines, while the plundered merchants simply had to eat the loss of their merchandise. The "bread riot" actually did nothing to alleviate the basic problem, however. Instead, when word of it spread through the Confederacy, other similar disturbances broke out in nearby Petersburg, at two or three places in Alabama including Mobile, and all across Georgia, especially Atlanta, where a pistol-carrying woman simply marched into stores with her friends and forced merchants to accept the prices she offered to pay, or else took goods at gunpoint. In Lafayette, Alabama, more than a dozen women bearing guns and knives staged an assault on a flour mill.[66]

While some met the hardship with violence, others turned to cruel satire. No doubt remembering Jonathan Swift's "Modest Proposal" to solve the problem of poverty and overcrowding among the Irish by having them eat their children, George W. Bagby, correspondent for the Richmond *Examiner* and the Charleston *Mercury*, launched a similar suggestion a few months after the riots. Viewing the tens of thousands of poor and refugees in the capital, he asked, "How to provide for them?" His answer was to take thousands of empty tobacco and whiskey hogshead barrels and turn them into "elegant and commodious" homes, each one able to accommodate a family of six if they squatted down. Packing peanut shells and old newspapers around them would provide insulation to preserve their body heat in the winter. By this and other means, Bagby thought the Confederacy could get off the streets some 60,000 blacks, 920,000 "men and women of pleasure," half a million Jews and extortioners, and a million of the poor. The blacks did not need to be fed, "for they will live on edible dirt," and if they needed more they would steal it. As for the rest, he proposed that they eat one another. "The common repugnance to human food is but a foolish prejudice, born of modern philosophy and political economy," he argued. Gamblers and whores should take it in turn to eat each other, while the Jews should dine on the restaurant keepers, and then themselves be fed to the poor living in the barrels. The blacks, of course, would eat the poor, "so that the dangerous classes will be destroyed at a blow, and nobody left but Government and negroes." That would finally and permanently see "the Sociology of the South established on the only firm basis possible—a basis which the slow cannibalism of modern antagonism between labour and capital would hardly reach in a century." Naturally the blacks could not be eaten. It would be an outrage to racial sensitivity, as well as a destruction of property.[67]

Not only did the bread riots send a shiver through the authorities. It also suddenly brought the men of the Confederacy up against the unalterable fact that the war was changing their women, cracking the pedestals and tarnishing the sheen that generations of idealization had carefully nurtured. When the war began, the inevitable DeBow had presented to the new nation yet another of his hyperbolic portraits of Southern life as people chose to believe it to be, in spite of what any critical intellect knew to be fable. "The Women of the South," he declared, were better than men, which "no true and brave and generous man will deny." They were more sympathetic and sensitive, more loyal and faithful, better educated, and all around "better, by nature." A woman had one-tenth the physical strength of a man, but ten times the moral might. She could resist the temptations of drink and vice that most men fell victim to, and whereas men fell prey to extravagance, "few women exceed their pecuniary means, because they have enough of moral courage to restrain them from improper indulgences and expenses." Clearly DeBow spent little time in the company of the well-to-do men who complained constantly that their wives were spending them into bankruptcy, or of those who so closely controlled the money available to their wives that even little extravagances were impossible.

"Man's passions are too strong for his reason," said the foolish editor; "woman's passions are under the control of her reason." She was, to be sure, not physically as brave as a man, nor as ready to throw herself in harm's path, yet she could meet death with greater calm. When it came to public affairs, of course, women had no business in government for they had less sense in that area than men. Yet DeBow did not deny that in the home, the Southern woman often exerted the guiding hand, perhaps even as a "power behind the throne," being her husband's closest counselor. "Nature intended woman as the helpmate of man," he said. In reality, of course, her rule of "the roost" was not nearly so much a sign that she did have independence and capability for management as an artifact of the abrogation men had long since made of leadership in the home. Running the family was "women's work" not because women had asserted themselves to take it, but because men had decided it should be theirs.

Women also led the South in its communion with the Almighty, one of the reasons they were less given to violence and crime than men. The ladies "possess fine instincts and little reason," according to DeBow, and somehow that made them idealistically superior, gave them more common sense refined by higher virtue. Those were just the sort of gifts needed in the present emergency. "Since our Revolutionary struggle there has been no crisis in public affairs which required so much of intelligence to comprehend and so much of self-sacrifice and fortitude to meet, as that in which we are now engaged," declared the editor. Indeed, it was the women who had been ahead of the men in embracing secession, he said, without giving any evidence of just where he came by that wonderful notion. "Too many of the men lagged behind," he went on, but now those men "say the women, from the first, were right." Their wisdom would be vindicated, and they would themselves wield a weapon in their deliverance. "Virginia will owe her delivery from the vile and vulgar despotism of Yankeedom almost entirely to her women," he said. Indeed, the Old Dominion would not have seceded but for them, and in the days ahead they would keep their men fixed to the purpose of independence.

In recent years great strides had been made in increasing the education and intelligence of Southern women, but happily it had not come at the expense of their delicacy and refinement. "They confine themselves exclusively to the pursuits and associations becoming their sex, and abhor the female lecturers and abolition and free love oratrixes, and Bloomers, and strong-minded women of the North," DeBow wrote. Never until secession had they interfered in public matters, which only made the purity of the cause the more. "No husband should ever act on his wife's advice, for she knows not all of man's affairs," the editor continued, but rather he should consult with her, and then form his own opinions, though DeBow added that once done, more often than not a man would find himself siding with his mate, even though she be prone to "a good deal of jealousy and rivalry, and some censoriousness," meaning, politely, that she could be a nag. Certainly women were more irritable than men, "but their irrationality does not often rise to anger or passion, and, under due and ordinary restraints, their little expressions of indignation, their querulousness and petulance, are the chiefest charms of their nature." Asserting that "they are as remarkable for their talent for quarreling as for their deficiency in argument," DeBow predicted that a woman would always lose in an argument with a man.[68]

Somehow DeBow's fatuous stereotype failed to embrace the image of a hatchet-wielding rioter battering down shop doors, screaming at soldiers and police, or going before the bench charged with civil disturbance, nor did it include the destitute wives and mothers who by 1863 were all but pleading with their governors to send their men home, or writing directly to their men practically encouraging desertion. "It is impossible to whip the Yankees," a poor North Carolina woman harangued her governor. "If we are to bee slaves, let us all bee slaves together, for there is, I see no other chance." Nothing else now mattered but staying alive. "The blood of our Dear ones is crying louder than the blood of Abel," she declared, and "you and some of the rest of those big bugs will have to answer for the blood of our dear ones who have been slain."[69] Missing from DeBow's portrait were the thousands of women actively abetting evasion of the conscript laws, and of the soon-to-be-common women in the factories and the women left to run the plantations who actually managed to step into the man's world and make it work. The war virtually forced new roles on most Confederate women, changes that worked strains on husbands and wives alike. In December 1861 twenty-two-year-old Ellen Moore, a Virginia wife with two children and one stepchild already, wrote to her husband to inform him that she was pregnant again after his last visit home, and having a hard time facing the raising of the family and running the household as well. "Do you wonder that I have the blues?" she confided to him. "Was there ever such a woman?"

In fact, there were hundreds of thousands, and in a scenario repeated innumerable times, what evolved was a gradual release of responsibility by the absent male. At first Ellen's husband tried to retain his control by telling her in his letters what she ought to do in managing the slaves, making expenditures, even disciplining their children, and demanding in return that she tell him everything that happened at home. When enemy troops threatened their home, at first her husband told her to get away, but then made the break that so many men in the army did when he told her that, in the end, she must decide for herself. Later another furlough and yet another pregnancy only made Ellen's lot the harder, and the more she thought and acted for herself, the more strain it placed on a marriage now chiefly sustained by intermittent correspondence. Toward the end of the war, each feared that the other had become too used to living alone.[70] By 1864 husbands with the army all across the front began to realize that they could no longer control affairs at home, nor make the decisions that once

had been routine for them. High and low, "you must decide" became a repeated refrain in letters from the army as the men recognized that they
had no alternative but to loose their control, at least for the time being, and
that their wives, having faced so much of hardship, sacrifice, loneliness,
and even danger from the proximity of the enemy and rebelliousness
among the slaves, were up to coping on their own. Even former governor
Milton Perry of Florida, forced to be absent from his plantation in the
summer of 1862, confessed, "I of course think of our interests at home, but
know that you will do all that can be done. These things do not therefore
concern me, or rather do not cause me the slightest uneasiness."[71]

Yet there was just cause for uneasiness, if not for the ability of the
women to cope with the ordinary challenges of keeping the family going
without their men, then surely for the special dangers and burdens caused
by the war, and none more so than the breakdown of law and order caused
by the siphoning of men away to the armies. Early in the war there was uncertainty just when the men were called away for a day or two for a militia
meeting or drill. "Our slaves were never more obedient, I believe," a Georgian wrote in January 1862, "but women & children sometime *feel* a little
insecure when left to themselves when not only the white man on the
place, but all his neighbors are gone for a day."[72]

Soldiers and their wives had to depend on each other and Reagan's
mails to sustain one another's morale and will to continue, and for many it
was increasingly an uphill struggle as the war dragged on. Charles George
went to war with the 2nd Georgia Battalion of Sharpshooters in 1861, full
of optimism and confidence. The first disappointment came late in the
year when, instead of fighting glorious battles, he found himself posted
pointlessly in what he called "this frog pond country" near Norfolk, Virginia. "I wish I was marching thirty miles a day where we could get good
water," he complained. Transferred to north Mississippi, he got his marching wish, only to be part of the Confederate evacuation of Corinth, where
even his uniform was lost in the hurried withdrawal. "There is no quiet or
peace untill after night and then I think that it is the most quiet lonesome
place I ever saw," he wrote during the retreat. "How would [you] like to
have a real bad head ache and a half a dozen field bands (drums and fifes)
blowing and beating all around you and three or four thousand men walking and kicking up the dust all over you."

By New Year's 1863 the optimism of earlier days became more and
more difficult to maintain. In places largely untouched by the armies, like

Houston, editors could still crow that "the heavens are bright above us; Earth smiles beneath our feet."[73] But closer to the continual scenes of action, even an event like the visit of President Davis to the Army of Tennessee camped around Murfreesboro could not cheer some. "He made no speech nor took any notice of the crowd of soldiers who came from their camps to see him," Charles George wrote. "No one cheered him—some one tried to get up a cheer for him but failed." This was evidence not only of growing war weariness, but also of Davis's peculiar unfitness for the role of inspiring Confederates. A few months later George would be with the army at Chattanooga, "the *lowest, dirtiest, filthiest* hole now in the Southern Confederacy," according to him. The merchants had sold out of everything they could speculate on, and now were offering the soldiers nothing but an abundance of cakes and strong ginger beer. "I dont know what kind of *beer* it is, but suffice to say that any of it would kill any man who wasnt a soldier," George wrote. And stronger spirits in town were seized by the provost and kept for private speculation at $20 a quart. "It takes all their wages and much more so that a great many of them are not half clothed, and because they have spent their money for whiskey," George continued. Such cynicism spread rapidly. By March 1863 he had seen enough of it that he told his wife, Mary, "I believe that every one is making so much money out of the war that they dont care much wheather it stops or not." Then he turned his discontent toward the noncombatants in the army and those at home evading conscription who boasted of battles they had never fought. "I usually find our greatest braggarts to belong to those departments," he grumbled.

He was even disillusioned with his new army commander, General Joseph E. Johnston, who had replaced the congenital failure Braxton Bragg. Hearing of his wife's destitution and the scarcity of hard money, he surmised that she would have "plenty of the *Confederate on hand to put into bonds* that will hardly be worth the paper it takes to make them." His cynicism had not long to last before a bullet ended it for him at Marietta in the spring of 1864 during the Atlanta Campaign. In his last letter he wrote to his darling Mary that "if it is God's will I want to live." For the rest of the war she carried those words with her. "When I read my Darling's *last letter,* and see those precious words," she wrote a few months later, "I feel like 'taking up the song where he left off the strain'—Death has no power here, oh our love was so much *stronger* than death so much stronger."[74]

The separation could be tantalizingly cruel. "We must keep trying to get

letters through for it is all the pleasure I have on this earth is what few lines
I receive from you," B.F.R. Jeffares wrote home from Virginia in December 1864. Worse was knowing that his native Georgia was largely occupied
now by the advance of General William Sherman's army, that Atlanta had
fallen and Savannah was about to be taken. "You cant imaggin how bad it
makes me want to see you all when I hear what a condition you are all left
in, in that country it seems to me that it is more than I can bear to stay away
from you & that Dear & sweet child, oh if I could just see you with the natural eye as plain as I imagined I saw you in my sleep last night I thought I
had you embraced in my arms but it turned out to be only a Dream when
I awoke up I was crying."[75] It was hard for soldiers who knew that their
families were in harm's way in besieged cities like Petersburg, Virginia, or
Atlanta, especially when they saw for themselves that Yankee shells could
kill civilians as well as soldiers. An Alabama man at Petersburg in June
1864 calmly reported the deaths of three women and children in the
shelling and the funeral that followed, then poured out his worry and loneliness. "If you had any idea what a source of satisfaction and how gratifying
to know and feel I am not forgotten I think you would write," he chided his
wife. "While the picket walks his post to and fro to protect me from our
deadly enemies, how cheering at that dark hour when nothing is heard but
his sturdy step, to think some loved one far away from these bloody fields
of strife had asked protection for him in her secret prayers."[76] There were
innumerable cases of soldiers on the front learning that a letter had arrived, and standing up and running heedless of enemy fire. "I got out of
the Ditch and ran threw the whistles of minnys and the bursting of Shells
to get my letter," David Denney told his wife from the lines around
Atlanta.[77]

Robert and Eliza Corry of Greensboro, Alabama, perhaps best reflected
the progression of the long-distance relationship that so sorely tried man
and woman alike. At the end of 1861 the family joked that Eliza's giving
birth to yet another baby girl might provide an excuse for her father not to
have to go to war. Indeed, he kept out of the military for several months.
Early in 1862, Yankee raids forced Eliza and the children to go to Decatur,
Georgia, outside Atlanta, for safety, and she urged him to come on after
her to find work in one of the government offices there. Eliza's mother had
rented her home to the government to be turned into a factory for making
army caps and had rented a slave out, too, giving them more than enough
income to rent a comfortable house. "We can have a nice time in Deca-

ture," Eliza promised. But Robert could not stay out of the army forever, and by early 1863 he had enlisted in an Alabama cavalry regiment, though with scant enthusiasm. "We have been favored more than I had any hope of and in this stage of the game am not anxious to win distinction or honors," he told her. "I don't care one cent if the war closes, and history leaves my name out of the book. All I want is peace and happiness with the privilege of being with you."

Soon enough Robert would witness firsthand the gradual deterioration of army morale. One evening in November an entire company of his regiment, including its captain, simply deserted. Soon thereafter they were camped near Okolona, Mississippi, unable to find pork or beef to eat, reduced to buying potatoes at $3 a bushel and collard greens. Worse, he knew, as did everyone else, that in the spring Sherman was likely to advance toward Atlanta, and Eliza and the children on their rented farm were right in his path. "The Yanks may visit you all again and drain you of your all," he feared, and gave specific advice on protecting the farm and the cotton gin, especially on what to do with the cotton bales already stored. "Let no one have any [as] this is all we have and may be of some service to us yet." Whether he was anticipating more shortages, or perhaps even what would come after defeat, he wanted to have a cushion for his family. He prayed that the people around Decatur were kind to his family while they lived there as refugees. "If anyone in that country who has anything to spare and suffers Mother and you to suffer or want for anything, I shall never cease disliking them and shall wish all manner of meanness about them," he promised. Then he made the same break so many other men in the army did. "I wish I knew how to advise you so as to make your pathway smooth and easy, but cannot—all I can say is keep in good spirits and never give way to the blues or evil forebodings." All he could give her now was assurance of his love. Otherwise she was on her own. "I would give up all my interest in the *Spirit* and *Glory* for the prestige of being near my wife and little ones," he told her, "but we may do our Country better service here and it is the duty of a good soldier to obey orders and not complain."[78]

The letters that came into the army camps reflected the same concerns, and often scarcely alleviated the anxieties that dogged the soldiers. Eliza wrote to her Robert at night when their three children were asleep "and I can't work for thinking of you." By Christmas 1863 she was so worn out from her struggle that she suffered recurring chills. "I don't know what I shall do dear, if I get very sick or even feebler than I am now, and you away," she wrote in words that impelled thousands of Confederate soldiers simply to leave ranks and go home. As for the cotton he wanted to hoard, she had already made a decision herself, and decided to sell it for a paltry ten cents a pound in return for payment in gold coin. That was far less than the bales' value, but it was hardly safe from Yankee raiders, and "I am willing to sacrifice a good deal to get something for it." She was only one of several women in her area who were thoroughly taking charge of their domestic affairs, many of them even taking cotton bales to town to barter for groceries. "We have little use only for the necessaries of life," she assured Robert, and even a little gold would go a long way, especially after her mother managed to barter for 1,500 pounds of pork. They would not starve. A year later she was still struggling, and still keeping the family together, even after the fall of Atlanta and the passage of Sherman's armies. "I am sun burnt quite brown attempting to dry fruit this hot summer," she complained. "I haven't a great deal dried, having so many other things to do in the mean time—I wished so much for your help—it is such a social enjoyment and we could have had many a cosy chat over a basket of peaches." Inevitably the brave veneer cracked from time to time, however. "I try to keep a cheerful heart and feel it won't last much longer, but oh dear husband you know not the thoughts I some times have to contend with—Sometimes it seems almost like a dream that I am your wife."[79]

No wonder men deserted. "How can a pour man stand it," moaned a North Carolina soldier who had not had a furlough in three years, on hearing of his family's deplorable condition. "I waunt to ast you or enny other conc[ion]able man what is the pour man fitting [fighting] for," he asked Governor Zebulon Vance. "We are fiting for the Rich mans property & negars—that [is] just what we ar fiting for—the pour man got nothin to fite for—what little he had is gon to Ruin & disstruction—An the Big men at home a setting studdying how to cheat & speculate out of the pour soulgers Wives." It was more than he could bear. "I had as liv dye as hear talk of my wife suffering," he went on. "I am Bound to go home som how." He would prefer to do it on a furlough, but if he had to go without one—desert—he would do so and he would not promise to come back. "A man cant stand evry thing."[80] A year later another Tarheel soldier claimed that two-thirds of the men from his state in Lee's army were saying they would not go into another campaign in the spring. They wanted the authorities in the states to do something to end the war or else the soldiers would take it into their own hands somehow. "They say plainly if they cant go home they will go somewhere to get out of this trouble."[81]

After Sherman laid siege to Atlanta in the summer of 1864, such expressions, when spread, added gloom over the army. "This is a dark hour with us dear," Corry told his wife. His only hope was that renewed active operations would repel Sherman long enough for war weariness in the North to defeat Lincoln's bid for reelection. If that happened "the old yankees will certainly lose some of their perseverance, and something will be said about peace." But Sherman took Atlanta in September, and by October the likelihood of a Lincoln victory seemed assured. "Last night I could hardly go to sleep for thinking of how much you are suffering," Robert wrote his Eliza after a brief visit home. "I am so anxious for you to look and feel as you used to do dear wife. You used to smile and look happy, but now you look so sad and low spirited that it pains me more than any thing in the world." With the world collapsing around him, he needed for her to remain the same somehow as she had been before the war. He begged her to do as he tried to do, to "pass things over and fret as little as you can well help." Yet even love could not halt the ravages of anxiety, malnutrition, and exhaustion.

By early 1865, Robert was run-down as his regiment could find only corn bread and old and bad beef to eat, and that was running out. Then in February Eliza told him that the latest enemy raid had hit their neighbors and cleaned them out, though the Corry farm was as yet untouched. "I am afraid we lack a good deal of being safe," she confessed. People were taking their livestock deep into the woods and camping out like soldiers to hide them from the Federals. Worse, a cold winter and scarcity of tools and draft animals meant that they had not yet been able to start plowing, "a poor prospect ahead for making a crop this year." Then there was Eliza herself. "I am afraid if you were to see me, you would think I wasn't looking as well as when you left, for with the nursing and yankee excitement I am not fattening much." Her teeth were abscessing, all the children had been repeatedly sick, and his last visit had been so brief and filled with anxiety that it did none of them any good. If she did not hear from him soon, she was going to go to the army herself to find him, "so look out." At the same time that she stepped out of DeBow's demure role in her determination to go to the front to seek the comfort of her husband, she also made it clear that after a few years' practice, she had become as sharp as any man in driving hard business dealings. Every time she spent any of that little hoard of gold from the cotton, she browbeat the merchants into a liberal discount for paying cash.[82] By April 19, 1865, Robert had had more than enough. "When will this dreadful war terminate?" he asked in probably his last letter. "I hope soon for I am growing sick of it especially as we are having reverses on every hand and have no encouragement in the world." Indeed, even then the wave of surrenders was under way that before long would sweep westward to engulf Corry, too. "The fact is darling I can hardly refrain from running right off and going to you." By that time, tens of thousands of others had already done exactly that.[83]

When invading Yankees finally took a community, the women left behind often suffered terrible emotional distress.[84] "I suffered too much, was to[o] crazed," said Flora George when Macon, Georgia, fell in April 1865. "I have no words to tell you how utterly wreched and broken my heart is." The men who were there, too, whether those had been too old for the army or those who were furloughed homesick or discharged for disability, suffered the same. Flora's husband, Parker, was destitute, desperate to find employment, and yet spent by the war. She found him "so much changed the *end* is so bitter for him."[85]

8

"We Are Done Gone Up the Spout"

THE STRAINS CAUSED by the war machine's hunger appeared early in the new nation, and did nothing but grow ever more oppressive as the conflict unfolded. They affected not just individuals and their relations with each other, but those of whole communities and states. Easily the most visible and pervasive of all was the drain of manpower brought about by the voracious appetite of the armies. At first, of course, tens of thousands of young men flocked to their county courthouses and village greens, eager to enlist and experience the excitement of a "war" surely destined to be so short and glorious that they might well miss it entirely if they did not sign up right away. Indeed, during the early months, President Davis and Secretary of War Leroy Pope Walker had no choice but to refuse to accept some regiments proffered by the states because the government had not weapons to arm them nor the wherewithal to support them.

Moreover, with equipment and weaponry in short supply, Davis rightly chose to try as best he could to put it in the hands of regiments that would enlist for terms of two or three years, rather than the nine to twelve months that many of the volunteers and governors preferred. That was a campaign in which he won most of the battles over enlistment terms, without ever completely winning the war, and the result was an army organization littered with a confusion of terms of service, and so many one-year regiments at the outset that in April 1862, when those terms expired, there was the real danger that much of the Confederate army would simply evaporate unless those men chose to reenlist, which in the end most did.

Yet within weeks of those reenlistments, and in fact well before, there were already problems arising in the shape of Southern men unwilling to fight for their new country, and anxious to seize upon any exigency to escape service. Despite the much exaggerated Minuteman tradition of service that the South shared with the North from the Revolution, the stark fact was that such voluntarism had always been primarily in the interest of immediate local defense, of protecting specific homes and hearths, and not those of the polity in general. Many a Georgian or Texan was simply unwilling to volunteer and leave his home and family unprotected in order to go defend Virginia or South Carolina. Confederate democracy was simply too new yet to have instilled in its young manhood a universal sense of civic obligation, especially since support for the idea of the Confederacy itself was so uneven and, in many areas, fragmentary at best. Hundreds of thousands surely would volunteer before this war ended, but just as certainly hundreds of thousands of others determined from the first to exert every effort to stay out of Confederate gray, especially after manpower demands pushed Congress and Davis to resort in April 1862 to the first of three conscription acts designed to compel men into the armies.

No sooner did the president sign that first act on April 16, 1862, in fear that otherwise expiring enlistments would dissolve his army, than pressure forced Congress to begin what would eventually be an avalanche of exemption provisions for certain occupations and classes of citizens. That, plus the active connivance of some governors and communities anxious to keep their own men in their own states, inaugurated a perpetual tug of war over men of conscription age. Even before the act, Florida complained in March 1862 of being destitute of soldiers and arms. The state armory had only enough ammunition for 5,000 additional men, plus a few swords and pistols, and one flag on a six-foot pike.[1] In June, Pontotoc County, Mississippi, protested that from a voter roll of 2,800 males, the county had already furnished 3,000 volunteers, with a mere 379 men left in the county, and most of them subject to conscription.[2] Within months Governor Francis Lubbock of Texas would complain to his friend President Davis that "Texas is almost denuded of her best fighting men," and extracted from the president a promise that he would ask Congress for no more men from the Lone Star State for the time being.[3]

In Georgia and elsewhere, men liable for the draft began enlisting in local and state militia or home guard units in the expectation that Richmond did not have the power to order them out of their states.[4] Knowing that militia officers were certainly exempt, in Crawford County, Georgia, seven innovative men already on the conscript rolls and awaiting orders organized themselves into a militia unit containing only themselves, and then promptly elected each other officers and asked Governor Joseph Brown to give them commissions, which he did.[5] It did not help that in the desperate need for manpower, Confederate conscript officers often overstepped their authority in violation not only of the civil law but also of the conscript act itself. Men of the 17th Louisiana Infantry, a twelve-month regiment whose term was long expired by the fall of 1862, found themselves being held in service against their will despite orders for their discharge. Worse, many of them were already over the age of thirty-five, even though the conscription act specifically said that such men should be discharged. "As citizens of Louisiana and as ardent supporters of the doctrine of States rights," said one, they appealed to their governor to protect them from the War Department's apparent contravention of congressional law.[6] Yet all too often they would discover that their civil authorities, their judges and their habeas corpus writs, and frequently even their governors could not protect them. Before long dark ancestral memories of British press gangs and the oppression that sent their grandfathers to war stirred in their brains, only now the oppressor was Richmond and their own new nation.

With Richmond and the statehouses in conflict over conscription and exemptions, and with the growing number of men determined to serve neither master, the loyal population felt even greater unease as enemy armies began to encroach on Southern soil. Even after the fall of Forts Henry and Donelson in February cost the South control of the vital Tennessee and Cumberland Rivers, many kept their spirits high. "Notwithstanding the great disasters the public spirits here do not seem depressed," declared one Louisianian, "but look forward confidently to a successful result."[7] But then in April, New Orleans fell bloodlessly to a Union fleet, and within weeks warnings came that Vicksburg and central Mississippi were to be a target by both land and river. "We have had flood, cotton burners, hog cholera, murrain with our cattle, and are soon to have Yankees," complained Mississippi planter James Lusk Alcorn to Governor John Pettus. "What we are to do heaven knows—we do not," he went on. "Oh, that the past lethargy of our Government had been changed to vitalized exertion."[8]

Even those who took pride in their achievements thus far in support of the war found themselves sobered. Most Texas planters, unlike others elsewhere, stopped planting cotton and sowed their fields with corn to feed the armies. A grower from Dallas exulted that "to contemplate the vast amount of flour & grain that this section of the state has afforded, & to now see the windows of every store house grinning, with white sacks, is most cheering for the support of our army." But sustaining those bulging granaries demanded the entire working force of the country, and so many men were enlisting and being conscripted that future harvests would be in peril. "If the agricultural pursuits shall fail," he warned Governor Lubbock, "our army must inevitably fail."[9] At the same time, industries like Georgia's Atlanta Rolling Mill, under contract to produce vital railroad rails and iron plating to armor Confederate gunboats, found conscription forcing so many men into the army that the shortage of workers would prevent it from fulfilling its orders.[10]

No wonder demoralization began to set in early, especially in those areas where support for the cause was never strong from the start. Following the Confederate defeat at Pea Ridge, Arkansas, in March, and at Shiloh in Tennessee in April 1862, and with them the loss of hopes to hold significant portions of both states, a group of citizens of Helena, Arkansas, protested that "we are now overrun by a brutal and unrelenting foe, our wives children and every thing dear to us is exposed to the wants and appetites of an unprincipled army who are now in force within our state." They had seen enough already to fear what was to come. "The desecration of our household Gods[,] starvation and unparralled suffering will be the fate of our people unless some relief is speedily afforded."[11] One Shiloh veteran of the battle just went home to Decatur, Mississippi, declaring that he had lost his mule in the fight, and if the government did not reimburse him, he would never return to his regiment. In fact, he never did go back, but instead became a lightning rod for other disaffected deserters.[12] As early as 1862, Louisiana, Mississippi, Alabama, and Georgia, especially, began witnessing the growth of bands of such dispirited and disenchanted men, augmented by those dodging the conscript officers, and even others who were avowed tories and Unionists. It was only a short step to their turning into predators rather than patriots.

A soldier's sister protested to Governor Thomas Moore in Louisiana of a band calling themselves Prairie Rangers who had been terrorizing the unprotected women of Bayou Chicot and elsewhere throughout the summer of 1862. "Prairie Banditti would be a far more appropriate name," she declared, saying even Lincoln's soldiers would not be as bad. "As often as that lawless band visits this part of the country, outrages of the deepest dye are daily committed in our midst," she protested. The renegades entered and pillaged their homes, often wantonly destroying what they did not steal. "They do not as much as respect private rooms, but enter in spite of tears and entreaties, and turn up beds, rip them open, search closets, brake open what happens to be locked, [and] in fact they leave no corner untouched." Local civilians expected that before the end of the war, the Prairie Rangers, their plundering done, would simply join the Yankees and attempt to incite the rest of the countryside to do the same. With all of the adult men in the area away in the army, the women were helpless to resist, though this wife hinted that if the governor or Richmond did not do something to protect them, then they would help themselves, "and I think that *Your Excellency,* will discover that soldiers do not all ware breeches."[13]

From Whitfield County, Georgia, a minister sent a similar plea to Governor Brown, detailing the depredations on the helpless citizenry by "so caled Partizan rangers who have formed them selves into companies in order to keep from the conscript law." By night the men stole horses from barns and corn from cribs, while in broad daylight they were "robbing little children who will have to suffer after Bread." Some farmers began to conclude that it was of no use to grow anything, since they could not protect themselves without more men being allowed to remain at home. "We look to you for protection," the minister complained to Brown, begging that more local men be exempted or else state troops be sent to their aid. "We must have help or our county is ruined."[14]

Similar expressions of community demoralization and outright terror came from most of the rest of the rural Confederacy beyond immediate reach and protection of the regular enlisted forces, and they only increased in number and volume as the war entered its later years. On New Year's Day 1863, even as Lincoln was issuing his final Emancipation Proclamation as testimony to the Union's determination, the governor of Texas was forced to promulgate a proclamation of his own that recognized just how uncommitted many of his citizens had become. "There exists within this state a spirit of Rebellion and insubordination," he declared. Bands of lawless men were openly wandering the state, advising citizens to ignore the laws of the state and especially to resist enlisting in Texan and Confederate regiments. In some counties they had actually armed and organized themselves, and while they were apparently not yet preying on the citizenry, it seemed probable that they would in time foment a clash of arms with the civil authorities, a small rebellion within a rebellion, a little war within a war.[15]

In fact, thanks to the absence of the best men in the armies, and the growing danger posed by those who were evading the draft and staying at home, communities in the less populated states felt increasing unease and vulnerability. Texans brought their pleas to their governor in growing numbers, and governors of adjacent states began to discuss their mutual problems and what they could do for themselves. In May 1863, Thomas Moore of Louisiana asked Lubbock to meet with him and the new commander of Confederate territory west of the Mississippi, General Edmund Kirby Smith, to address the problem. "The large proportion of the good material of our State is in the Army, pretty much *all* the bad left," protested Moore. The "bad" were using all their influence to prompt resistance to conscription on cries of unconstitutionality, and helping men fleeing the draft to congregate in the remote fastness of the swamps far from reach of what little law could be brought to bear. Worse, state militia sent after them often showed little stomach for acting against their fellow citizens. "I have almost despaired of accomplishing anything," Moore groused. "We can spare men, if they can be forced to do their duty, but the demoralization of the people at home from various causes is very great."[16]

This problem of getting the local civil authorities to act against their own friends and neighbors rapidly became widespread. While Moore and Lubbock were conferring, people in Lawrence and Marion Counties, Mississippi, complained to Governor Pettus that large numbers of deserters and conscript fugitives were roving in bands killing livestock, and local officers were doing nothing to stop them. If they did not do something to make examples of the offenders, it would only encourage desertion and evasion.[17] In Claiborne County planter Richard Archer lost seventy-five to eighty horses, numerous oxen, and all of his wagons. Worse, with the threats of a campaign against Vicksburg now a reality in May 1863, as a Yankee fleet bombarded the city and General U. S. Grant's invading army even then marched around east of the city to trap it between his soldiers and his gunboats, panic and disorganization worked to the advantage of the renegade groups, who encouraged slaves to run away to join them or go to the enemy, the design being to prevent Confederates from impressing their labor in further attempts to resist the Federals. Archer lost 160 blacks that way, and heard rumors that the people of Port Gibson, which Grant took on May 1, had actually encouraged their slaves to go to Union lines rather than see the Rebels use them, and then themselves arrested Confederate authorities who were sent to stop the blacks.

Loyal Mississippians spoke darkly of taking revenge by burning Port Gibson if they could, an ironic echo of Grant's own—perhaps apocryphal—declaration that the town was too beautiful for its conqueror to burn. "The difference between the Federals and our own citizens," complained Archer, "is that the latter if they had the courage to do so would possibly robb both enemies and friends but really robb our people only." The resultant demoralization was so great, he complained, "that no power can arrest it unless the Executive can do so."[18] In Texas local state militia were protecting their friends and neighbors from being sent to the army by enlisting men subject to the conscription act, and then refusing to release them when they were actually drafted.[19]

The governors did what they could, but it was little enough. Even with his own interior under invasion, Pettus had to try somehow to divert 7,000 of his state militia from local protection to War Department use in resisting Grant. In Georgia, Governor Brown appealed to General Braxton Bragg, then commanding the Army of Tennessee at Chattanooga, for assistance combating what Bragg called "organized bands for purposes of plunder," because Brown had not the wherewithal to halt their depredations himself. Bragg promised that he would show no mercy, yet then and for the next several months his attention would be occupied exclusively by the Yankee army in his front. In Texas the consumption of manpower by conscription had been such that the state was even trying to swallow citizens of other states who had come there as refugees from advancing enemy forces. A manufacturer making percussion caps for the Lone Star armory protested that he could no longer meet his orders because he could not find a workman over the age of fourteen. At the same time, in Florida poor Governor John Milton protested that his state, which had a voting population of males of 12,600 in 1860, had by now furnished 15,000 men for Confederate service and was now in the face of a call from Richmond for another 1,500 men, and he doubted there were that many left between the legal conscript ages of eighteen and forty-five. With all of them gone to the armies, there would be no one left to maintain civil peace except young boys, old men, and the lame.[20]

Sometimes all they could do was issue more futile proclamations, like Brown's September 5, 1863, plea for Georgians to rally to Bragg's army in the face of a new Yankee advance against Chattanooga, but even this only risked removing that many more men from maintaining local stability.[21] Moreover, by 1863 the marauders were not always just deserters and conscript dodgers. Langdon Cheves found that bands of regularly enlisted and serving soldiers broke into his plantation house just outside Savannah, plundered it of everything, stole his fence rails, took all the tools from his mill, and even robbed his slaves of their beehives and chickens. "They are habitually prowling about my fields & quarters, night & day, breaking trunks, letting water into & out of the fields so as to destroy the crops & doing all manner of wanton and malicious mischief," he said. Even in the act of protesting to their department commander, General P.G.T. Beauregard, Cheves confessed that he dared not complain for fear of reprisals from the soldiers, even that they might return and burn his buildings.[22]

No wonder, then, that as early as the summer of 1863 a growing number of civilian communities were feeling demoralized, disillusioned, and even defeated. Richmond felt the upset of inflation and limited shortages, and, of course, the bread riot, but was otherwise largely untouched directly by what the countryside experienced. Thus people like the journalist Littleton Washington could be optimistic. Despite Lee's crushing July defeat at Gettysburg, the strategic situation in Virginia remained unchanged and most of the state lay securely in safe hands. Even a disaster like the death of Stonewall Jackson in May he could view as an act of Providence. God had sent Jackson to the Confederacy as an example of courage, duty, and fidelity to his country, thought Washington, and as he walked the capital streets in Jackson's funeral procession, Washington concluded that Stonewall had accomplished his mission, and thus his Maker called him home.[23]

But away in Louisiana, Alabama, and other states feeling both Yankee pressure and their own inability to maintain stability in their communities, Stonewall's example seemed lost on lesser mortals bound more to their own safety and interests than to their new nation. The mere rumor of a new enemy invasion set officers and men in Texas to speculating that the war was lost and the only way for them to end it now was for all of them simply to leave ranks and go home. "If every man left his Regiment to go home to protect his family, the Army would soon be dissolved," complained General John B. Magruder in a special order to the men in his command.[24] He was right, of course, but the more the men in the ranks heard of the deprivation and depredations being inflicted on their families, the more their conviction in the cause diluted. That September a soldier in the 8th Georgia Battalion, at home in Fannin County on a furlough that had already been extended twice, declared that if it was not extended again, he would simply refuse to return to his command, even though that very day the Yankees occupied Chattanooga and set foot on Georgia soil. "There is no sens of fighting any longer no how for we are done gone up the spout," declared Private John Hopper. "The confederacy is done whipped it is sensles to deny it any longer." Many others from his unit were also home on furlough with no resolve to return, while numbers of others had simply deserted, and the people of their community showed no inclination not to support them. "The people here are nearly all unanimously against [the] war holding on any longer," Hopper wrote to a brother still with the army and encouraged him to desert as well. "There is no dificulty now in staying at home [and] no opposition from the citizens," he added. "I can tell you if you can only get here with out being took up it is all right—for in the place of opposition you will have protection."[25]

More than anything else it was fear that fed the loss of home morale that would make families condone desertion. Just such fear appeared early for the Confederacy, earlier, indeed, than it should have. In the fall of 1861, even amid the months of seeming peace and expectation of victory that followed the surprise Rebel success at First Manassas in July, and well before the denuding of the country by war demands and conscription, communities felt their safety and tranquility imperiled from within. In Marion County, Mississippi, one "rascally" man with the unlikely name Zachariah Kornegay refused to enlist, and instead preyed upon local livestock, burned houses, and encouraged slaves to run away, declaring that once the rest of the local men were all gone to war, he would boldly live off his neighbors. Though the county was trying to raise a company to send to the army, men balked at enlisting out of fear of what Kornegay would do after they left.[26]

The problem escalated rapidly when the deceptive "phony war" following Manassas turned into a very real war indeed early in 1862. By the summer, when Pettus had to call out the Mississippi militia in response to the new threat following Shiloh when Grant's army marched onto state soil at

Corinth and the first Yankee advance from New Orleans moved up the Mississippi toward Vicksburg, a wave of protest swelled from the state's planters and manufacturers, and especially from the wives. One wealthy cotton grower heard the small subsistence farmers asking "what is to become of my little crop," not needing to add concern for their families. At the same time, he expressed his own and his class's fears for their homes and families "when left in a land swarming with Negroes without a single white man on many plantations to restrain their licentiousness by a little wholesome fear or visit with condign punishment any act of wrong or insubordination."[27] Despite most states having laws requiring the residence of at least one white man on any farm or plantation on which there was even a single slave, the practical effect of national conscription, militia calls, virtual drafts, and enlistment worked in direct conflict with such statutes. By June some fifteen companies, totaling well over 1,000 men, had already left the area of Oxford, Mississippi, with 300 more ready to go. Pettus's call for militia would take 200 more from the remaining 259 men, meaning that there would be plantations with up to 100 slaves or more without a single white man to keep them in check.[28] In the Alabama counties along the Tombigbee River, there were nearly 230,000 slaves, yet some counties had not more than one white man left for every thousand of the blacks. By October 1862, Governor John Shorter had to warn the president that "a spirit of insubordination has already manifested itself."[29]

By the end of the year Governor Moore in Louisiana learned that conscription had virtually cleaned out some communities. Rapides Parish complained that with ninety-six poor and destitute families averaging five children each in one town, only five healthy men remained.[30] In Texas, Lubbock heard that Bryant's Station had eighteen women and thirty-five children, and not a single man except a shoemaker, and he was eligible for the draft at any time.[31] Jones County, Georgia, had one settlement of fifty families without a single man, and not one of the poor women or children with the means of going the twenty miles to the nearest mill to get flour. Even the disturbed and insane were not immediately beyond the grasp of the draft. One woman entreated Governor Brown to release her insane son, fearing he would kill himself if taken from home. "I wold beg for him on my bendid nees if I was thair," she pleaded. "I no you can send me Relief and you a lone for thair is no mercy hear."[32] In one county in Texas, three-fourths of the serving militia were drafted into Confederate service in September 1863, and on his own authority, Governor Lubbock suspended exemptions even for physicians when General Kirby Smith issued an urgent call for 10,000 more men, despite the fact that in some counties there would not be a single doctor left within a radius of twenty-five miles or more.[33] The drain was so great that in San Antonio, the police force evaporated to just one man who also acted as the stagecoach driver and postal agent, and he was about to be drafted.[34]

The pleas to spare men for protection, or to release sons and husbands from the army, only mounted as the war intensified in 1863 with no end in sight. Wives begged to have their husbands sent home, even if just long enough to bring in the crops to subsist the family, and all the while there were protests that no one was around to keep the unruly slaves in line. A mother with a son who had enlisted in the 1st Georgia Infantry when under the legal age, and who was now ill, begged the governor to secure his release and take her husband instead. "I love my country and are willing to make a sacrifice for the good of our country," she protested. "I will give up the father of my children to his god and country," she went on, "for my darling boy he has never been in a school room and aught to of been sent to school before becoming a soldier."[35] Plantation mistresses also wrote of fears for their own lives, not to mention the slowdown in vital agricultural produce needed by army and people alike with no one to keep the slaves from loafing.[36] In October 1862, Congress had finally addressed this problem by passing a specific exemption recognizing those state laws requiring one white man per plantation where there were slaves, and further providing that in states with no such laws, any plantation with twenty or more slaves should be exempted.

Yet even this contemptuously dubbed "twenty-nigger law" caused unrest, for it afforded special exemption and special protection to the wealthy. Their crops would be tended, their homes protected, their families left secure. The poor farmer who had no blacks, or even a dozen, had to still leave all in the face of the conscript officers. In May 1863, Congress sought to mollify the controversial law by limiting it to plantations belonging only to women, minors, the insane, or men already away in service, and further requiring that any man exempted to manage the slaves still had to pay a commutation fee of $500 to the Treasury. Moreover, the amendment empowered the president to grant special exemptions to poor and working-class men in those communities already stripped of their manpower. Even this, and subsequent modifications that all but ended exemptions for plantation owners and overseers alike, however, never removed the stigma of favoritism and special protection for the rich.[37] Democracy did not just require security in order to flourish; it needed equal security, but Confederate democracy, driven and yet compromised by the pressures of the war from the outset, could deliver neither.

The result was predictable, if unavoidable. By the summer of 1864, as a Union leviathan commanded by General William T. Sherman had marched south through north Georgia and stood poised at the gates of Atlanta, the only thing equal about protection was that it was impotent against either foe or friend. A planter wife told Governor Brown she had been burned out of two homes, though somehow she had managed to keep her blacks together. Her corn crop was planted late and only half grown, yet now she faced having her one white overseer conscripted. That would leave her and her two daughters "with hundreds of Negroes round & Yankees constantly seen in the woods." What was she to do?[38] In Tippah and Tishomingo Counties, Mississippi, all of the men but the old and infirm were in the military and all the slaves had been driven away or had run away. Women and children worked all the farms, wives and mothers drove the oxcarts to Okolona for salt and meal, and not enough men remained in one six-mile area to bury the aged and ill when they died. There were too few teams to plow the fields for what was going to be a short crop anyhow, and insufficient manpower to grind the sugarcane when harvested. "We are surrounded on two sides at least by a population in part disloyal & mixed with Bushwhackers & deserters," complained one old man, "ready at any time they may find us in a defenseless condition to pounce upon us & commit the worst acts of depredation & violence." What were they to do?[39]

The scramble for exemptions had been unseemly from the outset. Even before national conscription and some state militia drafts, anxious men asked if members of the legislatures would be protected.[40] Soon there came petitions to except doctors and pharmacists, ministers, teachers, millers and salt miners, and even makers of spinning wheels. In time Congress would grant many such exemptions, but still more sought to evade uniform. When Governor Lubbock saved men subject to the draft by placing them on special state details to tend livestock, one aggrieved citizen actually took out an advertisement in the Houston press and ran it for ten weeks in protest at the abuse of power.[41] Later in the war, even those who had enlisted in the state militia refused to appear for muster, fearing that it was merely a ruse to put them in the hands of regular Confederate military authorities.[42]

It was a predicament made all the harder to bear by the fact that in many places a number of men managed to secure exemptions, or simply evaded the conscript officers, yet did little or nothing to relieve the community's distress, most of them protected by connections of wealth or politics. In Catoosa County, Georgia, a poor farmer had all five sons in the army, while a wealthy doctor managed to keep all his boys at home, as did several other rich families. "They want other people to do all the fighting," he complained. "Such people aught to be drafted and made go." He begged Governor Brown to stop the operation of conscription, "or must myself and wife have our hearts tourn from us driping with patriotic Blood?"[43] Another aggrieved citizen spoke of his frustration at seeing "young men who have nothing to do here but promenade the streets, sit on boxes in front of the stores to comment on the passers by & drive in the afternoon *fast horses* & who will not aid with money services or any other way in the defence of our country." They even refused to help tend the sick soldiers who stopped in town.[44] In Georgia county court clerks appointed friends as deputies to grant them exemptions. "I have known instances of such appointments where I doubt if the Deputy ever wrote one line in the office during his life," complained a judge, who was himself besieged with applications to somehow get serving soldiers out of the army by giving them civil appointments, and to use habeas corpus writs to free others from service.[45] Soon enough the non-slaveowners who perceived the origins of the Confederacy in the oligarchy and its fears for its property came to dub the conflict "a rich man's war, but a poor man's fight."[46]

In Vice President Stephens's hometown of Crawfordville, a group of men paid a $1,500 bribe to a court official to certify fraudulent exemptions.[47] Out in Mississippi one George Harris, "as great a Clerical Ass as ever brayed," according to one citizen, had no church but proudly paraded his exemption as a minister supposedly received in return for his wife's entertaining a general and staff at dinner. Worse, four men in Jackson persuaded a captain to excuse them from the militia by substituting slave men instead, which not only outraged people on racial grounds, but also raised again the specter of the wealthy having the means to evade service, while the poor had no blacks to send in their place.[48] In Florida, Governor Milton found many men under the draft limit of forty-five who had themselves fraudulently elected justices of the peace and to other unessential offices in order to qualify for exemption, while all across the Confederacy young men simply left town when the conscript officers arrived and went somewhere else for the interim, as with many who left Savannah and Brunswick, Georgia, and sojourned in Marietta until it was safe to go home again.[49] In reaction, a few unscrupulous conscript officers actually told shirkers that unless they enlisted in the Confederate army, the military would simply arrest them and in the next battle put them in front of the soldier lines to be "made a living breastworks of."[50]

Yet when President Davis and Congress enacted yet another reform in the exemption laws in the spring of 1864, to make more overseers eligible, the protest from planters was just as great. "Without meaning to be disrespectful to the Confederate Govt," complained a planter from Thomasville, Georgia, in April 1864, "I must as a citizen say that the conduct of military affairs just at this time is in my opinion most unfortunate." His complaint was not that Sherman and his armies were poised on the verge of invading the state, but rather that in the face of such an emergency, Davis now had the power to draft men responsible for "the direction of Negro labor" and getting in their crops. "If the War Dept exercises the power given as I doubt not it will, we must inevitably go overboard shortly."[51] To tamper with the efficient management of the slave machine was to endanger the cause itself. Worse, in practice it created feelings of betrayal. Plantation mistress Mary Christian already had a husband called away from the farm by the militia. She had paid $500 in commutation for the exemption of her one male overseer in late 1863, but then the army conscripted him anyhow under Davis's new provision, and she had no husband, overseer, or money, and no way to manage her plantation and its twenty slaves. "I raley think I am treated worse than enny other person by the Government," she complained.[52]

Before long, every governor began receiving protests, often anonymous, sometimes including the names of the miscreants. From some communities like Spalding County, Georgia, came joint protests signed by whole committees of ladies over the exemptions and evasions. "Just look at our poor boys what has gone & died," they cried in June 1864 with Sherman approaching. "What account will our country be to us after all our friends are gone." The time to put absolutely every man in uniform was now or it would forever be too late. Old and young alike had to be made to go.

Just go round about these towns & see the men—they don't know the war is going on—they care nothing for nobody but themselves—they can speculate of[f] soldiers wives—make fortunes of[f] them. Just look at the women & children that are begging bread [with] husband in the war or perhaps dead . . . This has been an inholy war from the beginning—the rich is all at home making great fortunes. . . . Now will you go and take all the rest of the men & whip them at once & then we will have peace & if you cant go you must try & stop it some other way.[53]

It was not lost on many that an embarrassing number of the men who had called for war were now reluctant to fight in it. "Most of those who were so willing to shed the *last* drop of blood in the contest for separate Government," complained an Arkansan remembering early war blusterers, "are entirely unwilling to shed the *first*."[54]

The enormous diaspora of refugees from areas occupied by the Yankees added significantly to their hardships, as did sick and exhausted soldiers furloughed from the front, placing burdens of feeding, housing, and care on already strained communities. "It is hard to have to lose every thing," confessed the Spalding ladies' spokeswoman, "but I do think it the best to stay at home & take what comes—all cant run from them—the poor has to stay—they cant get away."[55] In fact, the refugees had been an increasingly burdensome drain on their civilian hosts almost from the beginning, for everywhere that a Union force advanced, there were those who refused to suffer occupation and enemy rule. Taking as much of their property with them as they could aboard trains or wagons, they moved to the proximity of friends or apparent security behind Confederate lines, and at first those friends were wholly sympathetic. "We who are in comparative safety, scarcely know the extent of the loss & inconvenience our friends on the coast are now experiencing," an acquaintance in Georgia told Langdon Cheves in February 1862 after agreeing to take for safekeeping the property Cheves sent from his tidewater plantation under threat of enemy advance.[56] Occasionally Southern authorities essentially evicted them for their own good, as when General Albert Sidney Johnston ordered the evacuation of women and children from Bowling Green, Kentucky, in December 1861 for fear of an enemy attack.[57] Elsewhere, as in New Orleans in 1863, Union authorities expelled those refusing to take an oath of loyalty. "Where they are to go, or what they are to do, is more than I can see," complained a sympathetic observer. "This entire country is in commotion and there is no such thing as procuring transportation for anything—scarcely for a person." Confederate soldiers so occupied the operating railroad in the buildup to meet Grant's advance on Vicksburg that not a single civilian could get a place on the cars.[58]

"It is a horrible thing to be compelled at our age to be forced from your homes," a friend complained to Louisiana's ex-governor Thomas Moore in January 1865 just after relocating to Texas. Moore had already preceded him, the impulse to escape the Union yoke gripping high and low alike.[59] Those who could took the means of their support with them. One Louisiana fugitive opened a store in San Antonio just as the war was closing and begged associates to "make my house known to your many refugee friends," adding that "we must stick to each other."[60] They took their slaves with them, for they represented not only their most valuable mobile property, but also the means of support away from home if customers could be found to hire their labor. Indeed, the Spalding ladies complained that the wealthy refugees "are afraid their niggers will be taken but don't care what becomes of the poor class of people [just] so they can save there niggers."[61] In February 1865, Robert Barnwell Rhett himself turned refugee as Charleston fell, and moved to Alabama. In his haste to "save" all of his more than one hundred slaves, he almost left his own wife behind.

Stories of outrages suffered by those who stayed at home under Yankee rule only fueled the impulse to become refugees. In Atlanta, following its fall and evacuation in 1864, scavengers and other refugees came in and occupied empty houses and appropriated furniture and any other loose property. Yet when Union authorities allowed citizens to return after Sherman left that fall to march on Savannah, the squatters refused to move. They claimed that the Federals had given them the property, or even that since it had been in Yankee hands, and was then abandoned, such property now belonged to any finder.[62] A woman in occupied Natchez, Mississippi, was, along with other ladies, robbed of everything, some even being imprisoned and physically searched by a black woman. "That is more horrible than any thing else," she grieved, "& you are subject to the insults of the negroes." Yet in some towns safely behind Confederate lines the wealthy would not help refugees, or even take recuperating soldiers into their homes for care, but left them to further burden the common folk. The Natchez woman openly prayed that such uncharitable people might have a visit from the Yankees in order to teach them to be more hospitable to those in need.[63] "The rich set back and seem to regard a wet and hungry soldier as something beneath their notice," grumbled an Arkansan in uniform. "They will certainly receive their reward."[64]

These well-to-do were many of the same men who so enthusiastically supported secession at the outset—the ones who so confidently blustered that independence would be so quick and easy that they would eat all the flesh of those killed in any war, and drink all the blood spilled. Now in mid-1864 still "those that brought the war on is at home & our boys are fighting for there property," complained the Spalding ladies' spokeswoman. While many invalid men sent home from the armies were actually willing and anxious to be detailed to perform some useful service, some of the wealthy and fit continued to hide behind their influence. Speaking for hundreds of thousands, the spokeswoman declared that the poor had borne the brunt of the rich men's war more than long enough. Now, she protested, "I think though some of the blood drinkers ought to."[65]

Such glaring inequities—no doubt exaggerated by many in their resentment—only fueled the estrangement felt from a system that could not protect civilians from either the enemy or, worse, their own onetime friends and neighbors now turned into predators. By 1864, Mississippi was a case study for such effects. In Jones County at least three hundred deserters from Confederate regiments had armed themselves and plundered loyal citizens at will. Near Yazoo City, Major S. M. Dyer led a company of conscript evaders, deserters, and layabouts, many of them described as professional thieves. "The whole command is a terror to the citizens and a disgrace to the Confederate Army," a local protested to the governor. And the local militia, to whom people should have been able to look for protection, were themselves being conscripted by Confederate officers in direct violation of the governor's exemption.[66]

The Jones County band became so strong and feared that other groups of renegades from neighboring counties began to ally themselves with Major Dyer rather than risk competing with him for plunder. "They have become quite bold," a judge complained in February, "and in some sections of the country have so intimidated the people that to save themselves and their property from depredation and pillage they are beginning to give them aid and comfort." This bowing to the threat of the renegades was such that almost every loyal man was afraid to say anything against the deserters for fear of retaliation, especially after they murdered one Baptist minister, forced another out of the county, plundered every house in the village of Trenton, and then brazenly fought and defeated a small force of state militia reserves. By this stage of the war the militia reserves were almost universally composed of the too old or the too young, the frail and even disabled, and those who sought a place in the home guard to avoid conscription and the regular army. Whatever their background, they were the dregs of Southern mobilization, many scarcely capable, and the rest hardly motivated to risk their lives. As a result, they avoided confronting bands like the Jones desperadoes as often as not. "They never interfere with anyone except a sick or discharged soldier," complained the judge, "or some man who darsent try to evade them." As a result, anarchy reigned, and the whole community lived in fear. "Unless it is checked," warned the judge, "all law and order will soon be suspended and every loyal man driven out of the country."[67]

Yet it could not be checked. The governor had to order his militia commanders to do their duty, only to be told by some that they could not help with the Jones insurrection because they were fully occupied dealing with similar bands in their own counties. The roving bands burned houses and barns, emptied corn cribs and torched cotton stockpiles, and robbed and beat citizens on the roads and even in their own homes. Many no doubt merely used the war and the breakdown of civil order to pursue old prewar grudges and feuds, but most were turning lawless out of simple opportunism in the legal vacuum. The spirit of dissolution even spread to other civilians, like the workers at the Mississippi Manufacturing Company at Bankston, where cobblers making shoes for the army rioted and threatened to burn their factory before Confederate cavalry arrived to quell the incident.[68]

Pettus's successor, Governor Charles Clark, tried to strike back. Some of the deserters were arrested in the Bankston area, even though some militia men simply refused to hunt for them. Clark authorized county sheriffs to appoint any number of deputies from among loyal men, and they made some headway with arrests.[69] Authorities sent the 20th Mississippi to Jones to attack the heart of the problem, and by May they had arrested some five hundred of the renegades, including four whom they tried and hanged for desertion and insurrection. It was the first time an example had been made, but at the same time the officers in charge could miss the fact that many in the citizenry were so demoralized and dispirited that they had encouraged sons and husbands to evade conscription, especially after earlier excesses by Confederate conscript officers. "Distress and want in their families induced many of these men to desert their colors," declared department commander General Richard Taylor," and the officers of the 20th Mississippi could see that in Jones.[70] The women especially feared hunger if their husbands went into the army.

"The females are decidedly the working part of the population," observed an officer in the regiment, yet they had seen other wives close to starvation when unable to work the fields while their men were in uniform. Provisions were scarce already, some had no cash crops like cotton to augment their meager subsistence, and one widow whose husband had been killed by Confederate cavalry previously sent to round up deserters was now reduced to making and selling combs of animal horn to avoid starvation. "These acts have done more to demoralize Jones County than the whole Yankee army," observed the same officer. If only the state could do something to ease the hardship of civilians like these "it would be productive of a much improved moral and political sentiment," he suggested. Full bellies and enough cotton and wool to clothe themselves would make patriots of them again. "It would convince them that we have a Government, a fact which they are inclined to doubt."[71] He was so right, and in that doubt, bred from fear and insecurity, lay the poison to cripple any democracy.

The problems in Mississippi were hardly unique, but rather represented the civil discontent all across the Confederacy among communities beyond the immediate protection of one of its armies. Even in Virginia, where the presence of the seemingly invincible Lee and his army kept morale more buoyant than anywhere else in the South, the decay still set in. Louis Wigfall found that the community of Oakland near the southern border of the state had become a conduit for deserters from Lee's army on their way to North Carolina, and the citizens condoned their action by giving them food and water as they passed through.[72] Loyal citizens of neighboring Carroll County protested to Richmond that their countryside was "the main thoroughfare for deserters from the army of Northern Virginia," and that "disorders and crimes of every kind are committed by them along the route they travel." In Lee's army itself there was a growing sympathy with those who simply went home, and who could be surprised? A county justice in Carroll asked Secretary of War James Seddon "what will be the conduct of the soldiers in the field, when they see the helpless and wretched condition of their families at home?"

Is it to be supposed that they will stand idly and indifferent with folded arms, looking calmly on, while their wives and children are freezing, starving, pining and dying from destitution and want, without clothes to cover the nackedness, without shoes to protect their feet from the frozen ground and snow, and the fearful frenzy produced by hunger unappeased. The man who reckons they would reckons idly. Would it not produce desertions, mutiny and rebellion?[73]

Rumors that Yankees were taking old men and young boys and arresting them to send north to an uncertain fate might have been untrue, yet they led to great unrest among sons and fathers in uniform.[74] Some stories proved to be unbearable, none more so than the plight of the women who worked in the textile mills at Roswell, Georgia. When Sherman's columns approaching Atlanta came upon Roswell, they destroyed the mills, which were producing cloth for Confederate uniforms, and then for reasons never adequately explained, arrested several hundred of the women and deported them and their children first to Nashville and later to Louisville, where they had no choice but to hire themselves out to stay alive. Some never managed to return to their homes, others were forced into prostitution to live, and a few simply died, leaving husbands in perpetual anguish and confusion at their fates.[75] In Milledgeville, Georgia, after Confederate authorities abandoned the town and almost all of the men were away in the army, the convicts in the local penitentiary got out to terrorize the remaining women, burning buildings, stealing livestock, pouring sorghum on the ground, and even stealing the children's clothing. The people had to ask advancing Yankees for protection. "Nearly every woman in the county is ruined," grieved Mrs. M. C. McCombs. "The men used them as they pleased." One woman was driven insane after repeated rape, and apparently a few others died as a result of the brutality.[76] The necessity of catching and bringing to military justice men demoralized by such strains on their families spread its own malaise in the army. Colonel David C. Glenn, once attorney general of Mississippi, served on the military court in the Third Corps of the Army of Northern Virginia, but by October he had had enough, complaining that "trying and shooting Confederate soldiers from one year to another is more than my disposition would stand."[77]

In Georgia, the imperious Governor Brown, who was disinclined to negotiate with anyone when it conflicted with his view of his sovereign authority, was finally forced by exigency to come to a compromise with alien citizens of Atlanta to grant them exemption from state conscription in return for their agreeing to form a company of their own to try to protect such unfortunates, while in Jefferson County, not far from the South Carolina border, citizens were so fearful of their inability to "subdue any insubordination at home" that they asked to have the enlistment age for local defense units lowered to just fourteen. Somehow they thought that arming children, along with some dog packs, would cow their insolent Negroes, who no longer feared the women.[78]

No palliative worked in the end, and right until the last days community unrest grew steadily as a direct function of the ability or inability of authorities to provide security and stability and to stave off fear. In August, as Union forces readied to an attack on Mobile, Alabama, the Confederate commander of the region, which included southern Mississippi, had to admit that he could spare no troops to protect the latter area, but pleaded instead for Mississippians to leave their homes at risk and come to aid him. Worse, he could not even arm them. Any who joined him must bring their own guns and ammunition.[79] At the same time, some 15,000 Union cavalry were advancing into Mississippi from the north. Clark and the state government had already abandoned Jackson and made their capital in Macon, almost at the Alabama line, a clear admission that the government could not protect even itself, and now Clark confessed that state forces were not adequate to meet the new threat, and that the part of his state not already conquered would likely fall.[80]

The best Mississippi militia could do was to make sporadic and opportunistic strikes. They began summarily trying and shooting renegades and deserters in the summer of 1864, with the inevitable result that some executions were no more just than the acts that had brought them about, and complaints were heard from some communities that entirely innocent men were put to death out of haste or prejudice, which served only to further alienate the civilians from a government that had always seemed distant, disinterested, and somehow unreal. And then when state forces left after visiting punishment, the outlaws often returned to exact their own vengeance on locals who had assisted the militia.[81] They destroyed bridges and ferries to keep militia from moving freely, at the same time trapping the civilians in their communities, and then boldly declared that they would not allow any further enrollment in state militia units to be carried out, even managing to destroy the county rolls that detailed eligible men.

No one could stop them. "This County has more civil officers at present than it ever had at one time," protested a justice in Jones, yet no legal business other than the probate court could be carried on. There were ten justices of the peace, five constables, three or four police commissioners in each district—all able-bodied men. Yet not a single justice's court or circuit court had met there since the beginning of the war, he grumbled, "and if a man is found dead the Civil authorrities pays no attention to it any more than if it was a dog."[82] By the end of the year the sheriff of Winston County, which was just as riven as Jones, confessed that "the deserters are emboldened," and he could do nothing to stop them, while the sympathy for them was such now that he thought the only hope for any success lay in requiring militia to hunt deserters in other counties but not in their own.[83] County officers began simply refusing to attempt to arrest miscreants.

By early 1864 the governors began receiving outright pleas for peace, and at any price. "We want this war stopped; we will take peace on *any terms* that are *honorable*," a North Carolinian told Governor Zebulon Vance in January. "We would prefer our independence, if that were possible, but sir we prefer *reconstruction* infinitely to *subjugation*." Clearly reflecting the attitude of the poorer class in the Confederacy, he declared that "this never was a war of the majority; with all its horrors it has been forced upon the people contrary to their will and wishes, and it is now perpetuated by the minority against the will of the majority." Their hearts had never been in this conflict, and with their country devastated, their crops subject to seizure, their young men pulled into the army against their will, "what we most want and need is *peace, blessed peace*." They seemed to win victories, yet everywhere the Yankee heel stood on their land, and the North had proven itself just as determined as the South, and with much more abundant resources. "The tide is against us, everything is against us," he warned. "I fear the God who rules the destinies of nations is against us."[84]

The only hope by January 1865 was that Congress would finally do away with all exemptions of any kind, requiring everyone to go into the army, a crowning irony in that communities that had started by pleading for exemptions had come around to pleading for their extinction. Townspeople still sent petitions begging for protection from the bands of blacks and renegades. Clark tried to call out the entire militia at the end of March to cope with the deserters, but was warned of the disaffection it would cause by forcing boys of sixteen and under and men over fifty-five to abandon the women and children and crops for which they were now the sole support. "Both the militia man and the soldier will therefore likely desert," warned a friend, "for say what you will, men are not going to remain in service if their families have nothing to eat."[85]

As late as April 9, the very day that Lee was surrendering hundreds of miles to the east, one militia officer promised Governor Clark that "the last man in the country is being caught, and sent to the army," yet that same day the endorsements by officials on citizen pleas for protection noted that the authorities were doing all they could and could do no more.[86] Even ten days later, having confessed that the militia's strength was inadequate to protect civilian security, Clark had to read reports that his militia was full of boys who had enlisted the moment they turned eighteen in order to evade conscription into the regular Confederate forces. Having escaped from national service, they were refusing to honor their state obligations as well. "Written orders will never get these men," Clark was warned. "They are protected by their officers, many of whom, to my knowledge are deserters."[87] In Texas, Governor Pendleton Murrah tried vainly to stir his supporters by declaring that "there are still good men enough left at home to arrest such outrages as you complain of if they would band themselves together for that purpose, and stand by the civil authorities."[88] But they would not.

That soldier who lost his mule at Shiloh and decided never to return to the army had by now become the leader of a deserter and dodger band of his own. "The party has now become so strong that the community in which they live have to submit to any demand they make," complained one Mississippian the day after Christmas 1864. The outlaws defied militia sent to arrest them, and even when the county sheriff summoned a posse, the deserters simply dispersed into the swamps and canebrakes. Their women made certain they had good warning of danger by blowing horns and trumpets whenever there was a sign of the law, each blast setting off another so that in only a few minutes the alarm could spread for twenty miles around. "They are growing more murderous and bolder each day," Clark was told; they were brazenly murdering and beating those who crossed their path. "Unless something is done soon we will be in as bad or worse condition than Jones county," came the warning, and in extremity one local man suggested that the wives and children of the deserters be arrested and deported to Yankee lines at Vicksburg to remove the base of their support. "They are all Union and oppose the Confederate Government and all that are in favor of it."[89]

The real point was not so much that they had been pro-Union all along as that they had been made anti-Confederate, and more and more that mood was being spread by out-of-control regular Confederate soldiers as well. "What the Yankees are unable to get, our own soldiers—or other men in the army—seem to think legitimately belongs to them as spoils of war," complained an Arkansas man.[90] In February 1865 the Mississippi state distillery found troopers of the 5th Mississippi Cavalry and soldiers of the 30th Mississippi Infantry along with some Texan infantry confronting managers with drawn pistols. They demanded whiskey, and when the operators refused, the soldiers sawed the hinges off the warehouse doors and plundered the contents. The manager refused to distill any more. "There is no use keeping a supply at the distillery for thieves & Robbers to take from me," he grumbled as he commented on the general breakdown. "Men have been engaged in the depredations here of good character and family who would have scorned such action previously."[91] At the same time, a commissary officer in Texas was caught selling supplies of Confederate beef to Yankees garrisoned in El Paso for his own personal profit, while the same department suffered from want of medicines for soldiers and civilians alike.[92] A Georgian captured the mood perfectly. "Do for Gods sake put an end to this unrighteous war!" he pleaded. "You are the representative of the yeomanry of the land—who are now helpless."[93] On April 16, 1865, a South Carolina woman begged authorities "for the love of Heaven look into our distressed situation," pleading for help on behalf of seventy-eight women and children in Beaufort who claimed that if they did not get some food they would either starve or be forced to go to the Yankees for aid.[94] In fact, in recognition of the desperate condition of far too many of that yeomanry, Union and Confederate authorities actually cooperated in places for their relief. In February a cartel was agreed between Northern General George H. Thomas and the Rebel cavalry commander General Nathan Bedford Forrest that the railroad track between their lines would be left unmolested so that destitute and starving citizens of northern Mississippi and Alabama could send some of their cotton north in exchange for desperately needed Yankee corn.[95]

Yet in spite of the near destruction of home, community, and order, a surprising degree of determination was still evident among many, and if the governors were given to dismay that the great majority of communications from their citizens brought tales of complaint and woe, surely they had enough philosophy to remember that men are more given to plaint than praise. In October the editor of the Houston *Daily Telegraph* told his readers, "Our motto is, 'fight this war out,'" and that same month the manager of a state asylum took time from his assessment of operations to reflect on patriotism, the war, and sanity.[96] "The birth of this Confederacy has brought with it a terrible baptism of blood, and has made this whole sunny Southern land, a house of mourning," he said. Nationally they had suffered the emotional loss of heroes like Stonewall Jackson, while hundreds of thousands endured individual losses of sons and brothers, husbands and fathers. "The very structure of our Society seems being destroyed," he reflected. In such a time of incredible strain on intellectual and emotional health, he found it surprising that not more people had been driven through his doors in madness. Some so afflicted simply could not reach asylums in the disruption of transportation, of course, while grief and mourning very likely supplanted more pernicious influences that could otherwise have sent them into the abyss of insanity.[97]

Still, in the face of the greatest trials of their generation, and amid hardship greater even than those suffered by many of their forebears during another revolution, most kept their wits, and some even kept their devotion to the cause. Nevertheless, even that lasting optimism of some might, in itself, have reflected the departure of rationality rather than a clinging to it, for in the last months only the most credulous and the most deluded held out genuine hope of victory in the face of increasing disasters on all fronts. Completely isolated from the eastern Confederacy, some Texans told their governor, Pendleton Murrah, in January 1865 that he was now the one great political power in the region, and that after a miraculous victory "you will shape the destiny of an empire."[98] After hearing a false report that Beauregard had been killed in battle in March 1865, Louisiana's governor, former general Henry W. Allen, lamented to his predecessor, Thomas Moore, that "one by one our great generals go." They were "paying dearly for liberty," he said, "but in the end, dear Governor, we will triumph—we will be free."[99] Somehow a few maintained their delusions even after the surrenders began. When the news of Lee's capitulation to Grant at Appomattox on April 9 first reached the western Confederacy, men clung to every irrational notion to keep hope aflame. "We do not believe here that Genl Lee has surrendered his army," Pettus advised his successor, Clark, on April 20. It was felt that Lee had yielded only a small part of his command and had gotten away to North Carolina with the bulk of it to join with the Army of Tennessee commanded by General Joseph E. Johnston, and even that together they had already defeated Sherman and would now turn about and crush Grant.[100] Others echoed Pettus's desperate hope, pinning their beliefs on the fact that their only real news came through newspapers circulated among the Yankee soldiers now occupying so much of Mississippi and Louisiana. "I would now doubt the Bible if coming *now* through that source," protested one. "I do not believe any material part of Lee's army has surrendered."[101]

In Texas, an editor who first scarcely credited Lee's surrender pretended still to be undismayed when it was confirmed, for Johnston was still at large. Despite that officer's consistent record of failure and retreat, the editor now called him "the man who has been regarded by many as the greatest warrior of the age." The message was clearly that even if they had lost Lee, they had a better general now ready for stage center. The same editor, consequently, was equally skeptical early in May when word came that Johnston, too, had surrendered to Sherman on April 26. Thanks to inaccurate reports of the number of men paroled in the two surrenders, he concluded that Lee and Johnston had yielded less than 40,000. "Is there not something remarkable in these numbers?" he asked. "Is there not something that both the Yankees and our own people have strangely overlooked? Where is Lee's real army? Where is Johnston's army? *Not surrendered,* by at least eighty thousand good men as ever shouldered a musket." Rationalizing that the two generals had surrendered only some state militia and a lot of officers to fool the Yankees, he concluded that there must be up to 100,000 unparoled Confederate soldiers somewhere in the East and that they "will yet be heard from in this war." To those soldiers who spoke now of disbanding and going home or trying to continue resistance as bands of guerrillas, he said, "No, no, our only possible course is to stay together, and share a common cause and common fate."[102]

A Texan officer called for all who could to rally to the Lone Star state and invited President Davis to come to lead them, unaware that in the wake of the collapse of April and the fall of Richmond and Lee's surrender, Davis was even then fleeing south with his dwindling government, intent on continuing the struggle in Texas if he could reach it in time. Led by the president, a heroic remnant could fend off all comers for two years, declared this optimistic officer, while a woman in Houston protested: "Stay in a conquered country? Never! I will take my son and fly to the islands of the sea first, and there live in everlasting solitude before I will live the subject of a conqueror."[103] With even greater resolve, and on the same day that a citizens' meeting in Austin met and resolved to fight on, another woman called for Texans to make their state a Thermopylae, "to win or die." They could be a wave in the breakers, gather to themselves all the remnants of the shattered and surrendered armies, and "finally burst with a sullen roar 'over the river,' and sweep from the face of the earth every Yankee soldier and garrison, from here to the mouth of the Potomac."[104]

Delusional as were such hopes and declarations, inevitably there were those who argued for a last act of vengeance, and even Armageddon or self-immolation in the face of defeat. "If we are in earnest, let our actions furnish the proof," a Mississippian declared in February 1865. No doubt frustrated that in six months of trying to recruit his own company he could raise only nine volunteers, and in spite of the evidence of his own experience, he argued, "there are men enough in the South, if brought together in an army, to burn up the North—at least to settle *the debt of vengeance*— which we so honestly owe them."[105] Another advised, "I say, yield not & advise individuals, no men of even 80 yrs or 100 yrs of age, never to surrender."

> What can the Yankees do with us if we refuse? They can take property, & put us in prison, or hang some; well let it be done, I say. I will never take the oath, never be a citizen of the Yankee Govt, never vote. . . . There are so many white livered folk at home, so many who think they will save property, so many who get sick at the sight of blood. . . . Let us wait until all are gone before us. I think as a brave man, I can wait until the choice is given *me*, to 'submit or die.' . . . Of course I am weary. Of course I cannot see what we can do without an army, but I think if we refuse submission God will take us through ere we are all slain.[106]

Surrounded by the debris of utter defeat, one hopeless romantic—or more likely, hopeless delusional—calling himself "Pacificus," sent a proposal to Murrah on May 1 for "A Golden Bridge" of peace to end the war by means of his poetry. Muddled among his lunatic verses were suggestions that in agreement for returning to the Union, the Confederacy should sell all its slaves to the Union at 1860 prices, after which the freedmen would still be held to service, the difference being that now they should be paid for their work, but only at the discretion of their employers! Thus the South would still have virtual slaves, only without literal slavery. The cost of their purchase would be reimbursed by export duties. Moreover, with the blacks now being free, they would no longer be counted for congressional apportionment purposes on the three-fifths basis, but would have their numbers fully taken into account in apportioning delegates in the House of Representatives, meaning the former slave states would gain seats, especially if they were also to encourage immigration. That would return the South to equality of representation and power in Washington. Further, in a dying gasp of experimenting with localism in democracy, he suggested that the reunited nation could operate on a basis of "sectional sovereignty," North and South, and that it should require a majority vote of the senators of both sections to pass any law affecting a local issue. Thus, with greater strength in the House, the South could impede hostile measures against its interests, while in the Senate it could stop cold anything that got past the House. Thus, declared Pacificus, would each section be secured against domination by a majority in the other. He hailed his delusion as "a new Union; on a new Basis."[107]

It was insane, and so were all the other impractical hopes and expectations, and many—in some places most—of the common folk knew it well before the end actually came. When the governors could bring out any men for the militia, they could not arm them, and they were forced to appeal to citizens to organize themselves into informal police squads that were little better than vigilantes. Seeking the furlough of men from the main armies in order to maintain some civil order at home, the governors were denied. Organized militia began to refuse to muster when called, for fear of reprisals from the deserters and renegades.[108] Once word of Lee's surrender was confirmed, militia commanders were ordered to keep those companies they could still manage on constant alert in the expectation of further civil breakdown as thousands of paroled soldiers came home to a civil vacuum.[109] "Language cannot depict the state of public affairs here," General Joseph L. Brent, commanding in western Louisiana, lamented on May 18, with all the surrenders confirmed and all hope gone except for the Pacificuses of the South. On the eve of leaving to start negotiations for his own surrender, he observed, "I think the state of sentiment among the citizens & soldiers is such that any Louisiana officer who refuses to support this course will be held as a wanton destroyer of the property & happiness

& honor of the State."[110] And so they surrendered. Yet so relentless and self-perpetuating was the march of paperwork that requisitions for conscripts to fill depleted ranks in the 2nd Louisiana Cavalry kept right on going through channels even as the generals were surrendering. One such request kept being forwarded from bureaucrat to bureaucrat until May 13, even after the surrenders of Lee and Johnston and almost every other Rebel army; after Davis had been captured; after Grant's and Sherman's armies were actually on their way to Washington to celebrate victory; and three days after President Andrew Johnson, succeeding the assassinated Lincoln, declared armed resistance to the Union at an end. And even then, in the end, the requisition was properly noted and denied, not because the war was over, but because the quartermaster could not provide sufficient forage for any more cavalry.[111]

Both that myopic quartermaster and Pacificus ought perhaps to have paid a visit to Robert Kells, the manager of that state asylum, though the poet-politician's rantings might have challenged Kells's conclusion that "there is a philosophy in every thing around us, and it is the part of wisdom and of duty, to gather every practical lesson that it teaches." Human societies engage in no greater or more demanding collective enterprise than making war, yet warfare is at the same time the most rigorous of all tests of the resilience of their institutions. The lesson offered by the breakdown of determination and morale on the Confederate home front was that democracy might be strong, but not strong enough to survive in the face of a sustained inability to keep peace and protect life and property. Protection proved to be the defining element in individual and community morale among the civil population. They would suffer hardship and scarcity, starvation and dislocation, and even the deaths of their sons and brothers, but in a culture that for generations had been accustomed to the maintenance of civil order by national, state, or local authorities, such a breakdown was near fatal. In the end, the greatest internal enemy of Confederate democracy was fear.[112]

The Year of Decision

If only Jefferson Davis could have stopped the hands of history's clock at the end of 1862. As bad as things were in the West, they could have been much worse, and it was hard to see how they could be better in the East. But then perhaps he would have let the hands tick onward a little longer, for early 1863 would bring his greatest victory. While Lee wintered his victorious army along the Rappahannock and sent part of it away for the spring, the disgraced General Ambrose Burnside resigned, to be replaced by the more intelligent, if more erratic, General Joseph Hooker. Hooker planned a brilliant campaign to catch Lee off guard, divert his attention, and then sweep around his western flank and trap the Army of Northern Virginia between two wings of his own massive army.

Late in April he was ready, and everything worked beautifully. One wing of his army made another threat to attack Fredericksburg, and Lee readied himself, unaware that Hooker was marching most of his army to upstream fords that he crossed almost undetected. The Yankees were sweeping toward Lee's exposed left. The graying general realized his peril in time, however, and daringly divided his army. Leaving just part of a corps to hold Fredericksburg, Lee marched with the rest to meet Hooker in the tangled second growth woods around Chancellorsville. For reasons still unaccountable, with Lee almost at his mercy, Hooker lost his nerve and started to pull back, afraid of making the push that would give him victory. Lee did not wait for a second chance. With incredible audacity, he divided *his army yet again, though outnumbered now more than two to one, and sent Stonewall Jackson and his corps on an exhausting flank march that brought them almost unseen around Hooker's own right flank. When Jackson's screaming Rebels suddenly appeared in their flank and rear, Hooker's right wing all but collapsed. This stage of the action was a Pyrrhic victory, however, for in the confusion of twilight, Jackson was accidentally cut down by his own men and would die of complications in less than two weeks, the greatest martyred hero of the Confederacy, and the one man whom future mythmakers would presume might have changed the outcome of the war had he lived. Meanwhile, Lee not only pushed the rest of Hooker's army from the field, but then turned to stop the advance of the Yankees that had pushed their own way through Fredericksburg and still hoped to crush him between themselves and Hooker's still strong, if demoralized, legions. It was the most incredible, if not the most complete, Confederate victory of the war.*

But it was the prelude to the most crushing defeat that Lee would suffer. Knowing he had the enemy off balance, with his reunited army strong and a whole season of campaigning weather ahead of him, Lee decided to move the war onto Northern soil again in hopes of further damage to Union morale, and to take the pressure off northern Virginia. His goal was the Susquehanna River in central Pennsylvania. He could cut the vital Pennsylvania Railroad, disrupt sources of coal for Union steamships, throw a panic into Washington, and perhaps at the same time draw troops away from Grant's army then besieging Vicksburg. There was even the possibility of breathing life into European consideration of recognizing the Confederacy.

Lee did not get to choose his ground. Chance and geography did that for him, but after crossing the Potomac and marching unopposed across Maryland into Pennsylvania, all of his roads led to Gettysburg. Other roads brought the Army of the Potomac, under Hooker's replacement, George G. Meade, to meet him. Meade had neither Hooker's brilliance nor McClellan's inspirational qualities, but he was solid, capable, and determined. And Lee was off balance. Unwell, missing the sure hand of Stonewall, and on unfamiliar ground for the first time, Lee simply did not manage his fight as he had in earlier engagements. He decided to take the initiative and attack Meade in good defensive positions on a low ridge flanked by substantial hills south of the town. Everywhere Lee struck, Meade held his ground, all the while grinding the Confederates down over three days until the climactic legendary frontal assault of July 3. It was an act of desperation by a commander who had run out of ideas, and whose army was so hampered by command losses that it simply did not work as once it had. Lee was beaten and had no choice but to withdraw into Virginia, having accomplished nothing but the exhaustion of his army and the near destruction of his structure of seasoned regimental, brigade, and division commanders. In the exhaustion after Gettysburg, the two opponents would do no more than feint at each other for the rest of the year, but the Army of Northern Virginia would never be the same for the rest of the war.

How much worse was it for Confederate hopes when the very day after Gettysburg, a twin disaster came hundreds of miles west. U. S. Grant had started his overland drive down the Mississippi Valley late in 1862, only to be stymied briefly that winter. But he did not give up on an objective, and in the spring of 1863 he moved his combined land and naval forces south toward Vicksburg. He tried one plan after another to get around the fortress city, but finally moved his fleet past its batteries by night, marched his army down the opposite side of the river, and used the fleet to ferry his divisions across below the city. Then came a masterstroke of strategy as he drove first toward the state capital at Jackson, then turned and pushed for Vicksburg from the east. He nearly managed to take it, but the defenders, commanded by another old friend of Davis's, General John C. Pemberton, held out long enough to force Grant to resort to a siege. When that happened, there was nothing to save the Confederates except a relief attempt led less than halfheartedly by Joseph E. Johnston, who got no closer than Jackson and was then brushed away by Grant's chief lieutenant, William T. Sherman. On July 4, starving, riddled with disease, and with no hope of aid or escape, Pemberton surrendered his 30,000-man command. It was a stunning victory, and five days later the other Rebel bastion on the river at Port Hudson also fell to General Nathaniel P. Banks. In one week in July, the Confederacy suffered major disaster on every front.

How strange, then, that the only bright spot in the year in this theater would come from that most unlikely of sources, Braxton Bragg, the most despised army commander in the Confederacy. From the time he took command from Beauregard of the Army of Tennessee, he fomented internal discord within his own high command, while on the battlefield he repeatedly disappointed. He remained in southeastern Tennessee and northern Alabama after Stones River, but in the summer General William Rosecrans brilliantly feinted him out of his positions and without a fight sent the Army of Tennessee back to Chattanooga. In the fall Rosecrans came on, intending to fight in earnest, but then Bragg himself left his defenses and took the field. In a well-planned but miserably executed campaign in which Bragg's chief subordinates repeatedly failed him, he caught Rosecrans with his army divided and spread out near Chickamauga Creek in September. Through a combination of luck, Federal ineptitude, planning, and hard fighting, Bragg managed to cut Rosecrans's army in two and send one-half of it streaming in panic for Chattanooga. It would be the most complete victory ever handed to a Yankee army, and it was, of all people, Bragg who had done it. But when he followed to besiege Rosecrans, the old Bragg reemerged. He and his generals began feuding anew. James Longstreet, on loan from Lee with part of his corps, left to conduct his own failure of a campaign to take Knoxville. Meanwhile Washington decided to break the siege by sending in Grant and Sherman. Within only a few weeks Grant turned the situation around, and had the Federal army ready to break out. On November 23–25 he launched attacks on Lookout Mountain and Missionary Ridge that caught the overextended and overconfident Confederates off balance. He routed them from the field. Chattanooga was relieved, the year was going to end on an unbroken string of Yankee victories, and a disgraced Bragg would be forced to resign, though not before one last campaign against his subordinates, including John C. Breckinridge once again. Most important of all, however, it left Chattanooga perched like a gateway into Georgia, ready to be used as a major base to launch the campaign to drive toward Atlanta and beyond, to slice the eastern Confederacy in two yet again. And the victory propelled Grant toward the goal that happy stars had seemed to want for him almost from the first. Lincoln would make him general in chief and give him direction of the entire war effort in the field. It was inevitable that in the spring it would be Grant who faced Lee in Virginia.

It had been a year of decision. The Mississippi was gone. The Confederacy was not just cut in two, but faced multiple subdivision. Loss of the Tennessee and Cumberland Rivers had hived off most of Tennessee. Now the Red River was open as a pathway of invasion to split western Louisiana in half and afford a doorway into east Texas should the Yankees choose to open it. Other tributaries would allow Arkansas and central Mississippi to be penetrated. Meanwhile the shuttling of livestock and agricultural produce from west of the river to the east was at an irrevocable end. From now on the Trans-Mississippi would be more a drain on than a contributor to

*the war effort. Just as important, if not more so, the surrenders at Vicks-
burg and Port Hudson cost the South more than 40,000 men it could not
easily replace and, combined with the defeat at Gettysburg, shattered any
remaining notions of invincibility. The Yankees would fight, and it was entirely possible for the Confederacy to lose.*

*The relief in the Confederacy at the replacement of Braxton Bragg was
evident everywhere, but none appreciated yet, nor could they, just what
a mixed blessing it was to be. By the very nature of the organization of
his army high command, Jefferson Davis had only two acceptable officers
of sufficient rank to replace Bragg, Beauregard and Joseph E. Johnston.
Beauregard he loathed as little better than an ingrate and egotist who
threw away Sidney Johnston's victory at Shiloh and then left his command
without permission. Joseph E. Johnston was a barracks lawyer who had
shown time and again that he did not like to take a risk or hazard his reputation on a fight. Moreover, he would not keep his commander in chief informed and let himself become the pawn of opposition politicians. Yet there
were no other full generals to turn to, and no subordinate officers who had
yet demonstrated that they might be capable of army command. In the
end, Davis distrusted Johnston less than he detested Beauregard, and thus
the decision was made. To be sure, Bragg had been inept and unbalanced,
a natural prey to sycophants and a paranoid conspirator who set his own
high command at war with him and itself. But he would work with the
president, and he would take the war to the enemy, and he was not afraid
to fight, however much he might lose control of a battle once it commenced.
Based on experience, Davis could not be certain that Johnston would go
even that far, and if he would not, then what hope was there for that hard-
luck Army of Tennessee?*

*In Virginia, though still strong and defiant, Robert E. Lee's once mag-
nificent army was crippled. There was valiant fight in that army yet, and a
spirit among the men that sustained them in the face of late or nonexistent
pay, inadequate rations, and sagging morale on the home front. Perhaps
that is what made them the finest army of the South. They had started out
to fight for youth and adventure more than for a cause. By 1863 they were
fighting for something else—loyalty to the god-man they called "Marse
Robert." In their expectations of him, and his of them, they were already in
the act of creating the most enduring legend of the Confederacy. Unfortunately, some very stark realities of mathematics were already starting to
catch up with them. Legends cannot defeat legions.*

9

The Enemy Within

THERE WERE PLENTY of other enemies all the same. The whole concept of democracy was based on the fundamental assumption of a right to preference, and perhaps more basically still, upon recognition of the right of opposition. Even in an oligarchy like South Carolina, still there was some scope for choices, even if not all segments of society had anything like equal voices in making them. Like any democracy, the Confederacy had its ruling majority and its loyal opposition, though the latter would always be amorphous and bound by no coherent alternative policy, but rather by the weak and shifting gravity of isolated issues and personal antipathies. Yet no matter how virulent that faction's attacks on the prevailing administration became, or how much damage it did to front parlor morale, still few if any would have accused its carping panjandrums of disloyalty to the cause itself, of actually wanting the Confederacy to fail and the Union to prevail.

There were such in the wartime South, however. They had been there from the beginning and everyone knew it, nor had they even attempted to disguise their sentiments, at least at the outset. They came from the same ranks of men opposed to secession in principle or practicality that had produced Alexander Stephens and others who were now incontestably enlisted in the cause. Most had been so-called Old Line Whigs, ideological descendants of the Federalists who felt less fear of central government than their Democratic neighbors on the plantations, and who had little or nothing to gain from Southern independence. While they were certainly a part of a society as a whole that had a cultural interest in maintaining slavery as a means of social control of the 3.5 million blacks in their midst, even that meant much less to the hill people since so few slaves lived there, and thus the threat, if any, to social order was minor at best. Ohio County, for instance, on the western border of prewar Virginia, had double the population of any other Old Dominion county west of the Shenandoah Valley, yet only one-fortieth the number of slaves that inhabited Berkeley County at the valley's northern terminus. The contrast was much the same in east Tennessee and north Alabama and wherever else the soil was too poor or the geography too broken for slave-driven plantation agriculture. Recognizing all too well that secession and independence offered them little of any benefit, but promised instead the likelihood of war in which they might be sucked into losing their lives to defend values and property they did not share, residents of such places had made their opposition to disunion known from the first.

The difference between them and men like Stephens was that he had fought against breaking up the Union as a matter of practicality. Secession to him was unnecessary but not necessarily treasonous. But those others held the Union more sacred, and at the same time felt no common cause with the planter and slaveholding elites who, they believed, had brought on the crisis to serve their own ends. For generations they had been accustomed to seeing their votes taken for granted or finding themselves all but disfranchised by property requirements that favored the landed elite, virtually allowing the latter to run the states to suit themselves. Thus there was little love descending from the hills and mountains to embrace the oligarchs, and certainly no sense of debt either of blood or favor to aristocrats who had abused the poor farmers for their own ends. It had been their delegates, sent from the mountain and hill country counties of the interior in western Virginia and North Carolina, north Georgia and Alabama, eastern Tennessee, central Texas, and elsewhere far from the affluent coastal cities and tidewater plantations, who stood and opposed disunion fruitlessly in the secession conventions, even though in Virginia at least they had helped defeat it four times before Fort Sumter made it inevitable. Added to their numbers were the small but vocally pro-Union pockets of immigrants from Ireland and the German states who had come to settle new lands in places like central Texas. Having come to a region where xenophobia ran strong among all classes, and where less than a decade earlier nativist parties briefly flourished on a platform of opposition to all aliens and non-Protestants, these new Southerners found little common cause with a leadership that silently objected to their very presence. Southern Unionists even had their defenders among the most hardened Confederates. "We all loved the Union once," Governor John Milton of Florida told President Davis in April 1863. If former love for the Union was a crime, "then what American does not plead guilty?"[1]

It was the votes of people such as these that the Confederate framers in Montgomery so feared when they quailed from seeing their Constitution submitted to popular referenda, for fear it would be rejected, and secession thus fatally humiliated and compromised. A leadership in the best of times suspicious of the will of the wrong sort of majority could hardly risk 260seeing its new Confederate democracy impaled on the irony of an unsympathetic majority within its own bosom. The mere fact that some men might have voted against a new nation did not mean that their attachment to the Union was unbreakably strong, however. Many simply did not view the matter as an either/or choice. Opposing the Confederacy did not mean they would necessarily work against it on behalf of the Union. Nonetheless, even among those thousands who were simply apathetic, there remained an ominous potential. If the new regime sought too hard to force them into its mold and fold, it risked alienating them to the point that they would make active resistance in the face of coercion. That, of course, is exactly what happened in the end.

It is no wonder that in the face of commitment and loss, most civilians in the Confederacy were early and adamantly intolerant of lingering Union sentiment in their midst. The old loyalty was dying out rapidly in Texas by June 1861, for instance, one citizen of Comal County reporting that "only those ignorant boys say frequently that they will not fight for the slave cause."[2] Any expression of Union sentiment was likely to be first exaggerated and then reported to the authorities, though sometimes the motive was as much business rivalry or old prewar animosity and feud as patriotism. "Finding persons in our midst who despise our cause, crave the sickness of the North, and express great delight at hearing of our southern soldiery meeting with misfortunes, such as sickness & death," a Mississippian in January 1862 argued that people should be prohibited from uttering such thoughts or else expelled from the Confederacy. "Shall we weight for action upon their part or should they be delt with for expressing such sentiments?" he asked.[3]

Eyes could turn in any direction in the first wave of suspicion. In Chattanooga, Tennessee, people warned authorities of a self-styled Union sympathizer who declared too loudly that he was "willing to submit to the action of the State as expressed at the Ballot Box" when Tennesseans held a referendum on secession, but the method of expression of his willingness to accept the verdict of the majority made him suspect.[4] A woman signing herself only as "A True Southern Girl" warned Governor John Pettus in Mississippi that around Kosciusko a Union party was forming by early 1862 that favored the North, its young men laughing and boasting of how they would run to the enemy if drafted, and one of their women even naming a new baby Lincoln. "I hate to breath the same air they do," said the patriotic belle, calling them all "Lincoln hounds."[5] Communities from Texas to the Atlantic suddenly began to take new notice of strangers passing through, some "giving very suspicious accounts of themselves," as one Georgian warned Governor Joseph Brown. Citizens organized informal companies and "committees of safety" for home protection as a "resort to some means that will insure us more safely," to prevent slaves and suspect persons from communicating with the Yankees, and sent petitions to their governors to place guards on railroad bridges and other necessary facilities in the face of rumors of cabals to disrupt communications.[6] In Florida the governor even authorized a citizens' group to undertake on its own to guard the Suwannee River and to place obstructions in it to prevent Yankees from using the stream, a function that ordinarily would have been undertaken by state or national troops had Florida not been so stripped of both.[7] More cities besides Richmond began to require passports to leave or enter, and Atlanta, Memphis, Nashville, and others learned that private watchmen employed to guard government storehouses could not always be trusted after apparent sabotage left warehouses burned to the ground. Only military guards could be depended upon, they concluded.[8] Indeed, more and more, as one portion of the population—the governors, the politicians, and the ideologues—complained louder and louder against the intrusion of army authority into civilian life, the broad mass of the people demanded that the military assume an ever greater role in protecting them not just on the battlefield but at home, in the market, and on the thoroughfares. Confederate democracy once again revealed itself to be a construct principally of interest only to its framers, while the Confederate people wanted and needed something at once more practical and effective.

Fears of active resistance emerged early. The male citizens of Bunker Hill, Mississippi, organized themselves into a company in April 1861, just days after Fort Sumter, for the purpose of "keeping down Toryism among the people" and arresting "anyone hostile to the institutions, and the interests of our common country." In fact, the first real concerns over active disloyalty to the Confederacy overwhelmingly connected it with the fear of attempts to incite servile rebellion. That was hardly surprising, considering that even before John Brown's raid on Harpers Ferry, Southerners had accused Yankees of attempting to bring about a slave uprising. Thus it seemed logical to assume that renegade Confederate citizens who would side with the enemy would naturally also try to catalyze Southern slaves to help undermine the new nation from within. Driven by that fear, Confederates from the first felt anxious to meet such behavior with swift justice. "In the event we find anyone hostile to the institutions, and the interests of our common country," the Bunker Hill company asked the governor, "will the law sustain us in arresting & handing over such characters to the officers of the law," or would they have to wait for the properly constituted civil authorities to take action? In short, could they meet disloyalty with vigilante justice?[9]

Barely had the Montgomery congress framed the new government before reports began coming to the authorities of suspicious characters who would bear watching. A Texan reported from San Antonio in May that two men suspected of abolition sympathies had recently gone to Washington on "a very suspicious errand," but that they were being watched and would not be allowed to return to their homes.[10] A man who had moved from Illinois to Texas in 1860 following Lincoln's election protested that he wanted to remain and would be a loyal citizen, but still he had to have a passport as an alien until he could go through the citizenship process, meaning that he would be constantly under the gaze of the authorities.[11] In Virginia that same month authorities ordered the stationmaster of the Richmond, Fredericksburg & Potomac Railroad to report the arrival in Fredericksburg of all strangers and persons of "suspicious character" to civil authorities who were to examine them, and if the travelers resisted, they were to be arrested and held by the military pending interview. The stationmaster was at least ordered to show prudence in exercising this power "to avoid any further interference with entire freedom of travelling on the part of citizens, than is absolutely necessary for our protection." Even more explicit was the avowal by the authorities that "the military authority is designed to be used in entire subservience to the civil authorities." When it came to dealing with disloyal elements, that would change, however, and soon enough, in yet another test of the true strength of their democracy.[12]

Some states adopted measures authorizing their governors to arrest and deport suspicious persons, and further empowering them to demand personal explanations from any alien, which also meant Northern citizens. Yet chief executives were to order an arrest only on the basis of strong evidence, even though justices of the peace all across the Confederacy were asking if they could on their own authority detain Yankees.[13] Some of those justices had excellent reasons for wanting that power, for outright flouting of the new government was not long in appearing. In Bandera County, Texas, just west of San Antonio and just south of a strong Unionist enclave of German immigrants in Fredericksburg, settlers refused to pay their property taxes to a Confederate state government. Worse, only one of the county officers would take the required oath of allegiance to the new nation, and citizens circulated a petition calling for reconstruction of the Union. One man was cursed simply for entertaining a secessionist judge in his home, and while he was there the judge's buggy was vandalized. Another resolution was circulated that no one should take the oath or enlist in the official county militia. But the Unionists did form their own informal home guard and there were fears that it would aid the Yankees if they invaded. Even the postmaster was a Unionist, and the secessionist justice of the peace in the county found that his mail was being ripped open and read before he received it.[14]

Texas offered an interesting example of Unionism deep within a Confederate state. Nothing spoke to that more than the fact that when secession broke out, its governor, Sam Houston, was the only outspoken Unionist chief executive of any of the states that would join in the rebellion. In spite of heavy pressure from the secessionist element in his state, Houston repeatedly stood in the way of calling a state convention. When a convention was summoned in spite of him, he tried to use a sympathetic majority in the state senate to outmaneuver the convention, but that failed, and on February 1, 1861, the secession ordinance passed the convention by a great majority. Houston hoped to defeat the measure when it went before a popular referendum, and when that, too, failed, he briefly toyed with engaging United States Army forces in Texas to militarily enforce Union rule until he saw that it would be futile. That done, Houston accepted defeat, even though the best estimates suggested that only one-third of Texans actually supported secession, while another third stood behind Houston and the decisive remainder stood in between. Of those favoring the Union, there were again three segments—the ones outspokenly pro-Union, others who kept their sentiments to themselves and remained publicly noncommittal, and a remainder who decided simply to yield to the prevailing power.

The openly declared Unionists soon found that many of their communities were no longer safe for them, especially the enclaves in towns like San Antonio and Austin. They escaped to the remote hill country or to communities like Fredericksburg, there to plot the restoration of Union rule in the Lone Star State. They had Houston's active encouragement for a time, for even though he left the capital after secession and simply went home, he did not yield the governorship until March 1861, when he was forced from office after refusing to take an oath of allegiance to the Confederacy. Thereafter he privately encouraged resistance to the new order, and discussed with others the means of getting control of the state and taking it out of the Confederacy, if not to rejoin the Union, then to resume its former independence as the Republic of Texas. Houston and others found their greatest support in the northern counties of the state, themselves settled largely by immigrants from the North, while Confederate sentiment ran strongest in the southern and eastern counties that had been the first settled, predominantly from the South and largely by slaveholders. Indeed, the desire to practice slavery played a large role in bringing on the original revolution in 1835–36, and the landscape between Austin and the Sabine offered good land for cotton, encouraging even more settlers to come from the Old South.

Thus Texas, like Alabama, Mississippi, and Georgia, and like the Union itself, lay chiefly divided between north and south, and it would be from those northern counties that most of the active resistance to Confederate rule would come. In fact, opposition erupted even before Texas joined the Confederacy, and before there was a new nation to join. On January 15, 1861, before the secession convention met, an anonymous call went out from Austin Unionists that, in the event that the convention voted for secession, they should unite the northern counties, declare themselves a new state, and apply to Washington for admission into the Union. Nothing came of the plan, nor was the attempt even made, but it revealed even before the birth of the Confederacy that there were groups of strong-willed Unionists within the state's bosom who would contemplate extreme measures to combat disunion. Once Houston was gone and the government firmly in the hands of Confederates, Governor Francis Lubbock ordered all alien enemies out of the state, and many of them went to Mexico.

Very likely some of the same unknown plotters emerged more than a year later with a new scheme in those northern counties. Now they called themselves the Peace Party, and after more than a year of war, with the defeats at Forts Henry and Donelson, Shiloh, Pea Ridge, New Orleans, Antietam, and others to spur them on, many of the once-neutral Texans were now with them, impelled not so much by love of the Union as a desire simply to end a war that they did not see the South winning. Indeed, all across the Confederacy, opposition sentiment would rise and wane in reaction to events on the battlefield. Every defeat brought the Unionists and the disaffected out more vocally; every victory drove them back toward the safety of the shadows, to await another opportunity to emerge again. Now in north Texas the Peace Party, infused with the comic opera melodrama that had already become emblematic of prewar groups like the Know-Nothings and the Knights of the Golden Circle, formed themselves with almost Masonic organization, including different degrees of membership, secret signs and passwords and handshakes, and the new name Loyal League. Headquartered near Gainesville in Cooke County, they pledged to aid invading Yankee armies, carry out espionage and sabotage, and help to interfere with the operation of conscription. Just what they might have achieved is uncertain, but little should have been expected. They were isolated, Confederate and state military authorities were too numerous, and their own organization was transparent in spite of all the panoply of secrecy. One drunken member gave it all away, and soon they were infiltrated and exposed, and that only brought down on the Unionists the outrage of the loyal Confederate citizenry. Without waiting for the military or state civil authorities to act, a mob gathered and took two dozen of the league members into custody near Gainesville and hanged twenty-one without the inconvenience of a trial. Then militia captured more than one hundred others, and hanged another nineteen of them, this time after perfunctory trials. Soon rumor escalated the hanged to more than 170, though the number was much smaller, probably no more than forty-five to fifty. Other counties like Hunt and Hopkins acted against their tories as well, lynching or simply assassinating more than a dozen, though most showed much more restraint. Still the effect was to drain the sap out of the Loyal League movement. The "Great Gainesville Hanging" became an admonition to all who would be disloyal to the Confederacy, yet even then north Texas would remain a primary problem area for Confederate sympathizers for the rest of the war.[15]

The concerns over disloyal citizens were nearly as great elsewhere, especially in San Antonio's Bexar County, which had been a hotbed of Unionism from the outset. In 1861 the local press had been brazenly anti-Confederate, calling President Davis an incubus "shapen in iniquity," and a traitor and bigot. By January 1862 a number of those who had fled to Mexico were coming back, some of them abolitionists "of the worst stripe," Lubbock was warned. In response he advised officials to keep watch on them, but to make no arrests unless the tories did something overtly treasonous.[16] In March 1862 an anonymous German-born citizen posted broadsides around the town in his native tongue, calling all of the sympathetic to arms and saying that "the revolution has broken out." It was probably a prank, for no such armed resistance erupted, though the German citizens had surreptitiously organized themselves into a small armed militia of seventy-three men. Just as likely, the placards were the work of a Confederate citizen hoping to arouse community and official hostility to the traitors in their midst by means of a little stratagem. If he hoped to foment another Gainesville, he would be disappointed, but soon the authorities did establish a Confederate Military Commission in San Antonio, ostensibly to deal with problems within the army and with its officers and men. In fact most of its work, especially with the judicial vacuum and the gaps in civil administration brought on by manpower shortages and the erosion of the war, was in adjudicating in civilian cases of disloyalty.

The commission sat on the remnants of one of the most notorious of all the Texas tory enclaves, in those counties surrounding the enclave at Fredericksburg in the middle of the state. Their sympathy had never been in doubt, from the date of the popular referendum on secession on February 23, 1861, when the vote there came out 25 to 1 in favor of remaining in the Union. At every step the Unionists tried to thwart Confederate activities. They got one of their own chosen enrolling officer for conscription, and he then impeded any attempt at signing up men, even refusing to attend gatherings of men who met in order to enlist, while at the same time refusing to give out an office address to prevent would-be Southern recruits from finding him. Those he did enlist were largely his fellow German Unionists, whom he hoped to form into a company with himself in command so that he could resist Confederate authority in the area. In the spring of 1862 some five hundred of them actually organized three companies of Union men in the area, and in response Governor Lubbock sent an officer to Fredericksburg to put down this new incipient threat. Yet he found so little cooperation among even the loyal citizens that he could accomplish little. The three tory companies dispersed, but then sixty-one of them banded together with a few others to go to Mexico. They were overtaken by ninety-five Confederates on the Nueces River and attacked by surprise on August 10, 1862, in the only real pitched—if one-sided—battle in the Confederacy between soldiers and tory civilians. Two Confederates were killed and eighteen wounded, while more than thirty Germans took wounds and as many more were killed. Reports soon circulated that wounded Germans were simply shot on the spot rather than being taken prisoner, while those fugitives who were captured were later shot or hanged without trial. Two months later seven of the German remnant were killed in another attempt to reach Mexico, while the Confederate officer in charge went on arresting and hanging tories in the Fredericksburg area for several weeks. Nowhere else in the Confederacy did the military put so many disloyal citizens to death.

Week after week names—some of them Anglicized—like Songworth, Schlickum, and Degener came before the San Antonio commission. Edward Degener was charged in September 1862 with being disloyal, specifically for failing to advise authorities of the band of Unionists forming with the intent of escaping into Mexico; for having communication with the Yankee enemy; and for spreading seditious falsehoods about the Confederacy itself with the intent of harming the cause. In the testimony it unfolded that two of Degener's sons were among the men killed on the Nueces. On the body of one of them was found a letter written by their father informing prominent German statesmen of the plight of German Unionists in Texas. Degener's defense counsel pointed out that there was nothing treasonous in the letter, and that if Degener did not show active sympathy for the Confederacy, the fact of his writing a newsy letter that revealed that lack of sympathy did not, of itself, constitute treason. At most, he said, Degener could be accused of "want of patriotism," which was hardly a crime in any nation. When found guilty he was ordered to post a bond for $5,000 that he would conduct himself loyally during the remainder of the war. The judge advocate said that "fortunately for our country, we have few such citizens & they wield little power to do wrong."[17]

More serious charges and consequences awaited those in active opposition, like Ferdinand Simon, who was accused of levying war against the Confederacy. He had been captured in the same skirmish in which Degener's sons were killed, bearing arms and resisting the soldiers of the Confederacy, and actually firing at them. Despite his pleas of innocence, the commission found him guilty and sentenced him to be hanged, one of the first instances in the Confederacy, if not the first, of a military court exacting capital punishment on a civilian even though the privilege of the writ of habeas corpus had not been suspended. Texas was then briefly under martial law, but nowhere else in the Confederacy that year, under similar relaxation of civil rights, were men put to death by army tribunals.[18] The civil authorities had simply given way to the military. Especially distressing were the number of men like Simon and the Degener boys who were trying to leave Texas for Mexico. Ordinarily a nation might say good riddance to traitors leaving. But these men raised a dual problem. Their manpower was needed by the conscription officers, while at the same time they could spread unfortunate stories about the Confederacy south of the border, even as the Richmond government had some hopes of encouraging sympathy in Mexico.

The military commission managed to dampen overt Unionism in the Bexar area, but never to drive it entirely underground. In January 1863 authorities uncovered another potential uprising in the Fredericksburg area, as between five hundred and eight hundred armed men met for inflammatory speeches resisting the draft and at the same time intimidating loyal Confederate citizens from speaking in opposition. "There is a secret organization and determination to make resistance hereafter," warned an observer. Within a month there had been large-scale arrests, and a dispersal of the miscreants to the several county courts for trial, but there would be no more mass executions.[19] By the fall of 1863 apathy toward the Confederate cause was so irritating that mass meetings were held to try to whip up Southern sentiment and compel tories to declare themselves openly. Those who refused to enlist or enroll either for active service or for the militia were to have their names published in the press in the hope that community pressure would force a change in their sympathies, but it did not work. In Houston one prewar Unionist was arrested after extracts of his private letters were published in the local paper.[20]

Meanwhile the flow of Unionists to Matamoros and Monterrey in Mexico remained so constant that United States consular officials in those cities believed that enough of them could be armed to go back and take Texas out of the hands of the Confederates. The Mexican-American inhabitants felt little or no sympathy for slavery or the Confederacy, either, and from the outset of the war they demonstrated their reluctance to wear the gray and an inclination to aid the Union instead. In time martial law would have to be declared along much of the Rio Grande to control dissident Hispanic citizens, while those Mexican men actually enlisted in Confederate units deserted at a high rate at the first opportunity. In November 1863 a whole company of them mutinied in cooperation with a Yankee thrust to take Brownsville. By then, conspiracies seemed to be appearing everywhere. The publisher of the Austin *Texas Democrat* was arrested by the military and charged with conspiring against the government with a secret society with its own rules and oaths and all the rest. Men from all the counties surrounding Austin were involved, but when they were released on $1,500 bond, they returned to their communities and went right on preaching sedition. Their purpose was to join with the Yankees if they should make a landing on the Gulf coast. So complicated was this business of the army arresting civilians in the absence of martial law that the department commander, General John B. Magruder, appealed to the governor to get the legislature to enact some stringent laws that would require the civil authorities to deal with the miscreants and relieve him of his difficulty.[21]

Unionists in many Texas communities like Austin were eventually forced to leave their homes to avoid conscription or the wrath of their Confederate neighbors. Others found different ways to deal with the problem. Determined not to fight against the Union, men in several of the lower central counties made a great show of turning out to enlist in and organize home guard companies that would keep them free of the grip of the state militia or national draft. In Fayette County alone they formed twenty-four companies, keeping more than a thousand Union men at home, while barely 150 men from the county went into Confederate service. Once the conscription act took effect, the prospect of Union men being forced into Confederate arms galvanized determination to resist, and by the fall of 1862 authorities feared an outright rebellion from Austin south to the Gulf coast. Shortly after the New Year came reports of hundreds of armed tories openly drilling as infantry and cavalry, while recent draftees were refusing to take their oath of service and enrolling officers were fleeing some communities in fear. One Fayette County community brazenly sent a declaration to a militia general in charge of its locality, saying its men would not serve, especially after they learned how poorly Confederate authorities treated and cared for the poor families of men who had donned the gray. Confederates responded with more declarations of martial law and hard-to-spare companies of soldiers were sent to impose Confederate will. In the end, only this diversion of scarce manpower managed to quell the threats of open outbreaks.

By 1864, Texan Unionists were publicly quiet, though still privately resentful, and they never stopped encouraging deserters and opposing conscription. In the end, their greatest injury to the Confederate cause was probably their overwhelming indifference to the cause, that same *"incivism,"* as Degener's counsel had called it, that lack of patriotism. By the fall of 1864 some Texas merchants were making their way through the lines to bring consumer goods back to sell for extortionate rates, one man going all the way to Illinois twice in order to profiteer off loyal Confederates driven to illegal trade by hardship and shortage. The governor wanted such people indicted by civil authorities, or even by the military, in a clear breach of constitutional law, but it was too late for anything effective to be done.[22] And when it became increasingly apparent late in the war that the South was going to lose, the Unionists became more open again in their sympathies, and even briefly challenged a state legislature resolution pledging unyielding resistance to Union and reconstruction, losing by only one vote.

The rest of the Confederacy, especially in the rural and hill country areas, echoed the Texas experience. In every state, of course, majority opinion gave varying degrees of loyalty to the Confederacy, yet everywhere the barb of disloyalty stung at and distracted civil and military authorities from their more pressing business. Even in Jefferson Davis's own Mississippi they faced the embarrassment of toryism. Of course there were the outspoken, if foolish, who simply said what they thought and dared authorities to act. A man in Jefferson County in June 1862, on hearing that a Union fleet was advancing along the Mississippi, publicly said that he "wished the Gun Boats would shell every God Damn plantation on the River." The planters were all thieves anyhow and he would not fight for them, and as for the slaves, if they would only rise up, they could defeat the Confederacy by themselves. Such men escaped the rope largely because authorities thought they had to be unbalanced to make such damning statements knowingly.[23] Nevertheless, reports came to Governor Pettus of men in high position who said privately that they would not hesitate to trade with the Yankees if Union forces occupied the state, and in the southern part of the state a number of whole families moved to the protection of Union lines extending from New Orleans.[24] Equally distressing reports came from communities like Canton, of citizens who spoke of joining the Yankees when they came, and of others determined to go to the hills as guerrillas and resist Confederate authorities if they had to. Meanwhile, as predicted, the slaves were getting more impudent as enemy lines grew closer, and they had the encouragement of deserters and the disloyal. "This last class is getting to be numerous," an official in Marion County complained to the governor, "and there seems at present to be no efficient remedy for the evil."[25] By late 1863 civilians in north Mississippi, hungry and discouraged, were openly trading with the enemy occupying nearby communities, even at risk of having their wagons and teams confiscated in punishment.[26] They simply no longer feared serious repercussions from their own government. Here, too, opposition to conscription had combined with inherent disaffection to encourage a peace movement early in the war, only to see it grow into more vocal toryism, especially in the rural northeastern counties.

By the fall of 1862, military commanders were shooting tories who cooperated too freely with the enemy in the northeast, while Jones and surrounding counties in the southeast of the state were in almost open rebellion with a fusion of deserters, Unionists, and conscript fugitives bound by the single issue of unwillingness to go to the army. If that did not make them all pro-Union, it nevertheless united them as anti-Confederate. Myths would arise that Jones had seceded from the Confederacy to form the Free State of Jones, though no such thing occurred, but certain it is that state and national civil administration all but broke down there, and in 1864 there were open skirmishes between state troops and the bands of combined tories and deserters, with deaths on both sides, though not on the scale of the Nueces skirmish.[27] A report from Macon in March 1864 complained that "the city is infested." The writer added that he was himself ambushed and shot near his own plantation, the county sheriff was a refugee, and "Union or Peace meetings are boldly held and Union speeches made." The tories were so bold that "no man's life is safe who dares to speak out against them."[28] Deserters appeared at the polls that fall and openly intimidated people from voting for candidates who supported the war, and soldiers sent to hunt them down often just joined them instead.

By the end of the year the officers in charge of conscription declared that their job was hopeless in the state, and in Alabama and Georgia the inability to protect citizens from the depredations of deserters was so palpable that even loyal people began to pass resolutions announcing that they would accept a return to the Union if Yankee soldiers would give them protection.[29] A Mississippi judge reported to his governor in October that the growing numbers of deserters "constitute by far the greatest common & public nuisance in the land—hardly inferior to so many yankee troops in the country," and implored him to "please put our house in order."[30] Predatory bands of deserters and tories were combining with their kind from across the border in Alabama, and even Tennessee, and spreading alarm through the countryside. A tax collector pleaded that "it will be at the risk of my life" to attempt to gather levies, and when Confederate cavalry was sent to try to bring order, the soldiers themselves broke ranks to "prowl through the county frolicing & stealing." The sheriff of Perry County declared that "I will venture to say that there are more deserters in this county today than was here when the cavalry came here & they are in formidable gangs a doing mischief they are a burning & destroying the property of all loyal citizens such as will not sympathize with them. If there is not a change soon the deserters will kill & burn out many loyal citizens."[31] General Samuel Gholson warned that if not successfully opposed and constantly watched, the deserter bands would "soon become far more dangerous and destructive than are the Yankees."[32] By that fall reports reached the governor of "Federal farms" operating in Issaquena County, ready to aid invading Yankees, and of a secret organization of shoemakers in the state boot shops determined not to fight but to welcome the enemy when they came. Tories in Hancock County organized on Honey Island to be ready to invade neighboring communities when Union liberation came, their announced object being to rob and plunder as soon as the state militia was engaged by the Federals.[33]

Neighboring Louisiana offered the same sorry sight, especially after its major city, New Orleans, and its capital, Baton Rouge, fell so early in the war. Governor Thomas Moore was forced to move his government to Opelousas, west of the Mississippi, and as early as the summer of 1862 was already trying futilely to combat his people's trading with the enemy. The Union commander in New Orleans required Confederate Louisianians to get a passport that included a pledge that they would in no way give aid or countenance to the Confederacy, and Moore protested against his people taking or using such a document, as it carried with it "incipient neutrality." He issued a proclamation denouncing such practice, though little good it did. Admitting the presence of tories in their midst, he claimed that "they are rarely to be met, but though very few in number, they exist, and with a hate of our government not exceeded by the hate of the predecessors to the Government of George Washington." Confederates could no longer tolerate them. "They have made their option," he said. "They cannot live here and disregard our laws." He forbade trade with the Yankees, any travel to New Orleans, enjoined vigilance against the disloyal, and required merchants to accept Confederate scrip as lawful currency. On almost every issue, Louisianians torn between subsistence and loyalty chose to ignore him, especially those of the merchant class who had always had strong ties to the North.[34] Besides, trade with the Yankees was easy. In less than a year, the Union blockade would make trade for Confederate Louisiana increasingly difficult, and the trade route to Texas required a dangerous ninety-mile overland trip so liable to attacks by marauding bands of deserters and the disloyal that the teamsters refused to risk the journey.[35]

It was the same in Georgia, where Governor Brown heard from one citizen in 1864 that "deserters and toreys are gitting thick and no person seams to take aney intrest in taking them up." Moreover, he warned that "they say they are waiting for linkon to cum and then they will cum in and Rule this countrey and Have the lands totted off to sute them selves."[36] Brown himself had much to answer for in this, for dedicated though he was to the Confederate cause, his constant and vehement objection to conscription and other national measures gave encouragement to the tories, while his overly liberal use of his executive authority to grant exemptions meant that inadvertently he was shielding many a Union sympathizer from Rebel service. As the war appeared to turn against the South in the summer of 1863, the disaffection increased apace, and after the fall of Atlanta in 1864, many actively pressed Brown to save Georgia by making a separate peace with the Union and abandoning the Confederacy altogether.[37] Though Brown might have quailed at that, he did for a time entertain the possibility of holding meetings with General William T. Sherman, their intent a mystery but the subject of frantic speculation. Worse, Vice President Stephens had gone over to the anti-Davis camp two years earlier, and now he joined Brown in supporting resistance to conscription. That fall in Augusta, Stephens even declared that Southern resources were exhausted and it was time to make peace, the implication seeming to be that he would accept peace short of victory or independence, a return to the Union in exchange for guarantees of rights in slave property. Neither Stephens nor Brown was disloyal to Confederate ideals, but certainly they felt no loyalty either to Davis or to his policy of no peace without independence, and their every word was encouragement to those Unionists in Georgia who were actually and actively tories by choice.

In Alabama the conditions created by deserters and conscription dodgers in Winston and other disaffected counties were only exacerbated by the Unionism that ran through those areas. A Peace Society achieved early prominence, and by January 1862 there were Union companies of militia organizing in at least two counties. After that spring, when Federal troops occupied northern Alabama and held it for most of the rest of the war, they became a rallying point for the disaffected. Some of those early bands of pro-Union men would flock to the Stars and Stripes and enlist. Alabama thus contributed two regiments of cavalry to the Union army and several other smaller companies. Indeed, before the war ended, every Confederate state but South Carolina would have white men constituting units in the Yankee army. Almost as embarrassing, whole units of Confederate troops like the 3rd Alabama Reserves simply went over to the enemy. Bolder than their counterparts in some other states, the tories, both organized and informal, practiced espionage on bridges and telegraph lines, and actively aided invading Federals as scouts and guides. So strong were the Unionists that by the fall of 1863 they put up a slate of candidates both for the legislature and for Congress, men secretly committed to ending the war with reunion if necessary. They actually managed to defeat J.L.M. Curry, one of the founding fathers at Montgomery and an ardent Confederate, when he sought reelection to Congress. Indeed, they managed to send no fewer than six Unionists to Congress, including one who was in almost constant contact with the Yankees. Though they were too few to accomplish anything, still they represented a stunning embarrassment, especially when their sentiments and activities were disclosed. When outside Confederate supporters like John Tyler, son of the late president, and Virginia congressman in Richmond, came to Selma, Alabama, to give a speech promoting the idea that the only path to peace was through prosecuting the war to victory, Unionist newspaper editors purposely misinterpreted his address in order to make him appear to be on their side.[38] The governor, Thomas Watts, could by then only complain that "Tories, instigated by the enemy, and wicked men incited by the love of plunder, have banded together and have committed many depredations," and though he tried to form volunteer vigilante companies to quell their outrages, he had no legal authority to arm them for the task.[39]

Of all of the Confederate states, only South Carolina did not develop a truly troubling peace and Union sentiment to interfere with civil operations, though even there by early 1865 the combinations of tories and deserters were brazenly looting barns.[40] By contrast, Florida had an active peace movement from the beginning, and in time some 1,300 Florida men would enlist in Union units after Federals established themselves in the state. The issues of loyalty to the old Union, antipathy to the slaveholding elite, and outrage at conscription were the same here as elsewhere, exacerbated by Florida being one of the largest livestock-producing areas in the South. After 1862, forced impressments of Florida beef to feed the armies turned many a stockman against the Confederacy. Moreover, the state's swamps offered some of the best hiding places for fugitives of anywhere in the Confederacy, and as a result deserters from as far away as Virginia and Tennessee made their way there to avoid capture and live off the land and the loyal Confederates as best they could. Some organized themselves into formal units like the Independent Union Rangers of western Florida. There was even a plot hatched to abduct Governor Milton in 1864, though it was exposed in time.

Disaffection was perhaps the worst of all in the region formed by eastern Tennessee, western North Carolina, and southwestern Virginia, all constituting much of Appalachia. There an organization appeared called the Order of the Heroes of America, whose tentacles extended loosely through most of the other states east of the Mississippi, and it became the pre-eminent association of Unionists and the disaffected. Slaves were few in these mountains, poverty widespread, and common interests with the planter elite and the oligarchies almost none. It is possible that the order actually predated the war and the formation of the Confederacy. It was devoted to preserving the Union, just as were the Knights of the Golden Circle, an equally comic-opera secret society that had been around since the late 1850s promoting Southern rights. As soon as secession became a reality, however, citizens' groups met to challenge its legality in all three states. When those men sympathetic to the Confederacy left to enlist, the mountain counties were left all the more in the hands of the tories. Before long Unionists from east Tennessee began to raid Confederate communities in western North Carolina.[41] In North Carolina anti-administration editors like W. W. Holden actively promoted disaffection, and when Zebulon Vance ran for the governorship in 1862, his outspoken stance for state sovereignty against Richmond's centralizing tendencies led to some referring to him as the Yankees' candidate.

Men like Vance and Holden, regardless of their basic loyalty to the Confederacy, encouraged the tories, just as did Brown in Georgia, by condoning opposition to Confederate authorities on principles of localism. Moreover, Vance stood up for men arrested on charges of disloyalty. Meanwhile, when there were strong reactions to the brazen Unionists, they were frequently extreme. In February 1864 at Kinston, North Carolina, some twenty-two men who had deserted from the Confederate army and enlisted in the Union blue were captured and hanged by military authorities. At Shelton Laurel in the western North Carolina mountains thirteen Unionists were hanged, and similar acts of retribution occurred elsewhere. All worked to urge tories and Unionists to even greater resistance. It is no coincidence that these acts came at the same time that the Order of the Heroes came out in the open to make a bid for control of their homelands. Peace meetings were held all across the mountains, desertion and resistance to the draft were more actively encouraged than ever, and in many places Confederate authorities feared to attempt to reestablish control. Deserters stopped and asked to show their furloughs or passes to be away from their regiments simply stroked their rifles menacingly and responded, "This is my furlough." By the fall of 1863, as in Alabama, elections sent eight peace men out of ten delegates to represent North Carolina in Congress, and in the following February, Davis had no choice but to ask Congress to suspend the privilege of the writ of habeas corpus to allow him to cope with the rampant disloyalty.

Soon Richmond had active agents infiltrating the Order of the Heroes and sending reports back of what they had learned. The tories were ready to declare a new State of Southwest Virginia, with its own governor and lieutenant governor, as well as militia commanders and a militia composed of deserters. When Holden ran against Vance for the governorship in 1864, he was widely believed to be himself a member of the order. "All the families of deserters & recusant conscripts will vote for him," charged a Vance supporter, and the rumor went the rounds that Holden sanctioned calling a state convention to make North Carolina secede from the Confederacy.[42] Holden was branded an outright traitor, and Vance won handily. A number of the leaders of the order were arrested and tried, though apparently none were executed, and almost all were soon released.[43] By that fall most of the people in six contiguous counties of southwest Virginia were believed to be involved in the order, including sheriffs, justices of the peace, and even militia officers. More alarming still, witnesses under interrogation alleged that the order had spread into Lee's Army of Northern Virginia, and that some regiments were thoroughly infected, so much so that Richmond warned Lee to watch out for active disloyalty in his ranks.

As with all of the peace societies and other secret tory organizations, the strength and influence of the Order of the Heroes was exaggerated, much of it blatant self-promotion, yet even such misconceptions spread the work of those opposed to the war and the Confederacy. Yet it is certain that in southwest Virginia, perhaps more than anywhere else east of the Mississippi, the Confederacy all but had to give up attempting to exert civil or military control by late 1864. The order controlled the courts, making convictions of the disloyal all but impossible, while the mountain fastness was sufficiently remote and the sympathy of the civilian population so strong that deserters could come to the region with impunity, with little fear that the military would ever catch them or be able to bring them to justice. Raids, sabotage, and espionage against Confederate installations and plans were carried on constantly, especially whenever a Yankee force invaded the area, as in May and again in October and December 1864. It was widely rumored that word leaked out by the order even led to the surprise attack that fall on the command of General John Hunt Morgan, who was killed.[44]

All across the Confederacy the same dynamics propelled significant portions of the population to seek their security and place their loyalty in the old order rather than the new. Tenacious attachment to the Union itself led the causes, but growing disaffection with their would-be Southern nation soon ran a close second. Conscription and impressment, limitations on civil rights, and an often imperious management from Richmond and state capitals drove those already inclined to waver in the direction of outright resistance. Battlefield failures, especially outside Virginia, made ever more pressing the impression that the Confederacy was destined to lose anyhow, and that when it lost conditions would become hard if they resisted the Union too long.

Confederate democracy was not strong enough to guarantee its men the constitutional right to speak their minds free of retaliation, nor to keep them from being forced into the army against their will. And once they were gone, neither could it protect their families at home from hardship and want, or from the depredations of deserters and profiteers. In short, it could not give them what they had been able to take for granted for generations from the Union, however much some of them objected to some of the political policies being pursued in Washington. Moreover, based on the experience they had under the Confederacy in the first two or three years of the war, when it seemed at times to be going well, wavering or disloyal civilians could see little to encourage them that after the achievement of independence, should it ever happen, they could expect anything better under a system simply too weak to run a continental nation. The evidence of the actions of men like Brown and Vance in defying Richmond sent further messages that this was not a strong nation, and no one, even a Southerner with grievances against the North, wanted to be a proud citizen in a weak nation. To those not steeped in the economic investment in slaves and large landholdings, a nation created primarily to protect the interests of an oligarchy simply had too little to offer. The tories did not cripple the Confederacy, nor is it likely that their cumulative influence shortened the life of the independent South by even a single day. Yet added to the problems of loyal political opposition, the disintegration of civil law and order, and all the other mounting wounds that bled the Confederacy from day to day, disloyalty spread its poison throughout a weakened system, ultimately taking its part in the final breakdown of the will and the ability to resist.

10

Cotton Communism, Whiskey Welfare, and Salt Socialism

SOME DEGREE OF CENTRAL CONTROL over the private sector was inevitable in the Confederacy, just as it would be in the Union. Rationing of staples and state redirection of manufacturing and production were old companions to nations at war throughout history, but chiefly among the monarchies and dictatorships where absolute authority lay unquestionably with the head of state. Neither had been seen before on any appreciable scale in a democracy, however, and not at all in America. The very ideas ran counter to the ideals of free enterprise and personal and business control of individual destinies, upon which the American concept of the relation of citizens and corporations to the state was founded. Nothing in either the Constitution of the United States or its statutes at large authorized the central government to control private industry, or even to involve itself as an investor or partner, and neither did the Confederate charters that virtually copied their progenitors. Though it was inevitable that scarcity and shortage, or difficulties in efficient transportation and distribution, would force both sides to address the potentially explosive issue of how far the state could intrude itself into the private sector, it was anathema to the leading secessionists. From the very outset there would be loud voices like Robert Barnwell Rhett's, William L. Yancey's, even Vice President Alexander Stephens's, arguing that no emergency justified trampling on personal rights of property, or encouraging or involving state or federal government itself with business and industry. The secessionist states had left the Union on issues of just such principles, these men and others would argue. How could they now contemplate betraying those very tenets themselves in the name of emergency and expediency? To do so called in question the very foundation of their movement. How could they preserve the rights they were supposedly fighting for by themselves becoming the violators?

Yet how could they not? Abraham Lincoln, when discussing his own in-fringements on his Constitution, supposedly said that it was more practical to cut off a man's arm to save his body than to sacrifice the body to save the limb and thereby lose everything. The same calculus applied to the Con-federacy. Confederate industry and society would have to be mobilized to have any hope of success, and that inevitably required management. Southerners could expect—and received—a remarkably high degree of voluntary effort in the first euphoric months of patriotic frenzy, but the longer the war lasted, the more that would abate, and what could replace the fruits of voluntarism but compulsion. Just as the Confederacy would have no choice but to turn all too quickly to conscription to fill its regi-ments, and impressment to feed those armies, so it would have to impose control at state or federal levels, or both, to draft individuals and industries into serving the cause. If that road led to other internal dangers, still they had no choice but to risk the journey.

The outpouring of patriotic voluntarism was staggering at the outset, es-pecially from the women who saw their men go to war and wanted to do their own part at home. Most prevalent of all was their work in spinning cloth and making uniforms and blankets to clothe the men in the field. "The family spinning wheel and loom have been resurrected from their hidden corners, brushed up, and set to work again," declared a man in Lexington, Virginia, who noted that woolen factories were also boosting their output. "A new impetus has been given to this business since the be-ginning of the war."[1] All across the new nation the governors' daily mail brought news of individual women and community organizations of them who were feverishly working away at their wheels, looms, and needles. "Wishing to aid in our country's struggle for her rights," declared a woman representing the Conway, Mississippi, Soldiers' Relief Society, and "know-ing that we could not bear arms, and being unwilling to sit idle, we now of-fer our services to our government through you to manufacture into clothing such cloth as you may be pleased to send us." If the state could not furnish them fabric, then they would try to weave their own.[2] "The ladies who are more than willing to further the independence of the country have every where organized sewing societies," Mississippi's Governor John Pettus learned in July 1861.[3] When Governor Joseph Brown of Georgia announced a call for women to turn their hands to sewing, it produced a race for distinction. One lady spoke to him of "the generous rivalry you have created by your announcement," and suggested that he should offer some award or distinction for the woman who furnished the greatest amount of soldier clothing by her own efforts. While it was assumed that the states would furnish the yarn or the fabric, many women were content to work to earn money to buy the raw materials themselves, and then work even more to turn them into clothing. "Every one will do all that may be in her power," a woman assured Brown.[4] Virginia's Governor John Letcher paid tribute to the women of the Ladies Soldiers' Aid Society of Natural Bridge for their work in tending the wounded after the first battle at Manassas in July, and stories soon circulated of the heroic work of two Alabama sisters who reputedly made all of the bandages used for the Confederates wounded in the action.[5]

Governor Andrew B. Moore of Alabama called on women of the state to make socks for soldiers, and the word went out to other governors from Congressman Alexander Clayton that "a similar call from you would put many fair fingers to work."[6] The women themselves called on their communities to contribute cloth or thread or buttons, as well as money to buy more. The Ladies Volunteer Relief Society of Edwards Depot, Mississippi, predicted that they would have ten bales—ordinarily worth $5,000—contributed by October 1861, and they would either sell it through the blockade in order to buy soldier clothing or else sell it to the state to be made into cloth at the penitentiary.[7] If they had to spend their own funds to buy material, they would do it, though soon some protested that they did not have enough money left to pay to ship the uniforms to the armies, and called on the governors to provide transportation.[8] Most of all, however, they begged for more cloth to work. As early as July 1861 there was already a shortage in some states. The Texas penitentiary inmates at Huntsville were manufacturing woolen cloth at the rate of 10,000 yards a month in February 1861, the month of Lone Star secession, but a year later the deterioration and overwork of their machinery had them seven months behind as the demand for uniforms steadily escalated. Worse, the emergency requirement that the Huntsville cloth be used exclusively for Texas soldiers led to the cancellation of contracts with other jobbers in the South just as the principal Confederate army in Tennessee commanded by General Albert Sidney Johnston was going into winter quarters. "It is next to an impossibility to keep our soldiers in this cold, damp climate from freezing on account of inadequate clothing," complained a Memphis supplier, who begged that large stores of clothing supposedly being held in Texas be made available for soldiers from other states.[9] Pettus of Mississippi put his prisoners, too, to work making wool cloth for distribution to the soldiers' aid societies.[10] At the same time, he put out contracts to a private textile firm to manufacture 100,000 yards of cloth for winter uniforms at a frantic rate of 1,000 yards a day.[11] "We are ready & desirous to do our part," one ladies' aid society assured him, if only he could get them cloth. Unfortunately, if understandably, most of the societies wanted to make clothing to go to their own locally raised companies, but that was impractical, and the governors had to insist that they distribute the goods at their own discretion.[12] Many suggested that factories in the Confederacy be persuaded or even forced to shift their production to fabric, and some companies volunteered their services, like the Mississippi Manufacturing Company, which proposed to convert its machinery and work force to making cloth, though the motive might have been muddied somewhat by wanting to hold onto workers who were volunteering at such a rate that only employing them in vital war work was likely to keep them on the job.[13]

By late summer 1861 the several factories in Mississippi and Alabama could not keep up with demand, nor could the penitentiaries, which sometimes produced inferior cloth. By October there came pleas that every available scrap of cloth had been sewn into uniforms and the women's fingers were idle.[14] Some women asked if they could be given passes to go to the front to act as nurses if they could no longer sew, while the "Thimble Brigade" from one community begged for a steady supply of cloth to "place the female department on [a] solid basis, so that its performance and eficiency shall be secured." There was also the added problem that citizens in many communities had contributed so much money to support the soldiers in the early months that now hardship loomed as consumer prices accelerated.[15] "When our ladies was making up soscities [sic] for the purpose of clothing the soldiers I told our soscity to let us all go to spinning an weaving but they said let us by the cloth," complained a Georgia woman. "Now wee have nothing to by with—what are wee to do for our soldiers—I for one am willing to spent and be spent."[16] Their frustration became only the greater when those at some distance from the front learned that the clothing they made, and often even the special bundles of things made by wives and sisters for delivery to particular soldiers, often did not get to the men, but were instead sold along the way by profiteering agents.[17]

The governors struggled with the problem for the rest of the war, and so did Richmond. Governor John Milton put Florida's women to work at sewing, and sometimes personally oversaw buying as little as two hundred yards of cloth to distribute to them.[18] In Mississippi, Governor Pettus often acted personally as the intermediary between delivery of uniforms from the societies and their distribution to the soldiers. South Carolina appropriated $20,000 to buy or build its own machinery for making cotton cards, and when Georgia established its own manufactory to produce the carding machines that furnished cotton for cloth, Milton sent his own machinist to observe so that he could return and build such machines for the state of Florida.[19] Women who somehow came up with wool themselves applied to governors to have it woven into jeans cloth at the penitentiaries and then returned to them for sewing.[20] The patriotic women could sometimes be more than just imploring, despite the fact that they were doing the states' and Confederacy's work for them at no compensation. "I am, one of the many, in these troublous times, who are sorely puzzled by the question 'wherewith shall you be clothed?'" a Georgia schoolteacher wrote Brown in November 1863. She did not earn enough herself to buy factory-spun thread for uniform making, and instead spent all her spare time at her own spinning wheel making thread from raw cotton when "cards" of the fiber were available. She begged the governor to find her just two cards of cotton so that she could keep her needle busy. "It is very mortifying to one's delicacy, or rather pride to thus beg," she complained, "but alas stern Necessity has trampled these down, or kindly hushed them to sleep."[21] As early as August 1861 the medical purveyor's office in the Confederate War Department at Richmond appealed to the governors to ask every family to contribute one blanket or comforter for the sick soldiers in hospitals and those in camp for the coming winter, and every community to form societies to raise contributions. It was only a request, and thus not an attempt to interfere with or impose upon state sovereignty, but nevertheless a clear sign that from the outset Richmond expected collective effort to supply the deficiencies in national capabilities.[22]

Unfortunately, for more than a year by this time, such private mills as continued in operation were so completely occupied with state and Confederate orders, or else commandeered outright, that planters and farmers

could not get their own cotton and wool woven into fabric to clothe themselves or sell at market, let alone make uniforms.[23] In Alabama the Confederate military authorities seized the cotton factory at Tuscaloosa that
provided clothing for the student cadets at the state university, forcing the
boys to cut up their bed linen to line their uniforms, even as the voracious
conscription officers were trying to take the boys, too, even though most
were under the military age.[24] In response to the critical situation, and the
ever-increasing demands for clothing to keep civilians from freezing and
exposure, some of the states turned to other expedients. With an irony
seemingly lost on Mississippians, their legislature actually appropriated up
to $100,000 for the importation of cards of cotton from other states or even
abroad through the blockade, in order to provide the raw material for
clothing for indigent refugees and poor soldiers' families. With commercial production of cotton all but curtailed as a result of the government-imposed embargo, Mississippi, the leading cotton state in the Confederacy,
would be importing foreign cotton to clothe its own people. As clothing
concerns shifted from exclusively military ones to providing for destitute
civilians as well, the state governments found themselves more and more
adopting an unaccustomed public welfare role. "Domestic cloths have gone
up to a point which renders it difficult for the poor," a South Carolinian
complained. "Although we feel much disposed to do something towards
relieving the needy, it will be impossible for us." In September 1863 when
the machinery of a defunct Georgia textile manufacturer went on sale,
agents from every state east of the Mississippi attended the auction, hoping to use it to alleviate their people's wants.[25] Never before had states purchased raw materials out of state funds and distributed them to private
citizens. By early 1864 it became a commonplace. Florida contracted with
the new Florida Card Manufacturing Company to spend $30,000 on buy-
ing cards to give to the needy, while in Louisiana in 1864 Governor Henry
W. Allen ordered the superintendent of the state penitentiary to loan its
looms to planters in eastern Louisiana so that they could turn their cotton
into cloth for the people, thus actually redirecting the operation of a state
enterprise to the benefit of the citizens. Declaring that "I shall do all in my
power to supply the wants of our people," Alabama Governor Thomas
Watts contracted with manufacturers in Selma and Montgomery, and also
managed to import 30,000 cards through the blockade to Wilmington,
North Carolina, only to find that then he could not get them on the railroad to Alabama.[26]

The shift to attempt to meet the needs of the people as well as the soldiers came at a time when the whole system was already approaching collapse. In Texas the Tyler County Card and Machine Factory could no longer operate because all of its workers had been conscripted.[27] On one raid in mid-August at another mill in Mississippi, the impressment officers took away wagons and teams and even one slave, while actually firing into the quarters of the other slaves who had replaced conscripted white workers. The works itself was so worn down that instead of piping for running water to the steam machinery, managers were using hollowed logs. The manager himself was uneasy lest he, too, be drafted and the whole operation simply shut down. "I am sorter afraid to come up now," he responded to his governor's summons. "As soon as I resign you will put me in the Militia."[28] The governors were even forced to contemplate dealing with the enemy. Men in west Tennessee who had friends behind Yankee lines managed in December 1864 to arrange for delivery of hand-operated spinning machines to Mississippi, and requested a permit to bring them through the lines. "It ought to be, the policy of the country to sanction and encourage by every proper means the importation of all such machinery as will reduce the amount of labor necessary to cloth the people and army," they argued, even if such machines came from the enemy's country.[29] As late as April 8, 1865, just hours before the final gasps of surrender commenced, Governor Pendleton Murrah in Texas still struggled to put clothes on his people's backs, but found not a single machine in his frontier counties. He had dreamed of making Texans self-sufficient, but instead now they were reduced to selling the few cattle that escaped the impressment officers, in order to buy fabric brought through the blockade, or misappropriated from the military and sold on the black market, and at grotesquely extortionate prices.[30]

Cotton was not the only object of considerable state interference in the normal operation of private enterprise and the free economy. Even so small an item as a crystal of salt could attract the attentive hand of centralizing authority. There was no more essential commodity in all the Confederacy, especially in wartime. Its use for seasoning quickly melted into the memories of other lost luxuries, as its necessity as a preservative became paramount. Armies required meat. Farmers' chickens fell prey to the armies as they marched past, and were as quickly eaten as taken. Hogs, too, found themselves liberated by foraging soldiers, but more often were collected by the impressment officers and marshaled alive or butchered at commissary depots. Beef was the great requirement, and herds sufficient for the demand could not practically follow the marching armies, while the armies themselves campaigned hundreds of miles from the major livestock-raising areas like Texas and Florida. Pig or steer alike, neither could practically be driven alive to feed hungry Johnny Reb where he camped or campaigned. The only practical alternative was to preserve the meat, whether for the soldiers or for their families at home. Sugar would work, but was itself in even shorter supply than many other commodities, too dear at the market to use in the uncountable tons needed to keep meat fit to eat, and its sources in Louisiana too far away and vulnerable to Yankee invaders. That left salt as the only practical preservative, as it had been for generations.

If not exactly abundant in the South, still salt had never been in short supply before the war. There were numerous sources west of the Mississippi in Louisiana, Texas, and Arkansas, and a couple along the Alabama and Tombigbee Rivers north of Mobile. There were several coastal sources along the Gulf and the Atlantic in Florida and Georgia, but the most abundant and dependable outlet of all was the extensive mines in and near the aptly named community of Saltville in southwestern Virginia. The rock salt deposit lying some 200 feet below the surface there was fully 175 feet deep, and extended over hundreds of acres. For nearly a century it had been the chief source of salt to most of the South, and with the coming of the war there were those who boasted that given enough labor to work the wells and pits, Saltville alone could supply all of the Confederacy's needs by itself.[31]

Yet competition for salt from the rather small number of commercial producers quickly led to problems. The Confederate government contracted for the supply needed for its armies, and would continue to do so until the end came. Before the war citizens had always purchased salt for themselves as needed or as they could afford, but now it remained to the individual states to manage the matter for their civilian populations. The same number of people were eating meat as before the shooting started, but the redistribution and concentration of hundreds of thousands of the men into armies meant that much more meat was now being preserved rather than consumed freshly killed. Thus the voracious appetite of the armies created a competition between soldier and civilian that was complicated by problems of transportation and distribution. It was not many months before Richmond and the statehouses alike realized that necessity made some form of central control essential. What developed was something far removed from the essentially libertarian ideals of the secessionist founding fathers: salt socialism.

In Congress some voices called for extreme measures from an early date. With the war scarcely more than a year old, bills and resolutions went onto the floor of the House and Senate that would have empowered President Davis to nationalize saltworks across the Confederacy for the needs of the military, or else to appropriate the production of such works for adequate compensation, or even to set price controls on salt. Nothing came of this first proposed threat of draconian centralization, but late in 1863 and into early 1864 the Congress again investigated government seizure and operation of saltworks to supply the army's needs. Once more, apparently, the acts seemed too radical, or sufficient support proved wanting, yet the portent of nationalization matched the kind of socialized management of salt that was already well under way within the states themselves.[32]

State action was swift, and in some instances dramatic. In the fall of 1861 the Alabama legislature passed a bill outlawing monopolies in salt production, and further prohibited the commercial export of state-manufactured salt as well as other commodities to other states in order to discourage speculation and profiteering. So dramatic was the action that Governor Moore immediately felt compelled to reassure his neighbor Governor John Pettus of Mississippi that Alabama had no intention of trying to interfere with the commerce of other states, and that there would be no interruption in the supply of salt contracted by the state of Mississippi for its people's private use.[33] But by the fall of 1862 the mismatch of supply and demand forced Moore's successor, John Gill Shorter, to renege on his predecessor's promise to Pettus, and he cut off the further shipment of salt contracted to Mississippi, even as Pettus monitored the progress of the production of Alabama salt that he planned on distributing to his citizens.[34] Pettus was using the county police courts to apportion salt to destitute families, meanwhile experimenting with measures for producing the necessity on his own soil. One of his agents tried extracting salt from the banks of brackish coastal streams, getting a few tablespoons of brine from a whole barrel of earth, while wells sunk near the coast could produce in a time-consuming and impractical process a single tablespoon of salt from every gallon of water. By early 1863 Pettus had agents experimenting with distilling salt from seawater on Mississippi's coast.[35]

In neighboring Georgia at almost the same time the legislature authorized Governor Brown to seize all supplies of salt in the state, both that in
the hands of outright speculators capitalizing on the increased demand on
limited production and that belonging to legitimate merchants and manufacturers. There came an immediate outcry that law-abiding people suddenly could not buy a single sack of salt. "What am I to do?" demanded a
farmer who protested that he was a planter, not a speculator. "My Pork will
soon be ready for slaughtering & no salt."[36] When the seizure first took
place, many assumed that it would be put on the market, and that henceforth consumers would simply buy from the state instead of from private
vendors. As a result, most farmers did not lay in a supply of salt from out-
of-state sources. But true to his hoarding instincts, whether of soldiers or
salt, Brown kept the commodity in state warehouses instead. Protests soon
came in claiming that whole communities were out of salt. Even a substantial town like Macon had only eleven sacks after the state seizure, and
several plantations were wholly without. Planters implored the governor to
put some of the state holding up for sale, warning of considerable suffering otherwise, especially among the poor farmers, and a few even raised
the portent of citizens storming state supplies. "Unless we have greatly
overestimated the necessity," advised the managers of the salt warehouse
in Macon on December 16, "Locks and Bolts will ere long not be sufficient
guard." By the summer of 1862, Brown had changed his policy and was
distributing salt to county agents for local sale, but only according to his
own distribution plan.[37]

In Florida, meanwhile, the legislature authorized Governor Milton to
assume complete control of the state's salt supplies; even state salt agents
could not disburse it to state militia officers without his authorization. In
desperation, by April 1862 people were forging the governor's signature on
orders in order to get a few sacks from the warehouses, and when any fell
into the hands of the unscrupulous, they quickly marketed it at extortionate prices.[38] Late in 1861 the Texas legislature empowered the governor to
take possession of a salt lake, at state-controlled prices, with the proceeds
going into the Treasury. The two Carolinas attempted to create works
within their borders, with only limited success in South Carolina, while in
its neighbor to the north the production was dogged by conflicts with the
national military authorities as conscription and impressment officers repeatedly drafted the men and equipment necessary to keep the state

works going.[39] The Palmetto State gave contracts for 5,000 bushels at a time, at $4 a bushel, imposing heavy state control through its own Department of Justice and Police, whose very name lent a powerful hint that the state meant business. It required suppliers to post bonds of $6,000 as surety that they would deliver, and when supplies in South Carolina ran short, the authorities began to investigate contracting for production in Virginia.[40]

Only in Virginia, thanks to Saltville, was the supply of salt truly abundant, and thus it was to be expected that other states sooner or later would attempt to contract with the operators there to supply their needs. Even there the state almost interfered when the legislature ordered Governor Letcher to seize the works and appropriate all of Saltville's output for itself through purchase or lease, but when that plan failed in May 1862, the other states, led by Georgia, quickly got in line. Rather than simply buying salt from the overtaxed existing manufacturers, Brown instead leased land above the massive salt layer and sent his own agents to construct wells and distilleries. Other states, including Tennessee, Mississippi, North Carolina, and even Alabama, which could not themselves supply all their own needs, put up their own works or negotiated contracts with existing producers at Saltville, paying seventy-five cents a bushel for the salt they produced. Pettus alone contracted for 40,000 bushels in September 1862, in the first of several such contracts.[41] But this new arrangement hardly ended the buyers' problems, for they still had to compete with the army for iron kettles for boiling the brine to produce the salt, and found the military impressing even the canal barges used for transporting the refined salt to railheads for shipment. As late as October 1862, with the Alabama source cut off and his Virginia contracts impeded, Pettus had only a single source of salt for his state, a well at Salt Mine, Louisiana, constantly vulnerable to Federal raid. No wonder he was also trying to bring in foreign salt through the blockade from Liverpool.[42]

By the summer of 1863, and from then on until the end, the interference of the national authorities in the states' salt procurement only worsened. In June 1863 some 130 men in the Cool Mountain vicinity in Georgia took up a subscription of $4,000 to buy 70 sacks of salt from the state works in Virginia, only to discover that they could not get it shipped home for distribution. They appealed to the governor for help, but he had problems of his own. Unable to get state salt shipped home from Saltville thanks to Confederate domination of rolling stock for military purposes,

Brown sent a locomotive of Georgia's Western & Atlantic Railroad to Saltville in May 1863 to haul the state's salt home for him. When it proved too weak, he sent another one, advised by his agent on the scene that "our only hope to get the salt from Virginia is to help ourselves."[43] Then in January 1864 conscript officers suddenly took all of the employees of the state's Georgia Salt Manufacturing Company near Saltville, leaving the manager to warn Brown that their operation could soon be dissolved "by the interference of petty officers unless we have some prompt means of getting rid of them."[44] Salt workers had once been exempt from the draft, but no longer, except on special request of the governors, and immediately Brown and others found themselves beleaguered with appeals.[45] It was not enough. By August a Mississippi operator at the state's own new saltworks located in Alabama complained that "our affairs are seriously deranged by the acts of the Confederate impressing officers." One night Southern cavalry surrounded the works at midnight and took eight slaves employed there, while the rest of the blacks fled to the nearby woods. When the manager showed the officer in charge that he had an executive order exempting his work force, the cavalryman ignored him. The result was the closure of every furnace in the vicinity engaged in distilling salt from seawater. "We are now stopped—not doing a solitary thing," complained the manager, while the remaining slaves were demoralized out of fear of being impressed into working with the army. "This conduct on the part of the Confederate authorities is resulting disastrously to the interest of the State."[46]

Worse, in Mississippi as elsewhere, much of what the works produced could not be carried to the soldiers or the destitute for whom it was intended. In Mississippi the governor apportioned it by county, but then had trouble even moving it about within his own state. First Confederate military traffic completely occupied his one operating north-south rail line, the Mobile & Ohio, with the result that early in 1865, 10,000 pounds of salt at Okolona apportioned to Calhoun County simply sat on a siding for want of transportation. Then while it waited for wagons, Yankee cavalry raided the countryside and destroyed the salt. Seeing their ration denied them, the citizens of Calhoun County appealed to the governor for another allotment. Unlike many in the now ravaged Confederacy, these Mississippians had no shortage of meat, but without that salt they faced the inevitability that it would rot within a few days.[47] By 1865 they expected their state government to relieve them of their difficulty.

It was a considerable journey from the individualism and self-help ethic of 1860. Other than the minimal alms- and poorhouses for the truly destitute, the future citizens of the Confederacy would scarcely have expected their state authorities to indemnify them against hardship or want. Yet four years of scarcity, emergency, and turmoil had turned almost every Confederate governor into a welfare agent in some degree. It could be argued under the doctrine of state sovereignty that the governors, with legislative backing, had the power to do so. Nevertheless, the extent of salt socialism was genuinely radical, embracing at least the authority to seize and "nationalize" private enterprises, and actually putting the states in the manufacturing and sales business at the same time that they set prices and oversaw distribution and rationing either free or at cost. The state might not have been taking "from each according to his ability," but when it came to salt they were certainly trying to provide "to each according to his need." That the citizens often still paid for the state salt once they got it did not obviate the fact that the state had inserted itself into the demand and supply equation, replacing both manufacturer and retailer. Moreover, given the highly inflated currency of the Confederacy, even paying for the salt hardly represented a genuine transfer of capital from buyer to seller. Throughout the salt story, the outward forms of traditional American and Southern laissez-faire capitalism draped themselves on a framework that represented something far more radical, something as remote from the intent and aspirations of the secessionist founders as emancipation itself.

Nor did this framework of socialistic policies and state intrusion confine itself to seasonings and preservatives. In South Carolina the governor banned the export of all foodstuffs from his state repeatedly during 1863, in the face of local scarcity and speculation in prices.[48] In Florida, Milton actually proposed that the state should assume control of planting and labor and crops, both to ensure that no cotton was grown in violation of the national embargo declared by Davis and Congress, and to make certain that corn was planted instead.[49] Giving a governor the unilateral authority to enforce such a policy was a much more intrusive step in a land where the right to control one's property had been sacred for generations. After all, it was the rights of property that propelled the secession engine itself, yet now in the emergency both national and state governments inserted themselves between a man—and almost all property holders were men— and his right to enjoy what he owned as he saw fit.

The growing number of refugee families who left their homes in advance of enemy invasion dramatically compounded the states' problems. At the same time that Milton called for extension of his powers over property, he also ordered that county judges make lists of the destitute families of soldiers in Florida, and then use state agents to purchase and distribute to them supplies of corn and molasses, potatoes and peas, bacon, pork, and beef.[50] As early as October 1861 he was trying to relieve the condition of Floridians forced to flee Key West for the interior, calling for private donations until he could engineer state aid, and for the rest of the war he tried to provide some assistance to people who fled the state for Alabama and elsewhere.[51] Governor Brown established corn agents in each of Georgia's counties and allowed them to use state troops to haul the grain to destitute families, thus involving the militia in relief work, while South Carolina established a Soldiers' Board of Relief that required reports of the destitute from each parish, with estimates of their needs.[52] The reports identified the needy by name, number of children, and the districts or "beats" in which they lived, and authorized disbursement of $3 per person up to a maximum of $7.50 per quarter, allocating $5,000 to $6,000 in state funds to each district. By late 1864 the system was breaking down, however, with no uniformity in the incremental payments from one district to another, leading to complaints of inequity, while refugee families shifted from one district to another when they heard payments were better elsewhere, making record keeping a nightmare, and the money was so scarce in any case that in some districts the welfare payment was down to $1 per person. Besides, the poor protested that money was no good to them in the grossly inflated market. They wanted the state to give them bread and clothing.[53]

At the other end of the Confederacy in Texas, relief committees to care for the families of soldiers appeared in 1862, and their demands grew rapidly. In October there were 150 to 200 destitute soldier families comprising some 1,800 women and children on Galveston Island alone, the best equipped of them subsisting on small garden plots and a few goats. Governor Francis Lubbock began a policy of directing the products of the Texas penitentiary to the soldier families first, and when he left office in 1863 implored his successor, Pendleton Murrah, to continue doing so.[54] In Mississippi men charged with helping the soldier families and refugees asked for a state tax for their relief, specifically calling for a "provision tax" based on the retail prices being charged rather than a money tax. This would strike a blow at the speculators who had bought surplus comestible goods when there was no scarcity, but who now sold them at exorbitant rates, men whom Governor Watts of Alabama condemned for trying to "fatten upon the life blood of their neighbors."[55] Such a tax would take provisions from them based on their profiteering prices and redistribute them to the poor, thus reducing demand, and thereby cutting the heart out of the profit in speculation. It was too radical an intrusion into private enterprise and the marketplace for governors like Pettus to go along, but still it revealed how far some influential men were ready to go in the emergency.[56]

From the first there was not enough relief to meet all needs. The police courts and county inferior courts charged with overseeing distribution soon had to make judgments. Distributing commissioners in Hog Mountain, Georgia, in 1863 decided that they could no longer pay out money to soldier families and would distribute only bread and meat. And they could not handle everyone, but instead began to single out only those most needy. There should be no discrimination between widows and wives, "they being all in destitute circumstances," declared the commissioners, who recognized that all these women were working hard to support themselves. Still, the failure to provide for all caused alarm with some officials. "I sincerely hope that the decision of the Inferior Court may never reach our Brave men from this county, that their wives and children should be compelled to live on bread alone," complained a distributing commissioner. "It is no uncommon sight here to see a child attending to two or three more little ones and their mother working in the field and fed on bread only while their husbands are Bravely defending there Countrys rights on the Battle feeld."[57] He did not need to say how demoralizing that could be to the men in the ranks. Not surprisingly, by 1863 the states were also forced to deal with the question of whether or not they should extend relief efforts to the families of soldiers who had deserted, and where they did, justices found great discontent when it was pointed out that by doing so, the relief funds were indirectly financially supporting the deserters themselves.[58] By the last year of the war, in Florida alone the majority of Governor Milton's appointments went to unpaid volunteer agents assigned to procure wool for soldier uniforms, and others to find and distribute corn for relief of soldier families.

Then there was the issue of the husbands, brothers, and sons from those families. Citizens and officials alike recognized from the outset that the Confederate government's resources would be simply too strained to be able to meet all soldier needs. The result was the speedy formation of soldier relief societies and funds in every state, even states like Kentucky and Missouri that had not seceded but had units in the Southern armies. Governor Lubbock set up a furnished office in Richmond that even had stationery for an agent who acted almost like an elected representative attending to the needs of constituents as he expedited mail and packages to and from Texas soldiers and their families, assisted men in applications for furloughs and sick leave, and sought a building for a Texas military hospital. Indeed, the agent soon found that the Texas soldier in the capital had come to "regard the Texas Depot as Home in a foreign country as it were," complaining that without it he would be "subject to the rapacity of the Yankee traders of this Town which he has come to defend." The agent even lobbied Congress and the Treasury for money to support his efforts, and when he failed he appealed to Lubbock to organize a soldiers' aid society in Texas to collect funds for the sick.[59] By December 1861, Mississippi, Louisiana, Alabama, Georgia, and South Carolina all had their own soldier relief depots in Richmond, with Arkansas and Florida about to pool their resources to form their own. Governors and their agents used every connection they could, as when Milton of Florida had his agent meet with native son Secretary of the Navy Stephen Mallory and the state delegation in Congress, in hope of gaining assistance in establishing a Florida hospital in the capital.[60] South Carolina actually operated a "soldiers' home" in Richmond, while the state's Central Association for Soldier Relief managed to take in private contributions of more than $32,000 by late 1863, and more than a quarter million dollars from all state and private sources.[61] Meanwhile, the Confederate government, if it could not offer them funds, did at least make available to them free transportation for the supplies being sent from the aid societies at home, thus placing the government's hand in their welfare efforts.[62]

Such efforts were not without problems, ironically sometimes caused by the state's willingness to aid in private philanthropy. When citizens created the Georgia Hospital & Relief Association in Augusta in 1861 to engage facilities in Richmond to care for the state's sick and wounded in the Virginia army, its agents solicited money and supplies in every county. One man raised $9,000 in commitments in just five days, and anticipated that in the state as a whole they would raise $100,000 or more. But there were 25,000 Georgia men in uniform, which meant only $4 a man to provide medicines, nurses, hospital beds, pillows, blankets, and more, not to mention "delicacies in the way of diet" for the healthy as well as the sick. Then Governor Brown issued a proclamation promising that the state would provide funds sufficient for the purpose, which threatened to stifle the impulse for public contribution, prompting protests from those who would otherwise be most anxious for state assistance.[63]

As the armies moved, so the state relief associations had to keep pace with them, and while the depots would remain in Richmond until its evacuation in 1865, state agents elsewhere went from front to front. After the fall of Fort Donelson in February 1862, and the resultant evacuation of Nashville, the Texan agent with the retreating Confederate army of Albert Sidney Johnston told Lubbock that "you have no conception" of the utter confusion of Texan soldiers scattered everywhere as he tried to find them and see to their needs, needs that Lubbock himself had supported by a personal check for $100 given to the Ladies Relief Society of Corpus Christi.[64] Soldier relief only became the more difficult after the Union gained control of the Mississippi in July 1863, and Texas, Arkansas, western Louisiana, and Missouri were entirely cut off from their soldiers on the eastern side of the river. Their agents in Richmond and elsewhere could go months at a time without receiving news or additional funds, while governors and citizens alike passed long periods in ignorance of the condition of their men or the needs of their relief agencies.[65] Nevertheless, in cities like Houston the fairs and balls to raise soldier relief money continued unabated, sometimes at the rate of two events a week, calling for contributions to support specific local units, or Texas regiments in general, hospitals, impoverished families, and more. The town's Jewish people even raised $500 at the circumcision ceremony of the son of a local merchant.[66]

By 1864, after a year of almost continual army reorganization in the western theater, with brigades broken up and regiments repeatedly reassigned, the states were increasingly challenged to get aid to their soldiers efficiently. Even little Florida, with only a handful of units in the armies, still faced huge challenges in getting aid from the state to the men in the field, while Mississippians had to create an entirely new Mississippi Relief Association in Atlanta to minister to their soldiers during the fight about to take place for the Georgia metropolis.[67] The agents themselves faced many of the same hazards as the soldiers. The man operating Georgia's Empire Hospital noted in his register one September that "Thomas died 8th professed religion a week before & died happy," and then added at the bottom of the page of himself that "I am still alive but very weak."[68]

Confederates did not forget their sons beyond their reach in Yankee prison camps. Hard as it was to get aid through the lines for them, still efforts were made. As late as March 1865 a bill passed the Mississippi legislature to send an agent through the lines to provide relief for its soldiers held in Northern prisons. Several Mississippians applied to their governor for the appointment as commissioner, many out of sincere intention, but some no doubt simply wanting to get out of the Confederacy before the collapse, and perhaps with some state money in their hands that they would not have to return. One surprising applicant was Tennessee Congressman Henry W. Foote, then in disgrace after he was captured just two months before trying to sneak through the lines to approach Lincoln on a private peace mission, and sent back to face censure and virtual expulsion from Congress. He had a son who was a prisoner of war who stood to benefit from such a mission, and Foote himself now desperately wanted to get out of a Confederacy where he was increasingly condemned and unwelcome. In perhaps the most confused imaginable concoction of public involvement in soldier welfare mingled with political influence and private self-interest, he sought now to capitalize on humanitarian relief efforts to serve his own selfish ends. He got the appointment, but instead of doing anything for Mississippi prisoners, he sought an audience with Lincoln, who rebuffed him. Presented with the choice of leaving the country or being forcibly sent back to the Confederacy, Foote went to Europe, the trip quite possibly financed by hard-raised relief money.[69]

Meanwhile, no one at the outset anticipated the strains that state involvement in war relief was going to put on those limited areas in which government was already by tradition involved in public welfare. Before the war the slave states had a long tradition of opposition to state-supported free public education. Even by 1861, with property taxes funding almost universal primary learning for white male children, in some states education still lay chiefly in the hands of the parents, who paid as much as $2,500 a year for tuition and board by 1865.[70] Still there were areas in which the legislatures assumed that the state had a predominant responsibility, particularly in the care and education of the deaf and dumb, the blind, and the insane. Mississippi, for instance, maintained an asylum for the deaf and mute and an Institute for the Blind, and actually kept both going during the war, even though they had to relocate repeatedly to avoid invading Yankee armies. Adding to such hardship, military impressment took almost everything from the pupils at the Institute for the Blind, including

mattresses and beds, furniture, washboards, towels, and even eating utensils. In 1861 an annual appropriation of $6,000 kept the school fully
funded, but after three years, in the face of trebled prices, the appropriation was still just $8,000, and half of that just met the cost of one attendant
at the school and firewood for heat. By 1864 pupils could no longer leave
their destitute homes to attend unless the institute could furnish them
with shoes and clothing for the term, which of course it could not. The superintendent actually had to send a board member to Richmond to remonstrate with the War Department over the impressment of their desks
and chairs, and finally got a settlement of $1,420, but it cost half that just
to pay the expenses of the representative, which he charitably paid from
his own pocket. The money was used to buy rice, some of which the students ate, and the rest was sold at a modest profit. Still in October 1864 the
institute stood $3,000 in debt and the superintendent wondered if it
should simply close its doors.[71]

Four months later there were only eleven pupils, with the possibility of
another four to come, while others simply could not attend for lack of
clothing. The institute's debt had mounted to $6,500 and money had dried
up. "Nobody is willing to lend money in these times of doubt and difficulty," the superintendent complained, and commodities cost ten times
their 1861 prices if bought with hard specie, and up to fifty times as much
if paid for in inflated paper currency. At the same time, legislative action
had forced overage pupils into the school, meaning that there were one or
two who were forty years old and looked on the institute as a permanent
home rather than a school. They refused to follow the rules that applied to
the children, which demoralized the younger students and made them insubordinate to the point that the superintendent begged that the legislature either limit admission to those between eight and seventeen or else
cease operation, for he saw himself accomplishing little good.[72] One teacher
was accused of excessive whipping of the boys, beating one until his back
was black with bruises, and though he was acquitted of excessive cruelty,
still the combination of shortages and insubordination probably manifested
itself in sufficient frustration that the staff lost their self-control and even
their concern for the students, reserving better food for themselves, eating
at separate tables, and leaving the blind students helplessly making a mess
of their meals.[73]

Virtually every state had an asylum for the mentally ill. Even if the institutions' mission was regarded more as incarceration than treatment and

rehabilitation, still citizens and legislatures alike long recognized that society at large had some obligation to provide care for the insane and at the same time some protection from them for the community. Almost at once, however, the superintendents of the asylums found themselves in competition with the military in providing for the basic needs of their inmates. Agents buying meat for them sometimes had to buy from other states to meet demands, while the inflation of currency and increasing scarcity of almost everything meant that after two years the Mississippi asylum alone projected needing $50,000 a year for a mere 170 patients and staff.[74] A year later, in 1864, the asylum found itself in a terrible condition, its books looted by raiding Yankees, everything in short supply, the inmates almost naked for want of clothing and shoes. The patients were in danger of starving if the asylum could not manage to sell through the lines some fifty bales of donated cotton to the enemy occupying Vicksburg. The director paid from his own pocket to buy corn, and with a complete absence of meat, he gave the inmates syrup as a protein substitute. By October he had only five remaining employees, and then the conscript officers came and took them, too, leaving no one to care for or control the patients but himself.[75] By 1865, with permission from the governor, he was trading with the Yankees to feed his patients, and arguing that the government ought to be lenient with all benevolent institutions and allow them to export their cotton in spite of the embargo, and further not require that they suffer imposition of the government duties on exports.[76]

In the end the superintendent, Robert Kells, expressed thankfulness that he had simply been able to keep the asylum's doors open during the war to keep ministering to "that class of our fellow-beings whose affliction are greater than all other temporal afflictions." He admitted more than two dozen new inmates in 1865 alone, some of them suffering for twenty years or more before coming to him. A third of those he took in the year before came from the army. "The birth of this Confederacy has brought with it a terrible baptism of blood, and has made this whole sunny Southern land, a house of mourning," he lamented. "The very structure of our Society seems being destroyed." In such a circumstance, he thought it a wonder that more were not driven to madness, and wondered if grief and mourning had not actually occupied and saved minds that might otherwise have been lost. "There is a philosophy in every thing around us," he concluded. Now a few of his charges showed hopes of recovery, but many others seemed "doomed to a perpetual insanity," and a few even came to him in

chains after being so restrained for months. Even in the face of Confederate and state collapse he pleaded for prevention and early treatment of
mental illness rather than neglect and incarceration, arguing that "early attention is mostly successful." Even as the Confederate armies were surrendering, Kells had his inmates planting gardens to feed themselves,
somehow found a hundred piglets for them to raise, and put them to making soap and turning hemp into rope, as well as sewing domestic goods, to
make money to purchase their other necessities.[77]

By then, virtually all relief and welfare efforts reflected the general collapse.[78] For almost a year it had been no longer possible in some areas
even to assemble a meeting of the commissioners appointed to provide
relief for soldier families.[79] Citizens in Tishomingo County, Mississippi,
protested to the managers of the Mobile & Ohio early in 1865 of "a large
number of Shuddering and Starving women and children" for whom they
were endeavoring to find corn, but having found some, they could not get
transportation on the railroad to take the grain where it was needed. They
saw suffering everywhere, with the countryside devastated by the retreat
of Confederate forces and the raids of the enemy. Their county alone had
15,000 or more inhabitants who were at or near destitution, and some
forty-six companies of soldiers had been raised and taken out of the
county. "We do lament to say that some of the Wives of the same has already written to their Husbands to come home and relieve them from
Starvation," pleaded citizens in the face of such encouragement to desertion. "For humanity we do most earnestly appeal to you to furnish us with
Transportation."[80] Yet there was none to be had. In February 1865, when
the legislature called for twenty commissioners to secure donations of
money or property to provide education for the orphans of soldiers who
died in service, one of the men so appointed frankly confessed that there
had already been so many appeals for other charitable causes over the
years that those who were willing and able to give were themselves broke,
while the wealthy who never parted with a cent before were hardly likely
to start now. He suggested instead a property tax like that used to fund the
public schools, but it was far too late for that now.[81]

Still the governors and their agencies tried right up to the last minute.
On March 13, Governor Milton issued his last proclamation of his tenure,
an appointment of a trustee to oversee shipment of corn and other supplies to soldier family refugees at Apalachicola.[82] A month later, with Lee
and his army surrendered and the Confederate government in flight from

fallen Richmond, Governor Murrah in Texas was still ordering investigations into failures to provide care for indigent soldier dependents. The state had made appropriations for the purpose, also designating profits from the penitentiary's products, and even gave county courts the authority to levy special relief taxes and distribute the funds, arguably the most comprehensive—and unprecedented—public welfare funding scheme of the war. And Murrah was ready to take the chief justices of some counties to task for their failure to act.[83]

In an ironic reversal of governmental social policy, when the states could no longer meet their historic obligation to provide for the insane and helpless during the war, the patients were forced to provide in some measure for themselves, even as private citizens who had always taken care of themselves without government assistance became increasingly dependent upon government aid and agency to survive. Other than asylums and poorhouses, welfare and charity in the slave states had always depended primarily on private philanthropy, but in the face of war those states came to view their obligations to their citizens through a newer, more active, even proactive, lens.

Indeed, state assistance had been remarkable—and revolutionary—across the map. In January 1865 the state auditor of Mississippi reported that in the fourteen preceding months state revenue had been $4,758,678.67, derived from property taxes, a special military tax, interest on school fund deposits, money raised by several special acts for indigent families of soldiers, sale of public land, advances on cotton held by the state, penitentiary income, and other special funds. Never before had the state placed such heavy burdens on its people, and never before had they been imposed to fund so many nontraditional efforts. More than a million dollars went to soldiers' family relief alone. More went to establishing state distilleries, payment for goods impressed by state officials, military hospitals inside and outside the state, distribution of salt to the citizens, and perhaps most revolutionary of all, $1,788,911.25 for investment in Confederate Treasury notes to fund the war effort. As 1865 dawned, the state had taken on the responsibility of feeding 72,000 of its people, for which available income was wholly inadequate.[84] With some 80,000 of the state's 350,000 white population away in the armies, that meant that Mississippi was providing food and other subsistence for a fifth of its population. In other states the proportion was not dissimilar, and state appropriations did not take into account the privately raised contributions of the innumerable relief societies. By February 1865 the Soldiers' Board of Relief for just Pickens district in South Carolina was providing corn, wheat, and sorghum as almost the sole subsistence for 4,670 people, practically half the district's white population.[85]

Still there were people starving. One woman in South Carolina complained in February 1865 that the Soldiers' Board of Relief had provided her with a meager six pounds of salt, six pounds of rice, and less than two bushels of corn since the beginning of the war.[86] In spite of such shortcomings, a few officials expected their obligations to extend even beyond the war. "The Confederate Government, at the end of the war," an optimistic Governor Watts proclaimed in November 1864, "will find itself without the means, if it has the constitutional power, to provide for these children of the Republic." Still he recognized the division of authority and responsibility between federal and state action. But that being the case, he anticipated that Alabama had to fill the need, and he proposed that six million acres of public land within the state be withdrawn from sale and reserved, to be parceled out after independence in the form of homesteads for every one of its veterans and his family, "and the widow and the orphan can be made to rejoice in the possession of a home they can call their own."[87] The Confederacy had become virtually a welfare state ahead of its time, and yet again the antithesis of the hands-off government ethic upon which so much of Southern political and social ideology lay based.

Each of the states used such ingenuity and resources as were at hand to raise capital, sometimes through the sale of remaining public lands as in Florida and Mississippi.[88] In an era when there were few if any state taxes, they made revenue where they could, as the business of the states seemed suddenly to be business. In the five years ending on November 25, 1864, Mississippi's state treasury took in more than $16 million, yet disbursed $15.5 million on state services and enterprises, most of them related to the war.[89] State buildings and facilities like the Chattahoochee arsenal in Florida were converted to war uses, while other states bought or rented private edifices like the Charleston Hotel in Memphis, usually as hospitals.[90] The states became contractors and sometimes even partners in war manufacturing, while in a surprising number of other ways crossing the once sacred line between government and private enterprise. When the blockade runner *Florida*, privately owned and funded, reached Governor Milton's coastline with a cargo of 1,400 rifles and other armaments, he authorized state seizure of a private schooner to act as a lighter in transferring the goods to shore.[91] In Georgia, Governor Brown confiscated distilleries rather than simply shutting them down, then turned them over to private leather tanneries for use in extracting acid from tree bark to tan leather for his soldiers.[92] Mississippi and other states entertained buying machinery to make their own percussion caps for their rifles and considered the further step of making inmates at the state penitentiaries do the work.[93]

Indeed, all across the Confederacy men in state prisons would be put to labor on a variety of products necessary to the war effort, like the looms in the Texas penitentiary at Huntsville that produced "jeans" cloth for uniforms. When the Texas Paper Manufacturing Company sought to capitalize itself in September 1863, no one would buy the stock, so its five directors subscribed for all of it, bought an existing gristmill, and made plans to convert it for producing paper. After more than a year, however, they could not afford the necessary machinery, and looked to the governor and the state to provide them with $10,000 to commence operation.[94] It did not matter that the governor could not help. By January 1865 the important thing was that, in spite of their hands-off tradition and ideology, state governments all across the Confederacy had become so involved with private enterprise that those in trouble—all of whom naturally deemed their businesses to be vital to the cause—had come to look on state involvement as a natural recourse to insulate them from failure. South Carolina literally considered beating its swords into plowshares late in 1864 when the superintendent of the state armory suggested converting his machinery from war production of weapons to the making of agricultural implements to be sold to planters in return for corn.[95]

When private enterprise offered a threat rather than a potential partner for state enterprise, it invited repercussions. Complaining of profiteering by lead producers, the Mississippi ordnance officer responsible for producing bullets to supply state units asked that the legislature make it a criminal offense to export lead out of the state for higher prices than he could pay. Not content with that, he demanded that Governor Pettus place a price control of ten cents a pound on what he needed to purchase, and that all lead in private hands after February 15, 1862, be seized by the state. Further to force owners of lead to sell to him at his preferential rate, he suggested a tax on lead of $1 per pound. "Some action must be taken by the State & that promptly," he argued, "or the traiterous, cowardly, yankee spirited note-shaving, money grasping knaves at home will deliver our

State to Lincoln while they are selling their souls to the Devil."[96] Neither were the banks, always regarded as sacred bastions of the private sector, to be immune. In Georgia, Governor Brown declared that "the condition of the Treasury is such as to require a call on Banks for the exercise of Patriotic Liberality." He asked them to extend interest-free loans to the state for up to six months, which meant in effect that the state would be taking money out of the pockets of the stockholders while also reducing the credit available to depositors.[97]

All such activities would have been unthinkable before secession in states that historically professed to regard the line between government and the private sector as inviolate. Yet necessity, expediency, and the self-serving inconsistency that had always permeated American, Southern—and now Confederate—notions of the role of the state, federal and local, brought an escalating sea change. In August 1861, for instance, seeing the growing demands on the horizon, the firm of Cook and Brothers in New Orleans, manufacturers of bayonets and rifles, estimated that their factory was worth up to $25,000. But it was too far away from the market. They approached Governor Pettus with the proposition that they would move their operation to Jackson and furnish Mississippi forty rifles a week at the rate of $30 each if the state would advance them $50,000 for building the necessary works, or 60 guns a week for $75,000. Beyond that, Cook and Brothers offered to rebore and refit old state muskets for modern service, promising to finish 400 a month at $20 each in return for an advance of $25,000.[98]

The preferential rate, in effect, made Mississippi a silent partner in the private enterprise. More to the point the advances, even if repaid, would use state revenues for the encouragement of a specific industry, a clear violation of the long-held Southern doctrine of opposition to bounties or preferments supporting private enterprise financed from public funds. Even more contradictory was the proposal from South Carolina that the Confederate government buy all of its privately owned lead mines, saltpeter beds, and coke furnaces, as well as the state foundry and armory, in return for $112,000.[99] Yet at the same time South Carolina was itself buying machinery from a Tennessee state factory, and then turning around and selling it to the privately owned Kalmia Mills Company in South Carolina.[100] It was just this issue of government involvement in business and industry in the 1830s, along with the tariff and internal improvements, that had fueled the original secession movement. Then, of course, the issue had been congressional appropriation of public money for such purposes, and a specific prohibition of any such action had been drafted into the Confederate Constitution. However, no such prohibition applied to individual, and presumably sovereign, states engaging in the practice, with only the doctrinaire secession theorists like Robert Barnwell Rhett maintaining that the principle applied on a local as well as national scale. He had even opposed state encouragement of building railroads or canals that presumably promised to boost business and prosperity for everyone.

It was a basic tenet of Confederate democracy from the outset that government ought not to spend one man's money to promote another man's wealth, but it was a principle that always contained germinated seeds of hypocrisy. After all, the oligarchs dominating the Southern political and economic landscape before secession were chiefly cotton, sugar, and rice planters, entirely dependent upon foreign markets for their wealth, which required well-maintained coastal harbors and navigable rivers. As in the United States Constitution, the new Confederate charter provided that public funds could be spent to maintain rivers and harbors, and that the dreaded tariff could be imposed on imports on a scale sufficient to provide the Treasury the money to carry out the work. Principled free-trade advocates like Rhett had argued against that, but accepted it in the end. Of course there was weight in the argument that ports for foreign trade and rivers for internal trade benefited everyone at least indirectly, but there was also no denying that the chief beneficiaries, by an overwhelming margin, were the same planter class who created the Confederacy. The subsistence farmer in east Tennessee, the clerk in Atlanta, and even the physician or attorney in Jackson or Nashville or Richmond derived little or no direct benefit to his trade or physical well-being from those ports, yet he paid duties on any listed imports that he purchased. Certainly the planters were also large consumers of imported goods. But their number was small, and thus their share of the wealth raised through duties was minuscule compared to that paid by the majority of the middle and laboring classes who derived so little from the commercial outlets they were almost unwittingly financing.

One might well have asked, if they thought maintaining rivers and harbors was a proper use of federal funds for the encouragement of trade, why then did they oppose federal money being used to support and encourage the building of railroads and canals? Some like Rhett had even opposed individual states granting bounties or loans to help construct tracks within their own boundaries. Their argument quite logically was that a rail-road or canal, unlike a river or harbor, was a private corporation. No one owned a harbor; federal money spent there benefited everyone, if un-equally. But a canal or railroad had stockholders, and bounties or subsidies directly enriched them particularly. Left unsaid in the argument against ei-ther federal or state support of transportation was another motive per-fectly in keeping with the elitism that undergirded the Old South and the new Confederate democracy. Virtually every proposed railroad in the slave states had shared the same goal from the outset—to connect navigable rivers or coastal ports with the cities of the interior and the agricultural products of their regions so that inland economy might flourish, too. At first blush that sounded fine, yet beneath it lay a disturbing reality. Expand wealth and commerce to the interior, and they inevitably shifted the power that followed the dollar. Spread wealth to those ignored and all but dis-franchised counties in western Virginia, and its population would no longer stand for having no say in Richmond over state affairs that would now materially affect them as never before. Spread wealth to the Up Country of South Carolina, and its people would no longer contain their resentment over state offices like the governorship and cabinet posts, and Senate seats in Congress, being passed around at the whim of the Low Country aristocrats.

Nevertheless, even the railroads were soon sharing sheets with gov-ernment, both state and national. The first and most dramatic incursion came, ironically enough, at the hands of that most insignificant branch of the new democracy, the Post Office. While the capital was still in Montgomery, Postmaster General John Reagan called together the presi-dents of all the railroads in the then seceded states, initially to discuss their rates for carrying the mail. Somehow he managed to browbeat them into agreeing to give him preferential freight rates, and while he was at it he stepped outside his brief by negotiating with them as well an agreement to carry soldiers at just two cents a mile and all military materiel at half the regular rates. Though ostensibly a negotiation, it amounted in effect to government-imposed rate controls on an entire industry, which state gov-ernments had previously been reluctant to encourage. Perhaps because of that, the railroads continued to charge their usual rates to the states for shipment of state munitions until the fall of 1861, when they agreed to bill the states at the national rate as well.[101] Some even volunteered to trans-port sick or disabled soldiers at no charge at all "as an act of charity," said

one line's president, even while they protested the proliferation of unauthorized passes from surgeons that certified healthy men as eligible for a
free ride.[102]

Moreover, the railroads rapidly found that the state and national governments became increasingly demanding bedfellows. Governor Brown
arbitrarily imposed his own wage controls on railroad employees of the
Western & Atlantic, in addition to the price controls already in effect
thanks to Reagan. In effect, this line, like many others, was all but nationalized, its stockholders and managers having at best minimal control over
the business they had built. Then the draft so reduced manpower that as
early as February 1862 the line protested that it had not enough men to
keep the trains running or the business in operation, until exemptions relieved the crisis.[103] Florida's legislature authorized Governor Milton to
seize and take up the rails of the Florida Railroad for use elsewhere if state
troops were withdrawn from its vicinity. And in Mississippi at the end of
1863, the governor entered into a contract with the Mobile & Ohio to have
the state pay for rebuilding up to $25,000 worth of the line torn up by raid-
ing Yankees, including building bridges, with the understanding that if any
profit was derived from the rebuilt road, it should be accounted for and
paid to the state at the end of the war.[104] By October 1863, South Carolina's state government had direct financial investments in all twelve of its
railroad lines.[105]

Later in the war President Davis would excite much criticism from
Rhett and the other purists when he asked Congress to appropriate money
to complete a gap between rail lines in North Carolina in order to facilitate
more efficient movement of men and munitions for the military, but long
before then Richmond had been interfering in what would ordinarily have
been regarded as the exclusive prerogatives of private enterprise. The war
was only nine months old in January 1862 when Quartermaster General
Abraham C. Myers in the War Department complained that the locomo-
tives on one line were wearing out and began trying to persuade other lines
to share or sell their engines. "It is all important to this Department and
the country that the motive power of the various roads should be so distributed as to render all routes efficient," he urged. Indeed it was, the old
argument of necessity once more, and rightly invoked. But it was also one
more iron band of governmental control gripping private industry in its
embrace.[106] And by 1863 the railroads were assumed to be willing partners
in unremunerative efforts by the state governments to relieve the desti-

tute. The Mobile & Ohio was carrying state wheat to feed the poor free of charge, and in the final months of the war, with its rolling stock run down or destroyed, the line was reduced to using handcars to transport corn to the needy in order to meet the governor's expectations. By then the governor had already entered into negotiations with General George H. Thomas, commander of occupying Union forces in northern and central Mississippi, in order to allow him to send trains on the Mobile & Ohio and the Memphis & Charleston behind Union lines to continue taking food to the destitute.[107]

The Confederate government itself took perhaps the most radical so-cialistic step of all in 1864 when it assumed to itself exclusive control of the exportation and sale of cotton, using the proceeds to finance the purchase or building of warships and armaments, while at the same time trying thus to limit or eliminate the importation of luxury goods and non-necessities that encouraged the speculators and black marketers, and even to build Confederate credit abroad with the produce of private planters of the in-dividual states who were required to sell their staple to the government at controlled prices. The result was a virtual government monopoly on pro-duction and distribution, prices and profits. At the same time, Davis's Feb-ruary 1864 ban on importing luxuries represented the most radical interference in the open marketplace ever seen in America. Henceforth, any blockade runner attempting to leave the Confederacy had to dedicate half its cargo space to government cotton or other goods like tobacco and sugar, and any private vessel seeking to enter Confederate ports had to carry Confederate necessities as half its tonnage, and at government-imposed rates. The individual states were allowed to import and export as they wished without interference, which is perhaps the only reason such measures did not arouse greater uproar in the statehouses, but the private shippers, who assumed the greatest risk, complained that their profits were all but erased, and many actually went on strike in the summer of 1864. Before long Richmond found itself in conflict with the states, too, as they competed for cargo space and control. By 1865, thanks to its social-ization of at least half of the Confederate import-export economy, the gov-ernment was actually in the act of building renewed credit abroad. To the cries that Richmond and the statehouses had gone into competition with private enterprise, the government responded that few if any private ship-pers had been put out of business, and the number of firms engaged in the blockade-running trade had actually increased.[108]

When government inserts itself into the production, management, control of supply, and even distribution and pricing of basic commodities, it is hard not to see the basic outlines of socialism peeking through. Of course, Southerners and now Confederates regarded any suggestion of socialism as anathema. They had seen and condemned forms of it in operation in some of the utopian and religious communes that arose in the North and upper Midwest from the 1830s onward. And men like Rhett exaggerated and misrepresented socialism in any form into essentially a forfeiture of all liberty in exchange for wage slavery, political servitude, and social disintegration and immorality. Yet ironically now here they were practicing it in some fundamental ways, a fact that many preferred to ignore, and which others deplored. To be sure, it was socialism born of necessity and not ideology, but that did not obviate the fact that for the first time in American and Southern history, the state had made itself a controlling participant in important aspects of Confederate life. It stepped through the doors of manufacturing and commerce and across the threshold of private homes, to cast influence and exert control. And its involvement did not stop there, for almost from the first the new Confederate democracy went even further, to mingle military necessity with a radical attempt to control public morality.[109]

Alcohol had always been an important ingredient in Southern and American society, especially in rural areas and on the frontier. Some of its prominence was due to very practical concerns having little to do with intemperance. With microbes and their influence yet to be discovered, water supplies were often unsafe, and every community at one time or another experienced its own epidemic of typhoid brought about by infested drinking water. Lincoln himself would lose a son in 1862, most probably as a result of the impure water of the Potomac, and in some areas like Texas in 1833, outbreaks wiped out whole families. Given the universal ignorance about sanitation, water could simply be too dangerous to drink. Milk was an alternative, but the ethic of the time saw it mainly as a drink only for children, and that left predominantly beer, wine, and grain spirits as the remaining alternatives for adults. Men and women alike consumed all three, much of it homemade. Moreover, with no regulation of distilling, whiskey was plentiful, selling for no more than a quarter a gallon on the frontier, while people made beer from anything that would ferment, including sweet potatoes. Some of it was potent enough to be dangerous, while most was actually rather weak, but the important feature was that the alcohol content, and especially the distillation process, meant that deadly germs in the water were killed and it was safe to drink.

Of course safety was not a concern with all consumers, and alcoholism had been a concern north and south for generations, generating an active temperance movement. The multiple sides of the matter were well represented in the Confederate founding fathers by Robert Toombs; Stephens, who drank only moderately but was still a virtual alcoholic because he constantly dosed his dyspeptic stomach with a remedy of whiskey by the spoonful, and Rhett, a self-righteously proclaimed teetotaler. With war on the horizon in the spring of 1861, among all the other matters occupying Jefferson Davis and his government, alcoholism scarcely loomed large enough to elicit mention, but those who reflected must have known that it would be a concern, for two reasons. First, if there was a war, there would be sick and wounded, and alcohol was going to be needed for its acknowledged medicinal effect. Second, anytime thousands or tens of thousands of men, young or old, were to gather away from the restraints of home and society, liquor was going to emerge as a chief source of entertainment. Some would be experienced and habitual drinkers on coming into uniform; others would be introduced to "the creature" for the first time by tent mates. Either way, liquor, with its benefits and pitfalls, would inevitably engage attention in high places if the war lasted more than a few months.

The attention came soon enough, and on the two fronts that would dominate the alcohol debate for the rest of the war. In early 1862 a Virginian noted that high prices for spirits had led to "quite a fever" for more distilling, with large quantities of grain appropriated, and "distilleries in abundance" appearing in the state.[110] But then just weeks after the disastrous loss of Forts Henry and Donelson in west Tennessee—and with them control of the vital Tennessee and Cumberland Rivers—an outcry rose that the defeats were due to high-ranking generals being drunk instead of remaining alert to the danger.[111] In this instance there was no persuasive evidence of liquor's involvement—simple incompetence on the part of the Confederate commanders provided more than sufficient explanation. Yet in the future there would be multiple instances of regimental commanders and men even higher in rank being inebriated on duty and during battle. One army commander, General Braxton Bragg, himself temperate and thus overly sensitive to drinking in others, would repeatedly blame his defeats on supposedly drunken subordinates. Scarcely was the war begun before some men who had been drinkers for years decided that it was time to stop. "I am heartily tired of the sin and vice of this world," an Alabamian told his wife a week after First Manassas. "I am perfectly free from that Arch-demon, and bane of my life—*Liquor*—and by Gods assistance never, no never, will I ever touch it again."[112] At the time of the Henry and Donelson rumors, protests emerged in public view. Alcohol in the South came from corn, yet that grain had long provided the bread staple of Southerners, now Confederates, and now for the first time shortages appeared as distillers and millers competed for supply sufficient for their consumers. The results were the beginnings of hardship on the home front and drinking problems within the military, aptly summed up by a Georgian who complained to Governor Brown that "I dont think they ought to be considered true loyal citizens that will in these times of distress take the corn out of the womans & childrens mouths and distill it to kill their husbands & Sons."[113]

The immediate response to the growing problem was proclamations and legislation in several states outlawing private distilling without official permit from the government. Lubbock prohibited spirit making in Texas late in May 1862, and with it the construction of new distilleries. Brown acted even earlier, in March, and soon ostentatiously patriotic distillers promised that after his proclamation "I did not consume another grain of corn."[114] Milton acted in Florida in June, asking a Confederate general to suppress stills that operated "to the prejudice of the public interest," and issuing orders to county sheriffs to seize all distilleries and arrest all distillers, making them post a $1,000 bond not to return to their trade without official permit, under pain of forfeiture and imprisonment.[115] In Mississippi the legislature enacted its own prohibition on January 3, 1863, banning distilling from grain and molasses, and in April 1864 extended the ban to distilling from fruits and vegetables as well, and in some measure all of the other states did the same.[116] Governor Francis Pickens revoked all distilling licenses in South Carolina late in 1862. "The free use of ardent spirits by our brave but thoughtless soldiers, has done more to injure the discipline of our armies and to introduce sickness and disease than any other cause," he declared in his proclamation. "The question is simply whether we are to keep bread for soldiers' families or allow it to be manufactured into poison, to be administered to their husbands and brothers in service."[117]

Though the driving intent was practical necessity rather than moral crusade, it amounted to de facto prohibition, and with it came new problems as the states and the military realized that closing distilleries would deny them the spirits they needed for their hospitals. "Alcohol is, as you are aware, a necessity to me," the Confederate medical purveyor in Atlanta complained to Brown. He was responsible for supplying alcohol to most of the forces in the Southern interior, and might even have to supply Virginia before long, "and without a considerable quantity of reliable & excellent quality being constantly supplied, the business of this department must be almost ruined." Moreover, Brown had fixed the price of whiskey at $2.50 per gallon in his proclamation prohibiting the use of corn for distilling, and that risked creating instant profiteering by unscrupulous vendors, of whom there was always a ready supply.[118] The War Department in Richmond, attempting to observe the proper protocols of state rights, began in October 1862 to contact the governors and ask permission to contract directly with distillers, asking that such providers be exempted from the state prohibitions.[119]

As soon as the legislation and proclamations were issued, of course, exceptions were made under state permits controlled by the governors themselves, and soon the statehouses were deluged with applications. The requirements were that all alcohol was to be made in specifically contracted quantities only, and sold exclusively to the state at fixed prices. Nothing more was to be made, nor was any to be made available on the local private market. Naturally that only made whiskey more coveted in the community, raising the possibility of higher prices on a black market, and profits that made many distillers decide that the risk was worthwhile. In no time authorities received complaints of the number of illicit stills operating everywhere. In March 1863, Monroe County, Mississippi, reported at least eleven of them "hurrying on the general distress that is fast approaching." The army needed the corn, as did the civilians, but this corn was reaching the army only in the form of bootleg liquor. "The cavalry (and lots of them at every still Home) are a drunken set," complained one citizen, "unless there is some unknown utility in drinking whisky at 50 cents per drink." The demoralization caused by a shortage of grain for bread on the one hand and rising drunkenness in the army on the other was palpable soon enough.[120] Following the impressment acts and prohibitions, black market whiskey went to $6 a gallon by October 1863, and rose steadily thereafter.[121]

Governors had to consult their attorneys general for advice on how to address a legal problem never before confronting them, and in the end many states like Mississippi concluded that the best plan was to remove private enterprise entirely from the equation and build state distilleries.[122] Then in the spring of 1864 acts were passed authorizing official dispensers of alcohol on a county by county basis, but even that did not stem the flow of illicit liquor. Distillers from Mississippi, shut down by the laws, simply moved across the line into Alabama, even though that state's laws were just as explicit, but its enforcement was not. Still, arrests and prosecutions of illicit distillers came to make up seven of every eight cases of arrest under the several suspensions of the privilege of the writ of habeas corpus. Meanwhile, in South Carolina and elsewhere, the state required hotel and inn proprietors to post bonds of up to $5,000 or more, liable to forfeit if they should be caught selling alcohol in their establishments. None could distill whiskey unless for the state, and they required a license even to transport legal spirits.[123]

The prohibition laws mostly applied only to grain distillation, which left fruit brandies and wines as an alternative.[124] Nevertheless, the outcry against alcohol abuse, especially within the army, only increased, finally separating itself from the matter of corn conservation. As a result, by late in the war drinking was widely regarded as a besetting sin, and in the religious revivals that swept the armies and the home front in 1864, haranguing preachers depicted Confederate defeats as a punishment for the crime of intemperance among other vices. Prohibition had become a moral issue supported and sustained by the Confederate government and the states as well. Alcohol itself was not evil, of course, for the states were still energetically engaged in its purchase or manufacture as a necessity. Florida put out contracts for up to 10,000 gallons at a time, to be provided at a rate of 300 gallons a week.[125] And alcohol had to have some strength to be effective; the Mississippi state distillery guaranteed that its product ran 50 proof at least.[126] But the authorities would maintain vigilance in trying to stop illegal distillation right to the end. Mississippi required quarterly returns of amounts produced and sold, by which time the official rate had risen to $10 a gallon, meaning the black market price was even higher. The state even required a statement of "leakage" in its accounting, suggesting that at such an inflated price, some of that missing whiskey might have "leaked" into the local market.[127] Indeed, official licensed makers and their agents were often suspect, both of appropriating some of their produce for their own consumption and private sale, and of watering down the remainder in order to conceal the shortfall in their deliveries.[128] Others who ran afoul of the authorities sought legal loopholes to escape, like the druggist arrested for violating the prohibition "to keep for sale spiritous liquors" who pleaded that he sold alcohol only once, and therefore was not "keeping" it.[129] After states passed new laws prohibiting all sale of alcohol and requiring that all future medicinal sales by druggists should be transferred to the state, more than one offending pharmacist protested that he had sold it to a patient to save a life.[130]

By late 1864 there simply was not enough medicinal spirit being made to meet the civilian demand. Since people could not distill their own, many of the poor simply had to go without, leading to increasing discontent. Opposition to the prohibition laws became so outspoken that judges and police feared it would be impossible to take action against offenders, for they would be simply too popular with the citizenry.[131] By war's end, some states like Mississippi heard calls to repeal the laws establishing state distilleries and to open the industry more to private enterprise without heavy regulation. Some citizens protested, especially in the wake of attacks by Confederate soldiers on some of the state warehouses where they took whiskey at gunpoint. If the authorities allowed whiskey to be made indiscriminately once more, feared one Mississippian in February 1865, "our country will be ruined on account of the use of it."[132] As if to punctuate his declaration, at that very moment across the Confederacy in South Carolina, military authorities had just finished quelling a small riot by drunken and insubordinate cavalry in Columbia. "Liquor is at the bottom of a greater part of the mischief," their officers concluded.[133] Within days of the first surrender, and with Charleston and Columbia in enemy hands and much of South Carolina overrun, one state-authorized distillery began selling whiskey indiscriminately to anyone in return for corn, while another openly commenced operation with no license at all, and the disrupted authorities were powerless to stop it, even though they were still trying to save corn to feed soldier families.[134]

As with so many other problems that dogged the Confederacy, authorities were never able to stem the flow of alcohol, either to keep it from the armies or to prevent it from diverting corn better used to feed men, animals, and families at home. Yet in what would amount to the Confederacy's only attempt at government-enforced social control, if indirect, its efforts proved not entirely futile, either. Indeed, it might well have laid the ground-work for the disproportionate support that temperance movements and eventually prohibition would develop in the South in the future. Of more immediate importance, however, it represented one more example, as with salt socialism and cotton rationing, of national and state government intruding their necessities on the rights of the private citizenry. The state of South Carolina even considered in 1863 a plan for statewide inocula-tions, as did Georgia, and at state expense, raising the breath of socialized medicine.[135] All such intrusions were antithetical to long-held values in the South, and even in America at large, but more particularly, they seemed to run counter to bedrock principles of Confederate democracy.

Or did they? That democracy lay founded in earlier dynamics within the several states, each of which to a greater or lesser degree accepted the idea of a natural leadership elite—the assumption that the oligarchies of land or wealth or profession knew what was good for everyone and by almost di-vine right ought to be followed by masses too unsophisticated to know what was best for themselves, and with too little stake in the sacred em-powerment of property to be trusted with a voice to gainsay the oligarchs. That being the case, there was a logic after all in those socialistic policies. Rationing, prohibition, control of production and the market were all de-signed by the oligarchs to sustain the war effort and the life of the Con-federacy, and it was only through Confederate independence that the rights and prerogatives of the oligarchy could be preserved, or so they had come to believe. Again and again the leaders would self-righteously de-clare that they would sacrifice their lives rather than compromise their principles. In the end they proved ready enough to sacrifice those princi-ples to preserve themselves, and as with so many other issues, it was not lost on the people of the Confederacy that the bulk of the hardship and in-convenience caused by government intrusion into the private sector fell on the common folk. From beginning to end, while boldly enrobing itself in the rhetoric of freedom, liberty, and individual rights, Confederate democ-racy was conceived and matured in the interest of preserving an ancient status quo.

But then at the very end, a few men, and certainly the president, were willing to upset even that to achieve independence. The most radical, the most intrusive, the most antithetical move of all to their libertarian princi-ples of state sovereignty and individual rights was the proposition to eman-cipate their slaves in return for European recognition. Just how Davis hoped to accomplish it is not entirely certain. The administration's position from the first had been that the central government had absolutely no power over the issue or the institution. That implied that only the states could address emancipation individually, and they would have had to do so by conventions. Even then presumably if one state balked, the enterprise would fail. The important feature, however, is that Davis and his attorney general, Judah Benjamin, did not even consult the governors before authorizing their envoys to make the offer. Richmond presumed to speak for the states, and then present them with a *fait accompli*. It was the very sort of usurpation of power that Confederates accused Lincoln of practicing. Moreover, if it actually came to pass, how could the slaveowners be compensated? Richmond could not simply force them to abandon their enormous capital investment. Yet compensation would have to come from some form of public revenues, meaning that through taxes or duties or any other means of raising the money, men who did not own slaves and never had would be helping to pay for those who did. It bordered on redistribution of wealth. It also seemingly violated their Constitution and their ancient antipathy toward public money being spent to aid or encourage a particular industry or segment of the population. Whether or not it could have happened at all, and without fomenting a revolution at home, is not the point. Fundamentally more significant is that Davis and his administration even thought of it, and were ready to make the effort. Never before had the central government North or South proposed to intrude itself so deeply into the rights of the states and the people. If Richmond could do this, what could it not do? Given that, what really remained of state rights and sovereignty?

The Struggle to Hold On

With the ascent of General Ulysses S. Grant to overall command of Union military forces, the initiative in the war passed irrevocably to the North. He had both the skill and the overwhelming military wherewithal to plan a coordinated offensive on all fronts designed to exhaust the Confederacy and make it impossible for one theater to weaken itself in order to bolster another, and that is exactly what he intended. When the spring of 1864 allowed renewed campaigning, Grant intended to send General Robert E. Lee back into northern Virginia to press him and Richmond, while General William T. Sherman would drive for Atlanta and then be guided by circumstances, and perhaps push onward to the Atlantic coast, completing the resegmenting of the South. General Nathaniel Banks would move up the Red River to occupy and disrupt the Trans-Mississippi, interrupting its cotton production and keeping its forces otherwise occupied, as smaller armies were to move into the Shenandoah and up the Virginia peninsula again, and eventually land forces would cooperate with Admiral David Farragut to attack Mobile. They did not all have to succeed. Each would help the other, and only Grant or Sherman had to prevail in their major campaigns to bring the Confederacy to its knees.

President Jefferson Davis knew that, and he also knew that the limited forces at his disposal were inadequate to the task, but that had always been the case. He had to keep Lee in Virginia to protect the capital and keep fighting on the ground that had brought the victories that nurtured South-

ern morale. General Joseph E. Johnston had to face Sherman, and at least he had the benefit of several rivers running perpendicular to the Yankee line of advance on Atlanta, making each one a potential Fredericksburg. General Kirby Smith could deal with Banks, and would handily, while to protect the Shenandoah he called General John C. Breckinridge from Johnston's army. Local defense troops had to try to stop General Benjamin Butler and his advance on the peninsula. Mobile would depend on its forts and small gunboat fleet.

It was Banks who moved first, in the early spring warmth of Louisiana, but his campaign was a bungle almost from the start. Kirby Smith and his troublesome subordinate General Richard Taylor, former brother-in-law of President Davis, managed to so discomfit Banks's inept advance that, despite a couple of battles in which the Yankees fought well, Banks was forced to retire and almost lost the gunboat fleet that accompanied him because of falling water on the Red.

Sherman moved next, launching his thrust south in April, and almost from the first it became painfully evident that Johnston was not going to hand him any repeats of Fredericksburg. Johnston simply gave up his winter quarters at Dalton, Georgia, without making any fight at all, and thereafter continually fell back in front of the Yankees with only token resistance. As he came to each of the rivers that seemed to offer so much potential, Johnston allowed himself to be distracted by a portion of the enemy army in his front, while Sherman sent another marching to cross above or below and then force Johnston to retire to avoid being hit from flank or rear. With every new withdrawal, Johnston's men became more disillusioned with "Old Joe," and in Richmond, Davis became ever more irritated. When was he going to stop and fight? Would he stop and fight? Would he even stop retreating when he reached Atlanta? Most of all, Davis wanted to know what Johnston intended to do, but time after time the general dodged questions and refused to reveal his plans, or even whether he had any. Only once, at Kennesaw Mountain, did Johnston stop and fight, and from a magnificent defensive position on the commanding eminence, he handed Sherman a bloody repulse. But then Johnston gave up that position, too.

Finally in July he had reached the environs of Atlanta itself, the major transportation center for the whole region. Once more Davis asked for the general's plans. Once more the general dodged. That was enough. Having been too patient for too long, Davis relieved Johnston of his command and

*turned it over to General John Bell Hood, who was jumped over other se-
nior officers, introducing yet more internal rivalry and animosity into the
already poisonous atmosphere in the army's high command. Hood had
shamelessly politicked to get the position, and now that he had it he knew
he was expected to fight. Fight he did. He launched one attack after another, stunning Sherman and disrupting the momentum of the Yankee en-
circlement of the city's defenses. But the Army of Tennessee was not strong
enough, and its commanders did not work smoothly enough with Hood, for
success to be more than a dream. Sherman finally laid siege, and in September, faced with being surrounded, Hood evacuated his works to save his
army. The victory might have gone a long way toward ensuring the reelection of Abraham Lincoln in November, an event that more than any other
sent south the signal that the Union had the will to keep fighting as long as
it took.*

*Sherman's was the one victory the campaign plan needed, for nowhere
else were they to be found. In May, Breckinridge met and decisively defeated the small army under General Franz Sigel sent to take the Shenandoah Valley, drove him out of the valley, and then moved east to reinforce
Lee. Lee needed the help. Grant, with General George Meade still nominally in command of the Army of the Potomac, began his campaign early
in May and slammed into Lee near the Chancellorsville battleground in an
area known as the Wilderness. For several days they slugged it out, Grant
too strong and determined to be repulsed like his predecessors, and Lee too
cagey to be fooled by the Yankees' attempts to get around his flanks. Grant
would have to fight for every foot of ground he took. When Lee finally had
to pull back from the Wilderness, he erected new lines around Spotsylva-
nia, and there they battled for several days more, and then Lee fell back,
river by river, to the North Anna, then the South Anna, and then to Cold
Harbor near the Chickahominy and close to the old Seven Days battlegrounds. There he handed Grant a brutal clubbing early in June that made
the Union general realize he was not going to get any farther by pushing
straight ahead. In one of the few times in the war when Lee would be utterly fooled, Grant removed his army from Lee's front and swung it around
below Richmond, secretly crossing the James River, and began a dash for
the Confederate capital itself. On June 19 he came within a hair's breadth
of marching into the city streets, but the fatigue of his army, and a brilliant
last-minute defense by none other than General P.G.T. Beauregard, now
returned to a minor command, saved the capital. Lee rushed his army to*

the scene, and Grant once again found no alternative but to commence laying siege. The small campaign under Butler moving up the peninsula had come to nothing, so he was no help.

Lee and his men began settling into and enhancing mile after mile of defensive works protecting Richmond and the neighboring rail center at Petersburg, and there for the rest of the year the Army of Northern Virginia would hold, unable to move, but strong enough to keep Grant out. The one thing Grant had achieved, however, was to take Lee effectively out of the war. He would never lead a campaign in the open field again, and Lee well knew, as did Grant, that if something did not happen to break the stalemate, time was all on the Yankees' side. Lee even tried detaching a corps of his army, Stonewall Jackson's old men now commanded by General Jubal Early, to move out to the Shenandoah where they beat back a fresh attempt to take the valley, and then drove north in the last invasion of Union ground in the East. Early crossed into Maryland and then drove for Washington itself, coming within sight of the spires of the city and sending waves of shock through the Union high command. But local defenses held, and Early was forced to retire. That fall Grant sent one of his most ruthless subordinates, Philip H. Sheridan, to drive Early out of the valley, and by November he had all but dispersed Early and his tattered "army." In Virginia now it would be just Grant and Lee, waiting through the winter for the spring of 1865.

Other theaters saw more movement. In August, Farragut's fleet had defied the forts protecting Mobile and taken its bay and soon the city itself. Soon Union forces would be carving up central Alabama and Mississippi. Only in the Trans-Mississippi did the Confederates strike back, that fall sending an army of cavalry under General Sterling Price on a doomed invasion of Missouri that drove all the way to the Missouri River before being stopped in battle at Westport near then tiny Kansas City. Price was a hopelessly inept commander, and his forces too ill-equipped and undisciplined to have much chance of success. It would be the last Confederate invasion of Union soil, and the last Confederate offensive of the war, save for one.

After giving up Atlanta, and knowing he was not strong enough to stop Sherman's massive army, Hood conceived the idea of leaving Sherman in his rear and striking northward on a bold drive into Tennessee, perhaps even to reach Kentucky. He expected Sherman would follow, thus relieving the pressure on Georgia, while at the same time Hood hoped that sympa-

thetic Tennesseans might come out to enlist as his army passed through, strengthening him as he marched. It was daring, perhaps foolhardy, but the Confederacy had only ever had a chance on the battlefield by gambling. Lee had gambled more than once and won against great odds. Hood hoped for the same. Unfortunately, Hood was no Lee. Moreover, Sherman refused to take the bait. He detached only one of the armies in his army group and sent it to protect Nashville and stop Hood, which it did handily. When Hood first approached Nashville, he encountered a strongly emplaced Federal force in and around Franklin, Tennessee, and there he battered his own army senseless against immovable defenses. With his army still reeling, he moved on to Nashville, where General George H. Thomas would be waiting. Hood was so understrength from losses by now that even a George McClellan could have beaten him, but still he launched an attack that was soon routed, and then Thomas counterattacked and so pulverized the sad remnants of the Army of Tennessee that it almost ceased to be. Hood could do nothing but pull his shattered divisions back into Georgia and resign in disgrace.

Meanwhile the Sherman leviathan was on the move again. After burning anything vital in Atlanta that could not be removed, he set out overland on his drive for the sea, his goal Savannah, an important port for blockade-running traffic. With Hood's army elsewhere, there was simply nothing to stop Sherman but Georgia militia and hastily assembled scratch forces that he brushed aside easily. He did not have to fight a single major battle, and by December he could smell the ocean air. Brief fighting took Fort McAllister, the principal work defending Savannah, and the Confederate garrison that had assembled to defend the city had no alternative but to withdraw. Sherman was in Savannah in time to offer it to Lincoln as a Christmas present.

After almost four years of war, the Confederacy had been cut into half a dozen pieces. One of its two major armies had nearly disintegrated, and though Davis would quickly seek to rebuild it, the result would be a shadow. Missouri was gone, and most of Arkansas. Texas and western Louisiana held out, but chiefly because Grant did not regard them as important enough at this stage to distract himself from the major theaters. Tennessee was all but lost, Georgia had been cut in half, Florida was penetrated and reeling, Mississippi and Alabama would soon feel Yankee cavalry raids in force, and newly formed armies were about to aim for the subjugation of all of these secondary theaters. Virginia was now little but the story of Lee besieged at Petersburg and Richmond. Only the Carolinas were largely inviolate, and they were next in Sherman's sights. Lincoln had been triumphant at the polls, and his armies were now unstoppable everywhere they moved. Grant had only to wait for spring to deal with Lee, and Sherman did not even have to wait for better weather to move into South Carolina. Only an incurable optimist or a blind man could look at the map and fail to see what was going to happen in 1865.

11

The States in Their Sovereignty

WAR IS THE SUREST ENEMY of democracy, and no such government can expect to emerge from war, especially a civil conflict, with its principles of individual freedom entirely intact. Founded in the rhythms of the war drums' beat, and by oligarchs whose private interests belied some of their publicly proclaimed democratic aspirations, the Confederacy was destined from the outset to fight an internal contest between the principles it presented to the world and the imperatives of self-preservation. It was a struggle that four years in the crucible of war was guaranteed to exacerbate, widening the fault lines all across the body politic, but nowhere more evidently than in the statehouses.

Within just days of the inauguration of Jefferson Davis as president on February 18, 1861, Louisiana Governor Thomas Moore confided to a friend that he found the political horizon before them "dark and the future gloomy."[1] Five months later, with Davis and Confederate officialdom moved to Richmond, a friend suggested to Moore that "our government has its hands full."[2] In the spring of 1862, Governor John Milton in Florida feared that prospects looked grim, indeed, but still trusted that the Confederacy would triumph and be independent.[3] Indeed the government did have its hands full, but no more so than the hands of those governors like Moore and Milton who had to try to make so much of Confederacy democracy work out in the states, and it was a task and a prospect that could make a man see gloom and darkness just over the hill.[4]

Just for a start, it was the governors who had to take responsibility for oiling those most vital machines of democracy, elections. The first congress, of course, was chosen by their state secession conventions, but once the Permanent Constitution was framed, naturally there had to be regular popular elections to fill its seats. The states were either to hold their elections as provided in their own legislation or else on the first Wednesday in November 1861 as specified by the Provisional Congress.[5] This meant that some states, like Texas, were choosing their delegates in August and other states, like South Carolina and Florida, in October, leading to some confusion as to which polling dates took precedence, the states' or the Congress's.[6] Even before then, of course, the first real ballot casting as Confederates took place in the spring and summer as those states that put secession to a popular referendum, Tennessee, Virginia, and Texas, held their polls.[7] In Tennessee, where thousands of young men who were already in the state militia made a speedy transition into the Confederate army, their commander, General Gideon J. Pillow, made certain to march them to the county courthouses so that they could vote in the referendum, thus addressing for the first time—but hardly the last in this war—the issue of soldiers being able to vote when away from their home precincts.[8]

At the same time, some states had legislators as well as new state constitutions to vote upon. There had been hopes of leaving partisan politics behind in the old Union, and many of those members of the Provisional Congress who sought reelection would run unopposed as a sign of unity and patriotism, but in the state contests the old political ways continued unabated, with jealousies, petty rivalries, and cabals among the factions.[9] In the spring and summer of 1861 some Mississippians feared that the ardent state rights "party" was going too far to appease the old submissionists in the name of unity, and that men who had been lukewarm on secession might capture all the important legislative and administrative seats. "When the time comes we will be compelled to speak to them in language they cannot misunderstand," fumed a true-blue state rights man. Otherwise, should state affairs go sour, the submissionists in power would lay all the blame on their predecessors in the old game of gaining power and evading responsibility.[10] In the emergency of 1861 the slowness of getting in returns from remote counties added to the anxiety of maintaining continuity in the democratic process, while at the same time causing worry in states like Georgia, where close votes continued to raise fears of shallow support for the new nation. Governor Joseph Brown, faced with a small

voter turnout and a very close vote in the July balloting on a state constitutional ratification, had to get involved personally in bringing the vote in for
a full count.[11] In Florida the difficulty of getting returns in from remote
counties forced Milton to consider whether or not he could even declare
winners in an 1862 contest.[12]

In Texas, Mississippi, and elsewhere, governors themselves faced reelection campaigns, and new challenges thanks to new nationhood. Governor Edward Clark in Texas was so busy with the extra demands of raising
volunteers and other requirements for the war effort that his supporters
feared he simply would not be able to canvass effectively in the face of his
official duties, his credentials as a good Confederate compromising his
ability to stay in office.[13] Brown had to run, and even some of his close supporters had feared that he would be defeated since he was bucking a
precedent against men seeking third terms, and most of the press and
politicians were in opposition. Still he gained a handsome majority, not
least because voters seemed reluctant to abandon an incumbent in a crisis. Even Vice President Alexander Stephens, sometimes Brown's foe, supported him in private, though observing fastidiously the propriety of taking
no side publicly.[14] Thomas Cobb privately opposed the idea of a third
term, but declared that "this is no time for division and dissension" and
kept quiet.[15]

Some races could be much more difficult. The peace element in North
Carolina had become so strong and vocal by 1864 when Zebulon Vance
sought reelection that it fielded W. W. Holden, an outright proponent of
peace at almost any price, and circulated a rumor that Vance had authored
a petition to secede from the Confederacy in an attempt to discredit him
with his supporters.[16] Still he won. In Mississippi, John J. Pettus sought reelection, encouraged by a number of prominent men who urged him to
run again, even promising that in some counties he would meet little opposition. But then there emerged rumors that state railroad interests were
combining to oppose him, while from some areas came word that even his
former friends opposed his reelection for no more specific reason than
that he had been too slow, too reluctant to exert his power, and not sufficiently attentive to raising volunteers. "In other words that you should
have usurped authority where you had none, and that you should have exhausted your private fortune or the State Treasury for the volunteers,"
complained his supporter Robert Hudson.[17] Yet as the campaign progressed, others assured Pettus that he had strong support from all but "a

few hungry aspirants for office," though one such promise came from a man who in the next breath asked for an appointment for himself. Moore in Louisiana warned his neighbor that men approaching the governors for action now were showing a disheartening propensity to have their own personal interests first at heart.[18] By late August 1861, Pettus's managers confessed that the campaigning was heating up. "The election is waxing a little warm," L. J. Jones told him, but Pettus was still popular and on the right side of popular issues, especially for a stay law that would freeze collection of debts in the emergency. Pettus did not actually declare his candidacy formally until August 31, himself spending the $10 to insert the announcement in the important press.[19] In the end, he, too, won reelection, but not before his experience revealed that the old ways of wirepulling and venal opposition were not about to disappear in the idealistic glow of the new order. Governor John Letcher of Virginia was perhaps the most unpopular, his face perpetually red from drink, and the stories of his appearing drunk in public too abundant not to have some basis in fact. Everyone in the state, down to young boys, knew that a visit to the governor's office in the statehouse would include a trip with Letcher to a liquor-laden sideboard.[20]

Their own elections past, the governors faced direct or indirect responsibility for filling several other offices that were cogs in the machine. Many sitting politicians resigned in order to go into the army, while other members of legislatures sometimes found themselves so bored with debate and committee work that they, too, would leave to seek military commissions. Robert Toombs, Howell Cobb, Francis Bartow, and Thomas R.R. Cobb, nearly half of the Georgia delegation to the Provisional Congress, would all resign to raise military units. Mississippi lost two state senators in a single month in 1861.[21] When special elections were not called for, the governors had to make appointments to fill the vacancies, awakening even more the calls for favors and the opportunities for strengthening allegiances to man and party. In Virginia, for instance, Governor Letcher would be criticized for handing out far too many of his patronage appointments to conservatives who had been submissionists before secession, greatly offending the small but vocal cadre of ardent secessionists who now wanted their share of the fruit.[22] Occasionally there were conflicts as to who was the lawful incumbent of an appointive office, and the governors had to decide. Even in such lowly affairs as elections of county probate judges and justices of the peace, the state chief executive found himself involved willingly or not.

Governors also had to help, where they could, in upsets to tradition brought on by the crisis. In Mississippi, for instance, the two counties of Winston and Noxubee had customarily alternated favorite sons for the state senate seat representing the two. Now, however, such a political "deal" had to be stopped, said many. "Introduced in the days of demagogues to subserve party purposes," complained one critic, it was "a custom that has often called on the people to abandon their interests and the best man, for the sake of consistency—a political phrase generally inconsistent with common sense."[23] Louisiana had long observed—with some interruptions—a tradition of alternating the governorship between a member of its Anglo community and one from the French, but this, too, would disappear. Thus, even as a result of turmoil and upheaval, political reforms were accomplished of necessity if not for their own merit alone.

With all of the resignations from the Provisional Congress by men who went into the military, dozens of new candidates had to be fielded to fill the vacancies in the first general election in the fall of 1861, and immediately some saw a dilution in the quality of the men being sent to Richmond. "I am disgusted with the candidates all over the Confederacy," an admittedly hard-to-please Tom Cobb complained in November 1861. "The Lord deliver us from this first Congress."[24] When the fall 1863 congressional elections approached, and the encroachment of Union armies put some counties behind enemy lines, the governors faced the question of whether or not even to issue writs for elections at all, though most people favored continuing with the forms of democracy even if many voters were now beyond reach. Facing this prospect, state legislatures passed acts continuing existing incumbents in office until changes in the military situation allowed elections to be held again, though that rarely happened. Instead, the governors simply held elections in as many counties as they could, and tried, as did Milton of Florida, to get ballots out to soldiers in the field so that their votes could be counted, or as in South Carolina, urged that citizens in occupied districts attempt to cross the lines and vote in neighboring districts in order to preserve democracy.[25] As in the Union, the soldiers generally were not able by law to vote unless they were actually in their home counties on the polling day, but as civil disruption became more of a problem, the governors tried more than one expedient to add uniformed ballots to replace those lost to encroaching Yankee control. Florida, more innovative than most, began declaring any soldier encampment in their home county a legally constituted precinct so that the men could vote when away from their county seat, and then passed a special ordinance allowing soldiers in or out of the state to vote for members of the legislature and Congress, something never before done in America.[26] Ironically, in a movement predicated on the assumption of the unfitness of the common people to speak through the will of the majority with a voice equal to that of the oligarchy, simple survival eventually forced states to expand that democracy in radical new directions to use the common people to keep the gears of democracy turning.

By 1864 the wear on the system showed increasingly, nevertheless. Protests came from citizens that the legislatures did not sit long enough, or that they sat too long; that they passed too little legislation, or too much.[27] In Georgia a deserter from the army actually managed to get himself elected to the legislature from a largely tory county, forcing Brown to try to get him arrested and tried by a military tribunal before he could take his oath of office and presumably rest beyond the jurisdiction of the army.[28] By 1864 candidates were fielded not just for being pro- or anti-administration, but also on the basis of whether they were for or against particular generals, as with General Kirby Smith, the almost dictatorial commander in the Trans-Mississippi. "I have no sympathy for those who are willing & knowing victims of his immeasurable stupidity," Judge E. Warren Moise complained to by then ex-governor Moore. "What we want now, of all other things, is to send to Congress a bitter opponent of Smith."[29] From such causes and others, not to mention war weariness and general disillusionment with the breakdown in civil order, voters showed increasing apathy that the governors had to combat in attempting to continue fulfilling their own mandates.[30]

The governors could easily find themselves facing a host of other tasks and challenges that were entirely new, thanks to the crisis. The sudden and dramatic need for much more money than they had ever budgeted before presented a constant challenge. They sold public lands, raised new war taxes, bought Confederate Treasury bonds, and, incredibly in some cases, even invested through the lines in United States Treasury notes and bonds.[31] Florida suspended trying to collect taxes in counties behind enemy lines. But in South Carolina it was determined that taxes had to be collected even from the unoccupied portions of counties currently invaded by the enemy, while taxes already paid by people whose property had subsequently fallen behind Yankee lines were not to have their money refunded. The state could no longer provide them services or security, but they still had to pay their levies.[32] Anyone who failed to file a return for the war tax was made liable to a doubling of the tax in punishment.[33] Hoarding for speculation was outlawed with stiff fines, and in Alabama in 1864 the governor proposed an increase in fines for felonies and misdemeanors in order to fund paying the state printer.[34]

There was yet one other unique circumstance facing some of the governors that none of their predecessors had been forced to handle. The state conventions originally called to debate and adopt secession ordinances sometimes remained in session, and in Florida, South Carolina, and Virginia especially they took on the form of autonomous governments themselves, sometimes working at cross-purposes with governors and legislatures. Virginia's convention continued sitting for some time after adopting secession, and continued to show the same conservative streak that had led it to defeat secession three times before the final successful vote. Worse, the convention used the appointive powers it had assumed to itself to appoint submissionists to important offices that ought to have been the province of the governor or legislature. On top of all, it proposed to revise the state's constitution, even though it had not been called for this purpose or any other than to consider the single issue of secession. "The Long Parliament of England was not more usurpative," complained the journalist J.D.B. DeBow, "and not half so silly."[35] The situation was just the same in Florida, where the convention took it upon itself to make foreign policy, impose taxation, select the judiciary, evict officeholders, install its own appointees, and even change statute law. And more ominously, it framed a new constitution and placed all telegraph lines in the state under surveillance and censorship, a considerable erosion of personal freedoms at the outset. It also enacted "interpretations" of certain clauses in the existing constitution, abolished state offices, and altered the structure of the civil service, extreme measures all.[36]

In South Carolina there appeared even a third authority, the Executive Council, ostensibly created to help the governor while the convention was not in session. In effect, it sought to all but supplant Governor Francis Pickens as it assumed by its votes to make the decisions that the governor himself had formerly made on his own. The council would make law, revise the constitution, set military policy within the state, and interfere with economy and finance. Its actions led to an increasing outcry that it was an arbitrary Star Chamber that Carolinians might have to rise up in revolution against as they had against the old Union. "It is amusing and degrading, trying and yet laughable," complained one Carolinian. "The laws passed by that convention, be they good or bad we will have to live under for many a long day to come."[37] In the end, the outrage was so great that the convention was reconvened to address the problem of its own creation, and decided to abolish both itself and the council at the end of 1862 unless the legislature chose otherwise. When the legislature met again, it so despised both council and convention that it abolished the council and severely castigated the late convention for its constitutional excesses. Having left the Union for more self-determination, South Carolina had only let itself in for two years of an authoritarian rule by bodies that stood subject to no control or safeguard.[38]

There was friction now and then between the statehouses. Late in the war when Governor Milton of Florida refused to allow removal of navigational obstructions at Apalachicola in order to allow a Georgia state blockade runner to pass through, Governor Brown fired off an angry response, saying that he would not forget and that Georgia might offer a similar lack of cooperation in the future. (Perhaps his ire was fueled by the fact that he owned the vessel.)

Yet for every time the governors clashed, there were more instances of cooperation, of setting aside temporal and local concerns in the interest of a greater goal that went beyond state borders. In short, they showed as never before the war just how much they could think as nationalists in spite of all their rhetoric over state rights. As early as June 1861, Clark appealed to Louisiana, Alabama, and Georgia to lend arms to alleviate his shortage. Three months later Isham Harris and Pettus were cooperating over shifting units from both their states to reinforce the movement into Kentucky to establish a forward position at Bowling Green, and well before then Governor A. B. Moore of Alabama had agreed with Moore of Louisiana and Pettus of Mississippi that the neighbors would accept each other's bank notes as legal tender for settlement of debts.[39] When reports of a Yankee fleet that might threaten his coast reached Milton in October 1861, both Alabama and Georgia offered help. A. B. Moore offered a new brigade of Alabamians if Milton could arm them.[40] Pickens and Thomas Moore combined on a scheme to get arms to the hard-pressed Louisiana governor from the West Indies. Moore encouraged him by declaring, "I feel deeply, as no doubt Your Excellency does, the necessity for the Executives of the states to bring to bear in the present contest those energies and resources of the several states which it is difficult for the Confederate

government to reach or beyond its power to control."[41] When the advance
of enemy forces endangered the security of prisoners in state penitentiaries, the governors helped each other out, sometimes requiring compensation but other times not, knowing the favor might have to be
returned. Pettus sent two dozen dangerous felons to the Alabama prison to
get them out of Grant's way during the Vicksburg Campaign, while after
the fall of Baton Rouge the year before, Louisiana miscreants from its penitentiary were sent to Texas.[42] They could even send relief to one another,
as when Georgia's legislature voted $100,000 to be sent to South Carolina
for the relief of Charlestonians who suffered a disastrous fire in December
1861.[43]

Most revealing of all were the governors' cooperative efforts stretching
beyond the immediate concerns of their offices and into the broader Confederate political arena. They were not attempts to appropriate Richmond's power to themselves, but they certainly revealed a common sense
that the sovereignty of the individual states gave them the power to combine in ways not specifically prohibited by their Constitution to promote
the general welfare and even political policy. In December 1861 the Georgia legislature passed a resolution promising never to countenance any
proposals for reunion, and called on the other states to follow its lead.[44]
The next month a convention met at Macon, Georgia, and passed resolutions calling for a "World Convention" to promote peace, itself a meaning-
less affair that came to nothing, but it seemed to inaugurate a passion for
convention proposals among the states.[45] In March, Pickens of South Carolina sent a letter to all the other governors suggesting that "unless the
States bring forward their power and resources to sustain the common
Government, and put forth all their local energies to defend our organization, we will feel the fatal consequences." He asked that they confer freely
on measures to support the central government, and the next month Milton, Letcher, new Alabama governor John Gill Shorter, and others agreed
to meet to talk about mobilization, industrialization for war production,
the blockade, and other issues. Pickens even envisioned a massive central
camp constantly inhabited by 100,000 or more soldiers sustained by the
states, ready at a moment's notice to go to any spot threatened. Most revolutionary, and certainly something never broached before the war, Pickens
even suggested that they consider the mutual sustainment of the separate
currencies of each of the states to impose some degree of financial order in
place of the complex and inflationary system of rates of exchange between

one state and another as if they were foreign currencies.[46] At almost the same time, Francis Lubbock of Texas and Moore of Louisiana proposed to meet and discuss mutual regional concerns with Governor Henry Rector of Arkansas and Claiborne Jackson, leader of a rump government representing Missouri, which like Kentucky never really seceded. "This is no time for bickering, heart-burning and division among a people struggling for existence as a free Government," declared Lubbock, and if any state leader wavered in patriotism, he promised the president, "I shall endeavor to get him right."[47]

Much more ambitious was Brown's interest in a proposal from out-of-favor General P.G.T. Beauregard in October 1862, just after General Braxton Bragg's initially successful invasion of Kentucky, during which Bragg captured the capital at Frankfort and drove almost to the Ohio River, taking the opportunity of installing yet another rump governor in office. This was the time to approach the North to make peace, said Beauregard. He approached Brown and Milton and no doubt others, and they appear to have favored his suggestion that Confederate governors—with permission from Richmond, of course—meet with the governors of Indiana, Illinois, Michigan, and other conservative northwestern states to try to conclude peace on the basis of Confederate independence. Nothing came of the proposal, yet in variants it would be revived again as the governors groped for some means to use their power in the national interest.[48] In the fall of 1863 it was even suggested that the Trans-Mississippi governors attempt to make their own separate treaty with England or France, since Richmond had repeatedly failed to achieve any diplomatic recognition or alliances, despite the fact that their Constitution clearly denied the individual or collective states any such power.[49]

Brown authored a call on Congress to remove restrictions on states exporting cotton in their own hulls without handing over half of the cargo or proceeds to the government. Only Milton demurred, thinking the governors had no legal right to ask Congress to legislate on anything, but ought rather to have their state delegations in Richmond present the case in the House and Senate.[50] Vance wrote to all the governors in September 1864 proposing that they meet in Augusta, Georgia, in October, "in order to attain this uniformity," and that "some general plan of action might be agreed upon for the relief of the country." He hoped to frame a plan of action to recommend to their legislatures and to the country at large, not only to meet their crisis at home, but also to produce more men for the armies.[51] The governors could force Davis and Congress to do nothing, but pressure from the legislatures, representing the states in their sovereignty, might exert enormous moral influence that the president would ignore at hazard. Most of them did gather in Augusta, but they stopped short of attempting to dictate policy to Richmond, though they did resolve that they were no longer happy with the government's monopoly on blockade running, and henceforth demanded to be allowed to run their own state runners without restriction, showing that they could flex their muscle. Only Milton demurred. They also agreed to seek repeal of laws in their own states that stood in the way of state militia from one being sent to another in an emergency, as well as other measures to impose upon themselves a degree of cooperation that some of them individually, especially Brown and Vance, bristled at when the president sought to impose it from central authority. They even addressed, though without unanimity, the question of raising black regiments.[52]

Inevitably, it was those same confrontations between gubernatorial prerogatives and presidential interference that produced the greatest and most public difficulties for the governors. The Constitution seemingly drew distinct boundaries between the power of Richmond and the powers in the statehouses, yet inevitably the crisis of being a nation at war for its life, especially a new nation lacking many of the inertial traditions of custom and habit in federal-state relations, led to one contention after another. The personalities of Jefferson Davis and some of the governors, especially Brown and Vance, only added to what became on both sides of the constitutional divide a constant irritant.

Jefferson Davis and his executive departments rarely if ever attempted to interfere with matters of justice, education, internal taxation, and the other areas that had traditionally been exclusively the province of the governors and legislatures. Overwhelmingly, the occasions grew out of national military policy, chiefly enlistments and conscription, and procurement of supplies, and they began early and escalated. All the governors had some degree of complaint over appointment of officers in the regiments they raised, for such commissions were a completely new and extremely useful bit of patronage that they were loath to lose because Davis or the War Department thought it knew better or had patronage of its own to dispense. Lubbock of Texas had early, but not disagreeable, complaints about such appointments, and the War Department obliged by overruling local commanders so that the men in the ranks could elect their company field officers as had been traditional among volunteers. Indeed, by spring 1862 it became universal throughout Confederate regiments for the soldiers to elect their leaders from colonel down to sergeants, the very imposition of military democracy that would lead some to bemoan the demagoguery and wire-pulling with the men in order to seek election. "The men have defeated almost *every good* officer and elected privates and corporals to their places, who have been electioneering by promises to favor them and have loose discipline," grumbled Thomas Cobb.[53] Indeed, the regimental commanders themselves protested such an excess of democracy. "The elective system is the destruction of all discipline," declared a South Carolina colonel.[54] Matters became more difficult when Congress authorized private individuals to raise regiments directly without going through the governor, for it then put the governor in competition with them for recruits as he tried to raise his own units to fill the quotas imposed by the War Department.[55] The problem of conflicting authority so frustrated some militia officers that they simply resigned in the face of seeing their commands all but appropriated by Confederate appointees. "I am weary. I don't understand this war," complained James Lusk Alcorn, who had command of some Mississippi militia that Confederate generals were taking from him. "I don't wish to be the tail of the kite any longer, an appendage that drags heavily in the mud, flapping and sloshing around, liable at any moment to have my brains knocked out without being able to see the reason of things."[56] The conflict with Richmond continued almost to the end. As late as September 1864, Governor Vance was complaining bitterly that the president had no authority to appoint officers over North Carolina troops, demanding a decision on the matter from the attorney general, who finely split some hairs to find legal power.[57]

Once those regiments were raised, however it was done or by whomever, the governors then almost universally complained that too many state troops were ordered out of the region, leaving home inadequately defended. Louisiana's Governor Moore was bombarded with complaints from one of his favorite sons, General Braxton Bragg, commanding Louisiana troops at Pensacola facing Yankee-held Fort Pickens. There was too much delay from Richmond, supplies were too scarce and inferior when they arrived, and if it came to a fight to take the fort, he had only enough ammunition to last half an hour. "The golden opportunity has been lost," he grumbled. Giving up on the government, whose attention was firmly fixed on northern Virginia and the Mississippi Valley, Bragg implored the governor, "if you can aid in removing this eye sore from the gulf."[58] By the spring of 1862, Pettus complained to friends that if Mississippi were to be defended at all, he feared that his state militia would have to do it, for Richmond was not leaving any regular troops for the purpose, and the legislation for creating and managing militia was itself "unintelligible, incongruous, and nonsensical," according to one of its generals.[59] This only made the governors the more touchy when the conscript officers began taking men out of their states. Pettus demanded that General Gideon J. Pillow actually cease conscription in Mississippi in the late summer of 1863 until he could produce an order granting him authority, while at the same time in Texas and elsewhere Governor Pendleton Murrah and others had equal problems with state militia being called out for Confederate service in an emergency and then being held in service well after the crisis had passed and their terms of service had expired.[60] Georgia's supreme court sustained the constitutionality of the conscript law coming from Richmond, but the governor himself sought at every turn to hinder its operation.[61]

Even the usually very indulgent and cooperative, like Milton of Florida and Moore of Louisiana, could become irritable and querulous. In 1862, Milton protested that Richmond had effectively abandoned eastern, southern, and middle Florida, and was still ordering new state regiments off to other theaters. "Florida seems to be considered of very little importance," he grumbled to the secretary of the navy, Stephen Mallory, and he was right.[62] Moore was even more irritated as he struggled not to lose any more of his state to the Yankees who had just taken New Orleans and Baton Rouge. Worse, when the states armed and equipped regiments to be sent off to Virginia or other fronts, the War Department in Richmond would not recognize the right of the states to demand the return of the weapons they had themselves paid for. They automatically became Confederate property, and the Confederacy had an obligation to pay for them, yet it had too little money for the purpose.[63] If that was not bad enough, Moore found the guns and equipment he imported to arm his militia being seized by one general after another "and afterwards by every petty colonel or captain who under the plea of excessive vigilance manages to abstract for himself and his command whatever they may need or their fancy may suggest as agreeable." Richmond had withdrawn almost every regular soldier from the state, and had yet to send one gun for its defense. "It is the smallest justice they can do to permit me to use what my own

State money has bought and what the Confederate Government has not in any manner helped me to get," he grumbled. "How much longer is Louisiana to be considered without the protection or beneath the consideration of the Confederate Government?" Richmond would not even assign a general to take charge of defending the state, but rather carved it up and assigned it to the commands of officers in neighboring states, who made matters worse by steaming south in boats and actually raiding and plundering the homes of his civilians. "I have taken measures to protect my people from the repetition of such raids," he warned the secretary of war, and demanded that the officers responsible for the raids be relieved. Should they come again, he declared that he had placed cannon on the riverbank and would sink their vessel. "You can refuse to dismiss them," said Moore in his outrage, "but my marksmen may save you the trouble if they come again. There is a point at which patient endurance can extend no further."[64] Moore then took his complaint directly to the president. "I do not propose to discuss at this time how far the principle of submission on the part of the separate States to the illegal exercise of authority by the Confederate Government or its agents is necessary to harmony of action in carrying out the common defense," he protested. "No free people can or ought to submit to the arbitrary and illegal usurpation of authority." Even though offended at Moore's tone, Davis could not risk losing the good will of one of his strongest supporters among the governors, and immediately ordered the arms returned.[65]

Brown clashed with the army over use—and misuse—of railroad cars belonging to the Georgia Railroad, his hackles rising when quartermasters threatened to impress rolling stock if he did not willingly loan it, though the cars were private property not even subject to Brown's authority.[66] When Richmond dragged its feet about supplying new rails to repair badly worn track, Brown could be equally haughty, though bending so far as to admit that the administrations in both Georgia and Richmond were "in no small degree dependent upon each other."[67] His argument was sound, at least so far as the governors' experience with Confederate treatment of state property when loaned. At first the governors tried to be accommodating, and Milton even stated that in peacetime he would oppose any interference with state property, but in the face of the current crisis he would willingly set necessity above principle.[68] By late in the war, that attitude changed, and when Richmond tried to remove the rails of a Florida line to use elsewhere, the state took out an injunction to stop it. When the rails were removed anyhow, the court threatened a contempt citation, and after that actually attempted to arrest the officers involved, who simply refused to be arrested. Again Milton took his case to the president. "Nothing can justify a conflict between the State and Confederate Government," he promised, "but an absolute necessity for the protection of civil liberty as intended to be secured by the Constitution of the State and of the Confederate States."[69] The response from Richmond was peremptory. "The Government will not, under any circumstances, enter the State Courts and go through a process of litigation whenever it is necessary to obtain supplies of any kind for the army," declared the Justice Department. Congress had authorized the War Department to seize supplies of any description under military necessity, and Richmond would not admit of any power in state courts to interfere with injunctions.[70]

The encroachments of the military on state prerogatives could be far more blatant, as when General Beauregard, on his own authority and without War Department sanction, had a private railroad connecting Virginia and North Carolina widened.[71] The governors involved chose not to raise strong objections in the situation, but such acquiescence was rare. The rolling stock Brown grumbled about had been loaned once and returned in deplorable condition. In Texas, Murrah would complain about animals and wagons being handed back in decrepit shape, so much so that he would refuse to accept their return and instead demanded a settlement for the damage. "The State has been insulted and outraged by some one," he protested.[72] There were even conflicts over scarce medicines as military authorities sometimes impressed limited quantities of quinine during the fever season, working an extra hardship on civilians.[73] The government also stopped state-owned blockade runners from leaving port until Richmond received its share of the cargoes.[74] At the same time, disillusionment with Confederate inattention or inefficiency led some governors to redouble their own efforts, even while complaining of Richmond. Murrah cooperated with army authorities in Texas in 1864 to feed the soldiers in the face of the proper authorities' inability to do so, and as much as he could sought to remove rather than erect obstacles.[75] But still there were limits. When the much hated General Braxton Bragg, now relieved of field command and acting as advisor to the president, came to Montgomery, Alabama, in the summer of 1864, Governor Thomas Watts frankly told him that he had no wish to meet or speak with him, but would do so out of duty. Bragg returned the note without reply, and an indignant Watts declared that "the dignity of the Office I hold will not permit me to notice, further, General Bragg, in any official manner."[76]

When Benjamin H. Hill learned in January 1862 that he had been elected to represent Georgia in the Confederate Senate, he told Governor Brown to "allow me to hope that during my short connection officially with the new Confederate Government, I shall find the actions of that government & the state government as harmonious as their interests are identical in the issue of this great contest for liberty."[77] Brown, however, was another case altogether. No governor clashed so consistently or intractably with the government. The man was an instinctive controversialist, at odds off and on with almost every prominent statesman even in his own state, and by late 1864 his clashes with the president and the administration became so widely known that some accused him of deliberately seeking to injure the greater cause, and others believed that whether or not he intended it, he was actually doing so. Even a staunch supporter of the governor's could still beg him to relax his intransigence. "I believe your policy is a correct one," A. A. Terhune told Brown in November just after the governor issued a message to the legislature calling for a convention with the states of North and South to find a way to peace. "Though I am a friend and admirer of President Davis, I believe anything emanating from you will not receive his blessing or support." He continued:

> We are all men of the same passions, both high and low, Envy, hatred, malice, love, friendship & revenge. Why can't you and Mr. Davis adjust your difference; Now is the time for 'the two horses in the team to pull together.' You are the Governor of the *Empire State* and he the President of the Confederacy; you are both good and true men, able men, men capable of doing a great deal of good and a great deal of harm; with united heads such as yours what could not be effected; I believe you are both willing to make any sacrifice for the good of the people; why not sacrifice a little private feeling, you don't know how much harm it does or you would I feel sure. Be the first to make the concession, oh! How noble how christian like it would be to ask of Mr. Davis a reconciliation, and then how great the good effected by it. . . . Every one now says look at President Davis & Governor Brown, they can't deliver a message or make a speech but they must cut and thrust at each other.[78]

The cut and thrust would continue right to the close of the war and the Confederacy, and as the situation grew steadily more dire, the tempers flared all the more readily, and not just in Georgia. "We are not getting on with the unanimity that you and I desire," a Texan legislator told Senator Louis Wigfall in November 1864. The best he could say was that "upon the whole we are doing better than we did last session."[79]

It was perhaps amazing that the governors maintained as much spirit as they did in the face of the continual erosion of their states' prosperity and physical and moral health. In 1864, with hardly anyplace to call his capital, Moore of Louisiana had to confess in his annual message that the legislature had been able to pass very few acts because of disruption, and those they had enacted could not be printed. As for the journals of debates, economic necessity forced him to ask for the first time that they be published only in English rather than in the long-standing tradition of two languages, English and French. He also felt convinced that no foreign power was going to come to their aid. "We must fight this battle alone," he declared, and yet he was still ready to fight it.[80] Even when disruption of his authority and respect for Louisiana's sovereignty was such that one of his state senators was conscripted into the Texas state forces, Moore kept his eyes chiefly fixed on the greater goal.[81] In neighboring Texas, despite the almost universal dislike of General Kirby Smith, still the legislature passed a vote of confidence in him in June 1864.[82] Despite being almost completely cut off from the rest of the Confederacy, even while their roads and bridges were breaking down from neglect, while state and federal agents could not get copies of the acts and laws they were to enforce, nor could Treasury funds from Richmond reach them, nor correspondence any longer come through regular postal channels, still somehow the Texans maintained their hope.[83] Milton would declare again and again that Florida would do its all for the cause, and did not want nor would it accept peace until every Confederate state was free.[84]

By the dawn of 1865, Louisiana, Tennessee, Mississippi, Arkansas, and Georgia had all lost their capitals, while Alabama's and Florida's were at the mercy of the Federals anytime the Yankees decided they were important enough to take. Of those remaining in the hands of their governors and legislatures, Virginia's was under siege and South Carolina's had a Yankee army heading for it with no substantial opposition. Despite all their sacrifice, all the turmoil and cooperation, and the efforts to keep democ-

racy alive while yet adjusting to meet the extraordinary demands of the crisis upon them, the state governments of the Confederacy simply could not
match the odds against them, either individually or collectively, whether
with the interference or collaboration of their national administration. As
their efforts showed, for every instance in which their now archaic adherence to the doctrine of rigid state rights did them harm, there were others
in which cooperation, adjustment, accommodation, and some sense of nationalism impelled them to rise above parochial attitudes to adopt a
broader view. They extended some rights and trampled on others. They
advanced justice and yet abridged some freedoms. They experimented
with measures that ran from the oppressive to the socialistic, and to the
very end their people never stopped looking to their governors and legislatures as the guardians of their security, more so than faraway Richmond.
All the while, amid the experimentation and cobbling, the underlying concept of who ought to have power never changed, however. The foundations of Confederate democracy in the states in 1865 still stood where they
had been in 1861, planted firmly in a ruling elite and shored up by the
trappings of republicanism that an acquiescent populace continued not to
challenge.[85]

Florida had taken up the carpeting in its statehouse in 1862 and sent it
to be used somehow for the comfort of its soldiers in the field.[86] Months
before then the capitol in Baton Rouge had burned, and even in untouched Montgomery the iron railings around the statehouse were taken
away to be melted into cannon. South Carolina was right in the middle of
building a new capital at Columbia when the war began. During the conflict it could ill afford the expense of the workmen to continue the job, and
so the shell of the building sat, protected by a watchman from vandalism.
The state actually sold most of the remaining construction materials, including 800,000 bricks, for other war purposes, while the state archives
languished in the unsecure vaults of the old capitol.[87] Somehow, amid the
devastation of the war, the grand edifices of state government seemed less
important than the cause they served, and yet like that cause, they had not
the strength to save themselves from the ravenous appetites of history.

12

The Power and the Ignominy in Richmond

THE FOUR YEARS OF WAR and civil turmoil, hardship, dislocation, and sacrifice were felt nowhere more than in Richmond. It became symbolic of the cause itself, at least for Confederates living east of the Mississippi and especially those east of the Appalachians. Just as the population fed on the news from their capital, in that city the survival of the young new nation became the daily bread of thought for president, cabinet, Congress, and people alike. A national capital always has a distinctive personality, composed of ambition and venality, the cosmopolitan influences of visitors from all over the map, its own parochial interests, and the sense of being a place in the eye of the world. For Richmond that personality was flavored by the knowledge that it was more especially a place in the sights of a Union juggernaut dedicated to the capture of the capital and the destruction of its would-be nation.

Within weeks of the capital and Congress moving to Richmond, both anxiety and euphoria had swept the city and those who came there to govern. Throughout the day on July 21, 1861, as the army under P.G.T. Beauregard and Joseph E. Johnston battled the invader in northern Virginia, the city trembled in excitement and trepidation. The nerve center was the War Department, where the most nervous of all was the secretary of war, Leroy Pope Walker. He paced his floor all day, damning his luck in being stuck in an office rather than out on the battlefield. Outside his door the hallways teemed with dignitaries and common citizens begging for news, and at the receipt of each new telegraphic dispatch from the army the ex- citement rose. Meanwhile Attorney General Judah Benjamin, clearly al- most frantic from anxiety, pushed his way out through the crowd around his own office and walked a few blocks to the Spotswood Hotel. The pres- ident had left for the front that morning, many thought, to take actual command as commander in chief, but in fact he went only to observe and be on hand if he could help in any capacity. His wife, Varina, was at the ho- tel, however, and any word coming back from Davis might reach her first, and so it did late that afternoon when she received a message from him of a glorious victory.

"Then joy ruled the hour!" declared War Department clerk John B. Jones. "The city seemed lifted up, and every one appeared to walk on air."[1] The Spotswood became, and remained, "gay and lively" to newly arrived Littleton Washington, now just starting a job writing editorials for a Rich- mond newspaper. "The rest of my time I gave up chiefly to society & amusement," he said. "My life was a holiday very nearly."[2] So was everyone else's, for in the wake of the victory along the banks of Bull Run, many in Richmond believed that this was all the war they would have to fight. The humiliating defeat handed the Yankees would make an end of the war. Even as the months rolled along, and it became well known that the North was rebuilding and regrouping rather than backing down, a sense of false security gripped many. It was a period of "phony war" that could not last, but while it did Richmond gleamed.

The men who made the government knew better. They had come to govern, and they got to it, even before the Congress reassembled in July. Already uncounted local concerns from the states were being sent to their delegations to bring to Richmond, whether it be coastal defense in Florida or customshouse suspension in Texas.[3] Governors sought the influence of cabinet ministers and their congressional representatives in disputes with other executive departments.[4] As soon as Congress convened, some mem- bers began the delicate act of mediating the conflicts that arose between their governors and the administration, and many a congressman went to Richmond with very special instructions to place special concerns before the president, the South Carolinians most of all. James Chesnut took on himself the task of representing his state's interests with his friend the president, and would continue to do so as a member of Davis's staff in later years.[5] Other Carolinians turned to William Porcher Miles, seen as the ablest of their delegation, and he got petitions for the appointment of favorite sons as generals and other matters before Davis, though he complained himself that it was almost impossible to get the Congress to turn its attention to any proposition not confined to military and financial matters.[6] Indeed, Miles stayed in Richmond even after the session of Congress adjourned in order to keep putting his state's interests constantly before the president. "I hope he may prove all that our Charleston friends believe he will," Miles said of Davis in August; "'the right man in the right place.'"[7]

The veneer of harmony in the wake of the victory continued for some time, even though underneath it the old dictates of ambition and politics made themselves felt. It took no longer than the fall congressional election to fill the seats to the first session of the Permanent Congress that would convene the following February for the velvet gloves to come off.[8] Despite many seats going uncontested for the current incumbents, others, especially the new Senate's chairs, saw the old wires pulled, nowhere more than in Virginia, so divided between its secessionist and submissionist factions. The former pressed Robert M.T. Hunter to run, which brought out a bitter opposition from supporters of the conservative James Barbour, including from the Richmond *Examiner* for which Littleton Washington worked, and which even he—a friend of Hunter's—described as a "scurrilous mouthpiece" of the anti-Hunter forces. "This paper stuck at no falsehoods & refrained from no calumny upon Mr. Hunter," said Washington, and before the election he stopped writing for the paper because Hunter felt his candidacy might be compromised. In the end Barbour withdrew and Hunter won the Senate seat almost unanimously, but the tone had been set, and it was clear that the men who sought office had lost nothing of the zest and passion of their prewar contests.[9]

Jefferson Davis, of course, ran unopposed for election as president under the Constitution, and on February 22, 1862—with all the auspicious connotations that George Washington's birthday could bestow on the new nation—he took his oath and delivered his second inaugural. "It was worthy of the occasion," wrote the reporter Washington, now a State Department clerk, "eloquent & heroic."[10] As late as January 1862 confidence still ran high in the national government. William B. Ochiltree managed to report a bill for frontier protection for his constituents in Texas out of the military affairs committee in January, and saw it passed unanimously by the Congress. That no doubt helped make him feel the more optimistic when he wrote to Governor Francis Lubbock that "affairs generally are beginning to assume a brighter hue than they have worn for some time past."[11] His colleague Williamson Oldham helped him pass the frontier protection bill, and he was even more confident when he wrote Lubbock at the same time that "our Government will rely upon its own power and resources to carry the contest in which we are engaged to a successful conclusion." The Confederacy was ready to meet and repulse the enemy at every point, he thought. "If we do the war cannot continue long after." Nevertheless, he warned, "we should however prepare ourselves for some disasters."[12]

Indeed, they should. Less than a month later the disasters began to hit, and they hit hard. First came the fall of Fort Henry on the Tennessee River on February 6, 1862. Then came the debacle two days later at Roanoke Island, North Carolina, when some 2,000 Confederates were forced to surrender. Not only was it the first capitulation by a Southern commander, and a terrific blow to Confederate morale, but it also gave the enemy a foothold on the Atlantic shore within striking distance of Richmond itself. And then came yet another blow on February 16 when Fort Donelson on the Cumberland River was forced to surrender, this time with the loss of more than 12,000 soldiers. Authorities in the area had no choice but to abandon Nashville and most of middle and west Tennessee. Some would later date the fall of the Confederacy itself to the loss of the river forts. Thus six days after Donelson, on February 22, when Davis was inaugurated and the first session of the First Congress under the Constitution convened, what should have been a festive occasion was severely sobered by recent disasters. "I struggled against the mournful feelings inspired by all these things as well as I could but it was impossible to resist their influence," Littleton Washington lamented. "I went out to parties & visited a good deal; but though I was apparently gay & cheerful I was far from feeling so." Suddenly foreboding replaced overconfidence, and with the enlistments of most of the army's twelve-month regiments about to expire, there was a fear that the men would not reenlist in the wake of the defeats, and the army would evaporate, and the cause with it.[13] Only Davis's resort to conscription and other carrot-and-stick measures kept the regiments full, but at some cost to him politically. Then came the loss of Missouri in a battle at Pea Ridge, Arkansas, on March 8; the failure of an ill-planned invasion of the New Mexico Territory; the defeat at Shiloh on April 6–7 of General Albert Sidney Johnston's attempt to regain Tennessee, which resulted in his death; and finally the catastrophic fall of New Orleans on April 25.

Now everything seemed stained, from Congress's point of view. Texas member Peter W. Gray noticed what Vice President Alexander Stephens and others would comment upon in later days, that the caliber of the members had declined somewhat from that of the Provisional Congress. It had been composed of the best and most patriotic, and many of them had chosen to enlist or raise regiments rather than continue to sit in a legislature, leaving their seats to be filled in too many cases by lesser men. Those inclined to wire-pulling and demagoguery were too many, the long-winded like Henry Foote too much indulged.[14] New member Franklin Sexton of Texas was appalled at Foote's penchant for making any comment last an hour, and attaching "stump speech preambles" to even the simplest resolution. "He tires everybody," complained Sexton.[15] Gray believed he could detect some who were disposed to create an opposition to the administration on issues like the recent setbacks. Yet among the better men, Gray found that "our recent disasters have only aroused all hands to the magnitude of the work before us, and has aroused the spirit of resistance more than ever."[16] They went to work and passed a bill providing for the destruction of private property in cotton and tobacco to prevent its falling into enemy hands, with compensation to the owners, a measure that Littleton Washington thought "showed firmness & pluck" even though it put the government between the planter and his sacred rights of property.[17] They also demonstrated their resolve by passing by unanimous vote a resolution repudiating surrender or negotiations on any basis other than independence. Even a few of those who voted for it, like Gray, thought it unnecessary, but perhaps politically expedient in the current downturn of their fortunes. And to address the criticism of uncoordinated and dilatory military operations, they created an office of general in chief to control field operations, subject to the president of course. "We have our hands full you may be sure," Gray reported to Governor Lubbock.[18]

It was hardly a time for yet more military setbacks, but the spring and summer of 1862 seemed to offer only unrelentingly dark hours. A Union army under George B. McClellan established itself on Virginia soil some fifty miles southeast of the capital. Though mired by its commander's indecision, still it eventually began to move, taking Yorktown, then Williamsburg, and finally posing a serious threat to Richmond itself. The gloom in the capital became palpable. Some believed the city would fall, and not a few members of the government, including the president, sent their families to the country for safety. Congress adjourned on April 21, not because its work was done, but because it seemed too dangerous to remain. The State Department packed some of its archives for removal, as did other executive branches. By mid-May some, like Littleton Washington, admitted to going to bed each night expecting to be awakened the next morning by the sound of Yankee shells exploding in the streets, and Secretary of the Navy Stephen Mallory privately confessed that "my mind is so depressed." But then on May 15 came a heartening repulse of a Union naval thrust up the James River toward the city, and though McClellan's army by now had reached within three miles of Richmond, people began to take more heart. The Virginia legislature, which refused to adjourn, showed its mettle by passing a resolution that the city should be destroyed rather than surrender.[19] Mallory told his wife that "the state & city authorities & even the women of the city desire that it shall be shelled rather than surrender," though hundreds of families had fled. "We are to have a fight for its possession, and will not abandon it so long as it can be held."[20] Then came the decisive battle at Seven Pines on May 31 when the hesitant and tardy General Joseph E. Johnston was wounded and Robert E. Lee took his place at the head of the defending army. After that there would be no more retreats, and Richmond was safe, though the shock to the country of the near miss had been critical. "Our Cause is nearly lost—public sentiment is deeply demoralized," complained Reuben Davis, newly elected congressman from Mississippi, in mid-June. "*Inaction* and disasters have cast a deep gloom upon every one." He blamed the president, as many others were beginning to do.[21]

When Lee struck back at the end of June in what became known as the Seven Days' Battles, he drove McClellan back toward an eventual withdrawal by sea, and greatly relieved the immediate pressure on the administration. Davis himself and several of his cabinet were frequently seen with Lee on the battlefield, sometimes even tending wounded, the civil and military authorities commingling at the point of crisis and emphasizing that this was one democracy whose life was bound up completely in its armies.[22] But when the delegates regathered on August 18, there were stiff demands for explanations for the past season of defeat and discontent, and the chief targets became immediately evident. Disgusted by what seemed a witch hunt, Sexton preferred to leave all talk of military policy to the generals rather than see it argued out on the floor by men like Foote and Louis Wigfall, who were willing to use anything as an excuse to pursue their petty personal vendettas. "Oh Lord," Sexton grumbled on September 12, "have mercy on all mankind."[23] Mallory too complained. "Congress having convened on the 18th is already at work carving our work for all the Departments & giving as much trouble as possible."

Well he should have protested, for Mallory himself had never been popular, and some thought him inefficient and lethargic, and his office ineptly run. Charles Conrad of Louisiana actually introduced legislation to abolish the Navy Department and merge it with the war office. There might have been no small quotient of spite in his proposal, for he had lost a lot of his property with the fall of New Orleans and blamed the navy in part for its fall. It was one of the first battles over a cabinet incumbent and revealed that these men had forgotten none of their old ways from Washington, in spite of their reforming pretensions. Foote soon seconded Conrad with what Sexton thought dreadful abuse, and both continued the attack on subsequent days. As soon as Conrad launched his attack, Mallory began politicking with three other influential members of the House, explaining to them the circumstances under which the navy labored, and revealing that much of the energy and money he had expended was on secret projects like commerce raiders and ironclads, and thus unknown to the people at large or even to Conrad. He asked them to institute an investigation at which he could reveal his industry to the Congress and the public, and even sat down with one of the members to help draft the resolution that would subject him and his office to inquiry, knowing that Conrad and his enemy Foote would be on the committee. He launched a similar movement in the Senate, even when some of his friends there were reluctant to put him through an investigation, but he insisted upon it as "the best means of meeting my enemies."

Such men could not hide the truth. He had no fears. "I have much to be proud of & nothing whatever to regret in my administration," he told his wife. He had revolutionized naval warfare with his introduction of the ironclad warship, and the assaults upon him now were only "the rage of the ignorant the rabble & the prejudiced who always constitute the majority of mankind." Conrad hated Mallory personally, of that he was certain, while Foote was simply "a fool & is crazy besides."[24] The ensuing debate on holding an investigation proved sometimes acrimonious as Mallory's defenders, chiefly Florida's Robert Hilton, clashed with Conrad and Foote especially. Foote denounced Mallory violently, demanding that if the president would not remove him from office, he should be impeached. Hilton welcomed such a threat, for at least an impeachment motion was more manly and straightforward than Conrad's "side blow" of trying to get rid of Mallory by eliminating his department.[25] So it went, to the credit of few, and when the committees finally sat, Mallory was proven right, though the investigation would take two years before he received a full vindication. "I am disgusted with deliberative bodies—at least with this," Sexton confessed after just one month as a congressman. "Oh judgment thou art fled to brutish beasts!"[26]

The ultimate target was Davis himself, of course, as the growing opposition sought to embarrass him through his cabinet. They also went after Benjamin, whom Davis had appointed to replace Walker as secretary of war the previous fall, and who had held the office through the spring disasters of March. Everyone seemed to blame him for Roanoke Island especially, and he had managed to become estranged from Beauregard and Joseph E. Johnston, who were flirting with the increasingly intertwined web of politicians, journalists, and others in the opposition. A motion of no confidence was introduced against Benjamin in the House on March 4, and soon thereafter word went out that Johnston had said the cause was hopeless with him in his current post. Faced with the near certainty of an embarrassing defeat if he sought confirmation of Benjamin as war secretary by the new Congress, Davis relented. On one of the few occasions when he appeared to bow to pressure, Davis decided not to retain Benjamin in the war office. Rather than dismiss him, however, the president promoted Benjamin to the State Department in March 1862, and he won confirmation with little difficulty. The opposition had made their point.

Of course the cabinet was always destined to be a focal point for criticism and discontent, a situation not helped by the fact that the longer the war went on, the harder it became for the executive departments to get something accomplished. "It is so difficult to get any business rapidly through any of the offices here," complained one of Beauregard's staff after days of waiting at the War Department.[27] When affairs went wrong, the population at large had only the administration and the generals to hold to account, while the generals themselves were only too happy to pass their failures on to their civil masters, and the Congress also knew where to lay responsibility for its own failures. Democracy might have depended on a chain of authority and responsibility, but when it came to blame, all fingers pointed upward toward the top of the power pyramid. The first cabinet appointed in Montgomery held office for scarcely two months before there were calls of incompetence and demands for removal, and thereafter there was scarcely ever a time when at least one of Davis's ministers was not afoul of the press, Congress, or both. No sooner did Walker leave office than General Braxton Bragg wrote to Benjamin to say, "I do not hesitate to say, 'I impugn the action of your predecessor.'" The harm Walker had done as a cabinet member was incalculable, Bragg continued, accusing him of rank favoritism and office pandering in his appointments. "We have not united in the 'On to Richmond,' seeking high places," he averred. "We considered it unmilitary and unbecoming. We were ardently serving the cause, not ourselves, but nevertheless, we did not suppose our government would so soon forget we were in its service, and degrade us." Such abuses were "a rankling sore" that only the president could cure by removal from office.[28]

The unpopular Benjamin himself was replaced in the War Department by George Wythe Randolph of Virginia, an ailing but intellectual grandson of Thomas Jefferson. Visitors found him "not only a gentleman in his manners, but exceedingly anxious to do all in his power to comply with your requests," said one early visitor.[29] Under his administration good works were effected, not least the seemingly minor yet vitally important—and potentially touchy—matter of setting a standard caliber for all weapons manufactured in the Confederacy. When the war began many different calibers were in use, and as weapons were imported from abroad the variety continued to baffle the best efforts of ordnance officers to supply the right ammunition. A single standard caliber could change all that, much to the improvement of the service. Richmond interfered in the prerogatives of the individual states, and they went along.[30] Yet Randolph would try too much to be his own man, and by the fall he and Davis had fallen out to the point that he resigned, and the president made no attempt to dissuade him. Another Virginian, James Seddon, replaced him, and proved to be far more pliant and amenable to Davis's imposition of his own will in the department. A well-meaning but largely ineffectual man, he would be used by Davis as little more than a glorified clerk until the outcry against him was such that in early 1865 Davis had to find yet another incumbent, and settled on the last and best of the lot, John C. Breckinridge.

In the State Department, Robert Toombs had been unhappy from the first, and made no secret of his disdain for the office or of his desire to leave it for the field, which he would do in July 1861. All who knew him knew what a loose cannon he could be. "As he does not remain on the track very long, he must demolish his enemies in a few weeks," quipped Quartermaster General Abraham C. Myers. And indeed, Toombs would make more enemies in the Confederate army than among the enemy, leaving uniform after a year to take his place among the administration's opponents.[31] He, among others, was largely responsible for General Lee's attempt to discourage the War Department from allowing elected state officials and congressmen to hold military commissions simultaneously, since they could do neither job adequately under the circumstances.[32]

R.M.T. Hunter replaced Toombs for a few months, and then came Benjamin, who would hold the office for the rest of the war. "Mr. Benjamin was a working man, and a man to make work," observed Littleton Washington, now a clerk in the department and one increasingly close to the secretary. Busy and efficient, Benjamin could also be curt and even unpleasant, but generally only when under the pressure of business. He kept his office door open to all and, when possible, operated a collegial sort of administration in which the views of many were welcomed.[33] "A man of society, his tact in personal intercourse was unfailing, his politeness invariable," said Washington. "I never saw his temper ruffled or embittered. His opinions were generally decided but courteously expressed." He loved work, kept office hours from 9 A.M. to 3 P.M., and often took in work from other departments, presumably at their behest, though some thought him an empire builder. With great perception, Washington remarked of the secretary's state papers, "I do not affirm that his compositions were wholly unstudied, but, whatever art there was, he had the art to hide."[34] Benjamin actually wrote some of the president's state papers for him, including annual messages to Congress. Art, indeed, was the essence of Benjamin, and there was much of it, too, in his chief assistant, William Browne, often called "Constitution" Browne from his time as editor of the Washington *Constitution*. A jealous Littleton Washington thought him "an adventurer of medium abilities & a foreigner [Browne was of Irish birth]." But when Browne resigned in 1862 to join Davis's personal staff, his office remained vacant for more than a year as Benjamin unsuccessfully sought a replacement. While in office Browne had shown particular attention to gathering copies of all the state convention ordinances and acts to use for reference, and "to preserve the historical records of the time," he told Governor John Pettus of Mississippi.[35]

In other departments there were often complaints of inefficiency and inadequacy. Christopher Memminger never pleased anyone as secretary of the Treasury. Certainly his office was lax about filling vacancies and even in collecting customs duties from some of the more remote places like Ea-gle Pass, Texas.[36] Still he probably performed as well as could be expected given the circumstances confronting him, and when he resigned to be re-placed by South Carolina's George A. Trenholm in 1864, his successor did no better. By its very nature, the Confederacy was destined to live its life amassing ever greater quantities of debt that only independence and years of tranquil prosperity afterward would allow it to repay. As for the Post Of-fice Department, few knew how it operated or cared, for it attracted no more notice in the new nation than it had in the old except for the stunning achievement of John H. Reagan in making it pay its own way. He put the postal routes out to contractors for bids, raised rates, bullied railroads into giving him preferential rates, and showed such frugality that as late as Sep-tember 1862 his office was still using up stationery printed for use at Mont-gomery sixteen months before. Ironically, the greatest complaints of Reagan's operation came from his own Texas, where he cut down the mail service to save money.[37] Nevertheless, by the end of the war he had be-come one of the president's most trusted advisors, and Texas continued to use him as an ally and liaison with Congress.[38] He was, along with Mallory, the only appointee to hold his office for the entire life of the Confederacy, and at the end, though it hardly mattered, Davis would make him Treasury secretary as well.

Almost as quickly as gloom set Congress against cabinet, a reversal of fortunes due more than anything else to Robert E. Lee changed the mood in Richmond. His stunning victories in the Seven Days, followed by even greater triumphs at Second Manassas, and the lightning campaign of Thomas J. "Stonewall" Jackson in the Shenandoah Valley, seemed to launch the Confederacy once more on the high road to independence, and if affairs to the west and in the Mississippi Valley did not entirely favor the cause, still the season of severe losses was past. When Lee finally suf-fered his first defeat, it was on Yankee soil in an invasion of Maryland, but Virginia remained intact and the enemy seemingly in shock. "The war seemed almost broken down at the North," Littleton Washington believed in November, and he began to hear people once more confidently express expectations that England and France would soon grant diplomatic recog-nition to the new nation.[39] Congress was discussing strong retaliatory measures against violations of rights of person and property by Yankees, and there were even suggestions from delegate Gustavus Adolphus Henry of Tennessee that they should escalate the war dramatically by raising the black flag of no quarter to intimidate the North into giving up.[40] Even more hopeful were expectations that the fall elections in the North would see a repudiation of Lincoln's Republicans and loyal Democratic supporters.

They were hopes that troubled some of the more thoughtful in the Confederate capital. "I fear that our people as usual are promising themselves peace from the elections of the North or foreign intervention," Robert Barnwell of South Carolina lamented to Wigfall. "This seems to me mere folly & cowardice." They would only get peace by fighting, he believed, and unfortunately the response to conscription was not what it should have been. Instead there were too many seeking exemption and personal advancement. "Every man wants an office," he complained. "I am pestered for the use of an influence which I neither have nor wish to have."[41] All that abruptly swung back toward anxiety in the spring of 1863 when another advancing Yankee army reached and crossed the Rappahannock, and suddenly clerks like Washington were enlisting hurriedly in home guard companies in case the capital suffered attack. Lee's incredible victory at Chancellorsville in May swung the pendulum back to confidence, only to have it swing yet again after his crushing defeat at Gettysburg, Pennsylvania, in July. "The prospect was a dark one," clerk Washington recalled a few weeks later. "Nothing could exceed the public depression," and this was on top of the loss of Vicksburg at the same time, and with it the last foothold of control on the Mississippi.[42]

As the public and political mood seesawed up and down in rhythm with Confederate military fortunes, the generals themselves found increasing cause for discontent with the administration and the administration with them. Joseph E. Johnston acquired a reputation with some for an officious and unpleasant demeanor.[43] Bragg, always carping and jealous, complained that Mansfield Lovell, a New Yorker to whom Davis gave command of New Orleans in the fall of 1861, had been "bought" by the president and was not to be trusted, his subsequent loss of the Crescent City through no fault of his own seemingly confirming Bragg's suspicion. "I am no aspirant for political honors, and if I were I know my chances would be small in these days of demagogues," he groused as others got positions he thought he deserved. "I hope to continue a soldier until the political demagogues are all killed off. The war ought not to end until then."[44]

Of course, once Bragg did rise to army command in the spring of 1862, he quickly found himself the object of the same vituperation that he poured so readily on others, and even Henry of Tennessee, who started by defending Bragg in the Senate, was forced to abandon him by that fall after Bragg's failed effort to take and hold Kentucky.[45] Congressmen complained that their own favorite son candidates for generals' stars were too often ignored. "In military appointments I do not think the President gives much weight to the recommendation of civilians, even if they are members of Congress," lamented Edward Sparrow of Louisiana. Indeed, after the first year of the war when expediency forced Davis, like Lincoln, to hand out a number of commissions to serve regional and political expectations, he almost ceased listening to congressmen entirely when it came to appointments in the army.[46]

This angered them all the more when controversial and unpopular generals like Kirby Smith in the Trans-Mississippi became themselves the issues in some congressional campaigns like that of Henry Gray of Louisiana, who was elected in the fall of 1864 in a special election after the death of an incumbent. There was only one issue, and that was the by now seemingly autocratic administration of Kirby Smith. Gray's opponent, Lang Lewis, completely misread the sentiment of the voters when he came out and supported the general. "Are you down there going to unite and send to Congress a man to support the character of Kirby Smith?" Judge E. Warren Moise demanded to know of former governor Thomas Moore. "By God, if you do, you deserve all you have suffered."[47] Further complicating things, Gray was then a brigadier general serving in Smith's command, so as a soldier he could hardly speak out against his general even though as a candidate that is what people wanted him to do. He was helped out of the conundrum by the fact that to the moment of his election, he did not even know that his name had been placed in nomination, and thus he never had to solve the problem. He won overwhelmingly on the single issue of his opponent's foolhardy endorsement of Smith, revealing just how conflated the military and political arenas could become.[48]

Some generals more than others expressed their discontent, and none more so than Joseph Johnston, who by 1863 had firmly established himself with the political opposition, and who unwittingly made himself their tool in their own battle with the president. He particularly attached himself to Clement Clay of Alabama and Wigfall of Texas. Clay was, in fact, a close friend of Davis's and one of his staunchest supporters, yet he recognized as well as anyone else the president's limitations, and applied himself to trying to bridge the gap between Davis's prickly personality and the equally contentious opposition. In the end, Clay mostly just succeeded in putting himself in the middle. He even found himself pitted against some of his own colleagues from Alabama, like Jabez L.M. Curry, with whom he clashed over a soldier pay bill in an exchange that ended with Curry trying to force Clay into a position that would cost him reelection in 1863, and Clay calling Curry a liar to his face.[49] Johnston, meanwhile, fed pet army projects to Wigfall, urging him to get them on the floor of Congress, such as his January 1864 plan to put all noncombatant soldiers in the front lines and replace them with impressed slaves, who would be kept in the army rather than returned to their owners when the army moved on. "Is this not worth trying?" he asked, and indeed it was, even though both knew it represented yet another assault on personal property rights. "Do now apply your energy and zeal to it," urged the general.[50]

Yet nothing in the confused political arena could become more strained than some of the relations between and among the civil leaders themselves. In 1863, Jefferson Davis and Senator William L. Yancey of Alabama became all but estranged over the silly issue of the patronage appointment of a postmaster in Yancey's hometown, Montgomery. The appointment was Davis's to give since it was a federal post, yet long custom in the United States had allowed representatives in Congress to expect that if they put forward their own favorites, an obliging executive would appoint them as part of the natural give-and-take of politics. But Davis bristled at Yancey's assumption that he was entitled to expect his own candidate to be appointed, and quickly the correspondence between two overly proud and disputatious men flew out of control. Quickly poor Clay got involved, hoping to save relations that could be vitally important to the cause, but to no avail, and it all became embarrassingly public. Only late in the affair, in July 1863, did Clay manage the beginnings of a rapprochement, with each contestant admitting that he wished to keep the good will of the other, when Yancey suddenly died and the episode ended. In his will Yancey left Davis a telescope that once belonged to George Washington, perhaps a sign that all was forgiven, though Yancey's wife actually blamed Davis for the illness that killed her husband. Sadly the glass did nothing to improve Davis's vision of how to deal with men as autocratic and independent as himself.[51]

Politics was becoming increasingly bitter by late 1863, and clashes like Davis's and Yancey's or the Lewis-Gray battle over Kirby Smith were more and more common. A few men like Clay and Sexton became positively outraged with what they saw in Congress and on the hustings. "Feel almost a disgust for legislative assemblies," Sexton told his diary in April 1863. He had no room to write all he felt, and concluded, in fact, that it was better that he did not.[52] "There is a strong feeling of dissatisfaction with those in office that is very natural & not entirely unfounded," Clay lamented, "that threatens to throw us all out, especially those regarded as the President's especial friends." By the fall of 1863, with elections pending, he feared that the governorships, legislatures, and Congress might all fall into the hands of old Whigs and Stephen Douglas Democrats, men soft on secession originally, and perhaps too prone to consider the idea of reconstruction with the North on some negotiated basis short of independence. Worse, Confederate currency was increasingly deflated and, in Richmond at least, people showed little sign of reduction in their consumption of goods and funds, or of their obsession with holding onto their property. "They cling to their flesh pots, while the country cries to them for help," Clay wrote. Refugees everywhere were "flying with their negroes to some safe place," placing increased strains on economies wherever they went. Before long he expected only the wealthy would have the altruism or be able to afford to serve in Congress, for few congressmen could subsist on their salary alone. "Our pay must boss us," he complained.[53] A trip to Montgomery that fall did nothing to alleviate his fears, for he found the legislature composed of new men he did not know, even in his home state. Their political beliefs and alliances were unknown even among themselves, representing as they did the second and third generations of wartime legislators who, with their counterparts in Georgia and North Carolina especially, were increasingly critical of the existing political leadership, and more and more skeptical of the prospects for independence. "Their acts indicate that they dissent from my views of public affairs & disapprove of my public course," Clay observed. The officers they chose to run their body were all prewar Unionists. Even Robert Jemison, whom they chose in a special election to fill Yancey's seat, had been an opponent of secession.

Clay suspected that in that fall's senatorial election for his seat he himself would be defeated, and he was right. The prospect did not altogether dismay him. "I am sick of the selfishness, corruption, demagogism & bigotry wh[ich] characterize so large a portion of those in office," he told Wigfall. "There is not enough intelligence & integrity in the country to appreciate & sustain men who act only fr[om] a high sense of duty without

regard [to] personal ends." Of course, Clay naturally saw himself as one of
those who had really met his own high standards, and to a large degree he
was right. Moreover, he had seen firsthand the growing corruption in Richmond—profiteers in the commissary department defrauding the government; men who never served a day in battle angling ever higher
promotions through political connections, perhaps even bribery; people
actually rejoicing at lost territory, credit, and resources, because each loss
drove up the prices of the goods they speculated upon to make their fortunes, allowing some who had opposed secession to take revenge on the
pocketbooks of others who helped bring it about. "How many are abusing
high trusts to justify personal applause or favoritism, or to deceive & en-
trap," he lamented. "I rejoice to think that I shall soon cease to be responsible for it beyond any other private citizen."[54] Even if Clay's lamentations
were a bit hyperbolic, still what corruption and venality there were in
Richmond and through the country did more than enough evil work just in
causing the disenchantment and cynicism of good statesmen like Clay
whose best efforts were desperately needed. It did not help when the new
crop of congressmen showed up in Richmond for the first session of the
Second Congress in May 1864 that some of them were outright avowed
Unionists. One from Alabama, W.R.R. Cobb, was actually denied his seat
because he was so outspoken, and his district spent the rest of the war un-
represented.

Minor disagreements could become bitter. Before his death, Yancey got
into a shouting match with Benjamin Hill on the Senate floor that turned
abusively ugly. Yancey accused Hill of being a man without ideas like a fox
without a tail. "We have disagreed always," said the Alabamian. "He attacks & portrays my intellect." But then Yancey himself "portrayed" Hill
and Wigfall together as "Thimble Nigger and Little Joker," only to have
Hill respond that when Yancey opened his mouth "words rush out like shot
from his bag." It ended with Hill throwing an ink bottle that caught Yancey
on the side of the head.[55] And the disagreements could turn deadly, as on
April 24, 1863, when the clerk of the House, Robert E. Dixon of Georgia,
was accosted and killed by a man he had had fired from his employ a few
days before.[56]

Adding to the bitterness were elements in the capital and national press
whose motives often seemed, at best, mixed. On the one hand there were
those like the Houston *Weekly Telegraph*. "The heavens are bright above
us," it proclaimed on January 5, 1862. "Earth smiles beneath our feet."

Even after the reverses of 1864, many sheets still maintained their optimism, along with their determined calls for renewed effort and commitment and sacrifice. At the opposite extreme were the carping, bitterly anti-administration journals like Rhett's *Mercury*, for whom neither the president nor the Congress, and sometimes not even Robert E. Lee, could do anything right. In between ran all hues of opinion, even a few papers that cautiously advocated peace at the cost of reunion.[57]

In Richmond itself, with several dailies and weeklies, the lines were more clearly drawn between pro- and anti-administration journals. Yet even there distinctions could be blurred. Littleton Washington came to the capital in September 1861 to write for John Daniel's *Examiner,* and act as editor in Daniel's frequent absences, chiefly because of Washington's presumed close ties to some in the government, especially Hunter and Benjamin. Daniel also hired Edward A. Pollard, who in time would be running the paper himself as one of the bitterest critics of Davis. Indeed, Washington would leave the *Examiner* before the end of the year after constant turf battles with the other editors, especially Pollard, whose editorials he found to be "malignant, unscrupulous & defamatory." Nothing if not contradictory, Washington had himself already authored sensational attacks on Vice President Stephens, intending to do more until he realized that he could not prevent the Georgian's reelection to the same position under the Permanent Constitution. After leaving the *Examiner,* Washington would write for the Richmond *Enquirer,* generally supporting the administration but more particularly endorsing the efforts of his new employer, Secretary of State Benjamin, even to the point of using the *Enquirer*'s pages to support diplomatic appointments. More columns in 1863 joined the chorus condemning any talk of reconstruction, and lent encouragement to the peace movements in the North.[58]

While President Davis disdained the press, others in his administration like Benjamin had no qualms about trying to enlist friendly journalists, and the *Enquirer* became virtually an administration organ thanks to men like Washington. But when word came that defiant articles in the *Enquirer* were being seen by peace elements in the North as authorized expressions of official belligerence and intransigence, Washington worried that this might discourage the efforts of Lincoln's opponents. As a result, he began writing articles for the Richmond *Sentinel* to conciliate friends in the North. "It was important to let the conservative men at the North know we were ready to meet them on reasonable terms & fair ground," he explained, blaming what he saw as a stiffening attitude in the Union on the *Enquirer's* uncompromising voice. "The effect of these articles was to take the ground from under the feet of the peace leaders."[59] He also worked with Curry of Alabama to draft resolutions that Curry would introduce in the House to extend for peace feelers, yet again blurring the lines dividing government and the press, while his simultaneous writing for both *Enquirer* and *Sentinel* seemed to have him speaking in two voices.

Moreover, he served multiple masters, not just the two papers and Benjamin, but also Secretary of the Treasury Christopher Memminger, when Washington pushed press support of a tax bill on which, he thought perhaps immodestly, his editorials exerted much influence on final congressional passage. He wrote editorials plumping for Curry and others in Congress whose measures he supported, and defended Davis from some of the *Mercury's* attacks. "The times seem to have disturbed the reason of many and a sensational press inspired by shallow and unscrupulous men are doing us infinite mischief," he complained in August 1863 after particularly hostile blasts at the president over the Gettysburg failure. "They debauch public opinion & unfortunately exert an influence on the government itself." It seemed not to disturb him that he was himself proud of the influence he thought himself able to exert. And he, too, could get involved in acrimonious disputes, as when he acted as a second in a difficulty between his former employer Daniel and another man. Daniel engaged Pollard as his second, which only added zest to Washington's involvement, and the affair was so difficult to settle short of a duel that congressmen—Wigfall, Clay, and James Orr—somehow took time off the floor to mediate. Clearly press and politicians could be not just strange bedfellows but rather intimate ones as well.[60]

The incumbents in the capitol were all too happy to have the use of compliant journalists like Washington and Pollard as the war dragged on and polarities became at once more stark and yet confused. The change in the complexion of Congress was made evident in its debates. James R. McLean of North Carolina, in almost his last appearance on the floor of the House in February 1864 before his term expired, protested that it was useless to try to disguise the conditions in his own state. "No doubt there is a hellish plot on foot among a portion of her citizens against the Confederacy," he protested. "They are moving for a convention—holding meetings attended by every disloyal citizen from the blue waves to the blue mountains." Henry Foote of Tennessee, serving his own ends as usual, tried to use the conditions in McLean's state as a weapon to defeat a judiciary bill sent in by the administration—his real objection was Davis's support of the measure—arguing that it would be so unpopular as to propel North Carolina to the enemy, and perhaps Arkansas, too, even though within a year he would himself be making peace overtures to the North that saw him branded all but a traitor.[61] "What a nuisance he is," Sexton complained of the long-winded Tennessean.[62] When mostly erroneous reports reached them that large numbers of Confederate prisoners of war in the North were taking an oath of allegiance out of despondency that they would never be exchanged and sent home, James Lyons of Virginia introduced a bill to try to restart the prisoner exchange cartel that had broken down when Richmond refused to exchange black Union prisoners, taking instead the stance that they were runaway slaves and therefore property. Lyons's bill passed handily, but immediately afterward Joseph B. Heiskell of Tennessee, himself a representative from an overwhelmingly Unionist district, resigned in protest.[63] The legislation went nowhere, nevertheless, and as late as May an exchange agent complained that exchanges were virtually abolished "by reason of the 'nigger' question."[64] The legislators were still unready to compromise on issues relating to blacks, it seemed, even when it stood to damage their ability to keep fighting.

The more crucial the issue, the more congressional debates reflected the pressures on the Confederacy. The debates on some specific questions could be especially contentious. In debate on a conscription bill of Foote's calling for another 250,000 men, word came that Governor Joseph Brown of Georgia threatened to stymie its implementation in his state. Augustus Kenan of Georgia stood to condemn Brown on the floor of the House and proposed another act calling on the governors to comply or else the Confederate government should enforce the draft directly. Then a Texas delegate threatened that his state would resist, even unto seceding from the Confederacy itself, while Sexton spoke in favor, and then yet another Lone Star member proclaimed that "there are no more loyal people in the Confederacy than those of Texas." A North Carolinian rose to proclaim that most of his state's people opposed conscription at all, after which Virginia's Charles Collier stood to condemn the entire debate, which had become so hot that Foote withdrew his original resolution. Foote himself occupied almost an entire day on the floor, and a frustrated Sexton complained to his diary that "we are wasting so much time."[65] Impressment of supplies could generate similar heat. "We impress the bodies blood & bones of all men between 18 and 40 and do you pay them a great compensation?" Hilton protested as he supported the policy. "Is property in wheat or corn or slaves more sacred?" They could make impressment a crime, but would not the soldiers who then went hungry just steal? "Will they not and should they not help themselves? What would you do then? Will you hang draw and quarter men who have left their all to come thousands of miles to fight your battles merely because they have taken that without which they could not discharge the service?" They had to either feed their armies or disband them. The government had a right, he declared, to fix the prices for what it would purchase, undemocratic as it might seem and much as it shocked the whole idea of a free market. Survival required it.[66]

Other recurring irritants were issues like exemptions from conscription, especially when it came to drafting their own kind, legislators. Governors argued that making civil officers like justices of the peace and judges liable for conscript risked destroying the operation of democracy. "Congress may have no power to destroy a state government by placing her officers into military service," claimed a Mississippian, whereas those in favor of the policy countered that exempting civil officers "simply constitutes an army of salaried idlers and refugees, who are not turning a wheel for their state or the Confederacy."[67] The secret sessions covering so much of their debate never lost their irritant effect for many members. "In Republican governments the proceedings of Legislative bodies should always be public," complained Sexton, but commonsense practicality never seriously endangered the cloak of confidentiality.[68]

Surely no issue more excited the members than the habeas corpus. Of course it was Congress itself that authorized the president to suspend the privilege of the writ on February 27, 1862, in certain areas, in the face of the recent disasters and the threat General George McClellan was about to pose to Richmond, and then again in the fall of that year. But by February 1864 when Davis requested it yet again, the mood had changed dramatically. In the face of the disasters of 1863, and with a more substantial element opposed to Davis and to the whole conduct of the war now sitting on the floor, members felt much less indulgent. When Davis's annual message containing the suspension request came to the House, Hilton observed that "the message was read amid profound silence." There were none of the cheers that might have met earlier messages. A Virginian immediately responded that passing a suspension now, especially if done out of sight of the people in secret session, "would be the last organized act of the Confederacy." Foote, distrustful as always, demanded more specific justifications for the action, though he did not say he would vote for it in the end. No one would dare call him a traitor to the cause, he declared. McLean wanted the rules suspended so that they could act immediately, and thereafter the members bogged down in measures for and against.

The next day they resumed debate, and it went long into the evening and became increasingly acrimonious. They enacted severe restrictions on how the suspension could be imposed, with strict procedures for the protection of the rights of those arrested. Men shifted positions. Some who opposed the two earlier suspensions now saw justification in the current crisis to support the measure, while others pointed out that those earlier suspensions went out to the public as "by order of the President," whereas the language of this legislation clearly stated that it was "by authority of Congress." Men sensitive to chances of reelection were not so happy to have the responsibility for an unpopular measure shifted to their own shoulders.

"Let us pause before we write this chapter in our history," a Virginian counseled, adding that his state's constitution did not allow suspension of the privilege of the writ. But another from the Old Dominion countered that their state had willingly entered the Confederacy and now it had to make its constitution abide by that of the higher authority and its mandated legislature, the Congress—a clear declaration that state rights must yield in conflict with the national government. This was the cue for Foote to stand and harangue the administration. If Davis had done his duty and weeded out the incompetent from the military, ended abuses of military authority by generals in the field, and been judicious in his application of martial law, then they would not have come to this pass. "If he had done his duty there would be no necessity for the increase of his power," claimed Foote, and now the president wanted the right to suspend "to prevent any opposition to his administration or strictures." The president claimed there were elements conspiring in North Carolina and elsewhere. Let him show proof. But Conrad and others countered in support of Davis, arguing that in the face of disloyalty everywhere, invaders' heels on every state in the nation, and the renewed threat of slave insurrections, the president would be a traitor to the Constitution if he did not impose suspension, and indeed if he did not, then Conrad himself would propose impeachment. Already angered at being so much ignored by Richmond, an Arkansas delegate threatened in response that if they passed a suspension bill, "you may bid farewell for a long time to any support from the Trans Missis-sippi."[69]

The habeas corpus debate was just one indicator that the renewed threat to Richmond that came with the spring campaign of 1864 caught their notice. A visitor to the capital late that month found that recent Yan-kee cavalry raids in the area had them all alarmed "if the consternation of Congressmen be taken as a criterion." The War Department transacted al-most no routine business for three weeks in the face of the threat, most of its clerks being out in the defenses with their city guard units, and Rich-mond itself felt in a state of virtual siege, even though the armies of Lee and Grant were still more than thirty miles to the north.[70] The fear became greater for a time as Grant inexorably pushed Lee back until, in mid-June, there were for a few days genuine possibilities that the capital would fall, and the Congress adjourned abruptly on June 14, not to convene again un-til November. By then, Lee was besieged in extensive works surrounding Richmond and nearby Petersburg, but the lines seemed secure at least for the coming winter, and the Congress could meet in some security once more. Besides, attention had been drawn to the threat to Georgia that summer and the capture of Atlanta in September.

Yet even after that some of the leaders found cause for hope. Congress-man Duncan Kenner of Louisiana, one of the founding fathers at Mont-gomery, confided to his friend Thomas Moore, "I do not look on the fall of Atlanta as gloomily as you do." They had been outnumbered all along and it had been all but inevitable. But the army that evacuated Atlanta, now under General John Bell Hood, was still intact, in good spirits, and had the approaching winter in which to recruit and prepare for campaigns to come, while Sherman's Yankee army now in Atlanta might starve if cut off from its supply lines. As for the situation at Richmond, "Grant is only hold-ing on for political effect on the Presidential Election," Kenner continued. His campaign had been an utter failure. "I am sanguine of McClellan's election & with it a change of policy," Kenner asserted. Once McClellan defeated Lincoln, the North would stop prosecuting an unpopular war and the Confederacy would have won by not losing.[71] Yet even as he wrote to Moore in September 1864, he was on the eve of leaving for Richmond, os-tensibly to resume his seat in Congress, but actually to meet with the pres-ident on their last desperate effort to win European recognition by offering the abolition of slavery in return.[72]

While Kenner was off on his mission, other last gasp efforts came from other congressmen, some even oblivious of the outcry they would raise at home. William W. Boyce, one of the staunchest of the early South Carolina secessionists, outraged many by calling on Davis to seek a convention of all the states, North and South, to negotiate a peace.[73] Then there was the issue of raising black troops from among their slaves. It passed, but only over considerable opposition. Hilton left Florida in October to come to the last session of the Congress, and on leaving believed that his state was overwhelmingly opposed to the idea, as was he. But as the weeks dragged on, seeing the disparity of numbers against them increasing, and Lee's responsibilities as newly created general in chief expanding, Hilton became convinced that arming slaves was their only recourse. "For our deliverance, I felt constrained to give it my support," he wrote in explanation to people at home, "though at the time that I did so without any assurance that one in a hundred of my constituents would approve my vote." Yet in explanation of his final vote in favor, he proudly pointed out that he had supported the president and the government to the full measure of his ability. "There have been no powers which the President and Gen Lee (between whom as far as I know there has been a thorough accord of sentiment and action from the beginning) would ask or accept which I have not been ready to confer."[74]

Had there been more men like Hilton in government, national and state alike, ready to take for granted the good faith and best efforts of the president and his administration, and support them wholeheartedly in spite of the inevitable mistakes and corruption attendant to any large-scale government, then the path of Davis and Congress together in the Confederacy might certainly have run more smoothly. But there were not enough to make that happen, and no certainty that in the end such unanimity would have brought them to success anyhow. Some who were intimate with congressmen believed that it did not really matter. "The minds and hearts of our people were too much occupied with the rushing events of the sanguinary and terrible war to give much heed to what was said in the Congress," argued a friend of South Carolina's Lewis M. Ayer, the man who, incidentally, had beaten Rhett in 1863 in his last bid to regain public office. Indeed, Ayer himself, soon after taking his seat, became increasingly convinced that Congress itself deserved little heed, and that "through the carping spirit and factious disposition of very many of its members toward

the Executive Head of our Government, was a hindrance rather than help-
ful." Worse, after the disasters of 1863, he saw the Constitution and their
very form of government itself as impediments to the swift action needed
to meet the emergencies before them. Davis had seemed patriotic and
anxious to observe the separation of powers and respect the Constitution
as much as was possible, and more than Ayer felt to be prudent. Looking
at the example of ancient Rome, Ayer sketched out a proposal to dissolve
the Congress altogether and suggest they make themselves more useful to
the cause by enlisting, while Davis himself should be proclaimed dictator
by the several states "with unlimited, absolute power to 'take care that the
Confederacy suffer no detriment.'" Interestingly, Ayer seemed unaware
that more than a year earlier exactly the same suggestion had been published in Mobile, and promptly condemned by Yancey and others. Wisely,
before actually bringing such a startling resolution to the floor, Ayer sounded
out a few fellow members for support, and found them so adamantly opposed that he concluded he could not even get a second on the floor to
bring it to a debate. He pocketed the proposal and didn't speak of it again.[75]

What Ayer reckoned without was that some of his colleagues already believed they had a dictator, and they did not like it one bit. Hilton's seemingly rosy view of the administration simply ran counter to the nature of
men and politics. "I will not dwell on the blots in our Statesmanship," a
South Carolinian wrote in disgust in 1863.[76] Confederate democracy could
not hope to escape the partisanship and mingling of petty jealousies and
ambitions and substantive disagreement on vital issues that ever carry the
potential for acrimony in any representative republic, as well as the power
to cripple it if good will cannot prevail. But in the Confederacy's echelons
of high government, good will could be in frustratingly short supply, as Jefferson Davis and the idealists who foresaw a nation without parties were
too soon to learn.

13

"Growlers & Traitors"

ANYONE PRESENT in the Exchange Hotel salons that first rainy afternoon in Montgomery back on February 3, 1861, could have guessed that this Confederacy was not going to be a one-party nation. As politics and partisanship lay at the very core of secession itself, so would they inevitably be dominant features of the political future. Yet if such an observer knew that the shadow itself would rise, still he likely would not have guessed its shape. For generations American and Southern partisanship turned primarily upon issues, no doubt because the issues themselves were so commanding. Free trade versus the protective tariff, internal improvements, and, most of all, the matter of slavery in the territories were all matters that decided elections, that made and destroyed political parties. Certainly personalities were associated with them, and in some cases—Andrew Jackson, Stephen Douglas, and Abraham Lincoln, among others—individuals were so identified with them that the man and the issue became synonymous in the public debate. Yet even in 1860 the Southern Democrats were far more opposed to popular sovereignty than they were to Douglas himself. In short, Douglas was not the issue—his platform was. Perhaps only Lincoln took precedence over his platform as an object of opposition polarity, but that was largely because Southerners knew so little of the man himself that it was hard not to make him one with his party. Moreover, when passions rise, simple human nature makes it far easier to characterize hostility toward the shape of a man rather than a set of ideas.

They had hoped to leave all that behind when they came to Montgomery. "In helping to establish a new Government I have endeavored to cast from my mind former party or political prejudices," Clement Clay told a friend, "and to regard and treat all men as political friends who earnestly desire and faithfully labor to prevent the restoration of the Union."[1] That was fine in theory, but the cracks in their unity opened even before they heard the first gavel. The same old issues came with them to the new nation—free trade or high tariffs, internal improvements, slavery in any new territories, and especially now the precise relations of the states and the federal government. But the crisis and the fact that they were a new nation starting from practically nothing, and then the war, imposed a whole set of new issues upon them, each with the potential—more likely the certainty—for creating opposing viewpoints that would be strong. Should they be strictly a slave nation or ought they to allow free states into their confederation? Ought they to engrave the right of secession literally into their charter? How were they to finance their new nation and then its war? How should they conduct their military policy? Who should raise and equip the armies and by what authority, state or federal? How should their generals be chosen? Should they stand on the defensive or might they take the war to the enemy? How were they to lure foreign governments into granting them the recognition and aid that many saw as essential to success? And in all of this and more, how far did the commander-in-chief clause give the president unilateral power? What voice—and power—was Congress to have, and with the power, who was to take the responsibility? The men who made the Confederacy were all over the map on these and other issues, and the fact that two men might stand on one side over the tariff did not mean that they would necessarily be in agreement on finance or on conduct of the war.

There were differing viewpoints on even so minor a matter as the import duty on hoopskirts and oranges, and much of it emerged first in the constitutional debates. Even before then, however, lines were drawn as men sought to define just what they had been sent to Montgomery to do, what they ought to do, and how they should do it. They were going to be aligning themselves in coalitions on an issue-by-issue basis, as Southern statesmen had been doing for two generations since the breakdown of the old Jeffersonian Republicans, the later collapse of the Whigs, and the vicissitudes of the Democratic Party for some thirty years. Yet if there were any discernible "parties" emerging, they were really the extension of extra-party factions that had existed for some time, and their Montgomery positions reflected their pasts: the ardent fire-eaters, the smallest group of all, led by Robert Barnwell Rhett and William Yancey, most of them former Democrats; the new nationalists represented by men like Robert Toombs and Wiley Harris—and soon Jefferson Davis—who wanted a strong new independent nation, chiefly John C. Breckinridge Democrats; the ambivalent who until recently had been called submissionists, men like Alexander Stephens who had grave doubts of the wisdom of their course and yet appeared committed to their future, most of them onetime Whigs or Douglas Democrats and John Bell supporters; and the reconstructionists, who had no real outspoken leaders in the early days, who yet hoped that secession and even forming the Confederacy would in the end be a bluff that would prompt the Union into making sufficient concessions to allow the seceded states to return to the old flag, an equal smattering of Bell and Douglas men and always a smaller faction than the Rhetts and Yanceys feared.

In varying degrees, they would maintain those same alignments through the life of the Confederacy, though the reconstructionists would fade from view until they reemerged late in the war as the prospect of defeat became ever more apparent. Some from the Stephens camp would follow, as indeed would men from all strata of the political geology once the certainty of disaster took precedence over their old ideologies. Yet at the same time, men from all of those factions, influential men at that, would shift in an entirely different—yet ironically complementary—direction, including Stephens, Toombs, and Governor Joseph Brown, for there was one island of opinion that could provide solid ground for all of them to stand on. There was one focus for all their disappointments to unite upon, from the extremists who had dreamed of Southern independence for years to the reconstructionists who saw failing Confederate fortunes as inevitable and only lamented the terrible wasted tariff in lives and treasure. It resided on East Clay Street in Richmond, just above the Twelfth Street intersection, in the old Brockenbrough house that was now the executive mansion. Its name was Jefferson Davis.

Opposition to Davis from start to finish revealed some of the fundamental contradictions within the Confederacy. Its founders wrapped it around a number of radical principles of self-governance—radical, that is, except for their predictable unwillingness to consider slaves as citizens. Yet it was an oligarchy imposing itself on a democratic form, and oligarchies depend upon a ruling elite that works together. Instead of that, however, these Southern oligarchs rapidly demonstrated just how unwilling they were to work with each other, maneuvering instead to establish any of a number of petty dictatorships of individual ideas or men. Scarcely was Davis installed as provisional president and the new administration under way before rumblings were felt across the South.

There were those who simply never liked Davis even before secession—the suspicious like Rhett or those viscerally incompatible like Toombs. The Mississippian's unwitting capture of the presidency solidified their personal antipathy, adding both Cobbs to a mix that included the odd crank like Thomas Withers. Davis's first cabinet appointments gave cause for others to join, as Douglas Democrats and Bell men felt frozen out, and with Rhett and his son already raising an outcry in the pages of their Charleston *Mercury*. Then when Davis began appointing generals to command the army about to be raised, disappointed would-be Bayards added their voices, seeing something sinister in the president's preference for men with professional military experience or even West Point training. That some of the appointees were his old friends from earlier days only added fuel to their resentment. Before long some men became convinced that this was to be an administration built on Breckinridge Democrats and nurtured by cronyism. "I feel myself degraded by the action of the Government," Braxton Bragg carped when he did not get a command commensurate with his own estimate of his abilities. "I am not surprised at the President, who, in his feeble condition is entirely under the control of a miserable *petticoat* government."[2]

Rhett saw the early signs of a division into dominant Davis and anti-Davis factions, lines that would cut across almost all other allegiances and cast an increasing influence on positions on even the most important issues except support for the war itself. "What a pity—these men have brought old hatreds & grudges & spites from the old Union," James Chesnut's wife, Mary, said in disgust as far back as February 28. "Already we see they will willingly injure our cause to hurt Jeff Davis."[3] When Davis seemed—and it was only a perception, not a fact—to favor Breckinridge Democrats in the growing number of patronage offices he had to fill, the loquacious but lightweight editor J.D.B. DeBow added his voice, complaining in August that "appointments under the new regime will be governed by the same political considerations as in the old one," and that "parties will form & are forming in the same way & party hacks will take the lead."[4] As the government was leaving to move to Richmond, a Montgomery editor protested in print that "it seems that secession has been accomplished merely to make offices for aspiring Democrats." The editor, of course, had been a Whig.[5] It was only one of many lines that became an increasing obsession of the *Mercury* as its owners pursued their personal resentments and disappointments in print. Mary Chesnut in October 1861 observed with no attempt to conceal her dismay that "if the Confederacy had chosen to elect Barnwell Rhett president instead of Jefferson Davis we might have escaped one small war, at least—the war the *Mercury* was now waging with the administration."[6]

Davis showed what was for him a remarkable degree of philosophy in dealing with the growing chorus of critics in the early days. Should their cause succeed, he told his wife, "we shall hear nothing of these malcontents." However, he was wise enough to know that if events ran against them, "then I shall be held accountable by the majority of friends as well as foes."[7] That applied across the board in dealing with the disappointed. The governors, too, would be accused of favoritism, as journalist Littleton Washington accused Virginia's John Letcher of handing out appointments only to men who originally opposed secession. Nor would Davis be the only recipient of mounting criticism. Indeed, perhaps the first really important blow at the administration in the press was directed at Stephens in the fall of 1861, when the disappointed secessionist office seeker Washington vented his anger at Letcher by scorching the vice president for his own lukewarmness on secession in an editorial in the *Examiner*.[8] Out in Georgia a concerned citizen that fall implored Governor Brown that "we must endeavor to keep all things straight," though he was not sanguine. "You may talk of no party lines as they please," he warned, "but in every movement you can see it sticking out and I awfully fear we will have much trouble yet before we get through this war." If the war did not go well it would get worse, "and from sources we would little think of," he feared. "We will have the worst kind of growlers & traitors."[9]

Of course, Davis's own manner could and did repel some men who found him aloof, haughty, even autocratic. He did not have the personality to win adherents, as he knew full well himself. The first time Franklin Sexton met with him he found the president irritable and undignified, and on a later visit Davis was again out of sorts, leaving the congressman to conclude that he would "not trouble him again," even though he at least gave credit to the pressure the president was under.[10] Dissatisfaction with the cabinet could as well repel those who would be friends. With the exception of John Reagan and at the end Breckinridge, none of the executive ministers escaped accusations of indifference or inefficiency. When Thomas Watts came to Richmond in March 1862 to take the justice portfolio, he found "red tape splurging on stilts and swelling swimmingly," and observed in all the bureau with disgust the way visitors were met by what he called "squirting attachés with curt incivility." Men with a very little authority put on the most offensively pompous airs of self-importance in dealing with the citizens who paid their salaries. In response, Watts had to issue orders in his department that "the penalty of incivility to even a beggar, in his department, would be a kicking down stairs."[11] He knew well enough that every rebuffed or offended visitor could become an ambassador of ill will for the administration.

Even those who had felt no special animus personally or politically toward Davis could still be propelled in that direction. No sooner did the army suffer its first reverses in February–April 1862 than the chorus of carping began. Just days before the fall of Fort Donelson, newly elected Congressman William Clark of Georgia declared that he was so disillusioned with Davis that he was ready to join the opposition. A month later, when the president vetoed a bill that sought to remove some of his unilateral power in appointing generals, the outcry in Congress in some quarters rose to a storm, involving some discussion of trying to remove him from office. Tom Cobb, never a reasonable judge where Davis was concerned, believed that "*he would be* deposed if the Congress had any more confidence in Stephens than in him."[12] In the gloom following the disasters, people on the streets of Mobile began suggesting that they needed a strong man, a dictator, to replace Davis and regain the initiative. Indeed, rumors even circulated that Yancey himself was plotting to overthrow the government to establish a dictatorship, perhaps with himself in the highest office, but he denounced such talk of "mad projects."[13] In the wake of the Shiloh defeat, the man who had served as the dead General Albert Sidney Johnston's chief of staff protested that "the present is certainly no time for a fair & intelligent judgment upon the conduct of the administration, & if it were our business is with the enemy in front." Critics would be more manly and patriotic if they would first attend to the foe "& leave the President to the verdict of the country when more is known than now can or should be."[14] It was a mature and sensible judgment, but he was offering it to the wrong man, for he was writing to Louis Wigfall. The Texan began the war as Davis's close friend and advisor, but relations rapidly deteriorated. Partly it was on personal grounds, as the two men's wives fell out, and daughter Louly Wigfall reflected her mother's prejudices by privately calling the dark-complexioned Varina Davis "the 'Mulatto.'"[15] More was due to the very nature of Wigfall the man. Fellow Congressman Sexton called him "a desperate man—a tyrant at heart." He often found Wigfall's manner and talk disgusting, fueled as it often was by drink. "He is surely a very bad man," thought the other Texan. "If he, W[igfall], was the 10th part as good as Curry he might have some hope of ultimate redemption." Wigfall's habit of lobbying in the House for his Senate measures against the president also cost him favor, even making the usually calm and prudish Sexton swear once during debate. "Whether he intends to be so or not," he said in a calmer moment, "his manner is very offensive."[16]

Before the end of June 1861 there were signs that Wigfall was feeling estranged, as a result of his own unfulfilled military pretensions, yet still he told a friend that "it would be disastrous for us, the head men, to engage in a row among ourselves." The friend, in fact the same man who later warned him to fight the Yankees first, replied that the new democracy ought to be strong enough to survive "a rupture between Mr. Davis and Mr. Wigfall."[17] But disagreements over military policy and appointments soon distanced Wigfall even more. It might have helped that Wigfall shared quarters in Richmond with men like James L. Orr of South Carolina, another Davis opponent, adding social relations to the family relations that tended to drive him from the president.[18] Such kith and kinship bonds had always exerted strong influence on political loyalties in the South, so it should be no surprise that they did in the Confederacy as well. Even though Wigfall would always support any administration bill aimed at enhancing or taking care of the armies for prosecuting the war, his personal antipathy to Davis would otherwise drive him inexorably into the camp of those coalescing around the single issue of Davis's unfitness for his office. By November 1862 rumors reached the army of the breach, and friends like General James Longstreet begged him not to differ with the president. "We think that all of our hopes rest upon you and the hopes of the country rest upon the army," said Longstreet. "You will readily perceive what weight you have to carry."[19] Wigfall agreed that "political consideration should weigh nothing in the movement of troops" and nurture of the army. When the two did conflict, "political considerations should be adjourned until after the victory."[20] Yet even such statements clearly revealed that the Texan believed an accounting would be due.

Others were even more outspoken. The attacks on Stephen Mallory, by Henry Foote especially, were blows aimed at Davis. Foote, said Mallory, "hates the administration & the President with an intense hatred," and he was right. The animosity went back for years in Mississippi when Foote lived there, and Mallory saw them come to blows at least once, and almost to the dueling field.[21] Another Mississippian, Reuben Davis, also a disappointed would-be general, refused even to approach Davis. "He is *mad* with me," concluded the aspirant. "I talk a little too plain to suit him." Davis did not dislike the president, he hastened to add. "I do not go about him, because his nature is such as not to tolerate opposition in opinion. I am more devoted to the country than to any one man, and if I *burn incense* at all, it must be to *Country*—not *Jeffy*." The nation owed its reverses to Davis and to no one else, he argued. "Had he discharged his *duty* with promptness, today the winter of our discontent would be glorious summer." The reason it was not, he said, was "*Jeffy's* imbecility."[22]

The imbecility of "*Jeffy*" presumably lay behind all of the unpopular administration policies, though then and later it needed remembering that for every complaining Rhett or Wigfall, there were scores in the Congress and hundreds of thousands in the country at large who either wholeheartedly approved of administration policy or at least recognized the logic of unpopular measures in the necessity of the hour. Certainly this was true of the foreign policy formulated by Davis and pursued consistently, if unsuccessfully, throughout the war. Davis had but one real diplomatic goal, and that was to win formal recognition of Confederate independence and nationhood, preferably from Great Britain but also from France. It would serve two ends. First and foremost, it could be a first step to alliances and then possible military intervention on behalf of the Confederacy, the threat of which could have been enough to persuade Lincoln to give up in the face of seeing the civil conflict in North America take on the proportions of a world war. Moreover, after recognition, attempts by the Union blockade to stop or even sink merchant vessels of such nations seeking to enter Confederate ports would constitute international incidents, the very sort of events that could rapidly lead to military intervention. England, as the great world power, would always be the primary goal, the assumption being common that France would follow its lead. Davis would send commissioners to other states like Denmark and Spain, and even try to establish relations with Mexico, but that effort was always to be badly compromised by Davis himself and many other Confederate leaders, who were on record as saying that it was their destiny to one day extend their dominion over Cuba and the northern parts of Mexico.[23] In 1861 the frequently silly DeBow predicted that within fifty years the Confederacy would absorb all of Mexico, while the British would absorb the Union into its Canadian dominion.[24]

Davis seemed to speak with two voices on his diplomatic expectations. To some he sounded almost overconfident that foreign powers would be eager to grant recognition, indeed that they would have no choice but to do so. Then at other times he would voice the far more realistic view that Britain had little or nothing to gain from embroiling itself in yet a third war with the United States, and much to lose as a growing Union navy of modern warships posed a considerable threat to British domination of the world carrying trade. Like most in the Confederacy—and like virtually every member of the extreme opposition—the president began with a high faith in the indigenous Southern monarch "King Cotton." The textile mills that were the lifeblood of English and European manufacturing would go silent without the crop, and the Confederacy dominated the world supply, or so they thought. The mere risk of cutting off that supply ought to bring England and France to their knees to beg alliances, and make John Bull willing to challenge Lincoln's ships on the seas to maintain a continuous supply of raw material. Whitehall simply could not risk the social and political turmoil of thousands of textile workers out of work, presumably rioting and even bringing down a government. Cotton alone would buy foreign support, and that would buy Confederate independence.

Unfortunately, it was a deeply flawed argument. It was typical of ideologues like Rhett simply to ignore facts that countered their self-revealed fundamental truths, but surprising that more reasonable men like Davis overlooked or refused to heed two very critical facts. The first was their own cotton crops in 1859 and 1860, the biggest in years. New Orleans alone exported more than 4 million bales in that time, 2.5 million of them going to England alone. Charleston had shipped another 375,000 bales in that time and Memphis 370,000 more. Exports were as much as half a million bales higher than in previous years.[25] Yet English consumption had not grown apace, meaning that warehouses in Lancashire and elsewhere

still bulged with inventory. Moreover, and what should have been especially unsettling, good-quality cotton had become increasingly available
from other places, chiefly India, Egypt, and Mexico. There would be no
immediate shortage of cotton to close the mills overseas if Confederate
supply dried up, and even after current inventory was exhausted, foreign
manufacturers had available other suppliers in volume and quality sufficient to keep them in operation. By 1861, King Cotton was a ruler without
a kingdom.

If Davis was consistent in his failed attempts to secure recognition from
Britain, he was not found consistent enough on other policies to please
Congress. Even before there was a Confederacy, when the presumptuous
Rhett had tried to make its foreign policy by approaching a British consul,
he had presumed that what the new nation would have to offer would be
unfettered access to the king on a basis of free trade and nominal import
duties on the manufactured goods that the South would buy in return. Duties would start as low as 15 percent and could go down to 5 percent, or
even be eliminated entirely on a "most favored nation" basis, Britain being
the preferred partner.[26] Once the new nation was born, and even before
Davis was inaugurated, Rhett and the free traders ran into opposition, not
so much from protectionists as from wise men who simply realized that independence and the likely war to come were going to be expensive, and
they had few other sources of revenue than duties. Free trade would have
to wait, but the free traders never stopped howling, charging Davis and his
administration with being either protectionists at heart or else too blind to
see the transcendent wisdom of their own policy. Events would demonstrate that once again, even with free trade, the South had nothing to offer.
So long as Confederates had money, they kept buying imports regardless
of the tariffs. It was the blockade that reduced the consumption of foreign
goods in the Confederacy, not duties, and again, England and France were
not about to risk war by a direct challenge to that blockade.

When Davis sent his first embassy abroad in 1861 under Yancey, he sent
it with no power to negotiate treaties, but more important, with nothing
persuasive to offer. There would be no free trade, no favored nation status.
The Confederacy simply expected that the great nations would see the obvious and act in their own interest by granting recognition and diplomatic
relations. Indeed, there were voices in the South that objected even to
sending envoys at all, fearing it looked too much like begging for what was

rightfully theirs.[27] But then Yancey himself concluded and announced within weeks that "important as cotton is, it is not King in Europe." If a shortage came at all, it would not be for six months or a year; meanwhile, the almost universal antipathy to slavery meant that popular sentiment was not that inclined toward the Confederacy.[28] Instead, he expected that England and France would stay neutral, and at best recognize North and South as belligerents, scarcely any concession at all. Seeing how pointless his efforts were, and how mistaken were Southern perceptions of sentiment abroad, Yancey suddenly regretted that he ever accepted his mission and resigned.[29]

The basic Confederate diplomatic effort would scarcely change for the balance of the war, and Yancey's successors would be no more successful than he. Indeed, necessity would instead force Richmond itself to start shipping cotton through the blockade just to keep financing the war. Secretary of State Judah Benjamin's diplomats could argue that Lincoln's blockade was illegal because it did not meet international definitions of effectiveness, and that therefore the stopping of foreign vessels was unlawful and cause for retaliation, but the protest was feeble. They could try to change foreign public opinion by representing Confederate viewpoints in the best possible light, even publishing their own propaganda organ, *The Index*, in London, but the receptive audience was small. When the successors to the Yancey mission were taken from a British vessel by a Union warship, Richmond tried its best to escalate the act into a major incident leading to war between Britain and the Union, the so-called *Trent* affair. Washington and Whitehall kept cool heads, in part because of Queen Victoria's husband, Prince Albert, and Lincoln ended the incident by releasing the envoys, whom Queen Victoria's foreign secretary refused to meet formally anyhow since they did not come from a recognized nation.

Even when the cotton supply did reach a critical low in 1862, with thousands of mill workers out of employ temporarily, the mill hands of Lancashire did not rise up. Meanwhile the sudden reopening of supply through Federally held New Orleans allowed a trickle of flow that, added to what the Confederates would ship, and the cotton from other countries, averted a major crisis. "I do not think there is any probability of France or England intervening in American affairs at present," lamented a Texan agent in Paris in June 1862. "England is waiting for France to act and France is waiting for England. Oh for one decisive victory for the South!"[30]

Certainly victories in the field would have helped, and Lee won them in Virginia that summer, but the Confederate disasters in the Mississippi Valley that spring, and then at Antietam in September 1862, raised serious questions in British minds of the ability of the Confederacy to maintain itself militarily. Whitehall had been ready to offer to mediate between the belligerents in the fall of 1862—even that a far cry from recognition or intervention—but shelved the idea rather than start a process that might end in alliance with a losing cause. Long-term world realities were far more important to as sophisticated a foreign office as the queen's than were transient commercial inconveniences and temporal unemployment. All the Confederates could do in their frustration was to expel British consuls in the fall of 1863 and then recall their envoy from London, virtually ending relations with Britain in what almost seemed an act of spite. It gave Davis's critics yet another issue to seize upon.

Confederate agents in France continued to try to make headway, but Emperor Napoleon III was involved in his own North American commitments after installing his nephew the Archduke Maximilian as a puppet ruler in Mexico, and as a result his relations with Washington were on shaky ground to say the least. To get involved with the Confederacy could be one provocation too many. By 1864, John Slidell, the Confederate agent in Paris, complained that no one in France even seemed interested in the conflict in America anymore and "our affairs are at a standstill in Europe."[31] Again, as with England, France had nothing to gain from an alliance or intervention, and too much to lose. Finally, all other enticements shown to be hollow, Davis sent Duncan Kenner to Europe with the last desperate hope that an offer of emancipation would win British help. But Napoleon finessed them, as usual, by saying he could not act unless England did so first, and Whitehall simply listened politely to a rather oblique hint of emancipation, and replied that British policy on the American war had not changed, and would not.[32]

Rhett especially, along with others, would never tire of casting the false conclusion that since Davis failed to offer trade concessions and commercial treaties to Europe at the beginning, and no recognition was ever forthcoming, therefore the one led to the other.[33] The same sophistry underlay their criticisms of the rest of administration policy. Davis did not do what they advised and the Confederacy was failing. It was easy to come to the self-serving conclusion that because events were proving Davis wrong, then presumably they were right. It was the false logic always born in un-fulfilled ambitions, wounded egos, and bruised conceits—in short, the logic of politicians, not patriots.

Such was the case with Confederate finance and cotton policy generally. The Confederacy did not begin in impoverishment. Even though there was not a cent in the Treasury on February 8, 1861, when the founders declared their government to be a reality, still their component states all had substantial funds of their own and immediately outright gifts were forth-coming from the statehouses to set the nation in motion. The gifts were only a stopgap, of course. "Economy is desirable in every government," Secretary of the Treasury Christopher Memminger said a few days after taking office, "but in ours it is a necessity." Even as he commenced raising a treasury, he put stringent staff reductions and salary limits in effect.[34] In the years ahead Memminger and his successor, George Trenholm, would try a variety of expedients including outright loans, the printing of Trea-sury notes, tariffs and taxes, sequestration and other confiscations, and simple donations. None of it would be adequate, but to a remarkable de-gree it succeeded in providing some media of exchange, if uncontrollably inflated, and at least enough real wealth to keep the armies armed and equipped, if not paid or adequately fed.

In addition to an initial loan from the state of Alabama, the Treasury put out a series of thirteen loans in the form of coupon bonds subscribed by state governments, business, and private individuals, paying quarterly in-terest rates varying from 4 to 8 percent, and one foreign loan subscription in France. Some loans took in only hard specie, others accepted agricul-tural produce, chiefly cotton and tobacco, and a few gave out bonds in re-turn for Treasury notes in order to get the glut of them out of circulation and provide some—ineffective—curb on inflation of the currency. From the first issue just ten days after Davis was sworn in as president to the last a mere two weeks before the fall of Richmond, the Treasury issued bonds to a total of $712,046,420.[35] The Treasury continued paying the interest when the coupons were presented to its offices, though many patriotic—and later cynical—citizens eschewed collecting even that. In December 1861, Wigfall felt so confident of the bonds that he boasted that after the war those of the United States would be worthlessly discounted, while Confederate bonds would be secured at full value.[36] More sophisticated at appraising public opinion than the president, Memminger even put Littleton Washington to work writing articles for the *Sentinel* promoting the produce loans.[37]

Moreover, during the course of the war the government issued just over $1.5 billion in Treasury notes in denominations from $1 to $500. They were all small loans in themselves, some bearing modest interest, and were to be repaid after the close of the war. In addition to the money they raised, they gave the coin-strapped Confederacy its only national currency, even though the several state banks each continued to print and circulate their own bank notes as well, as did even some corporations. The effect on inflation of such a mountain of unsupported paper was predictable, and it was not helped by a flourishing industry of counterfeiters, and even the introduction of bogus currency printed in the North with the intent of causing further depreciation. To combat just such an effect there had been a strong current in favor of the establishment of a national currency almost from the first, and with it much criticism of the dependency on loans and notes. "The impotency of Mr. Memminger's administration has lost the country millions," complained a Mississippian in November 1861. "His department is not an organism but is dependent upon the voluntary contributions of the people for its support."[38] Repeatedly Congress considered legislation to declare Treasury notes legal tender on a par with the bank notes of the several state banks in an effort to control inflation, but it always failed to act. Meanwhile the presses simply kept rolling. In 1864 people were exchanging devalued old Treasury notes at two-thirds of their face value to get new issues. By March 1865 a dollar in gold in the Union was worth $1.46 in its paper currency; in the Confederacy it took almost $70 in Treasury notes to buy that same hard coin.[39] The editorial wag George Bagby, in addition to suggesting the Confederacy solve its refugee problem by having Richmonders eat one another, proposed that the poor could be fed on paper money. "The cheapest and most abundant substance in this portion of the globe is unquestionably Confederate notes," he declared. They should be greased with bacon rinds and rolled in bran, which ought to make them quite palatable. And he could not help punning that "if Confederate notes will pass in no other way they certainly will in this."[40]

Toombs, who did not share Rhett's free trade mania, became one of the leading critics of Memminger's policy, and would in later years accuse Memminger, Benjamin, and others of running presses in their homes to print money for themselves. He supported the bonds, especially the produce loans, however, because he believed the goods thus collected could be shipped abroad and kept there to build more than sufficient credit for the Confederates to finance their war. If that failed, then he saw no alternative but a high direct tax.[41] Sure enough, Memminger did not wait for the loans to fail before resorting to direct taxation. The Confederacy was only a few months old when a commercial convention meeting in Macon, Georgia, adopted resolutions to send to Congress calling for the minting of a new Confederate currency—which would never be done—and some form of Confederate bank as both depository and safeguard on uniformity of exchange. That, too, would never happen, but then they also suggested "a permanent system of direct taxation."[42] The states already taxed their citizens, of course, chiefly on property, and in May 1861, Brown was already suffering criticism for his moves to increase tax rates on rail freight in order to defray the extraordinary new expenses of raising regiments.[43] By the end of 1864 the demands became so great that Alabama had a public debt of more than $18 million, with only $7 million in old and new Treasury notes and bonds in its treasury. Governor John Gill Shorter expected to raise more than $3 million from taxes in the next fiscal year, but even that would not be enough to meet his needs, and he confessed that he "had not the nerve" to try to raise taxes to a level fully to meet necessity.[44]

The burden of additional national taxation on top of all this seemed simply unthinkable, yet Richmond had no choice. Prior to the war, there were no national taxes. The national government was funded entirely by customs duties and sale of the public lands. Now on August 19, 1861, Congress enacted a property tax on slaves, real estate, stock, bank deposits, and more, at the rate of fifty cents per $100 of assessed value. For the first time in American history a central government had reached out from its capital to put its hand directly in the pocket of the citizen. It was revolutionary, and even the fact that the collection was left to the states did not change the fact. That it did not foment a great outcry in the Confederacy suggested to *DeBow's Review* that "it is possible, and perhaps even not altogether improbable, that this tax may never be collected." Many simply did not think the North would resist long enough to make the tax necessary.[45] It was cumbersome and slow, and eight of the states simply paid the tax on behalf of their citizens to protect them from the intrusion, but then themselves borrowed that money elsewhere, with the effect that the states took out of circulation money that the government needed to borrow. Still it was a milestone. Interestingly enough, old Rhett had argued for years for direct taxation for government funding in lieu of tariffs, placing him for once on the progressive side of an issue, even though many would argue the constitutionality of such a levy.

This was only the beginning. In 1862, Kenner would propose an even more revolutionary federal invasion of the private exchequer, a national income tax of 20 percent, with even a schedule of exemptions. His tax bill went nowhere, but in April 1863, Congress passed another act, this one calling for a tax in kind, meaning produce in lieu of money, and it was based not on property but on produce and income attached to it. It incorporated as well an occupational tax for a host of professions rated by their presumed levels of income, a graduated income tax with rates from 1 to 2 percent, and then another of from 5 to 15 percent on non-wage profits from sales, loans, bonds, and the like. Attached to it, Kenner's exemptions survived. A head of a family worth less than $500 would pay nothing, nor would any individual member of a family whose personal worth was less than that amount. Soldiers and officers and those discharged for wounds were exempted if worth less than $1,000, and so were widows of men killed in the service unless their property was assessed at more than $1,000. Farmers were taxed on the value of their crops as well as their land, but not on the grain that they needed to feed their animals and the produce sufficient to feed their families.[46] The authorized collectors would take cotton, corn, rice, peas, sorghum, potatoes, bacon, and other produce. The produce could supplement impressments in feeding the armies; the cotton would be sent through the blockade on government vessels to be sold abroad. This time there were serious challenges to the act's constitutionality, to whether or not Congress had the power to lay direct taxes. The Rhetts attacked in the *Mercury,* and the debate would continue until the end of the war, but still the tax in kind went into operation. Between them, the two tax acts—and two more supplementary value taxes on slaves, real estate, and bank deposits—would raise on paper nearly $200 million, though the actual receipts were dramatically less.[47] Congressmen like Hilton would lament in 1864 the fatal mistake of not instituting direct taxation at the very beginning. Their opponents, the followers of those like DeBow, complacently thought that no taxes would be needed.[48] At the end of March 1865, before adjournment, Congress passed two more bills levying even higher rates on income and property alike, but not a penny would be collected.

By comparison, the blockade proved sufficiently effective that import and export duties were almost minimal, less than $4 million during the four years of the war. At least sequestration and confiscation of Federal property in the South raised over $12 million. What gained the most notoriety of all, however, was impressment of goods belonging to civilians, chiefly livestock, machinery and wagons, and foodstuffs. This was not strictly a tax, for vouchers were given in return obligating the government to redemption at enforced market prices. Somewhere around $500 million in goods was acquired by such means, though for all too many it amounted in the end to a loan that would never be repaid. Along with conscription, the impressment acts gave Davis's critics one of their most potent weapons in the battle to accuse him of tyranny and destruction of personal and property rights. In any event, by 1865 the impressment system disintegrated of its own weight, because of the resentment and resistance of the producers, the inroads of the Yankee armies, and the simple inability to move the goods.

All this effort and failure would have been unnecessary, argued the opposition, if only Davis had adopted a different policy with their greatest single asset, their cotton. It was not just their weapon to coerce diplomatic recognition, or so they once thought. It was the currency that could fund their war without the need for taxation, and put sufficient weaponry of war in their hands as to guarantee victory on the field and leave the other nations no choice but to accept them as an equal. Rhett stated their case as well as any, and for him it became an obsession for the rest of his life. If cotton was king, he argued, then the only way to make Europe pay homage to the monarch was to force it to its knees by a strict embargo, and to sustain it until the nations howled for relief on Confederate terms. Not only conventional wisdom but also articles in the leading commercial press seemed to confirm that inventory abroad was critically low.[49] But Davis would not do as Rhett and others wanted, and instead allowed private firms to continue a trickle of exportation at their own risk through the blockade. Rhett tried to get a prohibition against private export through Congress but failed. Even before then, he also proposed that several million dollars' worth of cotton be purchased by appropriation and shipped overseas to fund the purchase of a navy, but Davis and Mallory demurred, arguing that they could not in any case afford to field a fleet to match the enemy's.[50] Besides, Mallory was already building ironclads and outfitting commerce raiders that should go some distance toward evening the odds. Toombs stood with Rhett on this issue, for finance was ever his special concern, and he, too, believed that if they acted quickly at the outset, they could get enough cotton overseas before the blockade became effective to buy all the ships, arms, and munitions they would ever need. But the president argued—or Toombs and Rhett believed that he reasoned—that there would be no war, or if there was it would not last long enough for all that materiel to be needed. Instead, by waiting until the cotton loan was in place and cotton could actually be collected, the blockade was too strong and the moment had passed.[51] Before long even one of Davis's diplomats in France, Edwin DeLeon, would decry the dependence on King Cotton for coercion and the feeling that there would be no war as blinders.[52]

Congress never would enact an embargo, though by 1862 some planters were doing so themselves as the staple began to accumulate for want of safe shipment. Both in the hope that a shortage would eventually coerce Europe into action and because they needed to put their ground to other purposes, they began to pledge not to plant their cottonseed. Then the governors and legislatures issued their own prohibitions against planting, but only because corn was what was needed now. Some planters ignored the prohibitions, and soon there were growing complaints against the selfish who flouted the laws while others sacrificed and suffered.[53] That resentment grew ever greater as a few were seen to build small fortunes at speculation and blockade running, and some felt in no way apologetic. R. T. Saunders, an employee in the Treasury Department, left through the blockade in September 1863 with some money to buy a runner of his own, intending to ply the route between Mobile and Havana. "If I can save but a few thousand Dollars," he wrote of raising the funds to buy the vessel, "it will be much better than working for Confederate money in this country."[54] Shares in blockade runners were being sold for $1,000 by March 1863, with the potential profits so great that one successful run could pay for the ship and return a profit.[55] By late 1863 the more hard-pressed citizens in Mississippi were even smuggling cotton across the lines to the Yankees in return for food staples they needed desperately. "I never would have attempted it if necessity *had not have* drove me to it," a farm wife protested.[56] Finally things got so bad that Governor Charles Clark ordered cotton burned rather than left in the path of the enemy. "Anarchy hovers over us, and Despotism—that bloodhound of humanity, is on the trail," another civilian complained. "Cotton is our all—without it we cannot live— without it we cannot pay our taxes." Many planters were in the army fighting for the right to plant that crop, and its destruction would be as demoralizing to them as it was to their families. "Destroy our cotton and you sever the tendon Achilles of the war."[57]

The smuggling in spite of prohibitions from the statehouses became blatant, and many did so without even paying lawful export duty. In more remote places like Florida there simply were not enough officers to enforce the laws.[58] Everyone, it seemed, was to get the benefit of Confederate cotton except the Confederacy. Finally Congress acted to the extent of prohibiting shipment of cotton and other restricted goods without Treasury sanction, but it was no embargo. Rather, the Treasury was to get half the tonnage on any blockade runner going out and coming back in, thus deriving both export and import income, and also space on the vessels for shipping government cotton at no cost in order to raise money overseas. By the end of the war, what had not been burned, loaned, or shipped through the blockade simply rotted in warehouses, as useless as the government it proved powerless to save. None could ever say with certainty whether or not the administration had squandered a great opportunity through its failure to use cotton effectively, or merely failed to buy into one of a host of after-the-fact myths based on hindsight and the acknowledged enmity of Davis's detractors. One thing it did reveal, however, was the inherent contradiction that bedeviled Confederate democracy. Davis and Memminger both had argued at the outset that the government did not have the authority to go into the cotton business as a wholesaler abroad, or any business trying, for it would be an interference with private enterprise and free trade. But then through their partial embargo they did just that all the same, and even more so when Memminger bought blockade runners and put the government directly in the shipping business in competition with private shippers. And then there were their direct taxes, most notable of all the income tax. How did the doctrine of limitation of federal power in favor of state sovereignty manage to rationalize that? Simply put, it did not, nor could it. Necessity was the driving engine, necessity and innovation, neither of which respected the hobgoblin of foolish consistency. In short, the extremes of Confederate financial policy, the uncertainty of a sure cotton policy, and the contradictions in both were just more examples of the underlying fatal weakness of that would-be Confederate democracy. Their ideals could not live with the realities necessary to their achievement, and neither could that carping, hovering opposition, ever-ready to heap on yet more justifications for its personal war with the president.

While the Davis opposition in Congress continued to grow as a result of doctrinal differences over all these issues and more, events in the field and the alienation of the president from generals like Joseph E. Johnston and P.G.T. Beauregard created a new political-military clique sharing the same basic resentments—antipathy toward Davis personally because of slights to ambition and pride, real or imagined, and differences over conduct of the war. The generals, especially the popular but woefully naive Johnston, readily became bedfellows with the opposition. Wigfall especially became the generals' man in Congress. Johnston, Longstreet, and others took their problems to him, and their grievances, whether it be over promotions not gained, independent commands not offered, or differences of opinion on strategy. Their friendship gave Wigfall and others added power in Richmond when they became known as spokesmen for the men in uniform. Indeed, Wigfall would go so far as to step well beyond his authority as a senator to give Johnston campaign advice late in 1862, telling him to concentrate his forces in his command west of the Appalachians for an offensive. Constitutionally only Davis had that power, yet Wigfall thought he could get around the president by enlisting the pliant secretary of war, James Seddon.

It did not work, but Wigfall would not stop trying to influence military policy, nor would Johnston stop trying to use him to gain his own ends. Unhappy that he did not know how to manage his large super-command between the mountains and the Mississippi, he chose to believe that it was inherently unmanageable and that the fault was Davis's, even that the president intentionally assigned him to the impossible in order to disgrace him. Johnston wanted Wigfall to try to get Lee sent west in his place so that Johnston could then resume his old command in Virginia. It was a shabby proposition at best, but by the spring of 1863, with Vicksburg about to be laid under siege, criticism of Johnston's inactivity was rising, including articles in the Richmond *Sentinel,* one of whose anonymous editorialists just happened to be Littleton Washington, himself the employee and confidant of Davis's henchman Benjamin, and known to make himself useful publishing unofficial administration attacks and defenses in the press. Soon rumors went around that the president's aide Constitution Browne was preparing a "Bill of Indictment" against Johnston for the loss of Vicksburg, and before long Wigfall got word from Charles Conrad that Benjamin himself was preparing the attack. It seemed that Davis was behind it, so Johnston could only defend himself, and Wigfall would be his armor.[59]

In time, other statesmen who had fallen into the opposition camp would also look to Wigfall when it came to military matters, not because he could accomplish much with the president but because he had become the de facto spokesman for dissent. Old R.M.T. Hunter of Virginia rapidly fell out with Davis, partly from his jealousy and partly from his transparent fawning to Davis's face while vocally backbiting in such an indiscreet manner that the president learned of it. As a result, by the spring of 1863, Hunter complained to Wigfall that "as *you know,* I am entirely without influence," and reportedly told William Porcher Miles in December 1863 that "no gentleman can stay in the cabinet with Mr. Davis."[60] If Wigfall in Congress and Rhett out of it but hammering through the *Mercury's* pages could not stop the president, still they could embarrass him by their public opposition. That, combined with bad news from the front at Gettysburg and Vicksburg, put some of the public in a mood to go along with their discontent. Seemingly everyone was willing to lay the losses of New Orleans, Vicksburg, and much of the Trans-Mississippi to the commanders he had appointed. The fact that these disasters came after Johnston and Beauregard had been removed from active command created in many minds the illogical conclusion that these generals would have won victories but for Davis's spite toward them. Weeks after the Yankees took New Orleans, the distinguished Louisiana diplomat Pierre Soulé would raise his hands in dismay and cry out, "If Jeff. Davis would only die!!"[61]

The fact, of course, as Davis and others well knew, was that Johnston had no stomach to risk a battle, and Beauregard could not subordinate his ego to the cause. In Davis's own Mississippi, the Meridian *Clarion* declared in July that if the presidential election were to be held then, "he could be beaten in Miss by any man of respectable standing in public life."[62] That summer Wigfall told Johnston that after the fall of Vicksburg the president "was blind as an adder with rage & ready to bite himself," and that in the administration itself "the whole concern when I reached Richmond was frantic & their first determination was evidently to immolate you." Even Lee did not escape Wigfall's criticism, as he castigated the general for his "terrible blunder" at Gettysburg. By that fall, as the criticism of Johnston for his palpable failure to attempt to relieve Vicksburg mounted—though the effort very likely would have failed in any event—Wigfall became ever more aggressive. He lobbied Seddon, arguing that if only Davis had listened to Johnston, they could have saved Vicksburg, regardless of the fact that Johnston never had a plan to relieve the besieged

city. Unable to make headway in the War Department, Wigfall began to
threaten. He would be heard on the floor of the Senate, he declared, "from
which place I could be heard throughout the Confederacy."[63] Good as his
word, when Wigfall took his seat for the fall session, he began gathering
papers to present Johnston's defense against the *Sentinel* attacks. "It was
very unfortunate that you ever trusted Davis," the senator told the general.
"I regretted it at the time & wrote you so."[64] For his part, Johnston's
protestations of friendship for Wigfall by early 1864 made it evident just
how dependent the two had become on each other for feeding their mutual antipathy toward Davis.[65]

The Texan was only the most vocal of Davis's critics. Others carped as
well. Stephens, after holding his seat as president of the Senate, essentially
became so disillusioned with Davis and the administration that he simply
went home to Georgia and left his chair vacant for all but brief visits. His
old foe Tom Cobb complained that the vice president was "demagoguing
low down" and "trying to build up an opposition party."[66] Toombs resigned
from the army in March 1863 after repeated conflicts with his superiors,
including one arrest for insubordination, and failure to win promotion, and
began to devote himself to correspondence with others in the anti-Davis
camp. Foote attacked frontally, if foolishly, in his long-winded floor
speeches in the House; the Rhetts fulminated in the *Mercury;* and the
lesser malcontents did their part. Tom Cobb was dead, mortally wounded
at Fredericksburg in December 1862, so his voice was stilled, and his
brother Howell seemed to lose some of what was always a lesser venom in
any case. Yancey, too, was dead. But perhaps the greatest enemy of the opposition was their dispersal. Too many, like Toombs, Rhett, and Brown,
were scattered across the country, with neither the concentration nor the
force of organization in Richmond to pose a real threat to Davis. Then, too,
it could not be denied that their own personalities worked against them.
Even Rhett's friends regarded him as a bigot and hypocrite, at best a dangerous crank and "one idea" politician. But then, what was to be thought
of a man who made declarations such as that "Jefferson Davis is not only a
dishonest man, but a liar," or that Davis was, in fact, the greatest traitor
since Judas Iscariot?[67] Toombs was a notoriously intemperate man, a braggart who had dared to criticize Robert E. Lee. Wigfall seemed too consumed by his own boast and importance to be taken too seriously, while
Foote, if not crazy as Mallory thought, was still an embarrassment to al-

most all in Congress. Even Stephens, by his petulant withdrawal from the arena, lessened rather than strengthened his position.

Taken in their all, they seemed too impractical, doctrinaire, and zany for their almost comic-opera movement to be regarded with enough respect to earn adherents. Perhaps that is why some others whose sentiments aligned them against Davis kept their views to themselves, for fear of being associated publicly with the extremists. Thomas Snead, a congressman representing Missouri, concluded even before reaching Richmond to take his seat in May 1864, "I have joined 'the keep your mouth shut society' & shall at least observe the rules so far as to avoid the expression, except in cases of unquestionable duty, or prejudices heretofore existing or opinions heretofore formed."[68] By their very nature, the opposition could never organize themselves, for though all in the same boat, each pulled his oar to suit himself. Indeed, in their independence not only from Davis but from each other, they were arguably Davis's greatest weapon against themselves. He never had to attack them openly and never would, for they could be counted on to do his work for him.

Certainly Davis felt the loss of those who abandoned him, and the sting of disapprobation was always especially bitter to a man as sensitive as he. Early in 1864 he told Clay how sorry he was to have lost Wigfall's friendship, and that he was "very much disturbed by the course of Stephens & those who have gone with him, & by the complexion of the present Cong[ress]." Clay implored Wigfall, "do keep the peace, if you can. . . . I think it important that we should at least seem united & harmonious to the enemy."[69] It was much the same advice that Robert Barnwell had given Wigfall eighteen months before. "The opposition in congress tells at home," he warned, "& if we are overrun, politicians will have to answer for it."[70] It was good advice, too, but the sort that Wigfall and the other outspoken opponents of the president would not heed if they could. By March 1864, Wigfall frankly confessed that he loathed the president, and prayed that he could get the Senate to start standing up to him more.[71] As a result, both the people and the foe knew of the friction in the government. "Jealousy and distrust of the Confederate Government has been excited, and causeless alarms at its designs been produced, as well as dissensions created against its authority," complained a Texas editor in June 1864, decrying the "spirit that is actuating some of our people, their legislators, and we must add the Governor, of opposition to the legislative and executive departments of the Confederate States."[72] Released from its bottle, the genie was not about to go back in quietly.

Especially not, as it happened, after the events of that spring and summer of 1864. As the campaigning season opened with Johnston again in command of the Army of Tennessee after replacing Bragg, and facing Sherman in north Georgia, Davis expected him to stop the enemy advance and protect Atlanta at all risk. But it would not happen. For a start, Johnston's own high command was just as riddled by the politics of animosity and jealousy itself, fomented under Bragg's hopeless nineteen months in command and not helped by Johnston's advent. He complained privately of "this army, which has the reputation, here in itself, of having the only general officers in the confederacy who practice here against each other, the arts to which they were accustomed to resort in electioneering before the war."[73] Indeed, he blamed that for much of its present demoralized condition. There were ardent Davis adherents left from Bragg's sycophantic regime, and others like Johnston himself, and for a time Longstreet, who sat in the opposite camp, their internecine war played out in the headquarters and bivouac. Johnston himself was powerless to combat the dissension, and some of it worked enough to his advantage that he might not have wished to do so, for it gave him the excuse he always sought to take no action. Thus when Sherman began his advance, instead of standing his ground, Johnston pulled back without a fight, starting a process he would follow all the way to Atlanta. "Why didn't he *fight!*" an infuriated Davis raged when handed notice of the general's action. He crushed the telegram in his hand and, as a witness recalled, "as it were, lifted himself from his chair by his hair," violently stamping the floor as he shouted over and over again, "Why didn't he *fight!* Why didn't he *fight!*" Before long he regained his composure, and later that afternoon even met with a delegation of Georgians led by Benjamin Hill who came to urge him to replace Johnston. Instead, he defended the general and deflected their objections, since he had no one else to put in his place. "Great God, Mr. President," one of the Georgians exclaimed, fearful for his native soil, "do give us some General who will stand up & make one manly fight before Sherman drives us into the sea." When they had gone, Davis confided to a friend that he was importuned almost daily to relieve Johnston at the same time that he was being attacked by Johnston's friends for not supporting him.[74]

Predictably, when Johnston finally wound up in the Atlanta defenses with Sherman at his throat, and with no plan of how to recover lost ground or save the city, Davis replaced him with General John Bell Hood. It was a poor choice, and Hood himself carried the heavy taint of politicking for the command, but at least he would fight, of that Davis could be certain. Hood held Atlanta until September, certainly longer than Johnston would have, but when it fell Johnston and his friends were triumphant. Even the disaster to Johnston's reputation helped Wigfall's cause if he could turn it to use against Davis. The equation was simple: Davis relieved Johnston and Atlanta was lost, and the president was to blame. Even before then Wigfall had tried to escalate his efforts. "It is the opinion of most leading men that Davis' bad judgment of men and bad temper together will ruin the country 'unless he can be controlled,'" Wigfall declared in March. "He has heretofore uniformly treated the Congress with contempt," he went on. "We have fears for the future unless he can be controlled."[75] For a start, the Senate should exercise its oversight powers and challenge the president's appointees. Then, in what was presumably Wigfall's own scheme, though it reflected an idea that had been around for some time, he wrote to James Henry Hammond, Rhett, probably Clay, and others to ask their opinion and support of the idea of inaugurating efforts to constitutionally check Davis's power over the military by interposing a general in chief to manage the war. It would still have to be a presidential appointee, but the Senate would have to advise and consent, and that would give them control over Davis's nominee, even though such a move would probably require changing the Constitution. Hammond ignored the question and just ranted about Davis, while even Rhett, much as he hated the president, advised that it was the wrong time for such a move and the process of summoning state conventions to amend would take far too long. "Establish a responsibility to the country by open sessions of Congress and published debates," the Carolinian counseled, returning to one of his earliest hobbyhorses. "We will win our liberties and independence I believe, but it will be in spite of the most terrible incompetency and perversity in our Executive, which have ever afflicted a noble people."[76]

Certainly Wigfall, and to a lesser extent the others in the opposition, were making names for themselves by their stand against Davis. General John Wharton of Texas flattered the senator by telling him that "you are the only civilian, developed by this Revolution, who deserves to have a history or an epitaph," a clear condemnation of Davis and all the rest.[77] Others among the public were also displeased. "Men may vaunt State Rights, or Confederate Rights; they may stand for this or that form of liberty; be jealous of this or that exercise of power," said a Houston editor, "but if, in war by a free people for self-preservation, the 'war power' does not command their entire resources; if the ranks are not full and the soldiers well supplied, where adequate men and means exist, then the government or the 'system of governments,' either in organization or administration, is bad; blame rests somewhere."[78]

The opposition in Congress, led by Wigfall, finally managed to strike their strongest concerted blow at Davis, but only long after it no longer really mattered. It began in December 1864 when Davis sent in another request for a suspension of the writ, but the Senate defeated it by one vote. Then on January 23, Congress passed a bill creating the position of general in chief to command all Confederate armies. The post had existed in name three years before, but it had no real power since the incumbent was wholly subject to the orders of the president. Under this legislation Davis's appointee would genuinely have the authority to set his own strategic policy, presumably removing at least some of the president's unilateral control, and the Congress would have some influence over the incumbent. Of course Davis vetoed the bill, citing it as a violation of his executive authority, but then gave the opposition a sop when he appointed Lee to the extant but vacant position of general in chief surviving from three years before. It was, in any case, the appointment that the Congress and the country expected, and it served to hearten the country at large.

That month the opposition struck again when the Virginia delegation, speaking through Speaker of the House Thomas Bocock, delivered an ultimatum calling on Davis to replace his entire cabinet or they would begin the motions for a vote of no confidence on the floor of Congress. Wigfall himself pushed a motion virtually calling for Benjamin to resign, failing passage by only one vote, but Davis stood his ground. Faced with the humiliation, the unpopular Seddon resigned anyhow, and the opposition was somewhat appeased when Davis appointed General Breckinridge in his place. The Kentuckian was in no way a member of the opposition. Indeed, he had largely stayed out of politics while wearing the uniform, but he was universally popular and on good terms with virtually every faction in the government and military save the disgraced Bragg and his coterie. Most important, however, Breckinridge's prestige with the people and the army was arguably greater even than Davis's, which meant that the president could not make a cipher of him as he had Seddon and the rest. When Breckinridge spoke, Davis might not have to act, but he would have to listen. More importantly, well known as a man of practicality and action, the new secretary could be expected to move on his own initiative, with Congress and the country ready to endorse him even if the president balked. Significantly, the Congress had even given Breckinridge an honorary seat on its floor. He could not cast a vote, of course, but his influential voice could be heard. Not surprisingly, no sooner did he take office than almost all factions began to call on him for their own ends. His office became a gathering place almost every afternoon for congressmen and others, especially Hunter of the opposition, but he kept his own counsel and committed himself to none of their schemes. As events would soon disclose, he had plans of his own for these factions and intended to use them, rather than they him. Yet the opposition could still take pleasure in his appointment, even if he kept them at arm's length. Between them, Breckinridge and Lee represented the greatest potential curb on the president's power since the war began.[79]

But then Davis stopped their momentum with the legislation to arm blacks in return for some promise of freedom. It passed the House on February 20 and the Senate on March 8. It was the final act that galvanized his opponents. Hunter, Foote, and others opposed it irrevocably. Out in the country at large they had strong support from Brown, Howell Cobb, the Rhetts, Toombs, and others. On this issue Wigfall even broke with his friend Johnston, the general seeing only the possibility of more soldiers to man the depleted armies but the senator unalterably opposed to putting guns in the hands of slaves. Stephens, generally the most reasonable of the president's foes, stayed uncharacteristically silent on the issue, but he did deliver a stinging critique of the administration in a special address that the Senate asked him to deliver, a move largely engineered by Hunter to give the vice president a forum.

Stephens told them that to save the cause they had to end impressment and conscription, reach out to those in the North who were sympathetic to seek negotiations, offer amnesty to deserters to get them to come back to their regiments, and change their military policy. Instead of dispersing their battalions trying to defend cities and territory, they should concentrate in numbers sufficient to defeat Yankee armies, and continue to do so until the Union finally grew weary and just let them go their own way.[80] It was largely the Wigfall program, reflecting yet again the wide streak of libertarianism that ran through the thinking of most of the staunch state rights men, and it was probably hopelessly impractical. But then, in what was for once a brilliant political move, Davis gave Stephens what he wanted. He allowed the vice president, Hunter, and others to attend a meeting with Lincoln and his secretary of state, William Seward, at Hampton Roads on February 3, ostensibly to explore peace options. Davis knew that Confederate insistence on independence, and Union determination on reunification, made the two sides' sine qua non positions mutually exclusive. The failure of the talks not only embarrassed the opposition by having one of its favorite issues deflated, but also briefly reawakened resistance sentiment in the country. Combined with the outcry in response to another opponent, William Boyce of South Carolina's, proposition for a convention of all states North and South to negotiate a settlement, virtually removing Davis from the equation, the failure at Hampton Roads threw the opposition back on the defensive.[81]

By 1865, Wigfall was reduced to private fantasies that "we are here on the verge of revolution."[82] There is no doubt that frustration with Davis could drive some men to extreme thoughts, though usually it revealed more about the character of his opponent. Those with disappointed ambitions were always the worst, the most intemperate and the most blind to their own selfish motivations. John T. Pickett was appointed a diplomatic agent to Mexico in 1861, but thoroughly bungled the job and embarrassed himself, resulting in Davis rebuffing his later efforts to gain a brigadier's commission. Instead the highest status he would achieve was as a lieutenant in a company of congressmen and clerks raised in Richmond in 1864 for emergency defense. So angry was he over his thwarted ambitions that one day when Davis rode past Pickett's company in the defenses, Pickett considered kidnapping the president and spiriting him across the lines to the Union. "Nothing had been easier than that capture," he would claim, "and it would have saved our cause."[83]

As far back as the fall of 1863 the ever-effervescent Toombs was hinting at the need for more than political or constitutional resistance. He had already said privately, in typical hollow bombast, that Davis should either be impeached or killed or else they were doomed. Commanding a state militia regiment at Savannah, Toombs spoke freely in January 1864 with his associates about his belief in the necessity of a counterrevolution. He made a speech at his tent in which he condemned all of the anti-libertarian acts of the administration. "*I was a revolutionist for liberty, and I will be one till I get liberty,*" he proclaimed, the hint being obvious as to where he might next revolt. "If domestic traitors stand in the way, I am their enemy," he went on. "There is no concord where there is no liberty; *and let discord reign until liberty be restored.*" Protesting Davis's recent call to arm every able-bodied man, he asked who would run their mills, factories, and farms, already so hard-pressed and run-down, and their wives and children exhausted from toil. Add total male mobilization to the evil of suspending the writ, and every man in the country would be subject to Jefferson Davis with no recourse to the protection of the law. That was dictatorship, for which there was only one answer. "When they put you all under one man and take away the *habeas corpus* it will be time to draw the bayonet," he shouted. As citizens, Confederate men had to defend themselves against anyone who threatened their liberty, whether the Yankees, their own Congress, or the president. They had to use the courts, but if that failed, still they had to fight in any way they could. "I ask for no mutiny," he cautioned, *"unless it be necessary in defense of constitutional rights."* Their rights and liberties were still not secured, and what they gained from the Yankees they could lose to their own government. "Maintain the revolution," he charged them. Privately he claimed that Beauregard and Johnston were of one mind with him, as well as other generals, as perhaps they were. But as if a sign were needed that Toombs had given way either to hyperbole or delusion, he even claimed that Stephens, Seddon, Breckinridge, and Lee were also in agreement, clear nonsense. All Toombs got for his outburst was another brief military arrest, though the charges were dropped before a trial could be completed.[84] Later he would advise "resistance, resistance to the death" against further suspensions of the writ.[85] Even a good friend concluded that "he has gone too far." His admittedly brilliant mind was driving him in the wrong direction. "It is violence & rebellion," and his passions had clearly become "stronger than the restraints of prudence & wisdom."[86] It was the same with Wigfall, Mary Chesnut decided by late 1864. She had been fond of him once, and confident of his abilities. The Confederacy had expected much from him, she said, but now she concluded that he "has only been destructive."[87]

There, of course, was the problem with the opposition from the outset. So much of what it said was nonsense, seen widely and in the main rightly as coming from the petty, the disappointed, and the cranks. Wigfall proclaimed that Confederate citizens were as much slaves to Davis as the serfs of Russia were to their czar.[88] Rhett was maintaining by the summer of 1864 that Davis ought to be deposed by Congress. He even wrote to Stephens to sound his opinion, since he regarded the vice president as being too soft on independence and privately still suspected him of wanting reconstruction. The Carolinian asked Stephens if he would stand aside from his constitutional right to succeed after Davis's removal, in favor of Congress installing General Lee as an interim dictator. Some had suggested this as early as the spring of 1862. Even Yancey declared that "nothing could be more unwise, and more completely demonstrate our unfitness for self-government." Such a course would ruin them. If Stephens responded at all now, he no doubt withheld any comment on the utter harebrained nature of the idea, but dismissed it—as did others—by pointing out that Lee himself would never go along with such a plan.[89] By March 1865, despite the reinstatement of Johnston and the presumed weakening of the president, they were all helpless. Stephens simply went home and kept silent, speaking out only to continue calling for negotiations and warning that if they depended solely on fighting to win their liberties, then "the only peace that the sword alone will bring us in fighting the united North will be the peace of death & subjugation."[90] Rhett, anticipating defeat, fulminated futilely in the *Mercury* and then in February escaped Charleston in the face of Sherman's advance, not to be heard from again during the balance of the war. He would never stop ranting, however, of how "I wish it placed on my tomb stone that the worst and most to be regretted act in [my] life was my voting for Mr Davis."[91] Wigfall kept his seat in the Senate right up to its adjournment on March 18, one of his very last acts a vote to override a Davis veto, a futile effort, as it turned out, as it had always been. Davis handed down more than thirty vetoes during the war, and the Congress successfully overrode only one of them, which dealt with a minor postal matter. And Wigfall still tried to continue the war over laying the blame for the loss of Atlanta on Davis for removing Johnston at the critical hour, even though there was no longer a quorum present to act or even take notice. Futility would never stop any of them from their chosen course. At the same time, Toombs was ranting to Stephens, who was now the only one who would listen. "There is but one remedy," he told his friend two days before Wigfall's last pointless effort. "It is begone Davis."[92]

Davis would later refer to what he called "the conflict of ambitious men around me," but he rarely stooped to counterattack during the war except in the feud with Johnston, and in the occasional endless quest for the last word in letter-writing exchanges with men like Stephens.[93] The president was wise enough to know that he had nothing to gain from engaging in public quarrels if he could help it, for he would only attract more attention to his tormentors. Moreover, for all his character and personality faults, he was much the better and wiser statesman than a Rhett or Toombs, and more practical than Little Aleck or Wigfall. On top of that, he was simply more mature than most of them. Jefferson Davis often in his life found it difficult to rise above petty squabbles when they touched on his honor or ideas, but however much he seethed within at the pricks and jabs of his foes as president, there was little outward challenge to rising above men of such puny stature as these. In the end he simply let them defeat themselves, for the broad public, for all its discontent and flagging morale, was still wise enough to see that the more one looked at the likes of the opposition, the smaller they became.

Though they harassed and sometimes embarrassed the president, the opposition was so fragmented themselves, so impractical, and in many ways so wrong-footed by their own similarities to the man they so despised, that they accomplished nothing as a faction. Nor did they accomplish anything for Confederate democracy. Indeed, they rather represented some of its inherent contradictions. Founded on the innate belief that a certain class was destined by birth to lead the masses, these men, most of them members of their own state oligarchies, simply could not agree on how to lead and how to follow. They would all be giants. They all distrusted absolute democracy, of course, but what they had to offer in its place was the chaos of a platform of conflicting ambitions, thwarted dreams, and unchecked jealousies. In the Confederate quest to enshrine the old order in a new nationality, they too often forgot who was the real enemy. Southern leaders had been squabbling within the Union for generations past, and often among themselves as well, and some men who could have contributed much simply could not leave the habit behind when their allegiances changed. Declaim as they might about principles and policy and high constitutional ideals, in the end they were all ready to compromise far too much of that, not for victory, but to serve the lesser ends of their own pride and conceit.

But that did not mean that they were an unimportant part of the Confederate story, for perhaps more than anything else, they represented the dynamics that had been in play for generations before secession. Theirs were the internal diseases that had not just crippled all of the efforts to bring about disunion as far back as 1828, but that so hampered the operational health of their Confederacy when finally they got it. For they could no more agree on when and over what to secede than they could unite on what their new nation was to be. Pride, ambition, individualism, and political culture had produced in them ante-bellum a disinclination, if not an outright inability, to suppress themselves in the greater interest of their country, for to them the two were identical. They did not need Jefferson Davis as the object of their discontent, for there was not a man among them, nor likely a man anywhere in the Confederacy, who could have given them satisfaction. Accustomed to being giants at home, they simply could not accept being lesser mortals on a grander stage. James Henry Hammond had been wrong about a lot in his life, but when it came to the fundamental flaw in too many of the big men of the Confederacy, no one ever coined a truer appellation than his "big-man-me-ism."

An End to Valor

Looking at the map on January 1, 1865, it must have been difficult for any Confederate to see cause for optimism. Lee was at bay in the works at Petersburg and Richmond. The tatters of the Army of Tennessee were recuperating in northern Mississippi while its commander, General Hood, composed his resignation. In South Carolina there were only scattered elements hurriedly trying to gather to offer some resistance to Sherman's march north from Savannah, while out west of the Mississippi, Kirby Smith simply had nothing to do but was too far away, and too isolated, to be able to give aid to the beleaguered forces in the East.

In preparation for the spring campaign, Congress and Davis finally appointed Lee general in chief on January 31, and three weeks later Johnston would be restored to command of the Army of Tennessee, which had come east to join with the assemblage of units trying to resist Sherman. The Confederates were far too few in number to offer serious opposition, and again under Johnston there were doubts that he would even try. Even before Johnston assumed command, Sherman pushed northward and in less than two weeks Columbia fell, and was soon in flames. That same day, seeing themselves cut off by the Yankees' move around them, the small body of Confederates in Charleston evacuated the city. Just days later Sherman entered North Carolina, and on February 22 Wilmington fell, the last Confederate blockade-running port outside Texas.

Lee ordered Johnston to concentrate everything he could. On March 10 a portion of Johnston's still-gathering command led by Bragg attacked and briefly stunned a wing of Sherman's army at Kinston, North Carolina, but they were not strong enough to follow up the initial success. That would be the Confederate story for the brief remainder of its life. Six days later at Averasborough, Sherman struck another portion of the scattered Confederates, who at least tried to impede the Yankee advance if they could not stop it, and stop it they could not. Finally on March 19, at Bentonville, Johnston had his army concentrated sufficiently that he could do what he had done so seldom before. He attacked, and at first he drove the Federals back, shocking them to find there was still some serious opposition in their front. But the next day Sherman got most of his army on the field, and when the fighting resumed, even though Johnston held his position, he had no choice but to withdraw to avoid being surrounded. It would be Johnston's last battle, and the final fight of the brave but troubled old Army of Tennessee.

That left only Lee. He did everything he could to augment his dwindling army, pardoning deserters if they would come back, supporting the enlistment of black troops, while at the same time pragmatically planning his route of retreat if and when he was forced to give up Richmond. The only real hope of any sort of successful continued resistance against the overwhelming Federal numbers was for him to move rapidly, leaving Grant behind, and to reach Johnston and combine their forces. Then, though still outnumbered, the two of them could try to stop Sherman, then turn around to face Grant. It was the only obvious alternative remaining, but that took nothing away from the boldness of the plan all the same.

To put the plan in operation, Lee needed to force Grant back a bit, to open a line of retreat. On March 25 he launched a surprise attack on the Yankees at Fort Stedman, hoping that if he broke through he could threaten or even cut Grant's supply line to his base on the lower James. At first the Confederates crashed through the Union lines, but they were too understrength to maintain their momentum, and a little more than three hours later they had been driven back. Four days later Grant seized the initiative and began the final stretch of his lines to encircle Lee and Richmond. After the loss of a critical road junction at Five Forks on April 1, Lee had no choice but to inform the government that he could not protect Richmond more than a few hours. The evacuation began the next day and the last Confederate units left the city and their earthworks late that night, barely ahead of the entering Yankees.

Now it was to be the race that Lee feared, to see if he could reach Johnston before Grant could catch and encircle him. There was only one route, and that was west toward Lynchburg, where there were supply warehouses that Lee would need to feed his army. But Grant managed to stay on his heels and worse, he directed Sheridan and abundant cavalry to race to get ahead of Lee and cut off his route. Exhaustion and disorganization set in, the Army of Northern Virginia became too strung out on the slender roads, and on April 6 at Sayler's Creek, Federal combined infantry and cavalry isolated and captured nearly a fourth of Lee's army. Now, to face Grant's 100,000 or more, Lee had less than 30,000 remaining. The next day Lee received through the lines a note from Grant suggesting that it was time to face the inevitable. Lee replied that he did not consider the situation absolutely hopeless, but nevertheless would be willing to consider what terms Grant would suggest for his surrender.

As if more was needed to convince him of just how pointless it was to go on, the next day Lee got to Appomattox Station, where supplies had previously been ordered to be ready to feed his men. The Yankees had gotten there first. Though Lee did not know it yet, Federal cavalry and infantry had reached the Lynchburg road ahead of him. He had nowhere to go, and an army too tired and hungry to be asked to do more. This same day there came a reply from Grant outlining generous terms. Lee agreed to meet with Grant the next day, but meanwhile that night authorized one last attack for the next morning to see if they could break through the Union cordon around them. If there was cavalry in their front, they could perhaps succeed, but if there was infantry backing the mounted enemy, then it would be hopeless. Despite initial success, the assaulting Confederates soon found more than enough infantry to stop them. Lee put on his finest uniform and rode into the village of Appomattox Courthouse to meet his enemy and his destiny.

Elsewhere the story was the same. After Bentonville, Johnston and his army could do little but continue to fall back before Sherman, comforting themselves that at least every step was taking them closer to the anticipated junction with Lee. By April 11 they were near Goldsboro, and learned of the arrival of the fleeing government at Greensboro. The next day Johnston went there to talk of their future plans with the president and secured

Davis's permission to open negotiations with Sherman. Two weeks later Johnston would surrender. Meanwhile Selma, Alabama, the Confederacy's last manufacturing center, had fallen, and the land defenses of Mobile were about to yield in a few days. Other than Johnston's army there was nothing left east of the Mississippi but a small army of about 12,000 some miles north of Mobile commanded by General Richard Taylor. There was nothing he could do with the forces arrayed against him, and in three weeks he would agree to a truce to begin surrender negotiations. Beyond the Mississippi the disintegration had set in to the point that Kirby Smith's army was simply dissolving. While he was on a tour trying to rally support and fresh forces, a subordinate took it on himself to surrender on his behalf on May 26, and Smith suddenly found himself a general without an army. Rather than surrender himself, he joined a party of other irreconcilables and left for Mexico and exile. That left only a few hundred Cherokee and related tribesmen from the Indian Territory who had enlisted and served under the only Indian general in the Confederate army, Stand Watie. Their isolation kept them from being an important target for the Federals, with the result that they stayed in the field fully a month after Smith's army was surrendered. Finally on June 23, Watie, too, took his terms and put down his arms. It was all over.

14

The End?

AT CHRISTMAS 1864 out in western Louisiana, the officers in the high command, including General Simon B. Buckner himself, seemed less concerned with events than they were in being what a local justice called "women-mad." To Governor Thomas Moore the judge complained that "I augured from their incessant companionship of the fair sex, they lacked that devotion to business, which in these times is the public man's first duty. The sight of a petticoat appeared to throw them in a tremer of ecstasy." Only the arrival of Buckner's wife apparently caused the general to "subside into that quiet, and obedient domestic animal which the ladis call a husband." Even then, they lived a life that Lee's poor veterans could scarcely dream of as they marched westward toward Appomattox. For Christmas dinner in Alexandria, Louisiana, the justice said that "the table groaned with a profusion of good things, and I am ashamed to say I ate until I made myself sick."[1]

The anger that most soldiers and civilians east of the Mississippi would have felt if they had seen that judge gorging and then disgorging his feast would have been towering, matched by their feelings toward Buckner and his generals cavorting with the ladies of Alexandria while the officers and men in Lee's army hunkered in muddy or frozen earthworks. Now was the time, if ever there was one, to set personal pleasures and comforts aside if the cause was to be saved. Yet four years of scarcity and making do, hundreds of thousands of empty chairs once filled by husbands, sons, and brothers, now buried in unknown graves in distant places, the collapse of civil order at home, an economy that was ravaged by worthless money and grossly inflated consumer prices on goods that were in any event scarce, and the stark reality that the Yankees had overrun most of their state capitals, taken all but two of their ports, captured most of their industrial infrastructure, and currently had Lee at bay in his trenches and the other Southern armies in retreat—all of these things and more made it starkly clear that the Confederacy was in desperate straits.

Indeed, the more pragmatic Confederates had known that defeat was all but certain at least as far back as November 1864, when the reelection of Lincoln signaled that the Union still had the stamina and commitment to stay with the war as long as it took. They always knew they were battling superior manpower and resources. In the absence of foreign assistance, their only hope had been to wear down or defeat Yankee will. Now all but the most zealous and deluded knew that was not going to happen. The people no longer had the emotional or material wherewithal to maintain their resistance, and the armies no longer had the power to protect them. Even Lee could not promise that he could protect Richmond once spring weather brought renewed campaigning. Few if any in high places would openly countenance what most privately feared, but the increasing desperation of their efforts spoke of the feelings of futility they must have harbored. Nothing could have been more eloquent of that than the Duncan Kenner mission and the proffer of emancipation. It did not matter that neither the administration itself nor Congress possessed the constitutional power to enact such a measure. Indeed, it was highly unlikely that the legislature could have passed anything of the sort coming on its floor, especially given the difficulty it had in passing the black soldier bill. And strictly interpreted, their constitution all but forbade individual states to abolish slavery, and perhaps did not even allow a convention of all the states to do so unless the Constitution itself was first amended. This slow, cumbersome process would be made even slower with the disruptions to travel and communications. Who, then, had the power? Did anyone?

Governor Andrew Magrath of South Carolina was so concerned about the question that in January 1865 he proposed to Governor Zebulon Vance of North Carolina and other governors that, assuming Richmond would fall and Lee's army disintegrate after capture, they should agree on some prearranged emergency plan to mobilize their remaining manpower to continue the struggle when the national government could no longer lead them. They had to have a "perfect understanding" for the anticipated crisis so that each would know what the other would do. Magrath's contempt for the administration in Richmond was implicit. Taken in himself by Joseph E. Johnston's hollow boasts of what he would do if he had a command, the governor proposed that all the governors pressure Davis to reassign the failed general to command of the Army of Tennessee—which Davis would do within a few weeks, but not because of the governors. "We should think alike, feel alike, and act alike," urged Magrath, in what amounted to a bold suggestion that the governors assume de facto power from the administration and Congress. Vance agreed, and with his support, Magrath took his proposal to Governors Joseph Brown, Thomas Watts, Charles Clark, and John Milton, whose states would form a compact last ditch of the Confederacy. During the course of the war, as Richmond assumed more and more power, it had become the mirror of the administration in Washington that they had despised enough to secede. "We have therefore presented in the whole progress of the war, the startling contradiction of States united in a league, for the support of their separate independence; called on to ignore if not abjure that independence," Margrath stated. Only by the states reasserting their supreme sovereignty did they stand any chance of survival. "The States, as States seceded; the States as States are to fight out this bloody war," he argued. "They are the realities of this grand drama."[2]

There was a brief flurry of renewed optimism in February thanks to some changes. The failure of the Hampton Roads peace talks gave a brief shot of adrenaline to resolve, at least in government circles. More important were the command changes. Making Lee general in chief was the best stroke of all, for many in the country now regarded the general and the cause as synonymous. People who in earlier generations had no idea even of who commanded their army in peacetime now hung on every move their gray chieftain made. Indeed, Lee himself well knew that his soldiers were fighting as much for him as for independence, and soon he would reveal just how perceptive was his sense of his place in Confederate popular confidence. The replacement of Seddon with Breckinridge also received universal approval. "He is a noble fellow, with a good golden thread of patriotism running through him, composed, courageous & cautious, & I know you'll like him in the end," General William Preston had told Louis Wigfall sometime before.[3] More important, Lee regarded him highly. Indeed, he was immediately disappointed that Breckinridge had not been

put in the war office much earlier. "He is a great man," Lee would tell
Davis's aide William Preston Johnston. "I was acquainted with him as Congressman and Vice-President and as one of our Generals, but I did not
know him till he was secretary of war, and he is a lofty, pure strong man."[4]
Then, too, the reappointment of Johnston to command the remnant of the
Army of Tennessee gave cheer to some, though even in that army itself
there were too many soldiers who remembered him only for retreat after
retreat.

Even such heartening news could not produce a sustained boost for
morale, for news of Lee or Breckinridge or Johnston seemed all too distant
when ordinary Confederates encountered in seemingly increasing abundance all the other signs of decay and disorganization. Even Johnston
started to complain, protesting that Lee could not be an effective general
in chief because the distractions of his position would take him away from
his own army's operations, and if he left that force to visit or lead another,
he would not carry the stature with the new command that he had with the
old.[5] Of course, as he still believed he rightfully was senior to Lee, Johnston's concern might have been that he should have had the general in
chief's portfolio instead. Far western regiments complained that they had
gone the entire war without a furlough to see their homes and families.
Breckinridge actually granted one such request from a Texas cavalry outfit
in February, perhaps reasoning that in so doing he would only be sending
them in a direction that the logic of the war suggested they would be going
soon enough anyhow.[6] Governor Pendleton Murrah kept right on trying to
get the army to pay for state mules it had purchased nine months before,
in the face of the quartermasters' refusal to do so. "The whole transaction,
Sir, I denounce as an outrage, and as a gross insult to the State," he blustered, "and some one is to blame."[7] Indeed, seeing the army trying to draw
even more men and supplies from his state in early 1865, Murrah joined
with Governor Henry Allen of Louisiana to remonstrate against sending
any more of their men east of the Mississippi. If they were taken, then
Texas would be lost, said Murrah, while Allen proclaimed in February that
"the fact is that Texas *is* the Trans Miss Dept, & her action is that of the
Dept."[8] In Mississippi the rumor that Congress might confiscate tobacco
and cotton caused an uproar of accusations of unconstitutional usurpation,
not to mention the complaint over their chaotic currency. "The condition
of the country is such that the Government should be held down to the
strict rule on this subject," assured one discontented planter. "As matters

now stand the Government can force a man to give up his property for paper which is worthless in his pocket, as he cannot force his creditor to receive [it] from him."[9]

Yankee advances only exacerbated the discontent and depression. Charleston finally fell to Sherman on February 18. Robert Barnwell Rhett and his son had already left, the father taking his more than one hundred slaves to Alabama, and the son taking the *Mercury* press to Columbia. Behind them the Federals entered Rhett's house and looted his furniture and papers.[10] The shock of the loss of the birthplace of secession and the Confederacy to the enemy far outweighed its military importance by now. "Separated from all sources of reliable information—without any idea where the state authorities are, with no means of reaching them, I am afraid that there will be a perfect paralysis of all vital energy," William Henry Trescot wrote to Governor Magrath, scarcely knowing if the letter would reach him. He wanted to know where the governor was and if the state government still even existed. "Bad news if reliable would be better than no news."[11] Poor Milton in Florida, seeing his state overrun and cut off, infested with tories and deserters, could only call their prospects "gloomy," and asked Robert Hilton to approach the president and Congress "to bring about a cessation of hostilities, in any practicable manner consistent with the honor and safety of the Confederate States."[12] It was not a call for surrender, or at least not yet.

Certainly there was still starch in some of the editors and soldiers and people. The 20th Texas Infantry showed it at Galveston on December 20, 1864. A group of them gathered to frame resolutions, only to be dispersed at first, for so worried were commanders now by desertions and demoralization that they feared what might come from any public assembly. "You can readily perceive how dangerous public meetings in military camps might become," General John G. Walker would warn Governor Murrah. "Oily tongued demagogues, in political life would easily gain such ascendancy over the simple minded soldiers as to destroy discipline and seriously impair the efficiency of our army." And a properly disciplined army, he averred, "is as far removed from democracy as it is possible to conceive."[13] Yet the meeting of the 20th Texas listened not to demagogues but to their own patriotism. Their response to Lincoln's reelection, they said, was to call for every man to go into uniform regardless of age or exemptions, and for all private property to be appropriated for the war effort. The government should stop printing worthless money and then stop wasting even that in paying officers and enlisted men—easy to say since it came so seldom anyhow—and just provide them the best food possible, tobacco to smoke, and stationery to write to their families. They would fight on indefinitely in return.[14] A Mississippian went even further. "If we are in earnest, let our actions furnish the proof," he declared. Let every man, young or old, sick or well, be called forth to make one last campaign. The Confederacy still had that in it at least. If they were destined to fail, then "the sooner we all close the scene of carnage the better." Even from the wreckage they might salvage something. "There are men enough in the South, if brought together in an army, to burn up the north—at least to settle *the debt of vengeance*—which we so honestly owe them."[15] In Alabama, Governor Watts spoke at a public meeting early in March to declare that if they had not resisted Yankee aggression in 1861 "we would have deserved to be the slaves of slaves." For all their losses, they were still holding out, even though voices in the audience hooted at that. "There is no occasion for depression—nothing to justify a disposition to go back to the old Union," Watts said. If they did, they would be conquered provinces at Yankee mercy. Who would be their governor and congressmen then, "some flat-nosed, thick-lipped sons of Africa, appointed by your conquerors?" They would be in a perpetual war as the Federals tried to place their blacks on a social equality with them.[16]

Where they could, civil officials still tried to maintain the workings of democracy amid the growing rubble. In Texas, Murrah was worrying about whether he should run for reelection even by late March, and already sizing up his potential opponents.[17] In April, days before Lee would be forced to surrender, Governor Charles Clark was being encouraged to run for reelection, and the remaining press in the state were already running banners for their favorite candidates. For some it seemed like an old-time political race, almost as if it would really matter now. "I see much to lament in the policy of our government, much to deprecate in the administration of its affairs, much to deplore," a Mississippian complained to Clark. "Still I am for my country now and forever." They could still gain their liberty somehow, he felt certain.

> We should forget all feeling, Resign all passion save our purpose, Behold no object save our country. I will not despair of the Republic. Though I must confess the blunders of our Rulers have been sufficient to ruin any people but the people of the South amidst all the tri-

als and hardships they have endured the sacrifices they have made the humiliations they have suffered from incompetency and obstinacy still their fortitude and manhood has not forsaken them, their patriotism predominates in their breasts, their will is not subdued, their persistence conquered or their spirits broken. The annals of history offers no record of the enslavement of such a people! God never permitted nor never will permit such a people to be subjugated or deprived of their freedom.[18]

Of course there were those who could not keep heart, or who were simply worn out by the war. After months of depression at the fate he saw coming for the Confederacy, sometime on the evening of March 31 or in the early hours of April 1, Florida's governor John Milton went to his plantation in Marianna and put a gun to his head. Friends tried to keep it quiet, even giving out the story that he had died of a stroke, while rumors soon spread among the people that he was not dead at all. He had simply hidden himself in a railroad car marked "meat" and been taken northward to try to join Davis and the remnants of the government. Two days later the president of the state senate was installed temporarily in Milton's place, and his first act was to schedule a special gubernatorial election for June 8. Somehow democracy had to go on.[19]

The thought of defeat was all but unthinkable to some. "What would become of our honor," asked a Carolinian of Governor Magrath. "To what a depth of infamy and disgrace we should sink."[20] Faraway in Houston, an editor decried the talk that now it was time for the several states to meet in convention to decide their fates for themselves. Such talk only weakened all the states. All might not be lost. After all, artisans were everywhere busy and so were mechanics in the Trans-Mississippi. Their wagons still moved on their roads and their ingenuity revealed itself in a host of inventive means to get around shortages and disrepair. They were not necessarily beaten yet. They had to stand or fall together. In Alabama, Watts decried the talk of a convention. "Our people are tired of war!" he declared in his annual message, but a convention was no answer. Indeed, he argued that by ceding the treaty power to the president in their Constitution, the states had no authority to meet and discuss negotiations leading to a peace treaty. Neither the president nor the Congress had the power to call such a convention, either. Sovereign conventions in the several states could meet and send delegates to meet with the Northern states, but to do that they would

first have to secede themselves from the Confederacy else they be in violation of the president's clear and unchallenged treaty power. In short, no
one had the authority to call a convention that, according to Watts, would
have no power to make peace anyhow. Having gone to war, the Confederacy simply had no legal mechanism to end itself other than voluntary disintegration, or military victory or defeat.[21] But should that unthinkable
eventuality occur, the Houston editor could counter Watts. "Should it ever
be our fate to take the terms of a conqueror," he said, "what can be clearer
than that those terms can be better obtained by our Confederate leaders
amidst unshaken fidelity to their cause, than by separate States bowing
their heads to the yoke." If they could not live, they could die with dignity.
"Defeat in war has been the fate of many a gallant people, and if they remain united and true to their cause, they exact respect even from the most
cruel victory,"[22] the editor averred.

That was exactly the sort of thinking going through some minds in Richmond, though they kept very quiet in the matter. One needed only to look
at history to discern that defeated peoples that held themselves together to
surrender as a nation generally fared better when it came to terms from
their enemies than did those who stubbornly fought on until utterly
crushed. It was clear enough to most that President Davis had no intention
of countenancing defeat or even a negotiated settlement short of independence, as his instructions for the Hampton Roads conference made
clear, and while only those in government circles knew of the Kenner mission, they understood that its very desperation only punctuated the president's determination to keep resisting. But people like Alexander Stephens
and R.M.T. Hunter, and Assistant Secretary of War John A. Campbell, all
three of whom had been at Hampton Roads, had seen glimmers of hope in
Lincoln's terms there, even if they extinguished Confederate independence. Lincoln had made it clear that all he wanted was for them to lay
down their arms and disband their armies, and his secretary of state,
William Seward, specifically made it clear that the Union did not demand
unconditional surrender. The seceded states would be welcomed back into
the Union with all their constitutional rights intact and unfettered. It
would be, in short, as if the war had never happened. Supporting this, Lincoln said he believed the courts and Congress would be generous in dealing afterward with property seized during the war, speculating that there
might even be restitution. Nothing was said of reprisals or prosecutions of
the leaders of the rebellion, though it had to have been implicit that since

there were treason indictments out against Davis and a number of the other principal leaders, either those courts would have to be persuaded to quash the charges or else the Confederate high command would have to face trial or leave the country. Lincoln would soon express his preference that Davis and his ministers simply flee the country and not put him to the bother and turmoil of trying them. Then he and Seward suggested that both the Emancipation Proclamation and the newly passed Thirteenth Amendment abolishing slavery had been chiefly war measures. Stephens and Campbell both believed they heard Lincoln hint that he could rescind the former, while Seward suggested that if the Southern states came back to Washington, they would have more than enough votes to defeat ratification of the amendment.[23]

It was almost too good to be true. After all the blood and sacrifice and in the face of virtually certain defeat, they had an opportunity to conclude the war with their full political and civil rights, no loss of property, no trials of political prisoners except presumably the president and cabinet, and most of all, they might even come out of it with their slaves! Though this last was a pipe dream, within days Lincoln did propose that all political crimes be pardoned and that Congress deal with slavery by appropriating enough money to emancipate all remaining slaves and compensate their owners at a low but not unreasonable price. In the end the Confederates would have won nothing to be sure, but all they would have lost as a nation would be their presumed nationhood. Such a solution was equivocal, and left unsettled some of the issues that propelled the South to secession in the first place, though the dramatic growth of the power of the Union and the power of Washington during the war could leave little doubt that the momentum in the struggle between state sovereignty and centralization was now all on the side of the latter. The South could never dominate the Union again, and clearly it would have to face the irrevocable loss of its stand for extension of slavery into the territories. Still, faced with the alternative of complete destruction and possible subjugation, coming out of the war with all of this under Lincoln's terms represented virtually a victory simply from not having to lose so much more.

Of course Davis rejected even such terms as these because of his own sine qua non of independence. Indeed, he tried to pressure the commissioners into falsifying their report of the meeting to claim that Lincoln had insisted on abolition and unconditional surrender, but they refused. Yet that is how the president succeeded in presenting the result to the public all the same, achieving the twofold end of concealing from the people just how remarkably generous Lincoln was being and averting the risk of a backlash from a war-weary country, and at the same time briefly reanimating their spirit by misrepresenting Union demands as harsh, insulting, and intransigent. Temporarily, Davis won. Stephens, Hunter, and Campbell, however, knew the truth. It was at just this moment that Breckinridge took office as secretary of war.

Four years earlier he had confided to a friend that he doubted the Confederacy would ever achieve its independence. Like Stephens and some others at the outset, he probably hoped that simply by making an initial stand, the Southern states could get sufficient concessions from Washington to allow them to put down their arms and come back, but that did not happen. Since then, he had seen on a wider scale than most the inexorable grinding down of Confederate resources. He had participated in the defeat at Shiloh. He had been with Johnston in the abortive attempt to relieve Vicksburg. He had fought in the setback at Stones River, seen his own corps crumble in the humiliating rout at Missionary Ridge, and was there at Winchester this past fall to see Sheridan rout Early. Breckinridge knew they were not going to survive this next season of campaigning, not with Lee all but surrounded, Sherman marching at will in South Carolina now, and only vestiges of other armies remaining at large chiefly because they were not important enough for the Union to give them more than secondary attention at the moment. The South was going to lose. That was no longer the issue. The only question was how. In parallel would be the last battle for Confederate democracy. Their movement had begun in politics, and so it would end.

In the natural course of familiarizing himself with his new office, Breckinridge met frequently with Campbell. Spending a long time with him on his very first day, the general first asked not about procedure or manpower or resources, however, but if Campbell thought the cause was gone, and the assistant said it was. It was no more than what the general himself already believed, so it was no shock. Undoubtedly Campbell filled him in on the discussions with Lincoln and Seward, and he also gave him a draft of the matters discussed. Breckinridge used that as the foundation for a campaign that would occupy him on and off for several weeks. He ordered reports from the several bureaus in his department on their status and ability to continue, and when the reports came in they told the story he expected of shortage, inadequacy, deterioration, and decay. He was building a dossier. Then he went to meet with General Lee. They discussed immediate military concerns, of course, and Lee made it clear that he could not hold Richmond for long. Breckinridge began preparations for an evacuation when the time came, even though it would be some time before he could get the president even to discuss the possibility of an evacuation.

But Lee and Breckinridge also discussed the broader picture. More than most generals, Lee had scrupulously observed the divide between the military and politics in a civil democracy, and rarely in the past stepped over the line. But certainly he was not hesitant to share his own conviction that the Confederacy was doomed. Indeed, it was his responsibility as general in chief to give his superiors his candid view, which he continued to do in a series of confidential closeted meetings the two would have, extending into early March.

Soon politicians like Hunter and some of the delegates from Kentucky and Missouri were calling, and finally Breckinridge's office became an informal lobby every morning for members of Congress. They discussed many things, but paramount was that of what to do. Finally Breckinridge and Lee met with Hunter. Unlike them, he could introduce legislation in Congress. He could make public an issue that neither Lee nor Breckinridge in their positions could do constitutionally, and he had also been at Hampton Roads. Among the three of them they planned to get Hunter to offer a resolution in the Senate calling on Davis to seek to open negotiations with Lincoln. Lee even said that if he were to come out in favor of negotiations after Hunter introduced the resolution, the men in the army and the people at large would take it as the general's own endorsement "almost equivalent to surrender." It was a brilliant plan to use Lee's prestige, Hunter's influence and voice in the Senate, and the dossier that Breckinridge was compiling to create a groundswell that Davis could not ignore. He could not even veto a resolution, since it was not legislation. Public disclosure, along with an honest representation of the terms Lincoln had suggested, would make it impossible for Davis to brush it aside. Now was the time. The Confederates still had two powerful if depleted armies in the field, and lesser forces elsewhere, perhaps 150,000 men under arms all told. That was not enough to win, but it was enough to cost a lot of Yankee lives and treasure if they chose to fight until defeated utterly. Saving the enemy that toll could go a long way in making Washington amenable to Lincoln's lenient terms. It would also allow the Confederacy to die with dignity as a nation, earning the respect even of their enemy for the present and the admiration of their posterity to come. And especially, it could make the transition back into the Union so much less difficult and rancorous than it would be if they kept the killing and the turmoil and the animosity alive longer by futile resistance.

Perhaps the most interesting feature of the plan was its attempt to stop a revolution by entirely constitutional means. No one was overstepping his rightful bounds, not even Lee really. Breckinridge and the others already knew what Davis's objection would be. As president he did not have the authority to negotiate for the end of his nation's life, nor for the fates of the separate states. But the plotters knew that North Carolina and Georgia already had elements anxious to call state conventions to discuss separate terms with the Yankees. What either or both of those two states did would set the tone for the rest since Florida and South Carolina, Louisiana and Tennessee, Arkansas and much of Alabama and Mississippi were already overrun by the Yankees. Virginia would likely be lost in the spring, and only Texas remained largely intact. Even if they could not get an armistice, still if either of those states called a convention and even one or two others followed, it could be enough. Since it was the states that began the Confederacy, it would be the states themselves that brought it to an end, and at least in that aspect Confederate democracy would have worked right to the end as it oversaw its own demise, not from Richmond, but from the statehouses and conventions.

Hunter refused to uphold his end of the plan, however, in part because he had always been a weak sister, happy to carp and preen behind Davis's back but never willing to challenge him frontally. That killed the plan, because it needed to come from Virginia, still symbolically the most important of the states, and it had to be pushed in the Senate, the constitutional forum for treaties and matters of diplomacy. Virginia's other senator, Allen Caperton, was simply too identified with the anti-Davis lobby to carry the weight that Hunter could have, had he so chosen. Instead, Breckinridge escalated his collection of reports for the dossier, including now a call for a frank report from Lee. He would present this to Davis in the hope that it would speak loud enough for itself, but he could also be assured through his contacts that members on the floor of Congress would demand that the file be made public. That, too, would be encouragement to the possible state conventions, and to an even wider mass audience if it hit the press, as surely it could be made to do. But then Lee balked, and turned in a report that was equivocal, lacking the force to make the case as it needed to be made. He painted a dire portrait of the armies' condition and prospects, but in the end he simply could not bring himself to put the case powerfully enough for it to work to Breckinridge's ends. The secretary of war still gave the dossier to Davis, and he passed it on to Congress, but in the rush of the last days of the session in March it got lost amid a final flurry of anti-administration squabbling. Interestingly enough, Davis had never shown himself a more able politician than in his continuing successful efforts to stymie efforts for a negotiated peace.[24]

Soon events, fate, and U. S. Grant caught up with the Confederates. Suddenly there was nothing else to think about but getting the government out of Richmond. At the end of March, Lee warned that he might be able to hold his lines for only a few days. Then on April 1 came word that in a few hours the last secure rail line out of the city would be lost. He had to evacuate his army to keep from being cut off and surrounded, and the city had to be abandoned. Of course, many who saw it coming had been preparing for some time. Postmaster John Reagan had sent his wife and children off to Texas on February 1, and it was clear enough that he was expecting Richmond to fall. Looking ahead to the possibility—probability?—that the Confederacy could not make a final stand anywhere east of the Mississippi, he sent along with them three tobacco boxes packed with $9 million in uncut sheets of Treasury notes and some $3 million in postage stamps for delivery to his agent in Marshall, Texas. Resourceful to the last, Reagan intended not to allow rain nor sleet nor gloom of night nor Yankees to stay the delivery of the Confederate States mail.[25] Congress, meanwhile, had adjourned and left ten days before Lee's dire announcement, with only a few of the more staunch and patriotic like William Porcher Miles of South Carolina remaining to attend to business. Davis had sent his family off toward South Carolina a few days earlier, though others like Lee and Breckinridge would simply be too busy to look to their own interests. Their wives would remain in the capital and trust to Federal chivalry for their protection.

The evacuation itself was a mixed affair, well organized and efficiently executed by Breckinridge and the other department heads within the confines of limited and unreliable transportation, but to the public it appeared a panicky shambles. Train after train left the Danville Railroad depot for the trip to the southwest. Much had already been sent out in the weeks beforehand, leaving mainly essential archives and materiel to be moved now. Breckinridge managed to save almost all of the War Department archives.

He was intent on preserving Confederate history even if records had to be turned over to the Yankees, which he expected to happen sometime anyhow. Davis and most of the cabinet went out on a late afternoon train, while the secretary of war remained behind with a few generals and the last of the city guard. Wagon trains also moved out carrying furniture, papers, and everything else they could hold. Breckinridge had to issue specific passes to get them through the retreating columns of Lee's army without military impressment officers seizing them, discarding their contents, and using them for their own purposes.[26] Looting and confusion were already under way, as rumors of everything including the death of Lee spread rapidly. People saw clerks burning money outside the Treasury, and bonfires at all the other cabinet offices consumed what could not be taken. Secretary of State Judah Benjamin had most of the State Department archives committed to the flames in the street. For some reason, the panic brought the prostitutes out for a last round of business, and an express company agent saw them "in every hole & corner of the city," even working the depot and the shops.[27] A disastrous fire that the army unwisely lit in warehouses soon spread on the wind, turning much of downtown Richmond into a single blaze. As the last Confederates crossed the one remaining James River bridge before it, too, was set on fire, a backward glance all too easily revealed their dying capital as a metaphor for their cause.

The metaphor stayed with them as they moved south. On April 3 the government went into a limited sort of operation in Danville, where it would remain for several days. Davis actually tried to make the best of the situation by issuing a proclamation that, dire as was the loss of Richmond, it now freed Lee to take the field again. With renewed determination, the Confederates could now take the war to the enemy once again, striking at targets of opportunity and not hampering themselves by having to protect cities and places on the map. It was a transparently empty gesture in that, in the end, few ever heard of it, since communications were now so disrupted. Meanwhile, more and more people started looking to their own interests. Agents of the Treasury, especially at some remove like Texas, were increasingly reluctant to part with money, some blatantly keeping it for themselves. Even the War Department's foreign purchasing agent Caleb Huse, now back in the country, refused to account to his superior for money in his hands, and simply kept it.[28] His attention never far from his own reputation, the day after Richmond's fall Joseph E. Johnston was still quibbling over his seniority in rank, and out in Mississippi on April 9 a licensed distiller was demanding payment of $20,000 for his product before it was too late and warning that he might have to water the whiskey a bit to make his quota.[29] That same day a cornered Robert E. Lee had no alternative but to surrender his army.

Now the government had to leave Danville almost as quickly as it had come, and it became an itinerant concern, moving south into North Carolina to Greensboro and then on to Charlotte. All along the way the dissolution was palpable. Most distressing of all was the open looting of government warehouses at Danville, Greensboro, and elsewhere by civilians and soldiers, sometimes even before the government moved on. In Greensboro the looters cleaned out twenty-four trains on the sidings, then went after warehouses bulging with cloth and more than a hundred barrels of sugar, bacon slabs by the thousand, and considerable quantities of corn. Most of it was taken by the local women—"dirty, slab sided snuff complexioned turkey buzzards," a government clerk called them—who had finally tired of their sacrifice. Aiding them were uniformed Confederate cavalrymen, slaves, and even a few government clerks themselves. A military guard at a warehouse ordered his men to shoot at the looters. They killed a lieutenant and wounded others, but could not stop the spree.[30] When Confederates were killing Confederates, even the most die-hard had to admit that they were nearing the end.

But that did not include President Davis, who had already left Greensboro before the looting and shooting. When he departed, it was still with a staggered confidence in his ability to continue. Greensboro gave the government a cold welcome for a start, fearing that the town could suffer from pursuing Yankees for harboring Davis and his ministers. There was little hospitality, and some of the cabinet leaders had to sleep in railroad cars. Then Davis got definitive word of Lee's surrender for the first time, a crushing blow that yet left him able to say that a lost army was not a lost cause. They still had Johnston and the Army of Tennessee, now not far away. Davis summoned Johnston and Beauregard, who was nearby, to come and confer with him, the cabinet, and Breckinridge, no doubt aware of the irony that in this extremity he was forced to turn to his two bitterest enemies in the military. They almost took pleasure in telling him what he did not want to hear: It was all over. The army was depleted, desertion was epidemic, and Sherman in their front had overwhelming force. The country was played out, the people exhausted. Resisting more was little better than suicide. After a tense cabinet meeting in which everyone but Benjamin sided with the generals, a dejected president agreed to allow Johnston to seek an armistice with Sherman to discuss the surrender of his army. Davis still had no intention of surrendering, but he recognized that an armistice would buy him time to continue organizing his plan now to get as many armed forces as he could across the Deep South to Texas to continue the war there with Kirby Smith's army. Johnston and Breckinridge, however, thought the military conference with Sherman might lead to one covering all Confederates in the field. If successful, it would result effectively in the laying down of arms that Lincoln had said was his only stipulation for reconstruction with full civil and property rights intact.

Johnston first met alone with Sherman, but then asked to have Breckinridge join them in his capacity as a general officer, since the Federals still did not recognize any civil officials of the Confederacy as having any official standing. Together, aided by Reagan, they quickly moved beyond the two armies now under a cease-fire. Sherman was anxious to end the war, too, and seemed receptive to proposals that came mainly from Breckinridge, which were an echo of what Lincoln had said at Hampton Roads, and what Breckinridge and Campbell had proposed to Hunter and Lee. There would be no unconditional surrender. Confederate armies, in fact, would disband, and the men would go home with their weapons and in their organized units to turn in their weapons to their state governments. That would be important to their pride, certainly, but even more it served the end of providing an immediate and trained policing force in a home front now almost devoid of civil law and order, for their governors could constitute them as militia until civil law could be resumed. It would be so much easier on the population to be policed by their sons and brothers than by occupying Yankees. And as for those state governments, as soon as their legislatures passed resolutions acknowledging the primacy of the U.S. Constitution and the Union, they were to be recognized as lawful. There would be no expulsions of Confederate governors and legislators. Reestablished Federal courts would start at once to settle disputes over property and personal rights, and the people themselves were to be free from interference or retaliation by Washington. Throughout the agreement they framed, there was no mention of the Confederate government itself, which Union policy did not admit to exist. With its armies disbanded and its component states back in the Union, it would simply evaporate, and thus there would be no formal surrender. It was defeat with honor, virtually the Confederate "reconstruction" plan that Breckinridge, Campbell, and others had worked out three months before, and Sherman agreed to it all. There was even a suggestion of universal amnesty extending even to the cabinet and perhaps Davis himself, and there was no mention at all of slavery or of acceptance of either the Emancipation Proclamation or the Thirteenth Amendment as preconditions. They might still lose the war and all but win the peace.

It was, nonetheless, the final tangled death throe of Confederate democracy. They had begun in 1861 as a movement dedicated to the professed belief that sovereignty lay with the states. For four years that democracy went through strains and wrenches testing its ability to resist centralization, through one compromise of its ideology after another over conscription, impressment, cotton policy, socialization, and other issues. The struggle battered it almost out of recognition. Confederate democracy could no longer protect the oligarchy that gave it birth to protect themselves, and it was increasingly forced to yield to greater democratization, to the tyranny of an expanding majority, simply in order to keep the popular will behind the cause. Through it all, however, it had at least managed to sustain the division between the civil and the military leadership, for all the accusations of military tyranny and despotism, especially west of the Mississippi. They were still a *constitutional* democracy, however torn their Constitution might be. But now here in North Carolina, what would be the closest thing to a treaty of peace between North and South was negotiated by a failed Southern general who hated his commander in chief and a general and cabinet minister of a government no one recognized, who had never wanted to be a Confederate in the first place.

Two officers in the army made civil and political policy not on behalf of their government but for the individual states themselves, as well as helped define the terms of the future peace to follow. It was a long way from what began in Montgomery. If the journey provided any lesson, surely it was that however natural Confederate democracy was as a necessary permutation in the evolution of republican government, the tide of affairs had demonstrated with tragic clarity that it was not strong enough to sustain itself in the critical test that Charles Darwin so eloquently described as the "survival of the fittest." In fighting for their past, they had all but destroyed their present. Men like Breckinridge, Reagan, and Campbell, and even the inadequate Johnston and Beauregard, could see that the struggle now was for their future.

Euphoria over the agreement soon collapsed when Sherman shared the news that a few days before President Lincoln had been assassinated. None could say if his successor would be as receptive to their agreement's generous terms as Lincoln had suggested he would be back at Hampton Roads. They could but try. Meanwhile, Davis was stunned when he saw how far afield the meeting had ranged, and how much had been yielded. He had expected nothing to come of the conference, yet now was confronted by everything they could ask for but independence—and it was not enough. While he pondered his response, he called on his cabinet to give him their written views, which proved to be unanimously in favor of accepting Sherman's terms. Even Benjamin bent to the inevitable. Still it took another day or two before Davis finally authorized Johnston to go ahead with beginning the agreement's implementation as soon as Washington gave its approval. But then came what Davis expected and Johnston and Breckinridge feared. Washington rejected the deal. Sherman could negotiate only for the surrender of Johnston's army and nothing more. Davis and the Confederacy were not dead yet. The government immediately prepared to leave Charlotte and continue southward, while Davis ordered Johnston to get his army in motion. The general, however, was through with the president. On April 26, without even informing Davis, Johnston sent Breckinridge a message that he was going to meet Sherman to surrender his army. Within hours it was done. Livid at this insubordination and the body blow of the loss of his second major army, the president rode out of Charlotte bent now on getting across Georgia and Alabama and on to the Mississippi to continue the fight. Once more the peacemakers had lost a battle to circumstances they could not control.

The Confederacy that awaited them out to the west was a hodgepodge of conflicting interests and motivations, some blindly committed to him continuing as their president and others seemingly just bouncing in the wind. In some places there was the sense that men were still dancing on a sinking ship. In South Carolina as late as April 10, Governor Magrath was complaining by letter to Reagan of poor postal service, and planters were still trying to get compensation for impressed slaves even though virtually all of the state was under Yankee control.[31] Faced with the imminent collapse, men still applied for pardons for their violation of the distilling laws from a government about to die. In Florida the secretary of state went on with distributing blanks for its soldiers to vote in the forthcoming gubernatorial election.[32] Mississippi state troops still futilely chased deserters, and farmers argued with the governor about impressment of animals needed to put in the spring crops. The inferior court at Athens, Georgia, complained that it could not find sufficient men to rebuild all the bridges washed out in a recent storm, while out in the Far West one of Reagan's agents insisted on continuing to run his mail route in Texas right up to the moment of surrender, and then he intended to hand over his operation to the Yankees and get a receipt. In Tyler, Texas, the local Masonic lodge assumed the guardianship of local army stores in the absence of the army, to protect the goods from looters until they could be distributed to widows and returning soldiers for their families. Faced with the fact that paperwork had to go on no matter what, officers at Natchitoches, Louisiana, resorted to using printed Mexican stationery when their own gave out.[33] As late as May 17 a Louisianian was still trying to collect his interest on a coupon bond.[34]

In the disruption of communications, news traveled slowly, but gradually the people of the Confederacy learned of the surrenders of Lee and Johnston and the loss of Richmond. At first there was incredulity. "We do not believe here that Genl Lee has surrendered his army," ex-governor John Pettus of Mississippi told his successor on April 20. Some imagined that Lee and most of his command somehow had escaped and joined Johnston, and that even now they were defeating Sherman in a great last battle.[35] "I have no idea what to believe," another Mississippian complained to Governor Charles Clark some days later. "All reports we have come through Yankee papers, & I would now doubt the Bible if coming *now* through that source. But enough is sent abroad to make the last man among us unhappy." He refused to believe that Lee had given up, and held to the hope that Johnston's army was still intact in spite of rumor. "But, *admit it all*, I say, yield not & advise individuals, no men of even 80 yrs or 100 yrs of age, never to surrender. What can the Yankees do with us if we refuse? They can take property, & put us in prison, or hang some; well let it be done, I say." He wanted no state conventions, no petitions for reunion. Micawberish, he advised that "we have but to wait & be the last to act, something may yet turn up." In any case, he wanted Mississippi and his native South Carolina, the first two states to secede, to be the last two to yield. "Let us wait until all are gone before us," he pleaded. "Of course I am weary. Of course I cannot see what we can do without an army, but I think if we refuse submission God will take us through ere we are all slain."[36]

When the reality became undeniable, men who had fought for four years faced a devastating emotional blow.[37] "I feel more *degraded* and *blue* than I supposed that I would ever feel as a Virginian," moaned Colonel Thomas T. Munford to his wife.[38] In Louisiana a patriot who had invested heavily in Confederate bonds and notes glumly told former governor Moore that "the prospects are by no means encouraging, and I apprehend that you will have to share the fate of myself and others of our friends, who received & have lost largely by investments in Confederate Securities."[39] A hospital attendant who had followed the government as far as Danville felt crushed, but finally made himself give his parole not to take up arms again, take the oath of allegiance to the United States, and start on his way home. "I reasoned in this way: our armies had surrendered, our government destroyed, and we had no longer a government or cause to uphold," said Dr. John Miller, "so I concluded that it would not only be mad folly but fanaticism for me to hold out any longer, and that it was best for me to make the best of a bad situation."[40]

Definitive word of Lee's surrender did not reach Texas until more than two weeks after the fact. Governor Pendleton Murrah announced it in a proclamation on April 27, but exhorted his people to renewed effort, saying there was still hope.[41] Some tried to hold on. "The clouds thicken around us from every quarter [and] every countenance is filled with gloom and despondency," a Louisianian wrote Moore as late as May 8. "What give up this contest now, my God, what can our people be thinking about?" he cried. "Let us strike now one and all or forever sink into oblivion." Yet even he closed his protestation by saying gloomily, "I have no heart to write more."[42] One day later Kirby Smith addressed the governors of Texas, Louisiana, Arkansas, and Missouri, announcing that the fall of Richmond and the surrender of Lee, along with the imminent but as yet unannounced fate of Johnston, meant that the war was over east of the Mississippi. It was up to them now, and he was ready to fight. He hoped the president could join them, but until then important political decisions needed to be made and he wanted to confer with them rather than be mistaken for a usurper. But that is what most of them thought he had been for some time now, and his communication carried with it the implicit announcement that he would do what he had to to keep the cause alive. A department so large that once it was known as "Kirby Smithdom" had shrunk until all he had was his army and most of Texas and western Louisiana.[43] Still the Houston press came out optimistically to say that the army would be all right and up to the job if only the people would continue giving their support.[44]

Finally came the time when they could no longer deny reality. Not only did confirmation of Johnston's surrender punctuate the undeniable truth of Appomattox, but then another piece of news began to filter westward. President Davis was a prisoner. The flight of the government south from Charlotte had continued on to Washington, Georgia, with cabinet members now dropping out along the way to go home and await their fates. By May 3 only Breckinridge, Reagan, and Benjamin were left. Breckinridge was managing the movement and commanding the cavalry escort of about four thousand troopers whose commanders only agreed to continue the flight this far in order to protect the president. When Davis asked them to accompany him to the Trans-Mississippi they flatly refused, giving the final brutal blow. And in the last spiteful blast from the opposition that had nettled him so long, Robert Toombs was also in Washington, his home, and made a point of offering the hospitality of his house to everyone but the president.

Now Benjamin left to try to escape the country, and on May 4, Reagan and Davis, and Davis's family, set off to the south while Breckinridge led a few hundred men off to the west to decoy pursuing Yankee cavalry. It did not work. On May 10 the Federals surprised and captured the Davis party near Irwinville, Georgia. Davis had wavered in his plans to the last, one day agreeing that he should escape the country to safety and the next renewing his determination to reach Kirby Smith somehow and continue. At least his capture put an end to any questions of continued resistance. As soon as he learned of the president's fate, Breckinridge himself set off to leave the country through Florida, not to escape but to get to Texas in order to arrange for the surrender of Kirby Smith's forces and put an end to all remaining resistance. Before he could get there, however, Smith had already been forced to capitulate. In a meeting with the Trans-Mississippi governors on May 13, they all agreed that it was time to yield, and so in the end the military subordinated itself to the civil authority and, in a peculiar way, a little bit of Confederate democracy had the last word in the decisions of the governors. Murrah still wanted to put it in some form of referendum, a final nod to the popular will, and even planned to hold elections for a state convention to bring Texas back into the Union, as if there was any question of it happening with or without state action.[45] Clark, too, had called a special session of the Mississippi legislature to address the new po-

litical landscape. His last order as governor was for a special wagon to
bring cornmeal, flour, salt, sugar, and cooking utensils to Jackson so that
the legislators could feed themselves when they met.[46]

And so it was over, with neither bang nor whimper, but rather with a series of halting gasps, the oxygen cut off in fits and starts, prolonging the
death agony. It was not the end the peacemakers and proponents of Confederate reconstruction had wanted, but neither was it the Armageddon
that Davis seemed to seek, especially when he considered asking his
armies to disband and take to the hills as partisans. In his meetings with
the senators in Richmond, Breckinridge had pleaded that "this has been a
magnificent epic; in God's name let it not terminate in a farce." The farce
he feared was the months or even years of pointless turmoil and hardship
that Davis's possible guerrilla scenario might have produced. To survive as
guerrillas they would have had to go to the hills and mountains of Appalachia, the remote places hard for Yankees to penetrate and control, and
then raid as opportunity allowed. But there was no way for them to sustain
themselves. The Confederacy had lost all of its ports. There were no
means for partisans to be supplied with weapons and munitions from
abroad, and the industry within the South was all but destroyed, and all in
Yankee hands in any case. Moreover, as Davis well knew, the remote and
high country was the region of the deepest-seated Unionism and opposition to the Confederate war from the start. Such people were hardly likely
to support partisans in their midst from their own exhausted larders. Inevitably, Confederate soldiers would have been forced to prey on Confederate civilians, as they had repeatedly shown themselves capable of doing
during the war anyhow, just as some citizens had shown themselves willing
to resist. The likely outcome of that could have turned Davis's partisan war
into the ugliest of all things—a civil war within the Confederacy, and at a
point when the Confederacy would no longer have been a geographical
entity but rather simply an idea in the minds of those willing still to resist.
With Yankees in their front and unsympathetic civilians in the rear and
midst, men who had fought honorably for four years would face the
prospect of a double war against the Federals and their own people in a
species of conflict that inevitably would degenerate into pointless barbarities. The lingering hatred generated by such a mode of struggle would
have set back reunification for generations, making reconstruction immea-
surably more painful and traumatic than it was already going to be. No
wonder that when he reached Cuba in his flight, and learned that Kirby

Smith had surrendered, Breckinridge made his last official act, arguably the final act of the Confederate government—a call through the press for all remaining Confederates under arms to "throw themselves on the clemency of the President and ask for pardon."[47]

In the weeks immediately following the collapse, the states began trying to feel their way in what seemed suddenly a vacuum, an interregnum between Confederate and United States allegiances. In North Carolina, Governor Vance issued a proclamation calling on everyone, including returning paroled soldiers, to stay at home, imploring them to band together under their county magistrates to keep the peace and stop the depredations of the deserters and renegades until civil authority could regain control.[48] Florida revoked the call for an election, seeing it now pointless until it knew what the Federals had in store. Instead it sent representatives to Washington to meet with authorities to learn what it intended to do regarding the former Confederate states.[49] In Georgia, Governor Brown intended to cooperate with Florida in the move, while William Yancey's old enemy Ben Hill confessed that he expected leniency from Washington because of "the completeness of our subjugation."[50] In Mississippi, Clark turned over all state records and even the statehouse and executive mansion to the Federal commander taking over, though he did so under protest. These things were not his to hand over, he said, but were entrusted to him by the people of his state. "I will not attempt to resist the Armed forces of the United States in taking possession," he told the Yankee, "but yielding to such power I will deliver the custody as demanded, protesting." The Yankees found him defiantly standing in the capitol on May 22. The last thing he was able to do was to arrange with the Union commander to get rations to the eleven pupils in the state institute for the blind. The children were given Federal rations, and General Peter Osterhaus gave $150 from his pocket for their assistance.[51] West of the Mississippi, Murrah told friends he expected a peaceful reunion, even though there appeared to be chaos all around.[52] Word came from several counties pleading for the organization of some militia or police to restore order. "Everything here is in a terrible state," one citizen complained. Paroled soldiers were wandering everywhere breaking into the remaining Confederate warehouses, and often into private property as well. They threatened to break into the bank holding remaining Confederate funds in San Antonio, and were generally looting and even killing. A man was shot dead in Austin, and another elsewhere. "Will it stop here?" asked the concerned

Texan. "If there is not some immediate organization, the country will certainly be utterly ruined."[53] Meanwhile the press appealed for calm, and for
the people not to lose heart. "Our house is destroyed, but the land remains," said an editor in June. "The people of Texas are not wanting in self-
dependence. They are versatile, full of resources, bold and adaptive. They
do not fold their hands when their house has burned down. They can build
another, and one safer than the one they have lost."[54]

In neighboring Louisiana, Governor Allen left office on June 2 to go
into exile in Mexico, and asked his people to form themselves into squads
to preserve order until civil law could be restored. He had resisted the encroachment of military power from Confederate authorities during his administration, he told them, but there was no way to resist the power of the
Union. Take the oath of allegiance and become good citizens, he advised.
"If possible, forget the past. Look forward to the future."[55] Of course there
were some who could not look forward or forget. No sooner did the surrenders begin than a scattered exodus commenced. Some like Benjamin
fled for their safety. Others like Allen simply could not stomach living under Union rule. Many more, seeing the ruination of their homes and property by the war, decided to start anew elsewhere. Many leaders spoke out
against exile. "Remain where we are I earnestly *implore* every one and go
clear through the furnace of suffering and come out clean & refined,"
General and Virginia governor Henry A. Wise begged fellow Virginians,
and even Lee strongly advised against exile. "Whither shall I flee? To no
country on earth that I know of where there is as much liberty as yet remains to me even in Virginia." Besides, the war had freed them of the aw-
ful responsibility of slavery, but now they had to stand their ground to
make certain that the peace did not make slaves of Southern whites. "That
duty is as stern, strong & imperative as was that of fighting for independence,"[56] said Lee. Nevertheless, in the end, as many as 10,000 former
Confederates would leave the country, to spread out in colonies in Mexico,
Venezuela, Belize, Brazil, and even Canada, while the rest simply wan-
dered. A few wound up in the Egyptian army, others spread across Europe. Most would eventually return when their bitterness abated.
Breckinridge lived as an exile for three years, lobbying through friends for
a general amnesty that would allow all who might have indictments against
them to come home in safety. On Christmas 1868 the amnesty would
come, and he went home to Kentucky. Benjamin, on the other hand,
would never go back. He "did not live in the past," he would tell Littleton

Washington in 1875. Adopting England as his new home, he all but severed connection with Confederates in a new life.[57]

For some even exile would not be enough. At St. Augustine, Florida, the mayor committed suicide, and on June 15 old Edmund Ruffin, the Virginia secessionist who had fired one of the first shots at Fort Sumter in 1861, put the muzzle of his rifle in his mouth and pulled the trigger twice. It misfired the first time, and so calmly he reprimed the gun and tried again. This time it worked. In the end, no one would ever know how many Confederates took their own lives rather than accept defeat. Fearing what Yankee captors might do to her, Jefferson Davis had even given his wife, Varina, a pistol before she left Richmond, showed her how to use it, and advised her to die, even if by her own hand, rather than be outraged by a vengeful enemy.

Happily Mrs. Davis did not have to make such a choice. While her husband was sent to prison to await trial, she began a campaign to raise money for his defense, even as the debate began in the North over whether Confederate leaders ought even to be tried. Certainly what they had done met the definitions of treason from the Union point of view. However, wise heads could ask what they had to gain from trials bound to be controversial and widely publicized, especially if they led to convictions and perhaps even death sentences. Would that not just make martyrs of these men, and make reconciliation that much more difficult? Some wondered at the same time if they could make treason charges stick. The question hinged on so many gray issues. Did the states have the right to secede? The U.S. Constitution certainly did not say that they could not. Was the Confederacy ever a "nation," or was what the states did always an insurrection? If it was a nation, then there could be no question of treason involved. If merely an insurrection, if the states never really left the Union, as Lincoln maintained, then how could the Union require them to apply for "readmission" and make passage of the Thirteenth Amendment a requirement? Were Davis and the rest of the leaders rebels or were they acting on the lawful instructions of their states when they left their seats in Congress in 1860–61, and if their states could order them to do that, then how could they be held to account for following the dictates of the states singly and severally in what the Confederate government did thereafter? Washington never had any designs on the military leaders of the lost cause. Lee was not even arrested, but paroled like any soldier and allowed to go home, and it was soon clear that Lincoln had been wise in hoping that Davis and the civil leaders would simply escape and spare him the trouble of facing the issue of trials. Within six months, Stephens and the other high officials were simply released. Davis would be held for two years. The victors were caught between the desire of so many in the Northern public for vengeance against someone, and the practical and political realities of what was risked if Davis went on trial. It would give him a forum to make legalistic arguments that could be embarrassing, or at least to ask questions that could not be answered unequivocally. If he was convicted what were they to do with him then? No sentence was safe; execution or lengthy imprisonment would outrage the South and even many in the North, while a light or suspended sentence would infuriate all those Yankee voters who had lost sons, brothers, and fathers in the army, as well as send a confused signal to the world. Why would the North spend all that blood and treasure to put down the rebellion and then let the leader off with a wrist slap? Even worse, what if somehow Davis made his case against treason successfully? It seemed unlikely, but there were those in high judicial councils who feared that, solely on the merits of case law, he might just possibly do it. If Davis was found not guilty, what would that say of the whole Confederate effort and the Union's struggle to bring its defeat? The simplest and the safest thing to do was not to bring him to trial at all. In May 1867, when he was brought into a courthouse in Richmond that once had housed the Confederate Treasury and some of Davis's own executive offices, the United States announced that it was not prepared to commence prosecution and simply released him on bail. Late the next year, when he still had not been brought to trial, his attorney petitioned for the charges against him to be dropped and they were. That was all, and the only man disappointed was Davis himself, who wanted his day in court.

There was no doubt that what came after defeat was going to be difficult. How were Confederates to face their uncertain future? Contemplating the question, Governor Watts's son believed that "when we contend, let us contend for all of our rights; the doubtful and the certain; the unimportant and the essential." It was as easy to struggle for the whole of them as for only a part. They must "at the termination of the contest, secure all our wisdom, valor and the fortune of war will permit." It would not be easy, he knew. "It is easier to prepare for war than to obtain union."[58] As early as June 1865, the isolated reprisals by new freedmen against their former masters began. Indeed, armed runaway slaves had been engaging in skirmishes with Confederate cavalry early in April before the collapse.[59] In

Rhett's old district in South Carolina at least three whites were murdered by former slaves in the first months of peace, and there were rumors that an organized raid by blacks against isolated planters was planned for the fall. It was exactly the sort of violence that Wise had feared, and it only highlighted the necessity for reestablishing not only law and order in the South but also some means of maintaining control of the blacks.[60] That was only one of the issues facing the former Confederacy. Their reunion with the North would not be as smooth as Lincoln, Breckinridge, and Campbell had hoped.

The states had to amend their constitutions to abolish slavery, while provisional governors appointed by Washington took over in five of the former states pending their reorganization. Then on November 13 the South Carolina legislature led the way once again by ratifying the Thirteenth Amendment, now made a precondition to readmission. Alabama, North Carolina, and Georgia followed in the next three weeks, but Mississippi stood its ground and voted to reject. It did not matter. Having received the necessary ratification of three-fourths of the states, the amendment became law on December 18, 1865, and it was onetime Confederate states that made it so, however much against their will. They had simply bowed to the new order of things.

Or had they? They had seen their country and their culture ravaged. More than a quarter million of their fathers, sons, and brothers had died, and uncountable others were maimed in body or spirit. Slavery was gone, and four million free blacks were now in their midst, without property or homes, most without jobs, many without even skills other than as day laborers. The potential for social chaos loomed threateningly. What industry the South had had was gone, its transportation was shattered, and its fields needed time before they would be back in production, assuming the planters could reach some accommodation with the freedmen to work. The war had drained more than $3.25 billion in money or goods from the South, leaving virtually everyone from the defunct government to the lowliest farmer deeply in debt to someone. Faced with this staggering ravishment of their entire world, what did they have left? Nothing, those who left for exile might have answered.

Yet other voices were already being heard. Slavery was gone to be sure, but the landowners still had their land. Far too many of their sons were gone now, too, yet the old families that had ruled several of the states were still intact, if badly perforated. Some of them had even managed to come through it all without entirely losing their fortunes. And even in a reunited country, they would still have the voice they once had in national councils, and much the same power to control their own affairs at home so long as they obeyed the laws of the nation. Confederate democracy was gone and would not be seen again—but the oligarchies had survived. In fact, a new and different one had been created during the war, formed not by birth but by distinguished service to the Confederacy in uniform. Many of these onetime generals were also sons of the old elites, but others were new, part of an aristocracy of achievement rather than blood, a leadership that the men in uniform had been accustomed to obeying. If that loyalty and obedience could be transferred from the military to civilian life, what might not be achieved?

The South could still be in the hands of the few, its rulers free to take for granted that the many who had been accustomed to following would still do so. That done, they might just be able to salvage more from the death of the Confederacy than their honor. Perhaps those who knew their Aristotle could find hope that even though the oligarchs might have lost some of their powers, still there could be more left to them than just performing pointless sacrifices before their household gods. The war had created a new pantheon for the South, populated by gods with names like Lee and Jackson. Perhaps in their name and in that of the lost cause, they could preserve the Old South in whatever new South was to come. Within just months of the end of the war, the old leadership and the old attitudes began to reemerge. One could be beaten without having to admit defeat, and nothing was truly lost until its believers gave up.[61] With a wonderful irony, for all that old Rhett had been beaten and rejected at every turn by his own Confederacy, his dark shade would loom again after Appomattox. Futile as it might have been, when Mississippi rejected the Thirteenth Amendment, it was a statement that the resistance had begun anew.

Abbreviations Used
in the Source Citations

ADAH   Alabama Department of Archives and History, Montgomery

CAH,UT   Center for American History, University of Texas, Austin

FHS   Florida Historical Society, St. Augustine

FSA   Florida State Archives, Tallahassee

GDAH   Georgia Department of Archives and History, Atlanta

Journal   United States Congress, *Journal of the Congress of the Confederate States of America, 1861–1865.* 7 volumes. Washington, DC

LC   Library of Congress, Washington, DC

LSU   Louisiana State University, Baton Rouge

MDAH   Mississippi Department of Archives and History, Jackson

NA   National Archives, Washington, DC

NCDAH   North Carolina Department of Archives and History, Raleigh

OR   United States War Department, *War of the Rebellion: Official Records of the Union and Confederate Armies.* 128 volumes. Washington, DC, 1880–1901

Rowland   Dunbar Rowland, ed., *Jefferson Davis, Constitutionalist: His Letters, Papers and Speeches.* 10 volumes. Jackson, MS, 1923.

SCDAH   South Carolina Department of Archives and History, Columbia

SCHS   South Carolina Historical Society, Charleston

SCL,USC   South Caroliniana Library, University of South Carolina, Columbia

SHC,UNC   Southern Historical Collection, University of North Carolina, Chapel Hill

TSL   Texas State Library, Austin

Notes

The Foretelling

1. William Jahnsenykes [Jenks], *Memoir of the Northern Kingdom, Written, A.D. 1872* (Boston, 1808), pp. v–47 passim.

Chapter One

1. Historian Richard McMurry argues precisely this, and only partly in jest.
2. Aristotle, *Politics,* Book II, Chapter 14, 1285a–1285b.
3. See Gordon S. Wood's review "Impartiality in America," *New Republic,* December 6, 1999, pp. 52–56.
4. For more on this see Joyce Appleby's *Inheriting the Revolution: The First Generation of Americans* (New York, 2000).
5. An excellent and succinct discussion of nationhood is Ian Baruma, "National Success," *Prospect* 36 (December 1998), pp. 36–40.
6. Benjamin H. Hill speech, June 30, 1860, Scrapbook F, George H.W. Petrie Papers, Auburn University, Auburn, AL.
7. Yancey to Wigfall, April 16, 1858, Louis T. Wigfall Papers, LC.
8. Crawford to Alexander H. Stephens, April 8, 1861, Alexander H. Stephens Papers, LC.
9. Stephens to James Madison Spullock, February 8, 1860, James Madison Spullock Collection, GDAH.
10. James E. Saunders to his wife, June 5, 1860, James E. Saunders Papers, Confederate States of America Records, CAH,UT.
11. Cleveland to Joseph Brown, October 22, 1860, Henry Cleveland File, Record Group 4-2-46, GDAH.
12. E. J. Arthur to Langdon Cheves, October 8, 1860, Langdon Cheves Papers, SCHS.

13. Col. C. S. Armee [Charles E.L. Stuart], "Rummaging Through Rebeldom," New York *Citizen,* April 6, 1867.
14. Littleton B. Washington Diary, July 30, 1863, copy in possession of Douglas L. Gibboney, Carlisle, PA.
15. Montgomery *Weekly Mail,* November 16, 20, 1861.
16. William L. Yancey to N. J. Scott, November 15, 1860, broadside in Scrapbook F, Petrie Papers, Auburn.
17. Pettus to L.Q.C. Lamar, November 12, 1860, Confederate States of America Records, CAH,UT.
18. Broadside, October 27, 1860, Holzman-Caren Associates Historical Collectibles Auction Catalog, April 28, 1996 (Poughkeepsie, NY), p. 34, item #208.
19. Thomas Moore draft message, n.d., Thomas O. Moore Papers, LSU.
20. Horatio Averill to Brown, December 19, 1860, Joseph Brown Papers, GDAH.
21. Stuart, "Rummaging," New York *Citizen,* April 6, 1867.
22. Ibid.
23. Littleton Washington Diary, July 30, 1863, Gibboney; Milledge L. Bonham to William Gist, December 3, 1860, Milledge L. Bonham Papers, SCL,USC.
24. F. L. Villepigue to William Winberly, December 15, 1860, Correspondence of the Secretary of State, 1845–1865, University of Florida, Gainesville.
25. *Address of Hon. W. L. Harris, Commissioner from the State of Mississippi, Delivered before the General Assembly of the State of Georgia, on Monday, Dec. 17th, 1860* (Milledgeville, GA, 1860), pp. 4–5.
26. Robert S. Tharin, *Arbitrary Arrests in the South; or, Scenes from the Experience of an Alabama Unionist* (New York, 1863), p. 62.
27. Louisa McCord to Cheves, December 4, 1860, Cheves Papers, SCHS.
28. Charleston *Daily Courier,* October 27, 1863.
29. A. Toomer Porter, *Led On! Step by Step* (1898; reprint, New York, 1967), p. 117*n.*
30. T. H. Spann to Annie Spann, January 27, 1861, T. H. Spann Papers, in possession of Lawrence Berry, Osprey, FL.
31. Charles E. Cauthen, *South Carolina Goes to War* (Chapel Hill, NC, 1950), pp. 84–85.
32. Drafts of ordinances, n.d., December 26, 31, 1860, Cheves Papers, SCHS.
33. Clipping in Charlotte Petrie Scrapbook B, Petrie Papers, Auburn.
34. Commission of John McQueen, January 1, 1861, Records of the Governors, Sam Houston, Record Group 301, TSL.
35. Littleton Washington Diary, July 30, 1863, Gibboney.
36. James Dowdell to William F. Samford, January 11, 1861, Petrie Papers, Auburn.
37. T. H. Spann to Annie Spann, January 27, 1861, T. H. Spann Papers, Berry.

CHAPTER TWO

1. Samuel Haycroft Journal, January 3, 1861, The Filson Club, Louisville, KY.
2. Col. C. S. Armee [Charles E.L. Stuart], "Rummaging Through Rebeldom," New York *Citizen,* April 6, 1867.
3. Clement C. Clay to Jefferson Davis, October 30, 1875, in Dunbar Rowland, ed., *Jefferson Davis, Constitutionalist: His Letters, Papers and Speeches* (Jackson, MS, 1923), 7:460–61.

4. James Dowdell to William F. Samford, January 11, 1861, copy, George H.W. Petrie Papers, Auburn University, Auburn, AL.

5. Robert E. Rodes to Francis H. Smith, January 13, 1861, Robert E. Rodes File, Alumni Archives, Virginia Military Institute, Lexington.

6. Ibid.

7. Anonymous to John Pettus, December 26, 1860, Volume 36, Record Group 27, MDAH.

8. G. Hall to Pettus, December 25, 1860, ibid.

9. Carey W. Stiles to Joseph Brown, December 31, 1860, Joseph Brown Papers, GDAH.

10. A. R. Lawton to Cheves, January 2, 1861, Langdon Cheves Papers, SCHS.

11. Commissioner of Roads to Cheves, January 17, 1861, J. R. Cheves to Cheves, January 18, 1861, Allen J. Izard to Cheves, January 18, 1861, ibid.

12. Clipping in Charlotte Petrie Scrapbook B, Petrie Papers, Auburn.

13. Charles Daniell to Cheves, January 30, 1861, Cheves Papers, SCHS.

14. Mallory to Angela Mallory, June 12, 1865, Stephen Mallory Papers, University of Florida, Gainesville.

15. Whitney to Pettus, December 21, 1860, Davis to Whitney, December 21, 1860, W. Maynadier to Pettus, December 26, 1860, Volume 36, Record Group 27, MDAH.

16. H. Gourdin to Cheves, January 12, 1861, Cheves Papers, SCHS.

17. Stuart, "Rummaging," New York Citizen, April 6, 1867. Stuart's account is certainly embellished in some degree, at least in language if not content, and he has a tendency to aggrandize himself in places. He is also writing as a man who felt himself ignored by Davis in parceling out Confederate offices, and thus has to be considered less than disinterested when remarking on Davis.

18. William M. Brooks to Pettus, January 11, 1861, John McGehee to Pettus, January 21, 1861, Volume 36, Record Group 27, MDAH; George Bramford to Sam Houston, January 22, 1861, Thomas O. Moore to Houston, January 28, 1861, John McQueen to O. M. Roberts, January 31, 1861, Record Group 301, TSL.

19. D. H. Hamilton to William Porcher Miles, January 23, 1860, William Porcher Miles Papers, SHC,UNC.

20. Spann to Annie Spann, January 27, 1861, T. H. Spann Papers, in possession of Lawrence Berry, Osprey, FL.

21. "Superiority of Southern Races," DeBow's Review 31 (October–November 1861), pp. 376–79.

22. "The Future of the Confederation," DeBow's Review 31 (July 1861), pp. 35–40.

23. Robert Bunch to John Russell, December 15, 1860, "Despatch from the British Consul at Charleston to Lord John Russell, 1860," American Historical Review 18 (July 1913), pp. 783–87.

24. Robert Barnwell Rhett, "Conversation occurring during the war," n.d. [1861–62], Robert Barnwell Rhett Papers, SHC,UNC. This is a first draft of another document in this collection written after 1865 titled "Conversation concerning the late war in the United States." In a few instances, material from this later draft has been included in the text.

25. One of the better studies of secession within a state is Walter L. Buenger, Secession and the Union in Texas (Austin, 1984).

26. Robert Gourdin to Cheves, February 3, 1861, Cheves Papers, SCHS.

27. The fullest account of the Montgomery convention is William C. Davis, "A Govern-

ment of Our Own": The Making of the Confederacy (New York, 1994). Except where otherwise cited, the account that follows is drawn primarily from this source.

28. Charleston *Mercury,* February 5, 6, 1861.
29. Robert W. Barnwell to James L. Orr, February 9, 1861, Orr-Patterson Papers, SHC,UNC.
30. Charleston *Mercury,* February 8, 1861.
31. Ibid., February 9, 1861.
32. William C. Davis, ed., *A Fire-Eater Remembers: The Confederate Memoir of Robert Barnwell Rhett* (Columbia, SC, 2000), pp. 22, 78.
33. Rhett to Robert Barnwell Rhett, Jr., n.d. [February 3, 1861], Rhett Papers, SCL,USC. Though undated, the content and context of the letter clearly establish that it was written after the discussions of February 3, and to accompany the February 3 report published in the February 5 *Mercury.*
34. Perhaps the best of several general histories of the Confederacy is Emory M. Thomas, *The Confederate Nation, 1861–1865* (New York, 1979). It is especially good on social issues, but its coverage of the origins of the government is now dated.

CHAPTER THREE

1. Betsy Fleet and John D. P. Fuller, eds., *Green Mount: A Virginia Plantation Family During the Civil War* (Lexington, KY, 1962), p. 48.
2. Beth Gilbert Crabtree and James W. Patton, eds., *"Journal of a Secesh Lady": The Diary of Catherine Ann Devereux Edmondston, 1860–1866* (Raleigh, NC, 1979), p. 35.
3. William Gilmore Simms to James Lawson, March 17, 1861, in Mary C. Oliphant, Alfred Taylor Odell, and T. C. Duncan Eaves, eds., *The Letters of William Gilmore Simms* (Columbia, SC, 1955), 4:352.
4. Howell Cobb to his wife, February 3, 1861, in Ulrich B. Phillips, ed., *The Correspondence of Robert Toombs, Alexander H. Stephens, and Howell Cobb* (Washington, 1913), p. 537; Alexander H. Stephens to Linton Stephens, February 5, 1861, Alexander H. Stephens Papers, Manhattanville College of the Sacred Heart, Purchase, NY.
5. Stephens to Linton Stephens, February 5, 1861, Stephens Papers, Manhattanville.
6. Charleston *Mercury,* February 9, 1861.
7. Thomas Cobb to Marion Cobb, February 3, 1861, Thomas R.R. Cobb Letters, University of Georgia, Athens.
8. Ibid., February 4, 1861.
9. Alexander H. Stephens, *A Constitutional View of the Late War Between the States* (Philadelphia, 1868, 1870), 2:326–27, 710–12.
10. Montgomery *Weekly Advertiser,* February 13, 1861; United States Congress, *Journal of the Congress of the Confederate States of America* (Washington, 1904), 1:19. Hereinafter cited as *Journal.*
11. *Journal,* 1:19–22.
12. Robert H. Smith, *An Address to the Citizens of Alabama, on the Constitution of the Confederate States of America* (Mobile, 1861), p. 5.
13. Lawrence Keitt to James H. Hammond, February 13, 1861, James H. Hammond Papers, LC.
14. Charleston *Mercury,* February 8, 1861. Rhett did not sign this and other open letters

and editorials that were noted simply as coming from a Montgomery correspondent, and when later accused of being their author, he had no hesitation in lying and protesting that he was not. However, his authorship was commonly known in Montgomery, especially among the South Carolina delegation. Memminger to Joseph Campbell, February 11, 1861, Joseph Campbell Papers, SCHS, says so explicitly when he complains that "we are annoyed by the chief of our Delegation being the correspondent of the Mercury, and undertaking through that paper to lecture the rest and the Congress."

15. Clipping from unidentified newspaper, March 1861, J.F.H. Claiborne Papers, SHC,UNC.
16. Barnwell to Orr, February 9, 1861, Orr-Patterson Family Papers, SHC,UNC.
17. *Journal,* 1:25–30.
18. New York *Citizen,* April 27, 1861.
19. Rome, GA, *Tri-Weekly Courier,* August 22, 1862.
20. New York *Citizen,* April 20, 1867.
21. Stephens to Linton Stephens, February 23, 1861, Stephens Papers, Manhattanville. The dating of this episode on the evening of February 6, while inferential, is the only date that fits into the context of events of February 5–8.
22. Ibid.
23. Thomas Cobb to Marion Cobb, February 5, 1861, Thomas R.R. Cobb Letters, University of Georgia, Athens; William W. Boyce to R.M.T. Hunter, February 5, 1861, R.M.T. Hunter Papers, Alderman Library, University of Virginia, Charlottesville.
24. Rhett claimed in the 1870s that the Florida *delegation* expressed such a view, though only Owens and Anderson were present, and nothing attests to Anderson's views, though he certainly was a Davis supporter in later years. Rhett also claimed that one of the Floridians—by inference Owens—specifically stated a desire that Rhett be nominated. This was all part of a case Rhett made that if only his own delegation had put his name forward, he might have been elected, or at least the election of Davis would have been stopped. This may be true, but as in any issue involving Rhett's ambitions, prejudices, or disappointments, it must be considered possible that he was simply lying, as he did so often. William C. Davis, ed., *A Fire-Eater Remembers: The Confederate Memoir of Robert Barnwell Rhett* (Columbia, SC, 2000), p. 116n.
25. A more extended discussion, with sources, of the election process will be found in William C. Davis, *"A Government of Our Own": The Making of the Confederacy,* (New York, 1994), p. 95ff.
26. Charleston *Mercury,* February 6, 9, 1861.
27. C. Vann Woodward, ed., *Mary Chesnut's Civil War* (New Haven, CT, 1981), p. 786.
28. Atlanta *Daily Constitution,* January 16, 1880; Richard M. Johnston and William Brown, *Life of Alexander H. Stephens* (Philadelphia, 1878), p. 390; Mobile *Daily Advertiser,* February 9, 10, 1861.
29. See Davis, *"Government,"* pp. 444–45n, for considerable evidence that Keitt did make substantially this approach to Stephens.
30. Cobb to Marion Cobb, February 8, 1861, Cobb Letters, Georgia.
31. Davis, ed., *Fire-Eater Remembers,* pp. 116–17n. This discussion of the dynamics and machinations in the election is drawn from Davis, *"Government,"* pp. 111–13, which is fully sourced and should be consulted for complete details on what is presented here only in summary.
32. Atlanta *Daily Constitution,* December 28, 1879; Memphis *Daily Appeal,* June 21,

1870; John Pettus to Jefferson Davis, February 7, 1861, in Lynda Lasswell Crist and Mary Seaton Dix, eds., *The Papers of Jefferson Davis* (Baton Rouge, 1992), 7:36.

33. For a full discussion of the sources and interpretations that undergird this reconstruction of these events, see Davis, *"Government,"* pp. 445–46n. The sources are admittedly few and open to much interpretation, but this scenario seems to be the only one that they fit.

34. Philadelphia *Weekly Times,* July 12, 1879.

35. Cobb to Marion Cobb, February 11, 1861, Cobb Letters, Georgia; Johnston and Browne, *Stephens,* p. 390. See also Davis, *"Government,"* pp. 116–18, 449–50n.

36. *Journal,* 1:40–41.

37. Howell Cobb to Joseph Brown, February 9, 1861, Record Group 1-1-5, GDAH.

38. Lawrence Keitt to David Jamison, February 9, 1861, David Jamison Papers, Washington and Lee University, Lexington, VA.

39. Curry to W. W. Anderson, February 20, 1861, Atlanta *Constitution,* March 1884 clipping in Scrapbook F, George H.W. Petrie Papers, Auburn University, Auburn, AL.

40. James T. Harrison to his wife, February 9, 1861, Charles C. Jones, Jr., Autograph Letters and Portraits of the Signers of the Constitution of the Confederate States, Duke University, Durham, NC.

41. Rhett to Robert Barnwell Rhett, Jr., February 9, 1861, in possession of Shinaan Krakowsky, Encino, CA.

42. Memminger to Campbell, February 11, 1861, Joseph Campbell Papers, SCHS.

43. Keitt to Susan Keitt, February 19, 1861, Lawrence Keitt Papers, Duke.

44. *Journal,* 1:49.

45. Hammond to M.C.M. Hammond, March 1, 1861, Hammond Papers, LC.

46. Augusta Bellinger Cheney, "The Inauguration of Jefferson Davis by an Eye Witness," ADAH.

47. *Journal,* 1:64–66.

48. Stephens to James P. Hambleton, February 22, 1861, James P. Hambleton Papers, Emory University, Atlanta; Stephens to Linton Stephens, February 15, 1861, Stephens Papers, Manhattanville.

49. Davis, *"Government of Our Own,"* p. 143.

50. Rhett to Robert Barnwell Rhett, Jr., February 11, 1861, Robert Barnwell Rhett Papers, SCL,USC; Rhett to Elise Rhett, February 11, 1861, quoted in Laura A. White, *Robert Barnwell Rhett: Father of Secession* (New York, 1931), p. 194n.

51. Davis, ed., *Fire-Eater Remembers,* p. v.

52. Washington *Evening Star,* March 14, 1861.

53. Varina Davis, *Jefferson Davis, Ex-President of the Confederate States of America: A Memoir* (New York, 1890), 2:63–64.

54. John Witherspoon DuBose, *The Life and Times of William Lowndes Yancey* (Birmingham, AL, 1892), p. 588.

55. Barnwell to his wife, February 18, 1861, Jones, Autograph Letters, Duke; Rhett to Robert Barnwell Rhett, Jr., February 25, 1861, in possession of Shinaan Krakowsky.

56. Cobb to Marion Cobb, February 20, 1861, Cobb Letters, Georgia; Charleston *Mercury,* March 9, 1861.

57. Rhett to Robert Barnwell Rhett, Jr., February 25, 1861, in possession of Shinaan Krakowsky.

58. Woodward, ed., *Mary Chesnut,* p. 142.

59. William C. Davis, *Jefferson Davis, The Man and His Hour* (New York, 1991), p. 245.

60. Johnston and Browne, *Stephens,* pp. 62–63.
61. Cobb to Marion Cobb, February 26, 1861, Cobb Letters, Georgia.
62. H.L. Clay to Clement C. Clay, February 11, 1861, Clement C. Clay Papers, Duke.
63. William C. Harris, *Leroy Pope Walker, Confederate Secretary of War* (Tuscaloosa, AL, 1962), pp. 20–21.
64. DuBose, *Yancey,* p. 588.
65. Leroy Pope Walker to Michael L. Woods, January 16, 1906, Michael L. Woods Papers, ADAH.
66. Toombs to Davis, February 20, 1861, Jones, Autograph Letters, Duke; Toombs to Robert Barnwell Rhett, Jr., December 20, 1882, Rhett Papers, SCL,USC.
67. *Journal,* I, pp. 105–106.
68. Report of the Secretary of State, August 31, 1861, Record Group 301, TSL.
69. J. G. McAlpine to Sam Houston, February 27, 1861, Record Group 301, TSL.
70. John H. Reagan to O. M. Roberts, March 2, 1861, John H. Reagan Papers, Benjamin H. Good Collection, TSL.
71. Cobb to Marion Cobb, February 21, 1861, Cobb Letters, Georgia; United States War Department, *War of the Rebellion: Official Records of the Union and Confederate Armies* (Washington, 1880–1901), Series II, Volume 2, p. 613 (hereafter *OR,* II, 2:613, etc.); Montgomery *Daily Post,* March 12, 1861; Columbus, GA, *Daily Columbus Enquirer,* February 25, 1861.

CHAPTER FOUR

1. P. Norton to Thomas O. Moore, February 23, 1861, Thomas O. Moore Papers, LSU.
2. J.L.M. Curry to W. W. Anderson, February 20, 1861, George H.W. Petrie Papers, Auburn University, Auburn, AL.
3. Thomas M. Alston to Joseph Brown, February 24, 1861, Governors' Papers, Joseph Brown, GDAH.
4. John Witherspoon DuBose, *The Life and Times of William Lowndes Yancey* (Birmingham, AL, 1892), pp. 588–90.
5. Ibid., p. 599; William C. Davis, ed., *A Fire-Eater Remembers: The Confederate Memoir of Robert Barnwell Rhett* (Columbia, SC, 2000), p. 37.
6. Stephens to Linton Stephens, February 24, 15, 1861, Alexander H. Stephens Papers, Manhattanville College of the Sacred Heart, Purchase, NY.
7. Yancey to Pickens, February 27, 1861, William L. Yancey Papers, ADAH.
8. *OR,* 1:135.
9. William C. Davis, *"A Government of Our Own: The Making of the Confederate Government"* (New York, 1994), pp. 212–14.
10. Davis, ed., *Fire-Eater Remembers,* pp. 44–46.
11. W.H.T. Walker to Brown, March 10, 1861, William Palmer Collection, Western Reserve Historical Society, Cleveland, OH.
12. C. Vann Woodward and Elizabeth Muhlenfeld, eds., *The Private Mary Chesnut* (New York, 1984), p. 49.
13. Davis, ed., *Fire-Eater Remembers,* p. 42.
14. Charleston *Mercury,* December 20, 1860.
15. Ibid., February 16, 1861.

16. Rhett to Robert Barnwell Rhett, Jr., February 11, 12, 1861, Robert Barnwell Rhett Papers, SCL,USC.

17. Rhett to T. Stuart Rhett, April 15, 1867, Robert Barnwell Rhett Papers, SCHS; Robert Barnwell Rhett, Memoir, Robert Barnwell Rhett, "Political Parties," Aiken Rhett Collection, Charleston Museum, Charleston, SC.

18. Constitution & amendments proposed for Confederate States, Rhett Papers, SCHS.

19. Charleston *Mercury*, February 20, 1861.

20. *Journal*, 1:851–58.

21. Fuller background on the committee deliberations will be found in Davis, *"Government of Our Own,"* pp. 225–29.

22. Rhett to Robert Barnwell Rhett, Jr., February 20, 1861, Rhett Papers, SCL,USC; Rhett to Robert Barnwell Rhett, Jr., February 25, 1861, in possession of Shinaan Krakowsky, Encino, CA.

23. Montgomery *Weekly Advertiser*, February 27, 1861; Thomas Cobb to Marion Cobb, February 25, 1861, Thomas R.R. Cobb Letters, University of Georgia, Athens.

24. *Journal*, 1:87, 92; Montgomery *Weekly Advertiser*, February 26, 1861.

25. There is some uncertainty about the precise dates of death of Ann "Nannie" Rhett and Catherine. Stephen Barnwell, *An American Family* (Marquette, IL, 1969), p. 172, says that both died on the same day, March 10, 1861. This cannot be correct, for Rhett wrote his first letter referring to Ann's death on February 20, which should place it within no more than a day or two previously, and would obviously be the occasion of his wife coming to be with him. None of his surviving correspondence makes reference to the death of Catherine, however. Genealogy of the Rhett Family, Rhett Genealogy Notes, SCHS, clearly compiled years later by someone other than Rhett, says only that Catherine died in February–March. However, the Rhett-Dent Family marriage notes, undated, in the Rhett Papers, SCHS, state that she died on February 27, and in the absence of better authority, this must be taken to be correct.

26. Woodward and Muhlenfeld, eds., *Private Mary Chesnut*, p. 5.

27. *Journal*, 1:95.

28. Charleston *Mercury*, March 6, 1861.

29. Cobb to Marion Cobb, February 28, March 2, 1861, Cobb Letters, Georgia.

30. Stephens to Linton Stephens, March 1, 1861, Stephens Papers, Manhattanville.

31. Ibid., March 4, 1861.

32. Cobb to Marion Cobb, March 5, 1861, Cobb Letters, Georgia.

33. J.L.M. Curry, "Political Quicksands," 1863, Curry Family Papers, ADAH.

34. *Journal*, 1:876–78.

35. Ibid., pp. 886–88; Stephens to Linton Stephens, March 8, 1861, Stephens Papers, Manhattanville. Marshall L. DeRosa, *The Confederate Constitution of 1861* (Columbia, MO, 1991), passim, argues that the Permanent Constitution, on this issue as on others, was not chiefly intended to preserve the old slave order, but rather was designed to halt the spread of centralization of power in the federal government. While preservation of sovereignty to the states was certainly a driving force, the presence of one clause after another aimed at preserving slavery and the control of slave interests as a driving force over the government renders such an argument unconvincing.

36. Curry, "Political Quicksands," 1863, Curry Family Papers, ADAH.

37. Stephens to Linton Stephens, March 10, 1861, Stephens Papers, Manhattanville.

38. Editorial, *DeBow's Review* 7 (January–February 1862), p. 163.

39. Drew Gilpin Faust, *The Creation of Confederate Nationalism* (Baton Rouge, 1988), pp. 14–15, passim, argues that the attempt to forge a new Confederate identity ironically contributed materially to the failure of the Confederate experiment.

40. J.L.M. Curry, *Civil History of the Government of the Confederate States, With Some Personal Reminiscences* (Richmond, 1901), p. 49.

41. *Journal,* 1:896.

42. "The Constitution of the Confederate States," *DeBow's Review* 31 (July 1861), pp. 13–17.

43. "Our Position and that of Our Enemies," ibid., pp. 21–35 passim.

44. Charleston *Mercury,* March 18, 1861; "Speech of A. H. Stephens," in Frank Moore, ed., *The Rebellion Record* (New York, 1861), 1, Documents: 45.

45. Columbia *Daily South Carolinian,* March 16, 1861.

46. Hammond to Ashmore, April 23, 1861, John Henry Hammond Papers, LC.

47. Ordinance, April 27, 1861, Record Group 1000, 1457, FSA.

48. Spann to Annie Spann, March 4, 1861, in possession of Lawrence Berry, Osprey, FL.

49. Jefferson Davis, *Rise and Fall of the Confederate Government* (New York, 1881), 1:292.

50. New York *Citizen,* April 13, 1867.

51. Littleton Washington Diary, July 30, 1863, copy in possession of Douglas L. Gibboney, Carlisle, PA.

52. John Echols to Francis H. Smith, February 28, 1861, John Echols File, Alumni Files, Virginia Military Institute, Lexington.

53. "The Times and the War," *DeBow's Review* 31 (July 1861), p. 1.

54. Moore, ed., *Rebellion Record,* 1, supplement: 149–50.

55. New York *Citizen,* April 6, 1867.

56. William W. Boyce to R.M.T. Hunter, February 5, 1861, R.M.T. Hunter Papers, University of Virginia, Charlottesville.

57. "Reflections on the Conduct of the War," *DeBow's Review* 31 (October–November 1861), p. 433.

58. Howell Cobb to his wife, May 3, 1861, Howell Cobb Papers, University of Georgia, Athens.

59. Thomas Cobb to Marion Cobb, May 4, 1861, Thomas Cobb Letters, Georgia.

60. Howell Cobb to Pettus, March 30, 1861, Volume 36, Record Group 27, MDAH.

61. Memminger to Alonzo B. Noyes, April 13, 26, 1861, Milton Perry to Noyes, March 25, 1861, Alonzo B. Noyes Collection, University of Florida, Gainesville.

62. C. H. Andrews to Brown, April 18, 1861, Joseph Brown Papers, GDAH.

63. Magrath to Pickens, April 20, 1861, Francis W. Pickens Papers, Duke University, Durham, NC.

64. *OR,* I, 2:783, 792, 805, I, 51, part 2:65–66; John Letcher to Josiah Gorgas, May 15, 1861, Executive Papers, Miscellaneous Letters and Papers, Governor John Letcher, Virginia State Library, Richmond.

65. Thomas Cobb to Marion Cobb, May 16, 1861, Thomas Cobb Letters, Howell Cobb to his wife, May 18, 1861, Howell Cobb Papers, Georgia.

66. Brown to the editor of the Brunswick, GA, *Advocate,* May 11, 1861, Brown Papers, GDAH.

67. Toombs to Stephens, July 5, 1861, Robert A. Toombs Papers, Duke.

68. Woodward and Muhlenfeld, eds., *Private Mary Chesnut,* p. 65.

69. Robert Smith to Robert Jemison, Jr., December 1, 1861, Robert Jemison, Jr., Papers, University of Alabama, Tuscaloosa.

70. Alexander De Clouet to Charles Gayarré, February 20, 1861, Charles Colcock Jones, Jr., Autograph Album, Duke.

71. Thomas Cobb to Marion Cobb, April 29, 1861, Thomas Cobb Letters, Georgia.

72. J.C.S. Blackburn to Brown, May 20, 1861, Brown Papers, GDAH.

73. Littleton Washington Diary, July 30, 1863, Gibboney.

74. *Journal,* 1:254–55.

75. H. McLeod to Edward Clark, May 29, 1861, Records of the Governors, Edward Clark, Record Group 301, TSL.

76. Stephens to Linton Stephens, May 22, 1861, Stephens Papers, Manhattanville.

77. Stephens to Henry Hilliard, September 12, 1864, Henry Hilliard Papers, University of Alabama.

78. Richard M. Johnston, *Autobiography of Col. Richard Malcolm Johnston* (Washington, 1900), p. 158.

79. Littleton Washington Diary, July 30, 1863, Gibboney.

CHAPTER FIVE

1. Samuel A. Cartwright, "Report of the Diseases and Physical Peculiarities of the Negro Race," *New Orleans Medical and Surgical Journal* (May 1851), pp. 691–715.

2. Declaration of Causes, January 1861, Record Group 577, FSA.

3. "The Right to Enslave," *DeBow's Review* 30 (May–June 1861), pp. 548–50.

4. New York *Citizen,* April 13, 1867.

5. James Lyons to Clark, January 17, 1865, Volume 57, Record Group 27, MDAH.

6. Robert Collins, "Essay on the Management of Slaves," *DeBow's Review* 32 (January–February 1862), pp. 154–57.

7. "The Duties of an Overseer," n.d. [ca. 1864], Bohemian Brigade Bookshop catalog, November 1998, p. 44, item 184-8216.

8. Montgomery *Weekly Mail,* December 14, 1860, January 4, 11, 1861.

9. Montgomery *Weekly Advertiser,* April 3, 1861; John W.A. Sanford, *The Code of the City of Montgomery* (Montgomery, AL, 1861), pp. 27, 29, 85–88; Montgomery City Council Minutes, February 25, 1861, ADAH.

10. Citizens of Aberdeen to Pettus, April 30, 1861, Volume 36, Record Group 27, MDAH.

11. B. A. Terry to Pettus, ibid.

12. Petition, April 29, 1861, Record Group 577, FSA.

13. P. Thweatt to Brown, July 11, 1861, Joseph Brown Papers, GDAH.

14. Montgomery *Weekly Confederation,* May 10, 1861.

15. Montgomery *Daily Post,* May 1, 1861.

16. Nashville *Union & American,* April 26, 1861; Frank Moore, ed., *The Rebellion Record* (New York, 1861), 1:94; New York *Herald,* February 23, 1861.

17. D.H.B. Troop to Brown, November 25, 1861, Brown Papers, GDAH; Pickens to General Walker, November 15, 1861, Francis W. Pickens Papers, SCDAH.

18. Thomas Drayton to Langdon Cheves, February 21, 1862, Cheves to Dear Sir, February 17, 1862, Langdon Cheves Papers, SCHS.

19. Cheves to C. J. Haskell, February 17, 1862, William P. Carmichael to Cheves, February 26, 1862, Haskell to Cheves, February 22, 28, March 24, June 16, 1862, Cheves Papers, SCHS. Florida, for instance, saw an act passed by its senate to remove slaves (Edward Judah to Milton, November 28, 1862, Record Group 577, FSA).

20. Joseph Tolbert to Pettus, September 2, 1861, Volume 46, Record Group 27, MDAH.

21. E. W. Beasley to Francis Lubbock, July 29, 1863, Papers of the Governors, Francis Lubbock, Record Group 301, TSL.

22. John Milton to J. H. Trapier, February 22, 1862, John Milton Letterbook, University of Florida, Gainesville.

23. Sarah Stowers to Pettus, June 2, 1861, Volume 49, Record Group 27, MDAH.

24. C. L. Buck to Pettus, June 7, 1862, ibid.

25. W. G. Rice to Pickens, September 9, 1861, Pickens Papers, SCDAH.

26. Isaac Applewhite to Pettus, June 8, 1862, Volume 49, Record Group 27, MDAH.

27. Robert H. Thach to Elizabeth L. Thach, July 27, 1863, Charles Coleman Thach Collection, Auburn University, Auburn, AL.

28. A. R. Farrar to Pettus, July 17, 1862, Volume 49, Record Group 27, MDAH.

29. A. T. Holliday to Brown, July 22, 1863, Brown Papers, GDAH.

30. Citizens of Issaquena County to Pettus, n.d., Volume 52, Record Group 27, MDAH.

31. Milton to Davis, May 23, 1863, John Milton Letters, Duke University, Durham, NC.

32. Ordinance, April 27, 1861, Record Group 1000, 1457, FSA.

33. See, especially, Judith Kelleher Schafer, *Slavery, the Civil Law, and the Supreme Court of Louisiana* (Baton Rouge, 1998).

34. Sam Rogers to Zebulon Vance, January 2, 1864, Zebulon Vance Papers, NCDAH.

35. Francis Parker to Magrath, December 24, 1864, Andrew G. Magrath Papers, SCDAH.

36. W. A. Rogers to Magrath, December 30, 1864, Joseph Cunningham to Magrath, January 3, 1865, ibid.

37. Brown to Cheves, March 2, 1861, John G. Barnard to Cheves, July 1861, Cheves Papers, SCHS.

38. James Jones to Pickens, May 2, 1861, Pickens Papers, SCDAH.

39. Houston *Weekly Telegraph*, September 3, 1863.

40. James McCutcheon to Pettus, February 21, 1863, Volume 51, Record Group 27, MDAH.

41. Milton to George W. Randolph, August 5, 1862, Milton Letterbook, University of Florida, Gainesville.

42. Milton to Davis, August 20, 1862, ibid.

43. Rufinia Lawrence to Pettus, February 17, 1863, Jane Pattison to Pettus, February 23, 1863, Volume 51, Record Group 27, MDAH.

44. Thomas Hiney to Pettus, June 4, 1863, Volume 52, ibid.

45. John Ransdell to Moore, May 24, 31, 1863, Thomas O. Moore Papers, LSU.

46. Sarah Elliott to Vance, January 6, 1864, M. L. Wiggins to Vance, January 1, 1865, Vance Papers, NCDAH.

47. James Seddon to Pettus, July 18, 1863, Volume 52, Record Group 27, MDAH.

48. Augustus Montgomery to Dear General, May 2, 1863, Volume 51, ibid.

49. Ransdell to Moore, June 3, 1863, Moore Papers, LSU; Richard Winter to Pettus, September 24, 1863, Volume 52, Record Group 27, MDAH.

50. H. Cassedy to Clark, September 12, 1864, Volume 57, ibid.

51. Circular, June 23, 1864, Papers of the Governors, Pendleton Murrah, Record Group 301, TSL.

52. Annual Message, January 18, 1864, Moore Papers, LSU.
53. Milton to Davis, November 1864, Milton Papers, Duke.
54. Robert Hudson to Clark, October 6, 1864, March 1865, Sarah Garrett to Clark, October 1864, G. H. Chandler to Clark, January 16, 1865, Volume 57, Record Group 27, MDAH.
55. Petition, March 1863, Bohemian Brigade Bookshop Catalog, July 1999 (Knoxville), p. 44, item 204-9515doc.
56. Ransdell to Moore, May 24, June 3, 1863, Moore Papers, LSU.
57. Petition, March 28, 1865, Magrath Papers, SCDAH.
58. N. M. Crawford, *Thoughts on Government. The Marriage of Negroes* (N.p., October 17, 1864), Vance Papers, NCDAH.
59. Resolutions of Yalobusha County, n.d. [1864], Volume 52, Record Group 27, MDAH.
60. Impressment receipt, March 3, October 23, 1863, John S. Powell Collection, Auburn.
61. Joseph E. Johnston to Wigfall, January 4, 1864, Louis T. Wigfall Papers, LC.
62. A. Macfarlane to Clark, September 23, 1864, Volume 57, Record Group 27, MDAH; Spencer Talley Memoir, 1918, in possession of Frances Martin, Lebanon, TN.
63. John Gilmer to Vance, January 2, 1864, Petition, January 23, 1865, Vance Papers, NCDAH.
64. F. W. Keyes to Clark, November 15, 1864, Volume 57, Record Group 27, MDAH.
65. Perhaps the best recent study of the dramatic shift in attitudes toward the potential role of slaves brought on by the pressures of the war is Clarence L. Mohr, *On the Threshold of Freedom: Masters and Slaves in Civil War Georgia* (Athens, GA, 1986).
66. O. F. Holladay to Clark, August 19, 1864, Volume 56, Record Group 27, MDAH.
67. Ransdell to Moore, June 12, 1863, Moore Papers, LSU.
68. Thomas Watts to John H. Dent, April 14, 1864, Thomas Watts Letterbook, ADAH.
69. Annual Message, November 1864, Thomas Watts Papers, ADAH.
70. David Williams to Magrath, February 15, 1865, Magrath Papers, SCDAH.
71. A. C. McDonald to his mother, March 15, 1864, Robert A. Siegel Sale 786 catalog, April 8–9, 1997 (New York), p. 91, item 2523.
72. Ethelbert Barksdale to Clark, November 6, 1864, Volume 57, Record Group 27, MDAH.
73. Robert Hilton Journal, n.d. [May 1865], University of Florida, Gainesville; *Journal,* 7:261, 393.
74. Charleston *Mercury,* November 19, 1864.
75. Hilton Journal, May 1865, University of Florida, Gainesville.
76. Seward to Clark, February 2, 1865, Volume 57, Record Group 27, MDAH.
77. James A. Lyons to Clark, February 10, 1865, ibid.
78. Charleston *Mercury,* January 13, 1865.
79. Hilton Journal, May 1865, University of Florida, Gainesville.
80. A discharged soldier to Murrah, April 17, 1865, Record Group 301, TSL.
81. P. K. Montgomery to Clark, April 4, 1865, Volume 57, Record Group 27, MDAH.
82. A Poor Woman to Vance, January 10, 1865, Vance Papers, NCDAH.

Chapter Six

1. Confederate States Congress, *The Laws of the Confederate States* (Montgomery and Richmond, 1861–62), pp. 242–47.
2. E. Anderson to Pettus, July 21, 1861, Volume 46, Record Group 27, MDAH.
3. Citizens of Smith County to Pettus, n.d., Volume 57, ibid.
4. J. Knight to Pettus, August 10, 1861, Volume 46, ibid.
5. B. Arbogast to Brown, December 17, 1861, Joseph Brown Papers, GDAH.
6. J. P. Cleveland to Clark, June 9, 1861, H. Castro to Clark, June 15, 1861, Record Group 301, TSL.
7. Jefferson Stubbs to Clerk of York County, February 22, 1862, Confederate States of America Records, CAH,UT.
8. Charles Maynhoff to Pettus, August 5, 1861, Volume 46, Record Group 27, MDAH.
9. *Laws of the Confederate States,* pp. 201–7.
10. Ibid., pp. 260–66.
11. Charles W. Ramsdell, ed., *Laws and Joint Resolutions of the Last Session of the Confederate Congress Together with the Secret Acts of the Previous Congresses* (Durham, NC, 1941), pp. 20–21.
12. T. R. Havins, "Administration of the Sequestration Act in the Confederate District Court for the Western District of Texas, 1862–1865," *Southwestern Historical Quarterly* 43 (January 1940), pp. 309, 311.
13. Receipt, February 20, 1863, E. J. Vann Papers, University of Florida, Gainesville. See, for instance, *Rules of Practice Under the Sequestration Act, for the Confederate States Courts, for the District of Florida* (Montgomery, 1862).
14. J. Hains to Pettus, August 8, 1861, Volume 46, Record Group 27, MDAH.
15. Grand Jury to Francis Lubbock, Record Group 301, TSL.
16. Order, March 14, 1862, John Milton Letterbook, University of Florida, Gainesville.
17. W. R. Poag to Lubbock, February 19, 1862, Record Group 301, TSL.
18. Oscar Hart to William Kincey, June 24, 1862, Correspondence of the Secretary of State, University of Florida, Gainesville.
19. Clay Alexander to Brown, September 15, 1862, Brown Papers, GDAH.
20. Sarah Hughes to Murrah, August 5, 1864, Record Group 301, TSL.
21. Arthur Lyon to Lubbock, February 27, 1862, July 9, 1863, ibid.
22. B. A. Terry to Pettus, April 30, 1861, Volume 27, Record Group 36, MDAH.
23. William Delay to Clark, November 27, 1863, Volume 56, Record Group 27, MDAH.
24. John LeGrand to Clark, November 30, 1863, Clark to LeGrand, December 6, 1863, ibid.
25. G. W. Bradley to Clark, February 8, 1864, ibid.
26. Thomas Watts to Davis, March 6, 1864, Thomas Watts Papers, ADAH.
27. Louisa Hillebrand to Murrah, November 24, 1863, Record Group 301, TSL.
28. F. M. James to Clark, October 10, 1864, Volume 57, Lock Houston to Clark, August 13, 1864, Volume 56, Record Group 27, MDAH.
29. E. C. Eggleston to Clark, June 28, 1864, Volume 56, ibid.
30. Alwyn Barr, ed., "Records of the Confederate Military Commission in San Antonio, July 2–October 10, 1862," *Southwestern Historical Quarterly* 73 (October 1969), pp. 246–72.
31. Florence Elizabeth Holladay, "The Powers of the Commander of the Confederate Trans-Mississippi Department, 1863–1865, II," *Southwestern Historical Quarterly* 21 (April 1918), pp. 354–55.

32. Ibid., pp. 356–57.

33. Milton to Thomas Jones, October 28, 1861, Milton Letterbook, University of Florida, Gainesville.

34. Quoted in George C. Rable, *The Confederate Republic: A Revolution Against Politics* (Chapel Hill, NC, 1994), p. 159.

35. Walker Vest to Charley Barnes, March 3, 1863, Lincoln Memorial Shrine, Redlands, CA.

36. The most recent, though incomplete, study of habeas corpus and civil liberties in the Confederacy is Mark Neely, *Southern Rights* (Charlottesville, VA, 1999).

37. Ibid., pp. 81–82.

38. George Kastner to Earl Van Dorn, n.d., Volume 52, Record Group 27, MDAH.

39. Clark to J.W.C. Watson, December 21, 1863, Volume 56, ibid.

40. T. J. Wharton to Clark, December 21, 1863, ibid.

41. Wharton to Clark, December 28, 1863, ibid.

42. Hilton to the editor of the *Floridian & Journal*, August 8, 1863, Robert B. Hilton Journal, University of Florida, Gainesville.

43. John Letcher to Joseph A. Hierholzer, December 3, 1864, John Letcher Papers, College of William and Mary, Williamsburg, VA.

44. Hudson to Clark, July 16, 1864, Volume 56, A. Groan to Clark, August 22, 1864, W. Brandon to Clark, January 19, 1865, Volume 57, Record Group 27, MDAH.

45. Receipt, November 6, 1861, Thomas O. Moore Papers, LSU.

46. Thomas Moore, Message to General Assembly, January 18, 1864, ibid.

47. E. Warren Moise to Moore, September 24, 1864, ibid.

48. Moise to Buckner, October 27, November 6, 1864, Buckner to Moise, October 27, November 10, 1864, in *Correspondence,* pamphlet in Confederate States of America Collection, LSU.

49. Thomas Manning to Moore, March 30, 1865, Moore Papers, LSU.

50. Hilton Journal, February 3, 1864, University of Florida, Gainesville; *Journal,* 6:744–46, 757, 804–6.

51. Watts to Leonidas Polk, April 1, 1864, Thomas Watts Letterbook, Watts Papers, ADAH.

52. E. J. Goode to Clark, November 17, 1863, Volume 55, Record Group 27, MDAH.

53. E. M. Devall to Clark, March 21, 1864, Volume 56, ibid.

54. William Quarles to Clark, March 28, 1864, William Crump et al. to Clark, April 16, 1864, ibid.

55. Robert Hudson to Clark, May 16, 24, 1864, ibid.

56. Hudson to Clark, May 2, July 1, 1864, ibid.

57. Alexander M. Clayton to Clark, April 8, 1864, ibid.

58. N. G. Nye to Clark, April 16, 1864, ibid.

59. William H. Kilpatrick to Clark, September 10, 1864, Volume 57, Record Group 26, MDAH.

60. Hudson to Clark, October 26, 1864, ibid.

61. Edward Burk to Murrah, July 1, 1864, Record Group 301, TSL.

62. George Sweet to Murrah, January 30, 1865, ibid.

63. Jesse Davis to Clark, February 27, 1865, Volume 57, Record Group 27, MDAH.

64. Statement, March 13, 1865, ibid.

65. Richard Cooper to Clark, March 25, 1865, ibid.

66. J. P. Reed to Magrath, March 30, 1865, Andrew G. Magrath Papers, SCDAH.

67. An Act to Prevent Monopolies and Extortions, December 14, 1861, Record Group 301, TSL.

CHAPTER SEVEN

1. The literature on Confederate women is increasingly broad and distinguished. Most recently it includes George C. Rable, *Civil Wars: Women and the Crisis of Southern Nationalism* (Urbana, IL, 1989); Drew Gilpin Faust, *Mothers of Invention: Women of the Slaveholding South in the American Civil War* (Chapel Hill, NC, 1996); and Laura F. Edwards, *Scarlett Doesn't Live Here Anymore: Southern Women in the Civil War Era* (Urbana, IL, 2000). All stress the expansion of independence from male domination, a growing political awareness, and a self-assertive redefinition of traditional female roles; while making excellent points, still each in some measure arguably overstates its case.
2. J. C. Blackburn to Brown, May 24, 1861, Joseph Brown Papers, GDAH.
3. Eliza Moses Journal, July 24, 1861, SHC,UNC.
4. J. M. Baker to Clark, May 30, 1861, Record Group 301, TSL.
5. J. K. McWhorter, "Caring for the Soldier in the Sixties," *Confederate Veteran* 29 (October 1912), pp. 409–10.
6. Mrs. John L. Manning to Manning, May 18, 1861, Williams-Chesnut-Manning Family Papers, SCL,USC.
7. William Butler to Gideon Pillow, June 3, 1861, Confederate States of America Records, CAH,UT.
8. Mrs. Manning to Manning, May 24, 1861, Williams-Chesnut-Manning Family Papers, SCL,USC.
9. Charles E. Munford to ——— Ellis, July 20, 1861, Munford-Ellis Family Papers, Duke University, Durham, NC.
10. John W. Erwin to Manning, July 22, 1861, Mary Fisher Hampton to Sallie Preston, July 22, 1861, Williams-Chesnut-Manning Family Papers, SCL,USC.
11. Colin Clark to Sally ?, May 13, 1861, ibid.
12. Jamie to My own Darling, July 4, 1861, Elizabeth Rudder Fearington Croom Collection, East Carolina Manuscript Collection, East Carolina University, Greenville, NC.
13. Erwin to Manning, July 22, 1861, Williams-Chesnut-Manning Family Papers, SCL,USC; George W. Harper to Pettus, September 4, 1861, Volume 46, Record Group 27, MDAH.
14. David Pemble to Pettus, September 10, 1861, Volume 46, Record Group 27, MDAH; James W. Asbury to Brown, March 23, 1862, Brown Papers, GDAH.
15. Robert Turner to P. W. Watkins, May 12, 1862, S. S. Taylor to James E. Saunders, December 29, 1861, James E. Saunders Papers, Confederate States of America Records, CAH,UT.
16. Moses Journal, October 13, 1862, SHC,UNC.
17. T. D. Crawford to Dear Father, July 22, 1861, James C. Galloway Papers, East Carolina Manuscript Collection, East Carolina University, Greenville, NC.
18. Invoice, July 3, 1863, Receipt, November 14, 1861, Thomas O. Moore Papers, LSU; Mallory to Angela Mallory, June 30, 1862, Stephen R. Mallory Letters, University of Florida, Gainesville; J. J. Allan to Brown, February 9, 1863, Brown Papers, GDAH.

19. F. W. Adams to Brown, July 22, 1861, Brown Papers, GDAH.
20. E. Halsey to Moore, May 8, 1861, Moore Papers, LSU.
21. Henry Whitehorne to Pettus, October 14, 1861, Volume 47, Record Group 27, MDAH.
22. C. Baskerville to Pettus, October 17, 1861, ibid.
23. Charles Shean to Lubbock, December 6, 1861, B. L. Peel to Lubbock, December 7, 1861, Record Group 301, TSL.
24. Anonymous to Dear Papa, October 1862, Confederate States of America Records, CAH,UT.
25. G. G. Torry et al. to Clark, February 20, 1864, Volume 56, Record Group 27, MDAH.
26. P. Thweatt to Brown, July 30, 1862, Brown Papers, GDAH.
27. William Yerger to Clark, April 15, 1864, Volume 56, Record Group 27, MDAH.
28. A. M. Burnham to Murrah, June 1, 1864, Record Group 301, TSL.
29. Milton Brown to Clark, December 11, 1863, Volume 56, Record Group 27, MDAH.
30. Stock statement, February 7, 1865, ibid.
31. Perhaps the best study of this subject is Rachel Bryan Stillman's Ph.D. dissertation at the University of Illinois, "Education in the Confederate States of America, 1861–1865" (Urbana, IL, 1972).
32. James Jackson to Pettus, September 28, 1861, Volume 46, Record Group 27, MDAH.
33. Anonymous to Pettus, n.d., Volume 52, ibid.
34. James Lyons to Clark, January 17, 1865, Volume 57, ibid.
35. Ashley Hurt to Pettus, November 6, 1861, Volume 47, J. Henry to Pettus, April 12, 1862, Volume 48, Henry to Pettus, October 29, 1862, Volume 49, ibid.
36. Milton to Josiah Gorgas, June 25, 1862, John Milton Letterbook, FHS; Proclamation, April 14, 1863, Record Group 301, TSL.
37. Joseph Bell to Clark, June 11, 1864, Thomas Gathright to Clark, August 18, 1864, petition, n.d. [late 1864], Volume 56, Record Group 27, MDAH.
38. "Education of Southern Women," DeBow's Review 31 (October–November 1861), p. 382.
39. Editorial, DeBow's Review 7 (January–February 1862), p. 164.
40. Paul A. Levengood, "In the Absence of Scarcity: The Civil War Prosperity of Houston, Texas," Southwestern Historical Quarterly 101 (April 1998), pp. 421–22.
41. F. Richardson to Murrah, January 25, 1865, Record Group 301, TSL.
42. S. R. Jones to Clark, November 15, 1864, Volume 57, Record Group 27, MDAH.
43. "Education of Southern Women," DeBow's Review 31, pp. 384–90.
44. Catalogue of the Library of the State of Mississippi January 1865, F. Whiting to Clark, February 6, 1865, Volume 57, Record Group 27, MDAH.
45. W. H. Mangrum to Pettus, February 22, 1863, Volume 51, ibid.
46. Editorial, DeBow's Review 34 (July–August 1864), p. 97.
47. Ibid., pp. 98–99.
48. "Disenthrallment of Southern Literature," DeBow's Review 31 (October–November 1861), pp. 349–59; Editorial, DeBow's Review 34, p. 98.
49. Oliver Fields to Pettus, July 9, 1862, Volume 49, Record Group 27, MDAH.
50. Houston Weekly Telegraph, August 13, 1862.
51. J.F.H. Claiborne to Pettus, August 4, 1862, Volume 49, Record Group 27, MDAH.
52. Milton to the planters of Florida, February 24, 1863, Milton Letterbook, University of Florida, Gainesville.
53. Receipt, December 15, 1861, Moore Papers, LSU.

54. Cheves to Dear General, May 17, 1862, Langdon Cheves Papers, SCHS.

55. Mobile and Ohio Railroad to Pettus, August 27, 1863, John Shaaff to W. E. Moore, September 5, 1863, Pettus to William J. Hardee, September 27, 1863, Volume 52, Record Group 27, MDAH.

56. Receipt, n.d., Haskell to Cheves, February 24, 1862, Cheves Papers, SCHS.

57. James F. Bozeman to Brown, March 5, 1862, Brown Papers, GDAH.

58. An outstanding study of the interrelationship between deprivation and the erosion of any spirit of Confederate nationalism is William Blair, *Virginia's Private War: Feeding Body and Soul in the Confederacy, 1861–1865* (New York, 1998).

59. Amanda Taylor to Brown, September 30, 1863, Brown Papers, GDAH.

60. John Bachlott to Brown, February 12, 1864, ibid.

61. Mary Bennett to Brown, October 13, 1864, ibid.

62. Carey W. Stiles to Brown, January 4, 1864, ibid.

63. Mallory to Angela Mallory, May 15, 1862, Mallory Letters, University of Florida, Gainesville.

64. W. Mason to Commissary of Impressment, June 16, 1863, Volume 52, Record Group 27, MDAH.

65. An innovative work on the experience of minors is James Marten, *The Children's Civil War* (Chapel Hill, NC, 1998). Its coverage of Confederate children and their hardships is slim compared to that of slave children and white Northern counterparts, but still illuminative.

66. The best account of the Richmond Bread Riot is Douglas O. Tice, Jr., "Bread or Blood! The Richmond Bread Riot," *Civil War Times Illustrated* 12 (February 1974), pp. 12–19.

67. Richmond *Examiner,* October 1, 1863.

68. "The Women of the South," *DeBow's Review* 31 (August 1861), pp. 147–54.

69. A Poor Woman to Vance, January 10, 1865, Zebulon Vance Papers, NCDAH.

70. Jonathan M. Berkey, "'Do You Wonder That I Have the Blues?': Ellen Moore's Wartime Negotiations," paper presented at Women in the Civil War Conference, Winchester, Virginia, April 2000.

71. Milton S. Perry to his wife, July 15, 1862, Milton S. Perry Letters, University of Florida, Gainesville.

72. Benjamin H. Hill to Brown, January 15, 1862, Record Group 1-1-5, Governors' Incoming Correspondence, GDAH.

73. Houston *Weekly Telegraph,* January 5, 1863.

74. Charles George to Mary George, August 5, September 22, 1861, June 10, 28, December 13, 1862, January 24, March 6, 1863, March 13, 27, 1864, Flora George to Mary George, June 22, 1865, George Family Papers, Auburn University, Auburn, AL.

75. B.F.R. Jeffares to his wife, December 3, 1864, Auburn.

76. John R. Dixon to Mattie Dixon, June 1, 26, 1864, John R. Dixon Correspondence, Auburn.

77. David M. Denney to Sinai Denney, August 24, 1864, Denney Confederate Letters, Auburn.

78. Robert Corry to Eliza Corry, January 26, 1862, Mary Corry to Robert Corry, March 16, 1862, Robert Corry to Eliza, November 17, 21, 25, 1862, February 14, 1863, Robert E. Corry Confederate Collection, Auburn.

79. Eliza to Robert Corry, December 4, 18, 1863, September 3, 1864, ibid.

80. John Robertson to Vance, January 13, 1864, Vance Papers, NCDAH.
81. North Carolina soldier to Vance, January 7, 1865, ibid.
82. Corry to Eliza, July 25, 27, October 14, 1864, January 25, 1865, Eliza to Corry, September 3, 1864, February 26, 1865, Corry Confederate Collection, Auburn.
83. Corry to Eliza, April 19, 1865, ibid.
84. An outstanding study of the life of Confederate civilians under Union occupation is Daniel E. Sutherland, *Seasons of War: The Ordeal of a Confederate Community, 1861–1865* (New York, 1995). For an equally meritorious study of life under occupation throughout the Confederacy, Stephen V. Ash, *When the Yankees Came: Conflict & Chaos in the Occupied South, 1861–1865* (Chapel Hill, NC, 1995), is path-breaking, though his conclusion that occupation tended to precipitate increased resistance on the part of Confederate civilians would seem to be at odds with their own expressions in their writings to their governors, legislators, and soldiers in the field.
85. Flora George to Mary George, June 22, 1865, George Family Papers, Auburn.

CHAPTER EIGHT

1. W. S. Walker to Milton, n.d. [March 1862], John Milton Letterbook, FHS.
2. Anonymous to Pettus, June 10, 1862, Volume 49, Record Group 27, MDAH.
3. Lubbock to Davis, November 13, 1862, Record Group 301, TSL.
4. S. S. Starnes to Pettus, July 24, 1862, Volume 46, Record Group 27, MDAH.
5. Anonymous to John Dunwoody, July 8, 1862, Joseph Brown Papers, GDAH.
6. S. P. Green et al. to Moore, September 30, 1862, Thomas O. Moore Papers, LSU.
7. Lancaster Brent to Moore, February 21, 1862, ibid.
8. Mansfield Lovell to Pettus, June 21, 1862, Alcorn to Pettus, June 13, 1862, Volume 49, Record Group 27, MDAH.
9. J. M. Crockett to Lubbock, February 7, 1862, Record Group 301, TSL.
10. Schofield & Markham to Brown, February 26, 1862, Brown Papers, GDAH.
11. W. K. Sebastian et al. to Braxton Bragg and Earl Van Dorn, May 14, 1862, Breckinridge Family Papers, in possession of Katherine Breckinridge Prewitt, Lexington, KY.
12. Hamilton Cooper to Clark, December 26, 1864, Volume 57, Record Group 27, MDAH.
13. A Soldier's Sister to Moore, August 9, 1862, Moore Papers, LSU.
14. Minister of Gospel to Brown, December 2, 1862, Brown Papers, GDAH.
15. Proclamation, January 1, 1863, Record Group 301, TSL.
16. Moore to Lubbock, May 25, 1863, ibid.
17. John Neal to Pettus, May 31, 1863, Volume 51, Record Group 27, MDAH.
18. Richard Archer to Pettus, June 17, 1863, Volume 52, ibid.
19. Elkanah Greer to Lubbock, September 17, 1863, Record Group 301, TSL.
20. Seddon to Pettus, n.d. [June 1863], Volume 52, Record Group 27, MDAH; Bragg to Brown, July 22, 1863, Brown Papers, GDAH; T. Cochran to Lubbock, July 5, 1863, James Browne to Lubbock, July 25, 1863, Record Group 301, TSL; Milton to Seddon, July 20, 1863, Milton Letterbook, FHS.
21. Proclamation, September 5, 1863, Brown Papers, GDAH.
22. Cheves to Beauregard, n.d. [1863], Langdon Cheves Papers, SCHS.
23. Littleton Washington Diary, August 21, 1863, in possession of Douglas L. Gibboney, Carlisle, PA.

24. Special Order 264, September 30, 1863, Record Group 301, TSL.

25. John Hopper to his brother, September 9, 1863, Confederate States of America Records, CAH,UT.

26. Citizens of Marion County to Pettus, October 26, 1861, Volume 47, Record Group 27, MDAH.

27. Richard Winter to Pettus, June 6, 1862, Volume 49, ibid.

28. A. A. Longstreet to Pettus, June 7, 1862, ibid.

29. John Shorter to Davis, October 22, 1862, John Gill Shorter Letters, ADAH.

30. Citizens of Staley's Precinct to Moore, December 1, 1862, Moore Papers, LSU.

31. Petition to Lubbock, n.d. [September 1863], Record Group 301, TSL.

32. J. F. Anders to Brown, November 8, 1862, Henrietta Stinchcomb to Brown, December 11, 1862, Brown Papers, GDAH.

33. Petition, September 16, 1863, Record Group 301, TSL.

34. P. Bugnor to Lubbock, September 8, 1863, ibid.

35. Catherine O. Stephenson to Brown, September 14, 1863, Brown Papers, GDAH.

36. M. M. Taylor to Brown, March 26, 1863, ibid.; Petition, n.d. [1863], Volume 52, Record Group 27, MDAH.

37. Albert Burton Moore, *Conscription and Conflict in the Confederacy* (reprint, New York, 1963), pp. 68, 74.

38. Mrs. J. M. Stevens to Brown, July 13, 1864, Brown Papers, GDAH.

39. W. D. Holden to Clark, September 15, 1864, Volume 57, C. A. Taylor to Clark, n.d. [late 1864], Volume 56, Record Group 27, MDAH.

40. F. W. Adams to Brown, February 20, 1862, Brown Papers, GDAH.

41. Houston *Weekly Telegraph,* September 10, 1862.

42. J. S. Lyons to Clark, March 9, 1865, Volume 57, Record Group 27, MDAH.

43. Anonymous to Brown, n.d. [post February 1862], Brown Papers, GDAH.

44. Anonymous to Brown, n.d., ibid.

45. S. P. Thurmond to Brown, October 15, 1864, ibid.

46. For a study of this problem in one region of the Confederacy, see David Williams, *Rich Man's War: Class, Caste, and Confederate Defeat in the Lower Chattahoochee Valley* (Athens, GA, 1998).

47. A. Acree to Brown, September 18, 1864, Brown Papers, GDAH.

48. M. Casky to Clark, September 3, 1864, Volume 57, Record Group 27, MDAH.

49. Milton to Seddon, October 16, 1863, Milton Letterbook, FHS; Anonymous to Brown, March 23, 1862, Brown Papers, GDAH.

50. Case files 11436, 11548, mm158, Record Group 153, Records of Military Courts Martial, NA.

51. John R. Alexander to Brown, April 12, 1864, Brown Papers, GDAH.

52. Mary Christian to Clark, September 1864, Volume 57, Record Group 27, MDAH.

53. Ladies of Spalding County to Brown, June 24, 1864, Brown Papers, GDAH.

54. John W. Brown Diary, July 31, 1863, University of Arkansas, Fayetteville.

55. Ladies of Spalding County to Brown, June 24, 1864, Brown Papers, GDAH.

56. William P. Carmichael to Cheves, February 5, 1862, Cheves Papers, SCHS. The standard work on refugees is Mary Elizabeth Massey, *Refugee Life in the Confederacy* (Baton Rouge, 1964).

57. Reuben Davis to Pettus, January 3, 1862, Volume 48, Record Group 27, MDAH.

58. Thomas Adams to Moore, May 11, 1863, Moore Papers, LSU.

59. Robert Hynson to Moore, January 3, 1865, ibid.

60. Frank Webb to Moore, April 29, 1865, ibid.
61. Ladies of Spalding County to Brown, June 24, 1864, Brown Papers, GDAH.
62. B. H. Bingham to Brown, February 27, 1865, ibid.
63. L. Julienne to My Dear Friend, May 22, 1864, Volume 56, Record Group 27, MDAH.
64. R.A.S. Park, ed., *"Dear Parents": The Civil War Letters of the Shibley Brothers of Van Buren* (Fayetteville, AR, 1963), n.p.
65. Ladies of Spalding County to Brown, June 25, 1864, Brown Papers, GDAH.
66. Isaac Anderson to Clark, January 28, 1864, H. M. Thompson to Clark, January 21, 1864, Volume 56, Record Group 27, MDAH.
67. W. H. Hardy to Clark, February 8, 1864, ibid.
68. Clark to W. R. Montgomery, March 16, 1864, D. Menim to Colonel, March 19, 1864, J. Nelson Bush to Clark, March 26, 1864, ibid.
69. P. Stull to Clark, April 24, 1864, D. Burton to Clark, May 12, 1864, ibid.
70. Taylor to Clark, October 8, 1864, Volume 57, ibid.
71. Unsigned to Clark, May 5, 1864, Volume 56, ibid.
72. Wigfall to James Chesnut, March 26, 1864, Williams-Chesnut-Manning Papers, SCL,USC.
73. Petition, October 12, 1864, in John Alderman, "The Civil War Period in Carroll County," *Carroll County Chronicles* 17 (Fall 1998), pp. 12, 14.
74. Case file nn2633, Record Group 153, Records of General Courts Martial, NA.
75. Tommie LaCavera, "The Roswell Women," *UDC Magazine* 62 (January 1999), pp. 12–13; Atlanta *Journal-Constitution*, January 7, 1999. Deborah Petite, currently working on a book on the Roswell women, kindly provided this and more material on this little-known episode.
76. M. C. McCombs to her sister, November 27, 1864, ADAH.
77. David C. Glenn to Clark, October 27, 1864, Volume 57, Record Group 27, MDAH.
78. Alien Citizens of Atlanta to Brown, June 4, 1864, Citizen to Brown, August 12, 1864, Brown Papers, GDAH.
79. Dabney H. Maury to Clark, August 14, 1864, Volume 56, Record Group 27, MDAH.
80. Wirt Adams to Richard Taylor, August 10, 1864, ibid.
81. Unknown to Clark, July 1, 1864, H. S. Van Eaton to Clark, July 12, 1864, ibid.
82. B. C. Duckworth to Clark, June 14, 1864, ibid.
83. John Hardy to Clark, November 17, 1864, Volume 57, ibid.
84. Old Friend to Vance, January 1, 1864, Zebulon Vance Papers, NCDAH.
85. T. Pegues to Clark, March 30, 1865, Volume 57, Record Group 27, MDAH.
86. W. H. Quarles to Clark, January 1, 1865, W. Strong to Clark, April 9, 1865, Volume 57, Petition, n.d. [February–March 1865], Volume 56, ibid.
87. J. McDonald to Clark, April 19, 1865, Volume 57, ibid.
88. Murrah to Citizens of Caldwell County, March 21, 1865, Pendleton Murrah Letterbook, Record Group 301, TSL.
89. Cooper to Clark, December 26, 1864, Volume 57, Record Group 27, MDAH.
90. Henry Hayes to Daniel Harris Reynolds, n.d. [1864], Daniel Harris Reynolds Papers, University of Arkansas, Fayetteville.
91. W. A. Strong to Clark, February 17, 1865, Volume 57, Record Group 27, MDAH.
92. John G. Walker to Murrah, March 16, 1865, F. Kalteyer et al. to Murrah, May 1865, Record Group 301, TSL.
93. Anonymous to Brown, n.d. [late 1864], Brown Papers, GDAH.

94. Margaret Anderson et al. to C.W.B. Peebles, April 16, 1865, John Jenkins Personal Papers, SCDAH.
95. F. J. Hening to Clark, February 15, 1865, Volume 57, Record Group 27, MDAH.
96. Houston *Daily Telegraph,* October 3, 1864.
97. Report of Robert Kells, October 1, 1864, Volume 60, Record Group 27, MDAH.
98. Guy Bryan to Murrah, January 16, 1865, Record Group 301, TSL.
99. Allen to Moore, March 15, 1865, Moore Papers, LSU.
100. Pettus to Clark, April 20, 1865, Volume 57, Record Group 27, MDAH.
101. P. Phillips to Clark, April 25, 1865, ibid.
102. Houston *Daily Telegraph,* April 22, May 11, 13, 1865.
103. Ibid., May 8, 1865.
104. Ibid., May 18, 1865.
105. E. S. Fisher to Clark, February 14, 1865, Volume 57, Record Group 27, MDAH.
106. M. Phillips to Clark, April 25, 1865, ibid.
107. Pacificus to Murrah, May 1, 1865, Record Group 301, TSL.
108. Davis to Murrah, February 25, 1865, Murrah to sheriff of Williamson County, March 17, 1865, Murrah Letterbook, Record Group 301, TSL; W. L. Brandon to Clark, April 5, 1865, James Gresham to Clark, April 15, 1865, Volume 57, Record Group 27, MDAH.
109. Clark to militia colonels, April 18, 1865, Volume 57, Record Group 27, MDAH.
110. Brent to Dear General, May 18, 1865, Confederate States of America Records, CAH,UT.
111. F. A. Prudhomme to S. S. Anderson, April 30, 1865, with endorsements, Simon B. Buckner Papers, ibid.
112. Report of Robert Kells, October 1, 1864, Volume 60, Record Group 27, MDAH.

CHAPTER NINE

1. Milton to Davis, April 15, 1863, John Milton Papers, FHS.
2. D. Bracht to Clark, June 17, 1861, Record Group 301, TSL.
3. W. J. Reeves to Pettus, January 5, 1862, Volume 48, Record Group 27, MDAH.
4. R. A. Anderson to Brown, July 1, 1861, Joseph Brown Papers, GDAH.
5. A True Southern Girl to Pettus, April 17, 1862, Volume 47, Record Group 27, MDAH.
6. R. A. Anderson to Brown, July 1, 1861, Daniel Aderhold to Brown, May 13, 1862, Brown Papers, GDAH; Notice, May 20, 1862, John Milton Letterbook, University of Florida, Gainesville.
7. John C. McGehee to Milton, March 13, 1862, Milton Letterbook, University of Florida.
8. Towson Ellis to Moore, November 18, 1861, Thomas O. Moore Papers, LSU; C. H. Alexander to Brown, March 17, 1862, Brown Papers, GDAH.
9. B. A. Terry to Pettus, April 30, 1861, Volume 36, Record Group 27, MDAH.
10. D. Bracht to Clark, May 18, 1861, Record Group 301, TSL.
11. Petition, June 24, 1861, ibid.
12. General Schriver to E. H. Chandler, May 30, 1861, Confederate States of America Records, CAH,UT.

13. George W. Munford to Jefferson Stubbs, August 8, 1861, ibid.

14. Charles Montague to Clark, July 19, 1861, Record Group 301, TSL.

15. This discussion of Unionism in Texas is drawn from Claude Elliott, "Union Senti-ment in Texas, 1861–1865," *Southwestern Historical Quarterly*, 50 (April 1947), p. 449ff.; Georgia Lee Tatum, *Disloyalty in the Confederacy* (Chapel Hill, NC, 1934), pp. 44–53; David Paul Smith, "The Limits of Dissent and Disloyalty in Texas," in Daniel E. Sutherland, ed., *Guerrillas, Unionists, and Violence on the Confederate Home Front* (Fayetteville, AR, 1999), p. 136ff. The Gainesville episode is best treated in Richard B. McCaslin, *Tainted Breeze: The Great Hanging at Gainesville, Texas, 1862* (Baton Rouge, 1994). David Pickering and Judy Falls, *Brush Men & Vig-ilantes: Civil War Dissent in Texas* (College Station, TX, 2000), covers the Hunt and Hopkins Counties killings.

16. J. H. Beck to Lubbock, January 31, 1862, Lubbock to Beck, February 8, 1862, Record Group 301, TSL.

17. Alwyn Barr, ed., "Records of the Confederate Military Commission in San Antonio, July 2–October 10, 1862," *Southwestern Historical Quarterly* 73 (October 1969), pp. 246–67.

18. Ibid., pp. 270–72.

19. Henry Webb to Lubbock, January 3, February 9, 1863, Record Group 301, TSL.

20. Mrs. B. Clarke to Murrah, November 30, 1863, ibid.

21. H. Conn to Lubbock, November 17, 1863, ibid.

22. P. Shelton to Murrah, August 13, 1864, ibid.

23. H. Hines to Pettus, June 5, 1862, Volume 49, Record Group 27, MDAH.

24. G. W. Fall to Pettus, July 11, 1862, J.F.H. Claiborne to Pettus, August 15, 1862, ibid.

25. Franklin Smith to Pettus, April 25, 1862, Volume 48, Isaac Applewhite to Pettus, June 8, 1862, Volume 49, ibid.

26. Stephen D. Lee to Joseph E. Johnston, November 23, 1863, Volume 56, ibid.

27. See Victoria E. Bynum, "Telling and Retelling the Legend of the 'Free State of Jones,'" in Sutherland, ed., *Guerrillas, Unionists, and Violence*, pp. 19–29.

28. William Quarles to Clark, March 28, 1864, Volume 56, Record Group 27, MDAH.

29. Tatum, *Disloyalty*, pp. 104–6.

30. R. Hudson to Clark, October 26, 1864, Volume 57, Record Group 27, MDAH.

31. G. W. Bradley to Clark, February 8, 1864, Volume 56, ibid.

32. Samuel Gholson to Clark, April 16, 1864, ibid.

33. J. Stutts to Clark, June 14, 1864, W. E. Montgomery to Clark, August 7, 1864, Volume 56, George Baylis to Clark, August 1864, Volume 57, ibid.

34. Proclamation, June 18, 1862, Moore Papers, LSU.

35. J. Macauley to Moore, April 14, 1863, ibid.

36. H. W. Blake to Brown, February 17, 1864, Brown Papers, GDAH.

37. Atlanta itself had a thriving underground Unionist community, as detailed in Thomas G. Dyer, *Secret Yankees: The Union Circle in Confederate Atlanta* (Baltimore, 1999).

38. John Tyler to Davis, October 19, 1864, Joseph Rubinfine C.S.A. List 69, Pleas-antville, NJ, n.d., item 27.

39. Thomas Watts, Annual Message, November 1864, Thomas Watts Papers, ADAH.

40. A. Duffie to Magrath, January 10, 1865, Andrew G. Magrath Papers, SCDAH.

41. Noel C. Fisher, *War at Every Door: Partisan Politics & Guerilla Violence in East Tennessee, 1860–1869* (Chapel Hill, NC, 1997), is an able overview of the turmoil

experienced and caused by Unionist East Tennesseans. An equally useful study
of the loyal Confederates from the region will be found in W. Todd Groce, *Mountain Rebels: East Tennessee Confederates and the Civil War, 1860–1870* (Knoxville, 1999).

42. C. Bannon to Vance, January 7, 1864, Zebulon Vance Papers, NCDAH.

43. J. G. de Roulhac Hamilton, "The Heroes of America," *Publications of the Southern History Association* 11 (January 1907), pp. 11–14.

44. Tatum, *Disloyalty*, pp. 160–65.

CHAPTER TEN

1. "What We Are Gaining by the War," *DeBow's Review* 7 (January–February 1862), p. 160.

2. Mollie Colbert to Pettus, September 2, 1861, Volume 46, Record Group 27, MDAH.

3. H. W. Stackhouse to Pettus, July 22, 1861, ibid.

4. Catherine Stubbs to Brown, May 21, 1861, Joseph Brown Papers, GDAH.

5. John Letcher to Jefferson Davis, September 24, 1861, Alexander Autographs Auction Catalog, April 29, 2000, item 84; "Prolonge" to the Editor, April 18, 1863, "Editor's Table," *Southern Literary Messenger,* May 1863, p. 317.

6. Clayton to Pettus, August 2, 1861, Volume 46, Record Group 27, MDAH.

7. Robert Smith to Pettus, July 25, 1861, ibid.

8. Thomas Allen to Brown, May 29, 1861, Brown Papers, GDAH; A. H. Raymond to Pettus, August 20, 1861, Volume 46, Record Group 27, MDAH.

9. Irby Morgan to Lubbock, December 2, 1861, John Besser to Lubbock, February 19, 1862, Record Group 301, TSL.

10. Soldiers Aid Society of Palestine to Pettus, September 7, 1861, Volume 46, Record Group 27, MDAH.

11. T. J. Roget to Pettus, August 23, 1861, ibid.

12. Lucy Banks to Pettus, August 15, 1861, ibid.

13. Stackhouse to Pettus, July 22, 1861, James Haynes to Pettus, August 3, 1861, ibid.

14. D. C. Grummond to Pettus, August 28, 1861, Volume 46, S. Butters to Pettus, October 1, 1861, Volume 47, ibid.

15. James Whitfield to Pettus, September 12, 1861, Volume 46, Almira McGee to Pettus, October 26, 1861, Volume 47, ibid.

16. Catherine A. Stephenson to Brown, March 9, 1862, Brown Papers, GDAH.

17. J. M. Stewart to Pettus, September 6, 1861, Volume 46, Record Group 27, MDAH.

18. Milton to Asa May, October 8, 1862, John Milton Letterbook, FHS.

19. Milledge L. Bonham to the Treasurer, June 30, 1863, Milledge L. Bonham Papers, SCL,USC; Milton to Brown, March 9, 1863, Milton Letterbook, FHS.

20. W. P. Millan to Pettus, August 1, 1863, Volume 46, Record Group 27, MDAH.

21. Lizzye C. Bachelder to Brown, November 22, 1863, Brown Papers, GDAH.

22. E. W. Johns to Pettus, August 6, 1861, Volume 46, Record Group 27, MDAH.

23. William Carmichael to Cheves, January 17, 1863, Langdon Cheves Papers, SCHS.

24. Watts to Seddon, February 1, 1864, Thomas Watts Papers, ADAH.

25. William Gregg to Bonham, September 21, 1863, Bonham Papers, SCL,USC.

26. Articles of agreement, June 30, 1864, Correspondence of the Secretary of State, University of Florida, Gainesville; Henry W. Allen to William F. Lockwood, July 6, 1864,

Miscellaneous Collection, LSU; Watts to Enoch Alldridge, April 21, 1864, Watts to Seddon, April 25, 1864, Annual Message, November 1864, Watts Papers, ADAH.

27. T. Clark et al. to E. Kirby Smith, August 4, 1864, Governors' Papers, Pendleton Murrah, Record Group 301, TSL.

28. T. B. Phillips to Clark, August 19, 1864, Volume 56, Record Group 27, MDAH.

29. W. W. Liddell to Clark, December 9, 1864, Volume 57, ibid.

30. Murrah to Kirby Smith, April 8, 1865, Pendleton Murrah Letterbook, Record Group 301, TSL.

31. Ella Lonn, *Salt as a Factor in the Confederacy* (University, AL 1965), pp. 25–26.

32. Ibid., pp. 58–60.

33. A. B. Moore to Pettus, November 14, 1861, Volume 47, Record Group 27, MDAH.

34. A. B. Longstreet to Pettus, October 3, 1862, Volume 49, Moody O'Ferrall to Pettus, January 11, 1862, Volume 48, ibid.

35. O. Osborn to Pettus, August 2, 1862, Volume 49, W. Turner to Pettus, February 24, 1863, Volume 51, ibid.

36. C. K. Ayer to Brown, December 9, 1861, Brown Papers, GDAH.

37. N. B. Atkinson to Brown, December 15, 1861, Messrs. Adams and Reynolds to Brown, December 16, 1861, A. J. Austin to Brown, August 26, 1862, ibid.

38. R. F. Floyd to Captain Hamilton, March 5, 1862, James M. Hunter to Milton, April 27, 1862, Milton Letterbook, FHS.

39. Lonn, *Salt,* pp. 100–102, 107–8.

40. J. McElmore to Isaac W. Hayne, October 22, 1862, Bonds and Contracts for Salt Manufacturing, 1862–1863, SCDAH.

41. N. S. Graham to Pettus, August 24, 1862, H. C. Dixon to Pettus, September 22, October 21, 1862, Volume 49, W. Alex Stuart to Allen Caperton, March 12, 1863, Volume 51, Record Group 27, MDAH.

42. Dixon to Pettus, September 22, 1862, George W. Randolph to Pettus, October 28, 1862, Pettus to Randolph, October 28, 1862, Volume 49, George Leovy to Pettus, December 6, 1862, Volume 51, ibid.

43. John Bailey to Brown, June 18, 1863, B. H. Bingham to Brown, May 16, 1863, Brown Papers, GDAH.

44. H. H. Tucker to Brown, January 23, 1864, ibid.

45. Bingham to Brown, August 8, 1864, ibid.

46. T. A. Phillips to Charles Clark, August 13, 1864, Volume 56, Record Group 27, MDAH.

47. A. McDonald statement, February 1, 1865, W. S. Hudson to Clark, February 13, 1865, Volume 57, ibid.

48. Proclamation, March 18, April 18, 1863, Bonham Papers, SCL,USC.

49. Proclamation, March 16, 1863, ibid.

50. William Lamar Gammon, "Governor John Milton of Florida" (Master's thesis, University of Florida, Gainesville, 1948), pp. 185–86.

51. Milton to John Darling, October 16, 1861, Milton to Benjamin F. Porter, January 15, 1863, Milton Letterbook, FHS.

52. James M. Black to George I. Foster, June 6, 1864, Brown Papers, GDAH.

53. Various reports in Soldiers Board of Relief Papers, 1862–1865, J. Fisher to James Tupper, November 10, 1864, SCDAH.

54. Philip Tucker to Lubbock, October 22, 1862, W. Haynes to Murrah, November 30, 1863, Record Group 301, TSL.

55. Clipping from undated issue of the Talladega, AL, *Reporter,* Watts Papers, ADAH.

56. John Humphreys to Pettus, June 13, 1863, Volume 52, Record Group 27, MDAH.

57. H. W. Blake to Brown, May 6, 1863, Brown Papers, GDAH.

58. J. W. Booth to Brown, September 14, 1863, ibid.; R. Hudson to Clark, October 26, 1864, Volume 57, Record Group 27, MDAH.

59. A. H. Canedo to Lubbock, November 3, December 10, 1861, Record Group 301, TSL.

60. Hugh Archer to Milton, September 23, 1862, Milton Letterbook, FHS.

61. Report of Bureau and Soldiers Home, October 1, 1863, Report of the Central Association, November 16, 1863, Central Association 1865 Miscellaneous Papers, SCDAH.

62. Report of the Central Association, December 10, 1861, ibid.

63. H. H. Tucker to Brown, September 6, 1861, Brown Papers, GDAH.

64. A. R. Rippetoe to Lubbock, February 24, 1862, Lubbock to Felicia Porter, February 8, 1862, Record Group 301, TSL.

65. K. Bryan to Lubbock, August 14, 1863, ibid.

66. Paul A. Levengood, "In the Absence of Scarcity: The Civil War Prosperity of Houston, Texas," *Southwestern Historical Quarterly* 101 (April 1998), pp. 418–19.

67. G. Dahlgren to Clark, June 27, 1864, Volume 56, Record Group 27, MDAH.

68. Statement for Empire Hospital, September 13, 186-, Confederate States of America Records, CAH,UT.

69. Henry W. Foote to Clark, March 4, 1865, Volume 57, Record Group 27, MDAH.

70. Report of the Institute for the Blind, February 1, 1865, ibid.

71. John W. Robinson, Report of the Institute for the Blind, October 1, 1864, ibid.

72. Report of the Institute for the Blind, February 1, 1865, Report of Board of Trustees of Institution for the Blind, February 23, 1865, ibid.

73. Affidavits of investigation, November 1865, ibid.

74. Milton to Thomas Green, August 25, 1863, Milton Letterbook, FHS; Robert Kelly to Pettus, October 9, 1863, Volume 56, ibid.

75. Report of the Trustees of the State Lunatic Asylum, October 1865, Volume 60, T. J. Wharton to Clark, March 16, 1864, Volume 56, Robert Kells to Clark, October 6, 27, 1864, Volume 57, ibid.

76. Kells to Clark, March 31, 1865, Volume 57, ibid.

77. Report of Robert Kells, October 1, 1864, Superintendent's Report, October 1, 1865, Volume 60, ibid.

78. Unfortunately, there is no full study of Confederate welfare efforts. Robert H. Bremner, *The Public Good: Philanthropy & Welfare in the Civil War Era* (New York, 1980), while an excellent work, is rather inaptly titled, since it is almost unaware that philanthropy took place in the South, devoting a mere five pages to the subject.

79. N. G. Nye to Clark, April 16, 1864, Volume 56, Record Group 27, MDAH.

80. Thomas Henderson et al. to M. Brown, n.d. [January 1865], ibid.

81. George Gordon to Clark, February 11, 1865, Volume 57, ibid.

82. Proclamation, March 13, 1865, Correspondence of the Secretary of State, University of Florida, Gainesville.

83. Murrah to W. H. Woodward, April 12, 1865, Murrah to Messers. Rochen et al., April 12, 1865, Record Group 301, TSL.

84. Report of the Auditor, January 1, 1865, Volume 57, Record Group 27, MDAH.

85. Report for Pickens District, February 1, 1865, Soldiers Board of Relief Papers, 1862–1865, SCDAH.

86. Nancy Owens to Magrath, February 11, 1865, Andrew G. Magrath Papers, SCDAH.

87. Annual Message, November 1864, Watts Papers, ADAH.
88. Milton to A. Corley, February 21, 1862, Milton Letterbook, FHS; A. Broughes to Clark, August 5, 1864, Volume 56, Record Group 27, MDAH.
89. A. J. Gillespie to Clark, November 30, 1864, Volume 57, ibid.
90. Milton to Joseph Finegan, April 22, 1862, Milton Letterbook, FHS; John Atwood to Pettus, September 23, 1861, Volume 46, Record Group 27, MDAH.
91. Milton to Isaac Widgeon, March 16, 1862, J. J. Finley to Milton, March 31, 1862, Milton Letterbook, FHS.
92. V. R. Tommey & Company to Brown, August 22, 1862, Brown Papers, GDAH.
93. C. Bradley to Pettus, August 5, 1861, Volume 46, Record Group 27, MDAH.
94. Stock certificate, September 19, 1863, F. Richardson to Murrah, January 20, 1865, Record Group 301, TSL.
95. J. Ralph Smith to Bonham, November 12, 1864, Bonham Papers, SCL,USC.
96. Edward Fontaine to Pettus, January 11, 1862, Volume 48, Record Group 27, MDAH.
97. Resolution, April 11, 1861, Brown Papers, GDAH.
98. Cook and Brothers to Pettus, August 2, 10, 1861, Volume 46, Record Group 27, MDAH.
99. Bonham to J. T. Trezevant, October 19, 1863, Bonham Papers, SCL,USC.
100. Extract from Journal of Executive Council, May 2, 1862, Bonham to Isham G. Harris, September 21, 1863, James Tupper to Bonham, October 27, 1864, ibid.
101. George W. Adams to Brown, October 21, 1861, Brown Papers, GDAH.
102. Ibid., October 26, 1861.
103. John Anderson to Brown, January 15, 28, 1862, Adams to Brown, February 14, 1862, Brown Papers, GDAH.
104. Resolution of Executive Council, March 13, 1862, Milton Letterbook, FHS; Contract, December 16, 1863, Volume 56, Record Group 27, MDAH.
105. Comptroller General to Bonham, October 4, 1863, Bonham Papers, SCL,USC.
106. Abraham C. Myers to H. Ranney, January 10, 1862, Confederate States of America Collection, LSU.
107. James Rives to L. Fleming, August 11, 1863, Volume 52, C. A. Taylor to Clark, February 11, 1865, George H. Thomas to whom it may concern, January 30, 1865, Volume 57, Record Group 27, MDAH.
108. Louise B. Hill, *State Socialism in the Confederate States of America* (Charlottesville, VA, 1936), pp. 3–31 passim. Hill makes the case, unconvincingly, that had the Confederate government gotten into the blockade-running and cotton-shipping business earlier, likely it would have won its independence, a shaky and highly speculative assumption at best, but one reflecting assumptions current when she was writing.
109. Emory M. Thomas, *The Confederacy as a Revolutionary Experience* (Englewood Cliffs, NJ, 1971), addresses several of the radical changes in Southern society and mores, but does not cover socialism as manifested in rationing, state control of supply and manufacturing, prohibition, and the other topics covered here.
110. "What We Are Gaining by the War," *DeBow's Review* 7 (January–February 1862), p. 160.
111. S. S. Taylor to A. Saunders, March 10, 1862, Confederate States of America Papers, CAH,UT.
112. Robert H. Thach to Elizabeth Thach, July 24, 1861, Charles Coleman Thach Collection, Auburn University, Auburn, AL.

113. Anonymous to Brown, March 17, 1862, Brown Papers, GDAH.
114. Proclamation, May 28, 1862, Record Group 301, TSL; Thomas Ames to Brown, March 17, 1862, Brown Papers, GDAH.
115. Milton to Finegan, June 20, 1862, Milton to sheriff of Holmes County, July 3, 1862, Milton Letterbook, FHS.
116. R. Hudson to Clark, October 26, 1864, Volume 57, Record Group 27, MDAH.
117. Proclamation, November 3, 1862, Francis W. Pickens Papers, SCDAH.
118. George Blackie to Brown, November 25, 1862, Brown Papers, GDAH.
119. J. M. John to Pettus, October 3, 1862, Volume 49, Record Group 27, MDAH.
120. M. M. Johnson to Pettus, March 18, 1863, Volume 51, ibid.
121. Blackie to Brown, October 18, 1863, Brown Papers, GDAH.
122. Milton to I. B. Galbraith, August 20, 1863, Milton Letterbook, FHS.
123. Petitions to Distill or Sell or Transport Liquor, 1862, SCDAH.
124. Thomas Watts to Clark, June 24, 1864, Volume 56, Record Group 27, MDAH.
125. Agreement, December 4, 1863, Correspondence of the Secretary of State, University of Florida, Gainesville.
126. W. A. Strong to Clark, November 8, 1864, Volume 57, Record Group 27, MDAH.
127. M. Vaughan statement, March 1865, Volume 56, ibid.
128. H. S. Cole to Clark, November 1, 1864, Volume 57, ibid.
129. J.A.P. Campbell to Clark, March 8, 1865, ibid.
130. T. C. Tupper to Clark, April 1, 1865, ibid.
131. R. Hudson to Clark, October 26, 1864, ibid.
132. W. A. Strong to Clark, February 17, 1865, ibid.
133. James Chesnut to Magrath, February 16, 1865, Magrath Papers, SCDAH.
134. Edwin Porter to Magrath, April 4, 1865, ibid.
135. William H. Cummings to Bonham, January 7, 1863, Bonham Papers, SCL,USC.

CHAPTER ELEVEN

1. A. Miltenberger to Moore, February 25, 1861, Thomas O. Moore Papers, LSU.
2. Braxton Bragg to Moore, July 25, 1861, ibid.
3. Milton to Lee, May 16, 1862, John Milton Letterbook, FHS.
4. The only work to date on the governors is Wilfred Buck Yearns, ed., *The Confederate Governors* (Athens, GA, 1985). It consists of essays by thirteen distinguished scholars covering each of the states, including Kentucky and Missouri, but is lacking in substantive synthesis of the gubernatorial experience and contribution.
5. Marshall, *Texas Republican,* clipping, n.d. [summer 1861], Record Group 301, TSL.
6. Milton to Lee, July 6, 1861, Milton Letterbook, FHS; J. M. Maxcy to Clark, June 30, 1861, Record Group 301, TSL.
7. An able study of state electoral politics in a Confederate state is Dale Baum, *The Shattering of Texas Unionism: Politics in the Lone Star State During the Civil War Era* (Baton Rouge, 1998).
8. Pillow to R. M. Russell, June 5, 1861, Confederate States of America Records, CAH,UT.
9. Carey W. Styles to Brown, November 11, 1864, Joseph Brown Papers, GDAH.
10. E. J. Marble to Pettus, n.d. [summer 1861], Volume 52, Record Group 27, MDAH.

11. Peterson Thweatt to Brown, July 31, 1861, Brown Papers, GDAH.

12. F. L. Villepigue to John R. Galbraith, November 17, 1862, Correspondence of the Secretary of State, 1845–1865, University of Florida, Gainesville.

13. W. M. Cook to Clark, June 12, 1861, Record Group 301, TSL.

14. Thweatt to Brown, October 7, 1861, Brown Papers, GDAH.

15. Thomas Cobb to Marion Cobb, September 26, 1861, Thomas R.R. Cobb Letters, University of Georgia, Athens.

16. C. Bannon to Vance, January 7, 1864, Zebulon Vance Papers, NCDAH.

17. John Kyle to Pettus, August 14, 1861, Reuben Davis to Pettus, August 20, 1861, W. Goodman to Pettus, August 20, 1861, Robert Hudson to Pettus, August 20, 1861, Volume 46, Record Group 27, MDAH.

18. W. R. Mosely to Pettus, August 21, 1861, John Marshall to Pettus, August 30, 1861, ibid.

19. L. J. Jones to Pettus, August 24, 1861, George Hillyer to Pettus, August 31, 1861, Volume 46, receipt October 1861, Volume 47, ibid.

20. Thomas Hughes, *A Boy's Experience in the Civil War, 1860–1865* (Washington, 1904), p. 21.

21. J. M. Thompson to Pettus, September 19, 1861, Volume 46, Joseph R. Davis to Pettus, October 11, 1861, Volume 47, Reuben Davis to Pettus, June 2, 1862, Volume 49, Record Group 27, MDAH.

22. Littleton Washington Diary, July 30, 1863, in possession of Douglas L. Gibboney, Carlisle, PA.

23. Broadside "To the Voters," March 1865, Volume 57, Record Group 27, MDAH.

24. T. Cobb to Marion Cobb, November 16, 1861, Cobb Letters, Georgia.

25. Proclamation, September 26, 1862, Francis W. Pickens Papers, SCDAH.

26. J. D. Barton to Pettus, August 18, 1863, Volume 52, Record Group 27, MDAH; B. F. Allen to Joseph Finegan, July 28, 1863, Milton to James Griffin, September 24, 1863, Allen to S. S. Smith, October 17, 1863, Correspondence of the Secretary of State, University of Florida, Gainesville.

27. Edward Jones to Pettus, July 3, 1861, Volume 37, petition of citizens of Franklin County to Pettus, n.d. [November 1862], Volume 56, Record Group 27, MDAH.

28. John Andrews to Brown, October 11, 1863, Brown Papers, GDAH.

29. Moise to Moore, n.d. [1863–64], Moore Papers, LSU.

30. B. F. Horsham to Clark, November 7, 1864, Volume 57, Record Group 27, MDAH.

31. R. D. Haden to Pettus, November 19, 1861, Volume 47, ibid.; Milton to John Boston, May 2, 1862, Milton Letterbook, FHS; certificate of deposit, April 15, 1863, Moore Papers, LSU.

32. Judah to Milton, December 6, 1862, Record Group 577, FSA; F. Moses to Joseph Farr, November 9, 1862, Pickens Papers, SCDAH.

33. Memminger to Milton, July 9, 1862, Milton Letterbook, FHS.

34. Thomas Watts, Annual Message, November 1864, Thomas Watts Papers, ADAH.

35. "The Women of the South," *DeBow's Review* 31 (August 1861), pp. 151–52.

36. Journal of the Proceedings of the People's Convention, January 3, 1861, Record Group 540, FSA; William Harris to F. J. Eppes, January 26, 1861, Resolution of Florida Convention, January 14, 1861, Madison Perry to John C. McGehee, January 16, 1861, Office of the Governor, Correspondence of the Governors, Record Group 577, FSA.

37. A. R. Stuart to C. S. Stuart, January 31, 1862, Stuart Family Papers, SCHS.
38. Laura White, "The Fate of Calhoun's Sovereign Convention in South Carolina," *American Historical Review* 34 (July 1929), pp. 759–71 passim.
39. R. J. McLeod to Clark, June 24, 1861, Record Group 301, TSL; Harris to Pettus, September 9, 1861, Volume 46, Reuben Davis to Pettus, July 13, 1861, Volume 37, Record Group 27, MDAH.
40. Mallory to Milton, October 29, 1861, Milton to Davis, October 29, 1861, A. B. Moore to Milton, October 30, 1861, Record Group 577, FSA.
41. Moore to Pickens, March 8, 1862, Pickens Papers, SCDAH.
42. Pettus to Shorter, May 2, 1863, Shorter to Pettus, July 6, 1863, Volume 52, Watts to Clark, May 4, 1864, Wharton to Charles Clark, May 27, 1864, Volume 56, Record Group 27, MDAH; Henry W. Allen to Murrah, August 10, 1863, Record Group 301, TSL.
43. Brown to Pickens, December 16, 1861, Pickens Papers, SCDAH.
44. Brown to Milton, December 16, 1861, Record Group 577, FSA.
45. A. O. Andrews to Brown, January 24, 1862, Brown Papers, GDAH.
46. Pickens to Lubbock, March 22, 1862, Record Group 301, TSL; Milton to Pickens, April 10, 1862, John Milton Letters, FHS.
47. Lubbock to Davis, June 27, 1862, Record Group 301, TSL.
48. Beauregard to Brown, October 31, 1862, Brown Papers, GDAH.
49. Lubbock to George Moore, July 28, 1863, John Tyler to Lubbock et al., October 27, 1863, Record Group 301, TSL.
50. Milton to Brown, April 14, 1864, Governors' Letterbooks, Volume 7, Record Group 32, FSA.
51. Vance to Clark, September 23, 1864, Bonham to George A. Trenholm, November 12, 1864, Volume 57, Record Group 27, MDAH.
52. Watts, Annual Message, November 1864, Watts Papers, ADAH; Milton to Vance, October 11, 1864, Milton to William Smith, November 19, 1864, Governors' Letterbooks, Volume 7, Record Group 32, FSA.
53. Cobb to Marion Cobb, May 1, 1862, Cobb Letters, Georgia.
54. P. F. Stevens to Pickens, March 12, 1862, Pickens Papers, SCDAH.
55. Thomas Waul to Lubbock, December 28, 1861, Lubbock to Davis, February 6, 1862, Lubbock to Benjamin, March 13, 1862, Benjamin to Lubbock, March 17, 1862, Record Group 301, TSL.
56. Alcorn to Pettus, January 4, 1862, Volume 48, Record Group 27, MDAH.
57. George Davis to Vance, September 16, 1864, Vance Papers, NCDAH.
58. Bragg to Moore, May 2, 7, August 13, 1861, Moore Papers, LSU.
59. Reuben Davis to Pettus, June 14, October 10, 1862, Volume 49, Record Group 27, MDAH.
60. Pettus to Pillow, August 24, 1863, Volume 52, ibid.; John B. Magruder to Murrah, November 9, 1863, Record Group 301, TSL.
61. Littleton Washington Diary, August 21, 1862, Gibboney.
62. Milton to N. A. Hull, March 17, 1862, Milton Letterbook, FHS; Milton to Mallory, November 2, 1861, Record Group 577, FSA.
63. R. S. Duryea to Pickens, February 1, 1862, Pickens Papers, SCDAH.
64. Moore to Randolph, July 8, 1862, Moore Papers, LSU.
65. Moore to Davis, July 23, September 12, 1862, Davis to Moore, September 29, 1862, ibid.
66. W. S. Ashe to Brown, October 3, 1861, Brown Papers, GDAH.

67. Brown to G. W. Smith, May 25, 1863, R. M. Smythe Sale Catalog #186, part 2, April 22, 1999, item 245.
68. Milton to Finegan, May 21, 1863, Milton Letterbook, FHS.
69. James B. Dawkins to Milton, June 9, 1864, James Banks to Milton, June 14, 1864, Milton to Dawkins, June 14, 1864, Governors' Letterbooks, Volume 7, Record Group 32, FSA.
70. Minor Merewether to Milton, July 14, 1864, ibid.
71. Joseph E. Johnston to Vance, March 2, 1865, Vance Papers, NCDAH.
72. Murrah to John G. Walker, January 29, 1865, Record Group 301, TSL.
73. Baskerville & Whitfield to Clark, January 9, 1865, Volume 57, Record Group 27, MDAH.
74. Telegram, January 8, 1864, Vance Papers, NCDAH.
75. Eli Baxter to Murrah, July 10, 1864, H. B. Andrews to Magruder, August 12, 1864, Record Group 301, TSL.
76. Watts to Bragg, July 22, 1864, Watts to Davis, July 30, 1864, Watts Papers, ADAH.
77. Hill to Brown, January 15, 1862, Benjamin H. Hill personal folder, GDAH.
78. A. A. Terhune to Brown, November 7, 1864, Collection 1-1-5, GDAH.
79. J. H. Parsons to Wigfall, November 8, 1864, Louis T. Wigfall Papers, LC.
80. Message to General Assembly, January 18, 1864, Moore Papers, LSU.
81. T. Weightman to Lubbock, September 1, 1863, Record Group 301, TSL.
82. Houston *Daily Telegraph,* June 8, 1864.
83. H. Washington to Murrah, November 12, 1863, P. W. Gray to Murrah, June 30, 1864, William Dunbar to Lubbock, March 13, 1863, B. Bloomfield to Lubbock, June 16, 1863, Record Group 301, TSL.
84. Milton to Memminger, June 26, 1862, Milton Letterbook, FHS.
85. May Spencer Ringold, *The Role of the State Legislatures in the Confederacy* (Athens, GA, 1966), is the only work to deal with the legislatures collectively, and deserves more attention than it has received for its generally sound and comprehensive analysis of the statehouses' activities. Less useful in its approach to the challenges faced by the states, and now badly dated, is Frank Lawrence Owsley, *State Rights in the Confederacy* (Chicago, 1925). More useful is Forrest McDonald, *States' Rights and the Union: Imperium in Imperio, 1776–1876* (Lawrence, KS, 2000), though its Confederate coverage is heavily dependent upon George C. Rable, *The Confederate Republic: A Revolution Against Politics* (Chapel Hill, NC, 1994).
86. Edward Judah to Milton, December 4, 1862, Record Group 577, FSA.
87. John R. Niernsee to Milledge L. Bonham, August 31, 1863, Milledge L. Bonham Papers, SCL,USC; Niernsee to Pickens, November 28, 1862, Pickens Papers, SCDAH.

CHAPTER TWELVE

1. John B. Jones, *A Rebel War Clerk's Diary at the Confederate States Capital* (Philadelphia, 1866), 1:34.
2. Littleton Washington Diary, August 3, 1863, in possession of Douglas L. Gibboney, Carlisle, PA.
3. Ebenezer Farrand to Alonzo B. Noyes, May 21, 1861, Alonzo B. Noyes Collection, University of Florida, Gainesville; Texas delegation to Lubbock, December 29, 1861, Record Group 301, TSL.

4. F. Mattington to Milton, May 10, 1862, John Milton Letterbook, FHS.

5. James Chesnut to Davis, June 4, 1862, James Chesnut Letterbook, Miscellaneous Manuscript Collection, LC.

6. Miles to Joseph Campbell, August 14, 1861, Joseph Campbell Papers, SCHS.

7. Miles to Cheves, August 11, 1861, Langdon Cheves Papers, SCHS.

8. The standard work is Wilfred Buck Yearns, *The Confederate Congress* (Athens, GA, 1960). It is now considerably dated, but still very useful. Useful also is Thomas B. Alexander and Richard E. Beringer, *Anatomy of the Confederate Congress* (Nashville, 1972), though its forays into statistical analysis sometimes provide statistical verities that are at odds with empirical reading of the evidence.

9. Littleton Washington Diary, August 3, 21, 1863, Gibboney.

10. Ibid., August 21, 1863.

11. Ochiltree to Lubbock, January 17, 1862, Record Group 301, TSL.

12. Oldham to Lubbock, January 13, 1862, ibid.

13. Littleton Washington Diary, August 21, 1863, Gibboney.

14. Gray to Lubbock, March 4, 1862, Record Group 301, TSL.

15. Mary S. Estill, ed., "Diary of a Confederate Congressman, 1862–1863, I," *Southwestern Historical Quarterly* 38 (April 1935), p. 276.

16. Gray to Lubbock, March 4, 1862, Record Group 301, TSL.

17. Littleton Washington Diary, August 21, 1863, Gibboney.

18. Gray to Lubbock, March 4, 1862, Record Group 301, TSL.

19. Littleton Washington Diary, August 21, 1863, Gibboney.

20. Mallory to Angela Mallory, May 20, 1862, Stephen R. Mallory Letters, University of Florida, Gainesville.

21. Reuben Davis to Pettus, June 18, 1862, Volume 49, Record Group 27, MDAH.

22. Mallory to Angela Mallory, June 4, 1862, Mallory Letters, University of Florida, Gainesville; Washington Diary, August 21, 1863, Gibboney.

23. Estill, ed., "Diary, I," p. 282.

24. Mallory to Angela Mallory, August 31, 1862, Mallory Letters, University of Florida, Gainesville; Estill, "Diary, I," pp. 278, 279.

25. Robert B. Hilton Journal, August 25, 1865, University of Florida, Gainesville.

26. Estill, "Diary, I," p. 283.

27. A. R. Chisholm to Beauregard, August 19, 1864, Confederate Autographs List 34 (Pleasantville, NJ, n.d.), item 26.

28. Bragg to Benjamin, October 30, 1861, Thomas O. Moore Papers, LSU.

29. H. Cone to Lubbock, March 28, 1862, Record Group 301, TSL.

30. Josiah Gorgas to Milton, July 5, 1862, Milton Letterbook, FHS.

31. A. C. Myers to Miles, November 20, 1861, William Porcher Miles Papers, SHC,UNC.

32. Seddon to Bonham, November 21, 1864, Andrew G. Magrath Papers, SCDAH.

33. Littleton Washington Diary, August 21, December 21, 1863, Gibboney.

34. Littleton Washington, A Memoir of Judah Benjamin, November 11, 1897, Gibboney.

35. Littleton Washington Diary, August 21, 1863, Gibboney; William M. Browne to Pettus, January 16, 1862, Volume 48, Record Group 27, MDAH.

36. Lorenzo Castro to Clark, June 26, 1861, Record Group 301, TSL.

37. Thomas Gregory to Clark, June 18, 1861, ibid.; Houston *Weekly Telegraph,* August 11, 1862.

38. Reagan to Lubbock, February 13, 1862, Record Group 301, TSL.

39. Littleton Washington Diary, August 3, 1863, Gibboney.

40. Anonymous to Dear Papa, October 1862, Confederate States of America Records, CAH,UT.
41. Barnwell to Wigfall, November 5, 1862, Louis T. Wigfall Papers, LC.
42. Littleton Washington Diary, August 21, 1863, Gibboney.
43. Ibid, July 30, 1863.
44. Bragg to Moore, November 14, 1861, Moore Papers, LSU.
45. Henry to Wigfall, October 25, 1862, Wigfall Papers, LC.
46. Sparrow to F. M. Herefard, September 20, 1862, Confederate States of America Records, CAH,UT.
47. Moise to Moore, September 24, 1864, Moore Papers, LSU.
48. J. Harper to Moore, September 30, 1864, ibid.
49. Johnston to Wigfall, November 26, 1863, Clay to Wigfall, November 15, 1863, Wigfall Papers, LC.
50. Johnston to Wigfall, January 4, 1864, ibid.
51. Clay to Wigfall, August 5, September 11, 1863, ibid.
52. Mary S. Estill, ed., "Diary of a Confederate Congressman, 1862–1863, II," *Southwestern Historical Quarterly* 39 (July 1935), pp. 34, 35.
53. Clay to Wigfall, August 5, 1863, Wigfall Papers, LC.
54. Clay to Wigfall, September 11, 1863, ibid.
55. Notes of Yancey speech in the Senate, n.d., William Lowndes Yancey Papers, ADAH.
56. Estill, ed., "Diary, II," pp. 35, 58, 59, 60, 63, 64.
57. For the best assessment of the press in the Confederacy, see J. Cutler Andrews, *The South Reports the Civil War* (Princeton, 1970).
58. Littleton Washington Diary, July 30, August 3, 21, 1863, Gibboney.
59. Ibid., August 21, 1863.
60. Ibid., August 21, 26, 1863.
61. Hilton Journal, February 5, 1864, University of Florida, Gainesville.
62. Estill, ed., "Diary, I," p. 293.
63. Hilton Journal, February 6, 1864, University of Florida, Gainesville.
64. J. G. Clark to Allen Thomas, May 25, 1864, Confederate States of America Records, CAH,UT.
65. Hilton Journal, August 23, 1861, University of Florida, Gainesville; Estill, ed., "Diary, I" pp. 277–78.
66. "Impressment of Property," Hilton Journal, n.d., University of Florida, Gainesville.
67. Hudson to Charles Clark, June 15, 1864, Volume 56, Record Group 27, MDAH.
68. Estill, ed., "Diary, I," p. 276.
69. Hilton Journal, February 3–4, 1864, University of Florida, Gainesville.
70. Clark to Thomas, May 24, 1864, Confederate States of America Records, CAH,UT.
71. Kenner to Moore, September 23, 1864, Moore Papers, LSU.
72. Ibid., September 25, 1864.
73. McCarter Journal, II, p. 61, n.d., LC. McCarter's first name is unknown.
74. Letter to the editor of the Tallahassee *Floridian & Journal,* May 1865, Hilton Journal, University of Florida, Gainesville.
75. Hartzog and Brabham, *Biographical Sketch of Gen. Lewis M. Ayer* (N.p., n.d.), pp. 22–23; Yancey to William M. Samford, June 20, 1862, Memphis *Daily Appeal,* July 18, 1862.
76. Richard J. Calhoun, ed., *Witness to Sorrow: The Antebellum Autobiography of William J. Grayson* (Columbia, SC, 1990), p. 197.

CHAPTER THIRTEEN

1. Clay to John J.W. Payne, August 26, 1863, Louis T. Wigfall Papers, LC.
2. Bragg to Moore, October 31, 1861, Thomas O. Moore Papers, LSU.
3. C. Vann Woodward and Elizabeth Muhlenfeld, eds., *The Private Mary Chesnut* (New York, 1984) p. 17.
4. James D.B. DeBow to Charles E.A. Gayarré, August 28, 1861, Charles E.A. Gayarré Papers, LSU.
5. Montgomery *Daily Post,* May 16, 1861.
6. C. Vann Woodward, ed., *Mary Chesnut's Civil War* (New Haven, CT, 1981), p. 206.
7. Jefferson Davis, *Rise and Fall of the Confederate Government* (New York, 1881), 2:163.
8. Littleton Washington Diary, July 30, December 21, 1863, in possession of Douglas L. Gibboney, Carlisle, PA.
9. William W. Anderson to Brown, October 15, 1861, Joseph Brown Papers, GDAH.
10. Mary S. Estill, ed., "Diary of a Confederate Congressman, 1862–1863, I," *Southwestern Historical Quarterly* 38 (April 1935), p. 286; Estill, ed., "Diary, II," 39 (July 1935), p. 38.
11. "Gov. Thomas Watts of Ala.," transcript of December 1863 clipping from unidentified newspaper, Thomas Watts Papers, ADAH.
12. Thomas Cobb to Marion Cobb, February 13, March 16, 1862, Thomas R.R. Cobb Letters, University of Georgia, Athens.
13. William Lowndes Yancey to William M. Samford, June 20, 1862, Memphis *Daily Appeal,* July 18, 1862.
14. H. P. Brewster to Wigfall, May 13, 1862, Wigfall Papers, LC.
15. Louly Wigfall to Charlotte Wigfall, May 19, 1862, ibid.
16. Estill, ed., "Diary, I," pp. 281, 282, 292; Estill, ed., "Diary, II," p. 59.
17. Alvy L. King, *Louis T. Wigfall, Southern Fire-eater* (Baton Rouge, 1970), p. 130.
18. Charlotte Wigfall to Halsey Wigfall, October 22, 1862, Wigfall Papers, LC.
19. Longstreet to Wigfall, November 7, 1862, ibid.
20. Wigfall to Seddon, December 8, 1862, ibid.
21. Mallory to Angela Mallory, August 31, 1862, Stephen R. Mallory Letters, University of Florida, Gainesville.
22. Reuben Davis to Pettus, June 18, 1862, Volume 49, Record Group 27, MDAH.
23. William C. Davis, *"A Government of Our Own": The Making of the Confederacy* (New York, 1994), p. 201.
24. "Our Domestic and Foreign Relations," *DeBow's Review* 31 (September 1861), p. 289.
25. "Commerce of New Orleans," *DeBow's Review* 31 (October–November 1861), pp. 455, 459, 460.
26. Robert Bunch to John Russell, December 15, 1860, "Despatch from the British Consul at Charleston to Lord John Russell, 1860," *American Historical Review* 18 (July 1913), pp. 785–86.
27. "Our Commissioners to Europe—What Are the Facts?" *DeBow's Review* 31 (October–November 1861), pp. 413–16.
28. Yancey to Samuel Reed, July 3, 1861, Yancey Papers, ADAH.
29. Yancey to R. Chapman, July 3, 1861, ibid.
30. JMS to Dr. Raymond, June 30, 1862, Record Group 301, TSL.

31. Slidell to L. W. Washington, May 5, 1864, Joseph Rubinfine Confederate Autographs List 34, item #140.
32. The standard work on Confederate efforts at diplomacy remains Frank Lawrence Owsley, *King Cotton Diplomacy: Foreign Relations of the Confederate States of America* (Chicago, 1931), revised in 1958 in an updated edition by his wife, Harriett Chappell Owsley. It is considerably dated, and half a dozen more recent works by Warren Case and Lynn Spencer, Frank Merli, Norman Ferris, Howard Jones, and others have refined and reshaped some of Owsley's thoughts, but in the main his presentation and assessment remain unchallenged.
33. William C. Davis, ed., *A Fire-Eater Remembers: The Confederate Memoir of Robert Barnwell Rhett* (Columbia, SC, 2000), pp. 38–39.
34. Memminger to Noyes, February 23, 1861, Alonzo B. Noyes Collection, University of Florida, Gainesville.
35. Richard Cecil Todd, *Confederate Finance* (Athens, GA, 1954), pp. 52–54. After half a century Todd is still the standard work on the subject.
36. Wigfall to Lubbock, December 9, 1861, Record Group 301, TSL.
37. Littleton Washington Diary, August 21, 1863, Gibboney.
38. Charles Johnson to Pettus, November 11, 1861, Volume 47, Record Group 27, MDAH.
39. Todd, *Confederate Finance,* p. 198.
40. Richmond *Examiner,* October 1863.
41. William C. Davis, *The Union That Shaped the Confederacy: Robert Toombs and Alexander H. Stephens* (Lawrence, KS, 2001), pp. 132–33.
42. "Commercial Enfranchisement of the Confederate States," *DeBow's Review* 31 (October–November 1861), pp. 346–47.
43. J.C.S. Blackburn to the editor of the Milledgeville *Southern Union,* May 1861, Brown Papers, GDAH.
44. Shorter to B. C. Pressley, December 12, 1864, John Gill Shorter Letters, ADAH.
45. "The War Tax," *DeBow's Review* 31 (October–November 1861), p. 439.
46. Tax in kind special exemption form, Confederate States of America Records, CAH,UT.
47. Todd, *Confederate Finance,* p. 156.
48. Bill to be entitled An Act to Tax Limit & Fund the Currency, Robert B. Hilton Journal, n.d., University of Florida, Gainesville.
49. "The Cotton Interest and Its Relation to the Present Crisis," *DeBow's Review* 32 (March–April 1862), pp. 283–85.
50. Davis, ed., *A Fire-Eater Remembers,* pp. 42–43, 65–69.
51. Toombs to Robert Barnwell Rhett, Jr., December 20, 1882, Robert Barnwell Rhett Papers, SCL,USC.
52. Edwin DeLeon, "Secret History of Confederate Diplomacy Abroad," New York *Citizen,* January 4, 1868.
53. Isaac Applewhite to Pettus, July 15, 1862, Volume 49, Record Group 27, MDAH.
54. R. T. Saunders to James Saunders, September 30, 1863, Confederate States of America Records, CAH,UT.
55. N. Habersham to Cheves, March 21, 1863, Langdon Cheves Papers, SCHS.
56. Martha Cragan to Clark, November 28, 1863, Volume 56, Record Group 27, MDAH.
57. John Ventress to Clark, February 6, 1864, ibid.

58. Thomas J. Winn to Memminger, May 8, 1864, Noyes Collection, University of Florida, Gainesville.

59. Wigfall to Johnston, n.d. [November–December 1862], August 8, 1863, Johnston to Wigfall, March 8, 1863, November 24, 1866, Wigfall Papers, LC; Richmond *Sentinel,* May 23, 1863.

60. Hunter to Wigfall, June 23, 1863, Wigfall Papers, LC; Robert Barnwell Rhett, Jr., "Fixed Ammunition in Reserve," ca. 1882, Rhett Papers, SCL,USC.

61. Elliott Ashkenazi, ed., *The Civil War Diary of Clara Solomon: Growing Up in New Orleans, 1861–1862* (Baton Rouge, 1995), p. 383.

62. Clay to Wigfall, August 5, 1863, Wigfall Papers, LC.

63. Wigfall to Johnston, September 11, 1863, Joseph E. Johnston Papers, Henry E. Huntington Library, San Marino, CA.

64. Wigfall to Johnston, December 18, 1863, ibid.

65. Johnston to Wigfall, March 6, 1864, Wigfall Papers, LC.

66. Thomas Cobb to Marion Cobb, January 12, 1862, Cobb Letters, University of Georgia.

67. Rhett to Robert Barnwell Rhett, Jr., December 17, 1861, Rhett Papers, SCL,USC; Davis, ed., *A Fire-Eater Remembers,* p. 118n.

68. Snead to Thomas C. Reynolds, May 14, 1864, American Historical Auctions Catalog (Boston, 1996), p. 66, item #293.

69. Clay to Wigfall, April 29, 1864, Wigfall Papers, LC.

70. Barnwell to Wigfall, November 5, 1862, ibid.

71. Wigfall to Johnston, March 18, 1864, Johnston Papers, Huntington.

72. Houston *Daily Telegraph,* June 6, 1864.

73. Johnston to Wigfall, January 9, 1864, Wigfall Papers, LC.

74. Robert Ransom, Reminiscences of Jefferson Davis, February 14, 1890, Confederate States of America Records, CAH,UT.

75. Wigfall to Johnston, March 19, 1864, Wigfall Papers, LC.

76. Wigfall to Hammond, April 1864, James Henry Hammond Papers, LC; Hammond to Wigfall, April 15, 1864, Rhett to Wigfall, April 15, 1864, Wigfall Papers, LC.

77. Wharton to Wigfall, September 18, 1864, Wigfall Papers, LC.

78. Houston *Daily Telegraph,* October 24, 1864.

79. For the secretary of war, the standard biography is William C. Davis, *Breckinridge: Statesman, Soldier, Symbol* (Baton Rouge, 1974).

80. Thomas E. Schott, *Alexander H. Stephens of Georgia* (Baton Rouge, 1988), p. 437.

81. Houston *Daily Telegraph,* November 11, 1864.

82. Wigfall to Johnston, March 3, 1865, Johnston Papers, Huntington.

83. John T. Pickett statement, August 5, 1882, John T. Pickett Compiled Service Record, Confederate Generals and Staff Officers Papers, Record Group 109, NA.

84. Henry W. Cleveland, "Robert Toombs," *Southern Bivouac* 1 (January 1886), pp. 454–57.

85. Toombs to Stephens, April 1, 1864, in Ulrich B. Phillips, ed., *The Correspondence of Robert Toombs, Alexander H. Stephens, and Howell Cobb* (Washington, 1913), pp. 638–39.

86. Sarah Lawton to her father, April 6, 1864, Alexander-Hillhouse Papers, SHC,UNC.

87. King, *Wigfall,* p. 467.

88. Montgomery *Weekly Advertiser,* August 29, 1862.

89. Davis, ed., *A Fire-Eater Remembers,* pp. 80–81, 142*n;* Yancey to Samford, June 20, 1862, Memphis *Daily Appeal,* July 18, 1862.

90. Stephens to Wigfall, February 13, 1865, Profiles in History Autograph Catalog #17, Fall 1992 (Beverly Hills, 1992), p. 40, item #56.

91. Barnwell R. Burnet to Dear Huger, November 8, 1913, Bacot-Huger Papers, SCHS.

92. Toombs to Stephens, March 16, 1865, in Phillips, ed., *Correspondence,* p. 660.

93. "Trusted as a Brother," 1886, transcript of remarks of Jefferson Davis, Watts Papers, ADAH.

Chapter Fourteen

1. T. C. Manning to Moore, December 27, 1864, Thomas O. Moore Papers, LSU.

2. Magrath to Vance, January 11, 26, 1865, Zebulon Vance Papers, NCDAH.

3. Preston to Wigfall, January 19, 1860, Louis T. Wigfall Papers, LC.

4. W. G. Bean, ed., "Memoranda of Conversations Between General Robert E. Lee and William Preston Johnston," *Virginia Magazine of History and Biography* 73 (October 1965), p. 479.

5. Johnston to Wigfall, February 12, 1865, Wigfall Papers, LC.

6. Officers of the 8th Texas Cavalry to Breckinridge, January 22, 1865, Confederate Scrapbook, CAH,UT.

7. Murrah to Horace Cone, February 2, 1865, Record Book 301, TSL.

8. Guy Bryan to Murrah, February 25, 1865, Allen to Murrah, February 7, 1865, ibid.

9. E. S. Fisher to Clark, February 14, 1865, Volume 57, Record Group 27, MDAH.

10. Robert Barnwell Rhett, Jr., to J. Franklin Jameson, May 19, 1899, J. Franklin Jameson Papers, LC.

11. Trescot to Magrath, February 20, 1865, Letters Received and Sent, 1864–1865, Governor Andrew G. Magrath Papers, SCDAH.

12. Milton to Hilton, January 9, 1865, Record Group 32, Volume 7, FSA.

13. Walker to Murrah, March 1, 1865, Record Group 301, TSL.

14. Thomas P. Aycock to Murrah, February 18, 1865, ibid.

15. E. S. Fisher to Clark, February 14, 1865, Volume 57, Record Group 27, MDAH.

16. Montgomery *Daily Advertiser,* March 3, 1865.

17. J. A. Dennis to Murrah, March 22, 1865, Record Group 301, TSL.

18. P. K. Montgomery to Clark, April 4, 1865, Volume 57, Record Group 27, MDAH.

19. William Lamar Gammon II, "Governor John Milton of Florida, Confederate States of America," Master's thesis, University of Florida, Gainesville, 1948, p. 270; A. K. Allison Oath, April 3, 1865, Correspondence of the Secretary of State, 1845–1865, University of Florida, Gainesville.

20. W. F. DeSaussure to Magrath, April 15, 1865, Magrath Papers, SCDAH.

21. Annual message, November 1864, Thomas Watts Papers, ADAH.

22. Houston *Daily Telegraph,* February 4, 7, 1865.

23. The most recent look at the Hampton Roads conference is to be found in Robert Saunders, Jr., *John Archibald Campbell, Southern Moderate, 1811–1889* (Tuscaloosa, AL, 1997), pp. 166–70.

24. Edward Younger, ed., *Inside the Confederate Government: The Diary of Robert Garlick Hill Kean* (New York, 1957), p. 199; John B. Jones, *A Rebel War Clerk's Diary at*

the Confederate States Capital (Philadelphia, 1866), 2:423-26; Varina Davis, *Jefferson Davis, Ex-President of the Confederate States of America: A Memoir by His Wife* (New York, 1890), 2, p. 592; Hunter to William Jones, [November 1877], in Dunbar Rowland, ed., *Jefferson Davis, Constitutionalist: His Letters, Papers and Speeches* (Jackson, MS, 1923),7:576–77. Much of this account of these events and the flight of the government is drawn from William C. Davis, *An Honorable Defeat: The Last Days of the Confederate Government* (New York, 2001), p. 28ff.

25. "From Richmond to Austin with Judge Reagan's Children," clipping in Confederate Scrapbook, CAH,UT.

26. Breckinridge to J. P. Hawkins, April 2, 1865, Robert A. Siegel Auction Catalog Sale #786, April 8–9, 1997, p. 82, item #2470.

27. J. P. Hawkins Diary, April 2, 1865, ibid., pp. 88–89, item #2513.

28. Murrah to T. C. Armstrong, March 21, 1865, Murrah to John Williams, March 21, 1865, letterbook, Record Group 301, TSL; Josiah Gorgas to Davis, February 3, 1878, Confederate States of America Records, CAH,UT.

29. Johnston to Wigfall, April 3, 1865, Wigfall Papers, LC; W. Strong to Clark, April 9, 1865, Volume 57, Record Group 27, MDAH.

30. J. P. Hawkins Diary, n.d., Robert A. Siegel Auction Catalog Sale 786, April 8–9, 1997, p. 89, items #2513 and 2514.

31. Magrath to Reagan, April 10, 1865, Henry Creswel to Magrath, April 8, 1865, Magrath Papers, SCDAH.

32. Allen to General Samuel Jones, April 19, 1865, Correspondence of the Secretary of State, University of Florida, Gainesville.

33. R. M. Butler to Clark, April 22, 1865, Daniel Dupree to Clark, April 24, 1865, Volume 57, Record Group 27, MDAH; F. W. Adams to Brown, April 18, 1865, Joseph Brown Papers, GDAH; "From Richmond to Austin with Judge Reagan's Children," clipping in Confederate Scrapbook, CAH,UT; W. G. Vincent to J. U. Galleher, March 29, 1865, Simon B. Buckner Papers, Confederate States of America Records, CAH,UT.

34. Daniel Avery to Moore, May 17, 1865, Moore Papers, LSU.

35. Pettus to Clark, April 20, 1865, Volume 57, Record Group 27, MDAH.

36. M. Phillips to Clark, April 25, 1865, ibid.

37. Karen E. Fritz, in *Voices in the Storm: Confederate Rhetoric, 1861–1865* (Denton, TX, 1999), argues that Confederates, through their oratory, were actually preparing themselves for defeat in the later years of the war. This is one of numerous overstatements in what is generally a weak case for the uses of oratorical analysis in understanding the Confederacy. Much more useful in identifying shifting Southern morale in popular culture is E. Lawrence Abel, *Singing the New Nation: How Music Shaped the Confederacy, 1861–1865* (Mechanicsburg, PA, 2000).

38. Munford to Sallie Munford, May 21, 1865, Thomas T. Munford File, Virginia Military Institute Alumni Collection, Lexington.

39. Daniel Avery to Moore, May 7, 1865, Moore Papers, LSU.

40. John Miller to Elizabeth Miller, May 23, 1865, in Charles F. Cooney, ed., "The Civil War," *Manuscripts* 27 (Spring 1975), pp. 128–29.

41. Proclamation, April 27, 1865, Record Group 301, TSL.

42. James C. Wise to Moore, May 8, 1865, Moore Papers, LSU.

43. Kirby Smith to Murrah et al., May 9, 1865, Record Group 301, TSL.

44. Houston *Daily Telegraph,* May 10, 1865.
45. Secret Instructions, n.d. [May 1865], Record Group 301, TSL.
46. Order Book, Volume 59, Record Group 27, MDAH.
47. Washington *Daily National Intelligencer,* June 29, 1865.
48. Proclamation, April 28, 1865, Vance Papers, NCDAH.
49. Proclamation, May 19, 1865, A. K. Allison to Brown, May 12, 1865, Correspondence of the Secretary of State, University of Florida, Gainesville.
50. Hill to James Johnson, July 14, 1865, Benjamin H. Hill File, 4-2-46, GDAH.
51. Clark to E. D. Osband, May 22, 1865, Volume 57, statement of rations, August 1865, William Merrill report, October 2, 1865, Volume 60, Record Group 27, MDAH.
52. Murrah to Ashbel Smith, May 24, 1865, Record Group 301, TSL.
53. John Ireland to Murrah, May 26, 1865, Magruder to Murrah, May 26, 1865, Crosby to Murrah, May 25, 1865, ibid.
54. Houston *Daily Telegraph,* June 23, 1865.
55. Message, June 2, 1865, Moore Papers, LSU.
56. Henry A. Wise to G. Julian Pratt, July 11, 1865, copy in Henry A. Wise File, Fredericksburg National Military Park, Fredericksburg, VA.
57. Littleton Washington, Memoir of Judah Benjamin, November 11, 1897, in possession of Douglas L. Gibboney, Carlisle, PA.
58. John W. Watts Journal, n.d. [April–May 1865], Watts Papers, ADAH.
59. R. C. Logan to Magrath, April 5, 1865, Magrath Papers, SCDAH.
60. Mary Delaney McConaghy, "Ordinary White Folk in a Lowcountry Community: The Structure and Dynamics of St. Bartholomew's Parish, South Carolina, 1850–1870," doctoral dissertation, University of Pennsylvania, Philadelphia, 1996, pp. 462–63.
61. Gary W. Gallagher, *The Confederate War: How Popular Will, Nationalism, and Military Strategy Could Not Stave Off Defeat* (Cambridge, MA, 1997), p. 158 and throughout, ably makes the point that Confederates quickly came to believe that only superior enemy resources and manpower had defeated them, and not weaknesses within their own resolve, a half-truth that would be the bedrock of the lost cause myth.

BIBLIOGRAPHY

PRIMARY SOURCES

Manuscripts

Alabama Department of Archives and History, Montgomery
  Augusta Bellinger Cheney, The Inauguration of Jefferson Davis by an Eye Witness
  Curry Family Papers
  M. C. McCombs Letter
  Montgomery City Council Minutes
  John Gill Shorter Letters
  Thomas Watts Letterbook
  Thomas Watts Papers
  Michael L. Woods Papers
  William Lowndes Yancey Papers

University of Alabama, Tuscaloosa
  Henry Hilliard Papers
  Robert Jemison, Jr., Papers

University of Arkansas, Fayetteville
  John W. Brown Diary
  Daniel Harris Reynolds Papers

Auburn University, Auburn, Alabama
  Robert E. Corry Confederate Collection
  Denney Confederate Letters
  John R. Dixon Correspondence
  George Family Papers

B.R.H. Jeffares Letter
George H.W. Petrie Papers
Joseph S. Powell Collection
Charles Coleman Thach Collection

Lawrence Berry, Osprey, Florida
T. H. Spann Papers

Charleston Museum, Charleston, South Carolina
Aiken Rhett Collection

Duke University, Durham, North Carolina
Clement C. Clay Papers
Charles Colcock Jones, Jr., Autograph Letters and Portraits of the Signers of the Constitution of the Confederate States
Lawrence Keitt Papers
John Milton Letters
Munford-Ellis Family Papers
Francis W. Pickens Papers
Robert A. Toombs Papers

East Carolina Manuscript Collection, East Carolina University, Greenville, North Carolina
Elizabeth Rudder Fearington Croom Collection
James C. Galloway Papers

Emory University, Atlanta, Georgia
James P. Hambleton Papers
Alexander H. Stephens Papers

Filson Club, Louisville, Kentucky
Samuel Haycroft Journal

Florida Historical Society, St. Augustine
John Milton Letterbook, 1861–1863
John Milton Papers

Florida State Archives, Tallahassee
Declaration of Causes, Record Group 577
Governors' Letterbooks, Record Group 32
Journal of the Proceedings of the People's Convention, January 3, 1861, Record Group 540
Office of the Governor, Correspondence of the Governors, Record Group 577
Ordinance and Resolutions of the Convention of the People of the State of Florida, Record Group 1000, 1457
Proceedings of the Executive Council, February 28, 1861, Record Group 82

University of Florida, Gainesville
Correspondence of the Secretary of State, 1845–1865

Robert B. Hilton Journal
Stephen R. Mallory Letters
Miscellaneous Manuscripts Collection
Alonzo B. Noyes Collection
Milton S. Perry Letters
Enoch J. Vann, Papers Relating to the Sequestration Acts, 1861 and 1862

Fredericksburg National Military Park, Fredericksburg, Virginia
Henry A. Wise File

Georgia Department of Archives and History, Atlanta
Joseph Brown Papers
Henry Cleveland File, Record Group 4-2-46
Governors' Incoming Correspondence, Record Group 1-1-5
Benjamin H. Hill Personal Folder
Eugenius A. Nisbet File, Record Group 4-2-46
James Madison Spullock Collection

University of Georgia, Athens
Howell Cobb Papers
Thomas R.R. Cobb Letters

Douglas L. Gibboney, Carlisle, Pennsylvania
Littleton Washington Diary, 1863–1864, transcript
Littleton Washington, Memoir of Judah Benjamin, November 11, 1897

Henry E. Huntington Library and Art Gallery, San Marino, California
Joseph E. Johnston Papers

Shinaan Krakowsky, Encino, California
Robert Barnwell Rhett Letters

Library of Congress, Washington, DC
James Chesnut Letterbook, Miscellaneous Manuscript Collection
James Henry Hammond Papers
J. Franklin Jameson Papers
McCarter Journal
William Porcher Miles Collection
Alexander H. Stephens Papers
William H. Trescot Papers
Louis T. Wigfall Papers

Lincoln Memorial Shrine, Redlands, California
Walker Vest Letter

Louisiana State University, Baton Rouge
Confederate States of America Collection
Charles E.A. Gayarré Papers

Miscellaneous Manuscript Collection
Thomas O. Moore Papers
Michael D. Wynne Collection

Manhattanville College of the Sacred Heart, Purchase, New York
Alexander H. Stephens Papers

Francis Martin, Lebanon, Tennessee
Spencer Talley Memoir, 1918

Mississippi Department of Archives and History, Jackson
Governors' Records, Record Group 27
Charles Clark
John J. Pettus

National Archives, Washington, DC
John T. Pickett Compiled Service Record, Record Group 109
Records of General Courts Martial, Record Group 153
Records of Military Courts Martial, Record Group 153

North Carolina Department of Archives and History, Raleigh
Zebulon Vance Papers

Katherine Breckinridge Prewitt, Lexington, Kentucky
Breckinridge Family Papers

South Carolina Department of Archives and History, Columbia
Bonds and Contracts for Salt Manufacturing, 1862–1863
Central Association 1865 Miscellaneous Papers
John Jenkins Personal Papers
Andrew G. Magrath Papers
Petitions to Distill or Sell or Transport Liquor, 1862
Francis W. Pickens Papers
Soldiers Board of Relief Papers, 1862–1865

South Carolina Historical Society, Charleston
Bacot-Huger Papers
Joseph Campbell Papers
Langdon Cheves Papers
Rhett Genealogy Notes
Robert Barnwell Rhett Papers
Stuart Family Papers

South Caroliniana Library, University of South Carolina, Columbia
Milledge L. Bonham Papers
Robert Barnwell Rhett Papers
William H. Trescot Papers
Williams-Chesnut-Manning Family Papers

Southern Historical Collection, University of North Carolina, Chapel Hill
    J.F.H. Claiborne Papers
    Alexander Hillhouse Papers
    William Porcher Miles Papers
    Eliza Moses Journal
    Orr-Patterson Papers
    Robert Barnwell Rhett Papers

Texas State Library, Austin
    John H. Reagan Papers, Benjamin H. Good Collection
    Records of the Governors, Record Group 301
        Edward Clark
        Sam Houston
        Francis Lubbock
        Pendleton Murrah

University of Texas, Austin
    Confederate States of America Records
        Simon Bolivar Buckner Papers
        James E. Saunders Papers

Virginia Military Institute Alumni Files, Lexington
    John Echols File
    Thomas T. Munford File
    Robert E. Rodes File

Virginia State Library, Richmond
    Executive Papers, Miscellaneous Letters and Papers
        John Letcher

University of Virginia, Charlottesville
    R.M.T. Hunter Papers

Washington and Lee University, Lexington, Virginia
    David Jamison Papers

Western Reserve Historical Society, Cleveland, Ohio
    William Palmer Collection

College of William and Mary, Williamsburg, Virginia
    John Letcher Papers

Manuscripts in Auction Catalogs

Alexander Autographs Auction Catalog, April 29, 2000
American Historical Auctions Catalog, Boston 1996
Bohemian Brigade Bookshop Catalog, November 1998
Bohemian Brigade Bookshop Catalog, June 1999

Holzman-Caren Associates Historical Collectibles Auction Catalog, April 28, 1996
Profiles in History Autograph Catalog 17, Fall 1992
Joseph Rubinfine Confederate Autographs List 34
Joseph Rubinfine C.S.A. List 69
Robert A. Siegel Auction Catalog 786, April 8–9, 1997
R. M. Smythe Sale Catalog 186, April 22, 1999
RWA Auction Catalog 41, March 15, 1997

Newspapers

Atlanta *Daily Constitution*
Atlanta *Journal-Constitution*
Charleston *Daily Courier*
Charleston *Mercury*
Columbia *Daily South Carolinian*
Columbus, GA, *Daily Columbus Enquirer*
Greensboro *Alabama Beacon*
Houston *Daily Telegraph*
Houston *Weekly Telegraph*
Marshall *Texas Republican*
Memphis *Daily Appeal*
Mobile *Daily Advertiser*
Montgomery *Daily Advertiser*
Montgomery *Daily Post*

Montgomery *Weekly Advertiser*
Montgomery *Weekly Confederation*
Montgomery *Weekly Mail*
Nashville *Union & American*
New York *Citizen*
New York *Herald*
Philadelphia *Weekly Times*
Richmond *Examiner*
Richmond *Sentinel*
Rome, GA, *Tri-Weekly Courier*
Tuscaloosa, AL, *Independent Monitor*
Vicksburg *Daily Evening Citizen*
Washington *Daily National Intelligencer*
Washington *Evening Star*

Official Publications

Confederate States Congress. *The Laws of the Confederate States.* Montgomery and Richmond, 1861–1862.
Ramsdell, Charles W., ed. *Laws and Joint Resolutions of the Last Session of the Confederate Congress Together with the Secret Acts of the Previous Congresses.* Durham, NC, 1941.
Rules of Practice Under the Sequestration Act, for the Confederate States Courts, for the District of Florida. Montgomery, 1862.
Sanford, John W.A. *The Code of the City of Montgomery.* Montgomery, 1861.
United States Congress. *Journal of the Congress of the Confederate States of America, 1861–1865.* 7 volumes. Washington, 1904.
United States War Department. *War of the Rebellion: Official Records of the Union and Confederate Armies.* 128 volumes. Washington, 1880–1901.

Published Diaries, Letters, Memoirs

Address of Hon. W. L. Harris, Commissioner from the State of Mississippi, Delivered before the General Assembly of the State of Georgia, on Monday, Dec. 17th, 1860. Milledgeville, GA, 1860.
Ashkenazi, Elliott, ed. *The Civil War Diary of Clara Solomon: Growing Up in New Orleans, 1861–1862.* Baton Rouge, 1995.
Calhoun, Richard J., ed. *Witness to Sorrow: The Antebellum Autobiography of William J. Grayson.* Columbia, SC, 1990.

Crabtree, Beth Gilbert, and James W. Patton, eds. *"Journal of a Secesh Lady": The Diary of Catherine Ann Devereux Edmondston, 1860–1866*. Raleigh, NC, 1979.

Crawford, N. M. *Thoughts on Government: The Marriage of Negroes*. N.p., 1864.

Crist, Lynda Lasswell, and Mary Seaton Dix, eds. *The Papers of Jefferson Davis*, volume 7. Baton Rouge, 1992.

Curry, J.L.M. *Civil History of the Government of the Confederate States, With Some Personal Reminiscences*. Richmond, 1901.

Davis, Jefferson. *Rise and Fall of the Confederate Government*. 2 volumes. New York, 1881.

Davis, Varina. *Jefferson Davis, Ex-President of the Confederate States of America: A Memoir by His Wife*. 2 volumes. New York, 1890.

Davis, William C., ed. *A Fire-Eater Remembers: The Confederate Memoir of Robert Barnwell Rhett*. Columbia, SC, 2000.

Fleet, Betsy, and John D.P. Fuller, eds. *Green Mount: A Virginia Plantation Family During the Civil War.* Lexington, KY, 1962.

Hughes, Thomas. *A Boy's Experience in the Civil War, 1860–1865*. Washington, 1904.

Inaugural Address of Gov. P. Murrah Delivered November 5th, 1863. Austin, TX, 1863.

Jahnsenykes [Jenks], William. *Memoir of the Northern Kingdom, Written, A.D. 1872*. Boston, 1808.

Johnston, Richard M. *Autobiography of Col. Richard M. Johnston*. Washington, 1900.

Jones, John B. *A Rebel War Clerk's Diary at the Confederate States Capital*. 2 volumes. Philadelphia, 1866.

Moore, Frank, ed. *The Rebellion Record*. 12 volumes. New York, 1861–1866.

Oliphant, Mary C., Alfred Taylor Odell, and T. C. Duncan Eaves, eds. *The Letters of William Gilmore Simms*. 4 volumes. Columbia, SC, 1955.

Park, R.A.S., ed. *"Dear Parents": The Civil War Letters of the Shibley Brothers of Van Buren*. Fayetteville, AR, 1963.

Phillips, Ulrich B., ed. *The Correspondence of Robert Toombs, Alexander H. Stephens, and Howell Cobb*. Washington, 1913.

Porter, A. Toomer. *Led On! Step by Step*. New York, 1967; reprint of 1898 edition.

Ross, W. D., ed. *The Works of Aristotle*. 2 volumes. Chicago, 1952.

Rowland, Dunbar, ed. *Jefferson Davis, Constitutionalist: His Letters, Papers and Speeches*. 10 volumes. Jackson, MS, 1923.

Smith, Robert H. *An Address to the Citizens of Alabama, on the Constitution of the Confederate States of America*. Mobile, 1861.

Stephens, Alexander H. *A Constitutional View of the Late War Between the States*. 2 volumes. Philadelphia, 1868, 1870.

Tharin, Robert S. *Arbitrary Arrests in the South; or, Scenes from the Experience of an Alabama Unionist*. New York, 1863.

Woodward, C. Vann, ed. *Mary Chesnut's Civil War.* New Haven, CT, 1981.

————, and Elizabeth Muhlenfeld, eds. *The Private Mary Chesnut*. New York, 1984.

Younger, Edward, ed. *Inside the Confederate Government: The Diary of Robert Garlick Hill Kean*. New York, 1957.

Articles

Barr, Alwyn, ed. "Records of the Confederate Military Commission in San Antonio, July 2–October 10, 1862." *Southwestern Historical Quarterly* 73 (October 1969), pp. 246–72.

Bean, W. G., ed. "Memoranda of Conversations Between General Robert E. Lee and William Preston Johnston." *Virginia Magazine of History and Biography* 73 (October 1965), pp. 474–84.

Cartwright, Samuel A. "Report of the Diseases and Physical Peculiarities of the Negro Race." *New Orleans Medical and Surgical Journal* (May 1851), pp. 691–715.

Cleveland, Henry W. "Robert Toombs." *Southern Bivouac*, New Series 1 (January 1886), pp. 449–59.

Collins, Robert. "Essay on the Management of Slaves." *DeBow's Review* 32 (January–February 1862), pp. 154–57.

"Commerce of New Orleans." *DeBow's Review* 31 (October–November 1861), pp. 454–61.

"Commercial Enfranchisement of the Confederated States." *DeBow's Review* 31 (October–November, 1861), pp. 333–47.

"The Constitution of the Confederate States." *DeBow's Review* 31 (July 1861), pp. 13–17.

Cooney, Charles F., ed. "The Civil War." *Manuscripts* 27 (Spring 1975), pp. 128–29.

"The Cotton Interest and Its Relation to the Present Crisis." *DeBow's Review* 32 (March–April 1862), pp. 279–86.

DeLeon, Edwin. "Secret History of Confederate Diplomacy Abroad." New York *Citizen*, January 4, 1868.

"Despatch from the British Consul at Charleston to Lord John Russell, 1860." *American Historical Review* 18 (July 1913), pp. 783–87.

"Disenthrallment of Southern Literature." *DeBow's Review* 31 (October–November 1861), pp. 347–61.

Editorial. *DeBow's Review* 7 (January–February 1862), pp. 161–67.

Editorial. *DeBow's Review* 34 (July–August, 1864), pp. 97–99.

"Editor's Table." *Southern Literary Messenger,* May 1863, p. 317.

"Education of Southern Women." *DeBow's Review* 31 (October–November 1861), pp. 381–90.

Estill, Mary S., ed. "Diary of a Confederate Congressman, 1862–1863, I." *Southwestern Historical Quarterly* 38 (April 1935), pp. 270–301; II, 39 (July 1935), pp. 33–65.

Floyd, Dale, ed. "I Have Severed My Connection with the North." *Manuscripts* 26 (Spring 1974), pp. 140–41.

"The Future of the Confederation." *DeBow's Review* 31 (July 1861), pp. 35–41.

McWhorter, J. K. "Caring for the Soldier in the Sixties." *Confederate Veteran* 29 (October 1912), pp. 409–10.

"Our Commissioners to Europe—What Are the Facts?" *DeBow's Review* 31 (October–November 1861), pp. 412–19.

"Our Domestic and Foreign Relations." *DeBow's Review* 31 (September 1861), pp. 287–96.

"Our Position and That of Our Enemies." *DeBow's Review* 31 (July 1861), pp. 21–35.

"Reflections on the Conduct of the War." *DeBow's Review* 31 (October–November 1861), pp. 427–35.

"The Right to Enslave." *DeBow's Review* 30 (May–June 1861), pp. 548–50.

"Superiority of Southern Races." *DeBow's Review* 31 (October–November 1861), pp. 369–81.

"The Times and the War." *DeBow's Review* 31 (July 1861), pp. 1–12.

"The War Tax." *DeBow's Review* 31 (October–November 1861), pp. 436–42.

"What We are Gaining by the War." *DeBow's Review* 7 (January–February 1862), pp. 158–60.

"The Women of the South." *DeBow's Review* 31 (August 1861), pp. 147–54.

SECONDARY SOURCES

General Works, Biographies, Monographs

Abel, E. Lawrence. *Singing the New Nation: How Music Shaped the Confederacy, 1861–1865.* Mechanicsburg, PA, 2000.

Alexander, Thomas B., and Richard E. Beringer. *Anatomy of the Confederate Congress.* Nashville, 1972.

Andrews, J. Cutler. *The South Reports the Civil War.* Princeton, 1970.

Appleby, Joyce. *Inheriting the Revolution: The First Generation of Americans.* New York, 2000.

Ash, Stephen V. *When the Yankees Came: Conflict & Chaos in the Occupied South, 1861–1865.* Chapel Hill, NC, 1995.

Barnwell, Stephen. *An American Family.* Marquette, IL, 1969.

Baum, Dale. *The Shattering of Texas Unionism: Politics in the Lone Star State During the Civil War Era.* Baton Rouge, 1998.

Blair, William. *Virginia's Private War: Feeding Body and Soul in the Confederacy, 1861–1865.* New York, 1998.

Bremner, Robert H. *The Public Good: Philanthropy & Welfare in the Civil War Era.* New York, 1980.

Buenger, Walter L. *Secession and the Union in Texas.* Austin, 1984.

Capers, Henry D. *The Life and Times of C. G. Memminger.* Richmond, 1893.

Cauthen, Charles E. *South Carolina Goes to War.* Chapel Hill, NC, 1950.

Davis, William C. *Breckinridge: Statesman, Soldier, Symbol.* Baton Rouge, 1974.

———. *"A Government of Our Own": The Making of the Confederacy.* New York, 1994.

———. *An Honorable Defeat: The Last Days of the Confederate Government.* New York, 2001.

———. *Jefferson Davis, The Man and His Hour.* New York, 1991.

———. *The Union That Shaped the Confederacy: Robert Toombs and Alexander H. Stephens.* Lawrence, KS, 2001.

DeRosa, Marshall L. *The Confederate Constitution of 1861.* Columbia, MO, 1991.

DuBose, John Witherspoon. *The Life and Times of William Lowndes Yancey.* Birmingham, AL, 1892.

Dyer, Thomas G. *Secret Yankees: The Union Circle in Confederate Atlanta.* Baltimore, 1999.

Edwards, Laura F. *Scarlett Doesn't Live Here Anymore: Southern Women in the Civil War Era.* Urbana, IL, 2000.

Faust, Drew Gilpin. *The Creation of Confederate Nationalism.* Baton Rouge, 1988.

———. *Mothers of Invention: Women of the Slaveholding South in the American Civil War.* Chapel Hill, NC, 1996.

Fisher, Noel C. *War at Every Door: Partisan Politics & Guerrilla Violence in East Tennessee, 1860–1869.* Chapel Hill, NC, 1997.

Fritz, Karen E. *Voices in the Storm: Confederate Rhetoric, 1861–1865.* Denton, TX, 1999.

Gallagher, Gary W. *The Confederate War: How Popular Will, Nationalism, and Military Strategy Could Not Stave Off Defeat.* Cambridge, MA, 1997.

Groce, W. Todd. *Mountain Rebels: East Tennessee Confederates and the Civil War, 1860–1870.* Knoxville, 1999.

Harris, William C. *Leroy Pope Walker, Confederate Secretary of War.* Tuscaloosa, AL, 1962.

Hartzog and Brabham. *Biographical Sketch of Gen. Lewis M. Ayer.* N.p., n.d.

Hill, Louisa B. *State Socialism in the Confederate States of America.* Charlottesville, VA, 1936.

Johnston, Richard M., and William Browne. *Life of Alexander H. Stephens.* Philadelphia, 1878.

King, Alvy L. *Louis T. Wigfall, Southern Fire-eater.* Baton Rouge, 1970.

Lonn, Ella. *Salt as a Factor in the Confederacy.* University, AL, 1965.

McCaslin, Richard B. *Tainted Breeze: The Great Hanging at Gainesville, Texas, 1862.* Baton Rouge, 1994.

McDonald, Forrest. *States' Rights and the Union: Imperium in Imperio, 1776–1876.* Lawrence, KS, 2000.

Marten, James. *The Children's Civil War.* Chapel Hill, NC, 1998.

Massey, Mary Elizabeth. *Refugee Life in the Confederacy.* Baton Rouge, 1964.

Mohr, Clarence L. *On the Threshold of Freedom: Masters and Slaves in Civil War Georgia.* Athens, GA, 1986.

Moore, Albert Burton. *Conscription and Conflict in the Confederacy.* Reprint, New York, 1963.

Neely, Mark. *Southern Rights.* Charlottesville, VA, 1999.

Owsley, Frank Lawrence. *King Cotton Diplomacy: Foreign Relations of the Confederate States of America.* Chicago, 1931.

———. *State Rights in the Confederacy.* Chicago, 1925.

Pickering, David, and Judy Falls. *Brush Men & Vigilantes: Civil War Dissent in Texas.* College Station, TX, 2000.

Rable, George C. *Civil Wars: Women and the Crisis of Southern Nationalism.* Urbana, IL, 1989.

———. *The Confederate Republic: A Revolution Against Politics.* Chapel Hill, NC, 1994.

Ringold, Mary Spencer. *The Role of the State Legislatures in the Confederacy.* Athens, GA, 1966.

Saunders, Robert, Jr. *John Archibald Campbell, Southern Moderate, 1811–1889.* Tuscaloosa, AL, 1997.

Schafer, Judith Kelleher. *Slavery, the Civil War, and the Supreme Court of Louisiana.* Baton Rouge, 1998.

Schott, Thomas E. *Alexander H. Stephens of Georgia.* Baton Rouge, 1988.

Stovall, Pleasant A. *Robert Toombs, Statesman, Speaker, Soldier, Sage.* New York, 1892.

Sutherland, Daniel E., ed. *Guerrillas, Unionists, and Violence on the Confederate Home Front.* Fayetteville, AR, 1999.

———. *Seasons of War: The Ordeal of a Confederate Community, 1861–1865.* New York, 1995.

Tatum, Georgia Lee. *Disloyalty in the Confederacy.* Chapel Hill, NC, 1934.

Thomas, Emory M. *The Confederacy as a Revolutionary Experience.* Englewood Cliffs, NJ, 1971.

———. *The Confederate Nation, 1861–1865.* New York, 1979.

Todd, Robert Cecil. *Confederate Finance.* Athens, GA, 1954.

White, Laura. *Robert Barnwell Rhett: Father of Secession.* New York, 1931.

Williams, David. *Rich Man's War: Class, Caste, and Confederate Defeat in the Lower Chattahoochee Valley.* Athens, GA, 1998.

Yearns, Wilfred Buck. *The Confederate Congress.* Athens, GA, 1960.

———, ed. *The Confederate Governors.* Athens, GA, 1985.

Articles

Alderman, John. "The Civil War Period in Carroll County." *Carroll County Chronicles* 17 (Fall 1998), pp. 12–14.

Baruma, Ian. "National Success." *Prospect* 36 (December 1998), pp. 36–40.

Dougan, Michael B. "Life in Confederate Arkansas." *Arkansas Historical Quarterly* 31 (Spring 1972), pp. 15–35.

Elliott, Claude. "Union Sentiment in Texas 1861–1865." *Southwestern Historical Quarterly* 50 (April 1947), pp. 449–77.

Hamilton, J. G. de Roulhac. "The Heroes of America." *Publications of the Southern Historical Association* 11 (January 1907), pp. 10–19.

Havins, T. R. "Administration of the Sequestration Act in the Confederate District Court for the Western District of Texas, 1861–1865." *Southwestern Historical Quarterly* 43 (January 1940), pp. 295–322.

Holladay, Florence Elizabeth. "The Powers of the Commander of the Confederate Trans-Mississippi Department, 1863–1865, II." *Southwestern Historical Quarterly* 21 (April 1918), pp. 333–59.

LaCavera, Tommie. "The Roswell Women." *UDC Magazine* 62 (January 1999), pp. 12–13.

Levengood, Paul A. "In the Absence of Scarcity: The Civil War Prosperity of Houston, Texas." *Southwestern Historical Quarterly* 101 (April 1998), pp. 401–26.

Tice, Douglas O., Jr. "Bread or Blood! The Richmond Bread Riot." *Civil War Times Illustrated* 12 (February 1974), pp. 12–19.

White, Laura. "The Fate of Calhoun's Sovereign Convention in South Carolina." *American Historical Review* 34 (July 1929), pp. 757–71.

Wood, Gordon S. "Impartiality in America." *New Republic*, December 6, 1999, pp. 52–56.

Theses and Dissertations

Berkey, Jonathan M. "'Do You Wonder That I Have the Blues?': Ellen Moore's Wartime Negotiations." Paper presented at Women in the Civil War Conference, Winchester, VA, April 2000.

Gammon, William Lamar, II. "Governor John Milton of Florida, Confederate States of America." Master's thesis, University of Florida, Gainesville, 1948.

McConaghy, Mary Delaney. "Ordinary White Folk in a Lowcountry Community: The Structure and Dynamics of St. Bartholomew's Parish, South Carolina, 1850–1870." Ph.D. dissertation, University of Pennsylvania, Philadelphia, 1996.

Stillman, Rachel Bryan. "Education in the Confederate States of America, 1861–1865." Ph.D. dissertation, University of Illinois, Urbana, 1972.

INDEX

Adams, James, 24
Adams, Wirt, 84
agricultural policy, 208ff
Alabama, secession of, 36
alcohol, 309–15
Alcorn, James Lusk, 227, 334
Allen, Henry W., 249, 285, 404, 424
Anderson, J. Patton, 52, 61, 435n
Anderson, Robert, 38
Archer, Richard, 230–31
Aristotle, 12–17
Arizona, 164
Arkansas, secession of, 36–37, 118
Ayer, Lewis M., 363–64

Bagby, George, 214–15, 378
Baldwin, John, 181
Banks, Nathaniel P., 256, 317–18
Barbour, James, 343
Barksdale, Ethelbert, 158, 159
Barnwell, Robert W., 48, 52–53, 70, 71, 80,
    81, 93, 130, 352
Barry, William, 60, 64, 104
Bartow, Francis, 59, 73, 74, 77, 88, 326
Beauregard, P.G.T., 88, 112, 126–27, 129,
    191, 196, 232, 249, 256, 258, 319, 332,
    337, 341, 348, 384, 385, 415
Bee, Barnard E., 126

Bell, John, 367, 368
Benjamin, Judah P., 83, 85, 120, 316, 342,
    348–50, 357, 375, 378, 384, 390, 414,
    418, 421, 424–25
Benning, Henry L., 114
Blackburn, J.S.C., 121
blacks in the Confederacy, 130–62, 363,
    391–92
Bocock, Thomas, 390
Bonham, Milledge L., 91, 126
Border states, 52, 62–63, 117, 145
Boyce, William W., 59–60, 68, 71–72, 74,
    99, 101, 114, 122, 363, 392
Bragg, Braxton, 191, 192, 219, 231, 232,
    257, 258, 310, 332, 334–35, 337–38,
    349, 352–53, 368, 388, 390, 398
Breckinridge, John C., 63, 192, 257, 318,
    319, 349, 367, 368, 370, 390–91, 393,
    403–4, 410ff, 416–18, 421–24, 427
Brent, Joseph L., 252
Brooks, Preston, 7
Brown, John, 7, 11
Brown, Joseph E., 85, 90, 91, 118–21, 144,
    147, 169–70, 210, 227–37, 244–45,
    262, 274, 275, 282, 284, 289–93, 296,
    303, 304, 307, 311, 312, 324, 325, 328,
    330, 332, 333, 336, 338, 359, 367, 369,
    379, 391, 403, 423

Browne, William, 350
Burke, Edmund, 16
Buchanan, James, 29, 51, 85
Buckner, Simon B., 180–81, 401
Burnside, Ambrose E., 193, 254
Byrd, Mary Lou, 197

cabinet, Confederate, 77–84, 348–51, 354ff
Calhoun, John C., 10
Campbell, John A., 408–10, 416–17, 427
Cartwright, Samuel, 131–35, 137, 138
Chesnut, James, 31, 48, 65–66, 69, 71, 91,
    96, 98, 102, 111, 120, 342, 352
Chesnut, Mary Boykin, 92, 120, 368, 369,
    393
Cheves, Langdon, 24, 48, 144–45, 149,
    209, 210, 232, 239
Cicero, 13–14
civil rights, 168ff, 360–62
Claiborne, J.F.H., 208
Clark, Charles, 158, 159, 171, 176, 177,
    204, 242, 245, 247, 250, 382, 403, 406,
    419, 421–22
Clark, Edward, 166, 325, 330
Clark, William, 370
Clay, Clement C., 27, 82, 121, 353–56, 366,
    387, 389
Clay, Henry, 9–10
Clayton, Alexander M., 96, 184, 282
Cleburne, Patrick R., 157–58
Cleveland, Henry, 24
Clingman, Thomas L., 27
Cobb, Howell, 27, 30, 35, 39, 48ff, 56, 58,
    65, 69, 70, 73, 74, 77, 81, 108, 117,
    119–20, 326, 368, 386, 391
Cobb, Thomas R. R., 57, 68, 73, 74, 82, 96,
    99, 103, 110, 117, 119, 120, 324, 326,
    327, 334, 368, 370, 386
Cobb, W.R.R., 356
Collier, Charles, 359
Collins, Robert, 137–40
Confederate nationalism, 20–23, 36
    Confederates as a distinct race, 40–43,
    45–47
Confederate States of America
    army, 88–91, 225
    capitol, move to Richmond, 115–17,
    121–22

church in, 33
civil rights in, 168ff, 360–62
civil unrest, 212–15
citizenship in, 33, 100
class conflict in, 240ff
congress, 345–47, 358–60, 362–64
conscription and exemption, 226–28, 238
constitutions, 44, 51, 59–63, 66–68, 75,
    77, 93–108, 438n
cotton policy in, 86, 308–309, 373–77,
    381–84, 456n
democracy in, 14–15, 18–19, 31–32,
    47–48, 59–60, 75, 85–124, 161–62,
    187–88, 278–79, 305, 339–40, 417
demoralization in, 355–56, 401ff
disloyalty in, 183–85, 259–79
dissent in, 49
elections in, 343
emancipation in, 376
finance, 377–81
foreign policy, 86–87, 373–77
formation, 31–32, 36, 40, 48–54, 55
free blacks, 142–43
fugitive slave law, 95
gag rule in, 67
governors, 90, 118–21, 228ff
ideological origins, 12–20
imperialism, 164
internal improvements in, 304ff
interstate cooperation, 169
judiciary, 32, 74, 118, 148–88
morale and disintegration, 212–15,
    228–53
navy, 92–93
oligarchy in, 15–21, 32–33, 106–107,
    123–24, 340, 427–28
opposition party, 28, 54, 57, 68, 81, 87,
    98–99, 120–21, 343–96 passim
origins, 7–11, 12–34
philanthropy in, 281ff, 292ff
politics, 341–96 passim
    in cabinet, 78–84
    parties in, 365–96
    see also opposition party
presidency, 5–6, 56, 63–66, 68–75,
    95–96, 101, 435n, 438n
race in, 30
rationing in, 280–316

secession in, 102
slaves in, 130–62
  resistance and insurrection, 145–53,
    155–56, 263
  use by Confederacy, 147–50, 155–61
socialism in, 280–316
states, admission of new, 102–104
state rights in, 32–33, 45–46, 118,
  323–40
surrenders, 250, 253, 397–400, 405ff
tariff, 74
toryism, 183–85, 259–79
Unionism in, 183–85, 259–79
women in, 194–224, 235ff, 243–44,
  283ff, 445n
Congress, 345–47, 358–60, 362–64
Conrad, Charles, 78, 347–48, 361, 384
Corry, Eliza, 220–24
Corry, Robert, 220–24
cotton policy, 86, 308–309, 373–77,
  381–84, 456n
Crawford, Martin, 22, 25, 77
Curry, J.L.M., 30, 48, 74, 85, 101, 104, 275,
  354, 355, 358
Cushing, Caleb, 166

Daniel, John, 357, 358
Davis, Jefferson, 27, 29, 35, 38, 39, 40, 42,
  50, 53, 85, 98, 103, 110, 112, 113, 116,
  178, 204, 213, 219, 250, 254, 258, 261,
  262, 271, 288, 302, 317, 318, 342ff,
  367ff, 435n
  and cabinet, 77–84
  character, 79
  and civil rights, 174–75, 178, 187
  first inaugural, 77
  foreign policy, 86–87
  and the governors, 333ff
  military policy, 88–91, 225–28, 384ff
  naval policy, 92–93
  and opposition, 394–96
  and the presidency, 50, 53, 56, 57,
    64–77, 435n, 438n
  relations with Rhett, 81, Stephens, 81,
    87–88, 121, Toombs, 81, 121
  and secession, 28
  on slave enlistments, 158
  on slavery, 137

Davis, Reuben, 346, 372
Davis, Varina, 80, 342, 371, 425
De Bow, James D. B., 41–44, 48, 49,
  108–10, 113, 115, 136–37, 205–6,
  208, 215, 223, 329, 368, 373
De Clouet, Alexander, 48, 50, 52, 96, 121,
  123
Degener, Edward, 172–73, 268
De Leon, Edwin, 382
Denney, David, 220
Dixon, Robert E., 356
Douglas, Stephen A., 23
Dowdall, James, 36
Dyer, S. M., 291

Early, Jubal A., 320
Echols, John, 113
education, 204–6
Election of 1860, 23–25
Ellett, Henry, 83
Ewell, Richard S., 126

Farragut, David G., 129, 191, 320
Fitzpatrick, Benjamin, 27
Florida, secession of, 36
Floyd, John B., 35, 39
Foote, Henry S., 157, 181, 298, 345–47,
  358, 359, 361, 372, 386, 391
Forrest, Nathan B., 248
Fort Sumter, 33, 38, 75, 87–88,
  112–13

George, Charles, 218, 219
George, Flora, 224
George, Parker, 224
Georgia, secession of, 37
Gettysburg, Battle of, 352
Gholson, Samuel, 273
Gholson, Thomas, 158
Glenn, David C., 244
Goode, E. S., 181
governors, 323–40
Grant, Ulysses S., 128, 129, 190, 255–57,
  317–22, 398–400, 413
Gray, Henry, 353
Gray, Peter, 345
Greenhow, Rose O., 29
Gregg, Maxcy, 24

Hall, G., 36
Hamilton, D. H., 40
Hammond, James H., 76, 111, 389
Hardee, William J., 210
Harris, George, 237
Harris, Isham, 330
Harris, Wiley, 48, 50, 52, 53, 60, 61, 64, 74,
    96, 101, 102, 111, 367
Harris, William L., 29
Heiskell, Joseph B., 359
Henry, Gustavus A., 351, 353
Hill, Benjamin, 21–22, 69, 102, 338, 356,
    423
Hilton, Robert, 158–60, 178, 347, 360, 363,
    405
Holden, William W., 277–78, 325
Hood, John B., 319–20, 362, 389, 397
Hooker, Joseph, 254–55
Hopper, John, 233
Houston, Sam, 84, 264–65
Hudson, Robert, 183–85, 325
Hunter, R.M.T., 63, 115, 117, 343, 350,
    385, 391–92, 408, 410ff, 416

inflation, 199ff

Jackson, Claiborne, 332
Jackson, Thomas J. "Stonewall," 126, 127,
    232, 255
Jahnsenykes, William, see William Jenks
Jeffares, B.F.R., 220
Jefferson, Thomas, 9
Jemison, Robert, 355
Jenks, William, 1–6, 11, 22
Johnson, Andrew, 253
Johnston, Albert Sidney, 126–29, 239, 283,
    296, 344, 370
Johnston, Joseph E., 126–27, 154, 157,
    171, 219, 250, 253, 256, 258, 317–19,
    341, 346, 348, 352–54, 384–85,
    388–89, 391, 394, 397–400, 403ff, 414
Johnston, William Preston, 404
Jones, John B., 342
Jones, L. J., 326

Keitt, Lawrence, 48, 68, 69–71, 74–76, 99,
    100, 103, 107

Kells, Robert, 253, 299–300
Kenan, Augustus, 359
Kenner, Duncan, 59, 60, 101, 167, 362–63,
    376, 380, 402, 408
Kilpatrick, William, 185
Kornegay, Zachariah, 233

law and justice, 118, 148, 163–88
Lawrence, Rufinia, 150
Lee, Robert E., 126, 128, 159, 189,
    192–93, 250, 253–55, 258, 317–22,
    346, 350, 351, 357, 362, 363, 376,
    384–86, 390–93, 397–99, 401ff, 414,
    419
Letcher, John, 115, 116, 179, 212–13, 282,
    290, 326, 369
Lewis, Lang, 353
libraries, 206
Lincoln, Abraham, 24–26, 29, 30, 39, 40,
    51, 55, 85, 86, 111–12, 117, 130, 319,
    392
Lipscomb, David, 153–54
literature and the press, 205–8, 356–58
Longstreet, James, 126, 257, 371, 388
Lovell, Mansfield, 352
Lubbock, Francis, 169, 226, 228, 230, 234,
    236, 266, 268, 293, 295, 296, 332, 333,
    343–44
Lyons, James, 159–60, 359

Madison, James, 16–17, 28
Magrath, Andrew G., 148, 402–3, 405, 407,
    418
Magruder, John B., 233, 270
Mallory, Stephen R., 35, 77, 83, 92–93,
    120, 199, 211, 295, 335, 346–48, 372,
    381, 386
Mann, Ambrose Dudley, 86
Manning, John, 196
Martin, Jeremiah, 113
Mason, James, 27
Mayo, John, 213
McLean, James R., 358–59, 361
McClellan, George B., 127, 189–90, 255,
    321, 345–46, 360, 362
McCombs, M. C., 244
Meade, George G., 255–56, 319

Memminger, Christopher G., 31, 48, 59–61, 71, 76, 77, 81, 86, 89, 93, 118, 120, 122, 143, 350–51, 358, 377–83
Miles, William Porcher, 48, 71, 72, 103, 123, 342–43, 385, 413
Miller, John, 420
Milton, John, 146, 150, 169, 174, 204, 209, 231, 237, 261, 276, 284, 289, 292–93, 295, 300, 302, 307, 323, 327, 330–39, 403, 405, 407
Mississippi, secession of, 36
Moise, E. Warren, 180–81, 328, 353
Moore, A. B., 25, 282, 288, 330
Moore, Ellen, 217
Moore, Thomas O., 25–26, 40, 85, 90, 150–51, 156, 166–67, 179, 181, 228, 230, 234, 240, 249, 273–74, 323, 326, 330, 332, 334–36, 339, 362, 401, 420
Morgan, John Hunt, 278
Morton, Jackson, 83
Moses, Eliza, 195, 198
Munford, Thomas T., 420
Murrah, Pendleton, 161, 173, 247, 249, 251, 286, 293, 301, 335, 337, 404–6, 420
Myers, Abraham C., 307, 350

Nisbet, Eugenius, 61, 77

Ochiltree, William, 343
Oldham, Williamson, 344
Orr, James L., 358, 371
Osterhaus, Peter, 423
Owens, James B., 68, 435n

Paine, Thomas, 16, 17
Pattison, Jane, 150
Pemberton, John C., 256
Perkins, John, 60, 67, 107
Perry, Milton S., 118, 218
Pettus, John, 25, 36, 65, 145, 146, 151, 176, 203, 210, 227, 230, 231, 233, 242, 249–50, 282, 284, 288, 290, 303, 304, 307, 309, 310, 324–26, 330, 335, 350, 419
Pickens, Francis, 33, 34, 75, 88, 144, 311, 329–31

Pickett, John T., 392
Pierce, Franklin, 10, 80
Pillow, Gideon J., 324, 335
Polk, Leonidas, 128
Pollard, Edward A., 357
Praed, William L., 18
Preston, William, 403
Price, Sterling, 320
prohibition, see alcohol

Quitman, John, 22

Randolph, George W., 349
Reagan, John H., 27, 84, 122, 199, 306, 351, 370, 413, 416–19, 421
Rector, Henry, 332
Rhett, Robert Barnwell, 22, 23, 28, 31, 40–41, 49–54, 56–57, 59, 61, 64, 67–77, 79, 81, 83, 87, 89, 121, 123, 130, 144, 158, 160, 187, 240, 280, 305, 357, 363, 367, 405, 428, 434–35n, 438n
   and constitution, 44, 91–108, 111, 117, 120
   and foreign policy, 44–48
   opposition leader, 81, 367–95 passim
Richmond bread riot, 212–18
Rodes, Robert, 36
Rosecrans, William S., 192, 256
Rost, Pierre, 86
Ruffin, Edmund, 425

salt, 286–92
Saunders, James, 24
Saunders, R. T., 382
secession, 24–40, 44–45, 47
Seddon, James, 25, 243, 349, 385, 390, 393, 403
sequestration, 166–68
Seward, William H., 112, 159, 392, 408, 409
Sexton, Franklin, 345, 347, 348, 355, 359, 360, 369, 371
Sheridan, Philip H., 320
Sherman, William T., 220, 223, 236, 238, 244, 250, 256, 257, 274, 317–21, 388, 397–400, 405, 416, 418

Shorter, John G., 234, 288, 331, 379
Sigel, Franz, 319
Simon, Ferdinand, 269
slaves
    resistance and insurrection, 145–53, 155–56
    use by Confederacy, 149–50, 155–61, 363, 391–92
slave trade, 62, 67, 95, 97–99, 100–110
slavery, 8, 42–43, 47, 97–98, 103–4, 106–11, 130–62
Slidell, John, 27, 376
Smith, Edmund Kirby, 126, 173, 175, 180, 202, 230, 235, 317, 328, 339, 353, 397, 400, 416, 420, 421, 423
Smith, Robert, 60, 96, 121
Snead, Thomas, 387
Soulé, Pierre, 385
South Carolina, secession of, 31–32
Southern nationalism, 20–23, 36
Spann, T. H., 31, 34, 40
Sparrow, Edward, 353
stay laws, 165–66
state politics, 323–40
Stephens, Alexander H., 24, 27, 37, 48ff, 52, 56–58, 60–62, 65–66, 69–75, 77, 81, 85, 87–88, 99–108, 110, 115–16, 120, 121, 123, 188, 237, 260, 275, 280, 310, 325, 345, 357, 408–10, 426
    elected vice president, 74–76
    influence as founder, 58–59
    in opposition, 367, 386–87, 391–92, 394
Stuart, Charles E. L., 24–25, 27, 29, 35, 39, 66, 113, 433n
Sumner, Charles, 7, 11
surrenders, *see under* Confederate States of America

Taylor, Richard, 243, 318, 400
Taylor, T. T., 173
Tennessee, secession of, 118
Terhune, A. A., 338
Texas, secession of, 45, 76
Thomas, George H., 248, 308

Thompson, Jacob, 27
Tocqueville, Alexis de, 21
Toombs, Robert, 27, 28, 48ff, 52, 56, 57, 65, 66, 69–73, 77, 81, 82, 85, 88, 89, 96, 99, 100, 103, 107, 120–21, 122, 147, 157, 204, 310, 326, 349–50, 367, 421
    in opposition, 368, 378, 381–82, 386, 391–95
Trenholm, George A., 351
Trescot, William, 405
Twenty Negro Law, 146, 235
Tyler, John, 275

Vance, Zebulon, 222, 246, 277, 325, 333, 334, 402, 423
Virginia, secession of, 113–15

Walker, John G., 405
Walker, Leroy P., 82–83, 85, 90, 119, 120, 225, 341–42, 348, 349
Walker, Richard, 60, 61, 82, 96
Walker, W.H.T., 91–92
Washington, Littleton B., 25, 28–29, 33–34, 113, 114, 122, 232, 342–46, 350, 352, 357, 424
Watie, Stand, 400
Watts, Thomas, 156, 171, 181, 276, 285, 294, 302, 337, 370, 403, 406–8, 426
Wharton, John, 389
Wharton, T. J., 177
Whitney, Eli, 38
Wigfall, Louis T., 22, 23, 27, 28, 33–34, 69, 120, 204, 243, 339, 346, 352–56, 358, 403
    in opposition, 371–72, 384–91, 393–95
Wilmot, David, 10
Wise, Henry, 115, 424, 427
Withers, Thomas, 67, 71, 121, 368
women, 194–211, 445n

Yancey, William L., 22–24, 25, 31, 36, 41, 65, 77, 80, 82, 86–88, 120, 280, 354–56, 364, 367, 374–75, 423